"Out of the Mouth of Hell"

Civil War Prisons and Escapes

FRANCES H. CASSTEVENS

McFarland & Company, Inc., Publishers

Jefferson, North Carolina, and London

ALSO BY FRANCES H. CASSTEVENS
AND FROM MCFARLAND

*George W. Alexander and Castle Thunder:
A Confederate Prison and Its Commandant* (2004)

Edward A. Wild and the African Brigade in the Civil War (2003)

Clingman's Brigade in the Confederacy, 1862–1865 (2002)

The Civil War and Yadkin County, North Carolina (1977)

LIBRARY OF CONGRESS CATALOGUING-IN-PUBLICATION DATA

Casstevens, Frances Harding.
"Out of the mouth of hell" : Civil War prisons
and escapes / Frances H. Casstevens.
p.   cm.
Includes bibliographical references and index.

ISBN 0-7864-2072-3 (illustrated case binding : 50# alkaline paper) ∞

1. United States— History— Civil War, 1861–1865 — Prisoners and prisons.
2. Military prisons— United States— History — 19th century.
3. Military prisons— Confederate States of America — History.
4. Prisoners of war — United States— History— 19th century.
5. Prisoners of war — Confederate States of America — History.
6. Prisoner-of-war escapes— United States— History— 19th century.
7. Prisoner-of-war escapes— Confederate States of America — History.
I. Title
E615.C37   2005   973.7'7 — dc22   2005000093

British Library cataloguing data are available

Cover photograph: Old Capitol Prison, Washington, D.C.
(Courtesy of the Library of Congress, LC-DIG-cwpb-00493)

Manufactured in the United States of America

*McFarland & Company, Inc., Publishers
Box 611, Jefferson, North Carolina 28640
www.mcfarlandpub.com*

Acknowledgments

I want to thank my special friend, Victor Seiders, for his help and advice over the years, and for the loan of several reference books.

This work could have not been completed without the untiring efforts of the staff of the Yadkin County Public Library and their help in securing books and material through interlibrary loan.

I am especially appreciative of the work Michael Gorman has done in transcribing old newspapers and creating a fantastic website about Civil War Richmond.

The Library of Congress has graciously furnished excellent black and white photographs which bring the people in some of the stories to life. The North Carolina Department of Cultural Resources has also been a source of information and photographs.

I also want to thank Ed and Sue Curtis for their work in preserving the history of the Salisbury Prison, and the information they share with interested persons on both prisoners and guards through a newsletter and a yearly seminar.

Last, but not least, I would like to thank Dr. Dave Bush and the archaeological team working to uncover and preserve the history of Johnson's Island. I know efforts are ongoing at other prison sites, but the limitations of space will not permit me to mention them all. I do encourage their efforts and urge others to do so, as well.

The Prisoner's Hope

In the prison cell I sit,
Thinking, mother dear, of you,
And our bright and happy home, so far away;
And the tears, they fill my eyes,
Spite of all that I can do,
Tho' I try to cheer my comrades, and be gay.

Tramp! Tramp! Tramp! The boys are marching
Cheer up comrades, they will come,
And beneath the starry flag
We shall breathe the air again,
Of the free land in our own beloved home.

In the battle front we stood,
When their fiercest charge they made,
And they swept us off a hundred men or more,
But before we reach'd their lines,
They were beaten back dismayed,
And we heard the cry of vic'try o'er and o'er.

So within the prison cell,
We are waiting for the day
That shall come to open wide the iron door;
And the hollow eye grows bright,
And the poor heart almost gay,
As we think of seeing home and friends once more.

— George F. Root

Table of Contents

Preface

This work follows my history of one Civil War prison, Castle Thunder (*George W. Alexander and Castle Thunder: A Confederate Prison and Its Commandant*). Captain Alexander also served briefly at Salisbury, North Carolina. Since I already had information on two prisons, I decided to continue and this book is the result. The research has proved even more fascinating than I at first believed it would be, and there was more information available than can be contained in one book. The sources ranged from fragile, leather-bound books written in the 1860s to web sites on the Internet.

It is beyond the scope of one book to document every prison (there were about 150 of them) or every prison break from 1861 to 1865. In fact, that would be impossible considering the length of time that has passed and the absence of records of some prisons. This book will instead focus on the major prison facilities, both in the North and in the South, and explore in detail the stories behind some of these extraordinary escapes and the men involved.

The book has been divided into two parts—the Federal prisons in the first part and the Confederate prisons in the second. Within these parts, the prison facilities have been organized alphabetically for easy reference. Each chapter opens with the basic facts about the prison: when it was established, type of facility, location, number and kind of prisoners held, known escapes, and other available data.

The book is designed to give the reader some idea of the obstacles the prisoner faced to prevent his escape. In addition to the buildings and grounds and fences, the prison personnel played an important part in how the prisoners fared and how far they would go to escape their cruel treatment. The surrounding territory played an important part in whether the prisoner managed to escape to safety, or whether he was caught by the search parties and bloodhounds.

An appendix lists the monthly Federal prison population from July 1862 through late 1865, and the escapes reported each month. The number of escapes does not always tally with the facts. Some prisons had large numbers of prisoners and escapes, while some had few prisoners and even fewer escape attempts. Many escape plots were reported before they could be carried out.

Being in prison at all during the Civil War was horrible, but some prisons were markedly worse than others. It is hoped that this book presents an accurate picture of Civil War prisons and escapes.

Introduction

During the American Civil War, more men died than in all the wars before or since that time. We honor those who died heroically on the battlefield, and erect monuments to their sacrifice. However, we tend to forget the thousands of men who were captured on the same battlefield and subsequently died in prison of starvation and diseases, or who were killed trying to escape. In addition, unsanitary medical practices probably killed more wounded soldiers than did the bullets that wounded them.

The Vikings believed that death on the battlefield assured the warrior eternal life in Valhalla. The ancient Greek believed it was better to be carried home on his shield than to live with defeat. Those who were held prisoners often came to believe death was preferable.

The Numbers of Prisoners

United States Secretary of War Edwin Stanton reported that Federal prisons held approximately 220,000 Confederate prisoners. Of those, 26,436 died. In the South, Confederate prisons held 270,000 Federal prisoners, of whom 22,576 died.[1] The deaths were from a variety of causes including, smallpox, pneumonia, typhoid fever, dysentery, diarrhea, and scurvy in addition to battlefield wounds and amputation. Contributing factors were depression, unsanitary conditions, polluted water, inadequate and unhealthy diet, and the lack of proper clothing, shelter, and medicine.

Suffering of Prisoners

Stories of dark dungeons, of solitary confinement, of brutal whippings, and of men being strung up by their thumbs sound like scenes from a horror movie. But these things did happen, and they happened fewer than 200 years ago in America. Many Confederate and Federal prisoners held between 1861 and 1865 soon learned that it would have been better to have died quickly from a bullet than to slowly starve to death in a cold, crowded, filthy prison.

Not since the time of the Spanish Inquisition in the 15th century have so many prisoners suffered such cruel and inhumane treatment as those men confined in prisons in both the North and the South during the years 1861 to 1865.

Those held in prisons were daily faced with life-threatening situations including starvation, freezing weather, cruel treatment, solitary confinement, and even torture.

Some suffering was purposely inflicted for infraction of the rules or for escape attempts. Other suffering was caused by shortages of water or food, deadly diseases, bad weather, and the despondency caused by confinement in cramped quarters and the denial of freedom.

Prisoners suffered because of ignorance, as a result of government bureaucracy and poorly thought-out rules and regulations, or deliberate cutbacks in rations, blankets and clothing. Sometimes, the plight of the prisoners could not be avoided because there was no food or clothing to give them — the numbers of prisoners simply overwhelmed most of the facilities set up to care for them.

To survive, some prisoners stole, murdered, and assaulted each other. Ironically, some prisoners held in the South fared better because they received more food (such as at Castle Thunder) than did the Confederate soldiers.

Under the best conditions, prisons are hellish places. The desire of a prisoner to escape is understandable, especially when there is no chance of being released, exchanged, or paroled. With every day spent in confinement, the prisoner grew a little weaker, and his chances of succumbing to disease or death from malnutrition increased. The desire to escape became the goal toward which the prisoner directed all his thoughts and efforts. The hope of freedom was sometimes the only thing that kept a prisoner alive, and if that prisoner wanted to see his home once more, he tried every way possible to escape.

Many never got the opportunity to escape, but died from one of the deadly diseases that ravaged prison barracks and compounds— typhoid fever, smallpox, pneumonia, scurvy, diarrhea, and dysentery. Even diseases that were usually not fatal, such as measles and mumps, could cause the death of the weakened, starving prisoners. Thus, those with the strong desire to live often found a way to escape their confinement quickly before they were incapacitated.

Many astounding stories attest to the fortitude, courage, and intelligence of men pushed to the brink of madness and with nowhere to go but over (or under) their prison walls.

The Prisoner's Duty to Escape

The desire to live was enhanced by the knowledge that it was the duty of every soldier to escape from his captors so that he might rejoin his unit to continue the fight against the enemy.

As one researcher so aptly remarked:

> Escape is the duty of any soldier taken prisoner. The threat of escape forces the captor to divert men from combat to guard duty; consistent attempts to escape necessitate larger numbers of guards. In this way, the prisoner, despite his removal from the theater of combat, can make a positive contribution to his cause.[2]

No exact figure exists of the number of prisoners who escaped their confinement. *The Official Records of the War of the Rebellion* contain numerous reports of prisoner escapes from the Federal prisons. Beginning in July 1862, the Federal facilities that housed prisoners included the number of escapes in their monthly reports. Whether their reports included the actual number who made their way outside or just those who were not caught is not clear. Often, an investigation was launched and the testimony of prison officials and guards was recorded in detail.

For southern prisons, no such factual information is available, though there are many published accounts in articles and books by soldiers who escaped and lived to tell about it.

The available information about both Federal and Confederate prisons has increased in recent years. Many older works have been reprinted and are now available. Many websites contain lists of prisoners who died and their dates of death, excerpts from first-person accounts of the prisoner themselves, and memoirs written years after the war.

Characteristics of Those Who Escaped

That so many prisoners died or were executed should make the few who did escape even greater heroes. Those who succeeded were, undoubtedly, the bravest, the boldest, the most courageous of those who were imprisoned. They were the ones who chose to live. They were probably the natural leaders, those gifted with greater intelligence than the average, or those who had a greater instinct for survival and who also possessed some trait that enabled them to succeed where others failed. Maybe they just got lucky.

Prison Facilities 1861–1865

A number of existing prison facilities were converted to hold soldiers captured on the battlefield as well as political prisoners suspected of disloyalty. As the war continued and the number of prisoners increased, so did the number of those facilities. Many facilities were only intended to be temporary prisons, and were not large enough to hold the number of prisoners assigned to them.

Prisoners were sometimes confined in an open field surrounded by guards, in houses, or in other buildings until they could be transferred to more secure and permanent facilities.[3] Some prisons, although overcrowded buildings, protected prisoners from the cold (Libby, Danville, Castle Thunder, the Federal forts); others did not and offered no shelter other than tents (Belle Isle, Andersonville, Camp Chase).

Some 150 locations were utilized to hold prisoners. They can be classified in six categories:[4] 1) an existing jail or prison (the Henrico County Jail for runaway slaves in Richmond, Virginia); 2) coastal fortifications (Fort McHenry, Fort Delaware); 3) converted commercial buildings (Libby Prison in Richmond, Virginia); 4) barracks enclosed by a high fence (Johnson's Island in Lake Erie; 5) clusters of tents enclosed by a high fence (Salisbury Prison; and 6) barren stockades (Belle Island, near Richmond, and Andersonville, Georgia.) While the Union modified many of the old coastal fortifications to hold prisoners, Castle Pinckney was the only costal fort used as a prison by the Confederacy. In the North, a few existing state penitentiaries were used to confine political and military prisoners, such as the Ohio State Penitentiary and the old prison at Alton, Illinois. Both North and South converted warehouses and other buildings into prisons.[5]

Both sides tried to separate officers from enlisted men because the officers were generally better educated, accustomed to giving orders and having men follow them, and were more capable of planning, organizing, and carrying out an escape. Thus, generally only Federal officers were confined to Libby Prison, in Richmond, Virginia, while the enlisted men were sent to Belle Isle. Confederate officers were sent to Johnson's Island in Lake Erie, while the enlisted men were packed into Camp Douglas or Camp Chase. Even when officers and men shared the same prison, the officers were often confined to a separate area, as was the case at the prison in Salisbury, North Carolina.

Many prisoners saw the inside of more than one prison, as the prison population was shifted from one facility to another to relieve overcrowding or because of the approach of enemy troops. Captain Bernhard Domschcke, for example, was captured at Gettysburg and interred in Richmond, Virginia; Danville, Virginia; Macon, Georgia; Savannah, Georgia; Charleston, South Carolina; and finally Columbia, South Carolina.[6]

Each prisoner is unique and each prison presents a different situation and varying obstacles the prisoner must overcome. The variety of formidable walls and barricades to be breached, all designed to keep prisoners confined and to thwart escapes, are as diverse as the methods devised by prisoners to escape those walls.

Conditions in the prisons and the treatment prisoners received varied as greatly as the facilities themselves. But most of the prison officials had one thing in common — the often justified fear that the prisoners would escape. Initially, both sides thought the war would be a short one, but as it continued, the numbers of prisoners increased. Some prisoners succeeded in escaping, but most did not.

Hoffman Placed in Charge of Prisoners

The prison system in the North was under the direction of Col. William H. Hoffman. Hoffman knew from experience what it was like to be held a prisoner. While in Texas, Lieutenant Colonel Hoffman was one of those captured when Union General David E. Twiggs surrendered his forces to the Confederacy in February of 1861. Twiggs was dismissed, so he joined the Confederate States Army and was appointed major general.[7] Hoffman was paroled but not exchanged until August 1862.[8] While on parole, Hoffman could not serve in the field, but he could accept a nonmilitary position. He was appointed commissary general on October 23, 1861.[9] Once appointed, Hoffman reorganized the prison system. He was a methodical, budget-minded administrator who pinched every penny. His policy was that if a prisoner had "clothing upon him," no matter what its condition, he would be issued nothing else to wear.[10]

Types of Prisoners

Prisoners held by the Union and by the Confederacy were not limited to soldiers. Many civilians were arrested on suspicion of disloyalty. Spies, both male and female, were held by both sides. Each government incarcerated its own soldiers for desertion and other crimes. Castle Thunder, in Richmond, held a mixture of prisoners, both male and female, white and black, Confederate and Union soldiers, along with spies and persons suspected of disloyalty or of aiding the enemy.

Col. William Hoffman, commissary general of prisoners (right), with his staff in front of his office at F and 20th Street, N.W., Washington, D.C. (Courtesy of the Library of Congress, LC-DIG-cwpb-03953.)

We are fortunate to have an abundance of letters from prisoners, diaries, published articles and books by the men who were confined in prisons during the Civil War. There was a plethora of literature published even during the 1860s, and the list continues to grow daily.

Suspension of the Cartel

During the first year of the war, captured prisoners were held in prison or released on parole. The first formal exchange did not take place until February 23, 1862, because the United States government refused to recognize the Confederacy as a nation and would not enter into negotiations for prisoner exchange. On July 23, 1862, an agreement known as the "Dix-Hill cartel" established points of exchange and ratios of prisoner exchange.[11] A general officer could be exchanged for 60 enlisted men, a colonel for 15, a lieutenant for 4, and a sergeant for 3.[12] The prisoner exchange system was suspended by General Halleck on May 25, 1863, and when Ulysses S. Grant took command of the Federal forces, he stopped the prisoner exchange system entirely.[13] Grant wrote to Gen. Benjamin F. Butler:

It is hard on our men held in Southern prisons not to exchange them, but it is humanity to those left in the ranks to fight our battles. Every man we hold, when released on parole or otherwise, becomes an active soldier against us at once either directly or indirectly. If we commence a system of exchange which liberates all prisoners taken, we will have to fight on until the whole South is exterminated.[14]

With no hope of parole or exchange, the need and the desire to escape became even greater for prisoners held on both sides of the Mason-Dixon line. The South soon became overburdened with prisoners, and northern prisons were filled beyond capacity. The curtailment of the prisoner exchange policy meant that the prisoners accumulated faster than the facilities to house them could be constructed, and resources became inadequate to care for them. Prisoners were kept in facilities never intended for prison quarters, which did not adequately protect them in subzero temperatures, such as the exhibit barns used for prisoners at Camp Chase. Southern-held Federal prisoners suffered greatly as food and medical supplies dwindled.

Escapes from Federal Prisons

Some idea of the number of escapes can be found in the monthly returns required from the Federal prisons from July 1862 and afterwards.[15] The total number of escapes listed in the monthly returns for Alton Prison was 120. However, during that period there was no report submitted for one month (or it could not be found). The number of escapes prior to July 1862 is also unknown.[16]

The required monthly reports began with submissions from 12 major Federal prisons: Alton, Camp Butler, Camp Chase, Camp Douglas, Camp Morton, Fort Columbus, Fort Delaware, Fort Lafayette, Fort McHenry, Fort Warren, Johnson's Island, and St. Louis (which included both Gratiot Street Prison and other facilities in the city). Over the course of the next four years, the number of facilities almost doubled and by December 1863, ten addition facilities submitted their reports: Allegheny City Penitentiary, Fort Mifflin, Fort Pickens, Fort Wood, Louisville, McLean Barracks, New Orleans, Old Capitol Prison, in Washington, D.C., Rock Island, and Wheeling, a total of 22 major Federal prisons.[17]

By September 1865, only seven Federal prisons remained open, and by November only Fort Lafayette, in New York, reported five prisoners still in custody, four of whom were citizens who were released in the spring of 1866.[18] No returns were published from Fort Monroe, in Virginia, where Confederate president Jefferson Davis was held until May 15, 1867.[19] Other prisoners, both military and civilian, were known to have been held at Fort Monroe occasionally.

Federal Prison Guards: The Invalid Corps — Veteran Reserve Corps[20]

Initially, detachments from regular troops were sent to the various Federal prisons to act as guards, and to fill the numerous other positions necessary to maintain a facility, house and provide for a large number of prisoners. Provost marshals served as escorts and guarded prisoners at various prisons.[21]

After the war had been in progress for a year, the United States War Department authorized the chief medical officer in each city to hire nurses, cooks, and hospital attendants from among those soldiers who were either convalescing or were too feeble to perform regular military duties. On March 20, 1863, General Order No. 69 decreed that those men who were not able for field duty be organized into groups to be detailed to assist the provost marshal, hospitals and other facilities to serve any capacity needed as guards, clerks, nurses, cooks, and other tasks that they were able to perform. Disabled soldiers were mustered into temporary positions and paid, but they were not dropped from the rolls of their regular companies, and sometimes, if they fully recovered, they returned to their regiments on the battlefield.[22]

General Order No. 105, issued on April 28, 1863, organized the Invalid Corps. Col. Richard H. Rush, of the 6th Pennsylvania Cavalry, became the colonel of the First Regiment Veteran Reserve Corps.[23] Once the Veteran Reserve Corps had been established, the men were assigned to wear a uniform which consisted of a dark-blue forage cap, sky-blue trousers, and a sky-blue jacket of kersey trimmed with dark blue that was cut long in the waist similar to those worn by cavalry officers. They were ordered to wear a sky-blue frock coat with the collar, cuffs, and shoulder-strap grounds of dark blue velvet. A double stripe of dark blue ran down the outer seam of the trouser legs. However attractive the men might have been, DeForest stated that they "did not like to be distinguished from their comrades of the active service by a peculiar costume," and would rather have worn the same uniform as regular troops.[24]

The Veteran Reserve Corps furnished guards for prison camps at Rock Island, Chicago, Indianapolis, Johnson's Island, Elmira, and Point Lookout. They guarded many general hospitals, worked as ward masters, nurses, and clerks, did clerical work in a number of military departments, and assisted in recruiting and enforcing the draft law.[25]

The assistance provided by the Veteran Reserve Corps relieved regular soldiers for active duty in the field.

Confederate Prisons

Official reports on prisons in the South are practically nonexistent. However, there are a number of published accounts that began appearing in print even before the war was over. With the exception of the prison at Andersonville, Georgia, there are no regular monthly returns. The major Confederate prisons were:

> *Alabama*—Cahaba, Mobile, Montgomery, Tuscaloosa
> *Georgia*—Americus, Andersonville (Camp Sumter), Atlanta, Augusta, Blackshear, Millen (Camp Lawton), Marietta, Macon (Camp Oglethorpe), Savannah
> *Louisiana*—Shreveport
> *North Carolina*—Charlotte, Raleigh, Salisbury
> *Texas*—Camp Ford, Tyler, and Camp Groce (Hempstead)
> *Virginia*—Danville, Lynchburg, Petersburg, Richmond (Libby, Castle Thunder, Belle Isle).[26]

Methods of Escape

There was a variety of methods by which a prisoner could escape the confines of a prison, death being the last resort. Many prisoners died from diseases, such as measles, smallpox, pneumonia, scurvy, etc. Others were shot by guards randomly or while attempting to escape.

Sometimes, prisoners were given a parole on the battlefield shortly after their capture. A parole, if accepted, was a pledge not to take up arms again against the enemy. While it existed, there was an exchange of prisoners that relieved over-crowding on both sides. When the exchange policy was curtailed, the number of escape attempts drastically increased.

Out of desperation, many prisoners agreed to sign the Oath of Allegiance (to either the United States or the Confederacy, depending on where they were impris-oned). By agreeing to fight in the army, prisoners could escape the horrors and forced confinement of prison. Sometimes, however, they found themselves in even worse situations.

Prisoners sometimes disguised themselves and, with forged passes, passed through the gates to freedom outside. Others hid in various containers and rode out to freedom undetected in coffins, in refuse containers, or in other types of boxes.

Escapes were made through tunnels constructed over many days and weeks of labor. Escapes were made by going over the fence or tunnelling under it. Prisoners stormed the gates, blasted holes in the fences, bribed their guards, and tried every conceivable means of escaping their confinement.

What the mind can conceive can often be achieved. Some of the successful escapes required massive amounts of physical labor, stamina, and sheer determina-tion. Yet even those who failed deserve our admiration for their ingenuity and cour-age.

PART ONE
FEDERAL PRISONS

I wish I was in the land of cotton…
—Daniel Emmett, "Dixie's Land"

I

Alton Military Prison, Alton, Illinois

Imagine, twelve hundred men shut up in prison in three rooms...
— Sergeant Jacob Teeple, Company H, 10th Missouri Infantry, C.S.A.[1]

Location: on Mississippi River, Alton, Illinois. **Established:** built 1833, converted to military prison February 9, 1862. **Type:** existing state prison facility. **Type of Prisoners:** Confederate soldiers, civilians, and Federal soldiers under sentence of court-martial or military commission.[2] **Capacity:** average 800, maximum 1,891. **Number of Escapes:** at least 120.[3] **Numbers of Prisoners Held:** estimated at 12,000.[4]

History

The building that became a "military detention camp" was the first state penitentiary in Illinois. Situated too close to the river on low ground, the site was criticized by Dorothea Dix, and a new prison was ordered to be built at Joliet. When the new state prison was completed, government authorities began using the old prison building at Alton in 1862 to house captured Confederate soldiers.[5]

The Facilities

This fortress-style building was a prisoner's worst nightmare. Formerly the state penitentiary, the main building was three stories high and contained 256 cells. Each of these measured 4 feet by 7 feet.[6] The main building was a low stone structure, surrounded by walls 30 feet high. It stood very close to the Mississippi River.[7] Within the wall, there were five large rooms partitioned to make two rooms, one 7 feet by 4 feet, the other 20 feet by 4 feet. There was also a large, two-story frame building and a stable, also two stories high. Two other buildings held Union soldiers under sentence from a court-martial, and civilian prisoners.[8]

Thus, a building that had been condemned and abandoned as the Illinois State Penitentiary was reopened to house Confederate prisoners of war. The poorly constructed building was adjacent to the Mississippi and the bad water drainage led to disease and death, hastened by a reduction or withholding entirely of the rations allowed prisoners.[9]

Yet, an inspection conducted in April 1862 by Col. Richard D. Cutts and Maj. John J. Key found that the quarters of the officers, privates and citizens were "excellent, certainly equal if not superior to those at Camps Butler, Douglas and Morton." At that time, 300 prisoners were housed in the main penitentiary building, not in the cells, but in the "wide passage ways running around the three different tiers of cells." Bunks were wide enough for two persons. The rest of the prisoners were quartered in various outbuildings that were large and "well-ventilated rooms heated by stoves."[10]

Prison Personnel

The prison's first commandant was Lt. Col. Sidney Burbank, of the 13th United States Infantry. Burbank was a graduate of West Point, and a soldier with experience on the frontier. He fought in the Seminole War. His tenure was short at Alton, however, and he was promoted to colonel of the 2nd United States Infantry on September 16, 1862, and later commanded a brigade at Chancellorsville and Gettysburg in 1863.[11]

The Prisoners

By April 1862, there were 300 prisoners in the building and 289 housed in outbuildings.[12] Shortly afterward, two Federal officers stated in their report that they heard only one complaint from the prisoners. That prisoner, Colonel Stone, had complained that there was no straw in some of the bedding, and that their blankets had not been transferred with them from on their move from Arkansas to Alton, Illinois. Cutts and Key recommended that the straw for the bedding be "more generally distributed and a few blankets supplied here and there, and when this was done, the prisoners would be "entirely comfortable and beyond the reach of reasonable complaint.[13]

An inspection report dated April 3, 1862, gave the total number of prisoners in Alton Military Prison under the command of Lieutenant Colonel Burbank as 719. Of these, 58 were officers (five colonels, two lieutenant colonels, three majors, one chaplain, 18 captains, 22 lieutenants, and seven surgeons. Eight surgeons (Captain Carey of Missouri and the seven surgeons) were on parole, allowed freedom as far as the town of Alton. Of the total number, 459 prisoners had been taken at the battle of Pea Ridge, 130 had been captured at or near Fort Henry, and the rest had been captured at Milford and were confined as "bridge-burners, soldiers arrested for pillaging, and disloyal citizens."[14]

Since both military and political prisoners were under his control, Col. William Hoffman, commissary general of prisoners, decreed that "as far as practicable, it is desirable that only such prisoners be sent to Alton as will probably remain in custody some time, for one can not be released from there without the authority of the War Department."[15] Hoffman had been a prisoner himself in Texas early in the war. His policies as commissary general of prisoners have been said to have killed more men than were killed on the battlefield, because he spent nothing unless absolutely necessary. Hoffman decreed that "So long as a prisoner has clothing upon him, however much torn, issue nothing to him."[16]

Six men from Illinois were being held in Alton Military Prison in April 1862 on the charge that they had helped prisoners escape. W. P. Brooks, N. T. Brooks, A. C. Gish, W. S. Hutton, W. G. Nabb and William Richardson were charged with giving money to a "rebel prisoner," and that the prisoner escaped from the railroad cars while being transferred from Camp Douglas. The prisoners admitted to giving the prisoner money, but they had done so because they believed him to be a "union man" who intended to return to his home and tell his friends of the malicious rumors circulating in the South about the people of the North. The prisoner also claimed that he would turn himself in to the proper military authorities. After being kept in solitary confinement for two weeks, Col. Richard D. Cutts recommended in his report that the men be released after taking the oath of allegiance and posting $1,000 bail for their appearance before the U.S. Circuit Court.[17]

Escapes

In July 1862, Alton Prison reported that 27 prisoners had escaped.[18] Actually, 36 had escaped, but some were recaptured. Maj. Franklin F. Flint, commander of the guards, sent search parties to recapture them. He notified Colonel Hoffman that "many have undoubtedly crossed the river at this place, as several skiffs are missing."[19]

One of the first prisoners transferred to Alton Military Prison was Col. Ebenezer Magoffin, of the 2nd Cavalry, Missouri State Guard. He and 1,300 Confederates had been captured by Gen. John Pope at Blackwater, Missouri, and taken initially to the Gratiot Street Prison in St. Louis, Missouri (see Chapter X). The newspapers called Magoffin "the boldest, most reckless and unscrupulous of the [captured] rebel officers." He was also noted to be a "tall, dark-complected, stoop-shouldered," man of 45 years.[20]

During an encounter at Georgetown, in Pettis County, Missouri, between Magoffin's men and Col. Henry M. Day's men of the First Regiment Illinois Cavalry, Magoffin shot and killed Union Sgt. George W. Glasgow with a double-barreled shotgun. Magoffin was found hiding in the attic of the Kid Hotel. The angry Union soldiers and members of the Home Guard threatened to execute Magoffin on the spot, but Colonel Day intervened, and Magoffin was taken to Lexington, Missouri.[21]

After the defeat of Union forces there by Gen. Sterling Price, Magoffin was exchanged for the former governor of Missouri, Austin A. King, and former Missouri Supreme Court Judge John F. Ryland, who were being held by Elijah Magoffin, one of Ebenezer's sons.[22]

Colonel Magoffin returned to duty with the Missouri State Guard, but he received word that his wife was dying. When he arrived home on December 7, 1861, he found Federal troops had been stationed in every room, except in the bedroom where his wife lay dying. He escaped capture but two days later, he sent word to the commanding Federal officer at Sedalia that he wished to see his wife before she died, and he was granted a pass.[23] He was captured by a force of Union soldiers on December 19, 1861, at Milford, Johnson County, Missouri, along with 684 Confederates under the command of Col. F. S. Robertson. His two sons, Elijah and Beriah, were also captured at that time.[24] After his arrest, he was taken to St. Louis. He was charged with the murder of Sergeant Glasgow, and with violating his parole by leaving his home to rejoin Confederate forces. The trial, conducted by a military commission of four Union officers, lasted from February 6, 1862, until February 20, 1862.[25] Magoffin was found guilty on both charges, and was sentenced to be taken to the prison in Alton, Illinois, and to be executed "at such time and place as the commanding officer of this department [Maj. Gen. Henry W. Halleck] may direct." Halleck approved the commission's verdict. The sentence was not carried out immediately, and his brother, Beriah Magoffin, sent a telegram to President Lincoln asking for a suspension of the sentence. The president complied and on March 25, 1862, he agreed to suspend the execution of Magoffin.[26] Subsequently, President Lincoln, concerned with Magoffin's welfare, sent another telegram on April 9, 1862, to Major General Halleck: "If the rigor of the confinement of Magoffin at Alton is endangering his life or materially impairing his health, I wish it mitigated so far as it can be consistently with his safe detention."[27]

Colonel Magoffin had previously been held at the Gratiot Street Prison in St. Louis, but he had led the inmates in an insurrection. Under sentence of death, he was moved to Alton and put in a cell on an upper floor with a padlocked door. A guard was stationed at the door.[28] Faced with certain execution, Magoffin had no choice but to attempt to escape.

On July 25, 1862, 36 prisoners made their escape from Alton Prison.[29] Shortly after midnight, a group dressed in civilian clothes was led through a tunnel under the prison wall by Magoffin. The men split and scattered into the town. Others made their way to Jerseyville, and still others boarded a train for Cairo. Two were caught that same day, but the rest escaped to safety.[30] Among those who escaped were Colonel Murrell and Captain Sweeney, a one-armed man.[31]

At dawn, the guards discovered the tunnel entrance in the wash house inside the prison yard. The escapees had cleverly hidden the opening to the tunnel on top of an old pile of brick masonry, beneath the roof of a shed which was used as a wash house by the prisoners. No evidence of digging was visible upon entering the shed. The dirt from the tunnel had been hidden between the top and the roof of the shed. Maj. F. F. Flint believed that the work on the tunnel had taken many weeks, and had been carved out with large knives through the clay and loam of the ground.[32]

A search was conducted, and eight of the escapees were soon recaptured. Several had taken small boats and crossed the Mississippi.[33]

The prison break distressed prison officials and there was much correspondence between Col. William Hoffman, and heads of the military regarding the prison break. Colonel Hoffman wrote on July 31, 1862, to General Thomas, stating that "proper precautions were not taken to discover the preparation of the means of escape," and it does not explain how so many men could "pass so near the sentinel without detection."[34] Undoubtedly, the prisoners had help from the guards, or at least the guards had been bribed not to notice the escaping prisoners. Questions continued to be raised, and a court of inquiry was ordered by President Abraham Lincoln.[35]

Public opinion expressed in the Alton *Telegraph* criticized the negligence and laxity of discipline among the prison guards.[36] Hoffman complained to Secretary of War Stanton, and urged that a more competent officer be sent to replace Colonel Hildebrand.[37] On November 27, 1862, Captain H. W. Freedley arrived to replace Hildebrand. Freedley found conditions lacking. He reported that the commanding officer had "not given as much of his personal attention to the prison as was required." He found a "terrible lack of system" in running the prison, and the records kept by Maj. W. B. Mason incomplete. The records were in such bad condition that when the roll was called, four persons could not be found, and there were three whose names were not on the rolls. Mason was replaced by Capt. I. B. Kinkead. Freedley also found the prison provost marshal, Lt. E. R. Moore, to be incompetent in that position. In addition to other prison deficiencies, there were four insane prisoners who needed to be transferred elsewhere.[38]

At a court of inquiry held regarding the escape, testimony by witnesses revealed that the tunnel was only 18 inches in diameter. It ran a distance of 50 feet at a level three feet under the surface of the ground. The tunnel cut through the solid limestone wall.[39]

Magoffin may have escaped with the help of political manipulation by his brother, Beriah Magoffin, governor of Kentucky. Sentiment in Kentucky was greatly divided during the war, and certainly President Lincoln would not have wanted to alienate the sitting governor by allowing his brother to be executed. Thus, Colonel Magoffin's execution was postponed, and four months after his trial and conviction, the colonel escaped, along with his sons, and 33 others.

Three weeks after Ebenezer Magoffin's escape, there was a sudden change in the executive office of the state of Kentucky. Governor Magoffin resigned and Sen. James F. Robinson became governor. Robinson was sympathetic to the Union cause.[40] Undoubtedly, Governor Magoffin had held onto his office long enough to see his brother free, and he may have made a deal with Lincoln to allow his brother's escape. Certainly, Lincoln did order the execution of Colonel Magoffin delayed, and he telegraphed Major General Halleck to secure better treatment for Magoffin while he was in "detention."

Sadly, after enduring so much, the daring colonel was murdered. Sources differ as to when this occurred. A report filed in September 1865 which described fortifications in the trans-Mississippi area mentioned that Fort Bliss had been on the "private grounds of a man named Magoffin, a brother to Governor Magoffin of Kentucky, and that he [Magoffin] had "gone South."[41]

Ebenezer Magoffin was stabbed to death by a man named Cordle, and probably his death occurred in Arkansas. A fight broke out in a tavern between Cordle and one of Magoffin's friends. When the colonel attempted to break it up, Cordle stabbed him. Magoffin's son, Elijah, followed his father's killer for 600 miles to Texas. There, Elijah caught Cordle and hanged the man himself to avenge his father's senseless death.[42]

Another Daring Escape

In November 1862, the number of prisoners had reached 522. They were guarded by 1,300 U.S. troops. Despite this ratio, another daring escape occurred. Prison officials hoped it would be the last escape.[43]

This escape occurred after the prisoners set a diversionary fire.[44] The fire department was summoned and it quickly put out the fire. However, the next morning, a fire broke out in the same room. In the light of day, the guards found a braided cord made from bedclothes tied to the top of a ladder which dangled on the outer side of the wall. Morning roll call turned up four prisoners missing.[45] This last break was attributed to "general neglect" by the prison authorities who were unable even to determine the number and names of the prisoners who were missing for several hours. Neglect was evidenced by the guards allowing a ladder to remain in the prison. Want of proper vigilance by the guards was decidedly a contributing factor.[46]

Escape During Transport

A group of 300 prisoners was being transported from Alton Prison to Johnson's Island, in Lake Erie. They were guarded by four companies (200 men) under the command of the incompetent Maj. W. B. Mason. One of the prisoners was a "notorious guerrilla chief," Colonel Faulkner. The Confederate colonel had publicly declared his intent to escape, and he carried out his plan. After his escape, Faulkner was believed to have written a letter using an assumed name to a prisoner still being held in Alton.[47]

Some Prisoners Keep Trying

Col. J. B. Douglas complained to Lt. Col. F. A. Dick, the provost marshal general, that John T. Singleton, an officer in Price's army and "a very bad and dangerous man" had been released from prison.

> He made his escape from Alton and was rearrested at Liberty, in this State. I know him well. He is a bad man and should not be set at liberty.... For God's sake do not let out the worst men and keep the poor ignorant boys in prison.

Colonel Dick forwarded the information to Col. William Hoffman in Washington, D.C., because Colonel Hildebrand, the commander at Alton, reported that Singleton had been released along with 90 others on Hoffman's orders. Dick thought it unwise for prisoners to be released on Hoffman's orders, and that he (Dick) had a better understanding of the charges and evidence against them. He warned Hoffman that "pretended Union men from Missouri are constantly applying for release of bad rebels."[48]

Escapes Continue

Six escapes were reported during August 1863, two in October 1863, four in November 1863, and 23 in December of that year. During 1864, one or more prisoners escaped monthly.[49] Undoubtedly, either security was lax, guards were accepting bribes, or the prisoners were extremely cunning and adept at escaping from their confinement.

Smallpox Decimates Prison Population

Those prisoners who managed to escape Alton Military Prison were among the fortunate few. Most of those who remained would die of smallpox and other diseases brought on by malnutrition, bad water, and overcrowding. Even before stricken by smallpox, prisoners were dying of pneumonia because, as reported by Freedley, of their "broken-down condition upon arrival, the change of climate and living, scarcity of clothing and bedding, together with the dampness of a portion of the prison."[50]

No one knows for certain just how many prisoners died at Alton. It has been estimated that between 1,534 and 2,218 inmates of the Alton Military Prison died during a smallpox epidemic alone. That epidemic began on October 15, 1862, and continued through September 1864. The death rate was six-10 daily. Among the dead were some 287 civilians and a number of Federal soldiers. Conditions were so bad and there were so many deaths that the citizens of Alton finally demanded that the sick men be isolated on an island in the Mississippi River.[51]

Alton Prison Today

After the war, the old prison building was sold and most of the stone blocks were moved to become incorporated into new structures. The site was then leased by the owners to the city and it was converted into a public park and playground for children. A stack of limestone rocks near the corner of Broadway and William Street in downtown Alton is all that remains of the state's first penitentiary. A portion of a cell block was restored in 1973 as a monument and a historical marker was placed by the state. In 1974, archaeologists from Northwestern University uncovered five brick-paved cells at the site. The cells were built back-to-back against a central wall. Measurements confirmed that each cell was only 4 feet by 7 feet 4 inches. From each cell, there was a 24-inch door opening through an outer wall two feet thick. In 1975, the site of Alton Prison was added to the National Register of Historic Places.[52]

II

Camp Chase, Columbus, Ohio

...it is almost a miracle that anyone could remain there for twenty months without losing his reason.
   — T. H. Henry, prisoner, Company E, Second Kentucky Infantry[1]

Location: Columbus, Ohio. **Established:** 1861. **Type:** barracks surrounded by high fence. **Kind of Prisoners:** Enlisted men and officers, plus officers' black servants, and political prisoners. **Capacity:** 3,500–4,000. **Most Held at One Time:** 9,423.[2] **Known Escapes:** 37.[3] **Number of Deaths:** 2,260.[4]

History

Camp Chase, located near Columbus, Ohio, was named for Secretary of the Treasury and former Ohio governor Salmon P. Chase.[5]

The camp was established as a training center for Federal troops, then converted to a prison camp for Confederate prisoners of war.

The Prisoners

The first prisoners were members of the 23rd Virginia Regiment who had been captured in the Kanawha Valley of western Virginia. They arrived July 5, 1861, but were soon exchanged.[6] According to one source, when the prison first opened, the Confederate officers imprisoned there were allowed to go into the town of Columbus, register at hotels, and receive money and food. A few even attended sessions of the Ohio Senate.

The new prisoners were an oddity, and citizens paid to take tours of the camp, which became an overnight tourist attraction. However, after a great number of prisoners were transferred from Island No. 10, the privileges of the Confederate officers were curtailed, and many of the officers were transferred to Johnson's Island.[7]

By July 1862, there were 1,500 prisoners confined at Camp Chase.[8] By December 1863, that number had increased to 2,448. There had been 28 deaths during October of that year.[9]

The Facilities

In August 1864, after an inspection of the camp, B. R. Cowen, adjutant general of the state of Ohio, reported:

This camp is situated on the National road, five miles west of this city [Columbus, Ohio], and consists of wooden barracks for the prisoners as well as for the garrison. The prisoners are surrounded by tight board fences twelve feet in height, surmounted by a parapet for the sentinels, from which a full view of the entire inclosure is obtained and any unnecessary movement on the part of the prisoners is observed. The prison inclosures are lighted with coal oil lamps at night to guard against any unnecessary collection of prisoners or any concerted efforts to overpower the guards. The prison buildings are similar in construction and material to the temporary military prisons in the Northern States, and, in my opinion, are as safe as wooden buildings can be made.[10]

A drawing of the camp showing the location of the buildings was done by A. Ruger, Company H, 88th O.V.I, and a map showing where the prison was appeared in the *Confederate Veteran*.[11]

Conditions Inside the Camp

Capt. Milton Asbury Ryan was captain of Company G, 8th Mississippi Regiment (the Tolson Guard). He survived the battle of Franklin, Tennessee (November 30, 1864). When the Federal troops retreated to Nashville, the Confederates followed, and during the fighting of December 15–16, 1864, Captain Ryan was wounded in the right thigh. He was taken to a house that was being used as a hospital. Gangrene set in and he underwent surgery twice. Once he recovered, he was taken to Camp Chase.[12]

Captain Ryan had vivid, unforgettable memories of Camp Chase. He described a wall 16 feet high. He also mentioned that a partitioning wall divided the camp into two main areas, known as prison No. 1 and No. 2, each of which covered about 7 or 8 acres, and each portion held approximately 4,000 prisoners. The gates to the two prisons stood side by side and opened into each prison. Upon his arrival, Ryan and others were asked to take the oath of allegiance, and if they did, they would be assigned to Prison No. 2, where rations were plentiful, and prisoners there were allowed sufficient blankets and heat.[13]

When a group of prisoners who had been captured at Nashville, Tennessee, arrived at Camp Chase, they were almost dead from lack of water after being confined inside boxcars for four or five days. The hydrants at the camp were frozen, and the prisoners had already eaten all the snow on the ground. The new arrivals were so desperate for water they lay down on the ground as close to the deadline as possible, and tried to scoop snow from across the line. The guards shot any who approached the deadline for any reason.[14]

Barracks

Captain Ryan described the barracks provided for the prisoners at Camp Chase as similar to those at Camp Douglas. In each building, three narrow bunks were stacked one above the other. Two men could sleep in one bunk. There was no bedding or straw, so the men slept on bare boards. No fires were allowed in the stoves at night, and many did not have sufficient clothing to protect them from the cold, which sometimes reached zero and below. They had no chairs or benches but had to sit on the floor. Barely enough food was given the men to keep them alive, and they were hungry all the time. One half loaf of bread, 8 inches in length, was divided between 8 men. In addition, they received one tablespoonful of navy beans and a piece of pickled beef or salt pork. The food was cooked outside the barracks and handed in a tin cup through the window.[15]

T. D. Henry, of Company E, Basil Duke's Regiment, Second Kentucky Cavalry, thought conditions were bad under Commandant De Land, but they got even worse when he was replaced by Col. B. J. Sweet as commandant with Capt. Webb Sponable as inspector of prisoners. The whole camp was rearranged, and "starvation was carried on quite systematically." Rations were reduced, and for even the slightest offense, rations were stopped entirely — a favorite punishment.[16]

Punishment

T. D. Henry, who was captured at Salenville, Ohio, with Gen. John Hunt Morgan, recalled the severe punishment handed out at Camp Chase. Although rations were of "good quality and quantity," he recalled "various and severe punishments which the commandant of the camp (Col. C. V. De Land) saw fit to inflict." If a prisoner bribed a guard or managed to escape by other means and was recaptured, he would be "tied up by the thumbs" and hung so that his toes would barely touch the ground. Henry saw men punished in this manner grow "deathly sick" and "vomit all over themselves," until their heads fell "forward and almost every sign of life became extinct; the ends of their thumbs would burst open;" but the surgeon standing nearby would feel the pulse of the prisoner and declare that the prisoner could "stand it a little longer." If this punishment did not induce the prisoner to reveal who had helped him escape, he was thrown into an "iron-clad dungeon," 10 by 10 feet square, with only a tiny window. After a prisoner had been so confined for 40 to 50 days, the smell from the hole in the floor that served as a privy was enough to kill him.[17]

Another means of punishment was to chain a 64-pound ball to the prisoner's leg, with a chain so short (about 28 inches) that the wearer had to carry the ball in his hand, or get "someone to pull it in a little wagon while they walked at the side. Some of the prisoners wore the ball and chain for as long as six months.[18]

Many prisoners tried to escape Camp Chase by tunneling, and the guards were always on the lookout for a tunnel. On one occasion, according to T. D. Henry, a tunnel was discovered under the barracks of Cluke's regiment from the 8th Kentucky Cavalry. Without even trying to find out who had dug the tunnel, the commandant had the whole regiment punished. They were ordered to form in a column of eight deep. A guard was placed around them and ordered to shoot the first man who sat down. This began just after sunup. By 2 P.M., a man who had just returned from the smallpox hospital and was still weak from the illness, fell to the ground. The guard shot him and killed him. Before this punishment ended, one man was dead, and two others were wounded, one so badly that his arm had to be amputated later.[19]

One of the "mildest" forms of punishments was riding the "horse." A piece of lumber, two inches wide, was shaved down until it was only half an inch thick on top. Underneath, legs 17 feet long were attached. For the slightest offense, prisoners were placed on top of the horse, with their feet dangling down, for hours. The guards would tease them and say, "I'll give you a pair of spurs," which was really a bucket of sand tied to each foot to increase the discomfort.[20] With that kind of daily treatment, the prisoners plotted and planned, defied orders, and risked their lives to escape.

Unrest at Camp Chase

In May 1862, Col. Henry B. Carrington, of the 18th Infantry, reported that the prisoners at Camp Chase "were threatening insurrection." For some reason, the guards were absent and only a few citizens remained to guard the prisoners. At the request of governors Tod and Dennison, Carrington took quick action and wisely moved some of his men from the 18th Infantry. Because he believed the situation so desperate, Carrington had spent the night at the prison, and probably averted an escape.[21]

When a fight broke out between two prisoners, the guard became alarmed and thought the prisoners were preparing to break out. After warning the crowd that had gathered, he fired and William Jones, of Ritchie County, Virginia, was shot and killed on November 1, 1862. Maj. Peter Zinn ordered an investigation, and concluded that Jones was a mere "looker on" and his death was regretted but the sentinel could not be blamed.[22]

Security Tightened

The fear of escapes may have resulted in several shootings of prisoners in the fall of 1863. Several rules were posted, and disobedience of the rules would results in the guards enforcing them with bullets.

> First. Not to allow prisoners to approach the prison walls nearer than ten feet. If any attempt to do so to halt them, warning them of the infringement of the rule, and if they persisted in approaching the wall to fire upon them.
> Second. Not to allow prisoners to collect together in large numbers; when they did so to order them to disperse, and if they disobeyed to fire upon them.
> Third. No lights allowed in their quarters after taps. If any were observed the sentinel should warn the mess in the building where it occurred to put it out, and if not obeyed to fire into the buildings.[23]

Guards with loaded guns were instructed to shoot to kill for any infraction of the prison rules. The prisoners were informed of this rule.[24] Yet, many prisoners preferred to chance being shot. Prison officials believed that the strict rules and the severity in enforcing the orders which resulted in subsequent shootings were justified because of the "apprehension which prevailed at the time of a revolt of the prisoners.[25]

Samuel Lemley, a citizen from Virginia who was confined in Prison No. 2 at Camp Chase, was fired upon by a sentinel on the parapet at 9 o'clock on the evening of September 16, 1863. The cartridge contained "one round ball and three buckshot." The ball passed through his right arm, fracturing the humerus. Two of the three buckshot lodged in his arm, and the third passed through the arm. Surgeon G. W. Fitzpatrick attended the patient in about 30 minutes after he had been shot. He noted his pulse as feeble, and his skin cold and clammy. He dressed the wounds, but the prisoner died after midnight on the morning of September 17, four hours after he was shot.[26] No circumstances surrounding the shooting were given by the doctor. Perhaps the guards were just "trigger happy."

It was known that the inmates of Block No. 3 were digging tunnels. They had been warned not to delay putting out their lights after the "tattoo" had been sounded. On November 16, 1863, the lights of mess 49 were still on at 11 p.m., when sentinel John White called and told them to put out the lights. Either the prisoners disregarded his order or did not hear him. White fired into the building and killed Pvt. Hamilton McCarroll, Company B, Welcker's Tennessee Cavalry, instantly.[27] Prisoners testified that because it had been extremely cold that night, McCarroll had opened the door to the stove to build up the fire in order to warm himself. He left the stove door open a minute while filling a kettle with water, which was why, according to C. S. Barnes, Company A, 4th Tennessee Cavalry, McCarroll did not hear the guard's order, "lights out." McCarroll was shot in the chest and died.[28] Another prisoner, H. P. Hathcock, Company B, 16th Tennessee Infantry, stated that McCarroll knew it was against orders to light the fire at night, but he believed that since McCarroll had no blanket, he was just trying to get warm.[29]

A month later on December 19, sentinel Frank Allen ordered those in mess No. 10 of Block 1 to extinguish their lights between 10 p.m. and midnight. After repeated warnings, Allen fired his rifle into the building and wounded prisoner Henry Hupman, a private from Company C, 20th Virginia Cavalry, in the arm. Several days later, the prisoner had to have his arm amputated and then he died.[30]

An investigation was launched because of the five prisoners who were shot in the months between September and December 1863. These events occurred while Col. W. Wallace, of the 15th Ohio, was in charge of the camp. The investigation revealed that Henry Hupman, who was wounded at about 9 o'clock at night, lay in his bed and suffered for a half hour before permission was granted for his fellow prisoners to bind his wound. He was not treated by the camp surgeon until the next day. Afterward, Col. William Hoffman then ordered that if additional shootings of prisoners occurred, an investigation was to be made immediately and a full report submitted.[31]

Richardson reported that during the summer months of 1864 a "very insubordinate spirit has prevailed among the prisoners for four or five weeks, manifesting itself in combinations to resist the prison rules and to escape from prison." Disobedience continued, and two more prisoners were fired upon by the guards for refusing to conform to a rule which forbade prisoners to throw refuse of any kind into a ditch inside the walls. Joseph W. Rutter, Company E, 23rd Virginia Cavalry was shot through the arm, and Mahlon Hurst, of Company C, 12th Tennessee Cavalry, was an innocent bystander who was shot in the thigh by the same ball that wounded Rutter. As a result Hurst's leg had to be amputated.[32]

Another prisoner, W. L. Pope, may have been attempting to escape. He was shot in the evening, about 8 o'clock, after the sentinel had ordered him away from the gate several times. The prisoner did not reply and was shot. Henry Glover, a citizen-prisoner from West Virginia, stated that Pope was standing at the gate for "looking into the key room.[33] Grover heard the guard's orders, and shortly thereafter the shot. Reportedly, Pope was attempting to get permission to burn a light because of a sick man in his barracks.[34]

Insubordination was the cause of the shooting of Pvt. Junius Cloyd, also with the 7th Tennessee Cavalry. His injury was so severe that it required amputation, according to a report submitted by the prison commandant, W. P. Richardson. In July 1864, Cloyd was shot in the left leg when he refused to remain in place at roll call. Rather than following orders to cross over a ditch after his name was called and remain there until the roll call was finished, guards claimed that Cloyd tried to remain with those whose names had not yet been called.[35]

To further tighten security, Hoffman ordered Richardson to be sure that in the future the guards were also armed with revolvers. Hoffman criticized Richardson for the lack of guards at the gate.[36]

B. R. Cowen reported to the governor of Ohio that when he inspected the prison he found "the discipline and morale" of the regiment who served as guards to be good, and their "vigilance is evidenced by the fact that while efforts to escape are often made they are very seldom successful."[37] Many attempts were made to escape from Camp Chase, but most were unsuccessful.

However, according to the monthly reports from Camp Chase, seven men escaped in September 1862, two escaped in January 1863, and one escaped in March 1863.[38]

Prisoner J. Coleman Anderson described how ladders were constructed from "planks taken from our bunks and hidden conveniently under the barracks." Prisoners armed themselves with stones, knives and forks, and, on a Sunday afternoon during one of the religious services held in the streets, the prisoners were going to attempt a breakout. However, they noticed that the guard had been doubled, so they abandoned their escape plan.[39]

Often the escape plans were thwarted before they could even get underway and leaked to prison officials by a spy among the prisoners. Col. August H. Poten, assistant commandant of Camp Chase, reported that there were frequent reports of conspiracies among the prisoners. Detectives working inside the prison reported that a conspiracy existed among the prisoners in connection with the Vallandigham sympathizers to overpower the guard and break out. In many places there was evidence that there had been digging under the walls. Guns were found in the possession of the prisoners, and mutinous conduct was increasing.[40]

Desperate to escape, the prisoners began using more drastic methods. On November 5, 1863, a group of prisoners rushed the guards as they entered the front gate. The sentries began firing randomly into the crowd. One prisoners was killed and several were wounded, and the escape attempt was foiled.[41]

On July 4, 1864, a number of prisoners tried to escape through the main gate. On that morning, only two guards, armed with muskets, were stationed when the gate was opened to allow a cart to enter. The 21 prisoners were soon recaptured with only one injury. Pvt. Ezekiel A. Cloyd, Company H, 7th Regiment Tennessee Cavalry, was shot in the right arm above the elbow, and was given medical treatment for the wound.[42]

The Easy Way Out

A civilian prisoner made his escape the easy way. A. J. Morey, editor of the *Cynthiana, Kentucky, News* had been incarcerated because of his political views. He learned that his wife was ill, probably from the shock of his arrest, and he pretended to feign "repentance," in order to get a release on parole. With a parole in hand, Morey traveled to his home in Cynthiana to find that his wife was dead and had been buried for four days. Considering the fact that he had been "dragged to Ohio" for his political opinions "in violation of the Constitutions of both the United States and Kentucky," he decided to take the opportunity to escape. He made his way to Memphis, Tennessee, where he wrote a scathing article to the newspaper there about the conditions in Camp Chase prison.[43]

Camp Chase Today

Now incorporated into the city of Columbus, nothing remains of Camp Chase except a cemetery for the Confederate soldiers who died there. The first prisoners were interred in the City Cemetery at Columbus. In 1863, a cemetery was established near the prison, and the remains of those in the City Cemetery removed to the new cemetery where, combined with later burials, the number reaches over 2,000. Camp Chase Confederate Cemetery is located on Sullivant Avenue. On June 7, 1902, a memorial was placed in the cemetery. It is a large arch made of granite blocks with a bronze statue of a Confederate soldier on top to guard those buried in the cemetery. Inscribed on the monument are the words: "2260 Confederate Soldiers of the War 1861–1865 Buried in this Enclosure," and beneath the arch is inscribed "AMERICANS."

In 1906, white marble headstones were placed on all the graves.[44]

III

Camp Douglas, Chicago, Illinois

*Many of the prisoners have escaped lately by tunneling but that is about
"played out" now for they are raising all the barrax [sic] 4 feet above ground.*
— Pvt. William D. Huff, A Prisoner's Diary, April 1864[1]

Location: Chicago, Illinois, near Lake Michigan. **Established:** February 1862. **Type:** wooden barracks enclosed by high fence. **Kind of Prisoners:** Confederate prisoners of war. **Capacity:** 6,000. **Total Number of Prisoners:** estimated at from 26,060 to 26,781 between 1862–1865.[2] **Most Held at One Time:** over 12,082 (December 1864).[3] **Known Escapes:** 317+.[4] **Nickname:** "80 acres of Hell."

History

Camp Douglas was originally created as a place to quarter and train Union troops from the Chicago area. The camp was located on part of "Oakenwald," the estate of Stephen A. Douglas, famous for his political debates with Abraham Lincoln. The camp was named in his honor. Camp Douglas was established to handle the influx of more than 15,000 Confederate prisoners captured at Fort Henry and Fort Donelson.[5]

The Prison Facilities

The camp covered 60 acres and was divided by partitions to create compounds of various sizes. Each of these compounds was named according to its purpose. Garrison Square, which contained about 20 acres, was lined on all four sides by quarters for officers and men, and had a level parade ground in its center. Hospital Square covered only 10 acres, and was the location of the prison hospital. Whiteoak Square was originally the prison of the army post, but was renamed Prison Square and enlarged when the facility changed over to a prison camp. Prison Square contained 64 barracks, 24 feet by 90 feet in dimension. Part of each barracks was set aside for a kitchen. The rest of the room held tiers of bunks along the walls. On an average, 95 men were housed in each barrack, but eventually that number increased to 189 men.[6]

The Prisoners

In addition to captured Confederate soldiers, five women and a child were imprisoned at Camp Douglas in 1862. The camp also had an assortment of nationalities:

Mexicans, Spaniards, half-blooded and full-blooded Cherokee Indians, full-blooded Negroes, as well as quadroons and octoroons.[7]

One of the first prisoners was Milton Asbury Ryan, a captain of Company G, 8th Mississippi Regiment. Captain Ryan saw the inside of more than one prison. He was captured at Fort Donelson on February 15, 1862. These prisoners were transport on old steamboats to Cairo, Illinois. After eight days on the boats, the prisoners were herded like "so many cattle and horses" into cattle cars in the middle of a blizzard. Since they were the first prisoners to arrive in Chicago destined for Camp Douglas, the group was a novelty, and thousands of people turned out to watch them. Followed by a crowd of people, the prisoners were marched from the train depot two miles to Camp Douglas Prison through ice-cold mud. Curiosity brought the crowds back to visit the prison every day until an order was issued to prohibit it. Someone built an observatory just outside the prison walls, and it was crowded with people peering over the fence at the prisoners all day.[8]

Famous Prisoners

Camp Douglas held many famous persons. Henry Morton Stanley survived his incarceration and became a journalist known for his statement, "Doctor Livingstone, I presume."[9]

Bates Washington, one of the prisoners, was related to our first president, George Washington. Sam Houston Jr. of Texas was also a prisoner. The camp also held sons of governors and congressmen, as well as sons of southern judges and politicians.[10]

Problems with the Prison Site

The first group of 3,200 prisoners that arrived in February 1862 was soon followed by thousands more. Initially, the prison was adequate to accommodate them. The prisoners were given stoves and cooking utensils and clothing, and they could purchase items from the sutler. However, by summer of 1862, the prison held 9,000 prisoners, and the conditions had deteriorated.

Even the prison guards deemed the site unsuitable. Col. Joseph H. Tucker reported that "the structure and form of this camp is very unsuitable for the confinement of prisoners...." Tucker was aware that the "insecurity of the fences is a constant temptation to the prisoners to attempt to escape, and numerous props and irregularities on the inside afford ready means of climbing over quickly."[11]

Situated on low ground, the camp flooded every time it rained. During the winter months, the ground, when not frozen, was "like a cattle-yard," according to Stanley.[12] The unsuitability of the site was noted by many Federal officials. Col. R. C. Wood, assistant surgeon general of the U.S. Army, ordered an inspection of the conditions at Camp Douglas. That inspection was done and a report made by Edward D. Kittoe, a surgeon with the United States Volunteers:

> The ground is low and flat, rendering drainage imperfect and difficult to effect. Its proximity to Lake Michigan, and consequent exposure to the cold, damp winds from off this large body of water, with the flat, marshy character of the soil, must of necessity

create a tendency to disease of the respiratory organs, which ... is clearly demonstrated by reference to reports of disease prevalent during the month of December.

During the winter months, the ground was covered with snow, and the foggy conditions of spring added to the cases of illness.[13] A report filed in January 1864 described the barracks which had housed Gen. John Hunt Morgan's men as "pre-eminently filthy."[14]

Morbidity and Mortality

Exposure to adverse weather conditions, coupled with the filth from bodily waste that seeped through the flooded grounds led to a high mortality and morbidity rate. In December 1863, Surgeon Kittoe reported, out of 5,616 prisoners 2,011 had been sick in the hospital, and there were 57 deaths (a 28 percent ratio). The prisoners' barracks were overcrowded, and there was a general "disregard of personal cleanliness," which led to an increase in the number of sick prisoners. Kittoe stated in no uncertain terms that the site and surroundings of Camp Douglas made it "highly objectionable and unfit for the use to which it has been appropriated...." He believed that even with a large expenditure of money and effort, the situation of poor drainage could not be overcome.[15]

Sustaining themselves on already meager rations, the prisoners faced starvation when their rations were cut even further in May of 1864.

Present Issue	Reduction	Amount Proposed
Soft bread, 18 ounces	2	16
Corn meal, 18 ounces	2	16
Hominy or rice, 100 men 8 pounds	8	—
Sugar, 100 men 14 pounds	4	10
Rio coffee, 5 pounds, ground	2	3
Rio coffee, 7 pounds, raw	2	5
Tea, 18 ounces, 100 men	18	—
Soup, 4 ounces (probably meant 4 pounds)	4	—
Adamantine candles, 5 candles 100 men	5	—
Tallow candles, 6 candles 100 men	6	—

Maj. L. C. Skinner, commissary of prisoners, recommended that rations of hominy, tea, and candles be entirely omitted in his proposal of May 10, 1864.[16]

Prisoners were deprived of clothing to discourage escapes. Blankets were confiscated. The weakest prisoners froze to death during the bitter cold winter of 1864. During a four-month period, 1,091 prisoners died, the heaviest total for any period in the camp's history and equal to the high death rate at Andersonville, Georgia, from February to May 1864.[17] When Dr. A. M. Clark, the medical inspector of prisons, inspected Camp Douglas, he noted a number of situations that needed improvement. Clark charged that the number of deaths was not reported properly. He reported that 1,200 prisoners were without blankets, and most were filthy.[18]

Cruel Treatment and Harsh Punishment

In addition to the harsh environmental conditions of the camp, the guards made life for the prisoners even worse. These guards, called "Hospital Rats" by Captain Ryan, were "overbearing and cruel in the extreme." They seemed to delight in making the prisoners suffer. On top of that, even for trivial offenses, prisoners would be punished in cruel and inhuman ways. One method of punishment was to put the prisoner in a guardhouse made of white oak logs, with only one small window. Inside was a pit 8 to 10 feet deep. It was entered by a trap door from which several steps led down into the dark hole. Ryan was put into the hole for some minor offense, that of trying to get a bucket of water at the hospital well while the hydrant that normally served the prisoners was out of order. He was confined in the hole for four days. It was pitch dark and he could see nothing. When he was finally removed by the same guard who had put him there, the guard cursed him.[19]

Riding the "Mule"

Another form of punishment were to make the prisoner ride one of Morgan's mules. This was not an animal but a wooden frame high off the ground (like a sawbuck used by carpenters, only higher off the ground). Prisoners were forced to sit astride the "mule" for hours, unless the unfortunate man fainted or fell off from pain and exhaustion. Sometimes weights were tied to the prisoner's feet. Fortunately for Captain Ryan, he was exchanged in September 1862, to rejoin his regiment in Mississippi.[20]

Escape Attempts

Early on in the prison's history, efforts were made to prevent means of escape. Lt. Col. William Hoffman, commissary general of prisoners, believed that the prisoners should not be allowed even small sums of money, because they could combine it and amass enough "to tempt disloyal persons to assist in their escape." He decreed that the prisoners' money should be held and the amount of purchases made should be subtracted from their account.[21]

Other preventive measures involved the number of the guard and their placement. In July 1862, the guard detail was one captain, seven lieutenants, 13 sergeants, 24 corporals and 382 privates. In addition, a patrol was on duty every night outside the fence which ran a distance of three miles.[22]

Those who even tried to escape risked their lives. As early as April 1862, orders were issued that any prisoner of war who attempted to escape and was recaptured, would be "put in close confinement in a prison or under guard."[23] At that time, there were 6,000 prisoners at Camp Douglas, with 1,500 guards. Governor Richard Yates believed that the prison could accommodate 1,500 more, but that the number of guards should also be increased.[24]

Despite all efforts by prison officials through tougher rules and regulations, nothing curtailed the efforts exerted by the prisoners to escape. Even during the time when prisoners were being exchanged frequently, escapes occurred. Federal adjutant general Lorenzo Thomas reported to Colonel Hoffman that he had learned from General Negley of a "number of rebel prisoners from Camps Chase and Douglas," who had been discovered in Columbia, Tennessee. The escaped prisoners had been aided by Mr. Smith of Chicago, and by the sutler at Camp Douglas who sold them "clothing for disguises." Thomas demanded an inquiry into the facts of this matter.

For the period of June 19 to June 27, 1862, no report exists, but there had been several escapes before that time, and many afterward. Undoubtedly, the prison did not keep good records of the escapes and escape attempts. Col. Joseph H. Tucker, commander of the 69th Illinois Volunteers, replaced Colonel Cameron as camp commandant. Tucker was asked to submit a list with the name and dates and the number of all prisoners who had escaped, but he was unable to do so. "I do not find any records on file from which I can furnish immediately the number and names of those who previously escaped." He promised to set up a system to record minute details of the prisoners of war held at Camp Douglas.[25]

Col. William Hoffman visited Camp Douglas to investigate previous escapes, probably those who had made their way to Tennessee. He found that Colonel Tucker had employed two detectives to go undercover as prisoners. The detectives discovered that the escapees had been aided by the sutler who sold clothing to the prisoners. Hoffman criticized the running of the camp and reported that there was "scarcely a record of any kind left," which made it difficult to determine who had been prisoners and what had become of them. He also noted that the camp was in "deplorable condition," which would take much work and money to make "inhabitable."[26] Certainly, poor recordkeeping would make it hard to call the roll and determine if all the prisoners were present, or if some had escaped.

Prisoners were often assisted in their escape attempts by some of the guards. A Lieutenant Higgins, of the 23rd Illinois Regiment, was charged with "aiding or attempting to aid" prisoners to escape. He was exempt from punishment, a fact which Colonel Hoffman believed encouraged others to engage in the same practice without fear.[27]

Twenty-one prisoners escaped on the night of July 23, 1862. According to the report filed by Colonel Tucker, a musket was fired by the sentinel at post No. 57, and a call for the guard was issued. Other shots were soon heard, and the soldiers outside the walls were alerted. A group of prisoners rushed the fence at post No. 57, and with "ladders constructed rudely of boards with cleats nailed upon them" tried to scale the walls. The sentinels fired upon the prisoners, but some escaped. In addition, a hole was found which had been dug under the fence at another point, and the sentinel, Pvt. Charles White, of Company C, 67th Regiment Illinois Volunteers, was gone. So were several prisoners. It was believed that the sentinel had helped the prisoners escape. Tucker concluded with a postscript informing Colonel Hoffman that "some of the prisoners who escaped last night are being retaken."[28]

In addition to the guards, civilians helped prisoners escape, sometimes inadvertently. During the summer of 1862, Dr. L. D. Boone was head of a committee of citizens who had "unrestricted communication" with the prisoners. This allowed Dr. Boone to distribute "considerable sums of money" to the prisoners. This was accomplished through a paroled prisoner who was allowed to visit the city of Chicago at will. Dr. Boone was arrested for giving money to a prisoner at Camp Douglas after the prisoner used the money to bribe a sentinel and escape. Dr. Boone claimed that he had no knowledge of a new regulation that went into effect May 2 prohibiting the prisoners from having any money. Any funds sent to them were to be placed in charge of the commanding officer.[29]

In October 1863, 26 prisoners escaped. They cut a hole through the plank floor of their barracks which stood close to an outside wall, and dug about four feet into the sink (latrines or toilets). From there, they dug under the fence to the outside, a total of 10 feet, all underground. This was done right under the guards.[30]

Repairs being made to the buildings and fences, and the installation of sewer lines and water pipes provided situations for prisoners to escape. Because of the construction, there were holes through the fences, and openings in the ground. A large number of workmen were needed to complete the repairs, and they passed freely among the prisoners. As a result, the prison commander, Col. Charles V. De Land reported that late in 1863 several prisoners "slid out the holes in the dark, have passed out as workmen, and in a variety of ways have eluded the vigilance of the guards.[31]

Colonel De Land, reported that several prisoners had been killed, and several others wounded, yet "some escapes could not be prevented." He was hopeful that once the new fence was completed escape would be "next to impossible." With the new fence, new sewers, and new water pipes, he believed that Camp Douglas would be "so safe and secure that not even money can work a man out." He thought that tunneling would not be tried very often. Yet, even with the improvements, pine-board facilities at Camp Douglas provided a "nest of hiding places," and it was not the "safe and compact prison" afforded by more permanent structures.[32]

Escapes were inevitable because there were not enough guards and the ongoing construction gave prisoners the opportunity to pass out as workmen, or to slip out of the holes unnoticed. De Land hoped that once all the new construction was completed, the prison would be secure.[33] This was not the case, and Colonel De Land's worst nightmare was about to become reality.

On October 13, 1863, Colonel De Land reported that he had lost 12 prisoners on Sunday and Monday nights, and that he suspected "collusion and bribery." Because some prisoners had escaped, the guards were nervous. On October 14, guards fired several shots at prisoners for trivial offenses.[34]

The number of escapes from the camp for the three-month period ending November 18, 1863, totaled 61.[35] After 151 escapes during his tenure, De Land had the worst record of any of the previous prison commandants. De Land tried to prohibit visitors because they might aid escapes. He was hampered by the small number of guards which was not sufficient to patrol the prison as well as search the city for escapees.[36]

After 75 prisoners managed to tunnel under the walls in November 1863, eight companies of the Veteran Reserve Corps and a regiment of Michigan sharpshooters were sent to the camp.[37]

The White Oak Dungeon

Confining those who attempted to escape in the White Oak Dungeon did not prevent the prisoners from trying to leave their terrible prison again. Dr. A. M. Clark described the White Oak Dungeon as "utterly unfit for that purpose." A small window gave the only light the room had. He found 24 prisoners confined there in a room, about 18 feet square, a room only large enough for three or four prisoners. Some of them in the dungeon had petitioned the prison commandant to release them and promised they would not attempt to escape again.[38]

Morgan's Men Lead Escapes

Some of the men from Brig. Gen. John Hunt Morgan's Confederate cavalry were often confined to the White Oak Dungeon. They had been captured in Morgan's unprecedented, unauthorized thousand-mile raid through Kentucky, Indiana and Ohio in July 1863. Morgan's Raiders were a breed apart.[39] A picture taken of a dozen of Morgan's men at Camp Douglas in August 1863 shows a fierce, rough-looking group dressed in a variety of clothing and wearing an odd assortment of hats.[40]

It was from that small room that 26 of Hunts' cavalrymen made a daring escape. At the end of October 1863, the prisoners cut a hole through the plank floor of the White Oak Dungeon, and dug about four feet into the sink. Then they dug another 10 feet underground until they were outside the fence. The prison commandant did not know what they had used for tools or how they were obtained.[41]

Another Escape by Morgan's Men

On December 3, 1863, the prison commandant reported a "serious break of the Morgan prisoners in this camp" that had taken place the night before.[42]

Morgan's raiders had been confined to Barrack No. 3, in White Oak Square. This particular unit was about 40 feet form the center of the building and only about 18 feet from the cook house. They dug a tunnel from the barracks to the outside fence, beginning with a small hole just under the frozen ground. They hid the dirt from the tunnel under the floors of the barracks and the cook houses. The tunnel was concealed during the day by a board covered with about 6 inches of dirt, and although the barracks were searched each week, the entrance to the tunnel was not discovered. The prisoners waited until a dark and foggy night, when the visibility of the guards was limited. They began to escape about 8 P.M. and continued at intervals until about 9:30 P.M., when an outside guard discovered the escape and sounded the alarm. Prison commandant De Land reported that, as far as he could determine, about 100 prisoners passed through the tunnel to the outside.[43]

A detailed report was filed by Brig. Gen. William W. Orme on January 20, 1864. Orme did not blame the prison guards or officials, but he did remark that the camp was "badly arranged." He recommended that the prisoners' barracks be removed from the southwest corner so that all the prisoners would be confined to one area.[44]

De Land sent out a mounted search party, and enlisted the help of the city police and military provost marshal's deputies, as well as his own detectives. They were successful in capturing a "large number." Those that were caught were found to have been entirely outfitted with civilian clothes given them by sympathetic friends on the outside. De Land telegraphed warnings to Detroit, Cincinnati, and Louisville to be on the lookout for the approximately 50 escapees that still remained at large.

Although there had been eight tunnels under the fences, only two attempts had been successful, De Land reported. To prevent future tunnels, he ordered the space under the barracks and cook houses to be filled up completely to the floor joists with dirt, so that the evidence from tunneling could no longer be concealed in this manner. Col. William Hoffman ordered a "strict investigation" into the escape.[45]

James Henry Shore was one of those in Camp Douglas at the time of the tunnel. A Yadkin County boy, James had been drafted and sent to Tennessee to join General Longstreet's Confederate forces. Captured at the Battle of Chickamauga in September 1863, Shore and other captive prisoners of war were marched to Strawberry Plains, near Knoxville, Tennessee. The prisoners were loaded into cattle cars and transported to Chicago's Camp Douglas. He often told his children stories about the hard life at Camp Douglas, and of trying to exist on a bare minimum of food, scanty clothing, and cold quarters. Disease was rampant in the camp and many died from not only disease but also from the cold and malnutrition.[46]

Shore described the barracks as having wooden floors about three feet off the ground, although the outside sheeting came down to the ground. Some of the prisoners dug a tunnel under the barracks by working at night, using anything they could find. They piled the dirt under the floor. Once the tunnel was complete beyond the prison fence, hundreds of prisoners escaped before being discovered by the guards. James Henry was not so fortunate. As a result of the escape, the guards tore off the sheeting boards from all the barracks from the floor to the ground so that the area underneath the structures was visible. This also made the barracks much colder during the bitter winter months. Shore managed to stay alive and make his way back home to North Carolina. He had to ride on top of the railroad boxcars all the way to Virginia because they were overflowing with returning soldiers inside. In Greensboro, he walked to Salem (now part of Winston-Salem), where an innkeeper gave him the first good meal he had eaten in two years. Then, he walked 30 miles to his home near Boonville. He arrived home at last, tired, weak, filthy, and covered with lice. He weighed less than 100 pounds but he was alive.[47]

Prisoners Unite to Escape

During the winter of 1863–1864, some of the prisoners confined at Camp Douglas organized into a "Supreme Council of Seven." Many of the prisoners believed that their only chance for survival was to escape. Six or seven of Morgan's cavalrymen planned a massive escape for the spring of 1864. The "council" was composed of Clayton Anderson, Harmon Barlow, Ottway B. Novell, A. W. Cockrell, Winder Monroe, John H. Waller, and E. M. Headelston. Members of the group had to be recommended and voted on unanimously before being accepted. Once accepted the prisoner had to swear to secrecy on the Bible.[48] One of the members of the council stated that about 2,000 prisoners were involved in a plot, while R. T. Bean believed the number was closer to 1,500.[49] The prisoners planned to smash through the fence, and then to free the prisoners at Rock Island, Illinois, 120 miles away from Chicago. When the two groups of prisoners had united, they would move on to Georgia to stop Sherman's army.[50]

In May 1864, Col. B. J. Sweet, the commanding officer of Camp Douglas, reported to Colonel Hoffman that he had instructed his commissary of prisoners,

L. C. Skinner, not to issue candles, because they were mainly used "to tunnel out at night. They [the prisoners] cannot dig much without lights. When a hole is once commenced and kept concealed, they then make rapid progress in the loose sandy soil where the camp is located."[51]

Even without candles, prisoners continued to escape. On the evening of June 1, 1864, some prisoners tried to escape by breaking the lamps and breaking through the fence. When the guards tried to fire at the prisoners, only one of five guns fired. Another guard arrived with revolvers in hand and ended the escape attempt. None of the prisoners got out. After that, all guards were required to carry revolvers, since they were more dependable when the need arose.[52]

Two months later, on August 10, 1864, two prisoners were shot trying to escape. The week before, six prisoners from the working party in Garrison Square attempted to escape. Three were shot, one killed, and two caught. Only one escaped.[53]

In August 1864, Camp Douglas was equipped with two howitzers, and 50 rounds of ammunition for each gun. Assistant Adjutant General Robert N. Scott thought that was enough. Yet, Scott suggested in a letter to Colonel Hoffman that the garrison at Camp Douglas was "too weak for safety," and he recommended sending a regiment of reserves. In Scott's opinion, the way the camp was laid out, more troops were required to prevent the "possibility of an escape."[54]

The September 1864 Escape

The prisoners at Camp Douglas continued in their efforts. Sweet's detectives failed to uncover a large escape plot which was tried on September 27, 1864, The plan involved men from several different regiments, but was not betrayed or uncovered.[55] The break began about 10:00 P.M. when a group of 30 prisoners ran out of their barracks. One man threw a blanket over the light on the fence, and he was shot in the face. But his fellow conspirators rushed bravely on and attacked the fence with axes and hammers.[56] They rushed the fence and guards surrounding the prison square. Twelve prisoners escaped: Joseph E. Adams, Company E, 3rd Georgia Cavalry; Thomas C. Cunningham, Company C, 3rd Confederate (?) Cavalry; James A. Cox, Company H, 4th Alabama Cavalry; A. H. Green, Company A, 4th Alabama Cavalry; W. R. Lay, Company K, 4th Alabama Cavalry; Robert B. Landman, Company C, 10th Kentucky Infantry; Lewis H. Moore, Company D, 7th Florida Infantry; J. W. Plant, 2nd Arkansas Battery; William Sparkman, Company K, 4th Florida Infantry; Isom Stone, Company A, 10th Kentucky Infantry; Berry Sexton, Company B, 10th Kentucky Infantry; and John E. Young, Company D, 1st Kentucky Cavalry. Pvt. Moore was shot during the attempt and would probably die. Some of those involved in the attempt were captured, and "placed in irons by way of punishment."[57]

Following this escape, some of the harsher prison regulations were relaxed, and prisoners were allowed to receive some clothes from home.[58]

Eight escapes from Camp Douglas were noted in the monthly returns for September 1864.[59]

The October 1864 Escape

On October 28, 1864, a massive escape plot was carried out. Prisoners rushed the fence and the guards fired. According to the official report, 18 prisoners escaped, but were captured. Ten prisoners were wounded only slightly. Colonel Sweet, the camp commander, had little use for the effectiveness of rifles, and he would have used cannon on them. If he had, many would have been killed.[60] For the month of October, 17 escapes were reported.[61]

According to the *Chicago Tribune*, the guards, members of the 8th Volunteer Reserve Corps fired on 25 to 30 prisoners after they began an assault on the fence. The fence was breached and four men escaped before troops could seal the hole from the outside. One prisoner was wounded. The *Tribune* attributed the escape attempt to the decreased number of guards, since 800 of the 196th Pennsylvania had left that day. One of the leaders of the break was John Shackelford. Shackelford had been involved in escape attempts twice before and wound up in irons. This would be his third time in the prison dungeon.[62] Colonel Sweet was so angry that he retaliated against the prisoners by taking their extra blankets and clothing. Sweet continued to ask Colonel Hoffman for more detectives to uncover escape plots before they could be carried out.[63]

Plot by Sons of Liberty Foiled

The Sons of Liberty, also called the Knights of the Golden Circle, was a secret organization in the North composed of men who were sympathetic to the southern cause. Originally begun in the South during the 1850s, its purpose was to extend slavery. Later, the name was changed to Order of American Knights, and by 1864 it was known as the Sons of Liberty. Clement Laird Vallandigham, a lawyer and former U.S. congressman from Ohio, was the last known supreme commander.[64] He was arrested by Gen. Ambrose E. Burnside and accused of violating General Order No. 38, which prohibited declarations of sympathy for the enemy. Vallandigham was court-martialed and sentenced to imprisonment for the rest of the war. However, President Lincoln commuted his sentence to banishment to territory held by Confederates. One of the most prominent of the Copperheads—northern Democrats who opposed the war and favored peace—Vallandigham was made commander of the Sons of Liberty.[65]

A plot to attack Camp Douglas on election night was discovered which involved members of the Sons of Liberty. Before the plot could be carried out, Federal officials arrested "rebel officers, escaped prisoners of war, and citizens" on the night of November 6, 1864. Col. J. B. Sweet reported those who had been arrested and were now imprisoned in his camp: Col. George St. Leger Grenfell (John Hunt Morgan's adjutant general); J. T. Shanks (an escaped prisoner of war); Col. Vincent Marmaduke (brother to General Marmaduke); Brig. Gen. Charles Walsh (a member of the Sons of Liberty); Captain Cantrill (a member of Morgan's cavalry); and Charles Travers. Travers and Cantrill were arrested at the home of Charles Walsh, where loaded guns and rifles were found. Judge Buckner "Buck" S. Morris, the treasurer of the Sons of Liberty, was arrested for helping Shanks escape and for plotting to release more prisoners from Camp Douglas.[66]

Colonel Grenfell had been assigned duty as assistant inspector-general of the Cavalry Corps of the Army of Northern Virginia by Maj. Gen. J. E. B. Stuart on September 14, 1863.[67] Other documents regarding the plot included a list of the names of 144 prominent members of the Sons of Liberty known to be in several Illinois counties.[68]

This November 6, 1864, raid was a major coup for the Federals. In addition to capturing some of the most daring men in the country, and some of Morgan's raiders, the raid yielded a large cache of guns and ammunition, and other items:

Shotguns (double-barreled), loaded	142
Revolvers (Joslyn's patent), loaded	349
Ball cartridges, caliber .44 and .46	13,412
Caps, boxes	344
Cones (extra) boxes	3
Bullet molds (for pistols)	265
Cone wrenches (for pistols)	239
Buckshot (No. 4) bags	8
Powder (partly filled) kegs	2
Holsters for revolvers	115
Belts for holsters	8
Shotguns (double-barreled)	47
Allen's breech-loading carbines	30
Enfield rifle	1[69]

The civilians arrested on November 6, 1864, in connection with the plot to liberate prisoners at Camp Douglas were tried by a military commission. Charles Walsh was sentenced to five years in the penitentiary. Morris and Marmaduke were acquitted. R. T. Semmes was sentenced to three years' imprisonment. Charles T. Daniel, alias Charles Travers, escaped from prison during the trial, but was convicted and sentenced to death. Benjamin M. Anderson committed suicide in prison, and G. St. Leger Grenfell, an Englishman, was convicted and sentenced to death. Grenfell was convicted mainly on the testimony of John T. Shanks who, it turns out, while a prisoner a Camp Douglas, was hired as a detective by Sweet to uncover evidence against those involved in the conspiracy to release prisoners and destroy the city of Chicago.[70]

Overall, the escape rate at Camp Douglas was only about 1.5 percent. Accurate figures are not available, but Charles Levy believes that between 1862 and 1865 about 25 prisoners were killed and 45 wounded in escape attempts. At least 20 others were also wounded who were not escaping. Thus, with such a low rate, the government did not feel obliged to invest the camp with more guards or weapons. Those who did escape were not a threat to private citizens or their property.[71]

The exact number of escapes remains unknown, but there were many. Some indication of the numbers can be gained from the fact that from August 1863 to August 1865, 245 escaped from Camp Douglas.[72]

Conditions continued to deteriorate at Camp Douglas. An inspection made by First Lt. M. Briggs, 8th Regiment Veteran Reserve Corps and special inspector for Camp Douglas, for the week ending December 15, 1864, noted that the hospital was insufficient for the number of sick prisoners, and that many were sick in the barracks that should be in the hospital. Many of the prisoners were poorly clothed, and many were barefoot and without blankets. The food was reported to be "scarcely sufficient for the winter season."[73]

Camp Douglas Today

Nothing remains of the infamous Camp Douglas. The 4,000 plus who died there were buried in unmarked graves in Chicago's City Cemetery. In 1867, they were disinterred and reburied at Oak Woods Cemetery five miles south of the prison site.[74] The exact number of Confederate dead buried in the mass grave at Oak Woods Cemetery is unknown. There is no monument at the camp site. However, the monument erected by Southern Veterans at Oak Woods Cemetery bears the following inscription: "Erected to the Memory of Six Thousand Southern Soldiers Here Buried Who Died in Camp Douglas Prison 1862–5." Bronze tablets attached to the monument list some of the dead, but by no means all.[75]

IV

Camp Morton, Indianapolis, Indiana

The two winters I passed in Camp Morton were the worst I have experienced
…the winds whistled and the rain and snow beat in upon us.
— Pvt. John A. Wyeth, "Cold Cheer at Camp Morton"[1]

Location: Indianapolis, Indiana. **Established:** 1861 as training camp, 1862 for prisoners. **Type:** converted buildings, converted fairgrounds. **Type of Prisoners:** Enlisted men of all classes. **Capacity:** 2,000. **Most Held at One Time:** 5,000. **Number of Known Escapes:** 150+.[2]

History

Camp Morton was unique among prison camps because of its appearance. Once the site of the Indiana State Fairgrounds, the buildings at the entrance were of the Victorian style, complete with gingerbread trim. This gave the camp a cheerful appearance. The fairgrounds had been established in 1852 on 36 acres of the Samuel Henderson farm. Methodist camp meetings were frequently held on the tract. In 1861, Gov. Oliver P. Morton converted the site to a training camp for Indiana volunteers.[3] However, after the fall of Fort Henry and Fort Donelson in February 1862, a facility was needed to quarter the captured Confederates. Governor Morton agreed to accept up to 3,000 prisoners and to house them at Camp Morton. The job of converting the camp fell to Capt. James A. Ekin, assistant quartermaster general of the United States Army. Additional barracks were hastily constructed, and the work was not completed when the first prisoners arrived.[4] According to Thomas Sturgis, one of the guards, the camp was originally established for the custody of wounded prisoners, but eventually was used for all classes of enlisted men.[5]

The Camp Site

Initially, the site appeared ideal for the location of a prison camp. It had a stream of water running through it and there were many shade trees, but it was also a large area and, therefore, required a large number of guards.[6]

The area that confined the prisoners covered five acres. It was dotted with maple trees, and bisected by a little creek the inmates dubbed "The Potomac." Water was provided by five wells.[7]

Prison Personnel

Col. Richard D. Owen and his 60th Indiana Regiment were put in charge. His regiment was not up to full capacity because 130 of them were sick.[8] Owen's tenure was shortlived. He was replaced by Indiana's U.S. marshal, Col. David G. Rose, of the 54th Indiana.[9]

The Facilities

The newly arrived prisoners were housed in five wooden frame buildings. One of the buildings was 40 by 24 feet; one 110 by 20 feet; two 100 by 20 feet; and one 120 by 20 feet. Three small buildings housed four commissioned officers, three female nurses, and eight noncommissioned officers, all attached to the prison hospital.[10] Four buildings served as quarters for the prisoners, while the fifth was used as a hospital. These flimsy structures had been the exhibit halls, stables, and barns used for during the fair. At first, the stables and barns had only dirt floors, and the prisoners slept in stalls. The whole area was surrounded by a board fence. A platform along the outside of the fence provided a walkway for guards.[11] A low fence inside the stockade marked the deadline and prisoners were forbidden to cross it. This was necessary because if they did get close to the walls, they were not difficult to scale with the use of a ladder or even a long plank taken from one of the buildings.[12]

John A. Wyeth survived Camp Morton, and became a surgeon. He wrote about some of the things he remembered in an article that appeared in *The Century* in 1891. Wyeth recalled the wall which surrounded the prisoners was about 20 feet high, and had a smooth surface. There was no ditch between the prison yard and the wall, but "later on we were forced to dig a ditch sixteen feet wide and ten feet deep to prevent ourselves from escaping." Only the heads and shoulders of the sentries could above be seen the top of the wall.[13]

The buildings near the entrance served as headquarters and quarters for the guards.[14]

One Prisoner's View

Wyeth, a private in Company I, 4th Alabama Cavalry (called "Russell's Regiment") was captured by a squad of Ohio cavalry near Chattanooga, Tennessee, on October 5, 1863. He was taken to Camp Morton. Wyeth remembered his quarters well: "The sides were weather-boards set on end and covered with strips when first erected, but as the planks shrunk, the strips disappeared, leaving wide cracks through which the winds whistled and the rain and snow beat in upon us." He remembered awaking many mornings with his blanket covered with snow. His quarters had no floor but did have large doors at each end. Along each side and extending seven feet toward a center aisle were four tiers of bunks. About two feet of space was allotted each man, so that each shed could house about 320 men. They had no straw for bedding, and each man was allowed only one blanket, so that they were forced to huddle together for warmth during the winter months.[15]

Wyeth was put in Barracks No. 4, which was "heated" by four wood stoves placed at equal distances along the passageway. He remembered that "Up to Christmas of 1864, I had not felt the heat from the stove." Many of the men were not used to a cold climate and suffered from the cold, especially when the temperature dropped to around zero. Many froze to death, and others died from disease brought on by exposure, and their debilitated conditions from lack of enough food. Wyeth counted "eighteen bodies carried into the dead-house one morning after an intensely cold night." In order to keep warm, the men slept "spoon fashion" in groups to share blankets and conserve body heat. Lots were drawn for the position in the center, where it was warmer. Wyeth stated that "the two winters I passed in Camp Morton were the worst I have experienced," although he had no means to accurately gauge the temperature.[16]

The Prisoners and Their Treatment

The first prisoners arrived at Camp Morton on February 24, 1862.[17] Three days later, 4,000 prisoners and arrived and there was no regular army officer available at the time to issue provisions. The prisoners were famished, so Adjutant General Lazarus Noble took matters in hand. He ordered rations to be distributed, and he contacted Secretary of War Stanton to see that the provisions were paid for.[18]

Some of the first prisoners, many under 18 years of age, were from the 1st, 4th, and 26th Mississippi who had been captured at Fort Donelson on February 15, 1862. During that siege, these Confederate soldiers had laid in the cold, wet rifle pits and ditches, and by the time they reached Camp Morton, many were quite ill. The Indianapolis *Journal* reported in March of 1862, that of the sick at the military prison and in the city hospital, most were Mississippians, Tennesseeans and Kentuckians.[19]

Shortly after the camp opened, Lt. Col. William Hoffman, the commissary general for prisoners, visited the camp and reported to the quartermaster general in Washington that he had found the prisoners "as well cared for as could be expected under the circumstances." Hoffman ordered several improvements and made some suggestions about the care of sick in the city hospital. Hoffman suggested that a bake house inside the camp could generate funds to provide many necessary items for both the troops and the prisoners which were now being furnished by the government. This system, he believed, would be much better than the current practice of paying an outside baker 22 cents for a return of 20 cents worth of bread.[20]

However, Dr. Wyeth recalled that at "no period" during his imprisonment was he given enough food to satisfy his hunger. Many of his comrades died from starvation. Many were reduced to stealing from their fellow prisoners, or to eat "like hogs" the refuse that was thrown into "swill-tubs" from the hospital kitchen. Wyeth was on a committee that tried to prevent men from eating the filthy garbage.[21]

When Hoffman visited the prison again, he recommended that there should be windows in the buildings used for barracks to let in air and light, and to prevent sickness. He believed the buildings would be too crowded when warm weather came.[22] The rough, temporary buildings used for the fair were also unsuitable to house prisoners during the winter months. The latrines soon overflowed and hundreds became ill and died. As a result, prisoners became desperate to escape.[23]

Colonel Owen reportedly treated the prisoners with kindness and compassion. He allowed the chaplain to distribute supplies on Wednesdays and Saturdays. He even permitted some prisoners to go into Indianapolis to purchase other needed articles, accompanied by guards, of course.[24] That permissiveness was a mistake. Some of the prisoners smuggled liquor back to the camp, and several drunken prisoners began to throw rocks at the guards. As a result, the guards fired upon the prisoners, and four were injured.[25]

When it became known that Owens allowed his prisoners to enjoy themselves in the saloons of Indianapolis, he was severely criticized. Owens defended his actions, but immediately rescinded the order that allowed prisoners to leave the camp.[26]

The rules Colonel Owens set for prisoners at Camp Morton were fair:

1. The entire camp prisoners will be divided into thirty divisions, each under the charge of a chief selected by the companies composing the division from among the first sergeants of companies. At the bugle call for first sergeants they will report themselves at headquarters.

2. These chiefs of divisions will draw up the provision returns for their divisions, care for and be responsible for the general appearance, police and welfare of their divisions. The first fifteen will constitute a board of appeal for the hearing of grievances, settlement and punishment of misdemeanors, subject to the approval of the commander of the post in their fifteen divisions. The other fifteen will form a like court for the remaining fifteen divisions.

3. Among the crimes and misdemeanors against which first sergeants are expected to guard and which they will punish on detection are counterfeiting the commandant's, doctor's, adjutant's or chaplain's hands for requisitions, making improper use of premises, refusing to take reasonable share in the details according to the roster, selling to the sutler any articles issued to them as clothing, appropriating things belonging to others or insulting sentinels.

4. The prisoners' returns will be handed in for approval at 10 A.M. each alternate day previous to the one on which the issue is made. The issues of tobacco and stationery will be made on Wednesdays and Saturdays at 2 P.M. by the chaplain, as well as the distribution of reading matter. Letters will be given out between 2 and 3 P.M. and mailed between 3 and 4 P.M.

5. Daily inspections will be made by the commandant or officer of the day to see that the policing so essential to health has been thoroughly performed, and facilities will be afforded for sports and athletic exercise also conducive to health, as well as bathing by companies, if permission can be obtained from the proper authority.

6. The first sergeants of companies will look after the general wants of their companies and maintain the necessary order, discipline and police essential to health and comfort, and will make requisitions, first on chief of divisions, and then afterwards at headquarters, for clothing, camp and garrison equipage absolutely necessary; also for tobacco wanted, and the like.

7. The inside chain of soldiers, except a small patrol with side-arms will be removed, and the quiet and good order of the camp as well as the policing for health

and comfort, the construction of new sinks when necessary and the daily throwing in of lime and mold to prevent bad odors will be entirely under the supervision of the sergeants of prisoners.

8. Vessels for the washing of clothing and ropes for clotheslines will be furnished, and no bed or other clothing will be put on roof tops or on fences.

9. Prisoners will carefully avoid interrupting sentinels in the discharge of their duty, and especially will not curse them, use abusive language or climb onto fences or trees, as the sentinels are ordered to fire if such an offense occurs after three positive and distinct orders to desist, even in daytime. At night only one warning will be given to any one climbing on the fence tops.

10. A prisoners' fund will be created by the deduction as heretofore of small amounts from the rations of beef, bread, beans, &c, a schedule of which will be placed at the commissary department. This fund will be used for the purchase of tobacco, stationery, stamps and such other articles as the chiefs of divisions may report, and which should be drawn on requisitions handed in by first sergeants between 9 and 10 A.M. each day.

11. Every endeavor will be made by the commandant to give each and every prisoner as much liberty and comfort as is consistent with orders received and with an equal distribution of the means at disposal, provided such indulgence never leads to any abuse of the privilege.[27]

Some of the guards were not as caring as the prison commandant. According to Wyeth, two men who were not even trying to escape were killed when a guard fired from behind them and the ball passed through both men. One of the dying men declared that he had been "deliberately murdered." Wyeth also recalled that on several occasions, shots were fired into the barracks at night. In the "Louisiana" Barracks, a "Creole" was shot through the pelvis while he slept.[28] Wyeth described some of the cruelty heaped on the prisoners, especially mentioning the guard named Baker.[29] Wyeth's comments were collaborated by Dr. Thomas E. Spotswood, of Fairford, Alabama, in *The Memphis Commercial*. That article can be seen on an Internet Web site.[30]

John Franklin Champenois also corroborated the story of the cruel guard named Baker. Champenois described Baker as "Cruelty personified." Baker made life miserable for the prisoners, and delighted in cracking prisoners over the head with his pistol, or firing into their barracks when they had gathered around the stove to warm. He would empty his gun in the passageway and shout, "Rats to your holes," and the prisoners scurried away like rats until the danger was over. It was either "be shot or freeze."[31]

Because of the harsh conditions at the camp, Wyeth remembered that the prisoners were always looking for means of escape, and many of them took "desperate, and some fatal, chances to gain their liberty." The walls were high, the sentries placed so close together, and the approach so well-lighted that even to attempt to scale the walls, according to Dr. Wyeth, was "virtually inviting death."[32] Yet many tried.

Escape Attempts

As early as April 18, 1862, Colonel Owen reported that as many as 13 prisoners had escaped. Some were recaptured and "placed in jail." Since he had charge of 4,200 prisoners, Owen thought that this low number of escapes reflected "favorably both for the vigilance of the sentinels and for the disposition of the guarded." In fact, Owen reported in an editorial to the local newspaper that a large majority of his prisoners had "signed papers pledging their honors not to endeavor to escape."[33]

Yet, despite their pledges, by their very nature, prisons are prisons, and prisoners are bound to escape.

On the night of July 14, 1862, 50 prisoners escaped. Captain Ekin reported that several were killed and wounded in the attempt, and some of the escapees were recaptured.[34] The monthly return submitted by Camp Morton for the month of July 1862 reported that only five prisoners had escaped.[35] Perhaps this number reflects those who were not recaptured.

Many Escape in 1864

Escape attempts began shortly after the new year. On January 16, 1864, a prisoner, Goacin Arcemant, was shot when he approached the fence. The prisoner was warned, and he halted, but did not return to his quarters. The guard fired upon him, in according with standing orders. It was noted that several attempts to escape at that same point along the fence had been tried during the month of January, and it was assumed that Arcemant had intended to do the same.[36] The returns for January 1864 indicated that three prisoners had escaped.[37]

Wyeth remembered an escape that succeeded that same month. A young Texan, about 20 years old, who had been captured along with Wyeth, said one night after they had gone to bed, "Boys, I am going to go over the fence, or die in the attempt." He asked his fellow prisoners to write his folks and let them know what happened if he didn't make it. Then, he took from his bunk a "slender ladder," which had been made by tying together fragments of planks with twine and strips of cloth and started toward the fence. Despite the falling snow, he could see the guards, and he waited until they had met, then turned to march in the opposite direction. He then placed his ladder against the wall and, in only a moment, he was over the wall. The sentries did not see him, and the ladder was not discovered until daylight. A few weeks later, the prisoners in his barracks received a letter and, although it was not signed with his real name, they knew he had made it to Kentucky and was on his way to "Dixie."[38]

Encouraged by the Texan's escape, Wyeth recalled that seven more prisoners decided to scale the walls. Two were killed in the attempt, and four were captured. The four who were recaptured were punished by tying being tied up with their backs to a tree. Their arms were tied at the wrists and pulled above their heads. In this position, they remained all night. They were cut down the next morning. Their hands were blue with "stagnated blood, and showed deep furrows where the rope had buried itself in the skin of their arms and wrists."[39]

The next month, the prisoners changed their method of escape. Instead of going over the fence, they decided to go under it through a tunnel. On the night of February 11, 1864, between 10 P.M. and midnight, prisoner James Barnhart was shot and killed by a guard while attempting to escape through a tunnel. The tunnel ran from the east end of Barracks No. 5 (or G), under the fence to the outside.[40] Upon investigation, Col. A. A. Stevens was told that there was a conspiracy among the prisoners, which was probably originated by some of the Confederate officers who had recently been transferred from Camp Chase to Camp Morton. The night before, several prisoners had escaped at that same point, and only two had been recaptured. While the prisoner Barnhart was being shot in his escape attempt, another attempt was made by prisoners to go over the fence. Several shots were fired at them, and they were stopped. Subsequent investigation revealed that an all-out attempt to escape was planned for the night of February 11. An inspection of the camp bought to light a unfinished tunnel running from Barracks A.[41]

During the breakout, Henry Jones and R. J. Phillips were shot.[42]

One of the prison guards was a witness to the breakout:

> I was ... on the east side of the ditch within 100 yards of the fence; heard stones striking the fence; heard firing and saw rebels running from the fence toward the barracks. Saw rebel prisoner named Phillips, who had been shot by the guard in attempting to escape, lying within fifteen feet of the fence. I found four ladders made by the prisoners, standing against the fence and five more lying near. I heard eight shots fired before I got up to the fence. The night was very dark. In my opinion, it was a combined movement of prisoners to escape.[43]

In an attempt to prevent future attempts to tunnel out, Colonel Stevens ordered a trench dug between the ends of the barracks and the fence.[44]

Colonel Stevens investigated the escape of 18 prisoners during the month of February 1864. From information gathered from the remaining prisoners, Stevens concluded that two had scaled the fence on February 3, because the tunnel was not completed until the night of February 10. Sixteen prisoners escaped on the night of February 10, and the remainder about daylight on the morning of February 11. Two were recaptured. The tunnel had been concealed by replacing the floor boards each day and nailing them back down. The tunnel exit was "under the guard walk and concealed from the sentinel by it." The tunnel was about 11 feet in length and had taken several weeks to dig. The dirt removed from the tunnel had been concealed in buckets mixed with ashes from the stove and from dirt swept up from the floor. Even the discovery of this tunnel did not stop the prisoners, and Colonel Stevens reported that he had found four similar attempts in different locations, but these had been unsuccessful in allowing prisoners to get out.[45]

Even though there were a few escapes, Colonel Hoffman had confidence in the commandant at Camp Morton, and described him as "a reliable and attentive officer and will spare no efforts to prevent the escape of prisoners."[46] The official report for month of February 1864 stated that 18 prisoners escaped, as admitted by Stevens in his correspondence.[47]

About 20 prisoners in Camp Morton made a bid for freedom on the night of September 27, 1864. They constructed ladders of tent poles and the short bunk ladders tied together to scale the fence. The plot was set in motion when prisoners began to throw rocks at the sentries. When the sentries turned to fire, the prisoners rushed the fence to escape.[48]

Again, on November 14, 1864, a prison break began at curfew when the prisoners began throwing rocks and other items at the guards. In the confusion, 60 prisoners rushed the fence, and although the guards fired upon them, 31 got away.[49]

The movement to end the war and free the prisoners was fueled by former Senator Charles Vallandigham and the members of the secret orders of the Knights of the Golden Circle (also called American Knights or Sons of Liberty). These secret organizations flourished with a large membership in the states of Ohio, Indiana, Illinois and Missouri. The headquarters of the Knights of the Golden Circle was in Indianapolis.[50]

Escapes Increase As Conditions Worsen

By August 1864, the conditions within Camp Morton were described by C. T. Alexander, a surgeon with the U.S. Army, as "anything but a favorable condition." Alexander stated that the five-acre inclosure was too small for the 4,885 prisoners being confined. All of the barracks were overcrowded. There were a number of tents, but these were overcrowded as well. He thought there were too many sick (327 in the hospital and 256 in the quarters) for the numbers of prisoners. There had been a large number of deaths, with 81 reported during the month of July. This was due to the "crowded state of camp, quarters, and tents, and want of change in position in tents, the foul condition of sinks, the want of good police, the want of vegetables until the 1st of August," all of which was in addition to the "inevitable nostalgia" among the prisoners.[51]

As might be expected under those conditions, efforts to escape increased. On August 23, 1864, Brig. Gen. H. B. Carrington reported that he had been asked to increase the number of guards at Camp Morton. Prisoners who had been used to obtain information reported that new tunnels were being constructed, and that there was a plan to attack the camp and "force their way to the arsenals," no matter how many were killed in the attempt.[52] The next day, Carrington telegraphed the acting assistant adjutant general, Lt. Col. S. H. Lathrop, that 2,000 prisoners had organized and had "sworn to make outbreak."[53]

That organization, also noted by Wyeth, resulted in one of the most daring escapes. It followed on the heels of an attempt that failed. Some of the men formed a group, selected a leader, and planned an escape. Ladders were made from planks taken from bunks and tied together with strips of clothing and blankets. They armed themselves with rocks, water-filled bottles, and pieces of wood. When the bugle sounded the call to retire for the night, the men rushed the fence, overturned a privy into the ditch for a bridge, and placed their ladders against the fence. Others detracted the sentries by pelting them with the stones and other missiles they had gathered. One guard fired his gun, another's misfired, so that the group of prisoners made it over the fence to the outside. A few were recaptured the next day, but most of them made it to Canada or to the South.[54]

Prison officials had been fairly successful in stopping escapes, but there were several each month during the summer of 1864. Six escapes were reported for July 1864, seven during August, and six during September.[55]

On September 16, 1864, prisoner George T. Douglass was shot At an inquiry into the shooting, testimony was given which described how this occurred. Capt. Robert C. Hicks testified that he had been ordered to furnish six men to guard nine Confederate prisoners who were taking out the hospital waste truck. Corporal De

Witt was placed in charge. After an hour, De Witt returned with only 8 prisoners.[56] De Witt testified that while he and the prisoners were at the creek, Douglass jumped over the fence. He was ordered to halt, but the prisoner kept on running. One of the guards fired his gun and the prisoner was killed.[57]

Despite the suggestions of Colonel Hoffman, conditions continued to deteriorate at Camp Morton as winter approached. Colonel Hoffman reported that many of the prisoners were without blankets and "almost destitute of clothing," and the camp showed "great neglect." He urged the camp commandant to send in his requisition for supplies of clothing, as authorized in a circular sent out in April. Hoffman also wanted to know if the extension of the hospital he had been instructed to build had been completed. Hoffman asked if the improvements to the old barracks had been made and, if more barracks were needed, said Stevens had only to submit a plan and a cost estimate. He ordered Colonel Stevens to acknowledge the receipt of his letter by telegram.[58]

Undoubtedly Colonel Stevens went to work to improve the camp. An inspection conducted by First Lt. J. W. Davidson the first week in January 1865 described the prisoners' conduct there as "very quiet, no attempts to escape." Clothing and bedding were good. The quantity of food was sufficient, and of good quality. The general health of the prisoners was good, and the guards, both officers and enlisted men, "have been very vigilant."[59]

The Tunnels

Although it became very difficult to dig a tunnel once the prison officials had the ditch around the barracks dug, that did not stop the prisoners from trying. A tunnel was completed and several prisoners escaped. The next night, more tried to follow, but the tunnel was discovered. When the first man stuck his head out of the tunnel, the guard put his gun against his head, and "blew the unfortunate man's brains out." Those behind him in the tunnel retreated quickly, according to Wyeth.[60]

Two more tunnels were constructed. One filled in with water, and the other, although completed, was reported by a informer within the ranks of the prisoners on the day before the escape was to take place. The informer was rewarded by being taken into protective custody, housed in the headquarters of the guards, and given plenty of food.[61]

Wyeth described the construction of a long tunnel in the summer of 1864. It began about 200 feet away from the fence. The opening was hidden by blankets. Sixteen men worked in regular shifts to dig a shaft about 10 feet down. Two feet from the bottom of the shaft, a tunnel was started running parallel with the ground until it encountered the ditch. There, it had to be deeper to go under the ditch. One man at a time worked in the tunnel, digging out the dirt with only a case knife and his hands. The loose dirt was put in a sack tied with a cord. When full, the digger jerked on the cord to signal those above at the opening to pull the bag out and empty it. The dirt was disposed of in a unique manner. At sunset, each man would tuck his trousers into the legs of his socks, then fill the trousers with as much loose dirt as he could. He would then "waddle" out to the little stream that bisected the compound. As he crossed the plank bridge across the stream, he would give his trousers a sudden pull and free them from the socks, and the dirt would fall into the stream. The work continued slowly but surely from July through September. However, one of their number turned them in, and thwarted the escape. Those who had worked so hard remembered what had happened when the previous tunnel had been discovered and a man shot as he tried to exit it. Wyeth and his fellow miners were not punished, but the informer spent the remainder of the war within the safety of the guards' headquarters.[62]

First Lieutenant Sturgis, one of the guards at Camp Morton admitted that there were several escape attempts during his tour of duty. They prisoners escaped at night, "probably not over a dozen at a time." He recalled several men escaped when they scaled the wall, overpowered the guard, and they vanished into the country. Outside, there were many small farms and many "sympathizers with the rebel cause." Sturgis remembered that the commandant at Camp Morton never sent out bloodhounds in search of escaped prisoners. He also believed that those who did escape had no trouble finding "food, clothing, shelter, and sympathy at every farm they approached."[63]

James Franklin Champenois, from Mobile, Alabama, was captured in Sequatchie Valley on October 3, 1863. He was later inspired by Dr. Wyeth's article to write one of his own. He told of the escape of three prisoners—Chase from Maine, White from Pennsylvania, and Lindsey from Texas—through a tunnel from the end of Barracks No. 5. The next morning the rest of the prisoners in No. 5 found the hole and the escape tunnel. Quite a few more escaped through that hole, according to Champenois. Some of those intent on escaping brought with them bundles strapped to their backs, crackerboxes filled with all their worldly goods, while others carried mess pans and kettles. They wanted to leave nothing behind, and "all [were] bound for Dixie via the tunnel route."[64]

One big prisoner, Aaronheart from Missouri, volunteered to lead the way through the tunnel. He had no thoughts other than to escape, despite the fact that the guards were waiting. Barracks 5 was only about 150 feet from the sentry line and the guards knew what was going on with the prisoners. Champenois and his comrade Barron decided to return and they "bolted for [their] quarters in barrack no. 4, and none too soon." They had no sooner made it back, when a barrage of shots rang out in the night. A long drum roll was sounded, and the guards poured into the camp from all sides. Those in Barracks No. 5 were ordered out and lined up. Several of them were taken from the lineup to the "black hole." The rest of the guards fired on one of the prisoners (Aaronheart?) until his body was riddled with bullets. The guards brought his body outside to serve as a warning to the rest of them.

Other Methods of Escape

Some prisoners were willing to try anything to escape the confines of a prison. Between 100 and 200 Irish Catholics were imprisoned in Camp Morton. They had formerly been conscripted into the Confederate Army, but they wanted to volunteer for the 35th Irish Indiana, a Union regiment. To hasten the process, W. R. Holloway, the private secretary to Governor O. P. Morton of Indiana, telegraphed the secretary of war and requested that he cut through the required paperwork and allow General Willcox to "facilitate the business."[65] Stanton replied quickly to Governor Morton and authorized him to enlist the 200 Catholic Confederates into the 35th Indiana, but "without premium, advance, pay, or bounty."[66]

Wyeth described a unique method used by one determined prisoner who escaped. A detail of prisoners was chosen to accompany the garbage wagons to a point some distance outside the walls, where it was unloaded. On one occasion, five prisoners sent with the garbage detail seized the guards, disarmed them, and escaped. Another time a member of the detail broke away and was killed.[67]

1865 Escapes

The winter of 1864-1865 was very cold. On New Year's Day 1865, the temperature dropped to 20 degrees below zero and the area suffered a severe snowstorm.[68]

Although two prisoners were reported to have escaped in February 1865, there were no more escapes reported until after the war ended.[69] The exchange of prisoners began in February and March, but by April 1, 1865, 1,408 prisoners still remained at Camp Morton. Some prisoners refused to be exchanged because they did not want to return to Confederate territory.[70]

The report for June 1865 listed two escaped prisoners. After July 1865, there were no prisoners being held at Camp Morton.[71]

The Controversy

Dr. Wyeth's account of life at Camp Morton did not go unchallenged. His account and its graphic illustrations was refuted in several articles which denied Wyeth's description almost word for word. However, many of Wyeth's statements, especially those about the escape attempts, can be verified in the many reports later published in *The Official Records of the War of the Rebellion*, as previously described within this chapter.

In the September 1891 issue of the *Century*, the Department Encampment of the Grand Army of the Republic took up the gauntlet. This group adopted a resolution and appointed a committee to investigate the statements made by Dr. Wyeth in his article entitled "Cold Cheer at Camp Morton." This lengthy article disputes Dr. Wyeth's statements almost line for line. Of value, however, is a drawing of the campgrounds showing the location of the barracks and other buildings.[72] In that same issue, Dr. Wyeth offered a "Rejoinder," to substantiate his initial article, including statements by a number of witnesses. Some even added more gruesome details. Dr. J. L. Rainey, of Cottage Grove, Henry County, Tennessee, stated in the "Rejoinder," that any "attempt to refute your [Dr. Wyeth's] narrative will be utterly futile. There are yet living hundreds of men who know that your statement falls short in details of many cruelties inflicted upon prisoners there by soldiers and officers, and many privations which were maliciously inflicted.[73]

Camp Morton Today

After the war, Camp Morton reverted to is role as the state fairgrounds, and was used as such until 1890, when a new fairgrounds was built. The old property was sold and divided into residential lots, and is now known as Herron-Morton Place.

Sumner Archibald Cunningham, editor of the *Confederate Veteran*, placed a bronze memorial tablet in Indianapolis in 1911 to honor of the camp commander, Col. Richard Owen. Contributions funded a bronze bust of Colonel Owen sculpted by Belle Kinney, which was put in the Indiana State House. Dedicated in 1913, it was inscribed:

> Colonel Richard Owen
> Commandant
> Camp Morton Prison 1862
> Tribute by Confederate Prisoners
> of War and Their Friends
> For his Courtesy and Kindness.

In 1916, students and teachers from Indianapolis School No. 45 marked the site by placing a bolder at Alabama and 19th Streets, inscribed:

> Camp Morton
> 1861–1865
> Erected by School Forty-Five
> 1916

A sign was erected in 1962 to mark the camp's location. Both of these are now located in the Herron-Morton Place Historic Park in the 1900 block of North Alabama Street.

On July 15, 2000, the Sons of Union Veterans of the Civil War, in cooperation with the Sons of Confederate Veterans, installed four boundary markers to delineate the boundary of the camp. A boundary-marker dedication ceremony was held on October 25, 2003.

Graves of Camp Morton Prisoners

Those who died at Camp Morton were buried in the city cemetery and at Greenlawn. It ceased to be used when a new city cemetery, Crown Hill, was opened. Some of the bodies of Confederates were exhumed and returned to relatives in the South, but most remained buried at Greenlawn. Some graves were moved in 1870 to make way for the Vandalia Railroad. In 1906, Col. William Elliot was authorized to locate the burial place of the Confederate dead. A plot about 45 feet by 200 feet was enclosed in an iron fence. In 1912, the Federal government erected a monument there, which was later moved to Garfield Park. It carries the names and regiments of the 1,616 dead Confederate soldiers and sailors, and to honor those whose graves could not be identified. In 1931, the War Department exhumed all those Confederate prisoners buried at Greenlawn and moved them to Lot No. 32 at the Crown Hill Cemetery. In 1993, additional markers were placed to list the names and regiments of those buried there.[74]

V

Elmira Prison, Elmira, New York

…Elmira was nearer Hades than I thought any place could be made by human cruelty.
— G. T. Taylor, Company C, 1st Alabama Battalion, Heavy Artillery[1]

Location: near Chemung River, Elmira, New York. **Established:** 1861 as training camp, prison in July 1864. **Type:** barracks enclosed by high fence. **Type of Prisoners:** Confederate prisoners of war. **Capacity:** 5,000. **Most Held at One Time:** 9,441. **Known Escapes:** 17.[2] **Nickname:** "Hellmira."

History

Because of its accessibility, Elmira was selected in May 1864 as a good place to confine Confederate prisoners of war. A second consideration was the "healthfulness" of the Chemung Valley.[3] Elmira is in western New York state, near the Pennsylvania line, 217 miles northwest of New York City. Although Elmira Prison was in existence for less than a year, its notoriety spread quickly. What were the reasons for this, and how did Elmira Prison gain such a reputation over such a short period of time?

Elmira is one of the oldest towns in the state of New York. It is in a valley of fertile farms and fields of corn and grains. The valley is surrounded by a range of hills and mountains. In 1776, the Battle of Chemung was fought between General Sullivan and the Iroquois Indian chief Thayendanega. The chief was of mixed race; he had been educated in Connecticut and had been given a military commission with the rank of colonel in 1775 by the English Crown. He was known to the whites as "Joseph Brant," and his cruelties in battle were motivated by the wrongs his people had suffered at the hands of the white people.[4]

The Facilities

The main entrance was through a set of double doors near the center of the enclosure on the north side. The area was enclosed by a plank fence about 14 feet high, around which had been constructed a narrow walkway or parapet on which the guards paced day and night. Large globe lamps were ranged inside the enclosure at

51

intervals and were lighted shortly after sunset, and extinguished after daylight. Thus, even on the darkest night, the guards could see anyone who approached the fence.[5]

Quarters for the prisoners were a series of long wooden buildings, 100 feet long by 10 feet wide. Behind the barracks were the buildings used by the camp officials and guards. The compound covered almost 40 acres of a flat plain on the bank of the Chemung River. The area was split by a long, narrow lake which ran parallel to the river. The lake began about 20 feet from the fence on one side and flowed under the opposite fence. Beyond the lake lay the sandy river bottom, which often was covered with flood waters.[6] The camp was surrounded by hills covered with tall trees. Water was pure and abundant, not like the "brackish, fever-ridden liquid" the prisoners had to drink at Point Lookout, commented one prisoner.[7]

By the end of July, after only a month of operation, 1864, 4,323 prisoners had arrived at Elmira, and by August 29, that number had more than doubled to reach 9,607. These prisoners were under the supervision of Maj. Henry V. Colt, of the 104th New York Volunteers. The barracks could accommodate only about half that number. Those that could not be housed in the barracks were provided with "A" tents.[8] Soon, prisoners were comparing the camp to hell. One prisoner remarked that it was not only a hellhole, "but a hellhole under siege."[9]

Pvt. Louis Leon, who was transferred to Elmira in July 1864, recorded in his diary that he "liked this place better than Point Lookout (see Chapter XIV for more about Private Leon). We are fenced in by a high fence, in ... a 200-acre lot." By September, he may have changed his mind, because he wrote, "It is very cold, worse than I have seen it in the South in the dead of winter."[10]

In addition to the cramped quarters and scanty rations, the prisoners were forced to provide entertainment for crowds of curious citizens. Two large platforms were constructed outside the walls of the prison which were an "observatory." For 15 cents, anyone could mount the platform and watch the prisoners inside the compounds, like watching wild animals in a zoo.[11]

The Prisoners

Anthony M. Keiley was defending Petersburg, Virginia, when he was captured. He recorded his five-month prison experience in a diary, published after the war in the Petersburg *Daily Index*. Keiley was taken first to Point Lookout, then transferred to Elmira.[12] On Friday, July 8, 1864, Keiley and 281 prisoners were put on board the *El Cid* and confined to the ship's hold. After 50 hours on the ship, the prisoners boarded a train near New York and were transported to Elmira. From the railroad depot, the men were marched about a mile to the prison. Along the way, they were stared at by curious citizens.[13]

Keiley was born in Paterson, N. J. He had moved with his father to Petersburg, Virginia, when his father obtained a position as the principal of the Anderson Seminary. In August 1864, he wrote home to his parents:

> I am well, not greatly discontented, want for little that a prisoner can expect. Have found many old friends; made some firm new ones. Am treated in the main here with a courtesy and kind indulgence that I can never forget, though it comes from foes.[14]

Miles O. Sherrill, from Catawba County, North Carolina, was a member of the 12th North Carolina Infantry, part of Gen. R. D. Johnston's Brigade, when he was captured at Spotsylvania Court House on May 9, 1864. Sherrill was shot in the leg and after it was amputated, he was transported to Alexandria, Virginia, then to Old Capitol Prison in Washington, D.C., before being transferred to Elmira. In November 1864, Sherrill wrote:

> We reached Elmyra, N. Y. Being in the mountains, the ground was covered with snow. Arriving at the barracks, we were lined up (I was on my crutches, and had to stand there on one foot for what seemed to me a very long time) just inside the gate, negro soldiers on guard. The commanding officer, Major Beal, greeted us with the most bitter oaths that I ever heard. He swore that he was going to send us out and have us shot; said he had no room for us, and that we (meaning the Confederate soldiers) had no mercy on their colored soldiers or prisoners. He was half drunk, and I was not sure but that we might be dealt with then and there.[15]

Prison Personnel

The commander of the camp, Major Henry V. Colt, was assisted by Major Beale. One prisoner wrote that they were at times, "not only unkind, but unjust and oppressive." G. W. Porter, of the 44th Tennessee, recalled that Beale called out all the prisoners on a bitter cold night and made them stand in line until he determined just how many had "United States overcoats, and where they got them." He then confiscated the coats and took them to his quarters where he cut the tails off each, then returned the mutilated garments to their owners.[16]

Cruel Punishment

Keiley noted that prisoners were punished for various infractions of the rules by being sentenced to solitary confinement in the guard house on a diet of bread and water, or they might be forced to wear a barrel shirt, or be locked inside a tall, narrow box (7 feet high, 20 inches wide, and 12 inches deep). When the door to the box was fastened, the prisoner could not move, and had to stand rigid inside the box until released.[17] This instrument of torture, known as the "sweat box," came in several sizes, each with different dimensions to fit different sized prisoners. When a prisoner was to be punished, he was marched to the various boxes until one was found that fitted, and he was then pushed inside, with his arms down by his side. An opening for the nose was the only concession to comfort. When the hinged door was fastened shut, the prisoner could not move and was confined for hours outside in the heat and the cold.[18]

Prison officials also punished men by hanging them by their thumbs to make them reveal "suppositious plots."[19]

High Death Rate

Elmira Prison had the second-highest death rate of any of the Civil War era prisons other than Andersonville. The majority of deaths were from diarrhea and dysentery, but many deaths were due to scurvy.[20] Smallpox also killed a great number of the prisoners. Miles Sherrill was one who survived smallpox.[21]

By the first of September 1864, there had been 386 deaths, a mortality rate of 4 percent for that month. During its brief existence, a total of 12,122 prisoners were confined at Elmira, and of those, 3,000 died.[22]

According to Clay Holmes, the death rate at Alton Prison in Illinois was 31 percent (2,218 prisoners out of 7,117), while Elmira had 24 percent (2,963 deaths out of 12,123). Stranger still, is the fact that the death rate at the hated Point Lookout prison was only 9 percent (3,446 deaths out of 38,053).[23]

Part of the higher death rate at Elmira undoubtedly was partly because of the condition of the prisoners that were received there. Many were poorly clothed, and were "pale, emaciated, hollow-eyed and dispirited" from months of imprisonment at Point Lookout and elsewhere.[24]

Another contributing factor was the pond inside the compound. It quickly become a cesspool filled with urine and fecal matter. The runoff from the camp and the seepage from latrines drained into Foster's pond, which shortly became the source of "disgusting odors," because the large sink used by the prisoners was over the pond. It did not take long for the pond to become filled with "nitrogenous materials, from the 2,600 gallons of urine passed daily by 7,000 prisoners.[25] At the hospital, since August, 2,011 patients were admitted and 775 deaths were reported from among "a mean strength of 8,347 prisoners of war." Thus, 24 percent of the prisoners were admitted to the hospital, and of those 9 percent died, according to a report from E. F. Sanger, the surgeon and the medical officer at the camp, to the surgeon general. Sanger foresaw the entire prison population being admitted to the hospital and a death rate of 36 percent.[26] As smallpox ravaged the weakened prisoners, pneumonia added to their woes. In the month of March 1865, almost 500 died, an average of 15 deaths per day.[27] Out of a total of 11,916 prisoners, there were 2,994 deaths, a rate of 25 percent. This rate only 3 points less than the 28 percent who reportedly died at the Confederate prison in Andersonville, Georgia.[28]

With so much sickness and death, a low number of escapes is understandable. Perhaps those intelligent, courageous men who might have attempted to escape died or were too weak to try.

Escape from Elmira

Officials at Elmira reported only 17 escapes during its short period of operation. Two prisoners escaped shortly after the prison first opened in July 1864. Eleven escaped in October, one in November, two in December, and one in April 1865, for a total of 17.[29] Among Federal prisons, only Fort Warren and Johnson's Island had fewer escapes reported.[30]

Prisoners were always plotting and making plans to escape, but few actually did. The number of escapes was probably kept at a minimum because of spies within the prison population. Melvin Mott Conklin, actually a 20-year-old Union soldier from New York, was placed inside the prison to report any tunnels or escape plots he could uncover.[31]

All but one of the escapes from Elmira were made in the first half of the year that the prison was in operation. During the last half, there was only one escape, and there were no foiled attempts. During the months of October and November several tunnels were started, but it was soon too cold to dig. When spring came, the idea of a tunnel had been discarded.[32] Once the war ended, there was no need for escape, because the prisoners were released.

The First Escape

The first known escape occurred July 7, 1864, the day after the first prisoners arrived. Two prisoners built a ladder and went over the fence.[33] Of those, one was caught down at the river and returned. His comrades refused to recognize him, hoping he would be released, but his manner of dress gave him away. It is presumed the other was not recaptured.[34]

A Unique Way Out

Among those to escape during the early days of Elmira was a man known only as "Buttons." This Georgia Confederate reportedly escaped by being carried out through the gates in a coffin with the dead bodies in coffins. He was called "Buttons" because of a number of brass buttons he had sewn on his gray coat, buttons he had taken on the battlefield from the uniforms of dead Federal soldiers. "Buttons" had bribed the coffin maker in the dead house to leave the nails in the lid loose so air could enter the coffin. The coffin was loaded on a wagon on top of several others and the wagon started toward the place of burial outside the prison. Once outside the gates and some distance away from the prison, he pushed the lid up, and jumped off the wagon. "Buttons" threatened the driver that if he told, he would come back and kill him. No one knows for sure if Buttons made it back safely to Confederate lines, but the story of his escape gave hope to others.[35]

Tunnels

M. T. Wade, a member of Company B, 12th North Carolina Infantry, had been captured at Williamsport, Maryland, on the retreat from Gettysburg in the summer of 1863. In 1911, he wrote from Atlanta, Georgia, to describe his imprisonment at Elmira. Wade was camped in a tent on the flat between the pond and the river, about 20 feet from the fence. Some prisoners decided to dig a tunnel from their tent under the fence, and then cut into the river. Once the river bank was reached, they could swim away to safety. He and his tentmates, Herth, French, and Cannon, dug down about six feet, then turned their tunnel toward the fence. They had not gone far, when a "lantern was thrown on us and our game came to a sudden stop." Luckily, Wade was away at the time in the process of carrying dirt in his haversack to empty into the pond.[36]

Wade recalled hearing about another tunnel that had been dug underneath Hospital Ward 14. Since he was a patient in the hospital at that time, he did not take part in that one.[37]

In his memoirs, Marcus Toney, a Tennessee boy confined to Elmira Prison, described how a tunnel was constructed. Some of the prisoners were housed in tents. One of those tents had a "false floor" which was covered over each morning with dirt so that it appeared just like the surrounding ground. Under this false floor the prisoners worked to dig a tunnel day and night. The tent's occupants had a routine set up whereby one man was in the tunnel digging at all times. The tunnel dropped down two feet, then ran parallel to the surface for another 60 feet to go under the fence. The only tool the men had was a large knife. A small box with a string attached at both ends was used to haul dirt out of the tunnel. When the box was full of dirt, the digger gave the string a jerk, and a prisoner close to the tunnel entrance would empty the box. At night, the men gathered the excess dirt and filled their haversacks. Then, they scattered the loose dirt along the streets. Once the tunnel reached the fence, it needed to go a foot lower. This was done, and when the moon set one night, several of the men escaped through it. The last six to leave were to notify as many other prisoners as possible so that they, too, could escape. However, only 15 prisoners got out, and those who remained learned that the 15 had reached safety in Canada.[38]

Successful Escape by Tunneling

Eleven men were involved in a conspiracy to escape by way of a tunnel are know, but only 10 of them escaped. The 11 were Washington Brown Traweek, John Fox Maull, and John P. Putegnat, all members of Alabama's Jeff Davis Artillery; S. C. "Cyclops" Malone, of the 9th Alabama Infantry; Gilmer G. Jackson and William H. Templin, of the Jeff Davis Artillery; J. P. Scruggs of South Carolina; Glenn Shelton, from Mississippi; Berry Benson, of the 1st South Carolina Regiment; James W. Crawford, 6th Virginia Cavalry; and Frank E. Saurine, 3rd Alabama Infantry. [39] Saurine, the 11th man, was eventually cast out of the group because he stopped taking his turn at digging the Traweek-Maull-Putegnat tunnel.[40]

Traweek, a plantation overseer near Selma, Alabama, had been only 16 when he volunteered.[41] Maull enlisted when he was 18. Putegnat was only 19 when he was put in the Elmira prison camp. Both boys had been in several major battles— Second Bull Run, Antietam, Chancellorsville, Fredericksburg, Gettysburg, and the Wilderness. Saurine, a Philadelphian by birth, had married a southern girl and was living in the South when the war began. All four of these young men had been captured at Spotsylvania in May 1864.[42]

Mull, Putegnat and Traweek decided to dig a tunnel from the tents on the north side of the prison to the city street, a distance of about 68 feet. They began digging with their pocket knives, working only at night, but found the work went faster if they dug during the day as well. The excess dirt was disposed of by putting it in little sacks which were emptied into the large pond in the compound. After a few days, additional men were enlisted to help. Each new man took a solemn oath, with his right hand on the Bible, not to divulge the tunnel, and each swore to kill anyone found guilty of revealing their plan.[43]

After digging for some time, when several new hospital buildings were constructed, the prisoners decided it would be closer to dig their tunnel from beneath Hospital No. 2. After they obtained a spade, the work went quickly. With only two nights of digging, the tunnel was completed by Traweek and Putegnat, but they decided to wait until another night in order to let those who had helped with the first tunnel know. Before they could enter the tunnel, a prisoner was caught going under Hospital No. 1 (James W. Crawford), and he was court-martialed and sentenced to a "dungeon during his imprisonment." Traweek's tunnel under Hospital No. 2 was discovered as well. The men switched back to their original tunnel. However, Traweek was taken before the prison commandant. Major told Traweek that he knew about the tunnel. Traweek was put in the "sweatbox" to make him talk. The "crank turned on" him until his breath was "squeezed out." It probably was only for a minute, but Traweek remembered it seemed more like 3½ hours. Traweek finally confessed to digging the second tunnel, but would not reveal the names of anyone who had helped him. Traweek was then taken before the court and sentenced to the dungeon which was in one of the old military barracks.[44]

After a camp inspection, one of the guards told Traweek that they had found 28 tunnels, but because Traweek had managed to warn his fellow conspirators, their tunnel was not discovered.[45] After three weeks in the "dungeon," Traweek and Crawford were released, and they immediately resumed work on the first tunnel. Within a short time, the tunnel was complete, and Traweek, Crawford, and Maull were the first to step out onto the streets of the town of Elmira on the night of October 7, 1864. Once out, the prisoners had planned to meet at a church, and from there, make their way in pairs away from the city. Traweek and Crawford waded across the river and went to the nearby mountains. From their position high above the prison, they could see the activity inside the camp that their absence had generated. A detachment of cavalry was sent out in search of the escapees. Their flight South is a story in itself. After several close encounters, Crawford and Traweek made it to Winchester, Virginia, within Confederate lines and safety. Traweek died in 1923 at Beauvoir, a home for Confederate Soldiers and Sailors at Biloxi, Mississippi. He was the last member of the Elmira tunnel escapees.[46]

John Fox Maull recalled that after he crawled out through the tunnel, he expected at any minute to be seen and fired upon by the guards. He walked past the guards and turned to the right, as if he was going to the city. He encountered fellow prisoners Gilmer "Hickory" Jackson and William Templin. Together, the three crossed river and rested in a wooded area. He recalled that they "lay on the side of the mountain watching and talking and planning all day." From their vantage point, they could see the prisoners gather around their old tent, and there seemed to be a lot of excitement that day within the prison walls.[47]

Once outside the prison fence, Malone and Putegnat headed northeasterly. They continued for about 30 miles and stopped at a small farmhouse near Ithaca, New York. That they could walk abroad without detection was because Malone had obtained civilian clothes for them while still in the prison. There, they were given breakfast. At the village of Varna, they took a room at the hotel. They then traveled on to Auburn, New York. Malone took a job as a machinist with Putegnat as his helper. They saved enough money to buy train tickets to New York, and from there to Baltimore. [48]

Berry Benson was another prisoner who made it out through the tunnel the night of October 7, 1864. Another account pertaining to Berry Benson has additional details. Three of the prisoners remained in the tent, afraid to go and thinking that some of the other men were stuck in the tunnel. Berry Benson had enlisted in Charleston South Carolina, and had been a first sergeant in McGowan's Brigade before he was captured near Spotsylvania and sent to Point Lookout.[49] Benson said he would go down and find out. He entered the tunnel to find it empty. He made his way to the exit and came up under the elevated sentry walk. Across the street from him was the observation tower from which the guards could look over the fence and around the camp. The guards did not notice him. He waited a few minutes, then walked across the street. At the end of the block, he jumped over a fence and into the front yard of a house. Then he made his way carefully toward a barn, the agreed meeting place. He called for Traweek, Maull, Putegnat, and Scruggs, but no one was there. [Traweek's account said the meeting place was the church.] Benson decided not to wait for them, but headed for the forests. He made his way through the village of Big Flats and the town of Corning. He continued south into Pennsylvania. He traveled various ways—walking, in a rowboat, and aboard a train carrying lumber. He slipped on board a train headed for Baltimore, Maryland, but was noticed by the conductor. He lied and told the conductor that he had received a telegram that his sister who lived in York was dying, and he needed to get home. The conductor bought his story, and allowed Benson to enter the cars and take a seat. At York, he got off and by October 16 he was in Cockeysville, Maryland, near Baltimore. He brazenly hitched another train and fooled the Federal guards into thinking he was a resident of Maryland. He got off the train at Baltimore and walked through the streets of the city. He went to the home of a woman he had heard was sympathetic to the Confederacy, but he could not locate her. He kept walking and made his way to Unity. He hoped to reach Leesburg, Virginia, and the home of Judge Gray, who he knew would help him. On the night of October 19, Benson lay in the woods watching a group of Yankee soldiers encamped at a crossroads. He heard the sound of cannon fire from Winchester. He was unaware that Union Gen. Phil Sheridan and Confederate Gen. Jubal Early's troops were engaged in battle. When night came, Benson swam the Potomac and finally made his way toward the home of Judge Gray. On October 23, he ran into a detachment of Col. John Mosby's cavalry.[50]

When he tried to tell the cavalry soldiers he had escaped from Elmira, they did not believe him, and suspected he was a spy. The Confederate cavalry officers continued to question Benson, and he finally convinced them who he was by telling the officer that he knew both Ben Crowley and Sam Underwood who had been in Old Capitol Prison when he was. After talking with Colonel Mosby, Benson was directed to move south through the Blue Ridge mountains. On October 27, Benson met the advance guard of Gen. Bradley Johnson's cavalry. He was welcomed by Johnson and his staff and given a pass to New Market and told to report to Gen. Jubal Early. He met a friend at New Market who told him that his family believed he had died at Point Lookout. In Richmond, Benson ran into his brother, Blackwood Benson, and they had a joyful reunion. Benson had traveled 600 miles in 20 days, an average of 30 miles per day. Barry Benson's escape was exceptional, and his skill at evading recapture almost miraculous.[51]

Benson's adventures and his journey to rejoin his regiment has been detailed in a recently published book.[52] His ability to take advantage of every opportunity and evade capture is to be commended.

Although there were rumors that anywhere from five to 25 men escaped on the night of October 7, the official report gave the correct number as 10.[53] Nine of those 10 men made their way back to the South. Only Glenn Shelton of Mississippi, who had escaped with the rest, was never heard from again.[54] The feat of these 10 was to be commended. Because of the tight security at Elmira, only 17 are known to have escaped. One prisoner, Marcus Toney, noted that after the 10 escaped, tunneling efforts ceased. There were more tunnels dug, but no one got out through them.[55]

The third escape was also in October 1864, shortly after the 10 had escaped via a tunnel. The escapee was Joe M. Womack, a member of Wade Hampton's famous cavalry. Womack had been captured in Virginia and sent to Elmira on August 1, from Point Lookout.

An enterprising prisoner, Sergeant Womack, took the easy way out. He had borrowed a book from one of the guards. When he opened it, he found a pass inside. Thinking it was a trap, he returned the book with the pass intact. Later, the temptation to escape became too great, and he borrowed the book again. Luckily, the pass was still there. Womack then set to work perfecting his disguise. Wearing a stolen Federal coat and blue trousers, he walked boldly up to the guards and presented his pass. In the dim light of evening, he was not recognized, and strolled calmly out the gates to freedom. Later, with the help of Confederate sympathizers in a nearby town, Womack was soon on a train bound for Richmond, Virginia.[56]

The last known escape from Elmira Prison came in April 1865, when a prisoner hid in the "swill" wagon which carried the garbage outside to be dumped. Although he probably did not go out smelling like French perfume, he managed to escape.[57]

Because of its high death rate, Elmira Prison came to be known as the "Andersonville of the North." Those few who did manage to escape were indeed fortunate.

Elmira Today

By the end of 1865, the prison camp at Elmira had been closed and the buildings either torn down or moved to other locations. All that remains of the prison is a memorial marker that was erected in 1992 within the camp site.[58]

Those who died in Elmira Prison are buried a mile from the prison site in Woodlawn National Cemetery. The graves are marked with headstones because of the efforts of John W. Jones. Jones, a former slave, kept meticulous records of each death and supervised each burial. Inside the cemetery is a monument, erected by the United Daughters of the Confederacy in 1937, to the memory of the Confederate soldiers buried there.[59]

VI

Fort Delaware,
Pea Patch Island, Delaware

*I'm still confined at this wretched place. God grant they may send us away
very soon, for this is the last place on earth to me.*
— Private Joseph E. Purvis, diary entry, July 13, 1863

Location: Pea Patch Island, Delaware River, New Castle County, Delaware. **Established:** 1859, converted to prison February 1861. **Type of Prison:** existing costal fortification of solid granite walls. **Type of Prisoners:** prisoners of war (commissioned and non-commissioned officer, enlisted men), and political prisoners.[1] **Capacity:** Unknown. **Most Held at One Time:** 12,600. **Known Escapes:** 52.[2] **Nicknames:** "The Death Pen"[3] and "Andersonville of the North."[4]

History

Fort Delaware was built on the island by Gen. George B. McClellan while he was a member of the Corps of Engineers.[5]

Imprisonment in Fort Delaware was feared by both northerners and southerners. It was deemed the worst of the Federal prisons. Second Lt. Randolph Abbot Shotwell, from North Carolina, recalled his first impression of Fort Delaware:

> As the long procession of prisoners staggered out upon the wharf at Fort Delaware, the universal thought was one of Despondency, as if each had been warned like the lost spirits of Dante's Hell, 'Abandon Hope, all ye who enter here!' The reputation of the place for cruelty was already familiar to all of us and it needed no more than a glance at the massive fort with its hundred guns, the broad moat, the green slime dykes and the scores of sentrys [*sic*] pacing to and fro in all directions to quench every lingering hope of escape.[6]

The Site

Fort Delaware is located on a 90-acre island at the upper end of Delaware Bay,[7]— Pea Patch Island, really a mud shoal. According to the local legend, the island was formed many years ago around the hulk of a sunken ship. The ship had been loaded with peas, hence the name. The island about 2½ miles from the mainland of both Delaware and New Jersey.[8]

Fort Delaware — West side sally port and bastion.(Courtesy of the Library of Congress. HABS, DEL,2-PEPIS,1–5.)

The Prison Facilities

This pentagon-shaped fortress has granite walls 30 feet thick and 32 feet high. The massive walls supported three tiers of cannons. Like a medieval castle, the fort was surrounded by a moat. Inside the massive walls three brick buildings housed troops. The parade ground covered two acres.[9] The fortress was poorly constructed, and it sat several feet below the level of high water. The interior was always damp and cold.[10] Drainage on the island was poor and after even a little rain, the ground turned into a muddy quagmire.[11]

Tom Jenkins recorded a vivid description of his prison in his journal:

> The fort is surrounded by a canal, which is full of water, our barracks are outside of this canal; then outside of us is another canal and outside of this and extending around the island is an embankment to prevent the overflowing of the island. This embankment is used as a guard line, which is doubled at night. There is a guard posted through the yard, in order to keep the yard clean. The principal parts of the washing is done in the outer canal, and the water is kept very filthy.[12]

Quarters for Prisoners

Early in the war, the surgeon general declared the fort unsuitable for a large number of prisoners. This was true, but prisoners were sent there for the duration of the war. Col. William Hoffman believed that Fort Delaware was an "excellent place to hold prisoners of war." He did order the construction of additional barracks. After the prisoners moved into the new barracks, the quarters on the lowest level, the dungeon, were used only for punishment.[13]

Some of the more fortunate prisoners, a number of majors, lieutenant colonels, colonels, and the political prisoners, were kept inside the fort. Several two-story barracks also had been built outside the walls of the fort which extended along the gorge on the side facing the Delaware shore. The first floor contained the mess halls, storage rooms, and offices.[14] The long barracks were divided into sections which housed 400 men each. Officers and enlisted men were separated by a wall, which had a platform for the guards. Inside the barracks were three shelves, about six feet wide, which served as bunks. Capt. Edwin W. Rich described the barracks as neither "pure Gothic nor Romanesque, but decidedly *Archaic*."[15]

Sgt. Warren D. Reid (11th Regiment, Mississippi Volunteers), was serving with A. P. Hill's Corps when he was captured at Gettysburg on July 3, 1863. He was among 1,500 prisoners who were marched to Westminster, Maryland, where they boarded a train to Fort McHenry. There, they were put on a canal boat and taken by the Chesapeake and Delaware Canal to Fort Delaware, where they arrived on July 6, 1863.[16] Reid was placed in the barracks, on the northwest corner of the island, which had a plank wall around it. The prisoners were never allowed outside the wall except occasionally to help load or unload a ship. A gate in the wall, about 12 feet wide, stood open during the day that allowed access to the wharf. A guard stood at each side, and no one passed in or out without permission.[17]

An Unhealthy Place

By 1863, C. H. Crane, medical inspector of prisoners of war, declared:

> I do not consider Fort Delaware a desirable location, in a sanitary point of view, for a large deport of prisoners. The ground is wet and marshy and the locality favorable for the development of malarious disease. There have been many deaths at this place from typhoid fever, the result of their being crowded together in large numbers in a confined space.[18]

The number of deaths from April to December 1863 was 1,262 out of the 14,599 prisoners who had been received at the fort. From January through December 10, 1864, 664 of 7,799 prisoners died. For the 17-month period, 1,926 died out of 22,398 prisoners received.[19]

Prison Fare

Capt. Griffin Frost, transferred from the Gratiot Street Prison in St. Louis in April 1863, described Fort Delaware as:

> the hardest prison we have seen ... this elegant and select little "Island Home" has refined ... their habits, the rigorous denial practiced upon our appetites is wonderful, we indulge freely in nothing except the water from the bay, which affects all who use it with diarrhea; many are sick, but our craving stomach must be filled, it cries out

continually, … and the table has almost literally nothing to offer. Five hundred and fifty-three of us starve around the same board.

Frost and his fellow inmates were permitted to purchase a barrel of oysters from an oyster boat. This sustained them until they were transferred to City Point. Unfortunately, when Frost attempted to rejoin his unit, he was recaptured in Missouri behind Federal lines, and returned to the Gratiot Street Prison in St. Louis (see Chapter X).[20]

Another prisoner could find little "to be said in praise" of the prisoner's fare. Two meals were provided each day, which consisted of only a piece of bread and a piece of meat "indescribable salt, yellowish-colored pork … that had its nutriment entirely boiled out of it in the making of soup for the garrison." Occasionally a "treat" was served in the form of soup, which contained an "ample portion of maggots." They never received coffee or tea.[21]

The First Prisoners

Political prisoners were held at Fort Delaware as early as February 1861. The first prisoners of war to be incarcerated there were eight Confederates captured at Harpers Ferry.[22] They were John A. Hibbs, John Wild, John J. Semen, George Seely, all of the 1st Virginia Regiment; Robert D. Chambers and Thomas D. Hollis, of the 2nd Virginia; John Ferris of the 5th Virginia; and John G. Godwin, of the 1st Virginia, who was captured a few days after the first seven.[23]

Later, Confederate soldiers of every rank were confined along with southern sympathizers—men who ranked from judges to friends of President Lincoln.[24]

Sgt. Charles W. Rivenbark (Company C, 1st Regiment North Carolina Troops), was captured at Gettysburg. He and others prisoners were taken first to Fort McHenry near Baltimore, where they were asked to take the Oath of Allegiance. Only two out of 250 did so, "and they were not Americans," Rivenbark declared.[25]

The prisoners who did not take the oath were conveyed by a steamer to Fort Delaware, situated on a low-lying island protected from flooding by a dirt levee. Sergeant Rivenbark described the conditions there as "filthy and poisonous," so much so that even slight wounds would "inflame and mortify—and then amputation or death, or both —was the consequence."[26]

Some Famous Prisoners

Many famous prisoners were held at Fort Delaware, such as Confederate Brig. Gen. Johnston Pettigrew. With him was his aide, Lt. J. Barroll Washington, who was a descendant of Lawrence Washington, brother of President George Washington.[27]

Another celebrity prisoner was Samuel W. Hardinge, who lost his commission in the United States Navy to love.[28] While sailing the prize ship *Greyhound* to Boston, Hardinge fell in love with one of the passengers, Miss Belle Boyd, the famous Confederate spy. In Boston, the *Greyhound*'s captain, George H. Bier, mysteriously escaped. Hardinge followed Miss Boyd to England and married her in August 1864. On his return to the states, he was court-martialed for neglect of duty, discharged from the Navy, and imprisoned at Fort Delaware until February 3, 1865. Upon his release, Hardinge walked to from Delaware City to New Castle in bitter cold weather. He then returned to England but died a few months later.[29]

Morgan's Cavalry Officers

On March 18, 1864, four months after Brig. Gen. John H. Morgan made his escape from the Ohio State Penitentiary, Secretary of War Stanton ordered the remaining members of Morgan's cavalry sent to Fort Delaware from the Ohio Penitentiary and Camp Chase. An ample number of guards accompanied the prisoners, and they were not allowed to communicate with anyone along the way.[30] These "First Fifty" officers were sent to Charleston for exchange. Another group (the Immortal 600) would be sent to be held on Morris Island and endure great hardship while under fire from both Confederate and Union artillery.

Col. Basil W. Duke, brother-in-law of General Morgan, was confined at Fort Delaware for a time. Duke had been captured in July 1863 with Morgan's cavalry on a raid through Indiana and Ohio.[31] Also transferred to Fort Delaware were Morgan's brothers—Col. Richard C. Morgan and Capt. Charlton Morgan.

Gen. James Jay Archer, the first Confederate general captured at Gettysburg, was taken to Fort Delaware on July 5, 1863. Archer was quartered on the second floor of the soldiers barracks which, in 1863, was used for Confederate officers. He was transferred to Johnson's Island (see Chapter XI). He remained on Johnson's Island, although he tried to escape, until Federal officials returned him Fort Delaware to become one of the "First Fifty" sent to Charleston on June 21, 1864.[32]

The Infamous "Zarvona"

Col. Richard Thomas (a.k.a. Zarvona) was held at Fort Delaware for some time. Arrested for piracy and tried for treason for capturing ships for the Confederacy, Zarvona was transferred from Fort McHenry to Fort Lafayette in New York. Zarvona languished in solitary confinement while Confederate officials tried to obtain his release. Confederate officials even threatened that if Zarvona remained a prisoner, they would select seven prisoners at Libby to serve as hostages.[33] However, Federal authorities did not want to release him since he was believed to be a dangerous spy.

Finally, Gen. John Dix intervened. After an interview with the prisoner, he determined that Zarvona was only a "harmless zealot." Dix, therefore, changed Zarvona's status to prisoner of war, which made him eligible for exchange, then recommended the prisoner be transferred from Fort Lafayette to Fort Delaware. In late 1862, Zarvona was moved to Fort Delaware, but it 1863 before he was released[34]

Although Dix believed Zarvona was harmless, his company of "Potomac Zouaves" was still working as scouts and covert operators for the Confederacy. The Federals feared that if Zarvona was released, his espionage techniques would become common knowledge.[35] They held him in custody in hopes that he would reveal classified information regarding Confederate undercover operations. After 22 months in captivity and solitary confinement, the Federals decided that any information he had was no longer relevant. After months in a dark, airless cell, Zarvona was so desperate to get out of solitary and be allowed to walk in the fresh air on the parade ground that he would have agreed to almost anything. Zarvona agreed that if he could be paroled, he would not escape from the fort or communicate with anyone except through the authorities of the post in coded correspondence. He even offered to leave the United States and not return until the war was over.[36]

Finally, Richard Thomas Zarvona left Fort Lafayette in chains and was taken to Fort Delaware, where he arrived on April 15, 1863. This was two years *after* General Dix had requested that he be transferred to Fort Delaware. Commandant Schoepf was warned to expect a dangerous prisoner, and Zarvona was met as he disembarked by Schoepf and a body of guards. Although Zarvona's health had suffered greatly, he was held in isolation until the exchange actually took place. On May 6, 1863, he was transferred via steamer to Fort Monroe, Virginia, and finally, legally exchanged.[37]

The Federal government had no idea just how dangerous Zarvona actually was, or that had been the originator of a "covert operations battalion" (now the 47th Virginia) which was created as an escape route of safe houses along the way to help escaped prisoners reach the South. John Wilkes Booth, a member of the Confederate Secret Service since about 1863, was one of the operatives. He and his assassins used Zarvona's network in an attempt to kidnap President Lincoln. When the kidnap plot failed, Booth and David Herold employed the established escape route to avoid capture.[38]

Prison Personnel

The first commandant at the fort, Capt. Augustus A. Gibson, was assigned to the garrison of soldiers on February 2, 1861. Gibson, a West Point graduate, treated the prisoners as he would like to be treated if he were a prisoner. After 19 prisoners escaped, he was replaced by Maj. Henry S. Burton on August 5, 1862.[39]

A subsequent commander was David Perkins. He was replaced by Col. Robert C. Buchanan, who built additional barracks and enlarged the hospital. When Buchanan was transferred, Brig. Gen. Albin Schoepf, a Hungarian refugee, took charge from April 1863 until January 1866. Schoepf allowed his men to treat the prisoners as they saw fit, and Fort Delaware soon gained a reputation of being the most brutal prison in America.[40]

One prisoner decided that because General Schoepf was a "Dutchman," he was better qualified than most for that type of duty. Schoepf was very kind to the men, and let some of them work near his house.[41] His assistants, however, were not liked at all, especially Capt. G. W. Ahl and Lieutenant Wolf.

> Schoepf ... has two unpopular and insolent officers, Capt. G. W. Ahl, Lt. Woolf [*sic*] as his assistants. The uniformed plebians delight in exercising petty tyranny over their superiors in prison. Woolf [*sic*] is generally drunk, boastful and boisterous. Ahl is more genteel in speech and manners but less obliging and more deceitful and cruel. Gen. Schoepf is disposed to be lenient and kind but is terribly afraid of Secretary Stanton.[42]

Another guard was named Adams, but nicknamed "Old Hackout" or "Hike" by the prisoners. Adams was an ugly, repulsive-looking guard. A Dutchman from Vermont, he had served time at Fort Delaware as a deserter from the Federal Army. Reportedly, after the Battle of First Manassas, Adams was the first to turn tail and run back to Washington.[43] After he finished his sentence, Adams was given the job of guarding the Confederate prisoners.[44] Sgt. Charles W. Rivenbark recalled that Adams seemed to delight in playing "villainous" tricks which caused them pain and suffering. He taunted prisoners with lies that Davis, Lee, and Jackson were dead, captured, or had deserted the cause.[45] Because of Adams' experience as a prisoner and his network of spies among the prisoners, few escape plans were made of which he was unaware.[46] The prisoners hated "Old Hackout."[47]

Treatment of the Prisoners

Sergeant Rivenbark and some of the prisoners saw a copy of the Philadelphia *Enquirer*. This particular issue carried a story about the experiences of a Yankee officer who had escaped from Andersonville, the Confederate prison in Georgia. The men passed the paper around, and it was read by jailors and prisoners alike — all admitted that "prisoners at Fort Delaware were faring worse, suffering more, and bearing greater indignities, hardships and privations than those of Andersonville.[48]

A copy of Schoepf's rules as of July 8, 1864, was preserved in the letter book of Dr. Isaac W. K. Handy, a Presbyterian minister held prisoner at Fort Delaware. Handy, a Virginian. had been arrested for making pro southern statements in Delaware.

> I. Roll call at reveille and retreat.
> II. Police call at 7 A.M. and 4 P.M.
> III. Breakfast call at 8 A.M.; dinner, 2 P.M.
> IV. Sergeants in charge of the prisoners will extract from them a strict compliance with the above calls, which will be regularly enforced, and must promptly report to the officer in charge, the number present and absent, sick, etc; and any who are guilty of insubordination, or any violation of the rules of this prison. They must also notify their men that if they do not promptly obey any order given them by a sentinel, officer, or men in charge of them, they will be shot.
> V. Sergeants in charge will be held responsible for the due execution of these rules, and for the regular accounting for the number of their men.[49]

Guards Quick to Shoot

As in all prison situations, the guards were sometimes quick to use their guns. Handy recorded in his diary under the date "July 3d, 1864" the shooting of Col. E. P. Jones. Jones was a physician from Middlesex County, Virginia. He arrived with some "affliction of the feet, causing lameness." According to Capt. J. B. Cole, a witness, Jones was shot as he was hobbling along, with one shoe, stepping with care near the water house, "buttoning his pants." Cole was within 10 steps of Jones, and heard no challenge or order to move on. The next thing anyone knew, Colonel Jones was shouting, "Oh, God! What did you shoot me for? Why didn't you tell me to go on? I never heard you say anything to me!" The wounded prisoner was taken to the hospital, but there was no chance of his recovery.[50] Handy confronted General Schoepf about the shooting. Schoepf defended the guard's actions, and told Handy that because of the many escape attempts, the guards had standing orders to shoot "any man who tries to get away."[51]

Punishment

Corporal punishment was common in the 19th century, and prisoners brought before the courts could expect to receive harsh punishment. A prisoner could be executed for desertion. One of the lesser punishments was to brand a deserters with the letter "D." A prisoner might be forced to wear a barrel shirt or have his head shaved for minor offenses or infractions of prison rules.[52]

At Fort Delaware, some convicts worked in the kitchens to prepare meals for the other prisoners of war. Some of those convicts had been sentenced to wear a ball and chain, and the sound of their iron balls rolling around on the granite floor was loud enough to wake the Confederate prisoners in the rooms above the kitchen.[53]

Second Lt. Randolph Abbott Shotwell was captured at Cold Harbor and imprisoned at Point Lookout before being transferred to Fort Delaware. In July, he wrote about seeing two political prisoners, Captain Gordon and Mr. E. J. Debett, marched outside, stripped of their clothing, and dressed in old Yankee trousers. Afterwards, they were confined to the chain gang along with Federal soldiers under sentence as deserters, bounty jumpers, murderers, thieves, etc. All those condemned to the chain gang worked hard labor to haul heavy stones or lumber for the repair of the buildings or the dikes.[54]

Torture

Prisoners were tortured at Fort Delaware in the area between the mess hall and the kitchen. Prisoners were punished by being bucked, gagged, or hung by their thumbs for the slightest infraction of the rules. Prisoner George Moffett declared that this "was a daily occurrence, and I have seen six or eight 'thumb hangers' suspended at a time ... [while] a guard stood by to shoot anyone who interfered." As a result, the prisoners' shoulders were sometimes dislocated, and their thumbs were cut to the bone, which often resulted in the thumbs having to be amputated.[55] Another painful means of torture was to have the victim stand on the edges of a barrel and to hold a heavy log for hours. If he dropped the log, he was shot.[56]

Prisoners who were "bucked and gagged" were then suspended by a rope to the ceiling of the sally port, where they remained for the duration of their punishment. Federal soldiers convicted of drunkenness were forced to wear the letter "D" cut out of red flannel, attached to their uniform. Thieves had their heads shaved or had to march carrying a placard around the parade ground for a specified time.[57]

One Confederate soldier was accused of being a deserter from the Union army. Many in Fort Delaware knew him, and knew he was a southerner and had never been in the U.S. Army. A mock trial was held and he was condemned to die. He was tied to a stake and the officer in charge urged him to confess. Instead, according to the eyewitness report of Confederate Sergeant Rivenbark, the man bravely defended himself and his cause.

> I am your prisoner; kill me if you will; I'd rather die than suffer as I do! But, so help me God! I am neither traitor nor deserter, I am a Confederate States soldier. Jeff Davis, and Lee and Jackson, and Beauregard and Johnston yet live and my death will be avenged.[58]

The trial probably had been a cruel joke from the first. The man was cut down and returned to his cell, according to Rivenbark's account, and he was finally released from the prison.[59]

Solitary Confinement

Another form of mental and physical torture was to confine prisoners alone in a small, dark, airless cell. Major Mills was confined in the dungeon, not for something he had done, but in retaliation for a similar confinement of a Union officer in a southern prison. The dungeon consisted of two small, narrow, low and dark cells on either side of the entrance to the fort. These rooms held the mechanism for raising the drawbridge. As the prisoners marched out each day to the river, they looked with sympathy at Major Mills crouching at the little door of the cell, the only opening for ventilation.[60]

A room without windows on the second floor over the sally port was also used for solitary confinement. Several rooms, originally powder magazines, could be used if needed.

When Brigadier General Archer first arrived at Fort Delaware on July 5, 1863, he saw immediately that the prisoners greatly outnumbered the guards. Archer planned to seize the weapons of the relief guard and instigate an insurrection. He planned to overpower the guards and then escape. But someone informed Commandant Schoepf. Archer was arrested and placed in close confinement in one of the empty powder magazines.[61]

The Dungeon

In a brief sketch for "Histories of Army Posts," Capt. F. W. Gano described one of the dungeons. On its wooden ceiling, a prisoner had written, "Thomas Wensley, Fort Delaware, April 5, 1862." The dungeon rooms, with wooden floors and ceilings, were used to punish prisoners who had tried to escape or who had broken the prison rules.[62]

According to Pvt. George M. Green, whenever prisoners got "sassy," they were put in the dungeons and fed on "bread and water until they get tame."[63]

Retaliation

Maj. W. P. Elliott, commissary of subsistence for Brigadier General Morgan's Confederate cavalry, was a prisoner at Fort Delaware In retaliation for Union officer Maj. Nathan Goff, 4th Regiment, West Virginia Cavalry, being placed in "close confinement in a cell," Major Elliott was ordered to be confined the same way. Elliott had done nothing to deserve solitary confinement. He was given two meals a day, and was not to be permitted to receive anything unless prescribed for the post surgeon for illness.[64]

Hostages for Exchange: The "First 50" Sent to Charleston

Fifty Confederate officers were chosen to be sent from Fort Delaware to Charleston as hostages on June 26, 1864. The next two months were a nightmare for the 50 Confederate officers who were to be exchanged for five Union generals and 45 Union field officers. Among those first 50 Confederate officers were Maj. Gen. Franklin Gardner, Maj. Gen. Edward Johnson, Brig. Gen. George H. Steuart, Brig. Gen. James J. Archer, Brig. Gen. M. Jefferson Thompson, Col. W. H. Forney, plus 11 other colonels and the rest lieutenant colonels.[65]

Col. Richard Morgan and Col. Basil W. Duke (Morgan's brother-in-law) were also sent to Charleston to be held under fire from Confederate guns.[66] Duke never envisioned the conditions he would undergo before he was released when he wrote Brigadier General Schoepf on March 11, 1864. Arrangements had been made for Basil Duke's release through a special exchange, but Duke asked for permission to be sent to City Point to be exchanged for a Federal officer of "equal rank." Naturally, Schoepf referred the letter to Col. William Hoffman for the approval.[67] Thus, by Duke being sent to Charleston, his exchange was delayed, but he was finally released and returned to serve the Confederacy until the end (see Chapter XII).

Civilian Hostages Held

In June 1864, Colonel Hoffman ordered eight civilian prisoners transferred from Old Capitol Prison to Fort Delaware to be held as hostages. The eight citizens had decoyed two Union soldiers across the Potomac River at Edwards Ferry and fired on them and wounded one in the thigh. Then, they captured and robbed the two soldiers. As a final insult, "for the gratification of the citizens," the two captive soldiers were paraded through the streets of Leesburg. Once arrested, Hoffman ordered the eight civilians be confined by themselves, and that special care be taken to prevent their escape.[68]

Escapes — Success and Failure

It was possible, although difficult, to escape from Fort Delaware, as recorded in a number of first-hand accounts. If a prisoner was in good physical condition and was a good swimmer, he could swim to escape. The first escape under Commandant Schoepf occurred only two months after he took command. The longer General Schoepf remained, the more determined the prisoners became to chance death by drowning or being shot in order to escape.[69]

The escape of one prisoner in June 1863 was the first escape reported in the required monthly returns for Fort Delaware.[70] Several escapes had occurred before that time.

Already facing sickness and subsequent death, the prisoners increased their efforts to get off the island. Several attempts succeeded because of the number of guards (300 to guard 10,000 prisoners) was inadequate.[71]

With a Raft Plus Canteens

During the night of July 15–16, 1862, 19 prisoners escaped from island on a dark and stormy night. The prisoners, aided by southern sympathizers from Delaware, escaped from the barracks outside the fort. They tied empty canteens under their arms to help them float across the Delaware River. The prisoners had been salvaging scraps of lumber to build a raft to cross the Delaware. Once the first raft was completed, the prisoners decided to go. After they reached the Delaware shore, a network of southern sympathizers and agents of the Confederate Secret Service passed them along to inside Confederate-held territory. One group succeeded by using the raft to get to the Delaware side. There, citizens clothed them and sent them on their way.[72]

Captain Gibson reported to General Lorenzo Thomas that 19 prisoners had escaped. Gibson knew that a break was planned, and he had taken extra precautions. The prisoners had used lumber from a "privy" being constructed on the shore about 400 yards from the quarters. The bank at that point was covered with thick reeds, and it was not until the next day that the partially completed raft was discovered concealed in the reeds.[73]

By the time the story of their escape had made its rounds in the press, the numbers who escaped had "multiplied" to around 200. Two gunboats were dispatched to patrol the waters around Pea Patch Island. The 19 escapees were never found.[74] The number who actually escaped during the month is unclear. The official report for the month of July 1862 does not list any escapes out of 3,434 prisoners held in the fort at the time.[75]

Other Raft Efforts Fail

A Fort Delaware guard, Alexander J. Hamilton, kept a diary during his tour of duty. Hamilton was 5 feet, 11 inches tall, with fair complexion, brown eyes, and light-colored hair. He was a member of Independent Battery G, Pittsburgh Heavy Artillery.[76] His diary entry for December 12, 1862, noted that three or four "deserters" got outside the prison, but they were caught by the patrol trying to build a raft to cross the river.[77] Hamilton noted that on November 14, 1863, that five "Rebels left on a raft. Three were drowned and two were picked up."[78]

The official report was that one prisoner escaped in November and one in December 1863.[79]

Canteens Used

As part of one plan, Sergeant Rivenbark was chosen to saw through a wall with a "jeweler's" saw close to a sentry's post. One hundred and 30 prisoners, with the help of two canteens each, made airtight with a cork and wax, escaped. Only one drowned. However, Rivenbark, being the last to leave, discovered that someone else had taken his canteens which were to have served as life preservers.[80]

One group of six prisoners escaped on August 12, 1863, and made it safely to Richmond, Virginia. That group consisted of A. L. Brooks and C. J. Fuller (Company G, 9th Georgia), J. D. Marian (9th Georgia), William E. Glassey (18th Mississippi), and John Dorsey (Stuart's Horse Artillery). The prisoners had tied four corked canteens around their necks as life preservers. The night was dark when they swam from the back side of the island to the shore. Three of the escapees swam for four miles to reach shore two miles below Delaware City. Two others, who could not swim, floated 16 miles to the mouth of Christine Creek. The sixth man drowned a short distance from shore. It took the escapees two weeks to reach the Confederate capitol.[81] That men who could not even swim would attempt to brave the deep waters of the Delaware River indicates just how desperate they were to escape.

The three men who went ashore near Delaware City hid in a cornfield all night, then started south the next morning. They were joined by five others escapees from Fort Delaware. The prisoners obtained a canoe at Quantico, Maryland, and crossed over to Virginia. They then took the train to Richmond. All along the way, the men were helped by southern sympathizers who furnished them with money, clothing, and advice.[82]

One of the more notable escapes occurred in August 1864.[83] Three prisoners decided to brave the water of the Delaware Bay. Joe Deupree, William B. Rodgers, and Benjamin Kelly eluded the guards, and began to swim across the bay with canteens tied to their bodies to help keep them afloat. They swam for six hours but with the incoming tide, the men became separated. Deupree saw a ship and was taken aboard. He was dismayed to find that he was only about 50 yards from shore. Very soon he found himself back in Fort Delaware Prison, to face his punishment. The other to men became separated, but both eventually rejoined their regiments.[84] The monthly reports for August 1863 reported that eight prisoners had escaped.[85]

Sgt. Warren D. Reid and his cousin, Joseph G. Marable, began to plan their escape. They first planned to swim across the bay with the help of canteens to keep them afloat. The route they chose, however, had been tried before, and was closely guarded. A new plan was devised, and on August 15, 1863, it was put into action. Reid and Marable passed out through the gate without even a glance at the guards. This fooled the guards into thinking they must have permission and were simply taking a stroll around the island as some of those who had taken the Oath of Allegiance were allowed to do. However, the two could not find a boat on which to leave, so they made do with a 12-foot ladder from an officer's barn. Then, they went back inside the fence, and passed the guards without any trouble. They boiled their clothes to get rid of the lice, and after the garments had dried, they went back through the gate to the outside. The two separated and hid until dark, then met at the little building used for a doctor's office.

Bravely, carrying the ladder, the two bluffed their way unnoticed past the sentinel to cross the levee that kept out the water at high tide. The levee was five or six feet high, and the canal that it enclosed was about 12 feet wide and three feet deep. They alternately crept forward and lay flat on the ground to avoid detection as the guard made his round to a certain point then turned and started back the other way. It took them about an hour and a half to cover about 150 yards.

Finally, they crossed the levee and reached the bay. They pushed the ladder into the water and used it as a raft. They tied their shoes to it, and picked up a piece of plank to use as a paddle. While one sat on top of the ladder and paddled, the other held on to the last round. A vessel passed but did not notice them in the dark. The two finally reached a small island and managed to cross over to the mainland of New Jersey about 12 or 15 miles from Fort Delaware. The two escapees then stole a small boat and recrossed Delaware Bay and made their way to Chesapeake Bay. They made several stops along the way, and kindly people gave them food. The two prisoners eventually reached Baltimore, Maryland, then headed up the Potomac River to just above Harpers Ferry. They had intended to go to Charlestown, but it was occupied by Union cavalry, so instead, they continued toward Culpepper and met the First Confederate Cavalry at the Luray Court House. A Confederate cavalryman paid for them to spend the night in a hotel, and the next day they took the stage to Culpepper. At Orange Court House, the two cousins rejoined their 11th Mississippi Regiment. Very few of their Company H were there to greet them.[86]

By the end of August, after the body of a drowned man was discovered, all canteens were ordered confiscated. The guards collected 8,000 canteens to prevent further escapes of the prisoners by using this method.[87]

Simply Swim Away

On July 18, 1863, several prisoners tried to swim the river. One was shot and killed by the guards; the others returned to the barracks.[88]

Four men attempted to swim the river and escape on August 13, 1863. Two nearly drowned men were picked up by Captain Thoroughgood of the schooner *W. H. Sherman.* No sooner had those two been rescued, when the ship's captain saw two more prisoners swimming past his ship. These two were captured, and all returned to Fort Delaware.[89]

In September 1863, the monthly returns noted 10 escapes, and four escapes the next month.[90]

Escape attempts continued into the new year. On February 16, 1864, Hamilton noted that the "Rebels are doing quite a good business in escaping in spite of the cold weather."[91] Officially, one prisoner was reported as having escaped in February.[92]

A plan by the prisoners to capture a steamer and escape failed in March 1864,[93] although one prisoner was reported to have escaped during the month.[94]

Five more prisoners were captured outside the prison walls trying to escape on July 6, 1864.[95]

Escapes continued through July 1864. Ten were reported to have escaped. The report form does not have a column for the number of escapees recaptured.[96] Guard A. J. Hamilton noted that on July 10, 1864, five more prisoners were captured while trying to escape.[97]

Just Board a Ship and Sail Away

One courageous prisoner, a member of Morgan's cavalry, took advantage of the 4th of July celebration. He dressed up as a Yankee officer and boldly walked out right by the sentinel. Once out, the Confederate-turned-Yankee continued to walk around the island to get his bearings and see what was available to facilitate his escape. He saw that the steamboat that had brought a large party of citizens down from Philadelphia for a picnic. The Confederate went back inside the prison, urged two of his friends to change to civilian clothes, obtained a forged pass with General Schoepf's name on it, and he and two companions returned to the boat where they were carried away when it left that night.[98]

On October 15, 1863, a prisoner named Johnson, who had already tried and failed to escape three times, got lucky. He boarded the coal boat when it landed on Pea Patch Island. Although a search was instigated, Johnson could not be found.[99]

On August 12, 1864, a ship landed with more prisoners. When the boat left the island, it was noticed that some of the prisoners were missing. A gunboat was sent to stop the ship, but none of the missing prisoners were found.[100] One prisoner was noted to have escaped on the monthly report.[101] In October 1864, two prisoners were reported as having escaped, [102] and one escape was reported in November 1864.[103]

Overpower the Guards

Some escape plans hinged on overpowering the guards. According to the Rev. Isaac Handy, two plots devised to overpower guards never materialized. Brigadier General Archer was to have taken charge of the first attempt, and Colonel Wicks was to be in charge of the second. In both cases, the plans were complete and would have succeeded, but there was difficulty in obtaining transportation for a large body of prisoners to cross the river.[104]

Lt. McHenry Howard's memoirs describe plans to overpower the guards and escape in the summer of 1864. As the men were marched out for their daily baths at the river, the guards would be overpowered, and the prisoners would seize the guns stacked along the inner wall, close the gate, and take possession of the fort. With the big guns at their command, they planned to release thousands of prisoners being held. Once this was accomplished, the prisoners planned to cross the river to Maryland where Confederate Gen. Jubal Early was conducting a raid. However, while waiting for the right time to make their move, the plan was leaked to General Schoepf. He immediately stopped prisoners from the daily trips to the water outside the fort. This plan was similar to that of General Archer in July 1863. Archer's plan, too, was discovered, and he was transferred to Johnson's Island in Lake Erie (see Chapter XII).[105]

Build a Boat

Rivenbark's second escape attempt involved building a boat. This was done with the use of a "knife-saw and screws." When the boat was finished in came the guards and tore up the floor, found the boat and destroyed it. If it had gone undetected, the boat would have carried as many as eight men to freedom.[106] Rivenbark did not reveal the "particulars of [his] escape, with all the adventures attending it," because "prudence forbids, even at this late day [April 9, 1901] that I should give the names of those who aided me to get out of prison or on the long route home—or the methods and means used."[107]

The inmates of Fort Delaware did not give up on the boat idea. Rev. Handy noted that a year later "about two hundred privates—favored by the extreme darkness—are reported to have gotten off, in two boats, constructed for the purpose, which they had managed to conceal under the floor of the barracks."[108]

Bribe the Guards

Bribery has always been a method used to effect an escape. If a prisoner had enough money, he could often bribe his way to freedom.[109] The prisoner trying to bribe his way out had to be very careful in his selection of the guard or official to bribe. Frequently, the guards took the bribe, then reported the prisoner. Sergeant Rivenbark knew two prisoners, one from Tennessee and the other from Maryland, who had bribed Lieutenant Campbell with a fine gold watch and $100 to help them escape. The two were smuggled aboard a steamer. Yet very shortly, Lieutenant Campbell went after them, hunted them down on the ship, and brought the pair back to Fort Delaware in handcuffs with his "cocked pistol leveled at them!" Even though many failed in their attempts, according to Rivenbark, " a good many did get away, although many perished in the attempt."[110]

When Sergeant Rivenbark decided to bribe his way out, he knew not to attempt to bribe a private or a subordinate officer. He went to "high officials with his offering." If the bribe was liberal enough, he knew his release was sure to follow." It was, and Sergeant Rivenbark finally won his release in March 1865, only a month before the surrender at Appomattox [111]

Or Steal a Barge

Sometimes the guards fled Fort Delaware along with the escaping prisoners. Hamilton reported that on the night of February 10, 1863, a sentry and 10 members of the 157th Pennsylvania Volunteers stole the "major's barge and deserted last night." Although a search party was sent out, the barge was recovered, but there was no sign of the 11 guards.[112]

Just Walk Across the Ice

On January 4, 1865, five prisoners in irons succeeded in cutting a bar out of the window and crossing the bay over the ice. A search party pursued them, but did not recapture any of the five.[113]

Out Through the Privy

The desperate men inside Fort Delaware spent all their time thinking of ways to escape. Some of the methods were not very clean. One "unsanitary" method was through the privy holes, which extended over the Delaware River. Even with strict security measures, prisoners continued to escape by this route.[114]

Go Out with the Dead

Another method of escape, not for the squeamish, was to replace a living body with the dead one in the coffin. Dr. W. H. Moon, of Alabama, wrote an account of one such escape. The coffin had to be one that was destined to be sent elsewhere for burial. This was done in one instance by a prisoner who was working in the hospital.

He decided to escape by removing one of the bodies from its coffin and hiding it under some old clothes. He then got in the box and had his friend replace the lid, but leaving it loose enough that it could easily be removed. The coffins were loaded on boats and rowed across the river to the New Jersey shore. Guards, accompanied by other prisoners, were sent along with the coffins to attend to the burial. When the burial site was reached and the coffins about to be placed in the ground, the undead prisoner pushed off the lid of his coffin, and jumped up. He ran as fast as he could to a nearby apple orchard. Both guards and prisoners were so badly shaken by the dead suddenly arising that, in the confusion, the prisoner made his escape.[115]

The last reported escapes from Fort Delaware came during the month of May 1865, after the war had ended. Eleven prisoners were reported as having escaped, from among the 8,270 prisoners still being held on the island.[116] These last escapees were men who grown tired of waiting for all the paperwork and red tape involved in their release and the problems of finding transportation for 8,000 prisoners.[117]

The Last Prisoners

After taking the Oath of Allegiance, most of the prisoners were allowed to leave. Still confined for some months after the war had ended was Lt. Gen. Joseph Wheeler, who had refused to surrender. Also confined were Texas governor Francis Lubbock; Burton Harrison, private secretary to Confederate president Jefferson Davis; and Col. William Preston Johnston, son of Confederate Gen. Albert Sidney Johnston, all of whom had been captured while fleeing with Davis. These men were placed in solitary confinement on the second floor of the administration building. Another man confined at Fort Delaware after the war was Maj. Henry K. Douglas, who had been arrested for wearing his Confederate uniform in Maryland. Douglas claimed he was going to have his picture taken. After several months imprisonment, these men were released. On January 16, 1866, Harrison, the last remaining prisoner in the fort, was released.[118] The fort reverted to its original purpose, and after new guns were installed, continued to defend the coast through World War II.[119]

Fort Delaware Today

Today, Fort Delaware is part of Fort Delaware State Park. It remains very much as it was during the Civil War era. The 8-inch Columbiads still guard the ramparts, and the "dark and damp corridors" echo with the sounds of prisoners and guards when life inside the prison is recreated by military and civilian reenactors. The fort is open to visitors on a limited basis on weekends and holidays from late April through September.[120]

VII

Fort Lafayette, New York Harbor, New York

For about five months I have been in close confinement....
— Zarvona (Richard Thomas), December 7, 1861.[1]

Location: island between Staten Island and Long Island, New York Harbor. **Constructed:** 1822, opened as prison in 1861. **Type:** costal fortification. **Type of Prisoners:** civilian political prisoners, and prisoners of war, soldiers, sailors, foreigners from Canada, England, Mexico, and elsewhere. **Capacity:** 50. **Most Held at One Time:** 163. **Number of Known Escapes:** 2[2] or 5 (monthly returns[3]). **Other Names:** Fort Diamond. **Nicknames:** The American Bastille.

History

Named in honor of the Marquis de Lafayette, the Frenchman who assisted with the American Revolution, this structure was one of the later costal fortifications to be built. The fort was located on a small rock island in the Narrows between the lower end of Staten Island and Long Island, opposite Fort Hamilton.[4]

The Facilities

The fort was a formidable structure. It had an octagonal shape and massive walls 25 to 30 feet high.[5]

Prisoners were confined in the fort's gun batteries and in four casements on the lower level. The batteries were about 60 feet by 24 feet," reported prisoner Francis K. Howard, editor of a Baltimore newspaper and grandson of Francis Scott Key. Part of the space was taken up by five big 32-pound cannons. There were five small windows, with iron gratings. Eventually, stoves were added to the battery rooms to provide heat.[6]

The four casemates rooms were 24 by 14 feet, and had vaulted ceilings. Light filtered in through two small loopholes, one on an outer wall and the other on the inner wall. The large wooden doors were locked at 9 P.M. and reopened at daylight. The casemate rooms were damp and dark, but did have fireplaces.[7] The conditions for prisoners at Fort Lafayette were deplorable. Howard described his imprisonment as "exactly like that of those who used to be held in the Bastille."[8]

The Prison Personnel

Fort Lafayette was under the command of Charles O. Wood, a former baggage handler for the Ohio and Mississippi Railroad. He was described as "brutal" by many prisoners. He was reported to have beaten and kicked prisoners.[9]

The Prisoners

Converted from a defensive fort to a prison in July 1861, Fort Lafayette was one of the first of the old forts to hold Federal political prisoners.[10] The first prisoners of war incarcerated at Fort Lafayette were officers captured by Major General McClellen, officers known to have recently resigned from the United States Army or Navy. As stated in Assistant Adjutant General E. D. Townsend's order, all those officers who had resigned their commissions to serve the Confederacy, if captured, were automatically sent to Fort Lafayette.[11] Townsend directed that those officers, along with "Marshal Kane and the police commissioners who are in arrest and such political prisoners as may not be under indictment by the civil authority" be sent to Fort Lafayette in New York Harbor. The prisoners arrived at Fort Lafayette on July 22, 1861. Townsend ordered a permanent force to the fort to guard the prisoners.[12]

Secretary of State William H. Seward ordered Major General Dix to arrest Richard K. Meade, of Virginia, when he arrived in Baltimore. Meade, a Virginian, had been minister to Brazil, but was now suspected of siding with the Confederacy. For national security reasons, it was deemed necessary to arrest Meade, confiscate his papers, and confine him in Fort Lafayette.[13]

James W. Ball, a member of the Maryland Legislature, suddenly found himself confined in Fort Lafayette.[14] A number of civilians were arrested in Kentucky in October 1861: William T. Castro, George Forrester, James H. Hall, William Hunt, Isaac Nelson, and B. F. Thomas. These men were subsequently transferred to Fort Lafayette on a variety of charges, ranging from treason to disloyalty or of being active secessionists and supporting the rebels. Most were released in December 1861 after taking the Oath of Allegiance to the United States of America.[15]

Early in 1862, a Union general was arrested for the fiasco at the battle of Ball's Bluff which occurred on October 21, 1861. Maj. Gen. George B. McClellan ordered the arrest of Brig. Gen. Charles Pomeroy Stone, who was already under arrest and confined in "close quarters" at Fort Lafayette, where he was to be allowed the "comforts due his rank," but not allowed to communicate with anyone by letter or otherwise, except under close supervision.[16] For months, Stone tried to get copies of documents and charges pertaining to his arrest.[17] Failing that, he applied to General McClellan to "serve with the Army ... even if only as a spectator."[18]

Stone was imprisoned for 189 days without being charged or tried. After his release, he awaited further orders in Washington, D.C., and was finally assigned as General Banks' chief of staff. Although he was in demand for responsible positions, he was kept under surveillance and in unimportant posts. He finally broke under the strain of suspicion that hung over him, and resigned on September 13, 1864.[19]

After the New York draft riots in July 1863, the leaders and some of the participants were arrested and confined to Fort Lafayette. A man named "Andrews," charged with being the "principal orator of the mob," as well as a southerner, was arrested by U.S. Marshal Robert Murray and taken to Fort Lafayette.[20] Since the fort was nearby, Lt. Col. Martin Burke, the prison commandant at that time, was immediately ordered to receive and "keep in safe custody" any more persons arrested for participating in the draft riots.[21]

Treatment of the Prisoners

Conditions at Fort Lafayette were harsh. There were a few iron beds, which were crammed between guns in the batteries. Prisoners housed in the lower casemates had no beds, bags of straw or blankets.[22]

As time went on, the fort was often filled beyond capacity with prisoners. John I. Shaver, a Canadian, was arrested in Detroit for helping the Confederacy. He was confined in one of the dark and unventilated casemates with 48 others prisoners, devoid, according to the *Montreal Advertiser*, of the common decencies of life."[23] The food was bad and the water even worse. The cistern from which water was obtained was often filled with dirt and "animalcules." There were even dry spells when prisoners had to go without any water.[24]

Lt. Col. Marshall J. Smith complained to James A. Seddon, secretary of war for the Confederate States, about conditions at Fort Lafayette.

> We were confined in the casemate without other exercise than the length of the room would allow; there we were not permitted to purchase or receive things from our friends; the guard was strict, but we were treated with respect.[25]

Typhoid Epidemic

While records of the number of deaths at Fort Lafayette are incomplete, newspapers reported a typhoid fever epidemic at the fort late in 1861, and so many prisoners died that the public was alarmed and there was an "outcry of indignation."[26]

The Way Out

Sometimes prisoners, especially civilians, were kept in the Federal forts, without being charged, without standing trial, and with little hope of being released. However, Senator Thomas J. McKaig was promised a parole if he took the Oath of Allegiance. He did so, and asked to be on his way to Philadelphia the day after his release papers were received on October 21, 1861.[27]

Henry M. Warfield seemed satisfied with his prison. He was interviewed by assistant surgeon R. D. Lynde. Lynde reported that at the present time Warfield "declines ... to make any application for his release on the score of health," because the prisoner did not "feel that he is now suffering from his confinement."[28] Sounds like he was offered a chance to get out, but did not take it.

Non-American Sailors Held

Capt. T. H. Baker and his crew from the *Savannah* were captured and arrested on June 3, 1861.[29] The seamen were indicted and held at Fort Lafayette until brought to trial at the October term of the U.S. Circuit Court for the Southern District of New York. The trial began on October 23, 1861, and continued for eight days, when the jury reported they could not agree and were discharged. Before a new trial could be held, the United States government made a formal agreement with the Confederate government to treat privateers as regular combatants, and the seamen were exchanged under the Dix-Hill Cartel.[30]

John Mack, a native of Ireland, who had been a crew member of a privateer, the *Petrel,* applied directly to Secretary of War Stanton to be released "on my parole of honor or by taking the oath of allegiance." Other non–American crew members made similar applications.[31] They were John Cronin, Edward Murphy, Hugh Monaghan, Thomas Woods of the *Petrel* crew, and Joseph Cruz del Cano, and others.[32] Twenty-four prisoners were released by the order of the secretary of the navy on May 30, 1862, and 59 "privateer prisoners" were sent away on the steamer *S. R. Spalding,* probably to an exchange point. The 59 privateers had been captured on the *Savannah, York, Sumter, Jeff Davis, Dixie,* and *Petrel.* [33] Order No. 8, from Edwin M. Stanton, secretary of war, permitted the release of those who had applied and agreed to take the oath of allegiance, on the condition that they "go South across the military lines of the United States, to Maj. Gen. John A. Dix," who was authorized to either grant or refuse their requests, and (2) that "all prisoners of war and other persons" who were subsequently released on parole or exchanged, should present themselves immediately upon their arrival at Baltimore to Dix, and be "subject to his direction while remaining in that city." Failure to observe those conditions would result in "forfeiture" of any parole or exchange granted.[34]

When nine British seamen were captured and imprisoned at Fort Lafayette, Queen Victoria and the British government were informed by the British Consul in New York. Subsequently, the British demanded that the seamen not only be released but compensated for having been treated cruelly and confined in irons and treated as common criminals.[35]

Seward replied immediately and elaborated on the details of how the British sailors came to be imprisoned. The British sailors claimed they had been shipwrecked and picked up by a another ship which, unfortunately, was the schooner *Henry Middleton*, a Charleston blockade runner. Some were also captured on a ship named the *Colonel Long.* After being captured, the ships and all on board were "condemned as insurgents against the Government … and become prisoners of war." As to the prisoners being confined in irons, Seward explained: "Being seamen and brought there simultaneously with privates who had been taken in battle in other vessels the officer in charge thought it prudent to put them in irons until his superior officer should direct what disposition should be made of a body of prisoners so large as to be deemed dangerous."[36]

The British consul to the United States applied for and was granted permission to visit the imprisoned British subjects. Seward also said that the nine British sailors claimed that they were "not only … subjects of the Queen of Great Britain but to have gone on board the vessels not from choice but necessity to seek a return to their native country." As soon as all the facts of the matter were considered, the men "were released from imprisonment and set at large," even before the demand from the British government for their release, according to Seward. The Queen's representative was told that President Lincoln did not feel obliged "to make any compensation to the persons to whom the clemency of the Government was thus promptly and without inquiry extended."[37]

Richard Thomas (Zarvona) Tries to Escape

Richard Thomas was born in Saint Mary's County, Maryland, on October 27, 1833, to a prominent Maryland family. He attended the United States Military Academy at West Point for a short time, but did not graduate. He was a nonconformist, an adventurer, and a wanderer. After leaving West Point, he is reported to have traveled to the Far East and was involved in war against Chinese pirates who were terrorizing the seas. He then traveled to Italy, and fought under Garibaldi during the war for Italian independence. It was in Italy that he assumed the name Zarvona.[38]

Shortly after Fort Sumter was captured, Thomas, a southern sympathizer, began to plan how he could serve the Confederacy. One way he could help was to capture Northern vessels plying the Chesapeake Bay.[39] He and several accomplices succeeded in capturing the steamer *St. Nicholas*.[40] The originator of this daring plan is unknown, but Zarvona, Capt. George N. Hollins, and H. H. Lewis, another naval officer were all involved, and a number of other officers and sailors.[41] Forty-six southerners took part in the capture of the *St. Nicholas*. A third of them were members of the Maryland Zouaves, headed by Colonel Richard Thomas (alias Zarvona).[42] The takeover of the *St. Nicholas* began when the ship was boarded by a "French lady," who was really Thomas (Zarvona) in disguise. The "French lady" excused herself, and emerged several minutes later from her stateroom dressed in full Confederate uniform and brandishing a cutlass and a revolver.[43] In a few minutes, the ship was taken, and the passengers and crew secured below the hatches.[44]

Encouraged by the ease with which they had captured the *St Nicholas*, Zarvona, Alexander and the others went on with their "piracy" and captured several more ships.

With the backing of Governor Letcher of Virginia, Zarvona set out to repeat his success. What he had in mind is unknown, but he may have planned to board another steamer and seize it.[45] However, Zarvona and a number of his men were captured aboard the steamer *Mary Washington* near Annapolis on July 7, 1861. When arrested, he was disguised as a woman — Madame La Force.[46] Colonel Zarvona was indicted by the grand jury for treason. Initially, confined at Fort McHenry, he was transferred to Fort Lafayette by orders of Maj. Gen. John A. Dix.[47] Thomas left Fort McHenry on December 2, 1861, and arrived at Fort Lafayette the next day.[48]

Despite all efforts, after nearly two years, Thomas was still being held prisoner. General Dix thought Thomas should have been treated as a "pirate and a spy." In February 1863, he was still in Fort Lafayette under "close confinement" because of escape attempts.[49]

After it was discovered that he was sending coded messages to friends outside the prison, he was placed in strict confinement, and allowed no visitors whatsoever.[50]

Zarvona continued his efforts to obtain release from prison, and he made repeated appeals for release on parole.[51] Numerous persons wrote in his behalf. Thomas Ingram, of Halifax, Nova Scotia, suggested Zarvona be exchanged for Colonel Corcoran. This was also proposed by R. W. Rasin, both prisoners at Fort Lafayette.[52] There was some correspondence between Dix, Secretary of War Stanton, and Secretary of State William Seward as to the possibility of transferring Zarvona to the list of prisoners of war, as requested by Colonel Zarvona.[53] Dix reminded Stanton that while Zarvona had been charged with piracy, he was indicted on "treason alone." Furthermore, Major General Banks never recognized those proceedings, and Banks believed Zarvona was a pirate "of the worst form." Dix believed that the prisoner "ought not to be classed with persons captured in open warfare," but rather should be treated as a "pirate and a spy."[54] Zarvona had not been treated as Capt. T. H. Baker and other privateers who were exchanged as regular sailors. Zarvona had done no more than the privateers arrested in July 1861 and released in May 1862. Federal officials considered Col. Richard Thomas Zarvona much too dangerous to be released, and thus they continued to keep him in solitary confinement.

Zarvona desperately sought help outside by sending messages in code. A recently released prisoner informed officials that Zarvona had a "cipher" by which he sent letters to a Mrs. Norris and others in Baltimore. The innocent looking correspondence actually was a request for acid, files, and other items which could be concealed and slipped to him. Lt. Col. Martin Burke, commander at the fort, was ordered to place Zarvona "in close confinement" and to keep a strict surveillance over his correspondence.[55]

Early in April, his mother, Mrs. Richard Thomas Sr., begged Colonel Burke for information about her son's condition. She feared that solitary confinement had affected his mind.[56] She may have been correct in her fears, because three weeks later, Richard Thomas Zarvona attempted to escape from Fort Lafayette.

On the stormy night of April 21, 1862, after being confined in prison almost a year, Zarvona attempted to escape.[57] By getting the guard to let him go to the "water closet," he managed to gain the top of the sea wall, and plunged into the waters of the harbor in the midst of a raging storm. He headed for the shore of Long Island. However, his freedom was cut short when the prison officials sent guards in a boat. They soon reached him and returned the prisoner "dripping but undaunted to his cell."[58]

The amazing thing about the attempt was that Zarvona could not swim. He had tried to overcome that disadvantage by making a sort of life preserver from corked tin cans suspended around his waist with a cord.[59] Although he did not drown, he probably wished he had. His failed escape attempt resulted in even longer solitary confinement, and he was allowed no visitors. His confinement eventually resulted in a breakdown of both his mental and physical health.[60] Secretary of War Stanton even revoked his mother's pass, so that she could not visit her son.[61] (For more about the short career of Richard Thomas [Zarvona], see also Chapters VI and VIII.)

One Conspirator Got Lucky

One of the last prisoners released from Fort Lafayette was Charles H. Cole, a member of Bedford Forrest's Confederate cavalry who had escaped Johnson's Island and fled to Canada (see Chapter XI). Cole had become involved in a plot to free the Johnson's Island prisoners with the help of a couple of pirated ships.[62] After Cole was captured he revealed the names of some prominent citizens and people involved in the plot. Cole remained confined at Fort Lafayette until finally released by Judge Gilbert at the Brooklyn Court House on February 10, 1866.[63] He was lucky he was not executed for treason or sentenced to a lengthy prison term.

The Last Prisoners at Fort Lafayette

In March 1865, the number of prisoners held at Fort Lafayette was down to 49 from a high of 122 in July 1863, and a like number in January 1864. The highest number of prisoners held at Fort Lafayette was 134 during the month of February 1864. The facility was not included on the monthly listing for April 1865. But by June, five prisoners had been added, among them the vice president of the Confederacy, Alexander Stephens. That number had increased to 10 by July 1865. Fort Lafayette continued to hold its prisoners, and by November 1865, it was the *only* prison still holding prisoners of war or prisoners of state, according to the monthly report. That month, the four prisoners in custody were joined by an additional prisoner making a total of five.[64]

Fort Lafayette Today

The fort continued to serve as a munitions magazine through World War II. In 1960, the old fort was demolished to make way for support beneath the east tower of the new Verrazano-Narrows Bridge. The rubble was dumped into the shore off Staten Island to help support the west tower of the bridge.[65]

VIII

Fort McHenry,
Baltimore, Maryland

A large portion of the prisoners of war are, while here, entirely without shelter.
— Maj. William W. Morris, commander, Fort McHenry

Location: Whetstone Point, on the Patapsco River, Baltimore, Maryland. **Established:** 1799–1805, converted to prison in 1861. **Type:** coastal fortification. **Type of Prisoners:** political prisoners, prisoners of war. **Capacity:** 600. **Most Held:** 6,957 at one time. **Number of Known Escapes:** 37. **Nicknames:** "Fort Mac."[1] **Total Number of Prisoners:** approximately 23,000 soldiers and political prisoners.[2]

History

Fort McHenry, a national shrine, is famous because its bombardment by the British on the night of September 13, 1814, inspired Francis Scott Key to compose the *Star-Spangled Banner*.

Located on Whetstone Point, about three miles from Baltimore, this site has been used as a defensive position since 1776.[3] A fort at this location was necessary for the defense of Baltimore. Similar in construction to Fort Monroe on the Chesapeake and Fort Macon on the coast of North Carolina, Fort McHenry was one of a string of massive, star-shaped, coastal fortifications constructed along the eastern seaboard between 1798 and 1812. It was named for Col. James McHenry, a resident of Baltimore who had served as an aide to Gen. George Washington during the Revolutionary War, and later as secretary of war from 1796–1800.[4]

The fort was garrisoned by Federal soldiers early in the war, and their presence helped prevent Baltimore and the state of Maryland from joining the Confederacy. Although many Marylanders were pro–Confederate, Maryland was never allowed to join the Confederacy, and was quickly occupied by Federal troops. The Federal troops kept the area under close surveillance.[5]

The Facilities

Designed by the Frenchman Jean Foncin, construction of Fort McHenry began in 1799 and was completed in 1805. The exterior walls are 15 feet high, and comprise

22,261 square feet. The length of the seawall is 12,500 feet. The fort has 30 rooms, two powder magazines, and the outer battery had four underground chambers.[6]

Inside the fort, five main buildings served as the commanding officer's quarters, junior officers' quarters, enlisted men's barracks which later housed guards, and a powder magazine with walls 10 feet thick.[7]

Fort McHenry could comfortably house 100 prisoners, with an additional 500 more quartered in the stables and the surrounding area. On an average, the fort held about 400 Federal prisoners, 250 prisoners of war, and 30 political prisoners.[8]

Captured prisoners of war were held in two large brick buildings, 120 by 30 feet. Injured prisoners were confined to the upper floor of one of the buildings. Captured officers and enlisted men were confined to the upper floor of a second building. Political prisoners were kept inside the fort in rooms 60 × 30 feet. The dungeons were beneath each side of the sally port. Prisoners who had violated the rules were sometimes kept in cells in the guard houses which could be entered only through narrow wooden doors reinforced with iron.[9]

The Prisoners

A number of political prisoners were confined at Fort McHenry. Maryland and the city of Baltimore was filled with Southern sympathizers. On August 15, 1862, Maj. William P. Jones, acting provost marshal in Baltimore, acted according to instructions and "suppressed the Maryland News Sheet and confined the two editors at Fort McHenry.[10] Early in the war, political prisoners were allowed to go out on a balcony for air, or they could roam the prison yard and parade grounds. This changed after a number of escapes.

Political Prisoners

Among the first prisoners at Fort McHenry were officers captured by Major General McClellan who were known to have recently resigned from the United States Army or Navy. Assistant Adjutant General E. D. Townsend directed that those, along with "Marshal Kane and the police commissioners who are in arrest and such political prisoners as may not be under indictment by the civil authority" be sent to Fort Lafayette in New York Harbor.[11]

Some of the prisoners held at Fort McHenry had done nothing, such as John Henry Bargfried, one the six sailors detained as witnesses in the case of Col. Richard Thomas (alias Zarvona).[12] Charles Wilson, one of the crew of the schooner *Margaret*, was confined at Fort McHenry in July 1861, and kept in custody as a witness against Thomas.[13]

On November 19, 1861, there were 10 political prisoners at Fort McHenry. In addition to Richard Thomas Zarvona, who was being held for piracy and treason, William Wilkins Glenn, editor of the *Exchange* was also a prisoner. Another civilian, Jonah Potterfield, had been arrested for "raising a rebel flag on his house. Other so-called crimes included correspondence with the enemy, disloyalty, and forwarding recruits to the Confederate Army. R. C. Holland had been arrested on November 4, 1861, for "Visiting Virginia."[14]

On February 17, 1862, Maj. Gen. John A. Dix submitted a report prepared by Col. W. W. Morris, commander of Fort McHenry, of all political prisoners who had been received at Fort McHenry since March 4, 1861. Of the 125 prisoners listed, most had been either released on parole, or sent to Fort Lafayette and other prisons. Several were sent to Fort Monroe. During that time, only one escaped prisoner was reported — George Washington Alexander.[15] Both he and Thomas were listed as political prisoners. Both were actually officers in the service of the Confederate States of America, and should have been treated as prisoners of war instead of political prisoners.

Other prisoners were held until the results of their trials were known. Capt. R. W. Baylor was being held at Fort McHenry while he awaited a decision in his court-martial. Capt. W. F. Gordon, who had temporarily been transferred from Fort McHenry to Fort Delaware, was back awaiting a decision in his case, according to Col. William Hoffman.[16]

An inspection report submitted to Hoffman by Col. P. A. Porter noted that as of December 19, 1863, there were "about" 69 surgeons, 29 wounded officers, about 130 other prisoners of war, and 26 offenders against the law of nations (including spies, pirates, etc., under sentence of death).[17]

Prisoners, such as spies, pirates, and others under sentence of death, were kept in two interior rooms of the fort. Some were in irons. The doors were opened during the day to admit air and light, and they were allowed to exercise on the interior parade ground for half an hour each day.[18]

The prisoners of war were held in two rooms on the upper floor of building No. 2. They were permitted to go out on the balcony for sun and air during the day, and to go downstairs to the prison yard for water, roll call, and to visit the sutler with a guard. Government blankets had been issued them during the winter of 1863. Soft bread was given to those who needed it. Eight prisoners of war who had tried to escape were held separately in another small room, but were not in irons, according to a report submitted by Colonel Porter in December 1863.[19]

Overcrowding

Fort McHenry was soon filled to overflowing. On March 10, 1862, Maj. Gen. John A. Dix wrote to advise the assistant secretary of war that there was "not room at Fort McHenry for any more political prisoners. There are only two rooms of moderate size and both are occupied."[20]

By July 1862, according to Hoffman, 500 prisoners were being held.[21] No monthly reports are available from Fort McHenry until March 1863, when the fort reportedly held 726 prisoners.[22]

Treatment of Prisoners

Overcrowding at Fort McHenry continued and became a major problem, especially after the prisoners taken at Gettysburg were sent there. The fort commander, Maj. William W. Morris, pleaded with Colonel Hoffman to erect temporary barracks at the fort.[23] While the prison population at Fort McHenry reached 658 prisoners in

July 1863, after a new Maryland prison was established, prisoners held in the fort ranged between 300–400 each month.[24]

Lt. Col. Marshall J. Smith wrote that while he was a prisoner at Fort McHenry he and several others were "confined in a hayloft of a stable for five months; were allowed to purchase and to receive the remnants of things sent us by our friends, after the provost marshal's employees had taken from the boxes or baskets all that they deemed desirable." This kind of treatment continued until their guards, members of the 8th New York Heavy Artillery, were replaced, and then they "were treated more kindly."[25]

In March 1865, Lieutenant General Grant ordered Brevet Brig. Gen. W. W. Morris to forward for exchange Capt. C. A. Marshal and other prisoners of war held there "in irons or in close confinement" However, since Brigadier General Hoffman had not been informed of any prisoners being held at the fort in close confinement, he "presumed that there were none so confined at Fort McHenry. Whether there were or not, he decreed that the last to be released should be those who had been arrested as guerrillas.[26]

General Hoffman was frequently asked about the whereabouts of prisoners. Some he knew nothing about, but he stated that "all these prisoners [at Fort McHenry] are treated with as much attention and kindness as is consistent with their position, and no harsh treatment is permitted."[27]

The Ways Out — Exchange

Prisoners tried every means known to escape their enforced confinement in prison. In answer to an inquiry from Robert Ould, the Confederate exchange agent, Colonel Hoffman wrote to give the status of several. He noted that if Mr. Ould would exchange Mr. J. Harvey Sherman, now being held at Richmond, he would release Henry A. Williams, who was being held in the Old Capitol Prison in Washington. Captain Compton, captured in Virginia with letters and other documents from the Confederate government, was tried as a spy, and sentenced to hang. His sentence was commuted by President Lincoln, and he was confined at Fort McHenry.[28]

Two Famous Prisoners

Among the most famous prisoners ever held at Fort McHenry were two daring Confederate "pirates," Col. Richard Thomas (Zarvona), and First Lt. George Washington Alexander. Both were listed as "political prisoners" on the report prepared by Colonel Morris.

Although listed as a citizen and charged with treason and piracy, both Alexander and Thomas were officers who had been working under the authority of the governor of Virginia. An article from the Baltimore *Sun,* dated September 9, 1861, referred to Alexander as "Major Alexander, formerly of the United States Revenue service, but late an officer in the Confederate army, and one of the political prisoners confined in Fort McHenry...." The next day's article correctly referred to him as "Lieutenant Alexander."[29]

George W. Alexander, Former U.S. Naval Officer

After 13 years in the United States Navy, George W. Alexander resigned his commission on June 15, 1861. With a group of men from Maryland, Alexander made his way to Richmond to offer the services of the group, on behalf of the Confederacy, to Gov. John Letcher.[30]

Because of his naval experience, Alexander was asked to take command of an expedition backed by Baltimore merchants to recapture the island of Sombrero in the West Indies. The island had been captured by a group of New Yorkers, and although it is worthless today, at the time it had large deposits of guano used for fertilizer.[31]

When Alexander and his crew sailed out into the Atlantic, they encountered a storm and the ship wrecked off Point Lookout. They

Capt. George W. Alexander, escaped from Fort McHenry, later was commandant at Castle Thunder in Richmond. (From Loreta Janeta Velazqauez, The Woman in Battle. Richmond, VA: Dustin, Gilman & Co., 1876, facing p. 288.)

reached land, and were given shelter by the Thomas family at their home, Mattaponi. Here, Alexander met Richard Thomas, who had served under Garibaldi in the Sicilian campaign.[32] Alexander and Thomas became friends and formed a team and embarked on a mission for the Confederacy that would forever alter their lives.

Thomas and Alexander decided to go to Baltimore to recruit a company of men for Confederate service. The men were transported on two steamers of the Patuxent line to Millstone Landing in Maryland. Back at the Thomas plantation, the new recruits were organized and drilled as a company of zouaves. Richard Thomas was chosen Captain, and George Alexander was made first lieutenant. J. W. Torsch was elected second lieutenant and Frank Parsons third lieutenant.[33]

Thomas and Alexander and their company of Marylanders approached the governor of Virginia with a plan to capture the warship *Pawnee* lying at anchor in the Potomac River near Alexandria. Thomas wanted to seize a steamer between Baltimore and Washington, and to use it to board the *Pawnee*.[34] Governor Letcher thought the plan good, and he provided money for arms. Thomas went to Philadelphia and got a supply of Sharps rifles and revolvers, which he had shipped to Baltimore.[35] The governor commissioned Thomas a colonel, and he took the oath before Joseph Mayo, mayor of the city of Richmond.[36] Governor Letcher also provided Colonel Zarvona, of the "Potomac Zouaves" a pass to travel freely over all the roads and rivers of the commonwealth of Virginia, together with his "men and baggage." The governor directed all officers, both civil and military, to afford him all respect, and to "give him such facilities as he may require...."[37] These documents would later be found on Zarvona when he was captured

Capture of the St. Nicholas[38]

On June 28, 1861, Richard Thomas and eight men boarded the *St. Nicholas,* a 1,200-ton side-wheel steamer,[39] in Baltimore bound for Washington, D.C. At Point Lookout, Lt. George Alexander and eight armed men, disguised as passengers, boarded the *St. Nicholas.* Alexander found Thomas in a cabin wearing the disguise of a "French lady," called "Madame La Force." Thomas gave Alexander the keys to the trunks in which the guns were concealed, then Thomas returned to his stateroom and put on his Confederate uniform. He slipped outside and signaled his men. Within only a few minutes, the ship's, captain, pilot, and engineer surrendered when confronted with the guns of Confederate soldiers. The lights were extinguished on the ship, and it was directed toward the Coan River on the Virginia shore for a rendezvous with Capt. George N. Hollins of the Confederate States Navy. Hollins, being the senior naval officer, came aboard and directed the subsequent activities.[40] However, Zarvona was the "key man" in the capture[41]

Hollins's Account of the St. Nicholas Capture[42]

Captain Hollins claimed that the idea for the seizure of the *St. Nicholas* "originated entirely with myself." He claimed it was he who proposed the idea to Governor Letcher, and that the governor gave him the draft for $1,000 to buy arms. At that time, Hollins was introduced to Colonel Thomas "as a person who could be trusted to go North to purchase arms, or transact other business."[43] Captain Hollins endorsed the bank draft from Governor Letcher and gave it to Colonel Thomas, who was to travel to Baltimore and Philadelphia to buy guns for the men. He was to return on the *St. Nicholas* with as many men as he could. Captain Hollins promised to join Thomas when the ship docked at Point Lookout. At noon, Hollins boarded the steamer with his small group of men. Thomas was already on board disguised as a woman. The disguise was necessary because the guns and ammunition were concealed in a number of large trunks, "such as milliners use." Hollins ordered Thomas to stay hidden until the ship left the wharf. Shortly, after the steamer got underway, Hollins gave the signal, and the large trunks were opened, and the Confederates took out the guns. Hollins grabbed a Sharps rifle and a pair of pistols and ran up to the wheelhouse where he told the captain of the ship that he and his men had captured the steamer. Hollins ordered the captain of the *St. Nicholas* to steer the boat to the Coan River, but the captain refused, and said that he was "no pilot." Hollins then threatened him and declared he would burn the *St. Nicholas.* This got results, and someone other than the captain, piloted the steamer to the desired location at Coan River Landing. Once safely across the Potomac, a group of Confederate soldiers and sailors came to help Hollins.[44]

Lt. George Washington Alexander described the capture of the *St. Nicholas:* "In a few minutes we overpowered the passengers and crew, secured them below the hatches, and the boat was ours."[45]

Other Ships Captured

In conjunction with the capture of the *St. Nicholas*, Colonel Bates of the First Tennessee was to assist in the attack on the *Pawnee*. However, he did not arrive until noon the next day, and this delay altered the plan. Since the captured *St. Nicholas* had already missed its regular trip, it would be under suspicion. A change in direction was ordered, and the *St. Nicholas* headed for the Chesapeake Bay and the Confederate "pirates" made several more conquests and captured three more vessels. Sailing with Captain Hollins, the group of officers, seamen, and Maryland Zouaves (all regular naval and army officers of the Confederacy) captured the *Monticello*, the *Mary Pierce*, and the *Margaret* in Chesapeake Bay on June 29, 1861. These ships were loaded with coffee, ice and coal valued at $400,000. The valuable cargo was taken up the Rappahannock to Fredericksburg, and the prisoners were sent to Richmond.[46]

One of the captured vessels contained some "excellent old whiskey." Another captured ship contained ice. Virginia's governor Letcher took charge of both ships, and "furnished mint." Soon, there were few sober soldiers in the executive mansion.[47]

On July 4, 1861, the first company of Maryland Zouaves was formed in Richmond and William Walter of Baltimore was elected captain. G. W. Alexander was elected first lieutenant and also served as adjutant of the zouave regiment.[48]

Zarvona (a.k.a. the "French Lady") Captured on the Mary Washington

In July 1861, Thomas and Alexander, along with Lieutenant Blackston, set out on a second expedition to seize Federal ships. They captured the *Georgeanna*. Then, at Millstone Landing, Thomas, again in disguise as a widow, boarded the *Mary Washington* to reach Baltimore to cash a bank draft from Governor Letcher. However, he was recognized by Captain Kerwin (the captain of *St. Nicholas* which had been captured only a few days before).[49]

No detailed report exists of the capture of Richard Thomas Zarvona, although reports appeared on July 9, 1861, in two Baltimore newspapers. The papers described the actions of two members of the Baltimore police force, John Horner and Lt. Thomas H. Carmichael who were on their way to Anne Arundel County to arrest Neale Green, a Baltimore barber. Green had been involved in the attack on the Sixth Massachusetts Regiment which had recently passed through the city. The two boarded the steamer *Mary Washington* bound for Baltimore. The boat had barely left the dock when Lieutenant Carmichael recognized the elusive "French Lady" traveling with a number of men. Zarvona's companions had tried to dissuade him from going to Baltimore so soon after the capture of the *St. Nicholas*, but the "daring Colonel" was set on carrying out his plans. So, rather than allow him to go alone into danger, his friends and comrades had accompanied him on the ill-fated voyage.[50]

Carmichael alerted the ship's captain to the presence of the "French Lady," and ordered him to set a course for Fort McHenry and let his passengers off there rather than at the regular dock. Zarvona became suspicious, and approached Carmichael, to inquire why the ship had been diverted. Carmichael replied that the change was due to police orders. One of the passengers recalled the action that followed. Zarvona called his men together, and drew a pistol on Carmichael, and threatened to throw him and Horner overboard. A woman screamed and ran out of her cabin. The police officers pulled out their guns, and with the backing of a number of male passengers, forced Zarvona and his comrades to surrender.[51]

Once at Fort McHenry, the police officers reported to Maj. Gen. N. P. Banks, and he sent a company of infantry to board the boat and bring the captives inside. While Zarvona's companions were being arrested, he managed to disappear. After an extensive search of the ship, he was found hiding in a large bureau in a ladies' cabin. A report made two years later to Secretary of War Stanton stated that at the time of his arrest, Zarvona was in female attire. However, Scharf, in his *History of the Confederate Navy*, denies that.[52]

Maj. Gen. N. P. Banks noted on July 8, 1861, that Richard Thomas was a "colonel of the Virginia army," and held a commission signed by Governor Letcher dated July 1.[53] It was not long before Maj. Gen. N. P. Banks, who commanded the Department of Annapolis, had doubts that Col. Richard Thomas Zarvona was being held securely. Zarvona was described as "a dangerous and desperate man." He was being held in a room only 20 feet from the sally port, an exit from the fort, with seven of his companions, all "equally desperate" to escape. The additional prisoners, including Lieutenant Alexander, had been brought to Fort McHenry on July 12, 1865. They had been captured "armed with weapons and ammunition sufficient for six or eight men...."[54]

Subsequently, Zarvona was held on a charge of piracy, but later he was indicted in the United States Court for the District of Maryland for treason only, and was held as a political prisoner.[55]

Alexander Captured

Alexander learned that Federal authorities were looking for the captured ship, so he made for the harbor and anchored the *Georgeanna* under the guns of Fort Severn at Annapolis. The following day, as Alexander sailed toward the Chester River, the ship's pilot ran ashore between Eastern Neck Island and the mainland. Alexander had heard nothing from Zarvona, so he boarded the *Arrow* at Kent Island expecting to find Zarvona there. There, he learned from the newspapers that his friend had been captured. Immediately, he split his men into two squads, and ordered one to remain under his command. The other squad was placed under the command of Lieutenant Blackiston. Blackiston then took a boat across the bay and escaped with his men. Alexander and his men tried to make the eastern shore. However, one of his men, Samuel H. Owens, was recognized by a relative who reported him. When they stopped to make camp that night they were surrounded by a company of militia under the command of Lieutenant Colghan. Alexander and his men were taken to the county jail. The next day, they were sent on a steamer to Fort McHenry and confined along with his friend and compatriot, Richard Thomas, alias Zarvona.[56] (For more about Zarvona, see Chapters VI and VII).

Initially, Alexander was confined in room 1837 of the sally port guardhouse-prison at the entrance of the old star-shaped fort. That room is still intact and now serves as a storage room.[57]

Fort McHenry — Sally port guardhouse-prison where George W. Alexander was confined on July 12, 1861. (Courtesy of the Library of Congress, HABS, MD,4-BALT,5-25.)

Alexander was charged with treason by committing piracy, and also charged with being a spy.[58] Both he and Zarvona awaited trial while imprisoned in Fort McHenry.[59] If convicted, they would be executed. It would take George Alexander several weeks to formulate an escape plan, but escape he did.

The time spent awaiting trial in Fort McHenry did not sit well with Lt. Alexander, and he was not a docile prisoner. The hot, humid weather made the small cells stifling and almost unbearable. To relieve some of the discomfort, the door to the cell in which both Alexander and Zarvona were kept was left open during the day and until 9 o'clock at night. However, one of the guards, a lance corporal, attempted to close the door one evening at 8:30 P.M. The prisoners asked by what right did he close the door early, and he replied, "Damn rebels have no rights," and he tried to close the door. Immediately, both Alexander and Thomas fell upon him and "beat him like the devil." The other guards were hesitant to come to the rescue of the corporal because they knew he was in the wrong. The guard had acted with unwarranted "impudence" toward Thomas and Alexander and, as a result, the two prisoners grabbed the guard and beat him.[60]

Alexander and Thomas were punished for their attack on the guard and placed in a dark, underground cell for six weeks, with only bread and water to sustain them.[61]

The prisoners were guarded by Companies I and K of the Second Artillery of the U.S. Army. Someone approached each of the guards and offered them a bribe of $1,500 in gold, but none would accept it.[62]

Alexander Plans to Escape

After six weeks, Alexander and Thomas were removed from the underground cell, and Alexander made up his mind to escape.[63] To do so, he would need outside help.

Susan Ashby Alexander, Alexander's wife, traveled from Richmond to visit him in prison. She had obtained an order from Secretary of War Cameron to allow her to visit her husband daily. She was determined not to let bad weather deter her, and she crossed the Potomac River on a night when any sensible person would have stayed ashore.[64]

Together, George and Susan planned his escape. On one of her visits, she brought her husband a life preserver in the form of a waistcoat and clothesline, which she had concealed under her hoop skirt. Standing in the corner, she cut the string that held the items under her hoop skirt, and kicked them under the cot. She had also obtained some letterhead stationery which had a picture of Fort McHenry and the surrounding area. On this, she had marked in blue ink the positions of various sentinels about the fort.[65]

Everything was set for Alexander's escape, but when his wife visited him on Saturday, she made him promise to wait until Monday, so that she would have another chance to see him before he tried to escape. It was a dangerous plan, and he could be killed in the attempt. But that night, Alexander could wait no longer. About dark, Colonel Thomas left the cell and walked up and down with the guard in front of the door to Alexander's cell. While Thomas distracted the guard, Alexander arranged his bed to appear that he was in it, and hiding behind the door, he put on the life preserver over a Federal uniform that his wife had smuggled into his cell. Then, he moved to the door, and as the guard's back was turned, he entered the corridor and walked away. When the guard turned around, Alexander saluted him and the guard saluted in return, not recognizing Alexander as his prisoner. [66]

Alexander moved quickly, but as he passed the mortar batteries, he knocked down a crowbar. The loud clang that resulted startled Alexander and he hurried to reach the ramparts on the Patapsco side of the fort.[67]

One account reported that Alexander was noticed by one of the guards, who fired at him. Then Alexander "leaped over the wall into the river."[68] The ramparts were high above the ground, and Alexander had forgotten to bring the clothes line his wife had brought him to use to climb down.[69] There was no other way to escape except to jump. He did not hesitate to do so, but landed on the hard ground, and he injured his right leg and shoulder. He managed to crawl to the river, and slipped into the safety of the water just as a guard was passing. The cold water helped ease the pain in his leg, but the sky was black and the wind was rising. He inflated his life preserver and began to swim. The prospects of ever seeing his lovely wife again seemed remote at the time. [70]

Alexander swam for about 2½ hours until he reached the shore near Riverside

Park. He crawled out of the river toward a light which shone from a cabin in which sat an old man. The old man asked him, "Are you drunk?" A cold and wet Alexander replied, "Not drunk but badly hurt."[71]

The old man and his daughters carried Alexander into the house. The girls had seen him at the fort and thus recognized him. The old man told Alexander that he must leave, because his property would be confiscated if it was learned he had harbored an escaped prisoner. The girls, however, begged their father to take Alexander away in their buggy. The old man agreed, and as he lay in the bottom of the buggy, the girls concealed him by covering him with their voluminous skirts. He was taken to the house of W. H. Norris. Norris then took Alexander in another carriage to Hoffman Street. There he was able to meet with his wife for a moment. He was then taken to the home of E. Law Rogers and was treated by a surgeon. Still later, Alexander was taken to the home of Charles Carroll in Carrollton, who gave him a warm welcome, and treated him with the utmost kindness.[72]

The escape of First Lt. George Washington Alexander is perhaps the first documented escape by a Confederate officer from a Federal prison.[73] According to the records of the United States War Department, George W. Alexander, "citizen" was confined at Fort McHenry on July 12, 1861, and listed as having escaped on September 7, 1861.[74] He the first of only 37 prisoners known to have escaped.

Alexander's escape was noted in the Baltimore papers.

> *An Escape from Fort McHenry.* — Major Alexander, formerly of the United States revenue service, but late an officer in the Confederate army, and one of the political prisoners confined in Fort McHenry, made his escape from his cell at the fort, sometime between ten o'clock on Saturday night and yesterday morning, and succeeded in getting off, eluding the guards and outposts. It is thought his escape was effected by means of a disguise of some kind, but nothing positive is known. Major Alexander was arrested at Cambridge about the time of the St. Nicholas affair.[75]

Undoubtedly, the fort officials soon learned that Alexander escaped with the help of his wife. The fort commander, Maj. W. W. Morris, immediately took steps to prevent further escapes by the political prisoners confined in the fort. Morris revoked the passes which had been issued to the friends and family of the prisoners, and decreed that in the future, "no such passes will be granted to any person whomsoever."[76]

Naturally, the Federal authorities were angry over his escape. Almost immediately, Maj. Gen. John A. Dix issued more orders designed to prevent further escapes, and detailed his suspicions to Captain Gibson at Fort Delaware:

> Put a stop at once to the visits of pleasure parties to the fort. The utmost caution should be practiced in regard to visits of prisoners. We have lost one of our most important ones [Alexander] within a few days and have no doubt his escape was facilitated by communication between him and his friends admitted to his room.[77]

A reward of $10,000 was offered for his capture. But luck was with him, and as soon as Alexander was able to travel, Frank Key took him in a buggy to a place below Fort Washington, and then, accompanied by a Confederate officer, they crossed the Potomac into Virginia. A Federal gunboat passed by several times as they hid on the riverbank awaiting a chance to cross. Finally, the pair made the crossing and Alexander traveled to Richmond.[78] He arrived about October 2.[79]

Once safely in Richmond, Alexander sent a report to Judah P. Benjamin, the new Confederate secretary of war:

> Having with Colonel R. Thomas Zarvona captured the Saint Nicholas I accompanied him on a second expedition. I was captured by Governor Hicks and the Dorchester Guards at Cambridge, Maryland, and confined with Colonel Z. In Fort McHenry about seventy days, when I effected my escape. Springing from the ramparts I sprained my ankle.[80]

Soon after Alexander arrived in Richmond, he chanced to meet General Johnston. The general smiled at Alexander and said, "Well, Lieutenant, I see you have saved us an exchange!" Alexander replied, "Yes, but lost you a soldier." True to his word, Alexander embarked on a new career that involved less danger, and became a provost marshal with the Eastern District of Virginia.[81]

Shortly after his escape from Fort McHenry, Alexander placed a notice in the *Richmond Dispatch* inviting people to come listen to him express the views of the imprisoned Col. Richard Thomas Zarvona. Zarvona hoped to see a battalion formed from Maryland for the Confederacy. The new company was to be called the "Zarvona Zouaves." Alexander noted that they already had one company, fully armed and equipped, but needed three more immediately. The meeting was scheduled for 8 P.M. on 10th Street, between Main and Cary, "two doors below Snead's Locksmith establishment."[82]

The meeting was held and a large party met at Adam's building on 10th Street in Richmond. Those who attended expressed their sympathy for the imprisoned Marylander, and pledged to organize a battalion to be named after him, the Zarvona Zouaves. The meeting was called to order by Captain Dugan. The object of the meeting was then explained by Adjutant G. W. Alexander, and Captain Lookerman was appointed secretary. A three-man committee was appointed to draw up resolutions, and then the men who wished to join were to be enrolled. Their departure was scheduled for Sunday. The article noted that Alexander, while still on crutches, was recovering from injuries to his leg incurred during his daring escape.[83]

Mrs. Alexander was safely lodged at Westmoreland. A newspaper article noted her role in her husband's escape from Fort McHenry, and that Colonel Thomas (Zarvona) was a heavily guarded prisoner there still.[84]

Repercussions for Zarvona — Solitary Confinement

Shortly after Alexander escaped from Fort McHenry, prison authorities discovered that Zarvona had set up an organization for the capture of the fort. As punishment, Zarvona was placed in a cell devoid of light for several months. The cell, as described by Captain Marks, had only a small source of light which came from a chink in the door barely wide enough for a knife blade. The prisoner spent countless hours at the door trying to peer out of the crack. Like a caged animal, he could be heard moving his head to and fro trying to see the light.[85]

The solitary confinement was detrimental to Zarvona's health. Even Major

General Dix became concerned, and he wrote to Major General McClellan on September 5, 1861, that Colonel Zarvona, was from "one of the first families in Maryland; is rich, intelligent and resolute. His nervous system is much broken by confinement and want of active occupation." The prisoner had asked Dix to obtain permission for him to walk outside.[86] However, permission was denied. Assistant Adjutant General Townsend replied that McClellan did not think "it prudent to extend [Zarvona's] liberty.[87]

Secretary of State William Seward reported that Zarvona had been allowed "the freedom of the public grounds [at Fort McHenry] and was treated in every respect as the men of the garrison were until he made his escape. Since his arrest he has been more closely confined [at Fort Lafayette] but only to such an extent as is deemed necessary to prevent him from escaping again.[88] [This refers to an escape attempt from Fort McHenry. He also tried to escape from Fort Lafayette in April 1862. See Chapter VII.)

Confederate agent Robert Ould tried to get Zarvona exchanged.[89] Although Colonel Zarvona was an officer in the Confederate service when he was captured, the Federals insisted in treating him as a political prisoner. He was registered as a prisoner at Fort McHenry on July 8, 1861, and he remained at Fort McHenry until December 2, 1861, when he was transferred to Fort Lafayette, New York.[90]

It was only through the efforts of Governor Letcher that Zarvona finally was taken out of the dark cell. However, the months of solitary confinement in total darkness had damaged his mind. Governor Letcher did everything in his power to obtain Zarvona's release. He wrote to President Lincoln and he even offered to exchange four Union colonels for the him. Letcher even threatened to hang four Federal officers if the indictments against Zarvona and Alexander were not dropped. The indictments were eventually quashed.[91]

Zarvona was considered such a important political prisoner that a number of the members of the captured ship's crew were also held as witnesses for his trial which never took place.

Few Escaped

It is not know just when 10 surgeons confined at Fort McHenry escaped but it was sometime after August and before December 19, 1863, when a report was submitted by Col. P. A. Porter. He noted that 65 surgeons occupied the soldiers' barracks for nearly two months, then they were moved to an upper room of building No. 1. Some 40 had arrived at Fort McHenry *in transitu* a couple of days before all were scheduled to be moved. When they first arrived, the surgeons were allowed the "freedom of the whole grounds of the fort," but after those 10 escaped, Colonel Porter had to "restrict the remainder" to a smaller area.[92]

One escape from Fort McHenry was reported in June 1863, one in July, and 14 in October 1863. One escape was reported for the month of November (with a prison population of 407) and one in December 1863, when the number of prisoners was only 240. However, in January 1864, 12 escapes were reported, none in February, one in March 1864, and five escaped two months later in May. The last recorded escape took place in May 1865, after the war had ended. By September 1865, Fort McHenry held only four prisoners.[93]

Tunnels

Some of the prisoners began digging a tunnel. The tunnel descended for 13 feet, and was 35 feet long when it was discovered based on information from an informer. Marshall J. Smith reported that "our officers and privates were prevented from making their escape by the betrayal of one of our own men, a renegade Virginian, whose home is near the White House, on the Pamunkey."[94]

Some estimate that of the approximately 15,000 Confederate prisoners of war held at Fort McHenry, approximately 7,000 were from the three-day battle at Gettysburg, Pennsylvania, in July 1863. There was also one execution by hanging and two by firing squad at the fort.[95]

Fort McHenry Today

Fort McHenry has played an important role the defense of America, from the War of 1812 until World War II. Today, it is a major tourist attraction, visited by over 700,000 tourists and schoolchildren each year.[96]

IX

Fort Warren, Boston Harbor, Massachusetts

…it seemed impossible to escape; and yet the escape was easily accomplished.
— Lieutenant J. W. Alexander[1]

Location: Georges Island, Boston Harbor, seven miles from Boston, Massachusetts. **Established:** 1845 (1861 for prisoners of war). **Type:** costal fortification. **Type of Prisoners:** prisoners of war (officers and enlisted Confederate soldiers), civilian political prisoners. **Capacity:** 175. **Most Held at One Time:** 500–800.[2] **Known Number of Escapes:** 4[3] (six or seven escaped, four recaptured[4]). **Nicknames:** "Hotel de Warren."[5]

History

Boston Harbor is dotted with a number of small islands, most of them "arid, treeless, and unadorned" by man-made structures. In 1634, one author described the harbor as "safe and pleasant … having but one common and safe entrance, and that not very broad…. The Harbor is made by a great company of Ilands [*sic*], whose high cliffs shoulder out the boisterous seas, yet may easily deceive any unskillful Pilote [*sic*]…."[6]

Writing in 1884, William H. Rideing described the islands as "picturesque in a wild and rugged way." A few islands are high enough to be habitable, but most are used only seasonally by the lobster fishermen. The only building of note is a most imposing structure perched on Georges Island at the edge of the narrow channel that allows ships to enter the harbor.[7] The pentagonal-shaped fortification is only one of several which dot the eastern coast of the United States. As a prison, this site, like Johnson's Island, provided maximum security with minimal chances to escape.

Construction of the fort began in 1834, and was completed in 1845. It was named for Joseph Warren, one of the heroes at the battle of Bunker Hill during the American Revolution.[8]

With sides 600 × 660 feet long, and walls 8 feet thick, the two-story fort covers about six acres of the 42-acre island. The fort is situated on the upper end of the island.[9]

The Prison Facilities

Initially, the fort was used to train Massachusetts regiments, but its value as a prison was soon evident. Massachusetts governor John A. Andrew requested that a battalion of three or four companies of infantry be stationed at Fort Warren "as a garrison and [to] guard to the prisoners to be sent there." His request was quickly granted.[10] On October 17, 1861, a battalion was ordered to be raised, and Bvt. Col. Justin Dimick, already at Fort Warren, was placed in command.[11]

Although the capacity of the fort was estimated at 175, from the first, both troops and prisoners were crowded. However, the fort offered better shelter than many prisons. When C. T. Alexander inspected the quarters of the troops in June 1864, he found them neat and orderly. In contrast, the quarters of the prisoners were "deficient in both neatness and order." Prisoners who were officers were kept in small rooms apart from the men, and "pay less regard to cleanliness." He did report that the quarters occupied both by the guards and their prisoners were "too crowded for comfort, but not for health," which was evident by the monthly sick report. Overall, he described all the prisoners as appearing "healthy, well clothed, clean, free from vermin."[12]

Fort Warren was and still is a formidable place. Many years ago, visitor James L. Homer, wrote his impression:

> You descend a long flight of stone steps. Having touched the ground, you walk about forty feet, and then turn to the left, when you find yourself in the "prison house" of the Fort, which extends, through several apartments or sections, a distance of over one hundred feet, and is capable of accommodating one thousand prisoners.[13]

The Prisoners

A large number of prisoners were captured on August 29, 1861, and sent to Fort Warren. These included commissioned and noncommissioned officers and privates from Company K, 10th Regiment, North Carolina State Troops Heavy Artillery. They were held until exchanged in February 1862.[14]

By November 21, 1861, over 700 "ordinary prisoners" were being held at Fort Warren. In addition, there were 100 "state" or political prisoners.[15]

In the first year of the war, exchange or parole of prisoners was common. In November 1861, Col. Justin Dimick, the commandant of the prison, was asked to furnish the adjutant general a list of names of 250 prisoners of war from among both the officers and privates held there "with a view to their release or parole." The list was to include the "most feeble and infirm" and "those who have families dependent upon them for support."[16] Even before this order was received, Maj. H. A. Gilliam, of the 7th [17th] Regiment, North Carolina Infantry, wrote asking to be released. He promised that if he was allowed to return to North Carolina to his "sorrowing wife and only infant son" that he would "undertake to procure the discharge of some prisoner of my rank now held by the Southern government." A few weeks later, the 250 prisoners listed were sent by sea to Fort Monroe, Virginia, to be paroled until exchanged. From there, under a flag of truce, they proceeded to Norfolk where they would take the oath of allegiance not to bear arms against the United States.[17]

Among those sent to Fort Monroe were 10 officers, and privates from several North Carolina regiments (Companies B, D, E, G, I, K, of the 7th North Carolina Infantry; Jonesboro Guards, Washington Greys, 2nd Regiment North Carolina Infantry; Lenoir Braves; and the North Carolina Defenders, North Carolina Volunteers).[18]

Many of the military prisoners at Fort Warren had been captured at Hatteras in North Carolina. One of them, Major Gilliam, continued to request their release on parole. On December 30, 1861, he wrote to Maj. Gen. George B. McClellan that one major, eight captains, five first lieutenants, 15 second lieutenants, one adjutant, and 350 privates from North Carolina regiments were confined at Fort Warren. Gilliam also knew that other North Carolina soldiers were being held at Fort Columbus, New York Harbor; Annapolis, Maryland; and Fort Monroe, Virginia. In addition there were 25 prisoners who had been captured on Santa Rosa Island.[19]

The exchange of prisoners continued and Colonel Dimick reported that he was sending "4 captains, 2 first lieutenants, 8 second lieutenants, 2 third lieutenants and about 370 rank and file" to Fort Monroe, because he was "certain of a reciprocal exchange of prisoners of war...." The group from Fort Warren included "four colored men," who wanted to return to North Carolina. Dimick believed that three were free blacks who had families in the South, and the fourth, although a slave, was "anxious to get home." In the process, Colonel Dimick requested that Frank W. Welch, a free colored man, who was a servant to a Connecticut volunteer officer, and "also any other free colored men who may have been taken while employed as servants to officers" be exchanged.[20]

On June 1, 1862, Colonel Dimick transmitted an alphabetical roll of all prisoners of war at Fort Warren as of March 1, 1862. The list totaled 126 officers and enlisted men, most of whom were commissioned officers who ranked from lieutenant to brigadier general. Twenty-eight were officers in the Confederate States Navy. No civilians were included in that number. [21]

Col. William Hoffman estimated the capacity of Fort Warren at 500 during the summer of 1862.[22]

A Repository for Political Prisoners

When President Abraham Lincoln suspended *habeas corpus,* anyone could be arrested and detained without being formally charged. Under that suspension, Richard Henry Alvey was arrested at his home in Hagerstown, Maryland, on June 18, 1861, on suspicion of disloyalty. He was first taken to Fort McHenry then to Fort Lafayette, and then confined at Fort Warren. Without ever having been charged with any crime, Alvey, like many other citizens, was imprisoned. Seven months later, Alvey was finally released on January 6, 1862, after he agreed to take the oath of allegiance.[23]

Many of the prisoners were wealthy, such a banker from Savannah who was being held in November 1861. The Savannah banker reportedly had made "one to two millions by speculations in cotton," according to information furnished by Boston banker George B. Blake to George Morey.[24]

Robert Renwick, a Scottish cabinet maker, lived in Baltimore, where he was very vocal in his opposition to the United States government. After he was observed enlisting men into the Confederate Army, he was arrested on October 6, 1861, by orders from Gen. John Dix. Although Renwick was never formally charged, he was taken to Fort Columbus in New York Harbor, then to Fort Warren. Based on information from a prisoner just released from Fort Warren, Renwick's stables were searched on November 11, 1861, and concealed arms were found. However, on February 7, 1862, an order was issued from the State Department for Renwick to be paroled for 30 days, and he was released.[25]

As was often the case with political prisoners, Thomas J. Claggett, a member of the House of Delegates of Maryland, was arrested in September 1861, and held for months. Claggett complained to the United States Secretary of War Edwin M. Stanton that he had been arrested "without any charge being made against me," and although he had been imprisoned for six months, he still did "not yet know what is charged against me."[26]

Everyone whose loyalties could be questioned was arrested, such as Col. A. Talcott, a citizen of Mexico, who was held at the fort in 1863.[27]

Notable Prisoners

Fort Warren served as a repository of many high government officials (such as Charles S. Morehead, the governor of Kentucky, and Charles J. Faulkner, minister to France), citizens suspected of disloyalty who could exert great influence (including Frank Key Howard, editor of the *Daily Exchange,* a Baltimore newspaper), and several police commissioners and mayors.[28] To prevent both Maryland and Kentucky from joining the Confederacy, many prominent men from those states were arrested, held without charges, and confined for months at Fort Warren.

Fort Warren is famous for its role in "the *Trent* Affair." Two Confederate commissioners, James Murray Mason and John Slidell, were on their way to England on the mail steamer *Trent,* when it was stopped by the United States warship *San Jacinto.* The two commissioners were arrested and taken back to Fort Warren, where they were held until January 1, 1862. Their arrest evoked great sympathy from England, and almost caused the British to declare war. However, Secretary of State Seward averted a crisis by ordering the release of the two men as "personal contraband" and he criticized Captain Wilkes for just capturing the two men and not the ship.[29]

Another international prisoner was Thomas T. Tunstall, ex-consul at Cadiz. Tunstall was arrested in Tangiers on February 19, 1862, on the orders of James De Long, the new United States consul at Tangiers. When arrested, Tunstall was with Henry Myers, paymaster of the ship *Sumter.* Both men were transported to the United States. They arrived in Boston on April 18, 1862, wearing "irons of several pounds weight firmly riveted to their ankles." A blacksmith was required to release them from the irons.[30]

Tunstall, a native and citizen of Alabama, had served as consul of the United States at Cadiz from February 21, 1856 until July 1861. Once he reached Fort Warren, he wrote to Seward to protest his arrest and confinement and to plead for his release. Tunstall told Seward that De Long had refused to tell him why he had been arrested, but did say that Tunstall had been "in bad company and that if [he] had been alone, he would not have been arrested."[31] On May 5, 1862, Seward ordered Colonel Dimick to release Tunstall, on the condition that he sign take the oath of allegiance to the United States.[32] The ex-consul was one of the more fortunate political prisoners. He was released after only three months' confinement.

Confederate Gen. Simon Bolivar Buckner from Kentucky and Gen. Lloyd Tilghman were captured by Grant at Fort Donelson and confined at Fort Warren.[33] Under orders from Maj. Gen. H. W. Halleck, the two Confederate generals were transported from St. Louis to Indianapolis, and thence to Fort Warren "closely guarded and not allowed to communicate with any person whatever." If they tried to escape, they were to be put in irons.[34] The two generals arrived at Fort Warren on March 6, 1862, and were confined in separate rooms.[35]

Buckner had taught philosophy at West Point, and was wounded during service in the Mexican War. He had returned to West Point and served as a tactical officer. He had been stationed on the western frontier before he resigned in 1855. In 1860, he was named a major general in the Kentucky militia, and worked with George McClellan for the neutrality of Kentucky. He was offered a commission by both the Union and Confederate armies, but refused all until Kentucky was invaded. He then applied to the Confederacy and was appointed a brigadier general on September 14, 1861.[36]

A Boston policeman described Buckner as weighing "over two hundred [pounds] and is solidly built." The general had a "round, hard face, high cheek bones, small gray eyes, and heavy over brows. His face was the exact counterpart of that of "Dumlin Tricks, the well known fighting man." Tilghman was "light and of nervous temperament."[37]

For some time, Major General McClellan forbade the exchange of any rebel generals who "had served in our Regular Army, without special orders from these headquarters."[38]

Care and Treatment of the Prisoners

In the fall of 1861, the prisoners transferred to Fort Warren from Fort Lafayette arrived without their bedding. Colonel Dimick was quick to correct the oversight, and procured bedding from the mayor of Boston. The fort commander reported that the prisoners have been "well quartered from the day they landed; very soon bunks were put up in their rooms and they think that everything has been done for their comfort." Dimick reported that he not had any complaints.[39] That would all change in the years to come.

As winter approached, so did illness and disease. Major Gilliam wrote W. N. H. Smith that his men suffered "greatly from disease." They have come down with "measles, typhoid, pneumonia, bilious fever, mumps, and finally smallpox, of which latter plague twenty have been the victims." Many of the sick were released, but there were still 400 men confined at the fort.[40]

In the summer of 1864, a hospital was set up in the room intended for the post chapel, but there was very little sickness. Surgeon C. T. Alexander, acting inspector of prisoners of war, reported to Colonel Hoffman that there were 180 prisoners, and that the "health of the prisoners has been so good that there has been no special hospital for their treatment." The few sick he did see were being treated in the "post hospital," which he found to be clean and the condition good. He did recommend that the hospital privy should be completed immediately "in accordance with the original design." As it was, the privy was a "close, offensive place, without drainage, unsupplied with water." [41]

Henry Harris, from Scottville, Virginia, joined Mosby's Rangers while still a teen. As a member of Company D, of Mosby's battalion, he was captured on October 17, 1864, near Bluemont, Virginia, and transferred to Fort Warren on February 6, 1865. There, he shared a cell with 63 other Rangers.[42] Harris remembered that the quality of food was better than he had received in Old Capitol Prison in Washington. However, near the end of the war, the rations given the prisoners were cut almost 20 percent. Harris recalled that Aquila Glascock, one of Mosby's Ranger from Fauquier County, Virginia, in the next bunk, had starved to death.[43]

In May 1862, when Edwin M. Stanton inquired of Colonel Dimick how the Buckner and Tilghman were confined. Dimick replied that the two Confederate generals were "confined in separate basement rooms, similar rooms as are occupied by half the prisoners of war. They converse with no one but myself and staff. Have one hour each day exercise on the ramparts separately."[44] Stanton, in turn, informed Major General McDowell that "General Buckner and Tilghman are not confined in dungeons."[45] Although not in a dungeon, they were in solitary confinement, a method of torture and punishment.

Prisoners Exchanged

One prisoner lucky enough to be transferred for exchange was Lt. Col. John R. Towers, age 37, of Company E, 8th Regiment, Anderson's Brigade. Towers was captured before Richmond on June 28, 1862, and sent to Fort Warren. He was for a brief time, transferred to Fort Monroe, Virginia, on July 31, 1862.[46] While Towers was imprisoned at Fort Warren, he started an "autograph album" of his cellmates. The album was filled with the names, date of arrest, address, and sometimes a brief note about how that prisoner came to be at Fort Warren.[47]

Because his wife was ill and was scheduled to undergo surgery, Col. H. B. Granby, of the 7th Texas Infantry, was allowed an early parole to go to his wife in Baltimore. Later, Granby was promoted to the rank of brigadier general. He was killed in the battle of Franklin, Tennessee, on November 30, 1864.[48]

Escape Attempts

Although prisoners plotted and planned, few escaped the prison on Georges Island. However, escape was always a possibility. Both officials and private citizens constantly looked for ways and means by which prisoners might escape the island.

As early as November 24, 1861, S. C. Hawley advised Secretary of State William H. Seward that the "number of prisoners in Fort Warren is large, the force is small and composed of inexperienced troops who are frequently changed." In addition, there was construction going on which necessitated a force of laborers and civilians going in and out of the fort. Hawley saw this traffic as an avenue through which correspondence could be smuggled out. It also would be easy for a prisoner to slip out with the workmen when they went home on Saturday. Hawley also believed that political prisoners, who had "money and intoxicating liquors enough to subdue the virtue of a sentinel or two," should be kept separate from the military prisoners.[49]

George Morey wanted warships stationed near Fort Warren to prevent "some strong iron-clad steamer" from coming to "co-operate with those prisoners."[50]

By 1862, Colonel Dimick was aware of several means of escape that prisoners might use. There were many small fishing boats that traveled between the numerous islands of Boston Harbor, and it would be easy for "a few strokes of the oar [to] bring them to touch the shore and in a moment" they could be away. He saw the need for a number of guards and sentinels to patrol the island "to prevent prisoners escaping by these boats."[51]

According to the monthly reports submitted from Fort Warren, four prisoners did escape in August 1863.[52] These were the only prisoners reported to have escaped during the period July 1862–November 1865.[53] Undoubtedly, although the fort never held the number of prisoners that other facilities held, its record is probably the best of any prison, either in the North or the South (see Appendix).

Some prisoners developed a plan to overpower the remaining guards while most of them were eating in the cook room. Prisoners would then grab the muskets, seize the transport steamer docked at the wharf, and escape. In order to stall pursuit, the prisoner planned to cut the telegraph line to the city. In 1864, The *Boston Herald* reported that an escape attempt had been "nipped in the bud" when one of the prisoners who had "taken the oath of allegiance" revealed the plan. The paper reported that since the discovery of the plot, "additional precautions had been taken to keep the prisoners more secure."[54]

The C.S.S. *Atlanta* was captured on June 17, 1863, and its crew taken to Fort Warren. From among those approximately 140 naval officers and crew,[55] only six dared attempt an escape, and only two made it off the island.

An account written by John A. Bolles which appeared in *Harper's New Monthly Magazine* in 1864, described how those six men planned and attempted an escape. Those involved were Lt. Charles W. Reed [Read], the captain of the Confederate privateer *Tacany;* J. N. Prydé, quarter gunner of the *Tacany*; First Lt. J. W. Alexander (a native of Lincolnton, North Carolina); and First Lt. of Marines James Thurston, of South Carolina, from the Confederate privateer *Atlanta;* Maj. Reid Saunders, quartermaster of the Confederate Army; and Thomas Sherman, a foreigner and sailor in the United States Navy imprisoned for making "treasonable statements" on board the United States brig *Santee.* The men made their escape the night of August 18, 1863. Prydé and Sherman supposedly drowned in Boston Harbor while attempting to swim to Lovell's Island. Another two, Saunders and Reed, were captured on the island. Only Thurston and Alexander managed to escape the island, but they were soon captured and lodged for a time in the Portland jail.[56] Bolles' account differs greatly from that written by Lt. J. W. Alexander, one of the actual participants in the escape.[57]

Alexander's Account

Lieutenant Alexander, one of the officers of the *Atlanta,* was confined to the casemates under the main battery. In the daytime, the prisoners were allowed outside to exercise in front of their quarters, but at sundown, they were locked in and sentinels were placed at the doors. Alexander and three others—Lt. C. W. Reed [Read], of the *Tacany;* Lt. of Marines James Thurston; and Reid Saunders, a political prisoner from Kentucky—planned to escape. Many plans were proposed and discarded. Finally, they decided to use the musketry loops that were in the wall of the basement. The loops were six feet high, and two or three feet wide on the inside wall, but they narrowed to a small point in the outside wall which was only seven inches wide.[58]

Alexander decided to see if he could get through the hole. By stripping off his clothes, he could barely squeeze through. He told the others, all of whom were small men, and when night came, they squeezed themselves through. Once outside, they hid in a dry ditch between the "main and water batteries." They made their way cautiously toward the seawall, and managed to slip past the notice of the sentinels. Once they reached the sea, they found the water rough, and it was too dangerous to try to swim to another island. The four returned to their quarter by means of a rope they had left hanging form the loophole.[59]

Lieutenant Reed suggested that two of his men be allowed to swim to a nearby island, get a boat, and return to Georges Island with it. The men tried again the next night. Alexander recorded that when Lieutenant Reed's two sailors swam off, the other four waited for the two sailors to return, but they were never seen again. (According to Bolles' account, the two sailors believed to have drowned were Prydé and Sherman.[60] Alexander does not name them, but said he believed they made it back to the Confederacy.[61])

Finally, the four prisoners decided that the two who had attempted to swim for the boat were not coming back. Alexander and Thurston decided they would swim to the island on which stood the lighthouse and get a boat. They would then return for Reed and Sanders, both of whom were poor swimmers. With the help of a practice target, the two believed they could float and swim to their destination. However, the sentinels noticed that their target was missing, and they moved to the edge of the wall and looked down. One thought he saw something in the water, and the other said "Stick your bayonet into it and see what it is." The sentinel lowered the muzzle of his musket down until it rested on Reed's chest. Reed never moved a muscle. Alexander remarked "That was the bravest thing I saw during the four years of war." The sentinels gave up, not wanting to ruin their guns with the salty water. After discussing the missing target for a few more minutes, the sentinels moved away.[62]

The two men, Alexander and Thurston, then tied their clothes to the target, and moved through the cold water toward the lighthouse. They found a small fishing boat, got in, and hoisted the sail, after which they headed back to Georges Island for Reed and Saunders. By this time, it was getting daylight, and they could see that the two men were not where they had left them. Alexander and Thurston thought perhaps their two companions had returned to their cells in the casemates. Later, they learned that was the case, and that Reed and Saunders had been discovered and put in "close confinement" for their efforts to escape.[63]

So, without landing, Thurston and Alexander sailed their little boat past the fort in view of the sentinels. The continued up the coast toward New Brunswick for a couple of days, until they were sighted by the crew of a schooner. The schooner, a revenue cutter, stopped and searched them. When the search revealed some Confederate money, revenue officers knew they had found the two escaped prisoners. The prisoners were taken to Portland Harbor and turned over to the United States marshal. The marshal handcuffed both men, and put them in the Portsmouth jail. Crowds of curious citizens visited the jail to get a look at the two pirates. Alexander wrote that onlookers "would come to the doors of our cells and discuss us as if we were a species of wild animals; and I suppose we were a kind of menagerie to them."[64]

During the month Alexander and Thurston were held in the Portland jail, they planned their escape from their cells on the second story. The cell doors had iron bars about an inch in diameter. The prisoners were permitted to go down to the first floor to wash. The windows of the washroom had the usual iron bars. The two decided that if they could remove one or two of the bars of the window, they could escape and go to Canada. They finally obtained something to saw through the bars, but before they could do so they were transferred back to Fort Warren.[65]

At Fort Warren, Alexander and Thurston were put in close confinement in a room with Reed and Saunders. They were joined by an officer of the Confederate States Navy, Capt. Samuel Starrett. A native of Baltimore, Starrett had been arrested along with other political prisoners and confined to Fort Warren.[66]

Read's Escape Attempt

Read's story of the failed escape attempt is basically the same as that of Joseph W. Alexander. After their capture, Read and Saunders were put in solitary confinement in the dungeon. A few days later, iron bars were placed over the loopholes of the casemates, and the two were taken out of the dungeon and put back in their former quarters inside the casemates.[67]

Read was still determined to escape. He may have tried at least twice, perhaps three times, but each attempt failed, and he was returned to the fort.[68]

An account published in 1915 in *Prince and Boatswain* by James Morris Morgan detailed possible another escape attempt by Read and Alexander that almost succeeded. Morgan had served with Read on the *McRae*. Morgan's story is similar to the first escape in parts, but there are enough differences to assume that this is a separate escape. Once the bars were put over the loopholes, Read tried another method of getting outside. He planned to take the schooner which one of the officers kept moored on the island and sail to Halifax, Nova Scotia. But first he had to get out. After studying every aspect of his cell, Read hit upon the idea of climbing up through an old chimney to the parapet. Using only a pocket knife and an old rusty ice pick, Read began chipping away at the mortar and bricks. He hid the debris under a pile of clothes.[69] Night after night he worked, and his cell mates helped by holding him on their shoulders. Higher up, he had to carve footholds in the walls of the chimney. Because of the dirt and debris that fell into his eyes, his right eye was damaged, and he had only partial sight for the rest of his life.[70]

Finally, Read broke through the last of the bricks and mortar. He and Alexander, the only two small enough to get through the opening, planned to escape the next night through the chimney. Read made his way to the top, and waited for Alexander. Alexander got stuck about half way up, and had to be literally pushed the rest of the way up by his fellow inmates. They crossed the roof and descended on the far side with the help of a blanket rope. Suddenly, they heard the guards. The two dived under a pile of old sailcloth and waited. As the sentries approached, one noticed that the blade of his bayonet was wet and would soon rust in the damp air. Again, as was the case in Alexander's account, the soldiers thrust a bayonet into where the prisoner lay hidden. This time he did not escape unscathed. The bayonet pierced his thigh, yet he did not make a sound. However, when the soldier withdrew his bayonet, he noticed that it was wet, not with water, but in the darkness he could not see that it was wet with blood. The guards left, and the two prisoners climbed the wall and let themselves down. Read left a trail of blood. When they reached the schooner, Alexander climbed in, and pulled Read up. Alexander had not known that Read was injured, but as soon as he was on the schooner, Read fainted. Thus, Alexander made little progress alone. At dawn, he revived Read, and they discovered they were among several hundred fishing vessels. Soon, the Federal revenue cutter was moving in and through the ships looking for the escaped prisoners.[71]

All was going as planned until something happened to one of the sails. Alexander tried to untangle it, but when he left the helm, the boat veered off course, and its odd movement was noticed by the Federal cutter. The two were captured. Read's wound was treated, and he and Alexander were put in the brig in double irons. They were returned to Fort Warren. Read, Alexander and Thurston were paroled on October 1, 1864, put on a steamer and sent south for exchange.[72]

Alexander also wrote of using a chimney to escape, but in his account they are stopped by a guard on the roof. Alexander and Read and the others continued to formulate escape plans, and once again had devised a plan to get out of the dungeon. Before they could put it into action, they were moved back to their old quarters in the casemates. There, they decided to use the chimney to escape. The chimney contained two flues, one for the fireplace in their casemate, and the other for the fireplace in the adjoining casemate. To remove the partition in the chimney would take months of work, but they were determined to escape. They removed enough bricks for one man to get into the fireplace, and he began enlarging the flue so that he could pass up. The bricks that were removed from the chimney were pounded into dust and carried out with the waste buckets every morning. Before they finished each night, to avoid detection, they put some of the bricks back with mortar made from bread dough. After several months, the work on the chimney was stopped because a sentry had been placed on the roof near the top of the chimney. The prisoners were greatly disappointed that their efforts had been in vain. Shortly afterward, they were told to prepare to go to City Point in Virginia for exchange.[73] Basically this is the same story as told by Morgan, while Morgan's seems to have incorporated elements of the first escape as well.

Prisoners continued to work at escaping through the chimneys or ventilators. Late in 1864, A. A. Gibson, post commander of Fort Warren, reported that about two weeks before, "brick was removed from a ventilator for the purpose of escape.[74] This is another attempt because Alexander and Read had already left the fort at this time.

Plot Discovered

The names of 14 men, probably those involved in the attempted escape through the ventilator, were compiled in January 1865, in response to a telegraphic inquiry concerning which prisoners (officers) were being held in close confinement, and if any of them were in irons. The list of those in close confinement for plotting to escape named the following: 1st Assistant Engineer William Ahern, Master G. D. Bryan; 2nd Assistant Engineer J. B. Brown; Capt. Frank Battle, Assistant Surgeon Thomas Emory; Master R. S. Floyd; Captain's Clerk W. D. Hough; Master T. T. Hunter; Lt. Col. John Hamilton; Capt. E. J. Patterson; 1st Lt. T. K. Porter; Lt. S. G. Stone; Midshipman G. T. Sinclair; and Chief Engineer W. S. Thompson.[75]

A footnote to the list indicated that Captain Patterson was the prisoner who had reported the plot to the prison officials. At the prisoner's own request, to prevent the others from knowing who had "squealed," and to safeguard his life, he was confined with the rest of the conspirators.[76]

The Lady in Black

There is a ghost story connected with Fort Warren which involved an escape attempt. How much of the story is true is debatable, but as the legend goes, there was a young Confederate lieutenant, Samuel Lanier, being held in the dungeon. He had been married only a few weeks before he was captured. He managed to smuggle a message to his bride, Melanie, and she, being very much in love with her husband, traveled from her home in the South to be with him. She disguised herself as a man and traveled to Boston. She obtained a small boat and rowed herself across the waters of the harbor to Georges Island one dark night.[77]

The young woman gave the necessary signal and was hoisted up to an opening that allowed her to enter the prison. After a tearful reunion, the couple decided to dig their way out of the dungeon. Their chosen route would allow them to come out on the parade ground. But they miscalculated the angle of the tunnel, and it was discovered by the sentinel. Colonel Dimick was informed of the scheme, and the brave little wife was confronted. She tried to fire her pistol at the colonel, but instead the pistol misfired, being the "old-fashioned pepper box type," and her husband was killed. She was tried and sentenced to hang as a spy. She faced it bravely, and her only request was that she be hung in women's clothing. Someone found a black robe and the woman went to her death.[78]

Over the years, soldiers have reported seeing a Lady in Black at various locations. Several men were court-martialed for firing upon a ghostly apparition while on sentry duty. One man deserted his post after he claimed to have been chased by a black-clad figure. On another occasion, footprints of a girl's shoe in new-fallen snow were seen under the huge arched sally port. The prints came from nowhere and led to nowhere.[79]

The Last Prisoners

Once the war ended, prisoners were released, but the process took some time. Soldiers from Mosby's Rangers were not released until June 15, 1865.[80]

Among the last prisoners was Confederate Gen. Richard Stoddert Ewell, who had been captured at Sayler's Creek on April 6, 1865. Once commander of a corps and then a division, Ewell had lost a leg at Groveton but returned to fight at Gettysburg, the Wilderness and Spotsylvania. He had been given command of the defenses of Richmond. Ewell was held at Fort Warren until August 19, 1865.[81]

Alexander Stephens, vice president of the Confederate States of America, and the secretary of the treasury of the Confederacy, John Henninger Reagan, were held at Fort Warren.[82] Stephens' book about his time in Fort Warren has recently been published.[83]

Fort Warren Today

Fort Warren is part of the Boston Harbor Islands National Park area. The island is accessible by ferry or water shuttle, and open to the public. It is visited daily by tourists and schoolchildren. Most of the fort is intact.[84] According to Massachusetts historian Edward Rowe Snow, Fort Warren "has more memories of the Civil War days than any other place in New England."[85]

X

Gratiot Street Prison, St. Louis, Missouri

Oh, for liberty, that my gallant steed
May carry me to the battle field —
There I can fight; I'll never yield!
Then away, away, to the battle field.
Dark and crimson is the tide,
Forms are scattered far and wide,
Death and victory will be won —
I'm a prisoner, I'm undone![1]
— seen by Griffin Frost, penciled on wall of prisoners'
room at Provost Office, St. Louis, MO

Location: 8th and Gratiot Streets, St. Louis, Missouri. **Established:** December 21, 1861. **Type:** Converted medical school building. **Type of Prisoners:** Confederate prisoners of war, political prisoners, bushwhackers, spies, Union deserters and criminals, and bounty jumpers (including both male and female, black and white).[2] **Capacity:** 500. **Most Held at One Time:** 1,800. **Known Number of Escapes:** 109+.[3] **Other name:** McDowell's Medical College.

History

The Gratiot Street Prison (pronounced "grass-shut"[4]) was originally McDowell's Medical College. This three-story, graystone building, one of the most unique of any prison building in the country, was erected in 1847 to house the growing medical college established by Dr. Joseph N. McDowell of Tennessee. The central octagonal tower, complete with cupola, of the fortress-like building was flanked by two wings. Dr. McDowell, a pro-slavery secessionist, had stored a number of muskets and small cannons in the cupola during the unrest of the 1850s.[5] When war was declared, he shipped his arms to Memphis, so when a detachment of home guard searched the building, they found nothing.[6] Because of McDowell's support of the South, his property was seized. The large building served in many capacities—a recruiting headquarters, Gen. John Fremont's headquarters, and a barracks.[7] It is remembered today as the Gratiot Street Prison.

The medical school was soon converted to a prison when Lynch's Slave Pen at Fifth and Myrtle Streets became overcrowded.[8] Very quickly, the Gratiot Street Prison became the principal place west of the Mississippi where prisoners of war were confined.[9]

The Facilities

At the McDowell Medical School, the central "round room" measured 60 feet in diameter, but was crowded when 250 men were crammed inside. This room had better ventilation than the smaller "square room," which was 60 by 15 feet. Many of the sick prisoners had been housed in the "square room." The officers' quarters were rooms 16 by 16 feet, and eight men were confined in each.[10]

Most of the quarters used to house prisoners had been classrooms. One of the wings was used for Federal officers and attendants, and the upper story was reserved for Confederate officers who were prisoners. The north wing also had a basement. The school amphitheater was converted to a hospital, and a dungeon.[11]

Capt. Griffin Frost was first confined in the upper room of the "round building" which he described as a "very dark gloomy place, and very filthy besides." He was moved to better quarters on the lower floor of one of the wings. A week later, he was moved to the officers' quarters, which were still better. Officers' quarters had bunks for sleeping, and the food was better and more plentiful. The officers were allowed knives, forks and spoons.[12] (Frost was a newspaper editor and may have rewritten or enhanced portions of his journal prior to publication in 1867. While one of few primary sources on the Gratiot Street Prison, the journal was published in response to the outcry against the treatment of prisoners held at Andersonville. Frost hoped to make it clear that northern prisons were just as bad as southern ones, but the conditions at Gratiot in no way compared to those at Andersonville.)

Prisoners were also housed in several other locations near the Gratiot Street building. The numbers kept in each facility cannot be determined because the monthly reports combined prisoners held at the McDowell College, the Myrtle Street Prison (formerly Lynch's Slave Pen), and the home of Margaret McLure on Chestnut Street, which was used to hold women.[13]

Setting up A New Prison

Setting up a new prison involved making many decisions. Questions arose about keeping the building clean and whether prisoners should be allowed to receive clothing and other items. Brig. Gen. Schuyler Hamilton advised Colonel Tuttle, of the Second Iowa Volunteers, who had been placed in charge of the new prison, that he was responsible for custody of the prisoners of war and it was within the scope of his duties to oversee "the internal police of the place of their confinement as well as provisioning" of those in his custody. He authorized Tuttle to request necessary cleaning supplies, such as brooms. Hamilton reminded Tuttle that the health of the prisoners was of "primary importance," and that prisoners should be given every opportunity to "wash themselves." Articles of clothing sent by friends were to be allowed, after they had been inspected, but that no "articles of luxury or ornament" would be allowed. Gifts of tobacco and pipes were to be regarded "as common stock" and divided among the prison population. General Hamilton suggested that, under proper guard, white prisoners should be allowed to bring in fuel. He also suggested that space be provided in front of the building where prisoners could exercise when the weather permitted.[14]

An inspection by Brig. Gen. William W. Orme in December 1863 noted an ample supply of food for the prisoners and facilities for cooking. There was an "abundant supply of pure water at this prison." Overall, the building and the yards were well maintained and clean and, although the prisoners were "generally in good health," there was a large number of sick prisoners. Orme found a "lack of personal cleanliness among the prisoners." He concluded that the number of guards was adequate.[15]

The Prisoners

Initially, 27 prisoners were transferred from the former slave auction house to McDowell's building. Among those were Max McDowell, the son of Dr. McDowell, who had been arrested in St. Louis for recruiting troops for Maj. Gen. Sterling Price's Confederate troops.[16]

Additional prisoners of war arrived at McDowell's Medical College on December 22, 1861. They were a ragged bunch, and the crowd that gathered at the train station was shocked by their appearance. These "western" Confederates had no uniforms, but the privates were clothed in blankets, coverlets, quilts, and buffalo robes, and the officers looked only a little better.[17]

Among the new arrivals was Col. Ebenezer Magoffin, the highest ranking officer, and the brother of Kentucky governor Beriah Magoffin. Colonel Magoffin was wearing a tall felt hat, and a blue blanket coat. He was tall, but stoop-shouldered, with a dark complexion. The *Daily Missouri Democrat* described Magoffin as "the boldest, most reckless and unscrupulous of the [captured] rebel officers."[18] (For more about Magoffin's escape from the Alton prison, see Chapter I.)

By July 1862, the Gratiot Street Prison held 400 prisoners.[19] By October 1862, the number of prisoners had increased to the point that Colonel Hoffman ruled that the Gratiot Street Prison should be used "for casual prisoners and for such as have their cases under investigation." Long-term prisoners of state, also under Hoffman's control, were to be sent to Alton.[20]

On December 7, 1863, Brig. Gen. William W. Orm reported that there were 382 prisoners of war, and 114 citizens being held on military orders.[21]

Although the prison was deemed unfit, unhealthy, and unsafe, more and more prisoners were sent there. One inspector wrote lengthy reports detailing the unhealthy conditions, and warned: "This state of things cannot long continue without producing the most serious results in the form of epidemics." He also noted that there was an insufficient number of guards. While the prison contained 480 prisons, there had been only 50 guards to watch them, and when the number of prisoners increased, no additional guards were assigned.[22]

Prison Commandant Convicted of Crimes

In December 1862, Capt. William J. Masterson, was placed in command of the prison. Masterson was a civilian who had been given the rank of captain by the provost marshal's department, and a monthly salary of $100 to manage both the Gratiot Street prison and the Myrtle Street facility. A small Irishman, who weighed only 120 pounds, Masterson was "one of the most hated commandants in the history of the prison." Griffin Frost, one of his prisoners, called Masterson "cruel, ungentlemanly, and insulting in a purely personal manner." Masterson remained in the post until August 1863, when he was charged with stealing commissary stores that were intended for the prisoners. He was arrested and confined in his own prison.[23]

Prevention of Escapes

In an attempt to safeguard the prisoners and prevent problems that might allow them to escape, H. L. McConnell, acting assistant provost marshal general in the Department of Mississippi, recommended to Lt. Col. B. G. Farrar that (1) prisoners of war be kept separate from other prisoners, and that officers be prohibited from communicating with privates; (2) those prisoners under sentence of death should be kept separate from other prisoners and it was advised that they should be sent to Alton, Illinois, for confinement; (3) one officer should be detailed daily as commander of the prison guard and should be required to remain constantly at the prison. He should not allow any of the guards to go beyond the lines. The constant presence of an officer would be more effective, and "preclude the possibility of escapes and outbreaks." McConnell was of the opinion that any escapes that had occurred at Gratiot were because of the "negligence of the guard."[24]

If death from disease was not enough, Maj. George Rex, the hospital surgeon, complained that a prisoner who was a hospital patient was standing before one of the windows when he was shot by the guards. The ball passed through his right leg and fractured both the tibia and fibula. The leg had to be amputated.[25]

In reply to Major Rex's complaint, the prison commandant, Capt. R. C. Allen listed the instructions regarding prisoners that had been given to the guards:

> No prisoners are allowed to stand at or sit in the windows at night.
>   If a prisoner works on the bars of the windows, and does not leave at the command, the sentinel will fire at him.
>   The sentinel will not allow any communication, such as letters, papers, signs, &c to be passed to the prisoners.
>   If a prisoner tries to break out, over, or through the fences, or in any other way, the sentinel will shoot him.
>   The sentinel will give alarm immediately in case a fire should break out in or near the prison.[26]

Escapes

By the summer of 1863, the old college building was in a sad state. An inspection by John L. Le Conte, surgeon of volunteers, and acting medical inspector, United States Army, found a number of areas that needed immediate attention. The building was not, at the present time, overcrowded, with only 249 prisoners. However, the floors and ceilings were "dilapidated," and, Le Conte reported, "when scrubbing is done the water leaks through from one story to another." He also noted that many of the windowsills were deteriorating, and that they should be replaced by wood, stone or iron. A number of windows did not even have bars, which would invite prisoners to escape.[27]

Despite all efforts, according to the official monthly reports submitted by the various Federal prisons (beginning in July 1862), Gratiot Street Prison had more than its share of escapes.

In August 1862, six escapes were reported. After that report, for many months afterward, no reports were published that could add to the statistics on escapes.[28]

Reports from Gratiot Street Prison are incomplete. However, a report for August 1863 noted that 836 prisoners were being held, and there had been two escapes. In October 1863, there were 10 escapes out of a prison population of 1,028. In November 1863, one prisoner escaped, but in December of that year, 12 escapes were reported. (Another source stated that 60 escaped in December 1863 through a tunnel. Others cut through the wall into the Christian Brothers Academy, and were shown the way out.[29]

In February 1864, seven escapes were reported. An attempt to cut through the wall into the building of the Christian Brothers on April 5, 1864, was discovered, and no prisoners escaped at that time.[30] Six escapes were reported in June 1864. The last reported escape was the only one in October 1864.[31]

The diary of Capt. Griffin Frost, a prisoner at both Alton Prison and Gratiot Street Prison, fills in some of the missing monthly reports. On March 13, 1863, Frost recorded in his diary that five Confederate officers escaped that morning. From the rumors Frost heard, the leader of the escaping prisoners had managed to obtain an overcoat that looked like those the Federal officers wore. The evening before the escape, the prisoner approached the guard, and represented himself as a "Federal surgeon." He asked the guard if he had seen the ambulance that was to transport three or four sick patients to the island where the smallpox victims were being kept. He seemed upset and told the guard that if the ambulance did not come in the morning he would have to walk. The next morning, the "Federal surgeon" approached the same guard, who informed him that the ambulance still had not come. The fake surgeon then went upstairs and told his patients that he was ready to leave. Frost recorded that they all "followed him down stairs, out the front door [and] into the street.... "The escapees were Maj. John F. Rucker, Captain Stemmons, Lt. James Harvey Rucker, and two others whose names he did not know. Because Frost and five or six others either could not or would not tell how the escape occurred, they were put into the dungeon and locked up. Frost spent his 29th birthday shivering with the cold and damp, with no fire, nothing to sit on, and hungry.[32]

Frost noted that two more prisoners escaped on March 31, 1863, one of whom had a ball and chain attached to his leg. Somehow, the prisoner managed to remove his ball and chain before leaving the prison. Frost rejoiced "with them, and [sent] my sincerest congratulations after them; would be pleased to do myself the honor of conveying them in person," because, and he quotes *The Prisoner of Chillon*, by George Gordon, Lord Byron:

> My limbs are bowed, though not with toil,
> But rusted with a vile repose,
> For they have been a dungeon's spoil
> And mine has been the fate of those.[33]

The prisoner who wore the ball and chain may have been William H. White, assistant adjutant general, Forrest's Confederate Cavalry. From Glasgow, Kentucky, White wrote to describe his escape from prison in St. Louis.

> I made my escape from prison on the 31st of March and have succeeded in getting this far from the city without any trouble and just as soon as I get money enough intend to return to Forrest in Tennessee. I have seen a pretty hard time. The damned scoundrels had a twenty-four-pound ball and chain on my leg for three weeks. I succeeded in sawing the rivets of the chain with an old case-knife some of the boys gave me, threw a handful of pepper in one of the guard's eyes, knocked the other one down, making my way to the river; got into a skiff and bid Saint Louis good by. I would have escaped sooner but tried to make them believe that I was a good Union man, thinking I would be released. [They] Got my Confederate money and watch. Finding I could not get my money I was determined to escape or die in the attempt. I effected the escape of six others with myself. I don't know what became of the others except one who is still with me, and he is a good soldier; belongs to Morgan's cavalry.... I am in good health and hope to live to kill 100 Yankees before I die.[34]

White criticized the prisoners confined in St. Louis for their lack of courage. He believed that if they had the "nerve they could all make their escape," but he knew, "they are all too damned cowardly." In addition, they did not protect their own. White said it was all he could do to keep the other prisoners from reporting his plan to escape.[35] White may have been recaptured. An endorsement was on the bottom of his letter from Lt. Col. Robert C. Buchanan, commander at Fort Delaware, as he forwarded White's letter to Col. William Hoffman. He noted that this copy was "furnished by Lieutenant Smith," of the 58th Illinois, "under whose charge White was brought to this post [Fort Delaware].[36]

A group of boys who were quartered on the lower level tried to escape in November 1863. They were caught and punished by being confined in the dungeon, on "half rations of bread and water." Frost thought that this treatment would weaken their "adventurous spirits."[37]

Absalom C. Grimes, of Hannibal, Missouri, was an acquaintance of Mark Twain. Noted for his many escapes, Grimes was skilled in escaping from prison. He reportedly was captured five times and managed to escape each time, twice while under a death sentence.[38] Once, he escaped from the guardhouse in Cairo, Illinois, and even managed to escape while chained in close confinement at the Gratiot Street Prison. Before the war, Grimes had been a steamboat pilot on the Mississippi, but because he refused to take the Oath of Allegiance to the United States, his pilot's license was not renewed. Grimes then joined the 1st Missouri Cavalry, and was captured near Springfield, Missouri. He escaped while being sent from the Myrtle Street Prison to Alton Prison. After his escape, he resumed his role as a courier and became the "Official Confederate mail carrier." He was commissioned as a major in Gen. Sterling Price's army.[39]

Grimes was confined to the Gratiot Street Prison on September 2, 1862, charged with being a "rebel mail-carrier and a spy." He was tried and found guilty and sentenced to death. He was placed in solitary confinement, handcuffed, with a ball and chain.[40]

Grimes was not idle as he lay on his mattress in a corner of a room. He cut a narrow groove across three of the floor planks. At night he removed the boards and crawled beneath the floor to work on the foundation walls. It took him two nights to cut through the 18-inch thick brick wall, and the two-foot foundation stones. Grimes recalled that "On the night of October 2, a few days before my execution, I disengaged myself from my shackles and a 32-pound ball [and made my] escape."[41]

An Aborted Escape Attempt

On December 25, 1863, several prisoners attempted an escape by burning a hole through the floor of the upstairs room. As they started to lower themselves down onto the next floor, they were greeted by some of the prison guards. The next morning the prisoners who had tried to escape were taken outside. Six were handcuffed to a post, but Samuel Clifford, the seventh man, was put in the dungeon.[42] Although the weather was extremely cold, they endured this treatment for several nights. According to Frost's account, the handcuffed prisoners stomped their feet, shouted and sang to keep from freezing.[43] The prison officials asked the men if they would agree not to try to escape again, then they would be brought in. All except Grimes and William Sebring agreed. They nearly froze to death in the -20 degree weather. Sebring finally relented, but Grimes refused to do so. Finally, two ladies who lived across the street from the prison, Miss Dora and Miss Cornelia Harrison, reported the plight of the prisoner to the provost marshal, who ordered him released. Grimes was fortunate to have escaped freezing to death. When he was released from the post, the temperature had fallen to 22 degrees below zero, after having been 70 degrees above during the daytime.[44] In his memoirs, Grimes said that they were brought inside each night at 11 P.M., and taken back outside each morning.[45]

Sebring's experience at Gratiot Street Prison while chained outside in the freezing weather is quoted in the "Report of the Joint Committee Appointed to Investigate the Condition and Treatment of Prisoners."[46]

An Attempt to Avoid Hanging

After making his escape, Grimes remained free for almost two years, until he was recaptured in June 1864. Again, he was confined at the Gratiot Street Prison where he was to be hanged. On June 20, 1864, he was in a room with five prisoners, four of whom were condemned to die. Grimes recalled that the men had mopped their room and the prisoners were taken outside by the guard while the floor dried. The men had already planned to attack their guards and escape. However, just as soon at the attack began, the sentries began firing at the prisoners. The alarm was given that an escape attempt was in progress and that the gate was open. Other prisoners (John Carlin, Jasper Hill, Alfred Yates, and several others) made a break for the yard.

During his bid for freedom, prisoner William McElhenny's kneecap was shot off, and several other prisoners were wounded. When order was restored, the score was five prisoners had escaped, two prisoners had been killed, two wounded, and the others recaptured.[47]

Grimes was shot in his right leg, the leg to which a 32-pound ball was attached. Although one report stated that Grimes was recaptured in Memphis, Tennessee, in his memoirs he recalled being recaptured lying on the woodpile inside the prison fence.[48] One report stated that McElhenny, a citizen of Washington County, Missouri, was captured while still in St. Louis. John F. Moshire, of the 6th Missouri Cavalry, was recaptured in Vicksburg, Mississippi.[49]

Afterward, while still on crutches, Grimes was transferred to the Missouri State Penitentiary. He escaped execution through the influence of Union friends and was eventually given a pardon by President Lincoln. He returned to his prewar career, married, and lived until March 1911.[50]

John C. Carlin was an interesting character. Having been captured in Illinois, Carlin, the son of the ex-governor of Illinois, had arrived at Gratiot Street Prison on November 14, 1863, with a ball and chain attached to his leg. During the war, he escaped and was recaptured several times. After having escaped with Hill and Sebring in 1864, he died of gunshot wounds received when he was recaptured near the home of his bride.[51]

Prisoner James H. Colcheasure, a 27-year-old private in Thompson's Regiment, managed to get outside the fence. He was found in Clay County, Missouri, where he was shot in the head and died instantly.[52]

The official report also stated that Lewis Y. Schultz, a citizen of St. Louis, was killed in the city.[53]

With Only a File, A Prisoner Could Escape

Robert Louden was sentenced to hang at the St. Louis city jail. All was in readiness for the hanging, but the priest, Father Ryan and a nun, Mother Meredith, managed to get General Rosecrans to delay the execution. Later, Louden and Pres Westerman were to be sent to Alton prison on a sternwheeler, the *Kate Kearney*. Grimes managed to slip a couple of files to Westerman before they left. Twelve prisoners, handcuffed in pairs, were taken aboard the ship and put on one of the upper decks. Louden managed to file the links off the handcuffs and then he took off his coat. When the waiters came to remove the supper trays, the prisoner, dressed in his shirt-sleeves, joined the waiters in gathering up the dishes, and walked away carrying a tray. Downstairs, he deposited his tray and went to the lower deck. When the boat landed at Alton, he jumped over the railing and swam to shore. He made it safely back to the South. Several days later, one of the guards at the Gratiot Street Prison brought in a newspaper that had an article titled, "Bob Louden; escape from the steamer *Kate Kearney* between St. Louis and Alton."[54]

A Different Disguise

Confederate Col. William H. McCowan had been recaptured after he escaped from another prison. He was being held in custody at the Gratiot Street Prison. McGowan had written Col. N. P. Chipman probably regarding release or parole (letter not found), but Chipman was told that this McGowan was the same person who had escaped prison by "resorting to the unchivalric system of blacking [his] hands and face."[55] Chipman was the inspector for the commissary general. He had been breveted a brigadier general in April 1862 for honorable service in the Bureau of Military Justice.[56]

With Just a Little Money

One prisoner escaped from the hospital at the Gratiot Street Prison. His plan was complete except he needed some money. To remedy the situation, he asked Mrs. Smith, an old lady, if she would exchange greenbacks for gold. She brought him $25, which he took and promised to return gold to her. Instead, he took the old woman's money, and left for "parts unknown."[57]

A Daring Escape

Captain Frost described the escape of 14 prisoners in December 1863 from the lower quarters. Some had even escaped from the "lock-up." Lt. Robert Lane LaValle was caught as he attempted to climb the fence. The guards were enraged and he feared they would shoot him after he surrendered. They questioned him and he said that 10 or 12 others had gone ahead of him. Those that had been upstairs in the "lock-up" had escaped by means of a "rope made of buckets." Those on the lower levels had exited through the "map house cellar," and out by an underground tunnel they had dug. The passage extended 40 or 50 yards to another cellar. From the second cellar, they could get outside in the yard, climb the fence and escape. Frost believed that it took the prisoners several weeks to complete their escape route, and he admired them for their skill.[58]

Frost learned the names of four of those who escaped from the "lock-up." One was W. Owsley, who had been tried for murder, robbery, bushwhacking, etc. Another was Watkins, who had charged the guards the previous spring and escaped. Watkins was recaptured, and had been in the lock-up ever since. There were also two lieutenants—Martin and Stewart.[59]

Needless to say, because of this escape, those who remained were placed under even more strict control. None were allowed to write members of their family. Other prisoners were punished because they would not reveal who led the escape, and put in the "strong room."[60]

Clifford — Talented, Handsome, Meanest, Most Dangerous Prisoner

Samuel Clifford was in the Gratiot Street Prison at the same time as Frost and Grimes. Grimes described Clifford as being 21 years old, six feet two inches tall, and weighing 200 pounds. Grimes said, "He was the handsomest man I ever saw. He was a pugilist, and was possessed of the meanest disposition imaginable."[61] Clifford could also play the banjo, and the prison authorities had a special pair of handcuffs made with a long bar between the cuffs especially so Clifford could play his banjo while wearing the handcuffs.[62]

On November 8, 1863, Frost noted the arrival of several new Federal soldiers who were locked up with Samuel Clifford. According to Frost, Clifford was "an awful chap," who escaped last summer "in open daylight, but was retaken in Illinois and brought back." Clifford got into an argument with one of the Federal soldiers and started a fight. For that, Clifford was confined to the dungeon. A born troublemaker, Frost hoped that Clifford would not give any of those already in the dungeon any trouble.[63] The "solitary dungeon" was the darkest pit in the prison.

Clifford had been playing his banjo when two drunken German soldiers were put in the room with him. They began to brag about how strong they were and how many guards it would take to make them drill. Clifford laughed at first, and told them, "You had better keep still or it will not take as many men to make you drill in here as it did at the Benton Barracks." The soldier asked just how many it would take, and Clifford replied, "I do not think more than one!" Then Clifford lay down his banjo and hit the man with his fist. As he lay on the floor, Clifford picked up the iron ball that was attached to his leg and struck the soldier on the chest. The guards rushed in and the wounded man was taken to the hospital where he died two days later. Clifford was not punished in any way for this "cold-blooded murder."[64]

Clifford took revenge on the man who had informed on their plan to escape through a hole in the floor. One day, while awaiting the guards to put him in the dungeon, he grabbed the man and carried him into the kitchen and set him on the large coal stove. The stove was almost red hot, and the man would have been burned to death had the guards not rescued him. The informer was, however, injured badly enough that he spent several months in the hospital.[65]

Sam Clifford also hated Captain Mosely. Grimes recalled that Clifford and Mosely (a German) had escaped from the same Room No. 3 by lowering themselves from a window using buckets and blankets. Mosely knew the area around St. Louis, but when they reached the street, he refused to guide Clifford. Mosely escaped, but Clifford was recaptured attempting to steal a boat to cross the Mississippi. Clifford vowed vengeance on "all Germans and on Mosely in particular."[66]

After the war Mosely became sheriff of Lincoln County, Missouri. About 1870, Grimes stole some books from a lawyer to give Mosely a reason to arrest him. Mosely found Clifford eating in a hotel at Moscow Mills. Although Clifford always carried a Winchester rifle, when he reached for it to shoot Mosely, the sheriff drew his revolver and shot first. The sheriff was quicker to the draw, and Clifford was killed instantly.[67]

Prisoners Executed in Retaliation

One event that stands out in the history of the Gratiot Street Prison was the execution of innocent prisoners in retaliation for the execution of a like number of Federal officers by Confederate guerrillas.

On October 23, 1864, seven bodies were discovered near Washington, Missouri. An investigation revealed the bodies to be those of Maj. James Wilson of the 3rd Missouri State Militia Cavalry and six other Union soldiers.[68] Union Gen. William S. Rosecrans, in command of the Department of Missouri, was enraged by the execution of Major Wilson and the Union soldiers by Confederate guerillas. In retaliation, in October 1864, Rosecrans ordered the execution of Maj. Enoch O. Wolf, of General Price's army, and six privates.[69]

In hopes of saving his own life, Major Wolf asked General Rosecrans to get Confederate Gen. Sterling Price to turn over Col. Timothy Reeves, the man who actually had killed Major Wilson, to Federal authorities. Wolf appealed to Rosecrans as a "soldier," a "gentleman," an "officer" and a "member of the Masonic Lodge."[70]

President Lincoln ordered a stay of execution for Major Wolf, and requested a full report of the case.[71] Because Wolf was a Mason, the local Masonic Lodge pressed authorities to delay his execution, until it was eventually dropped entirely.[72]

Efforts on behalf of the other six condemned prisoners failed, and on October 29, 1864, the condemned men were taken to Fort No. 4 in what is now Lafayette Square. After each was tied to a post, the death sentence was read to them and they were shot by a firing squad. The executed men were Pvt. Harvey H. Blackburn (Company A, Coleman's Arkansas Cavalry); Pvt. George T. Bunch (3rd Missouri Cavalry); Pvt. James W. Gates (3rd Missouri Cavalry); Pvt. Asa V. Ladd (Company A, Burbridge's Missouri Cavalry); Pvt. Charles W. Minnekin (Company A, Crabtree's Arkansas Cavalry); and Pvt. John A. Nichols (Company G, 2nd Missouri Cavalry).[73] All those executed were 21 or 22 years of age, except Gates, who was 34.

Mortality/Morbidy

Conditions at the Gratiot Street Prison continued to deteriorate. A report filed by surgeon George Rex on March 10, 1865, noted that during the four-month period from November 1864–February 1865, some 818 prisoners had been confined to the hospital because of illness. There had been 134 deaths. This, according to the surgeon, was a mortality rate of 50 percent for the year, 16 percent for those four months, and 4 percent per month.[74]

Many of the deaths were caused by smallpox. Most of the deceased prisoners were buried in the Jefferson Barracks National Cemetery, but a few were taken home by relatives for burial. Others, especially the smallpox victims, were buried on the Quarantine Island in the Mississippi River. [75]

By August 1865, there were no prisoners reported being held at Gratiot Street Prison.[76]

Gratiot Street Prison Today

The original building of the McDowell Medical College/Gratiot Street Prison was demolished in 1878. The property is now the headquarters of the Ralston-Purina Company, and the actual prison site is now a parking lot.[77]

XI

Johnson's Island, Lake Erie, Ohio

To the sweet, sunny South, take me home
— G.W.T (Johnson's Island prisoner), from poem
"Take Me Home to the South"[1]

Location: an island in Sandusky Bay, Lake Erie, Ohio. **Established:** February 24, 1862. **Type:** plank stockade, with two-story frame buildings for prisoners quarters. **Kind of Prisoners:** mostly Confederate officers, some enlisted men, and political prisoners. **Prisoners Held:** 300 to 2,000. **Known Escapes:** 12.[2]

History

In 1861, a 300-acre island in Lake Erie was leased by the Federal government for $500 per year. The lease included the stipulations that the government could build a prison large enough to house captured Confederate officers, and could control access to the island.[3]

The Site

Johnson's Island was the perfect site for a prison.[4] Situated in Sandusky Bay of Lake Erie, the island is about three miles from the town of Sandusky, which provided easy access to construction and maintenance supplies.[5] The enclosure which contained the prisoners covered about 15 acres.[6] Water and weather combined to present the most formidable barrier. One inmate, Col. R. F. Webb described his prison as "one of the most secure prisons I ever saw, yet sometimes our men manage to make an escape."[7]

The normally frigid waters of the lake usually froze over in the winter.[8] The severe winters affected the prisoners greatly. Many of the prisoners were from the Deep South and their uniforms were never meant to protect them from the deadly cold of the area of the Great Lakes. Occasionally, gales would sweep across the island, shaking the buildings and penetrating the rooms.[9]

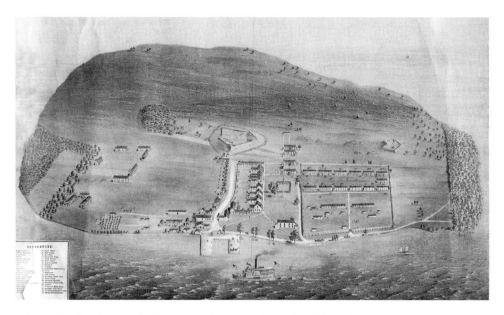

Johnson's Island — Sandusky Bay, Lake Erie, Ohio, sketch by Edward Gould, Co. B., 128th Ohio. The U.S. Steamer Michigan *is in the foreground. The straight lines are paths from the prison blocks to the pumps. (Original lithograph in the Geography and Map Division, Library of Congress, published ca. 1865 by Middleton, Strobridge & Co. of Cincinnati, Ohio, G4082.J6S5 1865.G6 CW 320. Reprint by Big-Web Development Corp., Loxahatchee, Florida.)*

The Prison Facilities

After Col. William Hoffman, the commissary general of prisoners, selected the site construction began. Local contractors were employed and by February 1, 1862, the majority of the buildings had been completed at a cost of under $30,000.[10]

Inmate Horace Carpenter described the prison as located on the west end of the island. The quarters of the prison officers were outside the stockade. The frame buildings for the prisoners were set in two rows on each side of a street about 150 feet wide. The buildings were weather boarded but unsealed on the inside.[11] An average of 187 were quartered in each of the 12 buildings.[12] The buildings that housed the prisoners were two stories, each approximately 130 × 24 feet.[13]

One prisoner described his prison as "a square lot of 16⅔ acres of land enclosed with a heavy slab of plank fence 15 feet high and very strongly made. The top of the fence was filled with spike nails, so you could not press the weight of your hands on them," wrote Capt. W. H. A. Speer. On the outside of the fence, 3½ feet from the top, was a platform which permitted the sentinels to walk around the compound.[14] The board fence was illuminated at night by lanterns to reveal any prisoners who attempted to violate regulations, or escape. On the south the lower portion of the fence was made of upright stakes with narrow spaces between each which afforded a good view of the bay only a few yards away The rest of the stockade walls were solidly planked. The whole enclosure was termed a "Bull Pen." The "deadline" was clearly marked by stakes set in the ground about 25–30 feet apart. The latrines, or "sinks," were on the north side behind the buildings, and about 10 feet from the fence, and inside the deadline.[15]

In addition to the barracks, one building served as a hospital. There was also a sutler's stand, and by 1864, two large mess halls inside the stockade.[16]

At the corners fronting the lake, two blockhouses held artillery and rifles. Another blockhouse sat at the main entrance to provide a view of all approaches to the prison.[17] Outside the stockade were buildings for stables, a lime kiln, barracks for the guards, and a power magazine. Two defensive forts were built over the winter of 1864-1865 to protect the island, and were in use by the spring of 1865.[18] The engraving made by Edward Gould in 1865 shows a total of 100 structures of all sizes.[19]

Water

The wells that provided water were very shallow, and in the summer the water was so bad that lake water was preferred. Water from the lake was piped into the wells.[20] One prisoner recalled that pipes ran from two pumps into the bay, but when cold weather arrived, the pipes froze. Two holes were then dug, about 8 feet deep, and the pumps placed in them. One prisoner recalled that many times he had been "painfully thirsty, and yet in sight of an ocean of fresh water."[21] In the winter when the lake froze, a hole was cut in the thick ice to obtain water.[22]

Prison Personnel

To get guards to serve on Johnson's Island, Colonel Hoffman offered a reward to men to enlist in the garrison, to be known as the "Hoffman Battalion." The first prison commandant, William Seward Pierson, was the former mayor of Sandusky. Although he had no previous military experience, Pierson was made a major and given command of the battalion.[23] Pierson was described as "gentlemanly and courteous in his deportment, very industrious, attentive and most anxious that everything should be done in a proper manner," but he lacked confidence in himself and his ability to command.[24]

The Prisoners

On April 11, 1862, a group of about 2,000 prisoners from Camp Chase arrived on Johnson's Island.[25] By July 1862, Johnson's Island held 1,184 prisoners. That number increased in December 1863 to 2,653. A year later, the island held 3,231 prisoners.[26]

First Lt. J. F. Cross (5th North Carolina Regiment) was captured at Gettysburg in July 1863. Cross kept a list of the prisoners while he was there. From among 2,437 Confederate officers, there was one major general, five brigadier generals, 50 colonels, 41 lieutenant colonels, 62 majors, 575 captains, 1,675 lieutenants, and 28 adjutants. The prisoners were officers from every state in the Confederacy, plus Maryland, Kentucky and Missouri.[27]

Some Famous Prisoners

The prison on Johnson's Island had been established to hold captured Confederate officers. Many outstanding officers were held there, including those captured at Gettysburg and Port Hudson about the time the exchange of prisoners was suspended.[28]

One of the most famous prisoners held on Johnson's Island was Gen. William Henry Fitzhugh "Rooney" Lee, the second-oldest son of Gen. Robert E. Lee. "Rooney" had joined the cavalry and fought with J.E.B. Stuart. Severely wounded in the leg at Brandy Station, Virginia, "Rooney" was captured June 26, 1863, while convalescing at "Hickory Hill," the Wickham family home. He was held a prisoner until March 1864, and while he was in prison, his wife, Charlotte Wickham Lee, died in December 1863.[29]

Col. Hoffman insisted that extra precautions be taken to prevent Lee's escape while being transported. Traveling with four guards from Fort Monroe, the young Confederate officer was not allowed to speak to anyone on the way.[30]

Maj. Gen. Isaac R. Trimble, of Ewell's Division, A. P. Hill's Corps, who had lost a leg at Gettysburg, was also a prisoner. Another captured at Gettysburg was Brig. Gen. J. J. Archer who headed Archer's Tennessee Brigade (see Chapter VI, and Chapter XII). Brig. Gen. William N. R. Beal of Louisiana was captured at Port Hudson on July 9, 1863.[31]

Lt. Col. John R. Winston and Lt. Col. Samuel Hill Boyd, both from the 45th North Carolina, were captured at Gettysburg.[32] Boyd was taken to Fort McHenry, then Fort Delaware, before being transferred to Johnson's Island. On February 9, 1864, he was transferred to Point Lookout, Maryland, and paroled for exchange on March 6, 1864. Returning to service wearing a bright new uniform, the 6-foot, 4-inch Boyd was wounded in the arm at the battle of Spotsylvania Court House. After he had the arm bandaged, he refused to leave the field. The big officer was killed "while gallantly leading his regiment in a charge upon the enemy lines" only a few moments later.[33]

Winston, of Rockingham County, North Carolina, was a teacher before he enlisted at age 23. He quickly rose in the ranks, and had just been promoted to lieutenant colonel on June 26, 1863, when he was wounded at Gettysburg. Winston remained with his regiment and received

Lt. Col. John R. Winston, 45th Carolina, was one of few to escape Johnson's Island, and also survive the war. (Courtesy of the North Carolina Department of Cultural Resources, Raleigh, North Carolina.)

a second wound while leading an advance upon the enemy. He was captured and hospitalized at Fort McHenry, and was transferred to Johnson's Island on September 28, 1863. Winston was one of the few who escaped the frozen hell of Johnson's Island. After he rejoined his regiment, he was wounded in the leg in the battle of Spotsylvania. Promoted to colonel, he was with his troops at Appomattox Court House on April 9, 1865. As evidenced by his actions, John R. Winston was "a man of deep piety, of stern integrity and the coolest courage in battle."[34]

Other Prisoners

Capt. William H. Asbury Speer of the "Yadkin Stars," Company I, 28th North Carolina Regiment, was captured at Hanover Court House on May 27, 1862 (Figure 7). He was first sent to Fort Monroe, Virginia, then to Fort Columbus on Governor's Island in New York Harbor.[35] After only a short stay, Speer was transferred to Johnson's Island.[36] Captain Speer and other officers were taken by train to Buffalo, New York, where they boarded a train for Cleveland, and Sandusky, Ohio.

Lt. Col. Samuel Hill Boyd, 45th North Carolina, survived imprisonment on Johnson's Island. After his friend John R. Winston escaped, Boyd was transferred to Point Lookout, Maryland, on February 9, 1864, and exchanged. (Courtesy of the North Carolina Department of Cultural Resources, Raleigh, North Carolina.)

He noted in his diary that the prisoners were marched from the cars to a boat "so quick no one hardly seen us." The steamer carried them across the lake 3½ miles to the island on June 21, 1862.[37] He was one of 1,300 prisoners confined there under Major Pierson.[38] Captain Speer was on Johnson's Island with his cousin, Lt. E. A. Speer from Tennessee.[39]

Life Inside the Prison

An inspection in December 1863 conducted by Brig. Gen. William W. Orme found that the facility held 2,381 "rebel prisoners of war," of which all but 59 were officers. The prisoners were housed in "very comfortable barracks," which were two-story frame structures. Orme found the barracks "mostly very clean and neat," but the degree of cleanliness depended "upon the taste of the occupants." He reported the supply of food abundant and the quality good. He stated that the bread was the "same kind used by our own officers and men composing the garrison." The men were organized into "convenient messes and have cooking stoves and other facilities for cooking," so that they got "along comfortably." Sutlers were yet not allowed on the island so the prisoners could not purchase other necessary items.[40]

Lt. Edward Ford Spears (Company G, the "Hamilton Guards," of the 2nd Kentucky Infantry), was sent to the new prison on Johnson's Island in April 1862, after he had surrendered at Fort Donelson on February 16, 1862. Spears was impressed and believed that "We have comfortable quarters and more ground and are in every respect better off than we were at Camp Chase. I think we will have better health here than any place in the Northern Confederacy." Spears had yet to experience winter on Lake Erie.[41]

Morbidity and Mortality

In 1862, there were 37 deaths, most from "diseases incurred before" the prisoners had reached the camp. At the time he visited the island, Orme thought that the prisoners looked "well and hearty." He

Col. William H. Asbury Speer, 28th North Carolina, was captured at Hanover Court House, confined at Fort Columbus, New York, then Johnson's Island in 1862. (Courtesy of Allen Paul Speer.)

also believed that Lieutenant Colonel Pierson's force of 400 men was sufficient.[42] Not only did Commandant Pierson worry about escapes, but he had to contend with smallpox. Smallpox had been brought to Johnson's Island twice by prisoners transferred from Alton Prison. After seven cases had developed, Pierson ordered the doctor to vaccinate every prisoner as quickly as possible, and to move those with the disease out of the barracks as soon as it was detected.[43] In December 1863, Brigadier General Orme reported only 69 deaths out of 2,695 prisoners, for an 11-month period.[44]

It has been estimated that over 300 prisoners died during their confinement on Johnson's Island.[45]

Treatment of Prisoners

After the prisoners arrived on the island, they were taken to the office, registered, and searched. Any money they had was taken and replaced by "sutlers' checks" which the prisoners used for currency. Then, the prisoners were marched through the gate into the prison compound.[46]

Each prisoner was housed in one of 12 buildings, and assigned a bunk with a straw mattress and a blanket on which to sleep.[47]

In the summer months, civilians flocked to the island in droves on "steamboat excursions," to gawk at the prisoners as if they were caged animals.[48]

One prisoner wrote in his diary that the prisoners on Johnson's Island were not allowed as much freedom as they had on Governor's Island. The guards continuously shot and killed or wounded prisoners.[49] Captain Speer saw what happened when sentinels fired into the prisoners' rooms. His diary entry for August 8, 1862, recorded the death of one of "our officers," who had been shot in his own quarters just as he was going to bed. Speer was appalled at the "cold, willful and premeditated murder," of an unfortunate "young man, a very peaceable, quiet fellow." The dead man was Gibbon from Arkansas. Speer described the shooting as "one of the most horrible things I ever seen in my life." Soon, a plot was devised to attack the guards, tear down the plank fence, and escape. The prisoners planned to capture the cannon, but even if they had succeeded, they were still surrounded by the deep waters of Lake Erie. Fortunately, reason prevailed, and the body of the murdered Gibbon was buried without incident. Gibbon, according to Captain Speer, was the third officer killed and there had been several incidents where the guards fired into the men's quarters without wounding anyone.[50]

Continuously in danger of being shot at by a cannon or from rifle musketry, Captain Speer vowed he had "rather be upon the battlefield every day than to be here in this miserable suspense and horrible condition of the mind."[51] Speer was later exchanged. He returned to his regiment by way of Vicksburg on September 1, 1862,[52] and was killed in the fighting at the Weldon Railroad at Reams Station, Virginia, on August 25, 1864.[53]

In August 1864, the prison sutler was stopped from selling anything edible to the prisoners. At that same time, all packages from friends and relatives outside were stopped. On November 20, 1864, prisoner William Norman arrived. Originally a member of Company A, 28th North Carolina Regiment, known as the "Surry Regulars," after his first tour of duty was up, Norman reenlisted in the 2nd North Carolina Regiment. He was promoted to captain, and served with the Army of Northern Virginia during the battles of Fredericksburg, Chancellorsville, and Gettysburg. Norman wrote to his wife, Letitia, in Surry County, North Carolina:

> This is the most fatal blow we have yet had to contend with, and at the same time and in the same order our rations from the government were cut down about one-eighth. *Starvation was now staring many a poor Rebel in the face.*[54]

These restrictive measures and the decrease in rations may have motivated some of the prisoners to increase their efforts to escape from the prison.

To Pass the Time

Prisoners tried to forget their misery and occupy their minds with more pleasant thoughts. One method was through minstrel performances. Charlie H. Pierce was one of the leading performers. The prisoners also organized baseball clubs — the Southern Nine (composed of those below the rank of captain), and the Confederate Nine (composed of officers with higher rank). Pierce was captain and catcher of the Southern Nine. A championship game was witnessed by a crowd of 3,000 people — prisoners, officers, and citizens from Sandusky.[55]

Other prisoners, including Robert Smith, carved rings and broaches from shell.[56]

Prisoners to Be Executed

A few soldiers were sent to the island under sentence of a court-martial to be executed. Pierson complained to Colonel Hoffman that he had received a "number of prisoners under sentence of death" and that more were expected. During the summer, the Federal soldiers could be held in the small guardhouse, but in the winter he would have to put them in with the Confederate prisoners in the barracks, which were not "secure." Hoffman urged Major General Burnside to discontinue this practice.[57]

First Lt. D. U. Barziza, of the 4th Texas Infantry, known as Hood's Brigade, recalled in his memoirs of his prison days the names of the Confederate prisoners brought there to be executed: Pvt. John Marr, Co. I, 2nd Kentucky Infantry; George P. Sims, of Bourbon County, Kentucky, a deserter from the 1st Kentucky Infantry, C.S.A.; William S. Burgess, of Harrison County, Kentucky, a member of Basil Duke's Regiment; and Thomas M. Campbell, of Nicholas County, Kentucky, who was awaiting sentence. On the day these condemned men arrived, May 15, 1863, two other men were executed by General Burnside's order. General Order No. 38, issued in April 1863, declared that anyone found within Federal lines who "commit acts for the benefit of the enemies of our country will be tried as spies or traitors and if convicted will suffer death." [58]

Until a building could be constructed, the doomed men had to be kept in solitary cells under the room of the officer of the guards. They were confined in an area about four feet high and five feet long, with only a crack for light. The men wore shackles on their ankles to which a 64-pound ball was attached by a chain six feet long. When the new building was finished, it contained eight small cells, each about seven feet high, and 2½ feet wide, and just long enough to lie down in, with only a tiny window to admit light and air. Although the executions of these men had been scheduled for May, President Lincoln postponed the executions several times.[59]

When a rumor circulated that some of the prisoners were to be executed, even Captain Speer made up his mind that if he were picked to hang, he would break out and swim the lake. Fortunately, he received news on August 23, 1862, that he and the others were to be exchanged.[60]

Escape Plans and Attempts Increase

There were many reasons to escape but few opportunities. As early as July 1862, Captain Speer reported that some prisoners tried to escape in the dark of night. They were discovered, and fired upon by two of the sentinels. The prisoners were not hit, but failed to escape. "Although some of us would be killed in attempting to escape" Speer wrote, "but yet we would try it."

Escape attempts increased in the latter part of 1863 after the Dix-Hill Cartel was suspended, and the exchange of prisoners was halted. In October 1863, Commandant Pierson reported that the prisoners had "exhibited much enterprise of late in the attempts to get out," although none of the recent attempts had succeeded. To prevent future escape attempts by way of the fence, Pierson installed lamps to illuminate the area.[61]

With the return of warm weather, prisoners' escape plans were hampered by the Federal gunboat which lay constantly near the island, her guns trained upon the prisoners' barracks. The gunboat guarded the island until it had to leave in the fall when the water of the lake froze.[62]

Many Plan to Escape, Few Do

Many prisoners tried to escape Johnson's Island through the usual methods of tunneling, bribing guards, obtaining Federal uniforms, and other means. Some employed unique methods.

Henry Shepherd survived imprisonment to become the superintendent of public instruction in Baltimore. He wrote several books, including *The Life of Robert E. Lee.* In a narrative about his own experiences, Shepherd noted those who tried to escape and failed, "as by far the greater number did," were subjected to the most "degrading punishments in the form of servile labor...."[63]

One prisoner tried to have himself carried outside in a barrel of slop, but was discovered. A prisoner named Deaton reportedly escaped on December 9, 1863. He had another prisoner answer his name at roll call, and escaped, but his method was not specified.[64]

E. A. Scovill noted in his inspection report dated January 8, 1865, that Lt. Amos C. Smith, of the 19th Tennessee Infantry, had been kept in close confinement and on a "low diet" since November 17, 1864, for his part in helping another prisoner to escape. That same inspection reported that Col. Daniel R. Hundley, 31st Alabama Infantry, escaped on January 2, but was recaptured on January 6, 1865.[65] Hundley's escape was not discovered until roll call the next morning. He was recaptured at Fremont, about 25 miles away on January 6, and returned to the prison. It was believed that Hundley escaped when he went with a party to the cemetery to bury a prisoner.[66] The two escapes reported as having occurred in January 1865 were the last from Johnson's Island.[67]

Escapes Using a Disguise

First Lt. J. F. Cross tried to escape by obtaining a Federal uniform from a guard. He was detected, however, returned to the prison, and punished.[68]

On June 30, 1864, two prisoners managed to escape dressed in Federal uniforms.[69]

Under the supervision of the new prison commandant, Col. Charles W. Hill, buildings were repaired and enlarged, and two additional buildings and a wash house were constructed. During the construction, several wagons were utilized to haul sand. Several prisoners obtained blue pants and caps, and they got in the emptied wagons and rode outside the gates. About 40 succeeded in getting out before their absence was discovered. Soon, all but two were recaptured.[70]

Pretending to be a workman. J. P. Murphy escaped on August 5, 1864, by walking outside the fence with the sand wagon. Once outside, he asked Colonel Hill for a pass to go see his mother, who was near death. Murphy got the pass and boarded a boat to Sandusky, then made his way to Canada. His absence was not noted for several days because he had a friend answer to his name at roll call, and another went to Murphy's bunk and pretended to be sick.[71]

On August 11, 1864, a young man managed to dress in civilian clothes and, with a forged pass, got by the officers and was making his way to the boat for Sandusky before he was recognized and arrested.[72]

Rufus C. Jones, of the 9th Alabama, escaped on the morning of January 5, 1865. Jones, described as about 27 years old, with light complexion, dark hair and hazel eyes, escaped over the ice in a Federal uniform, a fatigue cap and a light blue overcoat. Colonel Hill reported that Jones passed through the gates when those who had called the roll left.[73]

Tunnels

Commandant Pierson reported prisoners attempted to dig "under ground from the sinks" and also from the quarters, "commencing under the buildings." Three had tried to escape by sawing the pickets of the fences on the bay side of the island.[74]

A tunnel was begun from the "dead house," but it was also discovered before it could be used. As a result of these tunnels, the men were ordered outside while their quarters were searched. Several escape-related items were discovered, including ladders, sails, spades, and other digging tools.[75]

One prisoner wrote of a tunnel beneath one of the barracks in the summer of 1864. It ran about 30 or 40 feet, but just as the prisoners were planning to escape, the guards discovered it.[76] This tunnel ran from Block 11 which was near the fence. A loose floor board was removed and the tunnel was begun under the building. For weeks, the work continued late at night with case knives. Tin plates were used to remove the dirt and it was then spread under the rest of the house. The tunnel was supposed to end at the surface just outside the fence. However, before the tunnel could be completed, a spy in the midst of the prisoners reported it, and the tunnel was filled in with pieces of timber and other obstacles.[77]

A very hefty South Carolina lieutenant got stuck in an escape tunnel and had to be rescued when it began to rain and he was about to drown.[78]

Officials Fear Revolt

Commandant Pierson was overly concerned that the prisoners would escape. He wrote Colonel Hoffman on October 1, 1863, that there was a "bad spirit among the prisoners." Pierson explained that the prisoners believed "it would be a great thing for the Confederacy for them to escape, and they are talking about it being their duty to make the attempt, as they are superior in numbers to so great extent." Pierson was convinced that a revolt was imminent, and he asked Colonel Hoffman to send two more companies of soldiers. An added security measure would be the continued presence of the U.S.S. *Michigan*.[79]

Pierson overestimated the possibility of escapes. After talking with his officers, Pierson was convinced that his 2,452 prisoners were "a most desperate set of men, with great smartness and a conviction that their escape would be better than a victory in any battle," while they did not think the risk quite as great. Pierson feared that if the prisoners succeeded in getting hold of the guard's guns, they could also, "with the lumber from fences and buildings ... cross over back of the island" over less than a mile of shallow water, and be in Canada within two days. He reminded Hoffman that the "whole Canada shore, from the mouth of the river up, is filled with rebel sympathizers," who would gladly furnish boats to escaping prisoners. The prisoners, he told Hoffman, had the means available with lumber from their bunks and the stairs to scale the fences. Pierson closed his letter by requesting the presence of the *Michigan* again.[80]

Hoffman tried to allay Pierson's fears by telling him of the small steamer which operated as a ferry to Sandusky. The steamer had a "mountain howitzer" and with the guards armed with muskets and revolvers, "with ordinary vigilance" any escape by prisoners could be stopped. Hoffman suggested that if the guards already there exercised vigilance, no additional guards should be needed.[81] He continued to reassure Pierson and advised him of steps to take to maintain security.[82] Pierson continued to complain to Hoffman that "they [the prisoners] will do any act of desperation...."[83] Hoffman finally relented and sent three more companies of guards, making a total of seven companies.[84]

If at First You Don't Succeed

Lt. Charles Pierce, of the 7th Louisiana Regiment, tried several times to escape the island. He first tried digging a tunnel from Block 1 under the stockade. As the hopeful escapees crawled out of the tunnel, they were met by guards.[85]

In his second attempt, Pierce changed clothes with a cart driver who passed out inside the gate. Pierce took the driver's overcoat and cap, and drove out the gates with the cart. However, before he could get off the island, the deception was discovered and he was returned to the prison.[86]

Charlie's third try was successful, at first. On December 13, 1864, Pierce and Lieutenant Wheeler of Morgan's Cavalry, and J. B. Bowles, of Louisiana, scaled the fence with a ladder. Unfortunately, they chose a moonlit night, and were spotted by the guards. Bowles was shot and killed, and Wheeler was caught. Only Pierce succeeded in escaping. His freedom was short lived, and he was captured by a farmer on the mainland who received a $100 reward.[87]

The fourth and last attempt Pierce made took months of preparation, but he did not even succeed in getting out of the compound. He managed to obtain a Federal uniform, and he made a copy of a gun. He carved the stock from wood and made the barrel from discarded fruit tins. It took him five months to make the gun. When it was finished, he added a rusty bayonet he had found. The plan was to have someone tell the guards that an attempt was to be made to break out of Block 8 (the hospital block). The information was passed along and soon a group of soldiers came to inspect the building. Pierce, dressed in his blue uniform, fell in with them. As the members of the guard were ordered into formation for inspection, the officer in charge noticed that Pierce had no cartridge box. The guard became suspicious, and asked to see the fake gun Pierce carried. That was his undoing. For want of an easily-made little cartridge box, his plans were thwarted. The prison commandant, Colonel Hill, complimented Pierce on his courage and strategy, and did not punish him, except to confiscate the disguise and money that Pierce had, but kept the gun and it now resides in the archives of the state of Ohio. Lieutenant Pierce made no further attempts to escape, but remained on Johnson's Island until the close of the war.[88]

Plot Thwarted

A plot was reported to Pierson on October 24, 1863, by prisoners who had been sent for exchange. He was warned to expect an escape just as soon as the *Michigan* left the area. Fortunately, the steamer returned to the Sandusky harbor to remain through the winter.[89] Pierson was convinced that if the ship had not arrived, he would have had a fight on his hands. He had been informed that a large number of the prisoners had "bound themselves by signing papers to fight their way through...."[90]

Successful Escapes

Only 12 prisoners are known to have successfully escaped from the Johnson's Island prison. Those that did were aided by the deadly cold that enveloped the lake during the winter months.

One of the few to escape was Capt. Charles H. Cole, a member of Brig. Gen. Nathan B. Forrest's Confederate cavalry. Cole had arrived on Johnson's Island in September 1863. Shortly after his arrival, he was one of several prisoners sent into the hold of a steamer to get straw for bunks. Cole managed to remain behind in the ship when the rest returned to the island. He hid under the straw as the ship sailed into the port at Sandusky. By posing as a civilian, Cole left the ship and made his way to Canada.[91]

Cole contacted Confederate agents and supplied them information about the prison and its security system and he became involved in a plot to rescue prisoners by using a couple of passenger boats, the *Philo Parsons* and the *Island Queen*. On September 19, 1864, the plot was discovered when some of the prisoners tried to overcome the guard and make their escape. This plot was believed to have been connected to opposition to the draft law, which was scheduled to take effect that same day. Opponents of the draft law hoped that a prison break would deter the enforcement of the draft. After Col. B. J. Sweet learned of the escape plot, he decided to let the prisoners try, then capture them "in the act," and "make dispositions accordingly." Suspecting their plans had been discovered, the prisoners did not follow through.[92]

Cole was arrested in his Sandusky Hotel room before the plan could be put in motion. When questioned, Cole reveled the names of a number of men in high governmental positions and leading citizens and businessmen[93] who, he claimed, were involved in the plot to free the prisoners. Cole was held at Fort Lafayette until released on February 10, 1866.[94] A fellow conspirator, Acting Master John Y. Bealle, C. S. Navy, was not so lucky. He was hanged as a spy at Fort Columbus on Governors Island, on February 14, 1865.[95]

Henry Shephard remembered that a Mr. S. Cremmin, of Louisiana, made it off the island. Shephard did not report how Cremmin accomplished his escape, but he managed to reach the South by way of Kentucky. Cremmin, for many years a principal of a boys grammar school in Baltimore, cleverly represented himself as a "Union sympathizer." Mr. Cremmin lived until 1908, according to Shephard's memoirs.[96]

Escape Only to Die

Capt. Robert Cobb Kennedy (Company 14, 1st Georgia Infantry) escaped from Johnson's Island only to be caught later on a secret expedition to New York. Kennedy was captured near Decatur, Alabama. Years later, he was described by Lt. T. E. Fell as "a perfect dare-devil, and no situation, however perilous, seemed to daunt his courage." Soon after his imprisonment on Johnson's Island, Kennedy began planning his escape. After several unsuccessful tries, he finally made it out through a tunnel under a deep ditch and the walls of the prison. He slipped by the guards, stole one of the officers' boots, and escaped to the mainland.[97]

Perhaps his escape method had not been discovered, but Maj. Thomas H. Linnell, the prison commandant, reported that Kennedy had escaped the night of October 4, 1864, by scaling the fence between the blockhouse and Block 1. He then got in a small skiff and quietly moved away. Major Linnell blamed the guards who called the roll each morning. Because Kennedy had been reported present at roll call from October 5 through October 16, his escape went unnoticed, and no search was initiated. The commandant had the guards who called the roll arrested and charged with disobeying orders, because they failed to report Kennedy's absence.[98]

Traveling mostly at night, Kennedy made his way to Buffalo, New York, and crossed into Canada. There, he joined a band of exiles and other escaped prisoners. Kennedy wanted to rejoin his unit and was not satisfied hiding out in Canada. He joined a secret expedition to New York, but he was spotted by a detective. No sooner had he crossed over the border into the United States than he was arrested by the detective who had been following him. He put up a struggle, but was overpowered, and taken in chains to New York. On the train, he tried to escape by jumping out the window. In New York, Kennedy was tried as a spy, convicted, and executed late in 1864. In a letter he wrote near the time of his execution, Kennedy wrote that he "expected to die like a man," and that "death was a leap in the dark."[99]

Another who escaped during the winter was Capt. Robert McKibbin (or McGibben). After the roll of 3,204 prisoners names was called, Captain McKibbin, of the 31st Georgia Infantry, could not be found and was believed to have escaped.[100] An investigation revealed that McKibbin had escaped by going outside the stockade with a group of prisoners to get water from the lake at about 9:30 A.M. on December 24, 1864. He got about 20 hours' head start because the next roll call was not done until the following morning.[101]

Escape Over the Ice

In January 1864, Henry Shepherd watched 1,500 Federal soldiers "march in perfect security from Sandusky to Johnson's Island, a distance of three miles, across the firmly frozen harbor."[102] His was a simple plan — just walk across the frozen Lake Erie disguised as a guard.[103] He knew it could be done, and although he never got the chance, others did.

Just before Christmas 1863, when the ground was too hard to allow tunneling, Brigadier General Archer bribed a guard with $200 and a gold pocket watch to let him and several others out through the gate. However, the ice on the lake was too thin and Archer was forced to return to the safety of the prison. He demanded that his money and watch be returned, and claimed that the guard had pulled a "Yankee trick" to get his money. The guard denied the accusation and kept the money and watch.[104] Archer's brief taste of freedom encouraged others.

Success at Last

The winter of 1863-1864 was extremely cold, and temperatures often dropped to 22 degrees below zero for several days. Many prisoners suffered from cold and frostbite, and several died. Even the Federal gunboat which normally patrolled the waters around the island was absent during the time when the lake was frozen.[105] With the lake frozen, prisoners began to think about walking to freedom in Canada.

After a mild December, temperatures on New Year's Day 1864 fell below zero. Rain turned to sleet and a cold wind blew across Lake Erie. The guards on the catwalk sought shelter from the bitter wind and cold in their sentry boxes, content that no prisoners would escape in this kind of weather. They were wrong.[106]

Capt. Waller M. Boyd (19th Virginia) scaled the fence but was soon recaptured. Back in his quarters, he told his fellow inmates of his escape and his plan to try again. While the temperature was now 27 degrees below zero, Boyd believed that if he had enough clothing, he could make it off the island without being caught. After talking among themselves, five men were desperate enough to try — Lt. Col. John R. Winston (45th North Carolina), and Capts. Charles C. Robinson (9th Virginia Cavalry), Thomas H. Davis (1st Virginia Infantry), John E. Stokes (40th Virginia Infantry), and N. W. McConnell (11th Kentucky Infantry).[107] (The *Sandusky Register* listed six escapees with the addition of a Major Stokes to its list.[108] Another source named the five men as Winston, Robinson, and Davis, and added the names of three more escapees— Dr. Luke P. Blackburn, chief surgeon of the division of Sterling Price, of Missouri; and George Young and E. T. Osborne of John Hunt Morgan's cavalry.[109])

A prisoner who did not try to leave with these men recalled that Winston and his comrades covered their hands with pepper, and then put on thick gloves, to protect them from the cold.[110]

The men wore as much clothing as they could acquire — several pairs of trousers, shirts, socks, and gloves— until they could barely walk. They waited until 9 P.M. when the lights were turned out. Winston and Davis converted a bench from the mess hall into a crude ladder, to scale the walls. Winston was the first up the ladder, but found he was still four feet short of the top, but he bravely stepped onto the catwalk then jumped to the ground below. He landed unharmed in a soft bank of snow. He was soon followed by the others. Stokes, the last man, let the ladder scrape the wall and drew the attention of a guard. Thinking quickly, Stokes waved to the guard and, pretending to be a guard, walked toward the barracks used by the guard, while the other four made their way to the woods. The four waited for Stokes, but decided he must have been caught, so they made their way north toward the narrow channel between the island and Marblehead Peninsula.[111]

The fugitives slipped and stumbled but finally made their way across the ice. Following later, when Captain Stokes started north across the ice, he fell several times and lost his hat and gloves. By the time he reached the peninsula, his hands were frozen, and he sought shelter at a farmhouse. He was captured the next morning and returned to the island.[112]

Winston, the former teacher, had a good knowledge of geography. He planned a route to safety in Canada. The men made their way along the road to Port Clinton, and sought shelter in a haystack. They found a stable and "borrowed" a pair of old plow horses, and rode slowly off. McConnell fell from the horse, so they turned the horses loose and walked on until daylight. They obtained food and warmth for a while at a farmhouse, but left without paying the farmer, and made their way toward Toledo.[113]

Back at the prison, morning roll call revealed that some prisoners were missing. The recaptured prisoner, Stokes, was questioned by the commandant, and was forced to confess what he knew about the other four. Although Stokes was turned over to the prison doctor, he eventually lost several fingers and toes to gangrene from frostbite.[114] Colonel Hill telegraphed the surrounding cities with descriptions and offered a reward of $100 for their capture.[115]

The other four escapees continued in the subzero temperatures. McConnell fell ill and stayed behind at a farm house. Several days later, he boarded a train for Detroit but was arrested and returned to the island.[116]

The remaining three continued on their way, stopping at various houses as they made their way north. Robinson left his pocketbook behind at the house of a French-Canadian near Monroe. The pocketbook contained his identification papers and linked him to Johnson's Island prison. It had to be retrieved.[117] Robinson went back and got his pocketbook, then the trio continued. While crossing the icy Detroit River, Robinson fell into the water, but he was saved by the other two. The men made their way across the river on ice floes and reached land on the Canadian side near Gross Ile. It took four miserable days to reach safety in Canada, 125 miles across snow and ice in subzero weather.[118]

Once in Canada, the three found shelter with a French-Indian woman, Mrs. Warrior, who loaned them a sleigh so they could make their way to Windsor, where a hotel owner offered them free rooms. Former U.S. Congressman Clement L. Vallandigham, in exile from the states, was also a guest. Winston contacted a friend in New York who sent them enough money to book passage to Montreal. He also sent a letter to Captain Boyd and his cellmates back on Johnson's Island to let them know that the three had escaped.[119]

From Montreal, the three former prisoners made their way up the St. Lawrence River to New Brunswick and thence to Halifax, Nova Scotia. The last 500 miles was made by dog sleigh. When they reached Halifax, the men boarded the mail steamer

Alpha, destined for Bermuda. After only two days enjoying the warmth of the island, the former prisoners boarded the *Advance*, a blockade runner, and sailed to Wilmington, North Carolina. They were not out of danger yet. Their ship ran aground on a sandbar near Fort Fisher, but before the Federal gunboats could arrive, the blockade runner was free of the sandbar. The three men were finally safe in Wilmington.[120]

Ironically, Captain Davis returned to duty and was captured in the retreat from Petersburg in April 1865. He was taken first to Old Capitol Prison, then transferred to his former prison on Johnson's Island. He arrived there on April 19, 1865. On the prison ledger, the word *back* was scrawled above his name after his return. He remained only a month and was released after he took the Oath of Allegiance on June 19, 1865. Two years later he was killed in San Antonio, Texas.[121]

Three more officers escaped into Canada: Lt. William T. Williamson, of Benton, Florida; Lt. J. P. Murphy, of Columbia, Tennessee; and Lt. Archibald McFadyen, of Company A, 63rd North Carolina.[122]

Not So Successful

On January 7, 1864, James Gibbons struck a guard one dark night and escaped to the mainland. He was captured by a farmer and returned for the reward money. A week later, another prisoner feigned smallpox and escaped from the "pest house," only to be recaptured just 15 miles south of Sandusky.[123]

Other Methods

First Lt. Decimus et Ultimus Barziza (named because he was the 10th and last child in his family) was among those prisoners who were moved to Point Lookout. About 450 officers were chosen alphabetically by last name to take the train for Pittsburgh. Barziza was so determined to escape that he jumped from the train. Eventually, he made his way to Canada.[124] Taking a ship from Nova Scotia, he returned to Virginia via Fort Fisher in North Carolina.[125]

Changes in Administration

Pierson was replaced on January 18, 1864,[126] by Brig. Gen. H. D. Terry,[127] because of his inability to handle problems and maintain order, but possibly because of the escape of several prisoners. Terry's replacement, Col. Charles W. Hill took command on May 9, 1864,[128] and remained in command on the island until the end of the war.

Pierson's final report as to the status of the prison on January 18, 1864, from the date of its establishment in January 1862:

The whole number of prisoners has been	6416
Of which there have been exchanged	2983
Discharged on oath of allegiance, parole and otherwise	302
Transferred to other prisons	363
Deaths	149
Shot dead by sentinel	1

Executed	3
Escaped	3
Present, at this time, January 18, 1864	2612[129]

The new commandant, Colonel Hill, made many policy changes. Each man was held responsible for "any attempt to escape on the part of any prisoners," and as punishment, rations would be withheld from all. This was a crude method to force prisoners to "rat" on their fellow prisoners.[130]

Escape Totals

The official number of reported escapes from Johnson's Island was 12. Considering the number of prisoners, the climate, and other factors, this is not a bad record. In fact, for the period July 1862 until November 1865, only Federal prisons housed in the massive coastal fortifications of Fort Lafayette and Fort Warren had fewer escapes.[131]

When the war ended, prisoners were released from Johnson's Island in alphabetical order. Col. R. F. Webb was among the last to leave. He remained on Johnson's Island until June 25, 1865.[132]

Johnson's Island Today

The old prison buildings are gone and a number of residential homes have been built on the island. The cemetery where the prisoners were buried is maintained. It is surrounded by an iron fence. Just inside the entrance stands a statue of a Confederate soldier, named "The Lookout," who stands guard over the graves of his comrades. Legend holds that the statue changes position at midnight. Buried in the cemetery are 209 prisoners. However, is believed that there may be more than 100 more prisoners buried in graves across the island. [133]

Ongoing archaeological excavation has revealed artifacts and detailed information about the prison and the various escape efforts. Previously unknown tunnels have been discovered under the latrines.[134]

The records kept at Johnson's Island have been transferred to the Center for Archival Collections, Bowling Green State University Library, Bowling Green, Ohio. These rare records, which have been microfilmed, include six volumes of the camp sutler's financial records, one volume of receipts from the prison's commanding officer, and three autograph albums with signatures and notations by the Confederate officers held there. The autograph albums include name, rank, organization, hometown, date and location of capture of the soldiers on Johnson's Island from January 1863 to August 1864. The books also contain some poems and letters.[135]

XII

Ohio State Penitentiary, Columbus, Ohio

La patience est amère, mais son fruit est doux.
— From note Capt. T. Henry Hines left in the tunnel. [1]

Location: Columbus, Ohio. **Established:** 1863. **Type:** Existing prison. **Type of Prisoners:** non-military criminals, political prisoners, and some of John Hunt Morgan's Confederate cavalry officers. **Capacity:** Unknown. **Most Held:** about 79 (number of Morgan and his officers[2]). **Known Escapes:** 5[3] (seven escaped, two were recaptured). **Nickname:** "Castle Merion."

History

The Ohio State Penitentiary became famous because of a tunnel through which the Confederate hero Brig. Gen. John Hunt Morgan escaped. Morgan's daring escape with six of his officers received more publicity than any other escape, with the exception of the tunnel through which 109 Federal prisoners escaped from Libby Prison in Richmond, Virginia. Morgan's story cannot be omitted from any work on prison escapes.

The Site

The Ohio State Penitentiary was situated near the river in the downtown Columbus, Ohio. It covered the three blocks bounded by Maple Street on the north to Dennison on the west, West Street on the east, and Spring Street on the south. Construction on the building began in 1830, and it opened as a prison in 1834. The three-story building of "hammered limestone" was considered by the 1860s to be "seriously overcrowded and antiquated."[4]

The Cells

Prisoners were confined to cells, each with heavy iron bars at its door. The interior walls of the cells were brick. A massive wall, 4 feet thick and 25 feet high, surrounded the entire prison. On it were small rooms or "turrets" from which sentries could see the grounds.[5]

Ohio State Penitentiary, Columbus, Ohio— Brig. Gen. John Hunt Morgan and some of his Raiders were held four months before they tunneled out. (Courtesy of the Library of Congress, LC-D4-17365.)

The cellblock was about 100 feet long, 20 feet wide, and 40 feet high, and the exterior walls of hammered limestone were 11 feet from the cell block. The five levels of cells, one above the other, had 35 cells on each level. The doors of the cells, which opened outward, were a latticework of 2-inch iron bars. Cells on the opposite sides of the block in which convicts where held were separated by a brick wall which ran parallel with the fronts of the cells.[6]

Col. Basil Duke described the cells to which he and General Morgan's officers were confined. Each cell was 3½ feet wide, 7 feet long, and 7 feet high. The back wall of every cell had a 3–4-inch hole to admit air. Arranged in tiers, called "ranges, " each cell opened onto balconies three feet wide. Ladders led from each range to the one just above it.[7] Morgan and the men of his brigade were confined in the East Hall to Ranges One and Two.[8]

The events that led up to Morgan's capture are just as bizarre as his subsequent escape.

Who Was John Hunt Morgan

John Hunt Morgan was born in Huntsville, Alabama, on June 1, 1825. At age 17, he attended Transylvania College in Lexington, Kentucky.[9] He served in the Mexican

War. This Lexington, Kentucky, businessman was commissioned a captain in September 1861, and put in charge of a squadron of Confederate cavalry. In 1862, Morgan began the first of his famous raids. He was promoted to brigadier general in 1862 and given the command of a division of cavalry.[10] Most of Morgan's men were young, under 25 years of age. Morgan was tireless. In the summer of 1863, Morgan was 38 years old. Yet his "energy never flagged, and his invention was always equal to the emergency," according to Duke.[11]

Morgan was a striking figure, dressed in a clean uniform, with his long dark hair topped by a hat which sported a plume. Because of his daring exploits, he became one of the most respected and well-known Confederate officers. Fondly called by the nicknames "Thunderbolt of the Confederacy," The Great Raider," "The Guerrilla Chieftain," "The King of Horse Thieves,"[12] the tall, handsome, intelligent, debonair Morgan was a born leader. Standing six feet tall, Morgan had a muscular physique, and weighed about 185 pounds. His eyes were grayish-blue, and his hair, moustache, and beard were sandy-colored. (After his escape from the Ohio prison, Morgan reportedly dyed his mustache and goatee black and his hair a dark auburn to disguise himself.[13])

Morgan operated virtually independently of the rest of the Confederate Army. He even did his own recruiting and put up posters to attract volunteers. While technically subordinate to Gen. Braxton Bragg, Morgan hated Bragg.[14]

Morgan's Raiders wreaked havoc everywhere they went. They wrecked trains, blew up railroad bridges and tracks, sacked villages and towns, stole horses, and carried away tens of thousands of dollars paid to them to spare the businesses and homes in their path.[15]

Morgan's Last Raid

Morgan had made several raids into Kentucky, but his last and most famous raid, into Ohio, was unique, and it was his downfall. The purpose of the raid was to divert the forces of U.S. Gen. Henry M. Judah and General Rosecrans' cavalry away from Bragg. Bragg had authorized a raid but, although he gave Morgan *carte blanche* to raid Kentucky and capture Louisville, Bragg refused to give Morgan permission to cross into Ohio.[16]

From the time they crossed into Kentucky, Morgan's Raiders were engaged in 22 skirmishes and two major engagements. He and his men averaged 21 hours in the saddle each day.[17] Officially, the raid began on July 2 when Morgan and his command crossed the Cumberland River into Kentucky.[18] However, it actually started out at McMinnville, Tennessee, on June 28, 1863.[19] The raid ended on July 26, 1863, two miles west of West Point, Ohio, only nine miles from the Pennsylvania border. That point was the northernmost penetration of the Confederacy into enemy territory.[20]

Morgan, used to making his own decisions, ignored Bragg's orders because he believed that "the emergency justified disobedience." Morgan also had in mind that when he approached Pennsylvania he would join Gen. Robert E. Lee, if he should be in the state at that time. As luck would have it, on July 2, 1863, when Morgan's raiders were crossing the Cumberland River into Kentucky, General Lee was engaged in the second day of a three-day battle at Gettysburg, which would end in a Confederate defeat and subsequent retreat back across the Potomac to Virginia. Morgan was determined to cross the Ohio River to invade both Indiana and Ohio. With a force of about 2,500 men, Morgan set out from Tennessee on the longest raid during the Civil War — a distance of 1,000 miles across three states.[21]

Morgan led his 2,500-man cavalry force across Indiana, Ohio, and almost into Pennsylvania in a raid that lasted 25 days. Sometimes the Raiders traveled as long as 34 hours at a time, and covered a distance of 96 miles. They were pursued by a Federal army of 110,000 men.[22]

Morgan's raid was proceeding as planned but on their return, when they attempted to recross the Ohio River, they encountered the Federal forces of Hobson and Shackleford and local militia, supported by several gunboats. In the ensuing fight, about 120 of Morgan's men were killed, and 700 captured. Pursued by Hobson, Morgan and about 300 men escaped and tried to reach Pennsylvania, but they were captured near New Lisbon.[23] Captured along with General Morgan were 364 officers and men and 400 horses.[24] Morgan's brother, Thomas H. Morgan, was killed on the raid.[25]

Morgan's brother-in-law, Col. Basil Wilson Duke, rode with him on that raid. Before the war, Duke had been an attorney in St. Louis, Missouri. Yet, even though most of Morgan's Raiders were captured and many killed, Duke did not think the raid was not a failure:

> The objects of the raid were accomplished. General Bragg's retreat was unmolested by any flanking forces of the enemy, and I think that military men, who will review all the facts, will pronounce this expedition delayed for weeks the fall of East Tennessee and prevented the timely reinforcement of Rosecrans by troops that would otherwise have participated in the battle of Chickamauga.[26]

The Road to Prison

After their capture on July 26, Brigadier General Morgan and some of his officers were first taken by train to Cincinnati. When the train stopped in Cincinnati, huge crowds turned out to see the famous raider. Ohio governor David Tod and his staff were introduced to Morgan, and the governor shook hands with Morgan.[27]

A Night in the Cincinnati Jail

The prisoners were taken to the Cincinnati city jail, where Morgan and his men were divested of a "large number of pistols which they had been permitted to retain by the terms of surrender." Many of them still carried a "brace" of pistols, and a bushel of pistols, all loaded, were confiscated.[28]

Morgan asked his military escort what had become of his brothers. He was told that Richard and Charlton had been sent to Johnson's Island. Other officers, including Duke, who had been captured at Buffington were sent to the island prison, where they remained four days before being transferred to the Ohio Penitentiary in Columbus.[29] That information seemed to satisfy General Morgan, and after taking a drink of whiskey, he was content to spend the night in the city jail.[30]

Union Gen. H. W. Halleck ordered Morgan and his officers confined in the Ohio

State Penitentiary as hostages for the members of Col. Abel Streight's command who were being held by Confederates at Libby Prison in Richmond[31] (see Chapter XXIV). Governor Tod was informed of Halleck's orders.[32] Tod approved and agreed to house about 30 prisoners at the state penitentiary.[33] Morgan and 28 of his officers were selected and taken to the Ohio State Penitentiary in Columbus.

Arrival at Penitentiary

On July 30, when Morgan and his men arrived in Columbus, Ohio, a large crowd turned out to greet him. They saw a tall, middle-aged man who, despite having been in the saddle for 24 days, walked with dignity.[34] Eyewitnesses reported Morgan arrived wearing a linen coat, black pants, white shirt, and light felt hat. One reporter described him as having "a rather mild face, there being certainly nothing to indicate the possession of unusual intellectual qualities."[35]

Morgan's Confinement

The men were treated like convicts in some ways. Lt. Col. R. A. Alston, one of Morgan's men, complained to Confederate Secretary of War James A. Seddon that when Morgan and his men arrived at the prison, they were "shaved and their hair was cut very close by a negro convict." The prisoners were "marched to the bath room and scrubbed," after which they were taken to their cells and locked up. Alston reported that those who arrived a week later also had been "subjected to the same indignities." Col. D. Howard Smith, one of the second group, told Alston that Nathaniel Merion, the prison warden, had "apologized for such treatment," but Merion would agree to accept them "on no other terms" than the standard prison regulations.[36] Yet, some concessions were made, and Morgan and his men were allowed to keep their boots and wear regular clothes.[37]

Duke remembered how the Raiders "entered this gloomy mansion of crime and woe ... with misery in our hearts…. The dead weight of the huge stone prison seemed resting on our breasts."[38] Three of Morgan's brothers—Richard, Charlton, and Calvin—were confined with him.

Many expressed concerns about the welfare of Morgan and his men. Governor David Tod believed that they were a "band of desperate men under the lead of the notorious John H. Morgan," but because of the fears of Major General Burnside, the commander-in-chief of the Federal troops at that time, the prisoners had been sent to the Ohio state prison "as a place of safe-keeping for them until other provisions can be made." Tod ordered that they be searched, their valuables taken, and that they be kept "so far as may be possible, separate and apart from the convicts." Governor Tod also ordered that the prisoners be given everything "necessary in the way of food and clothing for their comfort, and impose only such restrictions upon them as may be necessary for their safe-keeping." The governor did not want Morgan and his men to "hold interviews or communications by writing" except under the express orders of General Burnside.[39]

Many complaints were received by Federal officials. Pressure was applied to Col. William Hoffman, commissioner general of prisoners. Hoffman, in turn, contacted

Brig. Gen. John S. Mason, commanding at Columbus, to ask about the treatment of General Morgan and his men. Because the prisoners had complained "they were treated as being convicts, in being shaved and having their hair cut short," Hoffman wanted to know the details and "the authority for any peculiar treatment which they may have received." Hoffman inquired if reports were true that the personal property of Morgan and his officers, such as money, watches, etc., had been taken from them. If so, he wanted to know the disposition of said money and property.[40] Brigadier General Mason sent a lengthy reply to Hoffman with specific details about their treatment at the Ohio Penitentiary.

> General Morgan and party, arrived from Cincinnati on the afternoon of July 30 [1863]. The train was stopped within a few yards of the prison, and the prisoners were marched under guard to the parlor of the prison. Each officer's name was called in turn and he was formally turned over to Mr. N. Merion, the warden of the penitentiary, when he was searched, and everything valuable taken from him…. This search was made in the presence of myself and staff, and also two of the directors of the penitentiary, and was done as delicately as possible. In most instances the officers delivered everything themselves.[41]

Mason reported that the money belonging to Morgan and his men was put in a package, labeled with the owner's name, and the package was put in the prison safe. A list of all articles inside the package was made.

Brigadier General Mason had not been aware that the prison officials were going to cut the hair and whiskers of Morgan and his men. He stated that "no order was given by any military authority" for this treatment on their arrival, but the warden was required by the directors of the prison to enforce their "usual sanitary regulations." When Mason went inside the prison, he found that about two-thirds of Morgan's men had already undergone the process. The prison warden informed Mason that he could receive prisoners no other way. The policy was meant as a sanitary measure and not to degrade the prisoners. The cells were clean and most of the prisoners were filthy and covered with vermin.

> Their hair was not cropped, but was cut in the style usually worn by gentlemen in this city, and was not more closely cut than my own. Their beards were cut close. No indignity was offered them. Many of them thought it a benefit, and quite a number requested afterward to renew the bath.

Mason verified that Morgan and his men were kept separate from the convicted criminals already in the prison. They took their meals by themselves, and were allowed to be together only during the day. At night they were locked in their cells.[42]

Mason denied that Morgan and his officers were being "treated as convicts, but [were treated] as nearly like prisoners of war as the circumstances of the case will permit." They were allowed to have "army rations" or as close to them as the facilities for cooking would permit, and that they were better cared for "than any of our prisoners can be at Camp Chase."[43]

During a routine inspection in November 1863, Brig. Gen. William W. Orme, at the Ohio Penitentiary, reported 79 "rebel prisoners here," including Morgan and his subordinate officers. They were quartered in cells and "have clean, comfortable beds and bedding. They have their washing done in the prison and their cells cleaned and swept by the convicts." Morgan and his men were given the regular prison fare, with the addition of coffee, at a table set for them "and cleaned away by convicts," Orme reported. They were allowed to wear their own clothing, and were not required to work. They were not allowed to have newspapers or communicate with anyone. Orme reported that they were in "good health and condition," and that only six had been "slightly sick," and they were being cared for in the hospital. Before Orme could turn his report, he learned that Morgan and several of his officers had escaped.[44]

The cavalry officers, accustomed to roaming freely, hated confinement. To make their confinement worse, in the summer months the heat was stifling, and in the winter, cold as the North Pole. Morgan complained to Brigadier General Mason that he and his men had been locked up the entire day for two Sundays. During the week, they were allowed to "go to our meals" and to exercise an hour at noon. They were locked up each night at 5 P.M., and released at 7:30 A.M. the next morning. Ordinarily, in a 24-hour period, the men were confined for only about nine and a half hours. Thus, by not allowing the prisoners out on Sunday, they were confined continuously for nearly 40 hours. Morgan did not like being confined on Sunday and having to stay in his cell for a longer period because as the "weather has grown cold," making the cells "extremely uncomfortable during the day."[45]

The Dungeon

Two of Morgan's officers had been confined to the dungeon, one for 24 hours and the other for 40 hours, on suspicion they violated some regulation, the said "offense unknown to the regulations of any military prison or any system of military law." Morgan wrote that the "rigors of confinement" they had been subjected was detrimental to the "health of my comrades." [46]

Warden Merion seemed to take pleasure in keeping Morgan's men in the dungeon. He made sure that Morgan's men broke his rules so they could be punished. The dungeon was a terrible place, dark and damp and infested with vermin. Another of Morgan's Raiders, Major McCleary, spent five days and nights in the dungeon. When he was finally released, the major could hardly stand. Others who were confined to the dungeon emerged with swollen feet, and with blood oozing from their fingernails and toenails. Even one of Morgan's four brothers, Calvin Morgan, was confined to the dungeon, and when he was finally released, he was covered in green mold.[47]

Morgan also protested being held hostage in retaliation for the Federal Colonel Streight and his men, and asked that he and his men be transferred to a military prison, where "the same favors that have always been shown to the prisoners taken by the general commanding will be shown us."[48]

Morgan continued to protest their confinement and the treatment of himself and his men in the prison. He wrote a lengthy letter to the United States secretary of war, Edwin M. Stanton, which he asked General Mason to forward. Again he complained that he and his men had been treated as convicts, their beards shaved and their hair closely trimmed. Undoubtedly, Morgan was proud of his beard and moustache, was not happy with being shaved.[49]

Indeed, Morgan and his men were in a unique situation, but Federal officials were not going to honor Morgan's requests. As the months passed, Morgan grew anxious about his wife, who was expecting their first child. In his letters to her, Morgan called his wife Mattie "My Precious One."[50] Prison officials had withheld letters from his wife, and Morgan was afraid she had died in childbirth like his first wife.[51] He became desperate to escape, and could no longer wait for news of his beloved. After four months in prison, Morgan and a few of his men escaped from the Ohio State Penitentiary.

The Tunnel

No one knows for sure who first came up with the idea of digging the tunnel that allowed Morgan to escape. Some accounts say that Capt. Thomas Hines got the idea after reading Victor Hugo's *Les Miserables*.[52] Other accounts credit the plan to Capt. L. D. Hockersmith.[53] Basil Duke's original 1867 version of *History of Morgan's Cavalry* attributed Hockersmith as being "another of the projectors of the plan." However, in the 1909 edition, Duke corrected his statement by saying, "Several plans were considered and abandoned, and at length one devised by Capt. Hines was adopted." In a footnote, he added: "Captain L. D. Hockersmith of the Tenth Kentucky claims to have originated the plan of escape, and I believe that he and Hines simultaneously conceived it. He would make no claim he did not think just. He had more to do than anyone with its practical execution."[54]

Brig. Gen. John Hunt Morgan and wife, Mattie Ready Morgan. The couple were married on December 14, 1862. (Courtesy of the Library of Congress, LC-DIG-cwpb-07516.)

Whoever envisioned a tunnel, the idea was quickly turned into reality. Thomas Hines discovered that the floor of the cells of Range No. 1 did not rest on the ground, but that there was an air space underneath. Once this was certain, Hines shared the information with General Morgan, and Morgan gave his approval. With the help of six of his officers, the digging began. Fortunately, because of the letter Morgan had written, there was a change in policy, and there were no more daily inspections of the cells his men occupied.[55] The Confederates worked for several weeks, undetected by the soldiers who guarded them during the day. Hines requested a broom and received permission to sweep out his own cell, and after a few days, the guards did not bother to come in his cell to inspect it.[56] To avoid having the guards slip up on them the night of the escape, they sprinkled coal dust in front of the cells so that when the guards approached they would be warned by the crunching of shoes on coal.[57]

Hines added other minute details to his story of the escape plans. He said that they had obtained some table knives, and candles and matches were obtained from their "sick comrades in the hospital."[58] Another item necessary for a successful escape was money. According to Hines., General Morgan had some money that was not discovered when he was searched. Hines also wrote to his sister in Kentucky and she sent books with money concealed inside. Another vital piece of information was the train schedule. This was obtained from a trustee who was allowed to go to town. Hines gave the old man, called Heavy, $10 to buy a newspaper which contained the train schedule, and a six-ounce bottle of French brandy.[59]

Morgan's Escape

Sometime during the night of November 27, 1863, Brig. Gen. John Hunt Morgan and Capts. J. C. Bennett, L. D. Hockersmith, T. Henry Hines, Gustavus S. Mayer, [J. S. McGee], Ralph Sheldon, and Samuel B. Taylor escaped.[60] The men had been imprisoned only four months, and had worked on the tunnel about a month.

The timing was perfect. Gen. John Mason had conveniently left on a trip to San Francisco on November 25, 1865, two days before the escape. In his place, Col. William Wallace, of the Fifteenth Ohio Volunteer Infantry, took charge until a successor could arrive.[61]

Over the Wall

After exiting the building, the prisoners scaled the wall with a rope ladder. The rope had been made of bed ticking and towels, torn into strips, and braided into loops about two feet in length and tied together to make a crude ladder.[62] A second wall still had to be scaled. Captain Taylor, the nephew of President Zachary Taylor, was boosted up and reached the top of the gate where he then got the rope over the wall. The rope that led to the warden's room was cut, and the men entered the sentry box to change clothes before letting themselves down from the second wall. In making the descent, General Morgan hurt his hands badly. Once on the ground, the seven men separated. Taylor and Shelton went one way; Hockersmith, Bennett and McGee went another way. General Morgan and Hines headed for the train depot and boarded the train, but they jumped off before it reached Cincinnati. They made their way to the house of a Confederate sympathizer, where they were given money, horses, and a good meal.[63]

After the Escape

Prison Warden N. Merion notified Wallace and gave him the facts of the escape as they appeared on November 28, 1863:

Seven rebel prisoners escaped from here last night. They were reported locked up by Sergeant Moon, but were not in their cells at the time. They undoubtedly hid out in the yard and scaled the wall with rope ladders. There has been bribery somewhere.[64]

Reward Offered

Governor Tod telegraphed Secretary of War Edwin Stanton that Morgan and five others had "dug under the walls." Tod blamed the warden and his guards for the escape, and authorized a reward of $1,000 for the capture of the escapees.[65] The War Department agreed that the reward might increase their chances of recapturing the escaped prisoners. Tod was authorized to take whatever steps were necessary to assist the capture.[66]

Officials in Washington feared that Morgan had gone to Canada, but Stanton suspected the rumor was only a "ruse to mislead and allay vigilance."[67] If the rumors were true, Stanton believed that he "would be a dangerous leader for the rebels there, and the utmost vigilance should be executed."[68] Stanton ordered Gen. John Dix to warn the British authorities at once.[69]

The mayor of Toronto assured Governor Tod that Morgan was not in Toronto.[70] Stanton believed Morgan might be in Columbus, "secreted with some copperhead." He authorized Governor Tod to increase the reward for Morgan's capture to $5,000, and authorized the arming and equipment for 10,000 volunteer troops within a 50-mile area of Lake Erie.[71]

How Did They Escape?

Officials soon discovered that Morgan and six of his officers had escaped during the night of November 27 by cutting through the stone pavement of the floor of their cells. They then burrowed under the sewer walls below their cells.[72]

The morning after the escape, Colonel Wallace telegraphed all the major cities in the area to the west and north to notify the chief of police in each city of Morgan's escape, and he dispatched two officers to the penitentiary to find out how the escape was made.[73]

Almost immediately Governor Tod asked Quartermaster General Wright and Secretary B. F. Hoffman to visit the prison and question both prisoners and prison personnel to determine who was responsible.[74] Governor Tod was told to find out if Morgan had been permitted to see or correspond with anyone.[75] General Mason promised that a full investigation would turn up evidence of "bribery and corruption."[76]

A thorough investigation was conducted to examine every aspect of the prison — policies, routines, personnel, and buildings — were examined.

The warden's records revealed details pertaining to Morgan and his men. On July 31, an entry stated that all correspondence to or from the prisoners was examined by General Mason. A notation on August 3 showed that General Mason had recommended the prisoners, "at their cost," be furnished with "a set of Waverly Novels and chewing tobacco." S. Loving, physician at the Ohio Penitentiary, had recommended that two of Morgan's men, Bennet and McLean, be allowed to purchase "a small quantity of ale daily," because they were both "in failing health." This also applied to prisoners Cheatham and Gibson, because both of them were "becoming feeble." It was recommended that Colonel Cluke and Major Elliot be allowed to "purchase small quantities of lager beer daily." Another entry noted that General Morgan's mother had sent Captain Merion two bottles of cordial, which he accepted for the use of the sick in the hospital.[77]

George B. Wright, the quartermaster general, concluded that the warden's record book presented a more accurate picture of the treatment and control of the prisoners than could be gained by personal interviews.[78]

Bribes and Corruption of Guards Suspected

The search focused on discovering those who had helped Morgan and his men to escape. Lieutenant Judkins, of Mason's staff, was in charge of disbursing any necessary funds and inspecting letters to and from the prisoners. Judkins was suspected of having been bribed, and he was relieved of his duties.[79]

Colonel Mason was instrumental in the personnel changes. He had conferred with the prison directors in October and suggested they send one of their physicians to attend the prisoners. He also asked permission to send one of the trusted Union officers to act as steward. As a result, Dr. Bailey was sent as surgeon, and Sergeant Moon was sent to act as steward. Moon was instructed to receive all communications to General Mason or the prison commandant. He was to see that the cells were kept in good order, and that the guards attended to their duties. Moon was authorized to conduct the prisoners from their cells to and from their meals, and "allow no communication with them."

Mason declared that Sergeant Moon was a "trustworthy and reliable soldier." Mason exonerated Moon from negligence because the sergeant "had nothing to do with the locking or unlocking of their cells," or when the prisoners should be in their cells or out of them. Sergeant Moon's duties were to monitor the guarding of the prisoners and to be sure they received no communication with anyone from the outside. In fact, Sergeant Moon believed that "arrangements were so complete" that he "could not conceive how prisoners could escape without aid from the outside." During the day, the prisoners were under the constant surveillance of either the guard, the steward, or one of the other prison keepers.[80]

How the Tunnel Was Made

A thorough search of the prison was made by F. N. Desellem. He found that the foundation of the cellblock was made up of three parallel walls, and end walls, all of uncut stone. The middle wall was the foundation of the brick partition wall. Desellem found that an "arch of twenty inches curvature [that] rests on these walls and runs from the extreme west end of the cell block to the east wall of the cell house, and formed the cover of an air chamber." This dark air chamber was divided by partition walls with an airway cut through each. An 18-inch opening, covered by an iron grate, that admitted external air into the chamber, was now closed by a "bank of coal." At the west end of this chamber under the cell block was an arch of about 30 inches, and on the east end, the space was only about 5 or 6 inches. The floor of the air chamber was covered in lime mortar 3 inches thick.[81]

To obtain access to the air chamber, the prisoners had made a small opening at the corner of Cell No. 20 (that of Thomas Hines), through about 26 inches of cement and lime mortar. The exterior foundation wall was 30 inches high at the point chosen to dig to the outside. The lower stone was removed by digging away the dirt underneath it until a hole was made through the wall almost five feet wide. A hole, 18 inches wide and 30 inches high, was begun in the dirt beneath the foundation. This was continued forward and downward for about five feet. There, it was widened to about 30 inches wide, and continued to the wall of the cell house. The stones taken from the hole were passed back into the air chamber. The exit hole was smaller than the opening in the floor of the cell.[82]

From the air chamber beneath the cells, openings had been cut into the floor of seven cells on the lower tier. Just enough brickwork and mortar had been taken down without disturbing the cement flooring of the cells to allow the passage of a large man. With the support underneath the floor removed, it took only a slight push to push the cement down and open the hole in the cell floor that allowed each man to enter the air chamber.[83]

The inspection revealed three candlestick holders, a small wooden box, two table knives, some pieces of candles, and two wooden wash dishes used by the prisoners had been left behind in the air chamber by Morgan's men.[84]

To add insult to injury, a note was found addressed to the warden:

> Hon. (!!) N. Merion, the watchful, the vigilant.
> Castle Merion, Cell No. 20
> Commencement — November 4
> No. of hours for labor per day — 3
> Conclusion — November 20th
> Tools — two small knives.
> "*La patience est amère, mais son fruit est doux.*"
> [Patience is bitter, but its fruit is sweet]
> T. Henry Hines, Captain, C. S. Army[85]

Subsequent interrogation of the prisoners did not reveal the exact time of escape, but it had occurred between 4:30 P.M. and 6 A.M. the next morning. Gen. John H. Morgan had been able to escape because he had switched cells with his brother, Col. Dick Morgan, who was on the lower tier. This switch went unnoticed because Dick Morgan was dressed in a part of the general's clothing and stood with his back to the door when the turnkey came to lock him in.[86]

Depositions were taken from several of the members of Colonel Wallace's staff. Robert Lamb testified that on the day of the escape he heard Warden Merion remark that the escape would never have occurred "if the cells had been swept out daily." When asked why this was not being done, Warden Merion replied that "One of the directors said let the God-damned rebels clean their own cells." Thereafter, the prison guard who had been sweeping the cells daily was told to stop and the prisoners notified that they must sweep themselves.[87] This was verified by M. W. Goss.[88]

Jesse E. Watson testified about the routine of the guards to check on the prisoners each night. The first rounds was made about 5 P.M. after the prisoners had been locked in their cells. The guard passed a light inside each cell and made a count. Another round was made at 6 P.M., and the guard checked to see if the prisoner's water buckets were filled. At 9 P.M. the guard made the rounds and directed that any light in the cells be put out. Additional rounds were scheduled for 11 P.M., 2 A.M., and 4 A.M.; each time the guard had a light in his hand and he could look inside the cells to ascertain that the prisoners were within. In between times, the guard walked about the block of cells. Such was the routine on the night of November 27. The guard had heard no noise and no disturbance, and it was only after the escape that he learned the men were not in their beds but had made "stuffed images of themselves wrapped up in their bedclothes." Watson stated that at no time before the night of the escape did he hear any noise that would indicate digging or see anything that would arouse suspicion.[89]

A contributing factor to the escape was the change in authority over the prisoners from the prison warden to the military. Warden Merion had been in charge until November 4, when Gen. John S. Mason, after getting permission from prison directors, decided it would be best if the military took charge. Mason sent two soldiers from his command to replace some of the prison guards. Sergeant Moon of the 88th Ohio Volunteers, became the new steward, and Sgt. John A. Conce, of the 9th Michigan Volunteer Infantry, was placed in charge of the guards outside the prison.[90]

Merion stated that after November 3, 1863, neither he nor the directors of the Ohio penitentiary had "any further care of said prisoners than to furnish food, fuel, &c, as above stated, and to watch them at night when locked up in their cells, and from that date until the 28th of November," he did not go into the hall where the prisoners were confined because he believed himself "freed from all care and management of same...."[91]

Who Was to Blame?

After all the testimony, Brigadier General Wright concluded that (1) had clear instructions been given to the warden, no conflict of jurisdiction or escape could have occurred; (2) that if the guards had maintained "proper vigilance" within the walls of the penitentiary, and a daily or even weekly inspection of the cells occupied by the prisoners of war, no escape could have been made; (3) the failure to make frequent and careful inspection of the cells came from the lack of definite and clear understanding between the military and prison authorities as to that inspection; (4) that the prisoners had complained about their confinement in a place designed for convicts only and, in trying to treat them as prisoners of war and grant them indulgences not allowed to convicts, discrepancies and embarrassments had occurred between the military and prison authorities. The bottom line was that the problems could have been avoided if there had been "distinct written orders and regulations by the military commander and the warden of the penitentiary, and the warden left to enforce their provision."[92]

Warden Merion wrote the editor of the *Ohio State Journal* to shift the blame for the escape to the shoulders of Brigadier General Mason and his military guards. Marion contended that just as soon as Mason appointed a surgeon, and a steward, and the steward given control of the money belonging to the prisoners, the situation changed. No longer did the officers of the prison examine the cells, nor did they consider it their duty to do so, since Mason controlled the military guards who were on duty during the daytime. The warden stated:

> We do not say that the prisoners would not have escaped had they continued under our charge, but we do say that they could not have escaped in the manner they did had they continued in our charge, for the reason that while in our charge every cell was examined daily.[93]

Repercussions

After the escape, the remainder of Morgan's men were treated more harshly. They were confined to the second and third tiers of cells, and were not allowed outside their cells except at meal time until December 12, when the warden resumed the practice of letting them outside in the hall for exercise.[94] Captain Lamb conducted a thorough search of the persons, clothes, and cells of the remainder of Morgan's men. The search lasted three days. The prisoners were stripped and their clothing and persons examined. The search revealed Confederate money, gold and silver watches, pocket knives, and pipes. One prisoner had $20 in U.S. money, while another had $42.75 in gold and silver concealed in a cravat and a boot. Three steel frames for using spring saws, and 35 saws of steel or iron were found. The frames and saws had been given to the prisoners by Lieutenant Judkins, an aide on General Mason's staff, to help them in making rings and trinkets from bone. The dirty cells were cleaned, and all surplus baggage and clothing was packed up, labeled, and removed.[95]

For even the slightest infraction of the rules, Morgan's men were put in the "black hole." According to what Dick Morgan had been told by those who had been incarcerated there, it was a place even smaller than the cells where one could "scarcely breathe." Some of the offenses for which men were put there included reading a newspaper or talking in loud voices. One prisoner was sent to the dungeon simply for asking his neighbor in the next cell what day of the month it was.[96] Those who remained continued to hope that once Morgan reached Richmond, he could arrange for them to be exchanged or sent to some other prison.[97]

The remainder of Morgan's brigade in the Ohio Penitentiary were watched closely. In February 1864, an escape plot was discovered based on information from one of Morgan's own men. The prisoners had planned to assault the guard with stolen weapons. A search revealed nine knives and two files. The prisoners were moved to the west wing, where they were entirely isolated, except for their guards. Meals were brought to them, and when removed, the implements would be counted, so as to remove any chance of theft. The informant's name was not revealed because if his identity were known, his life would have been in danger.[98]

By March 1864, the remaining 65 men of Morgan's command had been transferred to Fort Delaware. Those who had been held at the Allegheny Penitentiary were transferred to Point Lookout.[99] Basil Duke was moved to Camp Chase. Eventually, he was transferred Duke to Fort Delaware to become one of the "First Fifty" sent to Charleston as hostages (see Chapter VI).[100]

Some Escapees Recaptured

A little over a week after their escape, two of the captains who had gone over the wall with Morgan were recaptured. The two had hidden in a cornfield for 48 hours after they got off the train to Louisville, Kentucky, but were soon captured. Although they were offered a sizeable reward, Morgan's men remained loyal and refused to divulge any information.[101]

Captain Magee [McGee] made it back to his home in West Virginia. Bennet and Hockersmith fled together and avoided capture. [102]

Once they reached Tennessee, Hines saved Morgan from being captured by leading a detachment of Federal cavalry in another direction. Although taken captive himself, Hines escaped from the jail in Kingston, Tennessee, and crossed the mountains to Confederate lines near Dalton, Georgia.[103]

Subsequently, Hines was involved in a plot with the Sons of Liberty to cause trouble in Chicago. He evaded capture by slitting a mattress under a very sick woman and sliding in beneath her. When Union soldiers searched the house, they did not think to look under a woman sick with diphtheria.[104]

When Morgan finally reached his wife in Danville, Virginia, he was saddened by the news that on the night of his escape, November 27, their child had been born and had died.[105]

Morgan Is Killed

Nearly a year after his daring escape, on September 4, 1864, John Hunt Morgan was shot and killed by Federal troops near Greeneville, Tennessee.[106] He had attempted to flee, but when confronted by a Federal soldier, he had thrown down his gun and surrendered to his pursuers. He was shot at close range by Pvt. Andrew J. Campbell of Company G, 13th Tennessee Cavalry.[107]

After Morgan's death, Basil Duke took command of the remaining troops. Duke was promoted to brigadier general. At the end of the war, Duke and his cavalry crossed the mountains to travel to North Carolina, where they served as escort for Confederate president Jefferson Davis from Charlotte until he was captured at Irwinsville, Georgia.[108] Duke and his cavalry continued to serve the Confederacy until May 8, 1865, when Secretary of War John C. Breckinridge disbanded "Morgan's men," and told them to go home.[109]

Morgan's Legacy

John Hunt Morgan was first buried at Sinking Springs Cemetery, Abingdon, Virginia. Then, he was moved to Richmond for a state funeral, and his body was temporarily placed in a vault at Hollywood Cemetery. In April 1868, his body was moved to a Lexington, Kentucky, cemetery, for burial in the Morgan family plot.[110] He will forever serve as an example of courage daring, and fortitude in the face of all obstacles, a man with the willpower to do what was necessary, to improvise on the spur of the moment as needed, and to inspire others to follow him with undying devotion into hell if he asked it of them.

The survivors of Morgan's cavalry held a reunion in Lexington on the eve of Morgan's burial there. This group continued to meet annually until 1883. An association of the descendants of the men who rode with Morgan was formed by Gen. Basil Duke, who served as the president of the organization until his death in 1916.

More information may be obtained about the Morgan's Men Association from Samuel R. Flora, 1691 Kilkenny Drive, Lexington, Kentucky 40505 (Fax — 606-299-7000).

XIII

Old Capitol Prison, Washington, D.C.

"How I would like to stretch my limbs with a brisk walk over there."
— Gov. Zeb Vance, remark while in Old Capitol Prison[1]

Location: (1) Old Capitol, at First Street and Pennsylvania Avenue, and (2) Carroll Building, corner of Maryland Avenue and East First Street, Washington, D.C. **Established as a Prison:** 1861. **Type:** converted building. **Kind of Prisoners:** Confederate prisoners of war, spies, Federal prisoners, and civilians suspected of disloyalty. **Capacity:** 500 + 1000 in houses in adjoining block (Carroll Prison). **Most Held:** 2,763 (combined total of Old Capitol and Carroll Prison). **Known Number of Escapes:** 16.[2] **Nickname:** "The American Bastille."

History

The building has served in many capacities. A boarding house and tavern before the War of 1812, the building was leased by Congress to serve as the nation's capitol until the new Capitol Building could be constructed.[3] When the new capitol was finished in 1825, the building, now referred to as the "Old Capitol" again became a boarding house, and later a school.[4] John C. Calhoun stayed in the building when it was the most fashionable place for southerners to board while visiting in Washington.[5]

Both the Old Capitol and the Carroll Building were seized and converted into prisons, the doors to the many rooms fitted with locks, and iron bars added to the windows. With a force of guards of about 60 men from a regiment stationed nearby, the buildings were ready for occupancy once more.

The Facilities at the Old Capitol

The prison commonly referred to as the Old Capitol Prison was really two separate buildings— the Old Capitol and the Carroll Building. The first was named because it had served as a temporary meeting place for both houses of Congress, and the second building was the property of the Carroll family.[6] One of the civilians who spent some time in the Old Capitol described it. "On the principal floor of the building [are] the Halls of the Senate and House of Representatives, which are now divided

Old Capitol Prison, Washington, D.C. (Courtesy of the Library of Congress, LC-DIG-cwpb-00493.)

into five large rooms, numbered respectively from 14 to 18 — room 16 being the center and the largest." The rooms averaged about 30 feet square, and each held 18 to 25 prisoners. William P. Wood, prisoner D. A. Mahoney recalled, was the first superintendent. Although Wood ruled with an iron fist, the prisoners still believed him to be fair in his dealings with them. He, according to Mahoney, was especially lenient with "young attractive female prisoners."[7]

The Old Capitol Building was three stories, with the main entrance on First Street. A broad hallway served as a guard room. The first room was used as an office for the superintendent, clerk, captain of the guard, and the officer who commanded the guard. When prisoners arrived, they were taken to this office, questioned, and searched. A long room on the first floor also served as the mess hall.[8]

The rooms on the second floor opened onto a hallway. The largest had 21 bunks. There were also rooms on the third floor.[9]

The yard was about 100 square feet, partially paved with bricks and cobblestones. On the side of the yard was a one-story building of stone that housed the kitchen, guardhouse, and wash house. Behind this building were the sinks — trenches used by the prisoners as a latrine. There was also a sutler's shop, and a hospital.[10]

The Carroll Building

A row of houses, including the Carroll House, known as "Duff Green's Row" was used to house prisoners. These annexed houses became known as the Carroll Prison.[11]

Famous Prisoners

Old Capitol Prison held many famous and infamous prisoners, among them Miss Belle Boyd, and Mrs. Rose O'Neal Greenhow.

Many executions took place in the yard of the Old Capitol Prison — the Lincoln assassination conspirators, and Capt. Henry Wirz, commandant at the Confederate prison in Andersonville, Georgia. Anyone connected or even suspected of being connected with the assassination of Lincoln was arrested and held in the Old Capitol. This included the actor Junius Brutus Booth, brother of John Wilkes Booth; Mr. Ford, who owned Ford's Theater where Lincoln was shot; and Dr. Samuel Mudd, who set the broken leg of the assassin.[12]

At the end of hostilities, many of the southern governors were arrested and held at the Old Capitol, including soldier, congressman and governor Zebulon B. Vance of North Carolina; former U.S. congressman and governor of Virginia John Letcher; and Gov. Joseph Emerson Brown of Georgia.[13]

One prisoner recalled that when Belle Boyd was being held in the Old Capitol Prison, she would sing *Maryland, My Maryland* with great feeling. Her rendition moved the other prisoners so that it would bring tears to their eyes.[14] Bell was kept in solitary confinement on the second floor, but allowed to have the door to her room open. Those who were held on the third floor were citizens from Fredericksburg.[15] Her cell contained only a washstand, a looking glass, an iron bedstead, a table and some chairs. From the windows, she could see Pennsylvania Avenue.[16]

Belle Boyd, one of the most famous prisoners held in the Old Capitol Prison. (Courtesy of the Library of Congress, LC-DIG-cwpbh-03501.)

North Carolina's governor Zebulon Baird Vance was arrested after the war and held in the Old Capitol Prison. (Courtesy of the Library of Congress, LC-DIG-cwpbh-04049.)

Miss Boyd was allowed to go out into the yard on Sundays where there was preaching. She wore a little Confederate flag attached to her dress. The southerners gathered there doffed their hats to the regal lady.[17]

Belle did not attempt to escape, but through a slit in the wall, she passed notes back and forth to the prisoner in the next cell.[18] In the upper cell, a plank had been loosened to send messages to the prisoner below. When Belle wanted to communicate with prisoners across the hall from her cell, she wrapped a note around a marble and rolled it across the floor when the sentry was not looking. [19]

Since no specific charges had been filed against Belle, she was released and sent to Richmond. She continued her spy work and in May 1864 she sailed to England.[20] She carried dispatches for the Confederacy. Her ship was captured, but her captor, Lt. Samuel Wylde (Wilde) Hardinge Jr., followed her to England and married her. After the war, she became an actress and toured the United States, giving dramatic recitals of her wartime experiences.[21] Prison superintendent Col. N. T. Colby described Belle Boyd as "good-looking, with a fine figure, and merry disposition, and she could have been dangerous had she possessed equal good sense and good judgment."[22] She did manage to shift the loyalties of her husband, Lieutenant Hardinge. After he returned to the states, he was arrested and imprisoned at the Old Capitol and at Fort Delaware.[23]

Another famous spy for the Confederacy was the lovely widow Mrs. Rose O'Neal Greenhow. Mrs. Rose Greenhow had been held in the cell directly above that of Belle Boyd.[24] As an orphan, Rose O'Neal was sent as to live in the Old Capitol when it was her aunt's fashionable "Capitol Hill" boarding house.[25] Rose had married Dr. Robert Greenhow of Virginia and they and their four daughters lived only a few blocks away from the White House. After her husband's death, she used her friendship with prominent men of Washington to send messages to the Confederacy. She imparted her knowledge of the Federal troop movements to Gen. P. G. T. Beauregard in a coded message which prompted him to request reinforcements which gave the Confederates their first major victory at Manassas.[26]

Rose was arrested by Allan Pinkerton shortly after the first battle at Manassas, Virginia (First Bull Run), and placed under house arrest. On January 18, 1862, she and her eight-year-old daughter were taken to Old Capitol Prison, and held until June 1, 1862, for spying for the Confederacy. Rose managed to continue her spying activities for the Confederacy while confined in the prison, until she was released she was released for lack of evidence.[27] She managed to communicate through correspondence with innocent-looking phrases that gave the Confederates vital information. She also devised a system using different colors of yarn to represent the dots and dashes of the Morse code. After months of imprisonment, much of the time in solitary confinement, Rose was tried for treason, and in June 1862, she and her little daughter were exiled to the Confederacy.[28]

After her release, Rose sailed to England, where she met Queen Victoria and Napoleon III of France. She became engaged to marry the second Earl of Greenville. Unfortunately, Rose drowned off the coast of North Carolina in a shipwreck.[29] Her body was recovered and she was buried in Oakdale Cemetery in Wilmington.[30]

Less Famous Prisoners

The type of prisoners held at Old Capitol probably varied more than those held in any other Federal prison. The prisoners confined there were comparable, in some respects, to those held in Castle Thunder in Richmond (see Chapter XX). Prisoners held in the Old Capitol included prisoners of state; men charged with bounty frauds (enlisting in one regiment to collect the bounty and then in another to collect another bounty); counterfeiters of United States currency; contractors who had swindled the government; and men arrested by detectives on "trumped-up charges" in order to blackmail them. According to Colonel Colby, it would be unfair to assume that just because a person was being held in Old Capitol Prison he or she was a criminal. Colby claimed he met "*many* Gentlemen there, *as prisoners, too*, whose claims to regard as gentlemen and men of refinement and social standing is *to-day* widely honored." The reverse was also true. Colby believed that the civil prisoners held there were the "usual variety of humanity," but "generally of the better class." There were also privates from the Confederate army who were held awaiting court-martial or who had already been tried and sentenced.[31]

During the Civil War, the old building held prisoners from both sides and prisoners of state.[32] Provost Marshal William E. Doster believed that officials were too lenient on the guilty and too harsh on the innocent. To remedy the situation, a commission was appointed. The commission could release prisoners, but not acquit them.[33] Hundreds of civilians were also housed at Old Capitol because they were suspected of being disloyal. After President Lincoln suspended the writ of habeas corpus, these civilian "prisoners of state" were arrested on suspicion of being disloyal, without warrants, and imprisoned for months without ever knowing the charges against them, and without the benefit of a hearing or trial.[34]

Old Capitol Prison was a place of confinement for Confederate guerrillas, men who fought in loosely organized clusters for the purpose of harassing the enemy (i.e., William C. Quantrill and "Bloody Bill" Anderson, two of the most famous Confederate guerrilla leaders). A number of these guerrillas were confined in the Old Capitol Prison during the spring of 1864. The prisoners were described by Lt. Col. H. H. Wells, who was in charge of the defenses south of the Potomac, as "men of bad character" who "ought not to be exchanged, confined in some prison remote from Virginia, where they will not be likely to escape." Wells further warned that the prisoners were "generally rebels, cut-throats, and thieves," and they when released they would "return to their old avocation."[35] Maj. Gen. C. C. Augur agreed that the guerrillas should not be exchanged, "but kept closely confined during the war." He added that they were men "who have been selected for the particular duty upon which they were engaged by reason of their peculiar qualifications for it and their knowledge of the country." If any of them should escape, Augur feared he "would give more trouble to us than half a dozen ordinary soldiers."[36]

The Federal authorities were especially pleased with themselves when they captured some of Maj. John Singleton Mosby's Confederate cavalry officers. After scouting with J.E.B. Stuart, Mosby was permitted to organize a group of partisan rangers. Mosby engaged in guerrilla warfare in the Loudoun Valley, which came to be known as "Mosby's Confederacy." Known as the "Gray Ghost," Mosby dressed in a gray cape lined with scarlet and wore a hat with an ostrich feather. He was clean shaven, had sandy-blond hair, and was slight of stature. He was fearless and determined, and very successful in disrupting Federal operations. Mosby was held as a prisoner briefly in July 1862.[37]

Colonel Colby remembered that about 20 of Mosby's men were held in a large room on the fourth floor of the Old Capitol. He described them as "a turbulent and unruly set, and often amused themselves by throwing bricks (taken from an old fireplace in their room) at the sentinels" who were on guard below. To avoid injury to his guards, Colby ordered his guards to fire on "any one showing himself at the window.[38]

Life Inside Old Capitol Prison

Col. R. F. Webb, commander of the 6th Regiment, North Carolina Troops, was captured at the Rappahannock River on November 7, 1863. Initially, he was taken to Old Capitol Prison. In his memoirs, Webb described his quarters on the third floor as comfortable. Webb shared his rooms on the third floor with three other men. Colonels Godwin, Murchison, and Ellis. His suite of rooms had grated windows. One room was used for sleeping, the other was the parlor, dining and sitting room combined. It had a stove. The door was usually locked but could be opened quickly by the sentinel stationed outside. He was allowed outside to exercise for two hours each day, but generally no one but Miss Belle Boyd was allowed visitors.[39]

According to Colonel Colby, there was no "dungeon" at either building, and prisoners were never put in leg irons and were handcuffed only on a temporary basis, but not as a punishment. He described the fare as "full ration, cooked," and related that many prisoners bought food at nearby restaurants. They were allowed to buy wine and cigars, but it was usually only the civilians who could afford to do so. The soldiers and officers seldom had any money. All money and valuables were taken from prisoners as they were admitted, and a receipt given. Thus, the prisoners were allowed to draw on their funds for "legitimate uses." Knives were also confiscated. Colby reported that when he took over as prison commandant, he assumed control of $100,000 in money and United States bonds, and a bushel basket of pocket knives.[40]

The Rules

Prisoner James J. Williamson recalled that the prison rules were not posted, and the only information regarding the rules was obtained from talking with other prisoners or by seeing punishment inflicted upon "some poor wretch for a violation of an unwritten law."[41] Wiliamson did learn that "no more than 2 men were allowed to leave their rooms at a time, and that no lights were permitted at night."[42]

No one was permitted past the guardroom without orders from either the provost marshal or the secretary of state. Prisoners were not permitted to purchase extra food, and they were not allowed to communicate with each other.[43] All correspondence had to pass through the provost marshal.[44]

Escape Attempts from the Old Capitol

While few actually succeeded in escaping from the Old Capitol Prison, many tried. A citizen from Maryland was arrested and sent to the Old Capitol charged with having killed a Union soldier in a fight after a drinking spree. The man, whom Colonel Colby called "Brown," was a known southern sympathizer, and the killing was perceived as in aid of the southern cause. Colby described Brown as an example of southern "poor white trash." The man was put on the fourth floor in a room that was already occupied by a prisoner. The current occupant wanted to be rid of the newcomer, so he devised a plan. He returned from exercising outside in the yard one day and told Brown that he had overheard the colonel in charge of the prison giving orders to the guards to prepare to execute Brown the next morning. Brown went wild with anguish and despair, but finally calmed down enough to eagerly listen to his cellmate's plan. The cellmate told Brown that he had been an acrobat in the circus, and described how it was possible to jump with the use of a springboard from any place to a distant point, without injury. All Brown needed to escape was a board to use to jump into the yard, then he could scale the fence and escape. Brown was willing to try anything. That night, the two removed one of the floorboards. They secured the board to the window sill, while below the sentries patrolled the grounds. Brown told his cellmate goodbye, then crawled out onto the plank. When he reached its end, he stood, and following the instructions given him by his acrobat friend, he began to jump up and down on the board until finally he was impelled high enough, he thought, to thrust him through the air to where he could scale the fence. Instead, Brown barely missed the bayonet of a guard as he hit the pavement. The guard was frightened and fled. Brown, shaken but unhurt, got to his feet and ran to the steps which led to the top of a shed. There, he encountered another sentinel, who ended his flight.[45]

Although the drop from the fourth floor was between 40 and 50 feet, Brown was not injured. However, the fall must have damaged his brain, according to Colonel Colby, because he was soon shot and killed by a guard while attempting another escape.[46]

A member of John S. Mosby's partisan rangers, Henry Harris, was captured in October 1864, near Snickersville (Bluemont), Virginia. Harris was confined in Old Capitol Prison. Often prisoners signaled people passing by on the street. Prison guards tried to prevent this and they threatened to shoot any prisoners seen at the windows and to arrest any citizens who attempted to signal those inside. Harris recalled several escape attempts while he was there. Ranger John Munson successfully escaped by disguising himself as a hospital orderly. Then he simply walked out the door past the guards.[47]

Some time later, to prevent the escape of these daring Confederate rangers as they were being transferred to Fort Warren in February 1865, the officer in charge would take them only if they were handcuffed together in pairs. Thus, 86 of Mosby's men were taken by a lieutenant and 28 armed guards to the train depot for transport to Fort Warren in Boston Harbor. First Sgt. Hugh McIlhany, one of the prisoners, recalled that "A more enraged set of men were never seen than these, when standing on Capitol street, handcuffed together." The prisoners remained handcuffed until they arrived at Fort Warren. The officer there would not receive them until the handcuffs were removed.[48]

Prisoner Harry Stewart, the 23-year-old son of Dr. Frederick Stewart of Baltimore, tried to bribe a guard. Stewart waited for the night agreed upon to make his escape. He had just started to climb out of the window, when a guard shouted "Halt!" The guard fired his rifle and shattered Stewart's right knee cap. He was jerked back into his cell by some of the other inmates. A surgeon was called and the leg had to be amputated. Young Stewart died of the shock. The note he used to bribe the guard was found in his pocket, but no action was taken against the guard.[49]

According to Doster, two Confederate officers also escaped before the attempt made by Harry Stewart.[50]

Captain Wynne escaped on February 6, 1863, by breaking out a panel of his door. Captain Darling and George Adreon escaped on February 13, 1863, by bribing a sentinel. Two Federal prisoners escaped through the cellar on March 6, 1863, but one was caught. Also, in February 1863, there was some discussion by prisoners of rushing the gate when the delivery wagon pulled up to unload supplies.[51]

Lieutenant Colonel Wells learned that a Confederate guerrilla named "Shepherd," who had been captured "with great difficulty" in November 1863, managed to escape from Old Capitol, and return to his band of guerrillas.[52]

Union soldiers who had been court-martialed served out their sentences on the lower floor of the old Capitol Building. Although usually they were hindered by a ball and chain, they were constantly being caught trying to escape.[53]

To keep his identity a secret, a young man who was working for the Federals as a Confederate spy was arrested and sent to the Old Capitol Prison. The young man had brought a dispatch from Canada, addressed to Mr. Judah P. Benjamin, the Confederate secretary of state. The information concerned a military expedition by Confederates against Burlington, Vermont. The spy carried the document between two thicknesses of a pair of reinforced cavalry trousers, so that when he rode, the document was secure between his thigh and the saddle. He took it to Washington and gave it to Mr. Edwin Stanton, the United States secretary of war. President Lincoln was sent for. They decided that the message must be sent on its way. The only way to make public the fact that the Confederates were operating in Canada under the protection of the British government was to have the spy caught. According to Charles A. Dana, assistant secretary of war, the circumstances of the capture of the courier must be such that the British Foreign Office could not "dispute the genuineness of the document." But care must be taken for the young man's safety.[54]

The paper was returned to the courier's trousers, and he was instructed to start out at dusk along the road he usually took passing into Confederate lines. He was to stop at a tavern in Alexandria about 9 P.M. to water his horse. A description of the spy was sent through Major General Augur to General Wells, the military governor of Alexandra, to send troops to the tavern to arrest the young man. Wells was also instructed that he was "to do him no injury, but to make sure of his person and all papers that he might have upon him," and to bring him directly back to the War Department.[55]

The young man was taken back to the War Department, and each article of his clothing was searched, until the dispatch was found. The young man was taken to

Old Capitol Prison but the warden was told to allow him to escape. He did so and one day entered Dana's office.

Dana inquired, "Did they shoot at you?"

"Yes, sir, they did, but they didn't hit me," replied the young courier-spy.

"But," the young man explained, "I didn't think that would do, so I shot myself through the arm." He then showed Assistant Secretary Dana the wound in his forearm that had penetrated but not struck bone.

An advertisement offering $2,000 reward for the young man's capture was placed in several national newspapers. The young man returned to Canada where he was given new dispatches to carry south to Confederate officials.[56]

Escapes from the Carroll Building

When Miss Belle Boyd was arrested again and held in the Carroll Prison, she diverted the attention of the guard and of the warden to help three prisoners escape. When the cry, "Murder, murder!" was given outside, the guards rushed to see what was taking place. The three men who wanted to escape had made their way to the garrett, removed a portion of the roof, and while the attention of the guards was occupied, they descended by holding on the lightning rod wires to the street and scattered in the night.[57]

Colonel Colby recalled that a Virginia colonel escaped by lowering himself from a third-story window with a blanket rope. The rope was too short and he was nearly killed. He had chosen a dark and rainy night to flee his prison. He descended down the rope, hand over hand, until he came to the end of his crude rope. He was still far from the ground, but there was no way to go but down. He dropped to the pavement within a few feet of a sentinel with a loaded musket. The sentinel cocked his gun and fired, but it misfired. The prisoner jumped up and disappeared into the night. The colonel was, however, recaptured in Baltimore by Gen. Lew Wallace, and returned to the Carroll Building within a month.[58]

On April 14, 1865, the night President Lincoln was shot, there were 800 Confederate officers being held in the Carroll Prison. They ranked from second lieutenant to major general. While the search for the assassins was in progress, an angry mob attempted to storm the Carroll Prison. Someone had seen some Federal soldiers escort two prisoners, both civilians, from the provost marshal's office and word spread quickly that the two prisoners were Booth and an accomplice. A crowd soon gathered but the soldiers and their prisoners made it inside the building. The mob began shouting and throwing stones at the windows, but were disbursed with bayonets by the few guards at the prison. No prisoners escaped, and no one was killed, but a few were injured by the bayonets of the guards. The two badly frightened prisoners were not John Wilkes Booth or anyone connected with the assassination.[59]

After the War — The Fate of the Old Capitol

Two weeks after Capt. Henry Wirz was hanged in November 1865, the Old Capitol Building was dismantled. The site is now occupied by the United States Supreme Court. The Carroll Prison was also torn down and the lot is now the site of the Folger Shakespeare Library.[60]

XIV

Point Lookout, Maryland

And maby I will never live to see the last day of 64.
And thairfour I will try and do better than I have.
For what is a man profited if he shal gain the whole world
and loose his one Soul. Or what Shal one give in exchange for his Soul.
— B. Y. Malone, diary entry for December 31, 1863.

Location: on a peninsula at the junction of the Potomac River and Chesapeake Bay, in St. Mary's County, Maryland. **Established:** 1863. **Type of Prison:** tents enclosed by fence. **Type of Prisoners:** enlisted men and officers. **Capacity:** 10,000. **Maximum Number Held:** 22,000. **Number of Escapes:** 50. **Other Names:** Camp Hoffman.[1]

History

A hospital complex with a number of auxiliary buildings had been established at the end of the peninsula close to an existing lighthouse. The 1,400-bed hospital was near a wharf from which supplies and wounded soldiers could be unloaded. A 40-acre site northeast of the hospital was selected for the prison.[2]

The area along the Chesapeake Bay was and remains a resort area with many hotels, boarding houses, cottages, and businesses. The site that was to become one of the largest Federal prisons was leased to the Federal government in June 1862.[3] Thus, there were many comfortable buildings available to quarter the officers and prison guards, as reported by the *New York Times*.[4]

Gunboats always patrolled the waters to prevent prisoners from escaping by that route.[5]

The Facilities

The prison compound was enclosed by a board fence 14 or 15 feet high. Near the top of the fence a walkway had been built for the guards. This platform was about three feet wide, and as the guards walked it, they could overlook the whole camp.[6] There were guards stationed inside the camp, plus regiments of artillery and infantry were stationed near the camp to guard it from an outside attack

Another fence split the prison compound into two areas. An area of about 30 acres was for the enlisted men, and the remaining 10 acres was reserved for officers. Inside, the sandy soil was bare of trees or shrubs.[7]

Anthony M. Keiley, of Company E, 12th Virginia Infantry, described the interior of the compound and its few buildings:

> [There was] a row of eight or ten wooden buildings jutting out from the western face of the pen.... A street, twenty feet in width, ran along the front of these houses and at right angles to this street were long rows of tents of all imaginable patterns, and of no pattern at all, to within twenty or thirty feet of the opposite face of the enclosure.[8]

The only buildings were a cook house and mess hall combined. The smaller enclosure had only one, and the larger enclosure held seven. An eighth building was used as a commissary store. These wooden buildings were 160 feet long and about 20 feet wide. About 20 feet of each building was partitioned off as a cook house.[9]

Old Tents

The facilities were worse than primitive, and proposed barracks were never built to shelter the prisoners. As winter approached, Col. William Hoffman recommended building wooden barracks, but Secretary of War Stanton refused the request. The 9,000 prisoners spent the winter of 1863–1864 in 980 tents. Hoffman advised the commander at Point Lookout to requisition enough tents to accommodate 10,000 prisoners.[10] The tents, according to Assistant Medical Inspector C. T. Alexander, were "old and worn." Sixteen men were housed in one Sibley tent, and six in the common tents, another deficiency. [11]

Reverend J. B. Traywick, a prisoner, recalled that the tents they did have, "mostly bell or round-shaped," had been rejected for use by the Federal army, and that the ones they were given "generally leaked."[12]

Bad Water

Besides inadequate food and insufficient tents, the water was bad. An inspection was conducted in July 1864 by Alexander for the U. S. Army. Alexander reported that the water source, supply and quality was bad, the pumps deficient, and therefore there was much diarrhea and dysentery. He said that the causes of disease were mainly "bad water, and a deficiency of vegetables."[13]

Alexander reported that the water was "brackish and scanty," which caused a large increase in disease. He recommended that a supply of fresh water be brought by boats.[14]

A lengthy report submitted by W. F. Swalm of the Sanitary Commission detailed a number of areas that needed improvement, including the sinks. Swalm was amazed that there was not more sickness because the prisoners "live, eat, and sleep in their own filth."[15]

The Prisoners

Even before construction of the camp was completed, 136 prisoners of war arrived from the battlefield at Gettysburg, Pennsylvania.[16] Soon, prisoners were being transferred from Baltimore and from Old Capitol Prison. By the end of July, there were almost 1,700 men confined at Point Lookout.[17] That population rose almost continuously until by April 1865, 20,110 prisoners were confined there. The prison population was almost double that at Camp Douglas, near Chicago, Illinois.[18] (See Appendix.)

Traywick was captured at Fisher's Gap on September 22, 1864. He was taken by steamer to Point Lookout, where he arrived on October 3, 1864. Upon his arrival, he was stripped of everything he possessed except one blanket.[19]

It was extremely cold at Point Lookout beside the Chesapeake Bay. On the night of January 1, 1864, Bartlett Yancey Malone recorded that "five of our men froze to death before morning."[20] Malone, from Caswell County, North Carolina, a member of the 6th North Carolina Regiment, was captured at the Rappahannock Bridge on November 7, 1863. He was to remain a prisoner until his release on February 24, 1865.[21] He was one of the more fortunate who survived the harsh environment at Point Lookout.

Pvt. Louis Leon, of the Charlotte Grays, which made up Company C of the First North Carolina Regiment,[22] was captured at Mine Run on May 5, 1864. He and other prisoners captured at Chancellorsville were taken to Point Lookout. The camp, in St. Mary's County, was about 50 miles from Belle Plain.[23]

Female Prisoner Discovered

When Alexander made his report of conditions at the camp in July 1864, he concluded with, "Among the prisoners is a woman, Sarah Jane Perkins, whose removal is desirable."[24]

Daily Life of the Prisoners

The boring daily routine, according to Leon, began when the prisoners awoke at 5 A.M. to answer to roll call. At 6 A.M., 500 prisoners at a time went to breakfast until four groups of men had eaten. The prisoners were guarded as they marched to get their meals in ranks of four. Then they were free to walk around the compound. At 1 P.M., they received their second meal, and were free again until sundown, when the roll was called again. Each prisoner received "five crackers with worms in them" for breakfast, along with small piece of pork and a tin cup of coffee. For dinner, they were given four crackers, "a quarter of a pound of mule meat and a cup of bean soup," and every fourth day, they were given an 8-ounce loaf of white bread.[25]

Malone recorded in his diary that in November and December 1863, the prisoners were given five crackers and a cup of coffee for breakfast, and for dinner a small portion of meat, two crackers, three potatoes and a cup of soup. There was no supper. By January 1864, some of the men were so hungry they caught a rat, cooked it, and ate it.[26]

Leon asked for a parole to travel to New York to see his parents, but it was denied. His brother Pincus came to visit him, having gotten a pass from headquarters. But when he arrived at Point Lookout, he was refused entry, and so he returned home without having seen his brother.[27]

Private Leon survived for over a year at Point Lookout before being transferred to the prison at Elmira, New York, on July 25, 1864. After they heard the news of Lee's surrender, Leon and about 400 other prisoners took the Oath of Allegiance, and were released and given transportation to anywhere they wanted to go. He went to New York where his parents lived.[28]

Cruel and Unusual Punishment

Leon wrote in his diary on May 23, 1863, that the prisoners were guarded by "Negro troops, who are as mean as hell." They were not allowed to cross the deadline, but occasionally someone accidentally did. He was pushed across the line in the rush for food, and "a black devil shot and killed him, and wounded two others." Fearing retribution from the prisoners against the black guards, they were removed.[29]

Prisoners complained about the cruelty of the black guards. Private Malone recorded that the situation had become so bad that they had been replaced by white guards at night.[30] Finally, in January 1865, the black guards were removed.[31]

According to Traywick, someone threw a brick and hit one of the black guards. The guard fell off the parapet. Because no one would tell who had thrown the brick, 32 of the prisoners were aroused from their beds at night and taken to the nearest block cookhouse. The temperature was below zero, and the prisoners were dressed in only shirts and pants, and with no shoes or socks. They were confined in the house without food, water or fire, and were told they would be kept there until the person who had killed the guard confessed. If no one came forward, they would all be executed the next day. Sam Puckett of Waterloo, South Carolina, was one of the 32.[32]

The next day, the almost frozen prisoners were taken outside and questioned again. They were surrounded by angry prison guards, who were mostly blacks. The prisoners were preparing to meet their death, when several horsemen rode at full speed into the camp. A young man came forward to testify that he had been at the wood pile gathering chips for the fire, when he was struck on the leg by a brick. Not bothering to look, he had picked up the brick and tossed it over his shoulder. By chance, the brick hit the guard in the head, and he toppled off. The guard had been drunk that afternoon, so it was not certain whether he had fallen from the blow from the brick or because he was drunk. After the soldier's testimony, the 32 were sent back to their quarters, clothed and fed, but many suffered ill effects from their ordeal.[33]

Punishment for trying to escape was harsh and painful. Prisoners who were caught attempting to escape were strung up to a pole by their thumbs. They were tied so that their feet barely touched the ground. The pain was excruciating, and sometimes those undergoing this punishment would faint and had to be cut down.[34]

Private Malone recorded several instances when it seemed to him that the black guards were unnecessarily cruel and quick to shoot unarmed prisoners. Malone recorded that two of the prisoners were killed the night of February 24, 1864, "attempting to get away."[35]

Escapes and Escape Attempts

Because of the treatment prisoners received and the lack of shelter, there were many escape attempts. From the available monthly reports from Point Lookout (July 1863–June 1865), 41 prisoners were reported to have escaped. This does not compare to the 245 who escaped from Camp Douglas in Illinois or the 112 reported to have escaped from Camp Morton in Indiana. However, considering the number of prisoners held (over 20,000 in April 1865), it was a very good record and an extremely low number of escapes.[36] The most escapes for one month occurred in September 1863 when 11 escapes were reported out of 3,942 prisoners being held.[37]

To contain the prisoners and prevent their escape, by the summer of 1864 two regiments of veteran reserves had been moved to Point Lookout. One was a regiment of 100-days' men, the other a regiment from Massachusetts of black soldiers. The necks of land which connected Point Lookout to the mainland were bisected by a stockade and field work, "the latter to guard "against attack from without, and the former to meet any effort of the prisoners to liberate themselves," reported Colonel Hoffman. He believed that "with proper vigilance" by the troops stationed there, assisted by the presence of gunboats, "no successful attack [could] be made on the depot."[38]

One frequent method of escape, sometimes successful, sometimes not, was by water.

When the prisoners were allowed to go outside the fence to the beach to bathe, if a barrel or box was seen floating in the water, the prisoner would swim out to it and duck his head under it. Then he would drift with the river and get out on shore some distance away.[39]

Sgt. Berry Greenwood Benson was captured at Spotsylvania. He was taken to Point Lookout, which was not at all to his liking. One prisoner reportedly tunneled out the night before Benson arrived. He wondered just how that had been accomplished in the sandy soil. He heard that some other prisoners had put together a raft from pieces of wooden crates and boxes and any scrap lumber they could find. However, their plan was discovered before they could put it into effect.

Another story he heard was about a couple of prisoners who undertook a swimming match in the Chesapeake Bay, in full view of the guards. The match turned serious, when one of the contestants kept on swimming down the coast, and never returned.[40]

Encouraged by the stories of successful escapes, Sergeant Benson determined he would escape as well, as soon as he got the opportunity to do so. That chance came on May 25, 1864. Benson was watching the changing of the guards, when he noticed that the guards coming on duty failed to close the front gate. Word spread quickly through the camp. Normally, prisoners were allowed to move in and out through the gate during the day in order to swim in the Chesapeake under the close supervision of the sentries. However, at night the gates were closed and locked at dusk. Benson saw his opportunity and took it. He walked casually through the gate toward one of the privies which sat about 25 feet from the edge of the water. Once he reached the privy, he edged into the water, and used the privy to shield him from the view of the guards. He moved across the deadline, a row of logs driven into the shallows along the shore. Swimmers were not allowed past this line. Unnoticed, Benson swam away from the shore under cover of the approaching darkness, and was soon out of range of rifle fire. He had escaped after being at Point Lookout less than 48 hours.[41]

Benson moved northward a few miles and when it was full dark, he climbed out of the water and walked along the shore. Over the next few days, he traveled 50 miles. He crossed to Maryland's western shore, then swam the Potomac River to a point about 14 miles below Washington, D.C. He managed to swim with all his clothes on, carrying his shoes, his hat held under his Confederate jacket, and with three matches tied on top of his head. Once in Virginia, Benson found himself near Mount Vernon. There, he was discovered, captured, and jailed in Alexandria. He was then transferred to Old Capitol Prison.[42] All his attempts to escape the Old Capitol failed, and he was transported to Elmira Prison. He was signed in as Prisoner No. 1948. He chided himself for not escaping from the train which carried him to Baltimore, then on north to Elmira, New York. Because he hesitated, he missed a good opportunity to escape, which would have prevented the long months he endured at Elmira.[43]

Other Ways Out

On July 15, 1864, 833 prisoners were being transported from Point Lookout to Elmira, Pennsylvania, in the custody of 125 guards. They had just left Jersey City about 6 A.M. on the Erie Railroad when the train carrying the prisoners collided with a coal train near Shohola, Pennsylvania. Fatalities included 14 of the guards and 40 prisoners killed instantly. Three guards and eight prisoners were mortally wounded and died later. Sixteen guards and 93 prisoners were injured. Of the prisoners, 687 were unhurt. The prisoners were taken to Shohola then transported the next day to Elmira Prison. In the confusion of the train wreck, five of the prisoners were counted as missing.[44] They were assumed to have escaped.

The wreck was due to an error made by a telegraph operator who had signaled the coal train that the way was clear and to proceed. Someone had failed to mention that the prisoners' train was approaching along the same track.[45]

In January, President Abraham Lincoln sent a letter to Maj. Gen. Benjamin Butler regarding the prisoners. Lincoln and Secretary of War Stanton decided that, as announced in a proclamation on December 8, 1863, the prisoners at Point Lookout could be divided into two classes for discharge: First: those "who will take the oath prescribed ... will enlist in our service," and second, those "who will take the oath and be discharged and whose homes lie safely within our military lines."[46]

While prisoners continued to arrive at Point Lookout, others were shipped out. On September 21, 1864, all of the prisoners being held who were members of the Confederate States Navy were paroled. In February, certain groups of prisoners were released. Malone and all the prisoners captured at Rappahannock Station were released after they had signed the parole. Sent by the steamer *George Leary*, he and others were sent to Fortress Monroe, then to Akins' Landing. On March 2, 1865, after getting a furlough and his back pay of $237, Malone headed for Richmond.[47] He arrived just in time to see the Confederacy collapse.

Point Lookout Today

The peninsula that once was home to thousands of Confederate prisoners is now Point Lookout State Park. A visitors center and museum are open to the public. The museum contains photographs of some of the prisoners and artifacts recovered at the prison site. It has been estimated that over 14,000 prisoners died while imprisoned at Point Lookout, but only 3,384 bodies were found in a mass grave. The remains have been moved twice and now rest in the Point Lookout Cemetery.[48]

XV

Rock Island, Illinois

Prison life is very unpleasant to me. Were it not for my Testament and other books that I get to read, I don't know how I could stand it.
— A. P. Adamson, diary entry, June 27, 1864

Location: on an island in the Mississippi River, between Davenport, Iowa, and Moline, Illinois. **Established:** 1863. **Type:** barracks enclosed by high fence. **Type of Prisoners:** captured Confederate soldiers, civilian political prisoners. **Capacity:** 10,080. **Most Held at One Time:** 8,607. **Number of Known Escapes:** 41.[1] **Total Number of Prisoners Received:** 12,215[2]–12,409.[3] **Other Names:** Arsenal Island.

History

Rock Island is owned by the Federal government. It is a small island in the Mississippi River, three miles long and a half a mile wide. The government had claimed it in 1804, but it remained unoccupied until 1812. In 1816, a fort was constructed on the west end of the island and named Fort Armstrong, in honor of the current secretary of war. In 1840, the government established an ordnance depot on the island, but moved the arms and ammunition to St. Louis in 1842. In 1862, it was converted again into an arsenal for United States troops. A bridge connected the island to the Iowa side of the river, and to Illinois by two bridges. One of those bridges connected the island to the town of Rock Island, and the other to the town of Moline, both in Illinois.[4]

Preparing the Site for the New Facility

Capt. Charles A. Reynolds, assistant quartermaster, received orders on July 1, 1863, from M. C. Meigs, quartermaster general, to go to Rock Island to take charge of the construction of a depot for prisoners of war. He was to obtain the plans for the buildings to be erected from the quartermaster general's office. Meigs said that the plans were merely for the dimensions of the buildings, and that they could be modified as needed. A fence, 12 feet high, was to be built to surround the prisoners' barracks. A sentinel's walk was to be added to the outside of the fence, four feet from the top. Meigs also advised that if it was impractical to dig wells because of the rock bed of the island, then Reynolds should use pumps and pipe water from the Mississippi River. Meigs also warned that Reynolds should be "governed by the strictest economy consistent with the completion of the depot at the earliest practicable period."[5] Reynolds received a note a month later from Meigs directing him to construct barracks for the prisoners in the "roughest and cheapest manner." The barracks should be "mere shanties, with no fine work about them," and he wanted them built by contract in the "shortest possible time." He asked that Reynolds telegraph him to let him know if the contracts had been made.[6] Reynolds submitted a modified plan, which was forwarded to Colonel Hoffman. Hoffman approved the plan which now included a guard house. Acting Quartermaster General Charles Thomas notified Reynolds and also approved the construction of two guard houses if it "would render the place more secure." Thomas also suggested that coal-burning stoves should be used, if coal could be bought for the same cost as wood. Thomas also authorized that six wells, 25 feet deep, be dug.[7]

Colonel Hoffman visited the prison camp during the last weeks of November 1863. He described the vacant prison on Rock Island:

> The inclosure and the barracks for prisoners are completed and are ready for occupants, though there is yet some unfinished work. The extent of the inclosure and the less efficient character of the Invalid Corps than other troops the accommodations for the guards will have to be more extensive than was anticipated, and some little time will elapse before the additions which are in progress will be completed...."[8]

The Facilities

The barracks were situated near the center of the island toward the northern side. Eventually, 84 barracks were constructed, 100 by 22 by 12 feet in dimension. Each housed 120 men. The barracks were arranged in blocks of seven each, fronting streets that were 100 feet wide. Two avenues, 130 feet wide, intersected the center of the camp. There were four latrines (or sinks) in each street. The barracks were ventilated by two openings on the roof, 12 windows and two doors. Eighteen feet had been partitioned off in each barracks to serve as a kitchen; this area was furnished with a 40-gallon caldron, plus a table. Each barracks was heated by two small coal-burning stoves. The drainage within the camp was poor, and there was a swampy marsh in the southwest corner of the enclosure.[9]

The commandant in charge of the prison was Col. Adolphus J. Johnson, considered by his prisoners as "inhuman a brute as ever disgraced the uniform of any country."[10]

When Hoffman visited Rock Island he found four companies of guards present, but no medical officer. He subsequently applied to the assistant surgeon general in Louisville to send a doctor along with a supply of medicines and stores. This was done, and Hoffman requested additional medical officers. Hoffman also though it wise for the government to put the island under martial law, "in order that the commanding officer may have it in his power to prevent intrusion of persons who will take the advantage of every opportunity to enter into an illicit traffic with the guards or the prisoners." Hoffman also though it prudent not to allow the Chicago and Rock Island Railroad, which crossed the island, to allow passengers to leave the train at the island.[11]

Eventually, some of the barracks were put to other uses and fenced off from the barracks which housed the prisoners. Two were used as commissary-distributing storehouses, one for the quartermaster's distributing storehouse, 11 for the hospital, six were used to quarter six companies of the 37th Iowa Volunteers, and one was used for the quarters of the laundresses, for a total of 21. The buildings used for the temporary hospital were in the southwest corner of the enclosure. One of the 11 was used as a storehouse and carpenter's workshop.[12]

Dr. A. M. Clark also noted that, in general, the rations for the prisoners were good in quantity and quality, except for the corn bread. The Surgeon indicated in his report to Colonel Hoffman that the corn bread was so "poorly prepared as to become a source of disease."[13]

Hoffman, upon receiving Clark's complaint, issued orders to the prison commandant to limit the issuing of corn bread to one in seven days, and only then after the medical officer had inspected it and approved it. Undoubtedly, corn bread was issued in place of flour.[14]

It would appear from the official reports that Colonel William Hoffman was an able administrator. But, some have suggested that Hoffman's orders "killed more Confederate soldiers behind the lines than the orders of most Union generals engaged in legitimate warfare." Hoffman was so frugal that his lack of authorization for necessities caused starvation, disease, and death by freezing. His policy was backed by Union Quartermaster Montgomery C. Meigs who believed that prisoner-of-war camps should be constructed in the "roughest and cheapest manner, mere shanties, with no fine work about them."[15]

The Prisoners

Colonel Hoffman, the commissary general of prisoners, advised the commandant of Camp Douglas on October 17, 1863, that 1,000 prisoners would be transferred from that facility to Rock Island "in a few days."[16]

Although the buildings were finished, and everything in readiness, no prisoners had arrived by the end of November 1863, but they were expected and arrangements were being made for their reception. The barracks were ready to house 10,000 men, and a garrison of troops, under Colonel Rush, was in place.[17]

On December 1, 1863, Colonel Hoffman ordered 5,000 prisoners to be sent to Rock Island. He requested clothing to be sent there as well: 1,000 each of coats, pants, shirts, and pairs of stockings, plus 5,000 blankets.[18]

The official reports and correspondence between Hoffman, the prison commandant, and other governmental officials appear to show much concern for the welfare of the prisoners. Inspections were done and weekly reports submitted as to the condition of the camp and the prisoners and those in the hospital. However, the accounts of the prisoners tell an entirely different story, one of random shootings by the guards, disease, cold and hunger.

The first prisoners to arrive had been captured by Grant's Army at Lookout Mountain and Missionary Ridge on November 24–25, 1864. They arrived on December 3, 1863.[19] The 5,592 new arrivals were greeted by a temperature of 32 degrees below zero and two feet of snow. In addition, 94 of those prisoners already had smallpox, and General Hoffman had neglected to include plans for a hospital in the new camp. As a result, the sick slept with the well and by the end of December, 94 had died. Over the next four months, the camp would have an average of 250 deaths per month.[20]

Augustus Pitt Adamson, from Henry County, Georgia, enlisted at age 17 on September 25, 1861, in a company called the Clayton Invincibles. This company soon became Company I of the 25th Georgia Volunteer Infantry Regiment. A. P., as he was called, rose in the ranks to first corporal. He was severely wounded in the hip at the Battle of Chickamauga on September 19, 1863. He recuperated and returned to his command only to be captured near Calhoun, Georgia, on May 17, 1864. He was taken to a prison camp at Louisville, Kentucky then transferred on May 25, 1864, to Rock Island Prisoner of War Camp. Adamson remained a prisoner until he was transferred for exchange on February 25, 1864. He was one of an exchange package of 602 paroled Confederate prisoners, which included 97 officers.[21]

Adamson kept a diary from 1864–1865, which begins with an explanation of his capture and imprisonment. A number of letters from and to him survived the years and have been included in the edited version of his diary. Adamson wrote his first letter from prison to his father to inform him where he was to reassure him. He assumed his father had already learned that he was "missing." He told his father that he was "getting along," and also listed the names of several of his company who were at Rock Island with him. He encouraged his father to "rest easy on my account, for I will do the best I can."[22] The houses of his prison, wrote Adamson, "were all surrounded by a high plank enclosure and a strong guard placed around it." However, he found his quarters "much more comfortable than [he] had expected and our rations amounted to nearly as much as we obtained in the Southern Army ... ." Nevertheless, the "narrow space and the strict orders to which we were confined made me fully realize the nature of a prison life."[23] Adamson refused to take the oath and enlist in the U.S. Army as did 1,500 of the prisoners, who were subsequently taken out of the prison in October 1864. He remained and finally was taken for exchange on February 25, 1865.[24]

Charles Wright of Tennessee arrived at Rock Island on January 16, 1864, with about 50 other prisoners from Columbia, Kentucky. They were lined up and searched outside while standing outside in deep snow. He and the others were then escorted to Barracks No. 52, and searched again. The first search was for arms or contraband articles, the second for money and other valuables. A guard read them the prison regulations, and they were dismissed.[25]

Starvation

Prison guard John A. Bateson testified after the war that he was at Rock Island for 10 months. He said that the prisoners were "retained in a famishing condition by order of Edwin M. Stanton, Secretary of War," approved by President Abraham Lincoln. The order was read to the prisoners inside the garrison in January 1864. According to Bateson, the order regarding diminished rations was read to the guards on January 2, 1864, and "continued in force ... until the close of the war."[26]

Bateson recalled that a new group of prisoners arrived in January 1864. They had been captured at Knoxville. He had 60 of them in the barracks that was under his charge. When they arrived, one of the prisoners inquired when they would "draw rations." Bateson told him not until the next day. By evening, the prisoner exhibited signs of delirium, and attempted to grasp something from a table, thinking it was "loaded with delicacies." The next morning, he and two more were dead. It was a common occurrence. Bateson learned that the symptoms were the same: "There was no complaint; no manifestation of illness. Some drooped [dead] while standing on the floor; others fell from a sitting posture. All swooned and died without a struggle." Bateson believed that the "Knoxville prisoners were starved to death."[27]

Thomas R. McCormick, of Vossburg, Mississippi, enlisted in August 1861 in Company H, 27th Regiment, Mississippi Infantry, a company known as the Jasper Blues. McCormick fought in the battle of Missionary Ridge, then was captured at Lookout Mountain on November 24, 1863. He was taken to Rock Island. Confined to Barracks No. 8, McCormick fared fairly well, until the rations were cut to about a third "of a soldier's rations; it was so scant that we could hardly live on it, and we were told that they were retaliating for the way the Andersonville, Ga., prisoners were treated."[28]

Smallpox — A Deadly Disease

By February 1864, smallpox was rampant in the prison. Surgeon A. M. Clark, acting medical inspector of prisoners of war, visited Rock Island and conducted an inspection from February 4–11, 1864. Clark reported that the prisoners numbered 7,149. Col. A. J. Johnson was commander of the Invalid Corps, consisting of 1,361 troops in 16 companies, making the total population on the island 8,510. Water was obtained by pumping it from the river, and there was also one artesian well. The water quality was good, but the supply insufficient from the well. Each of the 84 barracks contained 60 double bunks, enough to accommodate 120 prisoners, for a total of 10,080. There were also two stoves in each of the barracks. The sinks, Clark found, were "very faulty" and would soon become a "seething mass of filth."[29]

Clark submitted a scathing report to Colonel Hoffman of his findings. Smallpox was prevalent. Clark found 38 prisoners with the disease, and they were lying "among their fellows in the prison barracks." He believed that the medical officers at the prison were remiss "in not taking proper measures to prevent the spread of smallpox." He criticized the commandant and reported that Captain Reynolds should have reported the sickness to the provost marshal and "should have directed their immediate removal, even without the request of the surgeon." One of the doctors at the camp, Dr. Temple, was not even aware of the "extent of his authority" as acting assistant surgeon, or his "duties as surgeon in charge," according to Clark. Another, Dr. Moxley, was "a very young officer" recently commissioned, who Clark believed was anxious to do his duty, yet was "entirely unfitted both by temperament and inexperience for a charge of this magnitude." Clark also blamed the prison officials in Louisville, Kentucky, for sending prisoners to the island who had already been exposed to smallpox, and even some who already had the deadly disease. Clark emphatically stated that a prison hospital was needed immediately, and a plan had been submitted for a building just south of the prison enclosure.[30]

Clark's report gave the mortality and morbidity—173 deaths in January 1864, 297 cases of smallpox, deaths from smallpox 62 (20.87 percent). From February 1 through February 8, there were 159 cases of smallpox, and 36 deaths from the disease (22.64 percent). Even some of the guards had contracted the deadly disease. The total cases so far were 456, with 98 deaths, although 3,613 had been vaccinated by February 8.[31]

Charles Wright, a prisoner, noted that by March 9, from his barracks alone, 29 men had died. Those who recovered from smallpox were detailed as nurses for the sick. The surgeons tried to vaccinate the men, but to little avail, according to the provost marshal's abstract, cited by Wright, on May 12, 1865.[32]

Shortly thereafter, Captain Reynolds reported that since the water and the sinks had been found to be inadequate, he had proposed to construct a sewage system and improve drainage. Reynolds believed that the prison could hold 12,000 men, and had 8,000–9,000 at the present time (February 25, 1864). He proposed also to build a "round reservoir of stone 150 feet in diameter and fifteen feet high" with the capacity to hold enough water for 15,000 men for 10 days. He also proposed a sewer through the center of the avenue to the river, over which there would be a "line of double privies," from the street to the prison fence. He proposed that the prisoners quarry the stone on the island. Surgeon A. M. Clark agreed with Reynolds' planned improvements.[33]

Sickness and disease continued to devastate the prisoners. A report submitted by A. M. Clark on March 1 showed a prison population of 7,260, of whom 1,555 were sick. There had been 331 deaths from all causes. However, Clark's report showed by numbers and percentages that smallpox was decreasing in virulence.[34]

The Guards

With the type of guards employed at Rock Island, it is remarkable that there were not more escapes. Probably, the smallpox killed or debilitated some of the more daring prisoners who might have tried it. The guards were "not properly instructed in guard duty or in the method of keeping their books...." In the spring of 1864, the garrison consisted of the 4th Regiment Veteran Reserve Corps and the 37th Iowa Volunteers. The 37th Iowa was described by Lt. Col. John F. Marsh of the 24th Regiment Veteran Reserve Corps after he made a routine inspection as "a regiment of decrepit old men and the most unpromising subjects for soldiers I ever saw." Not only did he find that the reports for March had not been finished, and Captain Reynolds, the quartermaster, "could not determine what balance was due the United States, but the "captain was somewhat intoxicated." It was this type of personnel who were charged with the care and guarding of 6,860 prisoners.[35]

Over the course of the next 20 months, the garrison at the prison would consist of the 4th Regiment, United States Veteran Reserve Corps; the 37th Iowa (Silver Grays), the 48th Iowa (100-day men), three companies of the 2nd Battalion; the 133rd Illinois (100-day men); 197th Pennsylvania Volunteers; and the 108th U.S. Regiment Colored Infantry, which arrived for duty on September 23, 1864.[36]

Join the Enemy to Escape

Some prisoners tried to get out by agreeing to take the oath of allegiance. They had written to Colonel Hoffman to express their desire to enter the United States

Navy. Hoffman, in turn, wrote the prison commandant, Colonel Johnson. Hoffman decided those prisoners were not to be released and he ordered that they "be treated with as much kindness as possible, while at the same time they must be held as prisoners." He advised Johnson to put them in a barracks by themselves, away from the other prisoners. In addition, whenever there were jobs to do, these men should be employed as laborers, "whether allowed compensation or not for it," if they wanted to work. Hoffman knew there would be repercussions against them, and he authorized Johnson to "punish severely any prisoner who threatens or insults them in any way for expressing a desire to return to their allegiance."[37]

Escapes and Escape Attempts

It was shortly after this that the commandant reported that 10 prisoners had escaped on the night of June 14, 1864, by tunneling under Barracks 42 (which had been used as a "variola ward" during an epidemic of that disease), "their egress being made directly under the parapet." The tunnel was made on the south side of the prison, the only side that did not have deep trenches to prevent such tunnels from being excavated. When the last two started out, they were discovered by a sentinel and he sounded the alarm. Immediately, Johnson had taken all necessary steps to recapture the escapees, and by the time he reported to Colonel Hoffman, seven had been recaptured. Three of the seven were found on the island, and four near the town of Rock Island. One drowned attempting to "cross the slough." The prison commandant sent out mounted patrols to track the remaining two and hoped to soon have them back in custody. Subsequently, a trench was dug on the south side of the prison compound down to the rock.[38]

Another escaped occurred while three prisoners were outside the compound working on the roof of a building. As they were returning to the camp, one of the prisoners remembered he had left his tools behind. He asked the guard to let him return for them. The guard permitted him to return. While the guard and the other two prisoners waited, the prisoner escaped.[39]

Thomas R. McCormick and three other prisoners, Fred Morgan, Joe Morgan, and Wesley Mayfield, planned to dig under the fence to escape. They selected a place where a new fence had just been built to separate 12 barracks from the rest. The new fence had no parapet and no sentinel. On the night of October 1, 1864, they approached the escape site. Joe Morgan volunteered to go forward and dig under the fence with a carving knife. He dug a hole and went out. The other three hid under a barracks and waited until the "lamp lighter" made his rounds. Fred Morgan then told them that Joe had been caught outside, and he heard the sentinel say, "The next one who comes we will bore him through." The three returned to their barracks and to bed. However, the report of Joe's capture had been false, and after some time, he returned to the barracks, woke the other three, and urged them to be ready to escape. It was about midnight, and after the four prisoners had said their goodbyes to their friends, they attempted to leave again. The sentinel walked back and forth, and their only chance was to wait until he turned his back to walk away. When he did, the prisoners crept across the deadline, 40 feet from the prison wall, by crawling flat along the ground. When the sentinel turned again to walk their way, they lay perfectly still in the darkness. They finally reached the hole under the fence, and went outside. Once outside, the four men planned to regroup and make their way together, but they had to separate.

Once McCormick was outside, he could not find the others. So, instead of waiting around to get caught, he made his way to the bayou. He undressed, tied his clothes to his back, and jumped into the water. In places, the bayou was not deep enough to swim, so he had to wade until he reached the opposite shore. When he emerged, he found himself in the suburbs of the town of Rock Island. He put his clothes on. Avoiding the roads, he headed south down the river. He concealed himself in the woods and bushes along the river, hoping to find a boat. Eventually, two men approached in a skiff and tied it up with a rope to a tree on the riverbank. McCormick took the oars from another boat that was chained to a rock to use in a boat he could untie. With oars in hand, in a stolen boat, he rowed silently down the river. After covering some distance, he pulled up to the bank to get some rest. McCormick was fortunate to evade capture and safely make his way home. It took him quite some time, but he finally arrived at his home on December 10, 1864. He approached his father with another man, and his father inquired, "Who is this you have with you?" McCormick replied, "Father, you do not seem to know me." McCormick had changed so much that his father did not recognize him.[40]

Prisoner Shot by Guards in Escape Attempt

Prisoner John P. McClanahan, of Barracks No. 8, was shot on the night of October 24, 1864. An investigation was launched by Colonel Johnson's Special Order No. 208. A military commission convened at the Rock Island prison the next day to hear testimony relative to the event. The prisoner had been shot by Peter Cowherd, a private in Company C, 108 Regiment, U.S. Colored Infantry. The officer of the day, Capt. Matthew H. Kollock, was asked what instructions were given the sentinels on the parapet at that time.

Kollock replied:

> The prison is arranged with a ditch surrounding it; also a row of stakes inside the ditch. My instructions were that if the prisoners passed beyond the line of stakes toward the ditch that they were to be warned back, but that if they deliberately crossed the ditch toward the fence that they should be shot and killed if possible. These instructions I imparted to my officers of the guard, and saw that they were imparted to the sergeants, corporals, and men comprising the guard.
>
> These instructions have been rigidly adhered to during the time we have been at this post, and this ditch is known and considered by both prisoners and guard as the dead-line.[41]

Cowherd, the guard who had killed the prisoner, testified that he had "no particular instructions." He said that the officer of the guard had asked him if he had been on duty before and Cowherd had replied that he had. When asked what were his instructions when he had been on duty before, Cowherd replied, "If I saw any one come across the ditch I was to halt them three times, and if they do not halt shoot them, and if they were across the ditch before I saw them to shoot without halting."

Cowherd further testified that when he first saw the prisoner, he was "lying by the end of the coal house. Then I went to the far end of my beat and turned around and missed him then, and I looked back and I saw him slipping across the ditch." The guard watched the prisoner who, undoubtedly, was attempting to escape. Cowherd continued, "when I got close enough to the man to be certain, I slipped off my shoes and crept right up over him and stepped right up on the rail and fired at him while he was scratching under the fence."[42]

Another guard, John Cowherd (a relation?), testified in support of Peter Cowherd's testimony. After hearing the testimony of three guards, the commission was of the opinion that Private Cowherd "acted only in accordance with the spirit of the instructions received by him while on duty as a sentinel on post No. 13," and they acquitted him of any blame or misconduct in the death of the prisoner. The commission determined that the guard was only doing his "duty as a good soldier and faithful sentinel."[43]

Charles Wright, a prisoner from January 1864 until June 1865, wrote in an article published in the Southern Historical Society Papers:

> 1864
>   April 17 — prisoner shot by sentinel
>   May 27 — one prisoner shot and killed one wounded in the leg
>   June 9 — Franks, of the 4th Alabama Cavalry, killed at Barracks No. 12, shot by sentinel on parapet. "His body fell into the barrack, and lay there until morning. The men afraid to go near him during the night."
>   June 22 — Bannister Cantrell, Co. G, 18th Georgia, and James W. Ricks, Co. F, 50th Georgia shot by sentinel from parapet. They were on detail working in the ditch and had stopped for a drink for fresh water which had just been brought to them.
>   June 26 — Prisoner shot in leg and arm while in his bunk at barrack.
>   September 26 — William Ford, Co. D, Wood's Missouri Battery, killed by sentinel on parapet. He was returning from the sink, and shot through the body at the rear of barrack 72.
>   September 26 — T. P. Robertson, Co. I, Twenty-fourth South Carolina, shot by sentinel on parapet and wounded in the back, while sitting in front of barrack 38, about 8 o'clock in the morning.
>   September 26 — T. J. Garrett, Co. K, Thirteenth Arkansas, shot by sentinel on parapet during the night while going to the sink.
>   September 27 — George R. Canthew, of barrack 28, shot by sentinel on parapet.
>   September 28 — Sentinel shot into barrack No. 12 through the window.
>   October 4 — Man killed in the frontier pen by negro sentinel.[44]

According to Charles Wright, who was there at the time, none of the men who were shot by the sentinels were attempting to escape or violating any of the known prison rules.

The Final Tally

In the overall scheme of prisons, some believed Rock Island to be the "Andersonville of the North," while others believed it offered more than the necessary comforts.[45]

Historians Abel and Gecik report that during the 19 months that Rock Island existed as a prison, 12,409 prisoners were confined there. Of those, 730 were transferred to other prisons, 3,876 were exchanged, and 1,960 died there. Forty-one prisoners escaped. A large number, 5,581, were released after taking the oath of allegiance, and of those who took the oath, about 4,000 enlisted in the Union forces. In addition, 213 civilians were held prisoner, of whom 197 were citizens prisoners from Missouri.[46]

Wright cites the provost marshal's abstract dated May 12, 1865:

Number of prisoners received	12,215
Died	1,945
Entered U.S. Navy	1,077
Entered U.S. Army	1,797 (frontier service)
Released	1,386
Transferred	72
Escaped	45
Exchanged	3,729
[Subtotal]	10,051
Remaining in prison May 12, 1865	2,164[47]

The difference in numbers of those received on Rock Island may be in the longer time frame of the first (12,409 vs. 12,215).

In June 1865, there were still 1,112 prisoners being held, but eight escaped, and 12 died. Of those, 12 were listed as citizens. By July 11, 1865, all the prisoners had been discharged, except two who were sick in the hospital, a force of about 40 guards and Colonel Johnson.[48]

Rock Island Today

Rock Island Prison ceased to exist in July 1865, after the end of the Civil War. A Federal arsenal was established on the island and buildings constructed. From that time until the present, the arsenal has made and assembled military equipment for the soldier in the field and in combat.[49]

There are two cemeteries on the island — the Confederate Cemetery, and the Rock Island National Cemetery. The Confederate Cemetery has the remains of 1,964 prisoners who died from 1863–1865 while in the prison on the island. Each has a marker with the name of the soldier, his company, and unit. The Rock Island National Cemetery was established in 1863 as the cemetery for Union guards. It covers 70 acres and now has approximately 24,000 grave markers, representing 29,000 burials.[50]

PART TWO

CONFEDERATE PRISONS

XVI

Camp Sumter, Andersonville, Georgia

Captain Wirz very domineering and abusive, is afraid to come into camp any more. A thousand men would willingly die if they could kill him first.
— Sgt. John L. Ransom, diary entry, May 10, 1864.[1]

Location: Andersonville, Georgia. **Established:** February 1864. **Type:** barren stockade. **Type of Prisoners:** mostly Union enlisted men, with some officers. **Capacity:** 10,000. **Most Held:** 32,899. **Known Number of Escapes:** 329.[2] **Nickname:** the "Southern Hades."[3]

History

In 1864, in order to relieve overcrowding at other prison sites, Camp Sumter at Andersonville, Georgia, was established. The camp was named for Fort Sumter, the first Confederate victory that began the war in April 1861.[4] It was in Sumter County, in southwestern Georgia,[5] which may also account for the name.

The location was chosen by Capt. W. Sidney Winder, son of Gen. John A. Winder. The plan was to build enough barracks at the new site to house 8,000–10,000 prisoners.[6]

The Site

The ground selected was on the side of a hill, part of it being in a marsh.[7]

At first, the site appeared ideal. It was close to a railroad, near an abundant supply of food, with a stream bordered by thick forests of pine and oak. However, problems were encountered in building the barracks, and eventually only a stockade was constructed. This was the cheapest form of prison, and the worst kind for the prisoners since it afforded no shelter from the elements of heat and cold, and forced them to fend for themselves as best they could. The stockade had a high wall of logs which enclosed an area of 16½ acres.[8] The hills were stripped of their timber to construct the stockade. The stockade was enlarged to cover about 27 acres, although several acres were swamp.[9] Additional security was provided by an outer wall around the stockade. A third wall was started, but never finished.[10]

Andersonville Prison tents in which prisoners existed. (Library of Congress, LC-USZ62-122695.)

It was a mean-looking stockade, about 17 feet high, the post being sunk into the ground some four or five feet. One prisoner described the prison as a "pen about two hundred yards long, and one hundred wide ...."[11]

Commandant Henry Wirz reported that although a large addition had been made to the stockade, the prison was still too crowded, and that "almost daily large numbers of prisoners arrive, and before two weeks it will be in the same condition it was before the addition was made...."[12]

The little branch, Sweet Water Creek, was initially pure, and the site was adequate for the number of inmates as planned.[13] Soon, as prisoner Ferguson related, the water in the stream was unfit for drinking or cooking because the "garbage, offal, refuse and dirt from the whole prison passed into the stream that supplied all with water."[14]

The Prisoners

The first prisoners arrived at Andersonville on February 25, 1864, even before all the stockade walls were completed.[15] On the day the prisoners were to arrive, Capt. R. B. Winder still had not received the 10,000 pounds of bacon he had ordered. Winder hoped to make arrangements to feed the prisoners on beef, if it could be obtained from Florida, and he believed he could obtain the needed corn meal locally.[16] Almost from the first, the huge numbers of prisoners presented insurmountable problems in providing them with food, water, shelter, and medical attention.

Because prison officials feared that the prisoners would break out, when those Federal soldiers arrived who had been captured in the fighting at Plymouth, North Carolina, on April 20, 1864, the officers were separated from the enlisted men. The enlisted men were ushered into the stockade, but Captain Wirz argued with the guards who had brought the new prisoners that he had no facilities for officers and they would have to be quartered elsewhere. The officers spent the night in a nearby church, and the next morning they were taken to Macon, Georgia.[17]

Lt. Alonzo Cooper, of the 12th New York Cavalry, was one of those captured by Confederate General Hoke's troops at the battle of Plymouth, North Carolina. He was transported to Andersonville. Upon arrival, he and the other officers were separated from the enlisted men. They were escorted, according to Cooper, to a small church where they remained overnight. The next day, they were put on railroad cars and sent to Macon, Georgia.[18]

Those same officers or other officers may have been quartered in smaller stockade, a half mile west of the main prison, was called Castle Reed. It was a pen with logs 15 feet high, surrounding an area 195 feet by 108. Within was an open-sided shed. Sixty-five Union officers were held there until May 1864, when they were transferred to Macon, Georgia. Afterward, the smaller prison was used only to hold Confederate soldiers who had committed various crimes and offenses.[19]

Captain Wirz's report for the month of June 1864 noted that on the first of June the camp held 18,454 prisoners (1,039 of them in the hospital). During the month, he received 9,143 more, for a total of 27,641, which included 44 prisoners who had been recaptured. Of that number, 1,203 died, 47 escaped, and 23 were sent to various other places, leaving a balance of 26,367 prisoners on July 2, 1864.[20]

The numbers of prisoners sent to Andersonville continued to increase at an alarming rate. By August 1864, there were 32,899. The available space per man was less than 36 square feet.[21]

Prison Personnel

The camp had a number of commanders. The first, Col. A. W. Persons, ordered a few barracks constructed for a hospital, but building materials were scarce.[22]

Capt. Henry Wirz, a native of Switzerland, was ordered to go to Andersonville and was soon placed in command. Whatever efforts Wirz and Winder made to improve conditions at the prison were thwarted by the increasing number of prisoners and the dwindling amount of food and other needed supplies. The lack of a proper diet, overcrowding, and filth brought disease and death to thousands.[23] Wirz reported on August 1, 1864, that they had an "inadequate supply of tools to put the interior of the prison in proper condition: we need axes, wheelbarrows, and such things; we need lumber, lime, iron, sheet-iron for baking pans."[24]

Wirz complained that the guards, with the exception of part of the 55th Georgia, were "undrilled and undisciplined" militiamen.[25]

The guards fared little better than the prisoners, being issued only a third of a pound of bacon, 1¼ pound of corn meal, or one pound of fresh beef in place of bacon. They occasionally received beans, molasses, and rice. However, vinegar and soap, "both very important articles" were seldom issued because the commissary could not obtain them.[26]

On June 17, 1864, Gen. John H. Winder arrived to take command of Camp Sumter and also the camp at Macon, while he was still in charge of the prisons in Virginia.

Winder, a West Point graduate, resigned and accepted a brigadier generals' commission in the service of the Confederacy. He was assigned as provost marshal and prison commandant in Richmond, and was in charge of internal security at Richmond. Winder took his duties seriously, but was often criticized. He was placed in charge of Andersonville and of all prison facilities in both Alabama and Georgia. In November 1864, he became commissary general of all prisons east of the Mississippi.[27]

By the time Winder arrived at Andersonville, there were 22,300 prisoners, most of whom were already in a weakened condition from months of imprisonment at Belle Isle and other prisons.[28r] Immediately, Winder saw the danger inherent in having too many prisoners and too few guards. The 1,205-man force of the Georgia Reserves had been detailed to guard the prisoners. These guards were "with the measles prevailing, badly armed and worse disciplined, to guard them." Winder feared that if the 25,000 prisoners were to make a successful massive prison break, the surrounding country would be devastated. "Every house would be burned, violence to women, destruction of crops, carrying off negroes, horses, mules, and wagons. It is impossible to estimate the extent of such a disaster." Winder recommended that another prison be established immediately, and that no more prisoners be sent to Andersonville. He saw that the "force is becoming too ponderous, and ... it is not possible with my present means to extend the post fast enough to meet the demands."[29]

By August, Winder had gained a reputation as being "a regular brute." When told the Yankees prisoners at Andersonville were dying at the rate of 100 a day, he is rumored to have replied, "God damn them, let them die. They don't die half fast enough; that's just what we want." Whether this was true or not, that statement made its way into the *Official Records of the War of the Rebellion*.[30]

Further details about the horrors of life inside the stockade at Andersonville will serve no purpose. The men lived in a filthy pigpen, and slowly starved to death on the meager rations, or succumbed to the ravages of disease.

Many southerners were not aware of the true conditions at the Andersonville prison. Miss Eliza Frances Andrews, a young lady of Washington, Wilkes County, Georgia, had heard some rumors. She recorded in her diary that Andersonville was rumored to have improved somewhat with colder weather. Miss Andrews heard other reports from Mrs. Brisbane, who had it from Father Hamilton, a Roman Catholic priest from Macon. Father Hamilton had been working with the prisoners. He told Mrs. Brisbane that "during the summer the wretched prisoners burrowed in the ground like moles to protect themselves from the sun. It was not safe to give them material to build shanties as they might use it for clubs to overcome the guard. These underground huts ... were alive with vermin and stank like charnel houses. Many of the prisoners were stark naked, having not so much as a shirt to their backs." According to Father Hamilton, prisoners were dying at the rate of "150 a day. Dysentery was the most fatal disease."[31] The ladies were not sure whether to believe him but, after all, he was a *priest*.

Escapes

Some prisoners could not endure the conditions inside the stockade at Andersonville. J. Nelson Clarke witnessed one prisoner who went insane and committed suicide. Another ended his life by hanging himself.[32] Others chose to escape.

Sometimes, escape attempts were numerous, but most prisoners soon were recaptured. Captain Wirz reported in June 1864 that he had "recaptured" 44 escaped prisoners.[33]

Martin E. Hogan recalled that one prisoner escaped, but was tracked down by the hounds. Another prisoner attempted to escape on October 8, 1864, and for his efforts he was fastened by the "neck and feet, and remained there sixty-eight hours." Per Captain Wirz's orders, the confined man was to receive no food. However, some paroled prisoners managed to slip some food to him.[34]

Sgt. Eugene Forbes enlisted in Company B, 4th New Jersey Infantry. The New Jersey man was 5 feet 7 inches tall, with blue eyes, light hair, and fair complexion. Captured at the Battle of the Wilderness on May 6, 1864, Forbes kept a daily diary during his imprisonment at Camp Sumter, Andersonville, Georgia.[35]

Although he died at Andersonville, a friend who survived carried Forbes' diary back to Forbes' former employers who published it in 1865. On May 27, 1864, shortly after his arrival at Andersonville, Forbes wrote in his diary that one tunnel was discovered and several more were suspected. The next day, three tunnels were found by the Confederate guards. One of them extended beyond the stockade.[36] A few days later, he reported that some of the prisoners had escaped, and that the dogs had been sent to track them. He also noted that inside the stockade there were 21,000 prisoners, and an average of 60 died each day. On June 4, he noted that the prisoners who had escaped a few days earlier had been recaptured. They all now wore balls and chains, as did about 100 others.[37]

Brigadier General Winder reported on June 24, 1864, that two tunnels had been discovered which reached the outside. One of the tunnels was 130 feet in length.[38]

A handsome, well-educated young man, Sgt. James E. Gillespie, of the First Kentucky Cavalry, was captured on October 20, 1863, along with his brother, John A. Gillespie, and some of Wolford's men. They were taken first to Atlanta, then moved to Belle Isle where they spent the winter months. The brothers were finally moved to Libby Prison where they were separated and James E. Gillespie was sent to Andersonville. In Andersonville, James made friends with an Englishman, and the pair tunneled under the walls of the stockade and escaped. They had not gone very far, however, when they were overtaken and captured.[39]

After their return to the stockade, the escapees were fitted with balls and chains. The Englishman, a blacksmith by trade, managed to get a small file. Gillespie managed to get a Minie ball from a soldier, and at night, the pair filed the rivets from their shackles and replaced them with leaden ones made from the Minie ball. During the day, they wore their shackles, but at night they took the heavy chains off. Gillespie was put to work on the "chain gang." Crafty as he was, he soon won enough money by throwing dice to buy some cotton sacking. He used the material to have a comrade make him a "Rebel suit of clothes with the Sergeant's stripes sewed upon the sleeves of his coat." With this uniform, Gillespie managed to get a "memorandum-book" similar to those used by the guards for morning roll call. With book in hand, he approached the guard at the gate, and limping to simulate lameness, asked to be let out. He was permitted to pass without through the gate. Once outside, Gillespie waited until night, then he started for Union lines.[40]

Gillespie had almost succeeded in reaching Union lines when he was recaptured and taken back to Andersonville. Captain Wirz happened to be in a good mood that day. He asked him, "Gillespie, why don't you stay in prison?"

The would-be escapee replied, "You can't blame a man for not wanting to stay in a place full of lice, filth, and impure air, can you?"

Wirz responded, "I don't blame you for trying to get away, but I blame you for getting caught."

Later, Wirz asked Gillespie if he would promise not to try to escape, he would parole him, and let him exercise outside the stockade walls. He also tried to get Gillespie to take charge of a work force of negroes, but the young cavalry officer refused. This refusal so exasperated Wirz that he threatened to have Gillespie shot.[41]

It was not long before Wirz was informed that Gillespie and his English friend were planning to steal two horses (one of them belonging to Wirz) and escape again. This angered the little captain and he put Gillespie in chains and sent him to the jail in Macon. He gave strict orders that if the guards even suspected Gillespie was trying to escape, to shoot him on the spot. This did nothing to stop the daring cavalry officer (see Chapter XXV).[42]

Prisoners Organize to Escape

James Wolfe, of the 89th Ohio Volunteer Infantry, recalled that during the month of August 1864, "an organization of eight thousand men was formed for the purpose of trying to affect their escape. They tunneled out to the line of pickets which they undermined for some distance. By rushing against them, they would fall and allow them to pass over at a point nearest to the Artillery, which they intended to capture and turn on the rebels ... ." However, the night before the plan was to be put in motion, the tunnel was discovered. When daylight came, the Confederate guards were ready and were "on their arms in line of battle all round the stockade." Wolfe wrote about other tunnels being dug on a smaller scale. But, when a prisoner did escape, the bloodhounds soon picked up his scent and he was caught. He was then either brought back to the stockade or "shot on the spot."[43]

During an archaeological examination of the grounds of Camp Sumter in 1990, an escape tunnel was found. It was small, about 35 inches at its widest, and only just big enough for a man to crawl through. The tunnel was discovered along the southern stockade wall. This site was apparently chosen because of the soft, sandy soil. Unfortunately, the same soil that was easily dug, was the reason the escape failed. The tunnel had been dug just deep enough to clear the bottom of the posts sunk for the stockade walls, but several of the posts had collapsed into the tunnel before it could be extended more than a meter past the stockade line.[44]

Many of the prisoners escaped when allowed to go outside the stockade to gather firewood. To curb that tendency, an order was issued that none would be allowed out without first giving a pledge not to escape. If, after pledging, the men escaped, the mess (group they ate with) they belonged to would receive rations only every other day until the prisoner was recaptured.[45] This did not seem to stop escape attempts, however. Forbes reported, on June 14, that after the order was issued, two men escaped from the wood squad. That night, 14 had tunneled out, and seven guards left with them.[46]

On June 17, 1864, several men out with the wood-gathering squads, overpowered their guards, took their guns, and escaped. General Winder decreed no more men would be allowed outside for wood.[47]

In a report for June 1864, according to Captain Wirz:

> It is proper to state that all those who made their escape during the month ran off from the guard while they were getting wood, &., on the outside; in fact, only one prisoner has got out of the stockade through a tunnel since the 1st day of April. The number missing up to date is 19.[48]

On July 15, Forbes recorded that several tunnels had been discovered and filled up. The next day, several more tunnels were discovered, one of which "undermined" four yards of the stockade wall. Prisoners took their revenge on the traitor who had informed about the tunnel. They shaved half his head and branded him with a "T" for traitor on his forehead.[49]

On July 20, 1864, another tunnel was dug by the prisoners, and several men escaped until daylight when a guard discovered it and sounded the alarm. At the entrance to another tunnel, a large group congregated in hopes of getting out. This crowd drew the attention of the guards. However, a few did escape only to be recaptured by the next night.[50]

Wirz reported in August that the prisoners used a variety of ways and means to escape. He had discovered and filled up 83 tunnels, "some 20 feet under ground," varying in length from 10 to 140 feet." Still, after all that effort, only one prisoner had escaped through a tunnel. All the others had escaped while being outside at work."[51]

Sgt. Maj. John McElroy was born in Kentucky, and eventually moved to Chicago. He enlisted in Company L of the 16th Illinois Cavalry in March 1863. McElroy was captured in western Virginia near the Cumberland Gap on January 3, 1864. Initially confined at Libby Prison, he and many others were shipped south to Andersonville on February 17, 1864. He survived the war, and became an editorial writer for the Chicago *Inter Ocean*, and later the editor of the Toledo *Blade*. It was while in this position that he began writing his war memoirs.[52]

McElroy and a boy about his own age, Frank Harney, decided to escape. In his memoirs, McElroy recalled that the two of them had been watching the moon and knew that there would soon be a moonless night. The weather was intolerably hot. The hounds were in their kennels, the guards were either "half or wholly drunken with villainous sorghum whiskey," and the 30,000 prisoners inside the barren stockade were lying "prone or supine upon the glowing sand, gasp[ing] for breath — for one draft of sweet, cool wholesome air that did not bear on its wings the subtle seeds of rank corruption and death." Harney and McElroy waited patiently for the sun to go down. As night fell, the master of the hounds brought out the dogs and began making his rounds. They knew the time had come, and they grabbed a little piece of corn bread, wrapped in a dirty rag, which had been saved from supper, and went over their plan. They were to stay in the little creek until it joined the Flint River. They drew twigs to see who went first, the one getting the longest was the first.[53]

The two young men crept silently toward the creek. The guard was not pacing as usual, but was leaning against a tree resting. They reached the creek and slid into the filthy water. Swimming in the creek, the two passed under the stockade fence. They made their way down the creek bed, and stumbled along in the dark with sore feet. They had to remain in the creek to avoid being tracked by the hounds. Others had tried to escape, but the hounds picked up the sent and resumed the chase when the prisoners left the safety of the water.[54]

Finally, they believed they had gone far enough to chance getting out on the bank, and they did so. They ran for about two miles along the creek bank. They could hear that the hounds were very near. Suddenly, the baying hounds were upon them. They ran back to the swampy creek, but the guard, mounted on a mule, soon found them and demanded they come back to the bank. The guard herded the two would-be escapees back to the hospital, and the next morning they were put back in the stockade with the rest of the miserable prisoners. Luckily, Captain Wirz was on sick leave, and the boys did not have to face him. Wirz was hard on recaptured prisoners.[55]

Other Means of Escape

When the Confederates offered escape from prison to those Federal soldiers who would take the oath of allegiance, many at Andersonville and in the Florence pen accepted out of desperation. It was reported that beginning in September 1864, 800 took the oath at Florence and at least that many at Andersonville. These "galvanized Rebels" only took the oath under the condition that they would not be required to fight against the Federal forces. Those who did take the oath were placed in different quarters and were given additional rations when possible.[56]

Overcrowding, exposure to the elements, poor sanitation, inadequate food and polluted water all contributed to exceedingly high rates of morbidity and mortality at Andersonville.

Andersonville Today

The area that once held thousands of Federal prisoner is now a national park and is open to the public. The national cemetery there has 13,737 graves, of which 1,040 are unmarked.[57] Estimates of the actual deaths are much higher.[58] When Union General Sherman invaded Georgia, all those prisoners who could still walk were transported to Charleston, South Carolina, so any of this group who died would not have been buried at Andersonville.[59]

XVII

Belle Isle, James River, Richmond, Virginia

Rations, escape, and exchange were the absorbing topics of discussion during the long, weary, cold winter nights of November and December, 1863, and January and February, 1864.
— James E. King, Company A, 1st Kentucky Cavalry.[1]

Location: an island in the James River, Richmond, Virginia. **Established:** 1862. **Type:** barren stockade. **Type of Prisoners:** prisoners of war, enlisted men. **Capacity:** 3,000. **Most Held at One Time:** 10,000[2] (10,500 on October 23, 1863[3]). **Known Number of Escapes:** ?

History

Belle Isle is an 80-acre island about a mile long and ¼ mile wide situated near the fall line in the James River.[4] The island was once an encampment site for the Powhattan Indians.[5]

Belle Isle means *Beautiful Island*, and it once was. However, by the time one prisoner arrived there after being captured at Gettysburg in 1863, he did not think the island so beautiful, but described it as "a miserable, hot place, an acre of ground, about 4,000 men in it, and full of lice and vermin."[6]

During the war, Belle Isle was used as a prison for Union soldiers. In the summer of 1862, after fighting near Richmond in the Seven Days' Battles of June 25–July 1, Confederate authorities contemplated moving all the Federal prisoners from the tobacco warehouses in Richmond to Belle Isle. The island would be suitable for a prison, and the "temptation to escape [by the prisoners] would not be enhanced by the change in position, while fewer men would serve as a guard," noted the Richmond *Daily Dispatch*.[7]

Thus, Belle Isle was occupied by prisoners until the end of the war, except for a brief period in September 1862, when all the prisoners were moved from the camp.[8]

Compared to those prisons that had been tobacco warehouses and other buildings, Belle Island was a paradise.[9]

The Site

The waters of the James River which surrounded Belle Isle were deep.[10] The terrain of the island rises 100 feet about the water from sandy beaches. Belle Isle had been used since 1815 to support an iron ore company. A village had grown up for the workers. A bridge linked the island on its south side to the Manchester District where the Richmond and Danville Railroad Depot was located.[11] The island could also be reached by boat from near the Tredgar Foundry, but few people were allowed access, other than those with official business.[12] Access to the island was allowed during the day over a walkway from the Manchester side of the James River. This 20-foot wide walkway was bordered by an 8-foot high fence. A gate at the prison end was bolted each night.[13]

Belle Isle did have some advantages as a prison over Libby Prison, however. There was an abundance of fresh air and sunshine, and water. However, being outside in the open, the prisoners had no protection from the bitter winds or the snow and rain.[14]

The Facilities

Facilities for prisoners were minimal. On the 15 acres of lowland, four or five acres had been set aside for the prison compound. Its boundary was marked by a ditch 3 feet wide and 8 feet deep, which served as the deadline. Earthworks were thrown up around the compound and guards were stationed every 40 feet. Inside the compound there were 60 streets lined with rows of Sibley tents. Prisoners were assigned to squads of 50 and the squads assigned to a specific row. Quarters for officers and guards, the hospital, and cook house were located outside the perimeter of the compound. The graveyard was placed near the hospital.[15]

Setting Up the Camp

Volunteers were enlisted from among the prisoners being held at Libby Prison to help set up the tents on Belle Isle in preparation for the arrival of the first prisoners who would be transferred there from other prisons. Early in July 1862, George W. Kremer, Company F, 11th Pennsylvania, from Uniontown, Pennsylvania, volunteered to help when a Confederate officer asked for some "Yanks" to go to Belle Isle. Kremer had been captured at Gaines Mill on June 27, 1862, and was eager to get outside the prison. Once sufficient volunteers were obtained, they were marched down Cary Street to join another squad of prisoners. These 100 men were given extra rations for the work — a small baker's loaf of bread. Kremer helped erect one Sibley tent, but the second one they tried to put up was too rotten.[16]

Tents were to provide protection from the summer heat. Pure water was available from numerous wells and, with permission, prisoners were allowed to bathe in the river.[17]

One prisoner who was brought over to help distribute food and clothing from Libby Prison on January 1, 1865, described his first impression of Belle Isle:

> Lines of tattered tents, holes dug into the wet sand and covered with roofs of raged canvas, shelters of earth and barrel staves, in which the prisoner crouched together from the cold, and where death kept his headquarters, and yet so crowded was the

island that only the fortunate ones had this protection, and many had to sleep out of doors.[18]

A building on the southern end of the island had been a foundry, and a few houses occupied the northern end. In between were the tents for about 3,000 prisoners, enclosed by an earthwork, a wide ditch, and guarded constantly by sentries.[19]

The Prisoners

In July 1862, some of the prisoners who had been confined at Libby Prison were removed to Belle Isle, which was, at the time, "a very pleasant spot." The Richmond papers noted that the friends of prisoners held on Belle Isle "may be perfectly satisfied that they will pass a pleasant summer at Richmond."[20]

One of those first prisoners was Pvt. J. J. Sneath, of Company I, 12th Pennsylvania Reserves. He was captured in the Seven Days Battles before Richmond that took place June 25 through July 1, 1862. In a letter to his mother, Sneath told of being captured and taken to Gaines Mill, then to Richmond. He did not receive any food until Sunday, when he received 5 ounces of "hard bread, without salt." He stayed 15 days in a prison in Richmond, before being moved to Belle Isle. At that time, there were over 4,000 prisoners on the island.[21]

The arrival of the new year also brought a large group of Yankees who had been captured after the fighting at Fredericksburg in December 1862. Tents were put up to house them, and plans called for constructing huts later, "if the timber can be procured."[22]

Another prisoner who lived to record his experiences was James E. King of Company A, First Kentucky Cavalry, captured at Philadelphia, Tennessee, on October 20, 1863. He was sent to Atlanta, Georgia, then Columbia, South Carolina, and then to Charlotte, North Carolina. From there, he was sent on a slow-moving train by Weldon to Petersburg, thence to Richmond. The officers in his group were sent to Libby Prison. He and other non-commissioned officers were taken to the Pemberton Building (Castle Thunder), before being sent to Belle Isle.[23]

Female Soldier Discovered

W. W. Sprague wrote in his diary on December 9, 1863, that a young woman named Mary Jane Johnson had been discovered in the camp. The 16-year-old female had been in the Union Army for a year, as a member of the 11th Kentucky Cavalry, because she had no parents to care for her. Once her sex was discovered, she was removed from Belle Isle, to be transported north.[24]

Smoked Yankees

There were a few blacks among the prisoners on Belle Isle. The Confederates called them "smoked Yankees." Many blacks joined the Union Army, and many had been captured. One of the reasons the Dix-Hill cartel was suspended was because the South would not exchange black soldiers, but insisted on returning them to their former masters. This did not make the "smoked Yankees" very popular with the prisoners on the island, who believed the exchange process had been halted on their account.[25]

Compared to the prisoners in Libby who were "bleached for the want of sunlight," a visiting prisoner noted that the faces of the prisoners on Belle Isle "were an ashy brown, and so lean and gaunt, so big-eyed and hollow cheeked...."[26]

Daily Life of the Prisoners

During the day inmates were allowed to use the walkway to reach the river, to bathe, wash clothes, and take care of other personal needs.[27] This was permitted because the high bluff of the river bank provided an excellent place for the placement of guards and artillery, which was aimed at Belle Isle. [28]

A Richmond paper reported that in the summer of 1862, the prisoners on Belle Isle seemed to be making the best of a bad situation, and attempting to enjoy themselves "in the best fashion possible. Most were quartered in tents, and between the tents, wells had been dug, either for better water or to bathe in. The prisoners were allowed to go by the dozen to the river.[29]

During the summer months, the prisoners enjoyed a pleasant life and greater freedom than those in regular prison facilities. They were content to await exchange. However, when that was stopped, the prisoners had to cope with being held longer than they anticipated. With winter approaching, survival on the island became the prime concern.

By September 1862, there were 5,000 Union soldiers confined on Belle Isle. Arrangements were made to send 2,000 to Varina for exchange. Those who had been prisoners the longest would be the first to be exchanged.[30] After the departure of some of the Yankee prisoners, the island underwent "fumigation for purification purposes." Tents were taken down and the space underneath cleaned. The removal of some of the tents revealed a number of good wells that had been dug by the prisoners. Good water was obtained in some with the use of a windlass, and a cup, tied to a string.[31]

Even the next year, in the spring of 1863, the papers reported that the prisoners on Belle Isle were "no doubt better satisfied than they would be if placed in houses, as they have good tents, plenty of water, and a large space to ramble about."

Prisoners Suffer from Cold Weather

A large number of prisoners arrived in January 1863.[32] Most of the prisoners who arrived in the first part of the very cold winter of 1863-1864 had no shelter. The James River froze over. To find shelter, former prisoner James E. King recalled, prisoners dug holes into the sand and "burred in them like wild animals." Those with tents fared little better.[33] The city of Richmond loomed to the north and east, and the glow from the chimneys of the Tredgar Iron Works looked warm and cheerful while the ragged, freezing, starving prisoners crowded on the frozen sands during the winter of 1863-1864, one of the coldest winters in recent history.[34]

During the winter months of 1863, Belle Isle had 3,000 prisoners living in tents.

Those tents did little to protect them from the elements. A plan was developed to build a permanent shelter to house up to 20,000, but this building never materialized, and the prisoners were forced to sleep on the cold ground. Many were even without blankets. Confederate officials distributed more tents, but many were tattered and torn. Prisoners were given straw and boards to sleep on, but they used the lumber for fuel for fires.[35]

Prisoners tried every means available to keep warm and survive. Some huddled 2 or 3 inside little "pup" tents made of a blanket held up by two stakes, and fastened to the ground with rocks or small pegs. Others burrowed in the ground with mounds of dirt thrown over boards. Some even lined their burrows with wood.[36]

Col. W. P. Kendrick, of the Third West Tennessee Cavalry, a Federal officer who had escaped from Libby Prison in Richmond, wrote to President Lincoln about the conditions of those remaining on Belle Isle. He reported that, although the treatment of the officers at Libby could be "tolerated," the enlisted men on Belle Isle were "treated brutally, cruelly." He told the president that many had frozen to death over the winter months, and even more had died from starvation. Kendrick told the president that 20 per day were dying from the cold and hunger, and if they remained confined into the spring and summer, he believed that more than half would "never be fit for duty." He pleaded with President Lincoln to do something for "these brave fellows."[37]

Smallpox and Other Diseases

Confederate officials were aware of the terrible conditions on Belle Isle, but could do little to improve the situation. William A. Carrington, medical director, inspected the prison camp and submitted a report in November 1863 to Gen. John H. Winder, who was in charge of the prisons:

> The camp at Belle Isle is as well managed as possible under the circumstances but I think that here may be found most of the causes of the severity and frequency of the sickness. The men are too much crowded. They have not sufficient quantity of blankets nor sufficient fuel supplies. They sleep on the ground and are exposed to all the vicissitudes of temperature incident to our climate, increased by the position and the winds blowing over the water…. Another class of causes is the depressing moral influence prisoners labor under, especially noticeable since they have been told there is no hope of exchange. They die from slight disease, having lost all hope.[38]

The medical director strongly advised that the prisoners be removed from Belle Isle and sent to facilities with buildings, such as Richmond, Lynchburg, Farmville, or Danville, or that they be sent to a warmer climate.[39] Those in the medical profession continued to inspect Belle Isle and continued to submit reports as to the crowded, filthy conditions in which the prisoners were confined, which led to disease — typhoid fever, diarrhea, dysentery, and disease of the respiratory system.[40]

After smallpox broke out on Belle Isle in December 1863, Union Gen. Benjamin F. "Beast" Butler sent enough vaccine to inoculate the prisoners. This helped prevent the spread of the disease and Robert Ould, Confederate exchange agent, sent Butler a letter thanking him.[41]

The condition of the prisoners was noted by Federal officials. Chaplain H. C. Trumbull, of the 10th Connecticut Volunteers, reported to Colonel Hoffman, in charge of prisoners in the north, of the terrible conditions, the number of men dying from starvation, and the lack of shelter.[42] Articles appeared in northern newspapers, such as the *New York Times*.[43]

When Walt Whitman, the poet, saw some of the prisoners from Belle Isle, he said in disbelief: "Can those be men? Those little livid, brown, ash streaked, monkey-looking dwarves? Are they not really mummified, dwindled corpses?"[44]

A decision was made to remove the prisoners on Belle Isle to further south. A Richmond paper noted that they were to be moved by rail to a little place between Oglethorpe and Americus, Georgia, called Andersonville.[45] The prisoners did not know it, but they were moving from the "frying pan into the fire."

By the fall of 1864, conditions were so bad inside the Confederacy and the necessities of life so scarce, that although orders were issued to the assistant quartermaster to provide shelter and blankets for the prisoners, the requisition could not be filled. The best that could be done was to send 600 of the prisoners away to Danville where they were housed in buildings.[46]

A popular song shows how the prisoners felt about their prison.

Belle Isle
Here in Belle Isle's rebel prison,
Pining through the live long day,
I'm dreaming, sad and lonely
Of the dear ones far away;
Comrades brave are sinking round me,
I like them may droop and die,
But though Tyrant-chains have bound me,
UNION! Still shall be my cry.
    Words by John Ross Dix,
    Sung to tune of "Just Before the Battle Mother"

Prison Personnel

Capt. Norris Montgomery was in charge of the prison on Belle Isle in the summer of 1862, at which time Henry Wirz was assigned to command the Confederate States Military Prison in Richmond.[47] Wirz, a native of Switzerland, had been trained in medicine in Berlin and Paris. He was tall and slender, with an aquiline nose, black hair, and a moustache. He spoke several languages. Wirz fought with the 4th Battalion of Louisiana Volunteers and his right arm was shattered at Seven Pines. While recovering, he met General Winder, and was persuaded to join his provost marshal force.[48]

Wirz tried without success to solve the many problems that confronted him. While Wirz was in command, security was tight. He changed the "countersign" each evening.[49] To relieve the overcrowding on Belle Isle, he ordered Captain Montgomery to enlarge the compound and extend the fence.[50] Wirz would later gain notoriety for his role as commandant at the Andersonville Prison in Georgia (see Chapter

XVI). There, he would see many of his old prisoners from Belle Isle. After the war, Wirz would be executed for his "crimes."

At some point, Lt. Virginius Bossieux was commandant of Belle Isle. A native of France, this officer and his brother Cyrus (who served at Castle Thunder), were more like Creoles than Virginians. Some thought Virginius brought a "compassionate attitude to his position," and tried to improve the situation of those in his care.[51] John W. Manning, of Salineville, Ohio, was a prisoner on Belle Isle for eight months after he was captured in September 1863. He recalled that Lieutenant Bossieux was in charge of the prisoners.[52]

Former prisoner H. J. Peter complained in a letter to the editor of the Toledo *Blade* about one of the guards, the "red-headed rebel Sergeant Hight, who had so unmercifully wielded his cudgel upon the heads and backs of feeble and sickly prisoners."[53] Hight (also spelled Hite) always carried a big hickory cane, to which was attached a heavy iron ring.[54]

Another guard was a one-eyed sergeant named "Marks." B. F. Jones, of Company B, 1st West Virginia Cavalry, remembered seeing Marks club sick men.[55]

One prisoner, W. S. Toland, described the lieutenant in charge as a "humane man, but he allowed a cruel and brutal subordinate to tyrannize over and persecute the unfortunate prisoners. However, Toland said that for the most part the guards were not cruel, but sometimes they would "shoot them [prisoners] down without provocation."[56]

The routine of the guards during the fall and winter months of 1863, was described by Pvt. Roland E. Bowen. At about 10 A.M. each day, a new group of 112 guards arrived from the city. At times they came in boats, and other times by the railroad bridge. The guards were divided into three groups and each stood guard for two hours before being relieved. The 36 relief guards were posted about 35 feet apart on the bank outside the fence. It was "not an easy matter to run the guard," said Bowen, but there was a "great traffic" carried on between the guards, who smuggled every item imaginable in to sell to the prisoners.[57]

There was always a sufficient number of guards to prevent their escape.[58] However, in the fall of 1864, when 1,800 new prisoners arrived within a 24-hour period, additional guards were definitely needed. Brig. Gen. William M. Gardner, who had been almost fatally wounded at First Manassas, recovered and was given command of all prisons east of the Mississippi, except Georgia and Alabama.[59] Gardner complained that, because of recent regulations, none could be assigned to the Invalid Corps but those who were permanently disabled. The Invalid Corps plus 250 additional men were badly needed for guard duty on Belle Isle.[60]

By the fall of 1864, the guards on the island were convalescent soldiers and officers from the various hospitals in Richmond. On September 24, 1864, 327 men and nine commissioned officers were stationed to guard about 6,000 prisoners.[61]

Food

Pvt. John J. Sneath (Company I, 12th Pennsylvania Reserves) wrote that many of the men had died from "want of food," and the dead were left unburied for three days in the hot sun. Sneath was lucky, and was exchanged after only 40 days of imprisonment.[62]

King and his fellow soldiers arrived at a time when the island was not very crowded, and they managed to get a tent. A sergeant was elected for each 20 prisoners whose duty was to draw the rations for his squad. According to King, those rations consisted of a small piece of bread, a water bucket two-thirds full of soup, and a small piece of beef to feed 20 men. Actually, the amount of food given was only enough for one man. Even though the men expected a little something extra on Christmas, the fare remained the same.[63]

Joseph Arnold, of the 28th Wisconsin, was captured along with Captain Domschecke and others at Gettysburg. The men were marched 175 miles to Staunton, Virginia, with meager rations to sustain them. Once he arrived on Belle Isle, he asked when they would receive any rations. A guard replied that they would get them in the morning. The men lay down on the ground both tired and hungry.[64]

When Arnold first arrived at Belle Isle, the prisoners were given 3 ounces of bread and 1 ounce of beef in the morning. In the afternoon, they were given another 3 ounces of bread and a half pint of soup. However, as the number of prisoners increased, by the end of August 1863, the quantity of meat began to diminish, and they were given cornmeal only every other day.[65]

The increase of prisoners on Belle Isle and other facilities in Richmond put a strain on the economy. By the fall of 1863, there were nearly 9,000 prisoners. General Winder was quoted in a Richmond paper as being of the opinion that the city would have to "entertain fourteen or fifteen thousand of the 'azure-stomached' [blue-bellies, a nickname for Yankees] race this winter. Because of the sheer amount of food required for that number, the paper compared Richmond to Egypt being devoured by the locust.[66]

What Became of the Man Who Killed the Dog?

The reports of the killing of Lieutenant Bossieux's dog are numerous and controversial.

The dog itself is described as a "fat little dog," "a fine pointer," one of "two bull-dogs," and a "fat, white bull terrier." Perhaps there was more than one dog involved.

James E. King recalled that they lured the "fat little dog" that belonged to Lieutenant Bossieux into the camp, killed the dog and ate him. As punishment, the prisoners received no rations the next day.[67] John Manning, writing years after the fact, said that the Lieutenant had "a pair of white bull-dogs," of which he was quite fond. The dogs mysteriously disappeared, and the "hungry fellows actually ate and relished the steaks sliced from their hams."[68]

Louis P. Lienberger, Company B, 76th Pennsylvania, who lived in Bainbridge, Indiana, after the war, wrote a letter to the editor, mainly to request information about the fate of the *man* who actually killed the dog.

> While on Belle Isle [after being captured during the charge on Fort Wagner, Charleston Harbor, July 11, 1863, until March 1864] the rations were so meager and of such poor quality, that anything in the shape of food was eagerly sought after. The officer in immediate command at the time was the owner of a fine pointer dog that came inside the prison frequently in company with his master. So it occurred to a member of the 13th Ind. and Comrade Lienberger that they would make the attempt

to capture and kill that dog, and thus procure food. Watching their opportunity they allured the dog into their excuse for a tent, when they suddenly threw a blanket over him to stifle his cries, and while Lienberger held the dog's hind legs, the Indiana man succeeded in cutting his throat. They dressed the carcass, selling some of the meat and giving some away, still retaining a good share for themselves.[69]

The two prisoners were just about to congratulate themselves, when the alarm sounded that the lieutenant's dog was missing. He knew that some of the prisoners had killed his dog, and he told them that if the guilty party or parties did not come forth, he would withhold rations for the entire camp for seven days. The prisoners were questioned one by one. The Indiana soldier who had killed the dog was the last to be called. No one knows what happened to him, because he never returned to the inside of the prison. When Lienberger was questioned as to why he killed the dog, he told the lieutenant that he was starving, and only wanted something to eat to keep alive. The lieutenant reprimanded him, but did nothing more at the time, and sent him back to his tent to "reflect on the past and wonder what was in store for him in the future."[70]

Another former prisoner, H. J. Peter, a corporal of Company E, 126th Ohio Volunteer Infantry, from Rogersville, Ohio, confirmed the killing of the dog, which he described as a "fat, white bull terrier." Peter added that after the dog was killed, he was skinned, cut up and cooked into a fine savory soup. He claimed he had one of the dog's paws that he carried with him when he was released to a hospital in Annapolis, Maryland, but there, the paw was burned along with his filthy clothes.[71]

Someone saw Louis Lienberger's letter to the editor about to the man who had killed the dog. W. W. Sprague, Company B, 13th Massachusetts, replied to the *National Tribune*. He said that the lieutenant had ordered that the dog killer punished: "Buck and gag him for four hours." Sprague claimed he had a photograph that he had been made from a sketch drawn by another prisoner which showed the dog slayer sitting on the ground near the gate. Sprague, also, had wondered for years who the man was, and Lienberger's letter had answered some of his questions.[72]

Ira E. Gosby wrote the *National Tribune* that the prisoners had "fasted three days" for killing the lieutenant's dog.[73] Seeing Gosby's letter, J. M. Emery wrote the newspaper to say that the slayer of the little "rat-and-tan" dog was caught eating the animal. As punishment, he was forced to eat the whole dog. Later, the dog slayer made a cap out of the skin, which he wore when he was sent to Andersonville.[74]

Cruel and Unusual Punishment

One prisoner who was nearly without clothes tore up a tent to cover himself. The commandant ordered him "bucked, then hung by the thumbs, then set on a fence post."[75]

John W. Manning, in a letter to the editor of the *National Tribune*, recalled seeing three men tied to the "horse" which sat about eight feet off the ground. (The horse something like a sawhorse, which sometimes was called "Morgan's mule." On Belle Isle, it was also called "Hite's cavalry."[76]) The horse was only about an inch wide on the top. Each man was gagged, his hand tied behind, and a rope was attached to each ankle. With legs stretched out, the ropes were tied to pegs in the ground. The men remained in this position until two of them died and fell off.[77]

E. C. Culp of Salina, Kansas, also wrote to the *National Tribune* in answer to the paper's request for information. He submitted his diary entry for July 22, 1862: "This morning a prisoner belonging to the 66th Ohio, and named Bowers, was shot dead by one of the guards for coming too near the guard-line."[78] It was standard practice at most prison camps to shoot those who crossed the deadline, but apparently if prisoners came even close, they risked death.

January 1, 1864, was an unusually cold day but, according to prisoner B. F. Jones, that did not prevent the commandant from having the prisoners stand in the "piercing cold wind on the bank of the river to be counted."[79]

Escape Attempts

Unfortunately for the prisoners, when prisons were located on islands in the middle of a body of water, the water presented an additional barrier that had to be overcome in order to escape. The Confederate prison on Belle Isle, as well as the Federal prisons on Johnson's Island and on Rock Island, had very few prisoners who were successful in their escape attempts.

When the prison life became to hard to bear, prisoners attempted to escape by diving into the river. They assumed the current would carry them downstream to Federal lines which had moved close to Richmond. Most discovered they were wrong, and were no match for the river or the "fishermen's nets strung across the waterway."[80] Of the five that attempted to escape by swimming the river in the summer of 1862, all were quickly captured.[81]

James E. King recalled that during that winter the prisoners talked constantly of escape. Plans were made and discarded. Tunneling was impossible, and although several had tried to swim the river to escape, they had always failed. A group decided to overpower the guards. One group was to "pounce upon and capture" the guards on duty, while another group was to rush the relief guards, overpower them, and take their weapons. Then, they would go up the hill and capture the artillery guns that were aimed at the prison compound. Once that was accomplished, then they would cross over the bridge to the south side of the James River, destroy both the railroad and the wooden bridge, and make their way along the south bank of the river to Federal lines. However, the plan was never put into motion, because of disagreement among the different groups.[82]

Orwin H. Balch, of the 142nd New York, who had been captured at Gettysburg, recorded in his notes that on August 12, 1863, "a large party escaped, with a few of the guards, who belonged to the 42nd N.C."[83]

Henry H. Ladd of Company D, 24th Michigan, was captured in the fighting for the Weldon Railroad, on August 19, 1864. Ladd noted his diary entry for September 29, 1864, that "Two of our boys retaken who attempted to escape."[84]

Outbreak Thwarted

In November 1863, prison officials learned of an escape plot, but suppressed it before it could be put into action. As a result several undisclosed precautions were taken to prevent future attempts to escape.[85]

Four months later, troops were alerted by the signal bell calling them to congregate as was the policy when a breakout was suspected. Several anonymous notes had been received that warned of a plot of some prisoners to escape. The authorities were taking no chances, and they increased the number of guards on the island and, according the Richmond *Whig*, "made other arrangements for promptly quelling any insubordination" that might occur. The paper ended with a note of confidence that only a few would ever escape and those would never "get back to the land of onions, wooden nutmegs and steady habits."[86]

That an escape was suspected is evident from the records of Company A and Company C, 1st Confederate States Engineers. On February 7, 1864, Company A marched across the James River and bivouacked opposite Belle Isle, where they remained in readiness to suppress any trouble or escape attempts. The records of Company C for February 7–12, 1864, noted that the steps were taken: "Fearing an outbreak of the Yankee prisoners at Belle Isle upon the advance of the enemy up the Peninsula, the company was ordered there on February 7 and remained until February 12." Afterward, Company C sent eight to 13 men and Company A sent four to eight men each day to strengthen the garrison of the guards.[87]

One of the preventative measures against escape was to move the prisoners to another location. Four hundred prisoners were sent in the latter part of February 1864 to Libby for transport to Americus, Georgia.[88]

The people of Richmond were getting paranoid about prisoners causing trouble and escaping. Someone reported that the prisoners had "mutinied" and that the guards had turned their cannons on them, fired, and killed about 300. The Richmond *Whig* published an article that put that story to rest and pacified the public by attributing the noise that had been heard to the guards firing "off their muskets which had been wet by the rain."[89] One would suppose, that if the muskets were wet from rain, they would not have fired at all. How many muskets would it take to sound like a cannon?

One night in August 1864, in the middle of a storm, two prisoners tried to escape by jumping in the river. As they swam away, the guards fired and killed one and seriously injured the other. Shortly afterwards, two more tried to escape by the same method and met the same fate — one killed, one wounded.[90]

D. J. Martin, a member of the 110th Ohio Regiment, from Covington, Ohio, was a prisoner on Belle Isle from August to October 1864. Thirty years later, in 1895, he wrote an account of his experiences for the *National Tribune*. Martin recalled that a corporal in his artillery squad was determined to escape. The corporal revealed his plans to Martin and another fellow inmate. Some 100 prisoners were on parole and thus were allowed to go outside the fence. They worked in the cook house, policed the grounds, or ferried wood from the shore to the island. The corporal planned to give his parole, get assigned duty on the outside, then, when he got the chance, he would escape, or die trying.[91]

Things went as the corporal planned, and he and a companion got duty outside. One day, they saw an officer's colored servant bring a little boat to shore and tie it to a stake. The servant then went to the officer's quarters. When night came, and the guard called "Ten o'clock and all's well," the two men made their way to the boat. The boat was locked and they did not dare make any noise breaking the lock or chain. Abandoning the plan to take a boat, the two spied a plank, which they took. They tied their little bundle of possessions to the plank, and waded into the water for about 50 yards, before they began to swim. The board with their bundle was soon lost in the dark, and the two men swam around in search of it until they were exhausted. They climbed out of the water to rest on a big rock and revise their plan. The river was swift and they did not have the strength to swim. They finally decided to call for help. They yelled loudly until a guard noticed someone in the river. When the guards arrived at the rock, they found two naked men kneeling and begging not to be shot. The guards cursed and fired their guns to frighten the boys, but put them in the boat and rowed back to the camp. As punishment, the two were made to ride the wooden horse and to sit for hours in an uncomfortable position for attempting to escape.[92]

Martin remembered another incident where some prisoners who had been to the river were marched back to the enclosure in single file to be counted. Two soldiers burrowed into a hole in the sand and their comrades covered them with a piece of old tent, then put sand on top of that. The boys were going to come out at night and swim the river to escape. An Irishman in the group was believed to be a spy because he had refused a parole in 1863 when Milroy's soldiers were paroled and sent home. The Irishman took a fishing rod and strolled along the edge of the water and discovered the prisoner's hiding place. He pretended not to notice but went to headquarters and told of his discovery. The commandant and two armed guards hurried to the spot and found the two still buried in the sand. The commandant hit both of the prisoners on the head with his sword, then told the guards to watch them. The commandant said, "I'll let them enjoy the beds they made for themselves." He ordered that the two were to be given nothing to eat or drink until he approved. The pair sat uncomfortably all day, through the night, and until noon the next day cramped in the sand, hungry and thirsty. If they moved, they would be killed. On the second day, the prisoners were marched outside as usual where they saw a circle had been drawn around the two buried prisoners. No one was allowed to come close to them or give them anything to eat or drink. Disregarding the orders, one of the prisoners threw a piece of cornbread to them. The guard grabbed it and threw it into the river. Eventually, the two were released, but in worse condition than they had been before.[93]

After several men escaped by swimming the river, the authorities on Belle Isle prohibited the prisoners to go to the sinks [latrines] near the river at night.[94]

Other Means of Escaping the Island

It appeared that the only way off of Belle Isle was either to die or to take the oath of allegiance to the Confederate States of America. Some chose the latter. As a result, by Christmas 1863, approximately 400 former Union prisoners enjoyed the Christmas holidays in the city of Richmond.[95]

Williams, of the 77th Pennsylvania, had been captured at Chickamauga. He found he could no longer endure the conditions on the island. One day, he climbed out of his dugout, ran up to a guard, and was immediately shot dead—a form of suicide. When told the story, another prisoner asked, "Was he out of his mind?"

The answer from an eyewitness came back, "No, sir, it was simply a choice of death, and he chose the easiest and quickest."[96]

Closure of the Prison

By the end of 1863, the island held about 10,000 prisoners. Because of the threat from the Kilpatrick-Dahlgren Raid and the drain on the food supply for the city of Richmond, the prisoners were moved to Andersonville, Georgia, when it opened in the spring of 1864.[97]

By late October 1864, most of the prisoners from Belle Isle had been removed to Andersonville, Danville or Salisbury. Only about a dozen prisoners remained, and those for maintenance purposes.[98] The property reverted to its original owners in February 1865.[99]

After Federal troops captured Richmond in April 1865, Belle Isle was designated as a temporary place of shelter for "Union refugees," persons who sought protection within Union lines.[100]

The island was sold to the Virginia Power Company around the turn of the century.[101]

When former prisoner Briscoe Goodhart, of the Loudoun, Virginia, Rangers, returned in 1892, the site where the prison pen had been located was covered by a rolling mill owned and operated by the Old Dominion Nail and Iron Company. The superintendent of the nail works, Mr. Baird, had in his possession the large kettle that had been used to boil the morning bean soup for the prisoners. It was now used to mix cement to lay firebricks.[102]

Belle Isle Today

Today, hundreds of tourists daily visit Belle Isle, walking across the pedestrian bridge at the bottom of Tredgar Street under the Robert E. Lee Bridge. From the island, they can get a good view of the Hollywood Rapids, part of seven miles of rapids that make up the Fall Line. They also see evidence of gunpits near the site of the Confederate prison camp. With its dense woodlands, open fields, the island provides a haven for birds and waterfowl.[103]

XVIII

Cahaba Prison, Cahaba, Alabama

By what strange and malignant destiny were cowards and cruel men so often placed in charge of prisons.

— Jesse Hawes, prisoner, 9th Illinois Cavalry[1]

Location: Cahaba, Alabama. **Established:** 1863–1864. **Type:** barren stockade, converted buildings. **Type of Prisoners:** Federal prisoners of war, civilians. **Capacity:** 500. **Most Held:** approximately 3,000. **Number of Escapes:** unknown.[2] **Other Names, Nicknames:** Cahawba, "Castle Morgan."

History

The town of Cahaba, Alabama, was located about 13 miles southwest of Selma, and about 60 miles west of Montgomery, the present state capital. It was situated near the junction of the Alabama River and the Cahaba River, and served as the state capital from 1819 to 1826, but flooding forced the removal of the capital to Tuscaloosa. The town remained the county seat for Dallas County for several more years.[3]

A thriving antebellum social and commercial center, Cahaba was the shipping point for cotton down the Alabama River to Mobile. When the railroad was extended to Cahaba in 1859, the economic success of the town seemed assured. However, the Confederate government seized the railroad and tore up the rails to use elsewhere.[4]

The Facilities

The prison was located at the end of Capital Street, in the town of Cahaba, on the bank of the Alabama River.[5]

An unfinished cotton warehouse owned by Samuel M. Hill was the core around which Cahaba Prison was built. The building covered 15,000 square feet. Only the brick walls and part of the roof had been completed when the war broke out, and the Confederate government took possession of the property and erected a 12-foot-high fence around the site.[6]

An inspection conducted in October 1864 by D. T. Chandler, assistant adjutant and inspector general for the Confederacy noted that the prison had been established

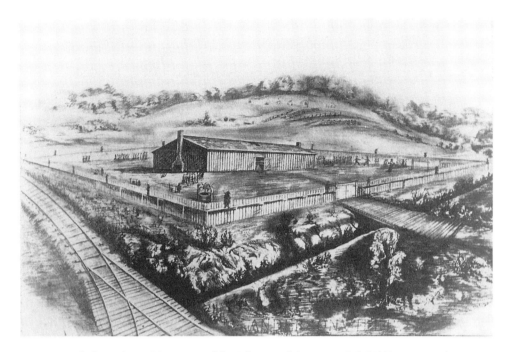

Cahaba Prison. (Courtesy of the Library of Congress, LC-USZ62-113562.)

to accommodate 500 prisoners. Around the "old brick cotton-shed" a stockade of 2-inch planks had been erected about 12 feet high. The planks had been set in the ground to a depth of three feet. Half the building was without a roof, and there were no interior walls. The water from an artesian well in the area was brought into the stockade through underground pipes where it flowed into three sunken barrels. The water also flowed into the sink [latrine] then into the river. There were bunks for only about 500 prisoners.[7]

R. H. Whitfield described the building as having "four open windows, and the earth for the floor," and it served as sleeping quarters with five tiers of bunks built along the walls. The "sleeping arrangements" were devoid of straw or other bedding, and could only accommodate 432 men. Thus, 228 prisoners were forced to sleep on the ground.[8]

Water was supplied by an artesian well outside the prison walls and was directed inside by an open trench. Along its course, the water was used for washing the hands, faces and feet of soldiers, civilians, and prisoners. It became the dumping ground for waste of all kinds.[9]

Chandler stated that in October 1864, 2,151 prisoners of war were confined in the stockade, and 69 in the hospital. Another 75 prisoners should have been in the hospital but there was no room.[10]

The building had only one fireplace, but because the floor was dirt, prisoners were allowed to build fires inside. Surgeon R. H. Whitfield saw about 40 small fires that had been built at intervals on the floor. Because the wood furnished for heat was of inferior quality—either green sap pine or decayed oak—those fires produced a dense smoke.[11]

The 10 Federal officers at Cahaba on parole in the fall of 1864 were not confined inside the stockade, but had been quartered in the town where they were more comfortable. Although the paroled officers were not allowed to communicate with the inhabitants of the town except for "prescribed purposes," they each stated they were content with their treatment.[12]

An area outside the building was surrounded by a plank fence 35 feet by 46 feet; the area was used only in the daytime because it would have been easier to escape from it at night. It was also the place food was cooked. Guards walked around an elevated walkway on the outside of the fence, and two small cannon were aimed at the prisoners through portholes on one side of the stockade. The cannons were primed and loaded with canister, ready to be fired at the first sign of trouble.[13]

The inspection of October 1864 determined that in addition to the poor quality of shelter, the prisoners had to live on a diet "exclusively of bread and meat." Rice had been issued only twice since June, and they had received no peas or beans in place of the absent rice. Chandler recommended and obtained a promise from the commandant that "anti-scorbutics (pumpkins, potatoes, etc.)" would be issued to the prisoners in the future. He also recommended that the stockade and the sink be enlarged, a suitable cook house and bake oven be erected, and the roof over the building be completed. A reservoir for water should be built. Captain Henderson promised to see to the improvements.[14]

Capt. J. J. Wheadon admitted that, while the guards had received rice regularly, he had not issued any for the prisoners. He gave as his reason the fact that he was in charge of purchase and collection of subsistence stores in four counties, and had been absent from Cahaba frequently.[15]

The Personnel

The commandant at Cahaba Federal Prison was Capt. Howard A. M. Henderson, of Company E, 28th Alabama Regiment. He also served as an assistant commissioner of prisoner exchange. Because of the duties connected with the exchange of prisoners, he was often away from the camp. Henderson was liked by the prisoners because he tried to be kind and courteous to them.[16] In his absence, Lt. Col. Samuel S. Jones, of the 22nd Louisiana Regiment, was left in charge. Jones, a former bookkeeper for a wholesale house in New Orleans, was hated by the prisoners. Jones had been captured twice, but each time was paroled and exchanged. Undoubtedly, his days as a prisoner had left him bitter. One prisoner recalled that Jones was guilty of "many, many inhuman acts." He appeared to delight in walking along the deadline and finding a prisoner sitting near it. He would then, without a word, kick the prisoner.[17]

Somehow, Jones managed to get himself appointed commandant. In October 1864, Brig. Gen. John H. Winder made some changes in prison personnel. Winder, formerly command of the Richmond prisons, had been given authority over all Federal prisoners in Alabama and Georgia in June 1864, and a few months later, he was named commissary general of all prisoners east of the Mississippi.[18] Winder assigned Col. George C. Gibbs to command the post at Camp Sumter, Andersonville; Col. Henry Forno at Camp Lawton; and Lieutenant Colonel Jones to the post at Cahaba,

Alabama. Winder was perplexed as to how Jones had gotten in control. He had received a letter from Jones which Jones had signed as "commander of the post." Winder was annoyed, and expressed his opinion that he should be informed "when a change is made in the prisons under control." As an afterthought, Winder decided to send an officer to inspect Cahaba and report on conditions there. Winder also advised that, based on information he had received, it would be better to "suspend work upon the defenses and push forward the winter accommodations for the troops and prisoners, especially the hospital accommodations."[19]

Early in December 1864, Captain Henderson was back at the Cahaba Prison, but performing his job as purchasing agent while Jones was in command at the post.[20] While in Memphis on November 15, 1864, Henderson entered into an agreement with the Federal Maj. Gen. C. C. Washburn, subject to the approval of Maj. Gen. Dabney H. Maury, in command of the District of the Gulf, for the distribution of clothing to Federal prisoners at Cahaba. The plan was for Capt. John Whytock to meet Henderson in Mobile when he went to obtain supplies, and return with Henderson to Cahaba. The Union officer would be a guest in the home of Henderson, and would not be allowed to visit the prison or converse with the prisoners. Henderson explained that any prisoners who required clothing would be brought "under guard, to my office, and the articles there distributed under the joint supervision of Captain Whytock and myself." Afterward, Henderson offered to escort Captain Whytock back through the lines. The camp commandant, Lieutenant Colonel Jones, did not object to the arrangement.[21]

According to the agreement between Washburn and Henderson, acting as an agent of exchange, 2,000 items each of coats, pairs of pants, drawers, shoes, and hats, and 4,000 pairs of socks would be distributed among the prisoners. In addition, five reams of paper and 2,000 envelopes were to be given to the men. Any leftover items were to be sent to the Federal prisoners at Meridian, Mississippi. A quantity of medicine was also included in the agreement. An addition to the agreement included 1,500 blankets and 100 mess pans.[22] The distribution hinged on the approval of General Maury. A veteran of the Mexican War, Maury taught at West Point for five years. He resigned to join the Confederate cavalry as a captain. Described as a "small, spare man ... with a sense of duty and honor worthy of the best of the traditional Virginia gentlemen officers."[23] Whether this distribution of clothing was made or not will never be known.

The Prisoners

Maury, in command of a prison at Mobile, Alabama, refused to accept any more Federal prisoners, and urged that any additional prisoners be sent to Cahaba.[24]

Undoubtedly, Maury was unaware of the true conditions at the Cahaba prison, but he may not have had another choice. By May 1864, there were 1,500 prisoners being held at Cahaba, and only 161 guards, plus a few local troops, and a small detail of 18 men with cannon. The prisoners called their prison "Castle Morgan," in honor of the dashing Confederate cavalry officer, John Hunt Morgan, who had been born in Alabama. Morgan had successfully escaped from the Ohio State Penitentiary (see Chapter XIII) in November 1863, about the time the Cahaba facility was established.[25]

By May 1864, the prison was closed and all prisoners, except the sick, were moved to Andersonville. However, because of the conditions and overcrowding at Andersonville, the Cahaba facility was reopened. By September 1864, there were 2,500 prisoners in a pen with the capacity to hold 500. Eventually, with the addition of more prisoners, the prisoners at Cahaba had less space per man than those at Andersonville.[26] To relieve the overcrowding, on October 19, 1864, the Confederate adjutant and inspector general, S. Cooper, ordered Brigadier General Winder at Millen, Georgia, to transfer "the surplus prisoners at Cahaba" to Millen.[27]

Not only was there no space at the Cahaba prison, but the little space available was shared with rats and lice. Prisoner Jesse Hawes recalled that he could hardly sleep for the rats "snuffing about some portion of my body." He would awaken all through the night to kick the rats away. Lice plagued the prisoners both day and night, crawling over their bodies and "into the ears, even into the nostrils and mouths by night."[28]

One of the prisoners at Cahaba was a Federal officer, Capt. John T. Young, of Company A, 24th Missouri Infantry. Young had enlisted in May 1861, and served until he was taken prisoner at Fort Pillow in April 1864. According to a letter he wrote to Maj. Gen. C. C. Washburn, commander of the District of West Tennessee, Young had first been at Cahaba, then was sent to Macon, Georgia. While in prison at Macon, a Confederate captain accompanied by two guards came to return him to Cahaba. Young did not know the reason they wanted him back, but his fellow prisoners urged him to escape on the way back, because he probably had been summoned in an act of retaliation. However, that was not the case. When he arrived at Cahaba, he was quite ill and was placed in the hospital under guard. To make him feel even worse, while in the hospital another patient, also a Federal officer, told him that he (Young) had been recognized as a Confederate deserter, and was to be tried by a court martial. To add to his discomfort, even the black hospital orderlies told him the same story.[29]

Three days after his return to Cahaba, Young was summoned to the provost marshal who asked him to sign some papers which endorsed Gen. Nathan Bedford Forrest's official report of the Fort Pillow affair, the battle which had occurred April 12, 1864. Young refused, although he knew that some of the newspaper versions of the Fort Pillow massacre were exaggerated. That same day, he was sent for again and asked to sign a paper with a few modifications. He refused again. He did agree, however, to send General Forrest a statement to the effect that he considered some of the "versions of the Fort Pillow affair which [he] had read in their own papers exaggerated" (said to be copies from Federal papers). Young was convinced that, in some respects, Forrest's report was exaggerated.[30]

Forrest had come under fire for his treatment of Federal soldiers captured at Fort Pillow. Southern accounts maintained that the approximately 231 Federal soldiers killed and 100 seriously wounded were the result of fighting as they attempted to make their way to the river. Northern accounts maintained that the fort had surrendered as soon as the demand was made, and that the troops inside had been murdered in cold blood by Rebels shouting, "No quarter! Kill the damned niggers; shoot them down!" The Committee on the Conduct of the War concluded the Confederates were guilty of "atrocities, including killing most of the garrison after they had surrendered, burying Negro soldiers alive, and setting fire to tents which contained wounded Federal soldiers. The southern view in House Report No. 65, 38th Congress, 1864, refuted those charges as "sheer propaganda," designed to stir up hatred.[31] The controversy over the events at Fort Pillow continues to the present time.

A week later, Young was brought before the prison commandant, Col. H. C. Davis. The colonel told Young that Judge P. T. Scruggs was coming to talk to him about the Fort Pillow battle. The judge arrived and informed Young that General Forrest believed him to be a "gentleman and a soldier." Judge Scruggs told Young the things that had been testified to before the military commission empowered to investigate the "massacre." Again, after reading the papers, Young refused to sign. Finally, the judge persuaded Young to sign with the promise that no one but General Forrest would see them and that they would not be used by Forrest as "testimony, but merely for his own satisfaction." At this, Young reluctantly signed. Later he wrote to say that his signature had been "extorted" while he was "under duress."[32]

Young had written that General Forrest had demanded "unconditional surrender" from the defender of Fort Pillow, Maj. L. F. Booth, and Booth asked for an hour to consult with his officers and the commander of gunboat 7. Forrest replied that he did not want the surrender of the gunboat, but only the surrender of the men and munitions in the fort. Forrest gave Booth 20 minutes to decide, and warned that he would assault the fort at the end of that time. Booth replied and declined to surrender.[33] A statement made five days later on May 16, 1864, by Young described the subsequent events.

> A majority of the officers of garrison doubted whether General Forrest was present, and had the impression that it was a ruse to induce the surrender of the fort. At the second meeting of the flag of truce General Forrest announced himself as being General Forrest, but the officers who accompanied the flag, being unacquainted with the general, doubted his word, and it was the opinion of the garrison at the time of the assault that General Forrest was not in the vicinity of the fort. The commanding officer refused to surrender. When the final assault was made I was captured at my post inside the works, and have been treated as a prisoner of war.[34]

Three days later, on May 19, 1864, Young wrote a letter to Forrest. There had been much talk and an investigation ensued over Forrest's treatment of the men at the fort. Rumors had led to the wide-spread belief that Forrest had "massacred" the defenders of Fort Pillow.

> Your request, made through Judge P. T. Scruggs, that I should make a statement as to the treatment of Federal dead and wounded at Fort Pillow, has been made known to me. Details from Federal prisoners were made to collect the dead and wounded. The dead were buried by their surviving comrades. I saw no ill-treatment of the wounded on the evening of the battle, or next morning. My friend, Lieutenant Leaming, adjutant Thirteenth Tennessee Cavalry, was left under the sutler's store [near the fort]; also a lieutenant of Sixth U.S. Artillery; both were alive next morning and sent on board U.S. Transport, among many other wounded. Among the wounded were some colored troops. I do not know how many.[35]

Young also stated he believed that the report submitted by Captain Anderson, aide-de-camp to Forrest, and appended to the report submitted by the general, was correct.[36]

Exchange

By September 1864, 350 prisoners, members of the 16th Army Corps who had been captured on the Sturgis raid, were being held at Cahaba. An exchange of the Federal captives for Confederates had been proposed. However, Major Washburn at Memphis had no Confederate prisoners to exchange, and asked that some be sent to him from other prisons so that the exchange might take place.[37]

Washburn also informed Col. William Hoffman that there were "no colored soldiers at Cahaba," but there was a "major of colored artillery" who was being badly treated, and he hoped that an exchange could be effected for him. At that time, there were also 30 to 40 citizens being held prisoner at Cahaba, most of whom had been governmental employees.[38] Hoffman submitted the request to the secretary of war. An endorsement on Washburn's request made by Union Maj. Gen. E. A. Hitchcock noted that Lt. Gen. U. S. Grant had ordered that "special exchanges are not to be made." For the exchange to take place, application would have to be made directly to Grant or expressly ordered by the secretary of war.[39]

Escapes

Escape attempts were continuous, although there are no surviving records of the number. Several prisoners crawled out through the floor of the latrine and thence continued through the drainage ditch. They were later caught and returned. At least 12 tunneled out from the dirt floor of the warehouse to the riverbank nearby. They were apprehended as well. Still others are believed to have cut their way out through the brick walls of the warehouse or through the plank stockade.[40]

Escape was always possible, and by a large number of prisoners. D. T. Chandler foresaw trouble when he inspected Cahaba in October 1864. The small number of guards assigned to control the prisoners, "badly armed" guards, the "discipline inferior," plus the fact that they were on duty every other day, made them totally "inadequate for the duties required of them." In his report, Chandler warned:

> The prisoners have a sufficient organization, having been divided into companies and squads for police and messing purposes, and need only a little determination and a leader to enable them at any time to overpower the feeble garrison. Some few might be killed, but the majority could easily effect their escape.[41]

If that did occur, and the prisoners escaped, they might get away without being recaptured. Chandler knew there were no other troops in the vicinity, except the provost guard at Selma, nine miles north of Cahaba.[42]

Revolt

Near the end of the war, on Friday, January 20, 1865, between the hours of 3 and 4 A.M., the prisoners rose up against the guards. As a group, the prisoners rushed the interior guards, disarmed, and captured them. They put the guards in the "water closets" (privies). The two guards outside heard the commotion and sounded the alarm. A courier was dispatched to the commanding officer of the troops stationed at the post, and the battalion was ordered out and the artillery set to fire. Soon, the prisoners had settled down. Henderson issued an order that all rations were to be suspended until the names of the ringleaders were learned. Five witnesses then came forth, and the information they provided led to the arrest of the ringleaders of the revolt. They were apprehended and put in irons.[43]

Several persons were arrested and witnesses called to testify what they knew about the mutiny. From the testimony of those prisoners, whether under arrest or not, it is apparent that the prison contained not only military prisoners of war but also a variety of civilians.[44]

ARRESTED: Captain Hanchett, alias George Schellar, was told that he did not have to give evidence against himself, but he could make a voluntary statement if desired. Hanchett said that he was a captain in Company M, 16th Illinois Cavalry. He was acting adjutant general on Colonel Capron's staff. He had been persuaded to dress as a civilian by Colonel Kofer so that he could quickly pass through the lines. Hanchett declared he "was not the instigator of the mutiny," but admitted he did take a part in it.[45]

ARRESTED: Robert Cox, of Company G, 115th Ohio, claimed he knew nothing of the plot, but heard a noise, got up, and went to the front entrance. There, Hanchett grabbed him by the arm and handed him a musket. However, he set it down a few yards away. Hanchett, said Cox, continued to run "to and fro from the entrance of the prison, calling for 100 men," but when he failed to get them, he "ordered everybody to their bunks." Cox further testified that he heard some men talking about an attempt to escape the week before, but did not remember their names. He swore that Hanchett was the man who gave him the musket.[46]

WITNESS: Francis M. Prim, Company M, 19th Pennsylvania Cavalry, testified that Cox was one of three men who "charged up to the entrance with a musket in his hand, but after they had "charged the guard they ran." He also swore that Hanchett was the one who had called for the 100 men to join in the breakout.[47]

ARRESTED: Pvt. John W. Lightbody, Company D, 18th Ohio Infantry, testified he knew nothing until the alarm was sounded, and when he arose from his bed, he saw three muskets lying between the bunks at the entrance. He said he knew nothing of the plan to capture the guards and knew nothing about Captain Hanchett. He said he heard men shouting, "the guard has been captured," and "get up."[48]

WITNESS: Pvt. George W. Salter, Company D, 3rd Iowa Cavalry, said he recognized both Hanchett and Cox as the two men who charged the guard at the entrance with muskets in hand. He also said that John W. Lightbody had told him the night before that there was to be an uprising in order for the prisoners to break out. He recognized Lightbody as the prisoner who was "busily engaged in the middle of the prison when 100 were called for." Lightbody had called out, "Come on, boys," and when the prisoners did not respond, Captain Hanchett had said, "Let them go; they are a damned set of cowards."[49]

WITNESS: Prisoner Jacob E. Lachler, who had been a civilian passenger on the steamer *Prairie State*, from Pennsylvania, testified that, although he belonged to the same mess as Hanchett, he knew nothing of the plot until he heard all the commotion in the night. He did say that Hanchett maintained he was a citizen, and did not inform the other members of the mess of his plans.[50]

WITNESS: Prisoner E. McCullough, pilot of the steamer *Prairie State* which ran a route between Nashville and St. Louis, supported Lachler's testimony.[51]

WITNESS: E. Baker, a citizen from New York who had been captured five miles from Nashville, Tennessee, was a government employee. He recognized Hanchett as the man who called himself Schellar, and stated that it was the consensus of the prisoners that Hanchett was the instigator of the plot.[52]

ARRESTED: Cpl. George W. Riley, of the 27th Illinois Infantry, claimed he knew nothing about the mutiny.[53]

ARRESTED: Pvt. G. Hammarberg, Company H, 9th Minnesota Infantry, testified that he told Salter that George Riley had told him that a "whistle would blow" and when he heard another whistle, he must arise and help. When asked if he thought the prisoner could have succeeded in getting out, Hammarberg did not think so. He had "seen so many trials made at it." He identified Corporal Riley as the man who told him about the whistle.[54]

WITNESS: Pvt. George Sherman, 4th Michigan Cavalry, testified that he saw a man named Becker running through prison calling for 100 men. He also saw James Morrison running around with a gun.[55]

ARRESTED: Martin A. Becker, Company D, 13th Wisconsin Infantry, and a prisoner who cooked for the sick, testified that he got up in the night about 4:30 A.M. to go to the spring. He saw four or five men holding a man, whom they believed had been stealing blankets. Almost immediately afterward, he said he heard someone calling for 100 men, and yelling, "The guards are captured." Soon afterward, he heard a man say, "Lay down." Becker denied that he was one of those involved, and that it was the opinion of the prisoners that Hanchett was the leader.[56]

ARRESTED: James Morrison, Company G, 19th Pennsylvania, also a prison cook, and one accused by the testimony of George Sherman, swore he knew nothing about the plan. He first learned of it when he heard someone calling out, "He will never steal anther blanket." Shortly afterward, he saw several men running through the prison with guns and heard one calling for 100 men.[57]

ARRESTED: Osmond F. Foster, Company I, 7th Pennsylvania Cavalry, swore that he did not even get out of his bunk the night of the "disturbance." The first he knew about it was when he heard some talk about a blanket being stolen. He said that Captain Hanchett was introduced to him as George Schellar, a "steward on a steam boat." Later he learned Schellar was a captain in the U.S. Army. Foster also testified that there had been a previous plot of about 200 men, which was never implemented. He swore he never told anyone that Martin A. Becker was the leader of that plan. Foster told his inquisitors that since the night of the revolt, he had heard that there were 20 to 25 prisoners involved, but he had no idea what their intentions were had they succeeded.[58]

ARRESTED: George H. Hoff, Company F, 114th Illinois Infantry, said he knew nothing of the riot until he saw the piece of artillery in the "door of the prison" aimed at his bunk. He knew nothing of the plot beforehand, and was not aware of anything happening until he heard someone say, "Steal another blanket, will you?" After that, someone called for 100 men. Then he saw a Confederate officer standing in the door with the artillery piece demanding the return of the muskets taken from the guards. Hoff said he got down from his bunk and retreated to another part of the prison out of the sights of the cannon. Hoff said, "I thought the plot to get out a very foolish one. I could not myself have escaped, as I was wounded."[59] To verify Hoff's testimony, Dr. Whitfield was called to examine him to see if he was "physically disabled to make a march." Whitfield reported that Hoff was capable of "making a march any distance, " and was not incapacitated because of his wound.[60] Hoff was recalled to the stand, and he swore that he "did not know a single man engaged in the plot, but that I would remain in prison 122 days before I would inform on the mutineers, if I knew."[61]

ARRESTED: Patrick Ponsonby, Company G, 13th Illinois Infantry, testified that someone named Miller had asked him early the night before if he knew anything about a breakout. He replied that he did not, and that it would be very foolish. Ponsonby testified that he had escaped from prison in Meridian, but gave himself up because he knew he could not make it to Federal lines. He had heard the conversation about the blanket, then the call for the 100 men, and then the order to "Lay down." About 10 minutes later, the Confederate officer was at the door with the cannon. He supported other testimony in placing the blame for the mutiny on Captain Hanchett.[62]

George Sherman was recalled. He testified that he saw Becker running about the prison calling for 100 men after Becker had said, "The guards have all been mugged — and my God, boys, ain't you going to stand by me?" He then identified the man under arrest as Becker. In answer to Becker's question, Sherman testified he said, "Lay down; did you never see a crazy man?" Then Becker went to the back part of the prison and Sherman did not see him again. Sherman also testified that Thompson Hanson told him that Becker was one of the instigators of the revolt. Sherman declared that only 20 men were involved in overpowering the guards, but that they had expected others to join in. He identified James Morrison as one of those with a gun at the front entrance. Shortly after leaving the entrance, two men turned off to the right and went to the deadline. Morrison moved in the direction of the privy. Sherman said he knew Osmond F. Foster, but did not see him that night. Sherman also referred to a previous plan Foster told him about in which a "large number were engaged," but before it could be executed, "some one turned traitor" so the plan had to be abandoned. That was why only 20 were involved in the attempt made the night of January 20. Sherman swore that Foster had admitted he was involved. Sherman also stated that George Hoff had told him he had not been involved but that he knew the originator of the plan was a "major-general."

The Verdict

After hearing the testimony of a number of prisoners, the prison officials concluded that the plan to revolt and escape originated with George Schellar (alias Captain Hanchett), and Robert Cox. Schellar had been captured near Nashville, Tennessee, by General Forrest on December 3, 1864. He was disguised as a private citizen and had been listed as such at each point in his transit as a prisoner along the way to Cahaba. His purpose appeared to have been to pass through the lines to be captured so that he might obtain information about the strength and movement of Confederate forces. Upon being identified by other prisoners, Schellar confessed that he was really Captain Hanchett of the 16th Illinois Cavalry. To complete his disguise, Hanchett had shaved off his moustache and whiskers and changed to civilian clothes. After being questioned by several officers, Captain Henderson, and the commandant of the post, they were convinced that Hanchett was the leader of the revolt. They also concluded that he was "an exceedingly dangerous and bad man." Lieutenant Colonel Jones believed that Hanchett's real mission was that of a spy. Thus, he and seven of his coconspirators were put in irons and taken to a "dungeon in the county jail."[63]

That action had the approval of Brig. Gen. John Daniel Imboden, but the adjutant and inspector general had ordered on January 24, 1865, that all except Captain Hanchett be released. Imboden ordered a new trial for Hanchett as a spy.[64] Brigadier General Imboden, a Virginia lawyer and legislator, had participated in the arrest of John Brown at Harpers Ferry before the war. After joining the Confederacy he was actively involved in military action in Virginia from the first major battle at Manassas (First Bull Run). He had captured Charleston, Virginia (now West Virginia), and fought at Piedmont and Newmarket during Early's Valley campaign, and he helped cover Lee's retreat from Gettysburg. In the fall of 1864 he was stricken with typhoid fever. After his recovery he was sent to Aiken, South Carolina, on prison duty.[65]

The Repercussions

With so many prisoners being held throughout the southern states, there was a great fear they would break out and ravage the county. As a result of the uprising at Cahaba Prison, Imboden issued strict orders regarding the results of any revolt in General Order, No. 2. These were distributed to every prison camp in his department by G. W. McPhail, acting assistant adjutant general, from the Confederate Military Prison Headquarters in Augusta, Georgia.

> I. In consequence of a recent mutiny and attempted escape of prisoners from the military prison at Cahaba, Ala., it is ordered that if any prisoner or prisoners of war confined in any of the military prisons in the States of Georgia, Alabama, or Mississippi shall engage in any mutiny or attempt by force to escape, the guard shall instantly fire upon the mutineers and, if necessary, upon the whole body of prisoners until perfect order is restored. And every prisoner found with arms in his hands at the time of any mutiny or forcible attempt to escape shall be instantly shot to death; and this penalty will in no case be remitted where such armed prisoner is overpowered by or surrendered to the guard on the suppression of a mutiny.
>
> II. The brigadier-general commanding directs that all prisoners of war who conduct themselves in an orderly manner shall be treated with that humanity becoming the Christian people of these Confederate States, who, notwithstanding the barbarous atrocities inflicted upon them by a cruel and merciless foe, have not yet learned to forget their own high civilization, but he is resolved that no ruffianism shall be tolerated amongst the prisoners under his control.
>
> III. This order will be published to those confined in the prisons of this department, and their own conduct will then determine whether their lives are to be spared or not.
>
> By order of Brig. Gen. J. D. Imboden, commanding.[66]

Release of Civilian Prisoners

When prisoners were released, they sometimes carried valuable information to the opposing side. Shortly after the mutiny, 78 prisoners were released on February 5, 1865, from Cahaba and transferred to Major General Washburn at Vicksburg. The citizens had been released "unconditionally." However, among the 78 were three paroled officers and some soldiers. Those reaching Vicksburg had reported that Confederate Gen. John Bell Hood and his entire army had gone to meet Union Gen. William T. Sherman. The former prisoners did not arrive at Vicksburg until February 23, because of the bad condition of the railroads. The prisoners also had been detained for three days at Jackson, Mississippi. They reported that on the train from Meridian to Jackson there were "six large launches [boats], each having a 12-pounder howitzer and a crew of fifteen men." After arriving in Jackson the boats were sent on the road toward Grenada. They also heard that the boats had been taken to the Yazoo River and might be taken to the Mississippi.[67]

The Cahaba prisoners seemed doomed to a watery grave. Disaster struck the prison in March 1865 when the Alabama and Cahaba rivers flooded the area. The prison was inundated and several prisoners drowned. The prisoners were left standing in hip-deep water for several days until help arrived. Lieutenant Colonel Jones came to the prison in a boat, but refused to do anything to relieve their situation.[68] After several days, 700 prisoners were moved to Selma, Alabama, while the remaining 2,300 were left to cope with the water and mud for about two weeks until the water receded and the land dried out.[69]

At the end of the war, the remaining prisoners at Cahaba were to be transported north. About 1,100 unfortunate prisoners were on board the U.S.S. *Sultana*, when it exploded and sank with a great loss of lives.

The Present

After a disastrous flood in 1865, the county government was removed to Selma, and the once-thriving community was abandoned. Within a short time, most of the houses had been dismantled and moved. By 1900, most of the commercial buildings had been burned or dismantled, and by the mid–1930s, only hunters or fishermen walked the once-busy streets.[70]

Today, with the exception of only a few solitary chimneys, nothing remains of the town of Cahaba or the prison. However, archaeological excavations have been undertaken. To visit the site, begin at the Cahaba Visitors Center, 9518 Cahaba Road, in the nearby town of Orrville.[71]

XIX

Camp Ford, Tyler, Texas

…there being no shelter for us, we were obliged to cut the pine trees and build
log fires in order to keep from freezing.
      — John W. Greene, 26th Indiana Volunteer Regiment.[1]

Location: four miles northwest of Tyler, Texas. **Established:** 1863. **Type:** barren stockade. **Type of Prisoners:** prisoners of war, Federal soldiers and sailors. **Capacity:** unknown. **Most Held:** 4,700+. **Known Escapes:** unknown[2] (600 per William Ryan[3]). **Nicknames:** Camp Ford Borough, Ford City.[4]

History

The town of Tyler, in Smith County, was the site of a large Confederate ordnance plant.[5] Camp Ford was established there as the need for facilities to hold prisoners of war increased. It was named for Col. John S. "Rip" Ford, an individual with a varied career as a Texas Ranger, state senator, newspaper editor, and commander of Confederate troops in Texas. The camp had originally been established as a training camp, but once it was converted to a prison, it became the largest military prison west of the Mississippi.[6]

The Site

Camp Ford was located in East Texas four miles northeast of the town of Tyler. Tyler is 90 miles west of Shreveport, Louisiana, 90 miles east of Dallas, and 199 miles north of Houston. The elevation is about 550 feet. Temperatures in modern-day times range from a high of 110 degrees F to a low of 5 above zero, with an average high of 94 in July. The average low is 36 degrees in January.[7] To the east, along the Louisiana border, flows the Sabine River. Further on is the Red River, and numerous other rivers, streams and swamps. To the north of Tyler is the Sulphur River which empties into the Red River.

The Facilities

A first, the prison compound was just an open area of four or five acres surrounded by guards. After Confederate officials learned that an escape was planned, the officers of the guard went to Tyler and called a meeting of the citizens. They told

Camp Ford — Federal noncommissioned officers, 19th Iowa Infantry, exchanged from Camp Ford. Notice that all are barefooted. (Library of Congress, LC-DIG-cwpb-01433.)

the people of Tyler about the "*awful* things the 'Yanks' might do, in case of an insurrection." They convinced the plantation owners to loan them some slaves and in about 10 days a stockade had been built of logs split in half, and set deep in the ground.[8] This was done in November 1863, and when finished the 16-foot high stockade enclosed about six to eight acres. A spring furnished good water, although it tasted of sulfur.[9] Outside the stockade, dirt was banked against the logs to provide a walk for the guards on patrol. Inside the stockade, all trees and shrubbery had been cut.[10]

The camp sat in the midst of prairies dotted by low, wooded hills. North of the stockade sheep and hogs roamed the plains. On the east lay woods and cultivated fields. To the west were hills covered with hardwoods. The Confederate cavalry had a camp and huts to live in. To the south was another hill on which the commandant of the prison had his headquarters, and from which he could look down on the stockade.[11]

No shelter was provided for the prisoners. They were simply placed in the open and left to their own devices. The prisoners were allowed to go outside the stockade and cut logs to build huts and cabins. Some of the cabins were quite elaborate with stacked clay chimneys. Some prisoners burrowed in the ground for shelter, as prisoners had done on Belle Isle and at Andersonville, all open, barren prison compounds.

Prison Personnel

The first commandant for the new prison was Capt. S. M. Warner. He was relieved by Maj. Thomas F. Tucker. The guard initially consisted of 45 men.[12] There

were a number of commandants assigned to Camp Ford. Colonel Allen followed
Tucker. Allen was a graduate of West Point, and the prisoners regarded him as a gentlemen who treated them fairly.[13]

T. Scott Anderson was in command by August 1864. Colonel Sweet and part of
the 15th Texas Cavalry were at Camp Ford, and he furnished men to help in guarding the prisoners. Anderson was looking forward at that time to being relieved of his
duty as commander of the post.[14] Lt. Col. J. P. Borders followed Anderson. He was
hated by the prisoners, and at least four prisoners were shot and killed by the guards
under his authority.[15]

The Prisoners

Prisoners were soon transferred from Camp Groce, formerly a cotton plantation near Hempstead, Texas.[16] The first prisoners, a group of 360 Union sailors,
arrived at Camp Ford on July 30, 1863. They were joined in October by 11 officers
and 203 enlisted men of the 19th Iowa Regiment.[17]

By the first of November 1863, as many as 500 prisoners were confined at the
camp, most of them without adequate clothing or shoes. Commandant Tucker wrote
to Maj. E. P. Turner, assistant adjutant general, to report on their plight. The men
were even without blankets and had no shelter. He had tried to obtain lumber to build
barracks but he had not been successful. Tucker also wanted to know if he should
requisition shoes and blankets from the quartermaster, and he begged that his previous requisition for "lumber, straw, &c" be treated with "respect."[18]

By December 1863, all but 65 of those prisoners, the enlisted men of the U.S.
Steamer *Harriet Lane,* had been marched to Shreveport, Louisiana, for exchange.
However, the officers were to be marched from Camp Groce and held at Camp Ford.[19]
This exchange never took place, and the prisoners wintered at Shreveport, and were
marched back to Camp Ford in the spring.[20]

By June 1864, Camp Ford held 831 Federal prisoners, most of them captured from
January 1, 1863, to September 29, 1863. Some of them had been prisoners for 8 to 17
months.[21] The naval prisoners at Camp Ford in June 1864 included 70 seamen from
the *Morning Light;* 15 from the *Velocity*, 90 from the *Clifton*, and 30 from the *Sachem*.[22]

It was not a bad location for a prison. Capt. William P. Coe, of the 176th New
York Volunteers, wrote on December 24, 1864, "It is a very healthy location and our
diet is simple and nourishing—corn bread and beef. We are as comfortable and as
well treated as prisoners can expect...."[23]

William Ryan, an Irishman, who enlisted in the 160th New York Volunteers in
the fall of 1862, was wounded at Pleasant Hill, Louisiana, on April 9, 1864. He was
captured and taken to Camp Ford. He saw prisoners from 17 states. From New York
alone, 18 regiments were represented. The naval prisoners kept their quarters separate from those who were in the army. Ryan wrote of the streets inside the stockade
with the names of Water Street, Front Street, Broadway, 5th Avenue, 10 Pin Alley,
and Mule Avenue. Along these streets, prisoners lived in A-frames, cabins and caves,
which held from 10 to 12 men. They called their crude shelters "shebangs."[24]

Another prisoner was Pvt. Xerxes Knox, from Company G, 3rd Iowa Cavalry.
Knox had enlisted at Keokuk, Iowa, on August 30, 1861. He was 27 years old, 5 feet

7¼ inches tall, with blue eyes and sandy-colored hair. Knox was taken prisoner on May 1, 1864, near Camden, Arkansas. The Federal forces of Union Gen. Frederick Steel lost 700 men killed, wounded, or captured between Camden and Jenkins' Ferry. They abandoned hundreds of wagons. Those that weren't captured made their way back to Little Rock. About 200 were taken to Camp Ford.[25]

In his application for an invalid pension, Knox said that he arrived at Camp Ford on May 10, 1864. Thomas H. Pace, another Camp Ford prisoner, supported in an affidavit to the Bureau of Pensions on January 7, 1889, the claim submitted by Knox. Pace also added that when they arrived at Camp Ford, "The weather being very hot and our rations being corn meal and occasionally some fresh beef which we had to cook and eat without salt."[26]

Daily Life of the Prisoners

Prisoner Ryan recalled that sometimes the prisoners entertained themselves by playing baseball games. They even produced a newspaper called the *Old Flag*. They gambled and fought among themselves almost daily. Wrestling matches were held between regiments. They made musical instruments, and whittled and carved all kinds of trinkets.[27]

The prisoners made combs, rings, chessmen, and other articles which they bartered for food.[28] They made baskets and built chairs from grapevines. One prisoner, Lieutenant Mars, became known for the beautiful banjos he carved from ash and hickory wood. Other prisoners made soap. Still others made items from the red clay: bowls, plates, coffee cups, and smoking pipes. All of these items could be traded to the guards or local families for food and dairy products.[29]

Prisoners Take Action As Conditions Worsen

In the spring of 1864, the prisoners who had wintered at Shreveport returned, and then came 340 prisoners captured in Arkansas from the 36th Iowa. Shortly thereafter, nearly 2,000 Federal soldiers captured at Mansfield, Louisiana, arrived. Many were without shelter, and soon all the shade trees had been cut down. The enclosure was too small for that many men.[30]

After being imprisoned for several months, many of the prisoners were in need of clothing, shoes, blankets, and other necessities. Many of the men had been imprisoned for as long as 17 months, and were practically naked. Clothing for 1,662 soldiers and 205 sailors was requested. Some of the prisoners at Camp Ford went so far as to write to the local United States Army commander to request clothing.[31]

To get their requests to the proper Federal authorities, the letters had to go through Gen. E. Kirby Smith. So, the letter was sent to him to forward. Those who signed their names to a plea for supplies for 3,700 men were: Col. Charles C. Nott, 176th New York Volunteers; Lt. Col. J. B. Leake, 20th Iowa Infantry; Lt. Col. John Cowan, 19th Kentucky Infantry; and Capt. E. B. Hall, acting assistant adjutant general of the Department of the Gulf. Those prisoners who had been there for several months needed blouses, trousers, shoes, drawers, shirts, socks and blankets. They requested medical supplies for 4,527 men for six months to include: quinine, calomel, blue mass, proto iodide of mercury, muriated tincture of iron, nitrate silver, nitrate potash, sulphate magnesia, a small quantity of assorted medicine, castile soap, opium, Dover's powders, morphine, ipecac, antimony, carbonate ammonia, camphor (gum), and stimulants.[32]

On February 8, 1865, Capt. J. M. McCulloch, from the 77th Illinois Infantry, who was a prisoner at Camp Ford, wrote to report that his fellow prisoners had "sufficient clothing to render them comfortable," but that they needed vegetables to "counteract the great tendency to scurvy." Scurvy, reported McCulloch, was the disease which was most prevalent at Camp Ford, and he requested a "lot of citric acid" which he believed would be beneficial to the health of the prisoners.[33]

Morbidity and Mortality

Lt. Frederick Crocker wrote in June 1864 to appeal to Federal authorities that many of the first group of prisoners had died of disease, and "sickness is now spreading with appalling rapidity among the remainder." Crocker stated that many were "destitute of clothing," and had "nothing but rags to cover their nakedness." Crocker stated that the Confederates were "unable to afford us clothing, or a full supply of medicines, and our necessities having become exceedingly great, we appeal to our Government, and to you [Rear Admiral David D. Farragut], to have them forwarded to us." Crocker included a detailed list of the number of men from the crews of four ships, and exactly what they needed in the way of clothing.[34]

Out of more than 4,700 soldiers imprisoned at Camp Ford, there were only about 286 deaths. This was one of the lowest death rates reported from any prison during the Civil War.[35]

Exchange

In November 1864, a specific number of U.S. naval prisoners at Camp Groce, Texas, were to be exchanged for those Confederates captured at Fort Gains. If the number at Camp Groce was not sufficient, then the balance was to be made up of prisoners from Camp Ford.[36] After the war ended, Capt. William H. Sterling, of the 1st U.S. Infantry, and agent of exchange, sent a list of Confederate blockade runners being held at Fort Lafayette and Fort Warren, who Major Szymanski, the agent of exchange in the Trans-Mississippi Department, wanted to exchange for the "steam-boat captains" now being held prisoner at Camp Ford. Sterling noted that there are "many steam-boat men, such as captains, pilots, engineers, &c, held as prisoners at Camp Ford for whom we have no other equivalents than blockade-runners."[37]

An agreement was reached whereby all the naval prisoners were to be exchanged. However, 27 naval prisoners were still at Camp Ford in late February 1865. The 27 were free Negroes who had been captured on the Federal ships *Clifton, Sachem, Morning Light,* and the ram *Queen of the West.*[38]

Escape Attempts

Getting out of Camp Ford was not as difficult as it was to remain out. It was at least 300 miles to Union lines, and the guards with their bloodhounds were efficient and swift in recapturing escapees. The terrain was rugged and there were many rivers to cross. The civilian population was pro–Confederate, and there was always the danger of encountering Indians.[39] In addition, bands of Confederate guerrillas roamed the country.[40]

Before the stockade was built, prisoners simply slipped by the guards at night. Some were soon recaptured by bloodhounds, others were gone for weeks traveling in circles. Some were never heard from again, and may have perished in the swamps.[41]

After the stockade was built, there were more than 50 attempts to escape from Camp Ford by tunneling. One tunnel was begun in March 1864. Fifteen men escaped through it, only to be recaptured within a few days by the Confederate cavalry and bloodhounds.[42]

William Ryan remembered that most of the escapes occurred on rainy nights. They men would escape by a tunnel under the walls and disappear into the night. Ryan stated that over 600 escaped, while only 46 were caught by the bloodhounds. To stop the tunneling, a deadline was established and if any prisoner went within 10 feet of the walls, the guards had orders to shoot without warning.[43]

There were at least four mass escapes planned. One which involved more than 50 men nearly succeeded. Once outside, the prisoners had to cope with the environment. One group evaded capture for three months, but were finally captured by some of Brig. Gen. Douglas H. Cooper's Choctow troops, returned to the stockade, and made to wear barrel shirts.[44]

When escapees were recaptured they were punished in full view of the remainder of the prison population by being hung up by their thumbs. Others were put in solitary confinement.[45]

John W. Greene and John A. Whitsit, of the 26th Indiana Volunteer Regiment, were captured during an engagement with Confederate forces near Morganza, at Mrs. Stirling's plantation. Out of the 854-man detachment, there were 515 casualties. Sixteen were killed, 45 wounded and 454 captured. Out of the 26th Indiana, Greene and Whitsit, and seven other officers, plus 209 enlisted men were captured. The Confederates loss was 26 killed, 85 wounded and 10 missing during the engagement. The prisoners were taken to Camp Ford.[46]

Greene lived to write of his experiences during his escape from Camp Ford. The pair actually escaped on Christmas Eve 1863. An out-of-date newspaper account in the *Indianapolis Journal* reported on January 6, 1864, that nine officers from the 26th Indiana were "in jail" at Tyler, Texas. They were listed as: Lt. Col. Augustine D. Rose, Lt. Calvin C. McDowell, Capt. Newton A. Logan, Lt. J. M. Robinson (or Robertson), Lt. Richard H. Stott, Capt. John Whitsett [sic], Lt. J. M. Collins [probably Elisha J. Collins], Lt. John Green, and Lt. William J. Wallace.[47]

However, Greene and Whitsit actually were not among these nine, but were in Shreveport, Louisiana, 100 miles away. Their initial destination had been Vicksburg, 180 miles east of Shreveport. When they started out, they crossed the Red River about 10 miles south of Shreveport. Then they crossed the Red Chute, and headed toward Sparta. They changed direction and headed southeastward to the Washita River and a Union outpost at Fort Washita. However, when they arrived there, they found it was held by Confederate troops. Eventually, the pair made their way to Vidalia, Louisiana, across the Mississippi from Natchez.[48]

Greene and Whitsit had developed a plan to escape. They knew that with paroles, they were allowed to pass in and out of the stockade to cut or gather wood. They thought to hide behind some large piles of brush. To keep their absence from being noticed, they had others answer the roll call for them. Then, they saw their chance when they learned that some prisoners held at Galveston and Houston were to be transferred to Tyler and Shreveport. After the new prisoners arrived, all officers, Greene got one of them to write a letter to some of the enlisted men being marched to Shreveport. With letter in hand, the pair passed through the gates at 3 P.M. on Christmas Eve. They hid until dark, then made their way to the group of prisoners being marched to Shreveport. They asked for the officer to whom the letter was addressed, and after explaining their situation, were welcomed in the group. The next day, the pair continued with those being marched to Shreveport, and passed unnoticed by the stockade of their former prison.[49] Thus, they traveled safely in the company of other Federal prisoners and their Confederate guards.

At the Shreveport barracks, the two stepped out of the line and joined those outside who were gathering wood, Then, they marched inside with their wood, as if they were old prisoners. At Shreveport, Greene and Whitsit met many members of their regiment, but they knew they could not remain long without being found out. So, they saved their rations, and managed to obtain a gray jacket and wool hat, and slipped out of the stockade early one morning on the pretense of gathering wood.[50] Their subsequent journey to freedom was made across rivers and swamps, through woods and thickets. They were helped along the way by slaves. Their flight was one of few successful attempts to escape Camp Ford.

The Destruction of Camp Ford

Camp Ford existed for 21 months. The last prisoners left in May 1865, to be turned over to Federal officials at Hog Point, Louisiana, on May 25, 1865.[51]

Two months later, on July 4, 1865, the stockade was burned by the men of the 10th Illinois.[52]

Camp Ford Today

The site of Camp Ford is now a public park, owned by Smith County, Texas, and managed by the Smith County Historical Society. There are walking trails and informative signs, a picnic area, and a replica of the cabin constructed by Lt. Col. J. B. Leak. Camp Ford Historic Park is located on U.S. Highway 271, .8 miles outside Loop 323 in Tyler, Texas. The park is open daily, and admission is free.[53]

XX

Castle Thunder, Richmond, Virginia

…we were placed in a dungeon, on the charge of attempting to escape. We were kept there ten days.
— Albert D. Richardson, newspaper reporter and prisoner[1]

Location: on Cary Street, between 18th and 19th Streets, Richmond, Virginia. **Established:** 1862. **Type:** group of three converted tobacco warehouses. **Type of Prisoners:** Confederate deserters, spies and political prisoners (both male and female), runaway slaves, Federal deserters, criminals under court-martial, and occasionally Federal officers. **Capacity:** 1,400. **Most Held at One Time:** 3,000+. **Number of Escapes:** unknown (numerous). **Other Names:** Rebel Bastille, Gleanor's, Palmer's.[2]

History

By the spring of 1862, Richmond's prisons were overflowing. The 13 rooms of Castle Godwin were so overcrowded that some of the political prisoners had been moved to Libby Prison. A larger facility was needed. What became known as Castle Thunder met that need, and as soon as it was ready for use, Castle Godwin was closed, and its 600 prisoners transferred to Castle Thunder.[3]

Castle Thunder opened as a prison in August 1862. The central core was Gleanor's Tobacco Warehouse. Attached to each side were Palmer's Factory and Whitlock's Warehouse.[4] The name was appropriate because those held there as prisoners were said to have evoked the thunder of the gods. Even the Richmond papers thought the name "indicative of Olympian vengeance" for offenders of the law.[5]

There is no doubt that during its day Castle Thunder was one of the most controversial prisons in both the North and the South.

Frank B. Doran, of St. Paul, Minnesota, wrote from experience gained while having been a prisoner twice in Castle Thunder:

> The frequency of public mention and private recital of occurrences relating to the various prisons of that eventful period have depended so largely upon the numbers confined in each that the names of Libby and Belle Isle, of Andersonville and Millen, of Salisbury, Columbia and Florence have become household words, while the location of some of the most tragic events of that great epoch are comparatively

Castle Thunder, Richmond, Virginia, held Confederate deserters, spies, Federal deserters, runaway slaves, and women. (Courtesy of Library of Congress, Washington, D.C., LC-B8171-3160.)

unknown. The Knoxville Jail, in Eastern Tennessee, and Castle Thunder, in Richmond are good illustrations.[6]

The Castle Thunder Complex

The prison complex was made up of three former tobacco factories and warehouses. The combination of Palmer's Factory and Whitlock's Warehouse attached to each side of Gleanor's Tobacco Warehouse formed a parallelogram.[7] Across the street was a smaller building called Castle Lightning, which held the overflow of prisoners from Castle Thunder.[8]

Behind Palmer's and Whitlock's, a high fence connected the two buildings. Water was pumped from the James River.[9]

The main building, Gleanor's Warehouse, faced Cary Street. The largest of the three, Gleanor's stood three and a half stories high, and could hold 650 prisoners. Palmer's could hold 400, and Whitlock's another 350, a comfortable total inmate population of 1,400.[10]

Upon entering the front door of Gleanor's, a passageway extended to the rear of the building. To the left of the passageway, was the prison office. On the right of the passage was the prison guards' room. A sentry stood at the end of the passage where two long flights of stairs led to the upper floors. Another set of stairs led to the upper levels.[11]

A door at the back of a room on the first floor where the balls and chains were kept opened onto the "execution yard."[12] A gallows stood in the yard on a side ledge. The brick wall that surrounded the yard was pock-marked from executions carried out there in full view of the prisoners who watched from their barred windows.[13]

Behind the three buildings was an enclosed yard where prisoners could exercise. The latrines were located here as well. Gaslights and water were available with the guards' approval. However, the quality of air inside the buildings was poor, and the odor of many unwashed bodies was most foul. Prisoners slept on blankets or straw. The second floor had a number of cells that were about 15 feet square. These had boarded-up windows. A long hall led to a big room that had four barred windows. This was called the "prison parlor" where prisoners could walk about without interference. The third floor was divided into two rooms, a larger one for prisoners of war, and a smaller room confined Confederate soldiers who were awaiting court-martial.[14]

The Dungeon

Also on the first floor were two cells for condemned prisoners. There was a foul-smelling latrine in the center of that room.[15]

The popular view of Castle Thunder was expressed by Joseph Ferguson in his work on Southern prisons published in 1865, when he wrote that prisoners were frequently "handcuffed, maimed, tortured, hung and shot, whipped until the weary soul winged its way to the creator, glad of flight from earth."[16]

However, the New York *Tribune* correspondent Albert D. Richardson was somewhat more honest, since he had been in both Libby Prison and Castle Thunder: "The prison's reputation was worse than that of Libby; but, as usual, we found the devil not quite so black as he was painted."[17]

The Prisoners

Castle Thunder held more desperate and dangerous prisoners than any other prison in the South.[18] Civilians and soldiers, men and women, were arrested and held for extended periods in Castle Thunder. Some inmates faced long-term incarceration or even execution as spies or deserters. Other prisoners were awaiting trial. Many citizens suspected of disloyalty were held indefinitely and were never allowed a trial. Confederate soldiers were sent back to their regiments once they served their sentence. They all had one thing in common — they were desperate to get out of Castle Thunder. But, it was far easier to get into this Confederate prison than to get out of it.

Capt. Thomas P. Turner, the commandant at Libby Prison, described the type of prisoners held at Castle Thunder as "the worst in the land…. Some of the most desperate men in the Confederacy are there."[19] Those held at Castle Thunder were, indeed, some of the most dangerous of prisoners—spies, double agents, deserters, traitors, and those under sentence of execution—desperate characters all. The counterpart of Castle Thunder in the North was, perhaps, the Old Capitol Prison in Washington, D.C., in which prisoners of state, persons suspected of disloyalty, those charged with bounty frauds, counterfeiters, government swindlers, spies, and others who may have been arrested by detectives on "trumped-up charges."[20]

Castle Thunder was used to confine those in the military who had broken military rules. Military tribunals sentenced offenders to incarceration at the Castle.[21] Military offenders from camps all over the Confederacy were sent to Castle Thunder to await sentencing. These soldiers were charged with such military crimes as impersonating an officer, falsifying place of residence, forging discharges or pay accounts, entering Richmond without a pass, and drunkenness. Whole companies were sometimes put under arrest. All the privates of Company D, 20th Virginia Battalion, were arrested on "mutinous conduct charges," because they had demonstrated against the "ill treatment of the battalion commander, Major Delagnel."[22]

Upon arrival at Castle Thunder, the prisoners were segregated among the three buildings. The Gleanor's Warehouse building was used to hold the social "outcasts," the Confederate deserters, and those civilians who had been declared enemies of the Confederacy. Blacks and women were assigned to Whitlock's Warehouse, while Palmer's Factory was reserved for Federal deserters and others.[23] As the war continued and the prison was packed beyond capacity, the segregation was not strictly enforced. By 1863, Castle Thunder held 1,500 prisoners.[24]

On September 2, 1863, all northern citizens who had been held in Libby Prison were transferred to Castle Thunder, including the New York *Tribune*'s Richardson. They were placed in the "Citizens' Room," next to the condemned cell. The Citizens' Room had four iron-barred windows, and the walls were whitewashed. It had gas lights and the floor was clean.[25]

Female Prisoners

An estimated 100 women were held at Castle Thunder as spies or political prisoners. One famous prisoner was Dr. Mary Walker, the first woman surgeon in the Union Army. Another woman, Mary Lee, gave birth to a baby while in the prison, which she named Castellina Thunder Lee. After her release, Mary often returned to show her growing daughter to the other prisoners.[26]

Another famous female prisoner was Madame Loreta Janeta Valasquez, also known as Lt. Harry Buford. She had served the Confederacy as a substitute, and as a spy. In error, she was arrested as a Union spy and placed in Castle Thunder.[27]

Many women were incarcerated in Castle Thunder on suspicion of being spies. Althea F. Harris was sent to Castle Thunder from Columbia, South Carolina, because she had been arrested as a spy. A newspaper article described her as "a very pretty girl."[28]

The Prison Commandant — Capt. George Washington Alexander

The new facility in Richmond was named Castle Thunder to instill fear and to terrorize evildoers. It did become a place of terror to many who were incarcerated there. Soon, the name of the prison would be indicative of the treatment the inmates received.[29] Some of the "thunder" heard within the walls of Castle Thunder came from one man — George Washington Alexander, the prison's first commandant. He was described in a report of Confederate prisons after the war as "harsh, inhuman, tyrannical, and dishonest in every possible way."[30]

Captain Alexander, a former United States naval officer, ran his prison as he would a ship. He had been a prisoner at Fort McHenry himself (see Chapter VIII), and had made a daring escape with the help of his wife, a Virginia lady, the former Miss Susan Ashby. Afterward, he came to Richmond and joined the provost marshal's office, and was put in command of the new prison in the fall of 1862.[31]

Richardson described Alexander as an "ex–Marylander, who had participated with 'the French lady' in the capture of the steamer *St. Nicholas*, near Point Lookout," and who had been captured and confined at Fort McHenry. He had few kind words to say about Alexander's "literary pretensions," and that he wrote "thin plays for the Richmond theaters, and sorry Rebel war-ballads." He thought Captain Alexander was "pompous and excessively vain," and that the captain delighted in "gauntlets, top-boots, huge revolvers, and a red sash." He had something of a temper and, according to Richardson, "was sometimes furiously angry," but for the most part, he was "kind to captives."[32]

Captain Alexander presented a formidable appearance as he galloped through the streets of Richmond on his black horse, his long black beard flowing in the wind. At his heels was always the magnificent black dog, Nero (Hero).[33] There were rumors that Hero, a Bavarian boarhound (descended from Great Danes), had more than once been turned into the cells of Union prisoners, and had killed or torn sickly prisoners apart.[34]

Based on appearance alone, both the citizens and the prisoners feared the commandant of Castle Thunder. Indeed, Alexander, with his coal-black hair, beard and eyes, completed the picture of terror. His normally fierce appearance was made even more formidable by the standard uniform required of the provost marshal. Instead of the elegant gray of the official Confederate uniform, each provost marshal wore a tight-fitting black suit. The trousers were buckled at the knee, below which he wore black stockings. The black of his attire was relieved only by a white collar on his black shirt.[35]

Castle Thunder Detectives

In addition to the regular guards, a detective force was stationed at Castle Thunder. They were employed to arrest deserters and suspicious persons, and to track down escapees. However, early in April 1863, that force was divided, and Detectives Crow, Causey, and Shaeffer were ordered to report to headquarters of the provost marshal in Richmond. Four of the detectives, Perdue, Folks, New, and Thomas, were to remain at Castle Thunder.[36]

Congressional Investigation Launched

Soon after the prison opened, complaints were heard that new arrivals were beaten and robbed. It was said that deserters from the Confederate army were routinely given 50 to 100 lashes upon Alexander's orders. Rumors were rampant that the brick wall at the rear was "chipped and scarred" from numerous executions by firing squads. It was reported that the dungeon in the prison contained 50 pairs of balls and chains, each with leg irons and handcuffs for the punishment of prisoners. Other methods of punishment were handcuffing the prisoner high on a post and leaving him dangling for hours. Bucking and gagging were also employed, or prisoners were chained to the walls and floors. Some were branded as well. Another method of treatment (one used extensively in the navy) was to hang a prisoner up by his thumbs. After a short time, circulation was cut off, and if the prisoner remained tied very long, he could lose his thumbs. The arms could also be dislocated from the shoulder joints.[37] These and other forms of punishment were common in all prisons, both North and South.

The extent of the rumors of cruelty finally resulted in an investigation. A committee was appointed by the Confederate House of Representatives and hearings were held. After numerous witnesses were called, Alexander was cleared of all charges.[38] (For more information about Captain Alexander and Castle Thunder, see Frances H. Casstevens, *George Washington Alexander and Castle Thunder: A Confederate Prison and Its Commandant,* McFarland & Company, 2004.)

Prisoners complained that punishment, especially under Captain Alexander, was brutal, and that the guards were careless and inexperienced.[39]

It is true that prisoners were often punished at Castle Thunder. Some of the prison records were found left behind in the commandant's office at the end of the war. The books listed the names of prisoners, their punishment, and the reason. For giving food to Federal prisoners, George Barton was sentenced to 40 lashes upon his bare back. The entry in the record book stated that this was approved and sentence carried out on July 2. Peter B. Innis was sentenced to wear a ball and chain for 12 months, and to receive 40 lashes.[40] However, most of those punished were by court order, and it was the duty of the prison commandant to enforce those sentences. Prisoners were also punished for attempting to escape or for infractions of the rules of the prison.

Some of the prisoners confined at Castle Thunder hated Captain Alexander so much they planned to assassinate him.[41] Others, such as Richardson, wrote that the "Commandant and *attachés,* unlike the Turners [at Libby Prison] treated us [the civilians] courteously, never indulging in epithets and insults."[42]

Others prisoners spent their time and energy attempting to escape, and some were successful. Others failed before their plans could even be put into motion, and were punished for their efforts.

Escapes, 1862–1863

There were many escape attempts at Castle Thunder. Breakouts began almost as soon as Castle Thunder opened as a prison. The Richmond papers recorded many successful as well as unsuccessful attempts by prisoners to put Castle Thunder behind them.

In December 1862, about 150 prisoners hatched a plot to assassinate the sentinels on Christmas Eve, and make their escape. The plot was discovered and the ringleader, David Welsh, was whipped, placed in irons, and reduced to rations of bread and water.[43]

The First Attempt

On August 24, 1862, the first week that Castle Thunder was in operation as a prison, John Farmer was shot by a guard at the rear of the building as he attempted to escape. The prisoner sustained a flesh wound in the arm and was taken to the hospital for treatment.[44]

Pvt. John R. Jones had deserted from Company C, 18th Battalion, Virginia Heavy Artillery, but a detective arrested him in Petersburg about January 14, 1863, and brought him to Castle Thunder. At his court-martial, Jones' statement about his escape was written into the record. Jones had said that as some 80 men were being sent to Jackson's Army from Castle Thunder, he went out of the prison with them. He did not board the train, but when it left the station, he hid and escaped without notice.[45]

Another clever prisoner escaped while on the way to General Winder's office. He told his guard that he was a "clerk of the Castle," and ordered the guard to wait for him at the next corner, while he visited the provost marshal's office. The clerk-prisoner promised to meet the guard within 15 minutes. The unsuspecting guard obeyed, but his prisoner walked away in the other direction.[46]

Some of the more popular means of escape, though not always successful, seemed to be climbing down from a window.

Out Through a Window

One crafty prisoner obtained some old clothing and an old slouch hat from a black person. He blacked his face with a piece of burnt cork and, with bucket in hand, followed a group of blacks down three flights of stairs and past four sentinels. He hid in the quarters where the blacks were kept until dark, then jumped out a window to land right before a sentinel. The sentinel was so surprised that the prisoner had time to disappear around the corner before the astonished guard could fire.[47]

The tools needed to carry out an escape were contrived from every available source. It is estimated that at least one third of all the blankets distributed at Castle Thunder were cut up and used to aid in an escape. Blankets were easily converted to ropes and thus were "zealously guarded by the prisoners."[48]

Bribe the Guards

It was very common for prisoners to offer to bribe their guards. Prisoners even bribed other prisoners. An officer might bribe an enlisted man to switch identities, if the enlisted man was soon going to be eligible for exchange.

In November 1862 there was an ingenious escape. A group of desperate prisoners decided there was no chance to bribe the sentinels, because they had no money with which to buy their assistance. So, they came up with a plan to fool the sentinels into believing that they had a large purse of money. The prisoners offered to give money to a guard to turn his back while they were escaping from a window. The prisoners selected a window in the northeast corner of the second story. The window overlooked a platform on which the sentinels walked, and there was a stairway which descended to the street, and a second sentinel was on guard there. At the appointed time, the sentinel who had been chosen was called to the window and the prisoners propositioned him. "If you will help us get out to night, we four will give you fifty dollars a piece — that'll be two hundred dollars!" The sentinel replied, "I'll see," which meant he had to check with his partner below. For the remainder of the day, the sentinels met and discussed the proposition. When they returned to their posts, the prisoners were told that the guards were in agreement, and preparations were begun for a "grand exit." A window was opened, and the leader stepped out. "Where's the money?" whispered the sentinel. The leader lied and said, "The last man has got it," and he left. Then came the second, third, fourth, fifth, sixth, and seventh man, and more would have escaped, but the sentinel began to get suspicious. He ran to the window to put a stop to the escaping prisoners, and gave the alarm. Meanwhile, the sentinel on the ground let the prisoners pass before the alarm was spread, and they got away.[49]

On Saturday, Captain Alexander and a force of detectives set out in search of the escapees. After much searching, they arrested two. He learned from those two the details of the escape, and which two sentinels had helped. The two sentinels were members of a corps who were usually on duty at a prison opposite Libby Prison and had been detached to duty at Castle Thunder. They were arrested and placed in irons to await trial for their offense, the penalty for which was death.[50]

On October 9, 1862, James Jennings, a substitute soldier arrested for desertion, escaped from Castle Thunder by jumping out a window on the western side. He had been gone for several days when Detective New saw him in a cigar store on Main Street in Richmond. The detective arrested him and returned him to Castle Thunder. The prisoner did not resist, although he could have probably escaped, because the detective had two other prisoners in tow at the same time.[51]

August Wile, a Yankee, escaped in November 1863 by climbing out of a window to the roof of an outbuilding, and from there sliding to the ground.[52]

Another conspiracy to escape Castle Thunder was discovered before the prisoners could use a long rope made from cotton sheets. A condemned prisoner scheduled to be shot on Saturday helped them out through the window, but they were spotted. After their discovery, the escapees were put in the dungeon. Richmond papers noted that the increasing efforts to escape could be stopped only by "increased vigilance, and the shooting of those seen escaping."[53]

Escape Through a Hole in the Wall

On January 5, 1863, about 70 prisoners plotted to escape through a hole in the walls. Each prisoner had managed to obtain either a knife or a revolver. Thus armed, they would kill any guard who attempted to prevent their escape. However, informers told prison officials of the plan, and the ringleaders were questioned and punished.[54]

J. Wrenn and M. J. Lemmon escaped by digging through the rear wall. They were recaptured after a short period of freedom as they attempted to board a train leaving Richmond, and were returned to Castle Thunder.[55]

A Richmond newspaper reported just before the hearings were opened into the treatment of prisoners at Castle Thunder: "This military rendezvous [Castle Thunder] was like an unpatronized hotel yesterday—few arrivals and fewer departures. A daily attempt or two on the part of the inmates to escape enliven the dull routine of the guard."[56] Two days later, another paper reported that "a number of prisoners" had attempted to escape by cutting through a wall. They had been discovered by the guards and "driven back to their quarters."[57]

Hard to Hold

William Campbell was hard to keep in prison, and he made repeated attempts to escape. An investigation was ordered to determine just how Campbell and Armstead, another prisoner, had escaped. Brigadier General Winder ordered a committee of officials at other prisons— Maj. W. M. Elliott, and Capt. L. J. Bossieux, and Capt. Thomas P. Turner — to meet in Richmond on January 14, 1863, to inquire into the matter.[58]

Prisoner Killed Trying to Escape

The news carried details about an escape that occurred on April 7, 1863, in which Charles Carroll, alias John Byas (or Byzas), was shot and killed. He and several fellow prisoners had cut a hole through the wall of the room in which they were held. They managed to get to another room and were actually out on the balcony, when discovered. One of the prisoners stepped back inside, but Carroll remained, was shot "through the heart," and died instantly. Another report stated that he was shot "between the eyes."[59] Carroll was a deserter from the 54th (or 53rd) Virginia Regiment.[60]

Another paper had a slightly different slant to the story. William Campbell and Charles Carroll were being held in the condemned cell, but they succeeded in cutting their way through a partition wall and were able to reach a window that faced Cary Street. Just as the men were about to jump, a guard called out a warning. The prisoners did not answer, so the sentinel fired. Carroll died instantly. His companion, William Campbell, ran down the main gangway and, because of the confusion, was able to get past a guard and into the street. Detective George W. Thomas ran after him and fired two pistol shots. The detective captured Campbell at the corner of 18th and Main. Campbell's attempt was again unsuccessful.[61]

Campbell Continues Escape Efforts

William Campbell continued to try to escape, and almost succeeded once. After this escape, he remained at large for some time. However, in July 1863, detectives

Thomas, Folks and Perdue found him in bed with a prostitute at a house of ill repute in Lombard Alley. He was hauled out of bed and returned to the Castle. The papers reported that this was his fourth attempt. Campbell swore that Castle Thunder could not hold him.[62]

Escape by Tunnel

Fifteen prisoners tried to dig out of the Palmer's Factory Building, which had been converted temporarily to a hospital. When the first man crawled out of the tunnel, Captain Alexander was waiting, with a gun. Alexander ordered the man to proceed, and then he captured the rest of them as each exited the tunnel.[63]

One prisoner did not even make it outside. James Howell was discovered digging in an old excavation which had been filled in. He was put in irons to prevent another escape attempt.[64]

In the fall of 1863, some prisoners decided to dig another tunnel. The site of their dig under the walls of the stable was discovered, although the diggers had tried to cover the entrance to their tunnel with a pile of rocks.[65]

On Saturday, November 14, 1863, 35 Yankee deserters escaped from Castle Thunder. They had been confined in a room on the second floor at the rear of the building, but they had cut a hole in the floor and descended to the storeroom below. From this room, they cut a hole through the fire place, and tunneled for 15 feet under an alley which ended in Sinton's lot beyond the alley. The exit was about a foot beyond the fence that connected the buildings. The tunnel was large enough for a man's body. The prisoners made their escape undetected. A reporter who saw the escape tunnel declared that the men who had constructed it must have been miners. By 12 o'clock that same day, two of the escapees had been recaptured attempting to make their way to the peninsula.[66] A week later, 29 of the prisoners had been recaptured; only six got away.[67]

Another group tried tunneling out, but were betrayed by a traitor within their midst. They were taken before the commandant who told them:

> There is no use, men, of trying to get out of here; it is absolutely impossible! You can make no movement; you can not breathe; you can not have a thought that is unknown to me. You might as well attempt to scale Heaven as escape from the Castle; so you had better behave yourselves, and become resigned to your situation.[68]

The commandant's talk had little effect on the determination of the prisoners, and the very next night, the first 10 plus another 12 prisoners escaped and "were never afterward heard of by the Rebels,"[69] according to prisoner Junius Henri Browne.

A Tunnel Plus a Backup Plan

Two captains from Indiana, working undercover for the Federal Secret Service, were captured in Tennessee inside Confederate lines. They pretended to be deserters, and were brought to Richmond. One of them told A. D. Richardson: "They offer to release us if we will take the oath of allegiance to the Southern Confederacy; but I cannot do that. I want to rejoin my regiment, and fight the Rebels while the war lasts. I must escape, and I cannot afford to lose any time." The next night he removed a plank from the floor in his room and descended to the basement where he began digging a tunnel. The tunnel was almost completed when it was discovered. Not to be bested, the Indiana captain started digging another tunnel. That one was discovered also. Finally, in desperation, he put croton oil on his face, which would result in skin eruptions that resembled smallpox. Following the method of several others, he escaped as he was being transported by wagon to the smallpox hospital.[70]

Another attempt was made on Monday night, May 18, 1863, by a prisoner who tried to saw the bars off a window. Even with the aid of a rope and a bribed guard, this attempt failed.[71]

Two days later, Patrick Garrack was caught trying to escape. He had tried to bribe one of the sentinels during the night, and the guard, while pretending to go along with the prisoner, notified the commandant. Garrack was seized the moment he descended down a rope. If he had succeeded, 15 more desperate men had planned to follow him.[72]

Forged Release Orders

Every possible means to escape was tried. One prisoner, Fleming Brazer, tried to get released with a forged special order. Presented by Lt. W. L. Soles, from a Florida regiment, the document appeared to be a release order from General Winder. When it was discovered that the order was forged, both the prisoner and the forger were soon captured and returned to Castle Thunder.[73]

Another man was actually a New Yorker who had been caught in Louisiana spying for the Secret Service. Incriminating documents were found in the lining of his valise. George W. Hudson moaned when he returned from being examined by General Winder: "There is evidence enough to hang me twenty times over." He knew he would die unless he could escape. After discarding a number of plans, he decided on one that worked. He sent out to buy a new valise, and then he washed his clothes so as to be more presentable. Then, he simply wrote out an order for his release and signed it with a close imitation of General Winder's signature. He got one of the black workers to place the document on the desk of the adjutant. A few days later, Hudson, valise in hand, appeared at the door of A. D. Richardson's cell. "I have come to say goodby. My discharge has arrived." After conversing with prison officials for a few minutes, the man who had forged his own discharge walked out of Castle Thunder. A lady who was sympathetic to the Union sheltered him for a while, and it was later learned that he was with the Army of the Potomac on the staff of Gen. George Meade.[74]

Another man who was successful in concealing his true identity and thereby avoiding recapture was Robert Slocum, of the 19th Massachusetts Volunteers. After being taken as a prisoner of war, Slocum escaped after only two days in prison. He obtained some clothes from some blacks, and made his way to Wilmington, North Carolina. He passed himself off as an Englishman who had just arrived on a blockade runner. Confederate authorities found some discrepancy in his passport, and he was arrested and sent to Castle Thunder. Still maintaining his alias as an Englishman, Slocum employed a Richmond lawyer to obtain his release. The Union officer-turned-Englishman remained in Richmond where he sent letters and provisions to the prisoners in Castle Thunder, and tried to assist them in escape attempts. He was so adept at maintaining his disguise, that he was invited to attend a social event with Confederate president Jefferson Davis.[75]

Sentinel Is Killed by Escapees

A successful escape was managed by E. D. Boone (or Booth), Edward Carney, Thomas Cole, and John A. Chipman, "all desperate characters," who were housed in Castle Thunder on serious charges. They had already tried to escape once, and thus had been placed in the condemned cell, with a guard on duty at all times.[76]

In his memoirs, Richardson calls the murderer Booth. The night before their execution, the condemned prisoners surprised everyone by "dancing, rattling their chains, and singing." Later that night, about 1 o'clock, the entire prison was awakened by the sound of shouts and musket shots. The men had cut a hole in the floor of their cell with a case knife while their comrades had made as much noise as they could. "Flinging off their irons," they descended through the hole into the store room, where they found four muskets. Under cover of darkness, they removed the lock from the door, and each taking a gun, moved out the street.[77]

After the escaping prisoners overpowered the sentinel inside the door, they encountered another a sentinel outside; one of the escapees put the muzzle of a gun to the sentinel's head and fired. The sentinel was a young man named Sutton Byrd, a private in Company C, 53rd North Carolina Regiment.[78]

A crowd of soldiers gathered around the body of their fallen comrade. Captain Alexander's dog, Hero (Nero), placed himself beside the body, and would let no one approach until the proper officer relived him of his duty. The dog then followed the corpse as it was carried into the building. Everyone was moved by this display of "canine affection."[79]

The prisoners ran up the street. At the long bridge across the James River, they knocked down another sentinel who tried to stop them. They continued to travel at night until they reached Union lines.[80]

The group separated just outside Richmond, and each took a different route By October 26, 1863, Boone (or Booth), "the Castle Thunder Murderer," had made his way to safety behind the Yankee lines at Williamsburg.[81]

Each successful escape attempt spawned more escape efforts by prisoners. The week of April 15, 1863, five prisoners escaped from Castle Thunder. This was only a day or two after Tim O'Brien was reported to have escaped from the county jail, where he was held for forging a check.[82]

Out on Oath of Allegiance

Yankee prisoners at Castle Thunder Alfred Turner, Edward Hill, Henry Page, William Fisher, J. Wilson and Eugene Delaney, took the oath of allegiance to the Confederacy, and were released "to earn, if possible, an honest living."[83]

Capt. Lafayette Jones, of Carter County, Tennessee, was being held for bushwhacking and recruiting soldiers for the Federal army within Rebel lines. If tried, he could be convicted and condemned to be shot. Jones managed to convince authorities that he was someone named Leander Johannes and, after enlisting in the Confederate army, he was released.[84]

Escape Through Winder's Legion

One means of getting out of Castle Thunder was to volunteer for "Winder's Legion" to aid in the defense of Richmond. The Winder Guards had been organized from among the Confederate prisoners held in Castle Thunder. Two companies, composed of about 150 men each, were on duty in May under the command of Major Vowels. A Richmond newspaper commented that only two "hard cases" had deserted, and the command was better off without them.[85]

After the battle at Gettysburg, Pennsylvania, in which the Army of Northern Virginia suffered heavy casualties, a group of the prisoners asked for and received permission from Captain Alexander to form a battalion in case of an emergency. Captain Alexander was appointed major of the unit, and he helped the men prepare in their efforts to help to expel "from Southern soil its ruthless invaders." The first company was armed and ready, having been drilled by Lieutenant Callahan, adjutant of the post. These 300 men were already veterans, and it was expected they would do their duty when faced with the enemy.[86]

The efforts of the former prisoners did not go unnoticed. The group of 300 prisoners who had volunteered to man the batteries were ordered to be "discharged and returned to their respective regiments without trial," just as soon as there was no longer a need for their "present organization." The Richmond *Examiner* noted that some of the prisoners had been confined on "very grave charges," but Jefferson Davis' order covered all "who have behaved themselves," and all had, except for one or two.[87]

On May 27, 1864, the Winder Legion returned to Richmond and was reviewed before General Winder's headquarters. The group had asked President Davis to "authorize the permanency of their present organization." The group, now about 250 men, were quartered in the Soldier's Home.[88]

Release by Flag of Truce

Thirty-one Yankee deserters confined in Castle Thunder made known their desire to return North. Their wish was granted. They were first sent to Libby Prison and then they were to be sent North under the first "flag of truce."[89]

Some Prisoners Just Walked Out

The easiest method of escape was to obtain civilian clothes and walk casually off the premises, unnoticed by the guard and mistaken for a visitor.[90] George Gerbert, alias Moore, tried this simple method to gain his freedom. He dressed in a nice suit of clothes, and passed by the guards unnoticed. He was captured by Detective Folks only a short distance from Castle Thunder while still on Cary Street.[91]

According to the Richmond *Whig*, two prisoners escaped from the castle in September 1864. John H. Scribener, the former keeper of the Rebel House on 14th Street in Richmond, had been confined to Castle Thunder for desertion. Scribener was well-known to officials. Three months before his escape he had had his mistress, Caroline Keepers (the Madame Danseuse of the Iron-Clad Opera Troupe) arrested for stealing his trunk. She had since "gone to the Yankees, where she and Scribener both came from originally."[92]

Scribener, along with a free black from Frederick, Maryland, who had been taken from a group of Yankees about 18 months before, simply walked out the front door of the prison. Undoubtedly they had bribed the guards. Their freedom was short lived. Authorities were informed that Scribener was hiding in Head's livery stable on 18th Street. A posse was formed and they found the prisoner hiding in the loft. The free black man was found at Stokes' jail where Scribener had left him to be sold.[93]

Escapes in 1864

In 1864, after Alexander had been replaced by Richardson, only 57 prisoners escaped from Castle Thunder. However, of those 57, only 18 were successful and were not apprehended.[94] Seventeen prisoners escaped on the night of February 9, 1864, the same night that Colonels Rose and Streight and 107 others escaped through the tunnel at Libby Prison.[95]

Attempts at Exchange

Brig. Gen. John Hunt Morgan, the famous Confederate cavalry officer, visited Castle Thunder shortly after his daring escape from the Ohio State Penitentiary (see Chapter XIII). Morgan wanted to try to effect an exchange of prisoners from the First Kentucky Cavalry (Union), who had been captured at Philadelphia and Rockford, Tennessee, for an equal number of men from his old regiment, the First Kentucky Cavalry (Confederate). This exchange never took place.[96]

Fake Death and Get Carried Out

James Hancock, held in Castle Thunder during the winter of 1864-1865 on suspicion of being a spy, was a "jolly, rollicking fellow having wonderful facial expression and great powers of mimicry." One evening, he suddenly staggered and fell to the floor. Some of the men inspected his body and said he was dead. The guards were notified and the surgeon called to determine if the man had fainted or if it was a true case of sudden death. The surgeon declared, he was "dead as a door nail!" In less than 20 minutes, the body had been loaded on a wagon and headed for the hospital, to be put in a cheap coffin and taken to a cemetery. However, when the driver reached the end of his journey, the body was gone. The driver thought the body had fallen out of the wagon, and he retraced his route looking for the lost corpse.

Hancock's "sudden death" was a part of his plan to escape. On the way to the hospital, he had simply gotten out of the wagon and started walking along the street. When the wagon driver returned to Castle Thunder, an alarm was spread all over Richmond. Hancock had some money in the lining of his vest, and he went to the best hotel in town and registered as being from Georgia. There, he spent a restful night, and the next morning he got new clothes, and walked around Richmond.

However, shortly after dinner, he was arrested on Main Street by the provost guards. But, no sooner had they taken him in custody than he crossed his eyes and pulled his mouth so it appeared drawn to one side. The confused guards let him go. Four days later, he was arrested again in the post office. This time, he drew his mouth to the right, squinted his left eye, and pretended to be deaf. He was taken to Castle Thunder, where neither the guards nor his fellow prisoners recognized him. He was locked up until he could be investigated. Finally, he got tired of holding his eye in a squint, and when he relaxed his face, he was recognized. Had the war lasted 10 more days, he would have been shot as a spy.[97]

Dangerous Spy Is Captured

Alfonzo C. Webster, christened Charles W. Brown at his birth in Maine, enlisted on October 3, 1861, when he was 23 years old as a first lieutenant in the 9th Pennsylvania Cavalry. He tried to get some of his fellow soldiers to go with him to Boston to raise a new company. For his efforts, he was court-martialed, and resigned. However, he followed his regiment when they moved to Louisville, and on board the ship, attempted to get some of the soldiers to join him. When the boat docked at Louisville, Webster (Brown) was arrested and charged with "inciting soldiers to desert." He escaped, and became a private in the Confederacy's 8th Virginia Infantry. In March 1862, Webster disappeared. With the help of a young Confederate, Charles Cooper, the pair ran mail across the lines. Webster's name was put on the Allan Pinkerton Detective Agency list of spies.[98]

At Waterford, Virginia, Webster was recruited by Capt. Samuel C. Means for Means' Loudon Rangers, a Union cavalry unit. Webster was described as rather tall, 5 feet, 10 inches, and he weighed 180 pounds. Proficient with a saber, pistol and carbine, the result of military training, he was made drillmaster for the unit in charge of training new recruits during July 1862.[99]

Webster and two of his company were sent to capture Confederate Capt. James Richard Simpson of the 8th Virginia Cavalry, who was at home in Loudon County on a recruiting mission. When Webster called Simpson to come out of his house, the Confederate ran out the back door. Webster tracked him down and killed him, probably to prevent Simpson from telling of Webster's former service for the Confederacy. [100]

While Means was on sick leave, Webster took command of the Loudon Rangers. He held elections, and had himself elected first lieutenant. Means returned and declared the election invalid. Gov. Francis Pierpont of West Virginia then signed an order to establish the "Loudon Rangers, 3rd Cavalry Regiment of Virginia Volunteers, with Webster as captain. During this time, Webster married Alice Downey, daughter of the former speaker of the Virginia House of Delegates. The announcement of their wedding on October 20, 1862, listed the groom as "Lt. Alphonso E. Webster, 2nd Massachusetts Volunteers."[101]

Early in December 1862, Webster was arrested in Georgetown for stealing horses, and was confined in the Old Capitol Prison in Washington. He was released on a technicality because the horses had been taken in Virginia, and the Washington judge had no jurisdiction there. He left Washington determined to find Means and punish him because he believed Means was behind his arrest. Still wearing a blue Federal uniform, Webster teamed up with his friend Charles Cooper and they, with several other Confederates went to the camp of Maj. Elijah V. White and his 35th Virginia Cavalry. Webster planned to use White's men to raid the camp of the Federal Captain Means. However, when Major White appeared, he went into a rage because he believed Webster was there to kill him, and ordered Webster bound and gagged.[102]

Webster was sent to Richmond as a "dangerous criminal, and put in Castle Thunder. Confederate officials could not decide whether to charge Webster with being a deserter, being a spy, or for the murder of Captain Simpson. On February 25, Secretary of War Seddon ruled that Webster should be tried by a military court. Confederate Capt. James Wampler, of the 8th Virginia, who had known Webster, wrote: "I can provide evidence in the persons of Major White and my wife that said Webster is a spy and has operated on both sides—the federal and confederate from Mississippi to Virginia. He is a villain and too dangerous a character to let go."[103]

Webster Tries to Escape

Webster had no sooner been put in Castle Thunder than he began to plan his escape. On Christmas Eve, he led a group in an aborted attempt. He tried again the next night, but found that armed guards were positioned to shoot any escapees. After that, he was put in irons but on March 9, 1863, he unlocked his irons with a key carved from bone. This attempt also failed.[104]

The court-martial began March 11, 1863. On March 26, Webster was found guilty of (1) the murder of Captain Simpson and of John Jones, of Hillsborough; (2) parole violation, and (3) horse stealing. He was sentenced to hang on April 3.[105]

Once he knew his fate, Webster became desperate to escape. On March 27, while handcuffed and under special guard, he jumped from his bed to a window and was about to exit. A guard took aim but his gun misfired, and Webster climbed out the window to the shed roof and jumped 15 feet (the jump was 27 feet according to one witness[106]) to the ground below. The impact broke both his ankles, and when he tried to hobble away, he was soon captured.[107]

Webster Finally Hanged

In a last effort to save himself, Webster appealed to President Davis, and Davis rescheduled the hanging for April 10. When the day arrived, Webster had to be taken to his hanging strapped in a chair because his ankles had not healed properly for him to stand.[108]

Dressed in his Federal uniform, he met his death with composure. An unusual man, the comments from those who knew Webster were as diverse and contradictory as his life. Captain Alexander, Castle Thunder's commandant, declared that Webster was "a master fiend." Fellow Ranger Briscoe Goodhart knew Webster as an "efficient drillmaster," and "brave and meritorious officer." Goodhart said that "nothing was too risky for him." Even Captain Means, when he wrote to Webster's father, admitted that the condemned man was "as brave a soldier as ever faced an enemy." Another who knew him called him the "daring Webster," and declared that he doubted if "in the annals of rascality a more finished character than Webster ever had a place."

The man known as Alfonzo C. Webster (a.k.a. Charles W. Brown) is still an enigma. While two Confederate regimental histories have much to say about Webster, he never appeared on the official rolls of the Loudon Rangers. There are at least 25 documents about Webster in the Confederate records, but the Federal records are blank, and there is no record of his service as a Union soldier.[109] Was he a secret agent for the Federal government? Or was he a double agent?

The Tables Are Turned

After the Federal forces occupied Richmond in April 1865, Castle Thunder became a prison for political prisoners, although a number of criminals were also confined there. These criminals had committed offenses against local civil law, and a few were deserters from the Union army. Under Federal control, the newspapers proclaimed that the "horror of these prisons are all of the past, thank God!"[110] By May 31, Castle Thunder had been emptied of all prisoners, except those held on specific charges, and they were few in number.[111]

Captain Alexander's Dog

Hero (or Nero), Captain Alexander's big black dog, was left behind when the Confederate forces fled Richmond.[112] The dog had been stigmatized by the Federal soldiers as a "monstrous savage Russian bloodhound." Others, such as the Reverend J. L. Burrows, who had petted the dog many times, described him as "one of the best-natured hounds whose head I ever patted, and one of the most cowardly. If a fise [feist] or a black-and-tan terrier barked at him … he [Hero] would tuck his tail between his legs and skulk … and he was quite a playfellow with the prisoners when permitted to walk among them."[113]

The dog that once guarded Castle Thunder was taken to Washington by Union soldiers. The Richmond *Whig* reported that the black dog had "taken a fancy to his captors, and is trying to be a good, loyal, Union dog."[114] George D. Putnam, who had seen the dog when he was a prisoner in Richmond, reported that when Weitzel's troops entered Richmond, the dog was caught and taken to New York. There, he was sold at auction on the steps of the Astor House. Putnam hoped the purchaser of the dog would be careful enough not to allow any of his family to wear army blue, because there could be trouble. The dog had been trained to attack anyone wearing blue.[115]

Hero was taken to New York and the New England states where he was exhibited for profit as "a specimen of the cruel devices of Southern officials to worry and torture prisoners."[116] The big dog and Jack, the bloodhound kept at Andersonville Prison, were on exhibit in Boston in September 1865.[117] Both dogs were reportedly shipped to the Chicago Sanitary Fair where an auction of the dogs raised $2,100 for the Soldiers Fund.[118]

The Last Prisoners

Maj. Isaac H. Carrington, the provost marshal of Richmond and Henrico County, was arrested and brought to Castle Thunder. Carrington had fled with the city along with President Davis, but had remained in the Danville area instead of going farther south. It was not know what charges were preferred against him, nor by whose order.[119]

Other Confederate prison officials, such as Richard Turner, were arrested and confined in Castle Thunder. Many fled to the country to avoid arrest, including Capt. George W. Alexander, the infamous commandant of Castle Thunder, and Capt. Thomas Turner, commandant at Libby Prison (see Chapter XXIV).

Castle Thunder Today

After it ceased to be useful as a prison, Castle Thunder was returned to the private sector. The *Combination Atlas of Richmond, 1876,* shows the building being used as Turpin & Brother's tobacco factory.[120] It was demolished in 1879 and over 100 years later was the site in 1990 of a paved parking lot for the employees of Philip Morris.[121]

XXI

Charleston, South Carolina

*We were treated exactly as well as the Confederates. We were hungry some-
times and so were they.*
— Maj. Orlando J. Smith, 6th Indiana Cavalry[1]

Location: various locations in Charleston, South Carolina. **Established:** 1861. **Type
of Buildings:** six existing buildings converted for housing prisoners, including a jail,
workhouse, hospital, and insane asylum, the O'Connor House, and coastal
fortification. **Capacity:** 1,100. **Most Held:** 1,100. **Number of Escapes:** unknown.[2]

History

The war began in Charleston, South Carolina, with the firing on Fort Sumter
April 12–14, 1861. For that and the subsequent casualties of the war, many persons
hoped for the destruction of the "Cradle of Secession."

The old city has withstood invasion and occupation by the British and by the
Yankees. It has withstood being bombarded by enemy forces, lashed by countless
hurricane-force winds, and shaken by a major earthquake in 1886. Yet, the city of
Charleston, like the Phoenix, rises each time from its ashes to emerge even more beautiful than before.

The First Prisoners

Initially, during the first year of the war, captured prisoners were held in the
Charleston Jail. When it became full, prisoners were moved outside to an enclosed
yard at the back of the jail. Tents were set up for shelter.[3]

Jail and Jail Yard

Lt. Alonzo Cooper described his new prison in the yard of the Charleston Jail:
"This was without exception the most filthy lousy, dirty place I saw. There were only
fifty 'A' tents for six hundred prisoners, and scarcely any wood with which to cook
our rations." It was at Charleston that Cooper witnessed his first "death by starvation" of a member of his company.[4]

In the center of the yard stood a gallows, a post about 25 feet high, with a horizontal arm which extended out about eight feet. At the end of the arm and at the

top of the post were pulleys to pull a rope. A weight tied to the end of a rope hanging from the post acted as a drop to elevate the body of the victim from the ground and lift him toward the end of the arm. The prisoners, desperate for wood, cut down the gallows.[5]

Joseph Ferguson thought the jail building "a splendid, commanding piece of workmanship," although now in disrepair and dilapidated. There were just enough tents for 125 prisoners, putting four and six to a tent. Thus, the remaining 400 prisoners were left without shelter of any kind from the elements of rain, wind, and sun. A cistern caught rain water and an artesian well provided brackish water. Those who had been transferred from Savannah had been forced to leave behind their cooking utensils, but some had been smuggled into the pen. For lack of wood, some meals were eaten uncooked.[6]

Also confined in the jail building were a number of black soldiers from Massachusetts, who had been captured in the assault on Fort Wagner in the summer of 1863.

O'Connor House

In July 1864, the O'Connor house and the Roper Hospital were also used to house prisoners. The O'Connor house, at 180 Broad Street, was a large, white, three-story structure with Corinthian columns which supported a porch on the front of the house.[7] The house was in the heart of downtown Charleston and exposed to the shells from the Federal fleet and from those on Morris Island, five miles from the business district of the city. During the summer and fall of 1864, the long-range artillery guns used by U.S. Gen. Quincy Gilmore to fire upon the city from Morris Island, were quite accurate.[8]

Eighty-six prisoners were taken from the jail yard and confined to the O'Connor house where, according to Maj. Orlando J. Smith, they were treated "exactly as well as the Confederates."[9] Another one of those who was moved to the O'Connor house was Edmund Ryan, of the 17th Illinois. After living in the filth at the Charleston jail yard, the O'Connor house seemed like heaven to Ryan.[10] The men being held in this house, exposed to the fire from Federal guns, would initiate a chain of events that would end with 50 being exchanged, while another 600 would suffer untold hardships.

The presence of Federal prisoners inside the city of Charleston did not deter the Federal guns, and a steady bombardment was kept up which rained ruin on the city. The building right across the street from the O'Connor house was destroyed.[11]

Other Charleston Prisons — The Work House

Some of the prisoners transported from Savannah on September 13, 1864, were put in a facility inside the city of Charleston. They were put in a four-story tall stone building which had an octagonal building attached. On the octagonal building was a tower which rose about 40 feet. The octagonal building faced a yard enclosed by a high wall. The yard was entered through a large iron gate. The 600 prisoners were put in that small area. Already in residence were a few prisoners from Andersonville who were to be sent on to Florence, South Carolina.[12]

Charleston, South Carolina, O'Connor House — Federal officers were comfortably quartered, but under fire from Federal guns. (Library of Congress, LC-USZ62-91674.)

According to prisoner B. S. Calef, from the outside the brick "work-house" was a "fine-looking building, built on three sides of a square, with two towers which gave it quite an imposing appearance." The prisoners were taken through the main entrance up a dark, narrow spiral staircase, only wide enough for one person at a time, to the second floor. There, the four prisoners were placed in a cell with barred windows. There was no furniture — they sat and slept on the floor.[13]

From the windows of workhouse, the prisoners could see the jail where more than 300 prisoners were being held. Some had tents, others were without shelter. In addition, 300 officers were in the nearby Marine Hospital, and a like number at the Roper Hospital.[14]

Roper Hospital

The three-story brick Roper Hospital building[15] was situated on the corner of Queen and Church streets. With a gift of $30,000 from Col. Thomas Roper to the Medical Society of South Carolina, Roper Hospital was begun in 1850 as the first

Charleston, South Carolina, Roper Hospital—Housed many Federal prisoners. (Library of Congress, LC-DIG-cwpb-03023.)

community hospital in the Carolinas. The mission of the Medical Society was to "treat the sick without regard to complexion, religion or nation."[16]

The building had a tower at each end, and towers flanked the entrance door. In front of the building was a large garden enclosed by an iron fence. The building that housed the insane was behind the Roper Hospital. To the right was the medical college building.[17]

On September 19, 1864, the Federal army began shelling the city of Charleston. One shell struck the Roper Hospital and did much damage. Several of the Federal officers who were prisoners there were wounded.[18]

Hostages Under Fire

Some of the prisoners being held by the Confederates in Charleston were told that if they would give their pledge not to escape, they would be furnished good quarters. About 86 of the prisoners accepted the offer, and soon found themselves housed in a three-story white house on Broad Street (the Colonel O'Connor House).

On June 13, 1864, United States Maj. Gen. John G. Foster was told of the presence of these officers by Confederate Maj. Gen. Samuel Jones. (Jones had succeeded Beauregard in command of the Department of South Carolina, Georgia and Florida.[19])

The Federal officers being held prisoner had been moved into the city of Charleston to a location that was within the range of the bombardment. Those officers consisted of five generals and 45 field officers from the United States Army who had been sent to Charleston for safekeeping. They had been turned over to Major General Jones by Brigadier General Ripley, with instructions that they were "to be given quarters in a part of the city occupied by noncombatants, the majority of which latter … are women and children." This particular part of the city had been "exposed for many months to the fire of our [Federal] guns." In his reply to Jones on June 16, Foster protested the action of the Confederates in placing the Federal officers in a position that was exposed "to constant bombardment." He deemed it an "act of cruelty" designed solely to stop the Federal bombardment of Charleston. Foster immediately forwarded Major General Jones' letter to President Lincoln. Foster promised the Confederate general that an "equal number of [Confederate] prisoners of like grades" would be placed in a position so that they would exposed to the fire from the guns in Charleston.[20] Thus, came about the "First Fifty." The Federals hoped to exchange 50 Confederate officers for officers being held in the O'Connor house who were in danger because they were within the range of the big Federal cannons bombarding the city.

The Exchange of the "First Fifty" (Confederate)

Much has been written about the "Immortal 600," but little about a group of 50 Confederate officers who preceded them.

After Federal officials learned that officers were being held by the Confederates in the city of Charleston, exposed to the bombardment from the guns in and around the harbor, a system to exchange Federal-held prisoners for Confederate-held prisoners was negotiated.

Federal officials selected a group of 50 high-ranking Confederate officers at Fort Delaware and then transported them to Charleston Harbor in June 1864. Many were Confederate cavalry officers and many were formerly Brig. Gen. John Hunt Morgan's Raiders. Among those 50 were Brig. Gen. Basil Duke, Morgan's brother-in-law. Morgan and his Raiders were famous for their 1,000-mile raid across Kentucky, Indiana and Ohio in the summer of 1863, and possibly even more famous because he managed to escape from the Ohio State Penitentiary four months after he was captured and imprisoned (see Chapter VI for more on Morgan). Another was Confederate cavalry officer Brig. Gen. Meriwether Jeff Thompson, called the "Missouri Swamp Fox." Thompson, a native of Virginia, who moved to Missouri with his family in 1847, has been described as a "lank and colorful Virginian with Yankee mechanical ingenuity and a love of deadly weapons."[21] He had been captured at Pocahontas, Arkansas, in 1863, and was sent to Fort Delaware in the spring of 1864, just in time to become one of the First Fifty.[22]

Once they reached Charleston, the Confederate captives were kept on board a ship in Charleston Harbor, exposed to their own fire from the mainland.[23] Correspondence concerning the exchange between Foster and Jones continued for over a month.[24]

The Exchange — The First Fifty (Union)

The names of the Federal officers who had arrived on June 12 to be placed under the fire of Federal guns were printed in the June 14, 1864, issue of the Charleston *Tri-*

Weekly Mercury. The paper also noted that the commanding officer on Morris Island had been notified of the presence of the Federal officers in the "shelled district," and if the Federal guns continued their fire, they would be the "peril of the captive officers." Among those 50 Federal officers were five brigadier generals: Seymour, Wessells, Scammon, Shaler, and Heckman. The other 45 were colonels and lieutenant colonels. The *Mercury* article stated that the prisoners would be "furnished with comfortable quarters in that portion of the city most exposed to the enemy's fire."[25]

The particulars of the exchange of 50 Federal officers for 50 Confederate officers were finally agreed upon. Brigadier General Jones agreed to send five generals and 45 field officers on a steamer to be exchanged on August 3, 1864, in Charleston Harbor.[26]

The Confederates wanted their officers back, and needed them badly. Another exchange of 600 men was in progress, but after an initial exchange of the 50 Federal prisoners for the same number of Confederates, the exchange process was halted. Once those 50 Federal officers had been returned safely, Major General Foster decided that "no more exchanges will be made through Charleston Harbor," as a ploy to get Confederates to move their prisoners to another location near Savannah. He wrote General Halleck of his plan to stop exchanges through Charleston Harbor.[27]

Prisoners continued to be moved to Charleston as Sherman's Union army drove deep into Georgia. On July 27, 1864, about 500 prisoners were transferred from Macon, Georgia. Macon was being evacuated because of the approach of Union Gen. George Stoneman's troops. Charleston soon became a "retaliation camp,"[28] and helpless prisoners suffered in a tug-of-war between the commanders and those in authority of the opposing forces.

The Immortal 600

Federal officials were convinced that prisoners were being held in the city of Charleston to prevent further bombardment by the Federal guns. The Federals did not give in, but retaliated by confining 600 Confederate prisoners, taken from Fort Delaware, to an open stockade on Morris Island.[29] Morris Island had been in the hands of the Federal forces since September 1863, but only after months of bloody fighting, and many casualties.

The 600 prisoners left Fort Delaware on August 20, 1864, in the hold of the steamer *Crescent City.*[30] Those chosen represented every state in the Confederacy plus Maryland and Kentucky, the border states. The prisoners were kept in the poorly ventilated hold for 18 days, in the extremely hot August weather. "The heat of the ship's boilers, the heat of the weather, and the seasickness" resulted in a situation almost as bad as the English soldiers confined in the "Black Hole of Calcutta."[31]

Escape from the Ship

As the ship carrying the 600 approached Cape Romain, the captain of the *Crescent City* steered a course directly toward the shore. Another Federal ship in the area, the *Admiral,* saw where the ship was headed and sent up rockets as a warning. The *Crescent City* ignored the warning and continued on its way until it ran aground. In the confusion, prisoner George W. Woolford (or Woodford) of South Carolina, made a bid for freedom. Others would have escaped, but Federal gunboats appeared and the prisoners were forced back down into the hold. The captain of the *Crescent City,* William Baxter, was placed in irons because of his attempt to ground the ship and allow the prisoners to escape.[32]

By the time the steamer reached Hilton Head Island, South Carolina, there was no water for the prisoners to drink. They suffered with thirst for 30 hours.[33] One prisoner, Capt. G. H. Ellerson of the 3rd Alabama, could take it no longer; he managed to slip overboard during the night and escape.[34]

Those reaming of the 600 were to be placed in a stockade on the abandoned Morris Island. They had to remain on the ship until September 7. The Confederates guns were aimed to fire high so as not to hit the prisoners with their artillery.[35]

To add to the misery the prisoners already endured, the Federal forces began the siege of Charleston in full force on October 1, 1864. The noise of the big guns was constant and terrifying, as the Federals pounded the city with guns capable of firing 200-pound shells. Scores of fires resulted, citizens were killed walking on the streets, and whole rows of houses were demolished.[36]

Out of the original 600, 558 were actually confined on Morris Island. Thirty-nine had been taken from the ship at Hilton Head Island and held in jail there before being transferred to Beaufort, South Carolina. Two escaped during this move, and one died. Three died on Morris Island, and two were shot by guards.[37]

A stalemate arose, and the Confederate prisoners of war remained for weeks on the little sandy neck under fire from both sides, with no shelter from the elements. They were confined in a stockade on Morris Island where such heavy fighting had occurred in the summer of 1863 near Batteries Greg and Wagner. Major General Jones was aware that these men were being held in retaliation for the Federal prisoners he held who were "comfortably housed" where they received the proper "treatment due prisoners of war."[38] There was no hope of escape from Morris Island for those brave men.

The "Immortal 600" endured weeks of hardship on board ships being transported to Charleston Harbor, then under fire on the hot, sandy, treeless Morris Island.[39] Finally, on October 23, 1864, the Federals decided to end the standoff, and the Confederates being held on Morris Island were moved to Fort Pulaski.[40] They arrived at Fort Pulaski on Cockspur Island near Savannah, Georgia, on October 22. In November, 222 of the group were transferred to Hilton Head Island and were kept confined in a large log house. The remainder of the original 600 continued to be imprisoned until March 3, 1865, when they learned they were to be exchanged. That involved being transported on the *Illinois* to Fortress Monroe, and then back to Fort Delaware. Two of their number died during the trip and 75 had to be taken off and put in hospitals along the way. Those who still survived remained at Fort Delaware until the end of the war.[41]

Other Escapes

Lt. H. Lee Clark, of the 2nd Massachusetts Heavy Artillery, managed to get a Confederate lieutenant's uniform. He put it on and casually walked out of the jail yard. He was captured and brought back. When he retold his adventure, he said he had no trouble passing by the sentry at the gate who noted his uniform and rank insignia. He saluted the sentry and went on. Outside, however, not knowing the city, he was at a loss as to which direction to take. He noticed two ladies watching him, and he approached them and asked for something to eat. The ladies invited him into their house and eventually he got up his courage to tell them who he was. He asked for their help and protection until he could devise a plan to get out of the city.[42]

Clark remained in the ladies' home for a couple of days until he was able to exchange his officer's uniform for that of a private. The ladies managed to get Clark a pass to go to Sullivan's Island, which was across the harbor from Morris Island, which was in Federal hands. From Sullivan's Island, Clark tried to find some way across the harbor. Without food, he became ill, and had to return to Charleston to give himself up. He was put in the hospital, and after he recovered, he was returned to the prison.[43]

Ferguson recalled that there were two successful escapes made by the prisoners in Charleston. These were accomplished through bribes. The guards were stationed every few yards from above Charleston down to the Port Royal Ferry. Captains Lee and Nash managed to escape, but after many harrowing escapades, and nearly drowning, they were recaptured.[44]

On the first of October, all the naval prisoners held in Charleston were exchanged by way of Richmond. Over 100 naval officers left just before the yellow fever epidemic struck.[45]

Yellow Fever Epidemic

Yellow fever raged in Charleston during September. Early in October, the prisoners being held by the Confederates in Charleston were moved to another location, to a healthier region near Columbia, South Carolina. The prisoners were marched through the streets to the train station. Along the way, several prisoners slipped away from the guards and disappeared in the crowd of onlookers. One of those who did was Capt. Eugene Hepp, of the 82nd Illinois, who also had been confined at Libby Prison in Richmond. He succeeded because he had managed to obtain some civilian clothes.[46]

Mass Escape from Train

On October 6, 1864, 1,500 prisoners were marched through the main streets of Charleston to the depot.[47] They were then put on a train and sent to Columbia, South Carolina. Several of the prisoners saw the ride on the train as their chance to escape. As the train passed a swampy area, Union Captain Cady and Lieutenant Masters jumped. Altogether, about 150 prisoners jumped from the cars and escaped into the swamp that night. Although Cooper did not get a chance to jump from the train, he was confident that the prisoners could have captured all the guards and taken the train, if they had made "an organized effort." The problem was in getting officers to obey orders—all wanted to be the boss.[48]

Charleston Today

Although there was much damage done by the bombardment and the subsequent fires to the city of Charleston, much remains to be seen. A boat ferries tourists daily to Fort Sumter. Morris Island is just a little sandy bump in the harbor, and Folly Island is being covered with resort houses adjacent to the popular Folly Beach.

The O'Connor house that once hosted Federal officers on Broad Street is gone. Yet, many beautiful structures give the city a grace of its own. The colorful old townhouses along Cabbage Row and Rainbow Row are distinctly Charleston. Most of the outlying plantations that existed in the 1860s were burned by U.S. Gen. William T. Sherman. Only Drayton Hall, built in 1742, survived destruction. It was spared because the residents told Union soldiers that it was being used as a smallpox hospital. The house is open to the public, and although without furnishing of any kind, its beauty, reminiscent of Stratford Hall in Virginia, still touches the soul.

Boone Hall Plantation, the setting for many motion pictures, has a fairly modern manor house, but the grounds and brick slave cabins are worth a tour.

The Roper Hospital suffered severe damage in the Charleston earthquake on August 31, 1886. Although structurally unsafe since the quake, it was not demolished until the 1920s. It was being used as an apartment house at the time. The Roper Hospital combined with Bon Secours St. Francis Hospital in 1998 to serve the health care needs of the area.[49]

The discovery of the Confederate submarine *H. L. Hunley* in 1995 was a historic moment. It was carefully removed from the bottom of Charleston Harbor where it had rested undisturbed for 136 years. This innovative submarine is undergoing a preservation and conservation process, and will be thoroughly examined and explored by professionals to uncover all its unique features. It currently remains in fresh water at the former Charleston Naval Base. It will eventually be on display in Charleston. The eight skeletons recovered in the submarine were buried with all honors and ceremony in Charleston's Magnolia Cemetery on April 17, 2004.[50]

XXII

Columbia, South Carolina

There is no soldier who can not flank pickets and elude guards in dark and foggy nights....
— Gen. John H. Winder,[1] Confederate provost marshal, commissary general of prisoners east of the Mississippi

Location: Columbia, South Carolina. **Established:** 1864–January 1865. **Type:** 1) jail, 2) open area, surrounded by guards, and 3) hospital building. **Type of Prisoners:** Federal prisoners of war, both officers and enlisted men, Confederate deserters, and some civilian criminals. **Capacity:** ? **Most Held:** ? **Known Number of Escapes:** 373.[2] **Nickname:** Camp Sorghum.[3]

History

Initially, when prisoners were first transferred from Savannah to Columbia, there was no prison facility available except the Richland County Jail. The jail was an old building in the center of the town.[4]

The Facilities — The Richland County Jail

By August 1864, the jail in Columbia, South Carolina, housed 132 officers, and 99 privates. There were about 30 Confederate deserters, some political prisoners, and some civilians being held on criminal charges. There was not enough room in the building, so some of the prisoners were confined outside in the yard.[5] Conditions at the Columbia jail were, according to an inspection conducted on August 3, 1864, "clean and sanitary," and "well policed." There were three kitchens in which food was prepared. The cooks were selected from among the prisoners. However, water had to be obtained from outside the jail, and four prisoners, with one guard, were allowed to go for the water each day. The rations seemed adequate, the same as allotted soldiers in the field.[6]

Captain Senn was in charge of the troops stationed in the city, 214 reserves and light-duty men holding surgeons' certificates. His duties included the prison, but he had little time to spare for the prison or the prisoners. He delegated authority to others, and was never at the jail more than a third of the time, according to Capt. John C. Rutherford's inspection.[7]

Thus, there was a discrepancy in the number of the prisoners being held when compared to the names in the books. Rather than prisoners being missing, there were eight more prisoners at the jail than were recorded. The books were in very "bad order and no dependence or certainty can be placed on them." Rutherford recommended the prisoners be moved to Charleston if a regular prison were to be established there. Rutherford did not believe that the number of prisoners at Columbia at the time of the inspection justified a new prison with a separate commandant.

One of the prisoners confined in the jail was George W. Dodge, chaplain for the 11th Regiment, New York Volunteers. Dodge had received word that he had been appointed president of a college in Oregon, and he wanted very much to accept. In order to do so, he had obtain his release from prison. In desperation, he wrote a letter to General Benjamin Huger and asked to be released. He also proposed that if Huger was unable to help him to "please communicate the facts to the authorities at Richmond and likewise at Washington."[8]

Escape Attempts from Jail Yard

Even before the prisoners arrived in Columbia, several prisoners eluded the guards and escaped from the hot, crowded railroad cars into the woods. Lieutenant Parker told Joseph Ferguson that as soon as it was dark, he was going to try to get away. About 10 o'clock that night, Parker rushed past the guard standing at the door and jumped into the darkness. The sentinel fired at the escaping prisoner but missed.[9] Parker was caught after the dogs tracked him down. The dogs almost tore him apart, and he died the day after his recapture.[10] Ferguson believed that many of the escaped officers, when found, were hung and murdered in the mountains.

It was not difficult for the prisoners to escape, Rutherford concluded. Most of the privates were confined outside in the yard which was enclosed with a rotten wooden fence. The sentinels were the only thing between the prisoners and freedom, and the sentinels "exhibit considerable ignorance as to their instructions," reported Capt. John C. Rutherford in his inspection report of August 1864.[11]

In a short time, the prisoners had dug three or four tunnels, and several had escaped, but were recaptured. One was wounded while trying to escape through the tunnel. Captain Rutherford reported in August 1864, that "four officers and three privates escaped, but have been recaptured."[12]

Camp Sorghum

The number of prisoners held at Columbia did not remain small, and as the numbers increased, a larger facility was needed. A stockade was built three miles from town to contain new prisoners that arrived from Charleston and other sites. The new arrivals were confined in a four-acre field just south of the Congaree River. The area had a sloping hill covered with scrub pine and a brook running near the base. When the first prisoners arrived, there was no fence, no water, except from the brook, and no shelter. Small branches were placed about every 50 or 60 feet to serve as a deadline.

The new camp was about two miles from the town. It was the most primitive situation for a prison camp. One Federal soldier described the camp: "There was no stockade, no fence, no water but from a brook, no shelter not even for the sick." Here, with no shelter whatsoever, 1,500 men were held.[13]

On October 5, 1864, about 600 prisoners arrived from Charleston where yellow fever was raging. The night B. S. Calef and other arrived from Charleston, a severe thunderstorm drenched the men, who were still at the train depot. The next morning, they were given a piece of hardtack and marched three miles to the pen in what had once been a grove of pine trees. In only a few months of holding prisoners, the camp was barren. Calef recalled that "There was neither wood nor water to be had in camp, and only six were permitted to go out at a time for either, and the same rule applied to attending the calls of nature." These rules proved very inconvenient to meet the needs of the approximately 1,500 prisoners kept there.[14]

The men were herded like cattle into the field. There were no tents, nor shelters of any kind. The prisoners built shelters as best they could from branches, which helped protect them from the sun but not the rain. When cold weather came, the prisoners were allowed to have a few axes and shovels so they could construct shelters. Some cut logs and fitted them together into crude log cabins, chinked with clay. Others, who had no better shelter, burrowed into the ground.[15]

Eventually, a 30-foot wide clearing was cut around the camp, and a line of guards were positioned ten paces apart. On the inside of this clearing, stakes were driven into the ground, about 30 feet apart, to indicate the deadline. In addition, there were bloodhounds to track down escapees, and the guards had several artillery pieces which were placed and aimed at the prison compound.[16]

The facilities at the camp were the crudest. The prisoners were not given meat, and about all they received to eat was a weekly ration of sorghum molasses, in addition to unsifted cornmeal. [17] Union Capt. Bernhard Domschcke wrote that the rations consisted of "cornmeal, a little rice, salt, flour (sometimes replaced by grits), and there was no meat. Sorghum being the chief article, the place was named Camp Sorghum."[18]

The prisoners were guarded by militia from both Georgia and South Carolina. The Confederate guards looked almost as bad as the prisoners. According to Domschcke's description, the guards were dressed in "gray rags, unwashed, unkempt, this corps looked like footpads and highwaymen." They were composed of the reserves, companies of boys and old gray-haired men. They were an undisciplined lot, and were sometimes punished by their officers by "tying them to trees or stretching them on the rack." During one such punishment, the guards mutinied. Order was restored, but not without difficulty.[19] The sentries sometimes fired at prisoners, and killed them. Their excuse was that the gun had discharged accidentally.[20]

Escapes from Camp Sorghum

Considering the number of prisoners held in one facility, Camp Sorghum probably holds the record for the greatest number of escapes. The prisoners confined there escaped by a variety of means: slipping past the sentries at night, bribing sentries, or during the day when out gathering wood. Domschcke wrote in his memoirs that on many days, "no fewer than thirty or forty disappeared, and their absence always ignited commotion among the Rebels at roll call."[21]

Some of the prisoners were "paroled," and allowed to go outside to gather wood.

These prisoners had given their word that they would not try to escape. Some of the guards were under the impression that all of the prisoners had been paroled, but this was not the case. Those who had shoes or were able to walk yet who had not been paroled attempted to escape. According to Ferguson, "The country was full of escaped prisoners, and the wildest excitement prevailed among the inhabitants." The citizens joined the soldiers to chase down the escaped prisoners. And they did capture some of them. Every day, prisoners were returned to the camp, but a few managed to make it to Federal-held territory.[22]

Because of hunger and the harsh conditions at Camp Sorghum, almost every night some "starving heroes would run the guard and risk their lives to escape dying by inches with starvation," recalled Ferguson. He estimated that sometimes as many as 40 prisoners would slip past the guards. The plan was that the leader would rush past the sentinel and draw his fire, so that the others could slip out while the sentinel reloaded his gun.[23]

Lieutenant Ekings, of the 3rd New Jersey Volunteers, escaped and made it into the mountains 150 miles away. Described by Joseph Ferguson as a "generous, kind-hearted gentleman, and brave Christian soldier," Ekings was recaptured and returned to the camp, where he was shot "through the heart while making arrangements with one of the guards for the escape of himself and companions."[24]

Domschcke believed that there had been at least 400 "runaways," and that the number would have been much greater if the prisoners had shoes or boots. The success rate for escapees, however, was not good. He estimated that two thirds of the escaping prisoners were recaptured, and some were shot while attempting to get away. Those who did make it headed in the direction of the Blue Ridge Mountains of North Carolina and Tennessee. A few went south to Augusta, Georgia, and a few escaped on boats down the Congaree River. No matter what the route the prisoners took, it was difficult to evade capture by the militia, the civilians, and the patrols with their bloodhounds. Some did make it, and many were helped by black people.[25]

In order to have enough firewood, the prison commander, Lt. Col. Robert S. Means, allowed some of the prisoners to go beyond the deadline to gather wood for their fires. This provided an opportunity for escape. Escapes soon became a nightly occurrence. Three escaped one night, and although several shots were fired at them, they got away unharmed.[26] Eventually, the Confederate officers had the men who were going out to gather wood sign a parole, but, as usual, other ways were found to fool the prison officials and guards.[27]

The prisoners grew bolder and even the bloodhounds failed to deter them. A number of prisoners who attempted to escape were bitten by the dogs, and at least one prisoner was killed by the guard dogs.[28]

Lt. Alonzo Cooper decided he wanted to go home. After enduring imprisonment at Macon, Savannah, and Charleston, by the time he was transferred to Columbia, he had had enough. Cooper had befriended one of the guards who, he believed, secretly held Union sentiments. One night when the guard was on duty, Cooper threw the guard a note wrapped around a small stone. The note contained an offer of $50 to the guard if he would let Cooper and some of his fellow prisoners slip past. Cooper took a big chance in attempting to bribe the guard. If the guard reported his attempted bribery, he would be punished. However, this was not the case. The guard wrote on the back of the note, wrapped it again around a stone, and tossed it back to the prisoner. The guard had written: "I do not want your money; but if you will come just as the moon goes down and throw a pebble at my feet I will leave my beat; but be very careful not to make any noise."[29]

Cooper and his friends busied themselves gathering food to take with them when they escaped. They filled their haversacks, and gathered their overcoats and blankets. Cooper turned over his tent to two prisoners who were ill and had not had the strength to construct a brush tent even. He waited until the moon had disappeared and all was dark before tossing the pebble as the guard had instructed. The guard muttered, "All right," and walked away from his post. Seven prisoners took that opportunity to leave. They were Captains Geere, Hock, Eastmond, Hays, Cratty, and Winner and Lieutenant Cooper. Before they got very far, one of the escaping prisoners stumbled and made a noise. Immediately a guard fired a shot in that direction. Other shots soon followed, but the seven soon were out of range and into a patch of woods. They continued and found another woods three miles away from the camp. They lay down and napped for an hour or two, then rose and ate.[30]

One of the seven, Captain Geere, had escaped once before, but had been recaptured. Thus, because of his experience, he was chosen leader of the group. They marched in single file, and if the leader saw any danger, he would signal, and those behind him would drop to the ground out of sight.[31]

The prisoners proceeded cautiously and tried to reach a road the next night. However, Captain Geere had just reached the middle of the road when he was attacked by a large white dog. Two armed men approached and silenced the dog. Cooper slipped back into the woods as fast as he could. He ran for about a mile until he came to a swamp. Alone, he walked about five miles before he encountered Hock and Winner. They continued to distance themselves from Columbia and by daylight the next they were about 15 miles from Columbia.[32] On the next evening, October 14, 1864, they started out but could travel only about 12 miles. By the third day, all their biscuits were gone, and Cooper's legs were swollen. He bathed them in cold water and felt much better. They found a road sign which indicated they were 34 miles from Columbia.[33]

On October 10, 1864, Capt. George H. Starr, of the 104th New York Volunteers, escaped from the camp. Starr had been one of the 109 Federal officers who tunneled out of Libby Prison in February 1864. He was recaptured. Because he continued to try to escape, he was sent to Macon, Georgia, from which he escaped but again was recaptured. He was then sent to Camp Sorghum in Columbia. He wrote a letter to his family from Camp Sorghum which was dated October 10, 1864, his third escape attempt. This time he was successful and made it safely to Union lines. He probably beat his letter home, because it was not delivered until January 1865.[34]

Col. T. H. Butler, commander of the 5th Indiana Cavalry, was captured with 400 of his regiment by Confederates near Atlanta on July 31, 1864. He was first taken to Macon, then moved to Charleston on August 15, 1864. From there he was transferred to Columbia on October 5, and confined in Camp Sorghum. Butler did not remain there long. With three other officers, he escaped on November 29. The men traveled 400 miles through enemy territory and finally reached Knoxville, Tennessee, on January 13, 1865.[35]

By December 1864, there had been 373 successful escapes from Camp Sorghum. There had also been a large number of prisoners wounded by shots from the guards, and several suffered from dog bites. The hospital board decided the prisoners should be moved to a more secure environment. Thus by the third week of December, the camp had been abandoned, and the prisoners removed to Camp Asylum.[36]

By early December 1864, there had been so many escapes from the open pen near Columbia that citizens had complained in an article in the *Advertiser*. The governor of South Carolina contacted Brig. Gen. John H. Winder, who was in charge of all prisoners east of the Mississippi, to see what could be done. Winder was not surprised at the number of escapes nor at the citizens' complaints, for they had been held in the open, with "no stockade, no intrenchments [sic], not even a fence around them." Winder replied that it was useless to try to guard a "large, or even small, body of reserves [prisoners] in an open plain." Winder asked that the male asylum in Columbia be used to hold the prisoners temporarily, until a proper stockade could be built. Winder also promised to remove the prisoners from the Columbia area as soon as possible.[37]

Camp Asylum

The South Carolina State Hospital had been a hospital for the mentally ill since 1822. Naturally, it was soon nicknamed "Camp Asylum." The building stood at Elmwood and Bull streets on the north side of Columbia.[38]

The garden of the asylum building was enclosed by a stone wall and divided by a fence 10 feet high. The prisoners' half covered two acres, with a ditch to mark the deadline. The boarded fence had holes through which two cannon were aimed at the prisoners. Water was piped into six troughs. Three were used for washing and bathing, a luxury the prisoners utilized.[39]

A two-story building near the gate was used as a hospital. There was also a small one-story building in which some of the sick were placed upon their arrival. The prisoners took shelter under the two buildings, and the rest slept on the ground without cover. A few barracks which could house up to 36 men were constructed. Three tiers of bunks provided sleeping accommodations. Prisoners cooked their own mush or soup. Someone constructed an oven outside in which to bake bread. Overall, rations were as meager as they had been at Camp Sorghum, and although items could be bought from the camp sutler, he charged exorbitant prices.[40]

Escape Attempts

Prisoners soon began attempting to escape. A tunnel was discovered, and the prisoners knew someone had squealed. The prisoners attempted to find out who had given their tunnel away. The camp commander then posted a notice from General Winder to the effect that "if tunneling does not stop," Winder ordered that all shelter—tents, barracks and permanent buildings—would be removed. Camp Commander Griswold also threatened to use force if any prisoner "suspected of having told headquarters about tunnels" was harmed.[41]

On February 8, 1865, the prisoners learned of the death of General Winder, and there was general celebration within the ranks of the prisoners. Whether dead or alive, Winder's order did not curb prisoners' efforts to escape. A new tunnel was begun under the barracks shared by Captain Domschcke and 35 other prisoners. They swore themselves to secrecy, and vowed revenge on anyone who told of their plans. The tunnel was then begun inside the barracks near the back door. It was dug down about six or seven feet, then ran horizontally. The men worked on it each night after 10 P.M. Blankets covered the barracks windows to prevent guards from seeing any light. Diggers worked in two-hour shifts. Every 30 minutes, two men carried the loose soil and hid it under the lower bunks. At dawn, work ceased, and a trapdoor was closed to hide the evidence. Just as the tunnel was about finished, the men were ordered to leave Columbia.[42]

Many prisoners escaped, but many were recaptured and returned to the prison. Because of the location, the distance was great to reach the Union lines and the local people were on the alert for escapees. The bloodhounds were used to track prisoners, and the prisoner who was in poor heath had little chance of escaping. Yet, according to one prisoner, "almost everyone pondered it more or less, and had sketches and maps ... of the surrounding country." Many slipped by the guards at night, and at the slightest noise, the guards fired their rifles. Two officers were killed and several more wounded attempting to escape. One night, the guards even shot two of their own men.[43]

Three prisoners escaped and made their way to the mountains. Along the way, the leader, dressed as a Confederate officer, stopped frequently at the homes of planters to ask for food. He always claimed that the two men with him, dressed in tattered Federal uniforms, were his prisoners. The three made it to the mountains of Tennessee when they were discovered by a band of guerillas. The three split up. One of them reached Federal lines, the second was never heard from again and presumably died or was killed, and the third was caught and returned to Columbia.[44] While they were unfortunate, many escaped Federal soldiers did make their way to the mountains of Tennessee where they were clothed, fed, and guided to safety by Union sympathizers.[45]

One of the favorite methods of escape was for those men who had not taken parole to go outside the area to get wood. Their friends would cover them with boughs of leaves, and those intent on escaping remained covered until dark. B. S. Calef recalled that he had "known a hundred officers to go out in one day in that way, provided with rations and blankets, their parties and plans all made up." This resulted in more guards being added and their area of patrol increased. The distance from the deadline was also increased so that "to run the gauntlets was next to impossible."

The prisoners did not remain at the insane asylum very long and as Union Gen. William T. Sherman approached, about 500 were transferred to Charlotte, North Carolina. Seven hundred more were transferred to Millen, Georgia, in February.[46]

A fire broke out in the city on February 17, 1865 (whether set by Confederates or Federals is still controversial). Confederate Gen. Wade Hampton charged, in a letter read before the United States Senate a year after the war ended, that Sherman had deliberately, systematically, and atrociously burned Columbia to the ground. Sherman countercharged that he and his men worked to prevent the complete annihilation of the city by putting out the burning bales of cotton fired by retreating Confederate soldiers. Whatever the cause, the wind spread the fire and half the city burned.[47]

XXIII

Danville, Virginia

Man may suffer with cold, pass through incredible hardships, endure fatigue,
and never murmur but let hunger prey upon his vitals and he becomes mad,
frantic and raving.

      — Cpl. J. F. Hill, 89th Ohio Volunteer Infantry[1]

Location: Danville, Virginia. **Established:** 1863. **Type:** six converted warehouses.
Type of Prisoners: Officers in some, enlisted men in other buildings. **Capacity:**
3,700. **Most Held:** 4,000. **Number of Known Escapes:** 70+.[2]

History

Danville is located in the south-central portion of Virginia, 143 miles southwest
of Richmond. It is only four miles from the North Carolina border in the heart of
the tobacco-growing territory. The economy of the town centered around the tex-
tile and tobacco industries.[3]

In 1863, the town had between 1,200 and 1,500 inhabitants. The thriving town
was a good site for a prison because it was at the terminus of the Richmond and
Danville Railroad.[4]

During the 1860s, Danville had a number of large buildings suitable for the con-
tainment of prisoners.

In November 1863, approximately 4,000 prisoners were transferred to Danville
to relieve overcrowding at other prison facilities.[5]

The Facilities

All the prisoners sent to Danville were held in former tobacco warehouses scattered around the city. Officers were kept separate from enlisted men, as was generally the practice.[6]

Prisoners were housed in six large brick buildings that had been used as tobacco
or cotton warehouses in the center of the town. The largest could hold 700. It also
had a bake house attached where rations could be prepared for as many as 3,000 men.
A large frame house across the street served as the commandant's headquarters.[7]

Three other warehouses were grouped together, and they held a combined prison
population of about 2,300. Two additional buildings nearby in the town's business
district were also converted. The last two buildings had the capacity to hold about

1,300 prisoners. The warehouses were all fairly close to the Dan River, and they were all three stories high with attics. They had no furniture and each floor provided a large open area for the prisoners. Prisoners were confined to the upper floors, with the guards on the ground floor. Wooden stairs inside the building gave access to the upper levels. The prisons were designated as Prison No. 1 through No. 6.[8]

The Prisoners

Although Danville was generally thought to be a prison facility for officers, initially enlisted men were also confined there as well. Prison No. 6 was used for black prisoners of war. All of the prisoners were under the supervision of Maj. Mason Morfit. It was not long before the buildings were overcrowded, and an average of 650 were quartered on each floor.[9]

Lt. Alonzo Cooper and other officers arrived in late fall of 1864, and were confined in a three-story tobacco warehouse. It was about 40 feet wide and 100 feet long, and stood near the Dan River. All the windows were fitted with iron bars. Prisoners were kept on the second and third floors. Sentries guarded the outside of the building around the clock, and two sentries were placed inside on the ground floor, where there was no stove.[10]

The sinks or privies were outside near the west end of the building and were surrounded by a high plank fence. The winter of 1864-1865 was extremely cold, so much so that the river froze over solid. Yet, during the daytime, prisoners were allowed to go down to the ground floor to exercise. They were forbidden, however, to come within six feet of a sentry or to talk to him.[11]

Maj. Abner R. Small, of the 16th Maine Volunteers, was captured in the fighting along the Weldon Railroad on August 18, 1864. He was first taken to Libby Prison, then transferred by train to Salisbury, North Carolina. After officials at Salisbury learned of his plot to escape, he was transferred to Danville, Virginia.[12] Small was placed in Prison No. 3 at Danville, a three-story, brick building in which only officers were contained.[13] This was the same building in which Cooper was confined, and Small recorded some of the same events in his diary.

Enlisted men were housed in similar facilities, and some of those buildings could be seen from the one in which Cooper was confined. Across the street was one in which enlisted men were kept, and some of them were assigned to work in the cook house, for which they received extra rations.[14]

George Putnam was transferred to Danville from Libby Prison in Richmond in late December 1864. He and a group were put in one of the tobacco warehouses near the Dan River.[15] According to Putnam, the tobacco warehouse might have been converted into fairly comfortable quarters. However, the glass was broken in many of the windows, and the wind blowing through made their quarters cold both day and night. The building he was placed in was three stories high, with prisoners restricted to the upper two floors. There were about 200 men on each floor at the beginning of winter, but the number steadily decreased through deaths of the prisoners. The rooms had two wood-burning stoves, one at each end. Spaces near the stoves were prized. The food ration was very small, only corn bread by the time Putnam arrived at Danville.[16]

Escapes and Escape Plans

While being transferred by train from Salisbury Prison in North Carolina to Danville, Major Small recorded in his diary that "Sixteen commissioned officers missing; escaped from train."[17]

Those who did not escape on the way were placed in converted warehouses. From their window the prisoners could see the river which ran south into North Carolina and also the Smoky Mountains, part of the Appalachian chain. This view generated much speculation about escape and how to reach the mountains, and if reached, how a man could survive in the wilderness in the winter and not freeze or starve.[18]

There was a large force of Confederate troops in the town to guard the railroad lines and to prevent prison escapes. Even if a prisoner escaped, he would have to avoid capture by those troops, and make his way a long distance to the Shenandoah Valley of Virginia in order to find safety with Union forces.[19]

According to Putnam, several tried to escape and two succeeded in getting through the lines to safety. Others, he heard, were "lost and were doubtless starved or frozen in the wilderness." One hindrance to escape was the inability of the prisoners to get any food to take with them. A second obstacle was that most of the men either had no shoes or their shoes were badly worn.[20]

Plot to Capture Town

In a letter to an Ohio newspaper, Cpl. J. F. Hill, of the 89th Ohio Volunteer Infantry, told of an escape plot that was planned while he was a prisoner at Danville. Captured at Chickamauga in September 1863, Hill had been had first been confined to Libby Prison in Richmond. In November, he was transferred to Danville. He began to plan how to get out. Hill took into his confidence "a brave and dashing young man" who was the sergeant major of the 19th Regulars (Ohio?) The two combined their ideas and came up with a scheme to make a general outbreak by bursting through all three doors of their prison. Then they would overpower the guards, capture the town, destroy the railroad bridge across the Dan River, destroy all the commissary stores, and take what arms and horses they could and head for the mountains. He believed the scheme would work because there were 700 men in the building, and about 700 more were expected to arrive that night. The guards at their building numbered only about a hundred and there were no Confederate troops nearer than Richmond.[21]

Hill and his accomplice picked a dark and rainy night. They chose to put the plan in action at the time when the railroad cars came in with more prisoners. The prisoners divided into three groups. The first group of 400 was to capture the guards as quietly as possible, then go to the guards' headquarters and overpower all there. Then they would go to the town and destroy anything of value. The second group of 200 prisoners was to burn the railroad bridge, and the remaining 100 were to go to the telegraph office and destroy it, then burn the train depot. After all was accomplished, the prisoners planned to obtain horses and about 75 or 100 would go to East Tennessee and Virginia and destroy the tracks and cut telegraph lines. They also planned to destroy bridges near Salem, Virginia, 60 miles away. Some of the group was to go to West Virginia to obtain aid from Federal forces there.[22]

A Hole in the Fence

The only problem was that most of the prisoners were so weak and feeble from lack of food they were not able to help. Hill was only able to get 60 men out of 700 to agree to help with the plan. The great escape plan had to be scrapped. Hill decided it would be best just to slip out and get as far away as possible before his absence was noticed. The quickest means was to cut a hole in the fence. The pine board fence was about an inch thick. They cut a board off about 18 inches above the ground with an old table knife. It took about half an hour. Once the hole was finished, the men settled down to wait for night. About 7:30 that night, they began going out in small groups of three to four men. They had to pass within 10 feet of the guards, but the guards did not notice the escaping prisoners. Hill emerged with Sgt. Solomon Stookey, and Cpl. Henry Thompson, all members of the same company. This escape occurred on Saturday, November 14, 1863.[23]

The journey that Hill and his companions embarked on is a remarkable story. It took them 16 days and nights to travel 250 miles. They crossed a dozen mountains, waded streams of all sizes, suffered from cold and hunger. They actually entered 22 homes, 19 of which were inhabited by Union supporters, and were fed 19 times. Although they generally slept during the day and traveled at night, they were lucky enough to spend three nights warm and comfortable in a safe house.[24]

Along the way, they encountered people who belonged to a network to help deserters cross over into Federal-held territory. There was an established route with stops all along the way, a kind of "underground railroad," but this one was for whites. Those involved belonged to a secret organization (probably the Sons of Liberty, or the Knights of the Golden Circle), and once the trio was initiated, they were given the signs and passwords so that they could recognize other members of the secret society. They finally reached Fayetteville, West Virginia, and were given letters to take to General Scammon at Charleston, West Virginia. He sent them, with passes, through the Union lines to safety.[25]

Tunneling to Freedom

Prisoners confined at Danville were so miserable from cold and hunger that they tried every means to escape. A few succeeded. Several tried digging tunnels, which would provide a way out for a large number. Several tunnels were begun, but were discovered or betrayed by squealers.[26]

Putnam described an escape plan that involved digging a tunnel from the basement toward a deep ditch not far from the building. If the men could exit through a tunnel, they could lie in the ditch until they saw an opportunity to slip away in the darkness.[27]

Once access was gained to the cellar, work on the tunnel was done in total darkness and only on stormy nights. Digging in the soft dirt was done with a couple of tin plates and a few shingles. A miscalculation resulted in a foundation stone tumbling down on one of the workers. A new tunnel had to be started, and in a few weeks it had been extended beyond the building and beneath the walk on which the prison guards patrolled.[28]

Since all work had been done in the dark, the men had no way of measuring direction, and the tunnel came too close to the surface of the ground. One morning, the ground gave way and one of the guards fell into the tunnel. The guard was badly frightened and in the process broke his arm. Another guard fired his musket, and the entire force of guards turned out. In the confusion, the guards thought that the Yankees were coming to capture the town.[29]

A tunnel was begun from Prison No. 5 in December 1863. No. 5 was a large, three-story brick building that had been a plug tobacco factory before the war. At the time several tunnels were excavated, this building held about a thousand prisoners, most of whom had been captured at the battle of Chickamauga in September 1863.[30]

The tunnel was not very long, but it ended outside of the guard line, albeit in plain view of the guards. However, by using the cover of darkness, about 70 prisoners escaped. Cpl. Jacob Eisenberger, of Company K, 77th Pennsylvania, was one of the leaders.[31]

Another tunnel was begun from that same building in January 1864. It took about six weeks to complete. To be sure that the tunnel was not reported, about 60 of the prisoners took an oath of secrecy. Sgt. John Obreiter, also of Company K, 77th Pennsylvania, was elected first assistant engineer, and John H. Shirk (Company E, 77th Pennsylvania), second assistant. The chief engineer of the tunnel was a man from the western states, who did not even inspect the work until it was finished, when he was the first to exit through the dig. The work was carried out under great hardships. Because of several previous escape attempts, guards were placed both outside and inside the building. Yet, the prisoners were determined in the effort, and when completed the tunnel ran a distance of 180 feet. Its exit outside was under a small outbuilding which had been used as a kitchen for a dwelling house on the adjoining lot. The kitchen building sat on posts about 2½ feet off the ground. From out of the ground underneath the little building emerged 160 prisoners. This would have continued until the entire building was emptied, but a lady passing by saw the men coming out from under the kitchen and reported them to the guards.[32]

Massive Prison Break Planned

In the fall of 1864, Lieutenant Cooper and three more Yankees, having escaped from Columbia, were recaptured and sent to Danville, Virginia. In Danville, Cooper met some old friends and they began plotting their escape. Daily conferences were held to consider various plans. The prisoners decided that a massive prison break was out of the question because it would prove disastrous and result in the deaths of many.[33] Cooper and his fellow officers bided their time and watched for an opportunity to escape. That chance came on December 9, 1864. Cooper had been in the Danville prison a little over two weeks, when a company of Confederate soldiers were lined up in front of the building where he was confined. With no idea what was taking place, all of the prisoners gathered at the windows to look at the troops. They appeared to be veterans by their rough appearance and tattered uniforms. After a few minutes, the soldiers were ordered to break ranks, and to stack their guns. A guard was left to watch over them. The prisoners looked at the guns and saw a chance to grab them, along with cartridge boxes. The prisoners organized under the leadership of

Col. W. C. Raulston, of the 24th New York Cavalry. Cooper described him as a "gallant Cavalry officer, whose coolness and courage could be relied upon, and whose military ability was well understood by all." However, all this organization and assigning of parts in the attempt to get the guns came to naught, as the soldiers returned and picked up their rifles. All was not lost, as the organization that had been built was kept in place for future escape attempts.[34]

Putnam reported that this event took place in January 1865. A company of about 150 Confederate soldiers was moved to Danville to prevent trouble from a band of Yankee raiders. The new soldiers were "the guests of the prison guard." When they entered the guardhouse for the noon meal, the guards always stacked their muskets together outside. One of the Federal officers saw the opportunity to escape, and a plan was developed to make a rush for the muskets. Volunteers were solicited, and they when they were outside getting water, they were to seize the muskets, and attack the guards.[35]

Four hundred officers organized themselves into eight companies, with a full set of officers for each, and the balance were to act as privates. Cooper's job was, once he was outside, to obtain horses as quickly as possible and to act as the advance guard. The plan was when the officers broke out, they would free the other prisoners held in Danville, which was about 1,800 at the time, overpower the guards, and seize their weapons. They were to take over the telegraph office and seize the entire town. Then, after obtaining supplies from the Confederate storehouses, they would march as an army to join General Sheridan in the Shenandoah Valley.[36]

The prisoners who were allowed to go to the river to obtain water had noted a two-story Confederate storehouse filled with hardtack, bacon, and other food supplies for the Confederate army. The prisoners, according to Cooper, received only a "piece of corn bread, or johnny-cake, made from unbolted corn meal, four inches long, three wide, and two inches thick," to last them for 24 hours. While once they had been given the "heads and lights of beeves," for a 26-day period they had received no meat at all.[37] The hungry prisoners grew desperate to escape.

One morning when several of the prisoners were poised to go outside with their buckets to get water, they distracted, seized and overpowered the guard. The prisoners grabbed the guard's gun. Another, hearing the scuffle, locked the outside door and sounded the alarm. The prisoners, armed with sticks and clubs, tried unsuccessfully to break down the door. Outside the building a crowd had gathered, and the prisoners retreated back upstairs. Colonel Raulston and Lieutenant Cooper were the last to go. As Raulston paused on the stairs to look out the window, he was shot by a guard outside. Raulston made it back up to the second floor, but he had been gutshot. He went to the place he usually slept, took off his overcoat, looked at his wound, and lay down. Soon, the prison guards arrived, led by Colonel Smith, who was in charge of all the Danville prisons. Everything appeared normal.[38]

Colonel Smith approached Raulston, and Raulston confessed that he was solely responsible. Raulston was removed to a hospital, but nothing could save his life, and he died December 15, 1864. Ironically, Raulston had been against the plan from the beginning,[39] but he took all the blame upon himself for the aborted escape attempt. There was no hope for the colonel, because he had shot in the bowels, and he died without naming the actual instigators.[40]

Successful Escapes — Through the Furnace

One other escape avenue proved successful for some. When the prisoners had to go to the river for water, they passed in back of a foundry. The front side of the foundry opened onto a street. The prisoners noted that the foundry operated only on certain days, the rest of the time the fire was out. It might be possible for a man to slip out of line and to hide in the cavity of the furnace until nightfall, then make his way across the bridge to North Carolina and possibly safety.[41]

Cooper and his fellow officers were allowed to go outside for water, wood and coal for the use of the prisoners. Just before dark each night, they would go out for water. In doing so, they had to pass an oven where cones for casting shells were baked. (Putnam calls it a furnace.) This oven was large enough to hold two men inside. The prisoners devised a scheme to stop near the oven and set their pails down so they could rest a minute. Someone would distract the guard at the rear of the line, the man at the front would slip into the oven, and the man next to him would pick up his pail. His absence would not be noticed for a while, because a head count was never made after the prisoners returned from getting water. When it was full dark, the prisoner could leave the oven, swim across the river, and walk away.[42]

In the early months of winter, the guards carefully supervised the water party, and counted them as the went out and as they returned. However, later, that degree of supervision diminished and, although their chances were slim, a few decided to try. Those that had shoes drew lots.[43]

To prevent their escape from being noticed, after the guards called the roll on the third floor, a prisoner was slipped through a hole in the floor down to the second floor, to make the head count correct. By this method, several prisoners escaped, and were not missed for several weeks.[44] Cooper named Lieutenants Baily, Quigley, Harris, Helm and Davis as the prisoners who escaped by hiding in the oven.[45] George H. Putnam wrote that only four men succeeded in getting away.[46] Of those four who escaped through the oven, two succeeded, one made it to the Union lines in Tennessee, and the other made it to the coast of North Carolina. The other two headed north through Virginia, but were captured and taken to Richmond. General Winder contacted the prison commandant to ask why he had not reported the escapes. The commandant did not believe the report at first, but after the second prisoner was caught, he decided to count his prisoners himself. He admonished the 350 that remained, and reminded them of the "pains he had taken to make them comfortable."[47]

Another Escape

The hospital had been set up about a mile southwest of Danville on the banks of the Dan River. There were three wards to accommodate about 50 patients. In addition, there was a cookhouse, a steward's office, and a dead house.[48]

W. H. Newlin, of Company C, 73rd Illinois Infantry Volunteers, was captured at Chickamauga, Georgia, on September 20, 1863. He and other captives were transported to Richmond, where they remained for a month before being sent to Danville. He and six fellow prisoners were allotted space on the second floor of Prison No. 2, a large frame building where they remained until December 15, 1863.[49] Then, Newlin came down with smallpox and was sent to the hospital. When he recovered, he was placed in charge of 64 men in eight tents. Newlin knew he had a better chance to escape from the hospital tents than from the building. Three of the nurses had previously escaped and headed for Federal lines. After those three left, Newlin was appointed wardmaster of Ward No. 1. He had the authority to choose men to assist him. He chose men he knew and could trust: Lucien B. Smith, William Sutherland, Watson C. Trippe, and John F. Wood. Robert G. Taylor was also added later to the nursing staff.[50]

As the smallpox epidemic abated, some of the hospital wards were closed and the attendants and the recovered prisoners were returned to inside the prison buildings. Newlin knew if he were going to escape it had to be soon.[51]

The would-be escapees made their plans. They got the cook to fill their haversacks with food, and clean clothes. That night, after the guards had gone to their quarters, the men and their full haversacks, and $200 in money, walked away from the hospital tents down the hill toward the wash house. They made their way individually to the place at which it had been decided to meet. As soon as all six had arrived, they set out through the woods until they found a wagon road. They then followed the railroad tracks that ran from Danville, Virginia, to Greensboro, North Carolina, for some distance.[52] The journey these six prisoners made from Danville, the dangers they faced, and the help they received would fill another book. Some of the six made it, others did not. Tripp was recaptured, and reportedly shot as an example. Nothing was ever heard of Taylor. Sutherland made it and in 1885 was living in Michigan. Smith lived at Dundee nearby in the same state. Wood escaped but was killed June 20, 1864, in battle. The sixth, W. H. Newlin, survived to tell the tale, which he published in a book in 1889.[53]

Freedom at Last

Those who remained in Danville, including Maj. Abner Small, were notified on February 15, 1865, that they would be returned to Richmond, where they again were sent to Libby Prison. They remained only a few days, and on February 22, 1865, they were released to board a steamer on the James River. The boat carried them to Aiken's Landing where they were exchanged and taken to Annapolis, Maryland.[54]

XXIV

Libby Prison, Richmond, Virginia

'Tis twelve o'clock! Within my prison dreary —
My head upon my hand — sitting so weary,
Scanning the future, musing upon the past,
Pondering the fate that here my lot is cast;
The hoarse cry of the sentry, pacing his beat,
Wakes the echo of the silent street:
  "All is well!"
    — Col. Frederick Bartleson, 100th Illinois, first stanza of
poem he wrote on wall at Libby, New Year's Eve, 1863-1864[1]

Location: between Cary and Canal streets, Richmond, Virginia. **Established:** 1862. **Type:** converted warehouse building. **Type of Prisoners:** black and white Federal officers (prisoners of war), Federal deserters, some civilians, and runaway slaves. **Capacity:** 1,000. **Greatest Number of Prisoners Held:** 4,221. **Known Number of Escapes:** 60+[2] (109 escaped through Rose's tunnel; half were captured). **Nicknames:** Hotel de Libby

History

Much has been written about Libby Prison, and much of it about the tunnel through which 109 Union officers escaped. But there are many untold stories about other escapes and the people who were confined there.

When the war began, there were 14 warehouses along the Richmond waterfront.[3] The most famous of those was the building at 20th and Cary streets, known as the Libby Prison. This building had a sad history even from the time of its construction between 1845 and 1852. John Enders Sr., one of the founders of Richmond's tobacco industry, fractured his skull and died after he fell some 20 feet from a ladder through a hatch during the construction of the central building. Enders' slaves burned all the buildings between 21st and 22nd streets when they learned that his will did not free them as they had expected.[4]

Capt. Luther Libby leased the west building for three years from the Enders family, and put up his famous sign, "L. Libby & Son, Ship Chandlers and Grocers." Libby was a native of Maine, and he had to close his business at the outbreak of the

Libby Prison, Richmond, Virginia. (Library of Congress, LC-DIG-cwpb-02249.)

war, but kept his lease. On June 27, 1861, Libby advertised that he had storage space for rent, enough to hold "20,000 bushels of wheat or corn." The building was taken over after the Battle of First Manassas to house the many prisoners and wounded.[5]

The three-story, 100- × 150-foot brick building leased by Libby stood near the Kanawha Canal, convenient for unloading supplies (and later prisoners). Each floor was divided into three large rooms. The ceilings were eight feet high, except on the top floor, whose walls ended just below the gabled roof. The basement was not visible on the front, but was exposed on the back side of the building.[6] The small, narrow windows were fitted with bars. The office was on the first floor, and there were damp cells underneath.[7]

George S. Palmer (who married John Enders's daughter Sarah) advertised the other two buildings for rent on "Water and Cary Streets," between 20th and 21st streets.[8]

A Richmond paper announced that the "Confederate States Military Prison" was to be moved from its present location on Main Street to Libby's building, "near the corner of 21st and Cary Streets."[9] After Luther Libby and his son, George W. Libby, were evicted, the building was opened as a Confederate prison on March 26, 1864.[10] The Libbys were given only 48 hours' notice. Several months later, the Confederate government rented the building for $100 per month or $1,200 per year.[11] Luther Libby would later be imprisoned in the Federal fortress of Fort Delaware. His wife took out advertisements in the personal column of the New York *Daily News* to let him know that she was safe at Smith's Farm.[12]

The Facilities

The three buildings were designated as East, Middle, and West. Interior doors were cut to connect the three buildings. The ground floor of the West Building was used as offices and guardrooms. The ground floor of the Middle Building housed the kitchen.[13] There were nine rooms 105 by 45 feet, each with ceilings eight feet high. Because of the slope of the ground, the buildings were four stories on the side near the canal.[14] Cellars contained cells for dangerous prisoners, spies, and slaves under a death sentence, as well as a carpenter shop.[15]

The cellar, shown in a drawing by Samuel H. Root (24th Massachusetts), was divided into three rooms. The center room had two double cells. One window served two cells, and faced the sidewalk on Cary Street. The back side faced Water (Canal) Street.[16]

Prison Personnel

Lt. Thomas Pratt Turner, of White Post, Virginia, was placed in command of Libby Prison. He had attended the Virginia Military Institute, but left in 1861 to join the 1st Virginia Battalion. Turner was thin, with dark hair and gray eyes, and was always clean-shaven. With his deep voice and stiff posture, he presented a formidable appearance in his Confederate uniform.[17] The Richmond *Dispatch* described him as "a most polite and accommodating officer."[18] Lieutenant Turner was the provost marshal at Lynchburg, Virginia. In the fall of 1862, he was promoted to captain and ordered to return as commandant of Libby Prison.[19] He was promoted to major for his excellent record as prison administrator.[20] Unlike Alexander, who ruled Castle Thunder with an iron hand and was criticized for his treatment of prisoners, Turner believed stern measures were necessary for maintaining discipline. However, at Libby, "where all are Yankees I have no need for such modes of punishment."[21]

Second in command at Libby Prison was Richard R. Turner, usually called "Dick" Turner. Dick had attended West Point for six months, but was dismissed after being convicted of forgery. He had been a plantation overseer in Henrico County, Virginia, before the war. He had dark hair and blue eyes, and was a man of considerable size and much heavier than Thomas Turner. Capt. Dick Turner was disliked by the prisoners because he was prone to inflict physical punishment.[22]

Former prisoner Capt. Frank Moran wrote that "Dick" Turner was a civilian whose status was that of "Inspector." He described Dick as one of the "Plug-ugly or blood-tub breed," from Baltimore.[23]

Although the prisoners nicknamed Dick Turner "The Libby Lion," his son William remembered him as a kindly man whose eyes "had a merry twinkle when he laughed," and who risked capture to return to Richmond after the war to see his wife and child.[24]

Some said that Thomas P. Turner and Richard R. "Dick" Turner were cousins; others said they were *not* related. They did not look alike, but were often confused by the prisoners in their narratives and memoirs.[25]

Third in command was Lt. George Emack, hated by the prisoners for his cruelty. He was 6 feet tall, fair complexioned, with blue eyes and short light-colored hair, and a moustache. He always wore a light-blue cap, blue trousers with black stripes, and carried a sword in a scabbard.[26]

Erasmus Ross, a big, heavy-set man, was in charge of registering the prisoners. Another of his duties involved visiting the prisoners' quarters each day for roll call. Accompanied by two armed guards, Ross, one of the most despised prison officials, always armed himself with an array of weapons, a revolver and a Bowie knife, for his own safety.[27] After the war, Ross was staying at the Spotswood Hotel in Richmond when it caught fire.[28] His remains were recovered in time for his memorial service on December 31, 1870.[29]

Famous Prisoners

Albert D. Richardson and Junius Henri Browne, two correspondents for the New York *Tribune,* were captured near Vicksburg on May 3, 1863. They were brought to Richmond to begin 19 months of captivity, first at Libby Prison, then Castle Thunder, and finally at Salisbury, North Carolina (see Chapter XXVI).[30] Captured with them was Richard T. Colburn of the New York *World.* Colburn was released in a few days, but Richardson and Browne were kept in prison, despite efforts from various citizens and officials.[31] Richardson was still in Libby Prison, in 1864 when a move was made to exchange him for Dr. James P. Hambleton, a prisoner being held in Fort Monroe.[32] Even Maj. Gen. Benjamin F. Butler tried to arrange this exchange.[33] Confederate exchange agent Robert Ould declined the exchange, but remarked that Daniel Gerhart (a wealthy citizen of Ohio), Richardson and Browne "seem to be the only citizens for whom the enemy show any solicitude."[34] Browne and Richardson were put on the third floor. They scrubbed the floor of their room two or three times each week, and it was "fumigated" every morning. A huge wooden tank contained water in which they could bathe.[35]

Another prisoner was Col. Michael Corcoran, of the 69th New York. He reportedly owned a saloon in the Bowery in New York and was well known in that city. He was seen by the Reverend J. L. Burrows while in Libby Prison as a "course-looking man in his shirt sleeves, sitting in a corner, with a crowd of cronies around him playing cards on the head of a barrel...."[36] Corcoran was transferred from Salisbury, North Carolina, in August 1862.[37]

Col. Neal Dow had been instrumental in getting the "Maine Law" enacted, the law which banned the sale of liquor in that state. Wounded at Port Hudson, the former Quaker was captured and sent to Libby. He was exchanged for Confederate Gen. W. H. F. "Rooney" Lee on March 14, 1864.[38]

Col. A. D. Streight, of the 51st Indiana, had been captured during "Streight's Raid" by Confederate Gen. Nathan Bedford Forrest near Rome, Georgia, but only after losing a third of his regiment, most of them mounted on army mules.[39] Streight become famous for his escape through the tunnel with 108 other officers, a great embarrassment to the Confederate officials.

Shortly after the tunnel incident, prison officials were pacified for the loss of Streight and the others from the tunnel by the capture of Maj. Gen. Eliakim Parker Scammon and his staff. Scammon was in charge of Scammon's Division and the 3rd Division, West Virginia troops, when he was captured and sent to Libby.[40]

Union Gen. Hugh Judson Kilpatrick, who led a raid on Richmond early in 1864, was a prisoner for four months.[41]

On April 20, 1864, at Plymouth, North Carolina, a number of Federal officers were captured and sent to Libby Prison, among them Brig. Gen. Henry Walton Wessells.[42] This veteran of the Seminole and Mexican wars was promoted to command Wessells' Brigade. He was in command of the Subdistrict of Albemarle, North Carolina, when he surrendered at Plymouth.[43]

Civilian Prisoners

After the fall of Richmond and its occupation by Federal forces, some of the defeated Confederates were held in Libby Prison. Among them were Judge Robert Ould, the former Confederate commissioner of exchange, and William H. Hatch, his assistant.[44]

Mr. Philander A. Streator, of Holyoke, Massachusetts, was believed to have been the first prisoner held at Libby Prison. Over the course of the war, more than 50,000 passed through the prison doors.[45] The inscriptions carved by the prisoners on the walls, doors and windows were copied and published in 1884 in a book titled *Walls That Talk*.[46]

Black Soldiers in Libby

Major Turner reported that he had received 148 black soldiers from the 5th, 7th and 13th U.S. Colored Troops. All were dressed in Federal uniforms and were reported to have been captured "in arms." Turner reported to exchange agent Capt. W. H. Hatch that 12 had died in the hospital since their captures, and 54 were in the hospital sick on October 14, 1864. The remaining 82 had been sent to work on the fortifications.[47]

Daily Routine of the Prisoners

First Lt. Thomas Sturgis (5th Regiment, Massachusetts Veteran Volunteers) was captured near Petersburg at Fort Haskell. He and other prisoners were sent by train to Richmond.[48] When Sturgis arrived at Libby Prison, his money was taken from him at the door. The officers were separated from the enlisted men, and he was sent to a room on the second floor. The room had three barred windows on each end. There were no sashes or shutters, and no way to keep out the cold. The windows on one end overlooked the street, and the other the James River. There was an iron stove, and a table, and a toilet sink and a water faucet.[49]

Capt. Thomas Simpson (Battery F, 1st Regiment, Rhode Island Light Artillery), described his life in prison after his capture in October 1864. New arrivals at Libby Prison were taken to the office where their name, date and place of capture was recorded in a ledger. Each new prisoner was searched for concealed weapons, and asked to surrender any money he had. Prison officials claimed that the money would be returned whenever the prisoner was transferred. The prisoner was then taken to the two stories on the west end of the building, which was reached by wooden steps. After going up them, the steps were lowered to the floor by a pulley, so that none could descend. All the glass had been removed from the barred windows, and replaced by worn and tattered canvas screens which did little to keep out the cold wind. Furniture consisted of a long table and two cast-iron, wood-burning stores for heat. Most of the prisoners slept on the bare floor—few had blankets.[50]

Reveille was sounded at 6 A.M. each day by a drum band of some of the Federal black soldiers. Fifteen minutes later, the prisoners lined up for roll call. Instead of answering to a name, the prison inspector, R. R. "Dick" Turner, counted them. After the count, the rooms were searched, then the prisoners returned to their quarters. Those who were sick were examined by Turner, and if he thought necessary, they were sent to the hospital. A piece of corn bread and perhaps a pint of black bean soup were issued shortly after roll call. The beans were filled with little black bugs. The next meal was issued at 3 P.M., and sometimes it included two or three ounces of beef. Those who had money could invest in a clay pipe and smoking tobacco, "the only cheap article in the Confederacy," at the price of a dollar a pound, according to Thomas Simpson.[51]

Cruel and Unusual Treatment

When the Federal government captured Captain Baker and 14 of his crew from the schooner *Savannah*, tried them as pirates, and threatened to hang them, the Confederates retaliated. On November 6, 1861, Gen. John H. Winder ordered a like number executed. They were to be chosen from among the Federal officers of highest rank, held in close confinement, and executed if Baker and his crew were not released. The first name drawn was Col. Michael Corcoran, who was to be a hostage for Captain Smith of the privateer *Jefferson Davis*, another captured Confederate vessel. The convictions were not upheld and the captured Confederates classified prisoners of war. Subsequently, those hostages held at Libby were released and exchanged.[52]

A similar incident was described by Capt. Bernhard Domschcke (26th Wisconsin).[53] After Union Gen. Ambrose Burnside captured two Confederates near Knoxville, Tennessee, and ordered them hanged as spies, prison officials at Libby were ordered to select from among Streight's and Milroy's officers "two captains by lot" and hang them.[54] Major Turner called all the "Yankee captains" to come to one of the lower rooms in which there was a table with writing materials. Turner announced: "Gentlemen, an unpleasant duty devolves on me this morning. I am instructed to select two of your number, by lot, for immediate execution."[55]

Lots were drawn, and two unfortunate Federal officers, Capt. Henry W. Sawyer (1st New Jersey Cavalry) and Capt. John Flynn (51st Indiana Infantry) were the losers. Turner put Sawyer and Flinn in "the underground cells." Daily, the two expected to be executed. However, Confederate Gen. William H. F. "Rooney" Lee, son of Gen. Robert E. Lee, and Capt. William S. Winder, son of Gen. John H. Winder, were captured. The Federal government promised that if Sawyer and Flynn were executed,

Lee and Winder would be hanged. The two Federal officers were released from the dungeon and no more was said about their "execution."[56]

The Dungeon

As with most prisons, the dungeon at Libby was a dark, damp, cold subterranean cell. Joseph Ferguson reported that he knew several officers who were kept in the dungeon for attempting to escape. When they came out, according to Ferguson, "their beards and hair were long and matted. One officer's beard had rotted from the effects of damp and mold. Another lost his eyesight on coming to the light after the long confinement in midnight darkness. There was little flesh on their limbs or bodies. They were living skeletons."[57]

Special Treatment for Some

Lt. Col. James M. Sanderson owned a hotel in New York which was popular with southerners before the war. He "toadied" up to the prison officials, and was allowed to leave the prison to visit in the city. His privileges, however, gained him disfavor with other prisoners, especially Colonel Streight.[58]

Prisoners Refuse Transfer

For some unknown reason, the prisoners in Libby did not wish to be transferred to Danville. In May 1864, when a thousand Federal officers were ordered to prepare to be moved to Danville, the Richmond *Whig* reported that the prisoners swore they would not go. They even refused to have their names registered. At the point of bayonets, they were forced to comply. However, while they were being registered, they had set fire to the boxes of supplies on the second floor. The fire was extinguished, and the prisoners spent their last minutes in Libby throwing all the sugar, coffee and other supplies recently sent to them from the North into the latrines. The prisoners vowed to escape from the train on the way to Danville, but, the paper reported, that "did not make good on their vows."[59] Perhaps they knew they were better off in Libby, or perhaps they had plans to escape.

Escape — Massive Plot Discovered

One unsuccessful escape plot hinged on the combined efforts of the prisoners in Libby with those in Castle Thunder. They planned to break out at night, surprise the guards, seize weapons, and reach Union-held territory. The prisoners planed to destroy Confederate property,[60] including the Tredgar Iron Works. They even planned to hold the Confederate Congress and President Davis hostage until they could be rescued by Federal forces. The plan was thwarted when Lieutenant Colonel Sanderson informed on his fellow prisoners. After several threats against his life, Sanderson was removed from the prison and kept secreted. Shortly thereafter, Sanderson was either paroled or exchanged. One of his fellow prisoners believed that he fled to London before being court-martialed. Sanderson was later indicted on several charges, including disloyalty to the Union and the betrayal of an escape plot. He was dismissed from the Union army on June 8, 1864. After hearing testimony from several witnesses a military commission reversed Sanderson's dismissal and reinstated him.[61]

The Easy Way Out — Exchange or Enlist

The exchange of prisoners began in February 1862, and continued until it was stopped in May 1863. Both sides obtained release of prisoners through an exchange at designated places—City Point in the east, and Vicksburg in the West.[62]

To guarantee they would be exchanged, Union officers courted the favor of Confederate officers and prison officials. Others used influential relatives and friends to help them get exchanged. After a Catholic bishop began visiting the prison to preach and share their meals, Domschcke recalled: "Catholic and all who claimed to be Catholics were exchanged."[63]

After the exchange process was stopped, prisoners tried other methods to get out of the prison. John Williams (Company M, 1st New York Cavalry) was captured in the Shenandoah Valley and taken to Libby Prison. He claimed he was a citizen of Fairfax County, Virginia, and so he was conscripted into the 61st Virginia Infantry. One morning while on picket duty, he escaped and made his way to Union lines.[64]

Escape Attempts

A group of five prisoners escaped but two, Lieutenant Colonel Hatch and Lieutenant Masters, were recaptured and returned to Libby Prison on August 7, 1862. No

mention was made in the newspaper account of how they escaped.[65] Hatch and Masters were placed in "close confinement" until exchanged.[66] The other three were recaptured by Confederate scouts in Essex County.[67]

Colonel Abel D. Streight attempted to bribe a guard with a gold watch. The guard took the watch, but caught the colonel as he tried to make his escape. Streight was put in irons and kept in the underground cell for three weeks on a diet of bread and water.[68] Colonel Streight's spirit was not broken and he emerged from the cell more determined than ever to escape.

Major McClellan and Lieutenant Aking, of the 22nd New York Cavalry, both patients in the prison hospital, forced a door open and rushed the guard. The guards fired at them, but missed. The two prisoners ran up 21st Street, but were

Colonel A. E. Streight was one of 109 prisoners to escape through the tunnel from Libby Prison. (Courtesy of the Library of Congress, LC-USZ62-90936.)

captured and returned to the prison. One of the shots fired by the guard had passed through Aking's clothes and grazed his left side. Maj. Thomas Turner, who was sleeping in a tent near the prison, was awakened, and he returned to make sure the prisoners were more securely confined.[69]

Maj. H. A. White of Pennsylvania, a former member of the Pennsylvania Senate, attempted to get out along with the physicians who were being exchanged. He made it to City Point, the place of exchange, where he was recognized and returned to Libby Prison.[70]

First Successful Escapes

Domschcke believed that Major Houstain and Cavalry Lieutenant Volziehn were the first to escape Libby Prison. Their escape inspired others.[71]

Domschcke recalled that one prisoner simply walked out the kitchen door into the street. Several others disappeared by way of the hospital. One Federal officer, dressed in a Confederate uniform, walked down the steps of the west wing to the ground floor. He walked casually past the guard and into the office. There, he asked directions to the office of a captain outside Libby Prison. The adjutant accompanied the disguised Federal officer to the street, where the guards seeing the two together, made no move to stop his escape.[72]

Captain Hyndman, of Company A, 4th Pennsylvania Cavalry was captured in October 1863. When he decided to escape, he planned to go out when the detail of prisoners was marched daily to the bakehouse for rations. Hyndman confided his plan to members of his company, but none thought he could succeed. Only one agreed to go with him, Cpl. Alex Welton. The two managed to get Confederate caps and old gray jackets. With a piece of blanket around their shoulders, and their caps under their arms, the two edged into the center of a double line of the prisoners. The prisoners were to be marched out with only one guard in front and one in back, and one Confederate guard near the center. The two whispered to their comrades to quickly fill up the gap when they stepped out of line. Just at the column reached the corner of 19th Street and turned down Main, the two left the ranks, donned their Confederate caps, and walked back the way they had come whistling *The Bonnie Blue Flag*. As soon as they were out of sight of the guard at the rear, they hurried to the river near the navy yard. They remained for a few minutes to settle their nerves and catch their breath, then started toward the suburbs. They hid in a ravine about five miles from the city limits. They asked an old black man with a horse-drawn cart filled with coal for direction to Harrison's Landing where the Federal troops were stationed. After they told the old man that they were escaped prisoners, he then gave them all the information he could. He advised them to hide until night, and to "keep clear of all white men, as the whole neighborhood were in league in order to capture escaping prisoners." But, he assured them, "you need not fear the colored people," because "they are your friends." The pair made it to Federal lines near Williamsburg.[73]

Four or five officers decided to take "French leave." They obtained Confederate uniforms, which allowed them to pass the guards.[74]

Capt. John F. Porter Jr., of the 14th New York Cavalry, escaped on January 29, 1864. Porter went to the surgeon's room and told the surgeon he had the "chills." He then passed by the commissary's room, shaved his beard and darkened his eyebrows and hair to disguise himself. He waited until the 3 o'clock roll call, then he went downstairs with the guard. When the guard went inside the building, and before the new guard could come on duty, Porter walked outside, right by the sentinels, who supposed him to be a clergyman or simply a Richmond citizen. He kept going until he reached the city limits along Nine Mile Road. He spent the night in the woods, and returned to Richmond to await a more favorable time to escape. He waited nine days, while he checked the fortifications of the city. At the end of that time, he obtained a passport from a Confederate officer and, with a family of Irish refugees, started the long trek to the Army of the Potomac. Once, he was nearly caught when he was suddenly surrounded by a force of Confederate cavalry in Hanover County at Cat Tail Church. The cavalry looked at his passport, and took his money, $100 in Confederate bills. They left him $50. Two days later, Porter and his group reached the Rappahannock River, and crossed over into Richmond County. After they reached the Potomac, Porter and the others were hidden in the home of a Union supporter, and for $20 in gold, the man carried them to St. Mary's County, Maryland. Porter luckily encountered a detachment of Union cavalry, and they gave him transportation to Point Lookout.[75] Porter sent messages to his comrades and asked for money, which they immediately sent. Once he reached home, Porter married the young lady who awaited him.[76]

Mr. and Mrs. John H. Quarles had hidden Captain Porter for nine days. Quarles enlisted in the Union army, and his property in Richmond was confiscated. His wife and children were turned out. The oldest was four, the youngest only four months. She escaped and came to New York with the children, and Captain Porter tried to help her and her family.[77]

A New York newspaper described how Porter had escaped wearing a "rebel uniform," and was thus able to remain in Richmond without being discovered.[78]

Maj. E. L. Bates, of the 18th Illinois Volunteers, who escaped Libby only a few hours before Porter, was not so fortunate and was recaptured.[79]

Thomas J. Orr and William Cummin escaped and made their way to Williamsburg. They passed numerous heavy guns, all unguarded. The Yankees thought about spiking the guns, but since they were trying to avoid capture, they did not have time.[80]

When Pvt. Charles Goodwin, a deserter from the 32nd New York, escaped, Major Turner called on Capt. George W. Alexander of Castle Thunder to lend him John Coon, one of Alexander's detectives, to aid in the prisoner's capture. Turner described Goodwin as being "a very trim, neat looking fellow," who was 20 years old, with gray eyes and fair complexion. He stood about 5 feet 4 inches. He usually wore light-colored pants, and a blue jacket, with "N.Y. state buttons" and a "round felt hat."[81]

Major Turner reported to Capt. W. S. Winder that nine Negroes had escaped from Libby Prison "at different times" on February 16, 1863. They had been placed in a "secure room with a sentinel at the door," and counted twice each day. During the daytime, they were used to work in the kitchen and do chores, such as cleaning, cutting wood, etc. Their escape, Tuner said, was due to the guards' "gross neglect of duty."[82]

Three Yankee prisoners escaped from Libby on Saturday night, April 30, 1864. Two Richmond papers reported the next week that they had not yet been recaptured.[83]

Col. Charles A. De Villiers was as unique as his escape story. When first taken to Libby, the colonel became ill with brain fever. Being knowledgeable about medical practices, De Villiers was asked to help in the hospital after he recovered. He was given a red ribbon to put in his buttonhole, and was occasionally given permission to go out into the city. Once, however, he was stopped by a guard and forbidden to pass. Angered, the "French Yankee" wrote out a note which said he had permission to go outside the prison. This forgery was discovered, and he was taken from the hospital and put back with the prisoners, and placed in irons. [84]

De Villiers confided to Colonel Woodruff that he was determined to escape, and he proceeded to get the coat and hat of a Confederate officer. Thus disguised, he passed by the guard. He hid for two hours in order to learn the countersign which was necessary to pass out the gates. When the guard called out, "Who comes there?" De Villiers replied, "A friend with the countersign." About six miles out of Richmond, he was again challenged by a guard, who was armed with a double-barrel shotgun, a revolver, and a Bowie knife. The guard questioned him, and became suspicious. The Confederates took him into custody and marched across a bridge over a stream. De Villiers was desperate, and in the middle of the bridge, he struck the out and knocked both his guards in the water. He then continued on to Petersburg, a distance of 65 miles. [85] As he approached the area controlled by Magruder's Confederate forces, he was shot at several times. The gunfire aroused the whole brigade. With the use of a board, he swam the James River and landed on the far side of a swamp.[86]

The crafty Frenchman decided the best way to avoid notice was to get a job. He took a position with a German blacksmith for $1.50 per week. Thus, secure, he could learn of the location of the Confederate forces when he continued on his way. He stayed for two weeks, and after explaining his true situation to the German, he adopted another disguise. De Villiers pretended to be a blind man who desired to return to France. The German was to act as his companion and guide. The two approached the headquarters of Gen. Benjamin Huger, a French Huguenot who had served as chief of ordnance in Mexico under Gen. Winfield Scott.[87] Huger promised to sent De Villiers to Fortress Monroe under a flag of truce. Thus, the escapee was transported north to safety.[88]

Or Dig a Tunnel

Confederate Brig. Gen. John Hunt Morgan visited Libby Prison, and made a tour and inspection early in January 1864.[89] Morgan, with his reddish beard and hair cut short from his imprisonment in Ohio, knew many of the prisoners from Kentucky who were being held in Libby. Morgan had brought the war to the North with his 1,000-mile raid across Kentucky, Indiana and Ohio. When he bragged about his escape through a tunnel under the Ohio State Penitentiary, he unknowingly inspired the Libby prisoners to dig their own tunnel.[90]

The Great Libby Prison Escape

The Libby Prison tunnel has probably received more publicity than any other escape route from northern or southern prisons. Indeed, the escape of 109 Yankee officers out of Libby Prison on the night of Tuesday, February 9, 1864, was one of the greatest escapes of all times.

On the morning of February 10, the head count turned up a number of missing prisoners and the search began. Captain Hayward's cavalry was immediately sent in pursuit.[91] Since prisoners were counted only when it was discovered that some were missing, a roll call by name was done, which took four hours and gave the prisoners an additional advantage.[92] The fugitives included 11 colonels, seven majors, 37 captains, and 59 lieutenants.[93] The prison population at that time was 1,200.[94]

A list of the principal officers who escaped included:

Colonels—J. F. Boyd, 20th Army Corps; W. G. Ely, 18th Connecticut; H. C. Hobart, 21st Wisconsin; W. P. Kendrick, 3rd West Tennessee Cavalry; W. B. McCreary, 21st Michigan; Thomas E. Rose, 37th Pennsylvania; J. P. Spofford, 97th New York; C. W. Tilden, 16th Maine, T. S. West, 24th Wisconsin, A. D. Streight, 51st Indiana; and D. Miles, 79th Pennsylvania.

Majors—J. P. Collins, 29th Indiana; G. W. Fitzsimmons, 30th Indiana; J. H. Hooper, 15th Massachusetts; B. B. MacDonald, 100th Ohio; A. Von Witzel, 74th Pennsylvania; J. N. Walker, 73rd Indiana; and J. Henry, 5th Ohio.[95]

As soon as General Winder learned of the escape, he immediately ordered the guards arrested. Major Turner also assumed the guards had been bribed to let the prisoners escape. He followed orders and the guards were arrested and incarcerated in Castle Thunder prison. Upon further investigation, the guards were exonerated and released.[96]

Turner and Lieutenant La Touche made a thorough inspection of the prison.[97] They discovered the entrance to a tunnel hidden by a large rock which fit the hole exactly. Once removed, a small black boy was sent into the hole to explore. The tunnel had been dug directly beneath the place where three sentinels daily marched back and forth. It ended at the rear of Carr's warehouse, where the escapees emerged, one by one, at least 60 feet from any of the sentinels on duty. To reach the tunnel, the prisoners cut through the hospital room and a closed stairway which led to the basement. The authorities surmised the work must have been done at night, and the debris cleared away before daylight. They also surmised that the completion of the tunnel must have required several months of digging.[98]

How the Tunnel Was Made[99]

Most authors credit Col. Thomas E. Rose with devising the plan and organizing its completion.[100] Although Colonel Rose was in charge, he was assisted by Maj. Andrew G. Hamilton, who apparently came up with the idea of getting to the cellar by way of the fireplace in the kitchen.[101] Hamilton, a member of the 12th Kentucky Cavalry, had been captured at Jonesborough, Tennessee. He credited Rose with being the leader of the tunnel party. A. D. Streight was involved in no way other than as an escapee.[102]

It was years before Colonel Rose told his story. In a short article published in 1885, Rose described how the plan was devised and the work carried out. He organized a party of 15 men to work in shifts in the cellar the prisoners called "Rat Hell." Rose gave special credit to Lt. F. F. Bennett who helped rescue him from a dangerous situation, and Capt. John Sterling, who furnished the diggers with candles.[103] One of those who escaped through the tunnel recalled that the only tools they had to dig with were a table knife, a chisel and a spittoon.[104]

They had several false starts before a tunnel to the outside was successfully completed. The first tunnel was stopped when bedrock was struck. A second tunnel had to be abandoned because of the sewer which ran between the prison and the canal.[105]

Finally, a plan was developed to tunnel under the street east of the prison to the yard of the warehouse opposite. Their only tools were a chisel with a long handle, and a square wooden spitbox, which was used to haul the dirt from the tunnel by a rope.[106] Once the actual digging of the tunnel began, it was completed after 14 days, and 52 days from the start of making a way through the kitchen fireplace.[107]

Initially involved were: Colonel Rose, Capt. A. G. Hamilton, Capt. J. F. Gallagher, Major Fitzsimmons, Lieutenant Bennett, Capt. John Sterling, Captain Lucas, Capt. I. N. Johnson, and one or two others. It took them 12 nights just to complete the entrance to the basement through the fireplace.[108]

Johnson missed roll call one morning. Prison officials thought he must have escaped. He hid out in the basement for many days in the dark and cold. Eventually, he began coming back upstairs at night to sleep. His ordeal is another unique aspect of the tunnel story.[109]

Rose and his crew overcame all obstacles—lack of tools, distance required, avoiding the attention of the guards and prison officials, and keeping the plan secret from other prisoners. The entrance to the cellar from the kitchen was covered in the daytime by the cookstove. The tunnel then ran from the cellar under the street to the yard of a warehouse. A big block of granite hid the tunnel's entrance, which had to be broken out of the foundation of Libby before the digging of the tunnel could begin.[110]

A letter written at the end of the war detailed the excavation of the tunnel:

> The officers were confined on the 1st floor in the middle room & took up the brick fire place some 15 ft. back from No. 6 & digging down passed through the brick partition into the basement landing in the outside room, then began the hole, carefully covering the earth removed under bales of hay & forrage that was then in this room until the distance after many weeks was traversed & ready for use, then they passed out one at a time, letting the sentry just turn about to march back while they popped out & as one fellow came to view he had just sung out 12 o'clock & all is well.[111]

At one point, the tunnel was angled upward because it was believed it reached far enough. However, when the person in the tunnel cleared a small hole, he could see two guards practically upon him. One of them said, "I have been hearing a strange noise in the ground there." They listened a while and decided it must be rats. The tunnel continued another 15 feet further to a point under a shed. It ran eight feet below the street a distance of between 60–70 feet, and was just barely large enough for a grown man to crawl through.[112]

When the tunnel was completed, Colonel Rose went out one night to reconnoiter.[113] The next night the prisoners began slipping out one at a time. Once outside, each crossed the yard and disappeared in the dark down the streets of Richmond.[114]

The Flight

Next out after Colonel Rose and the original 15 diggers was Colonel Streight, and he headed for the house of a black woman who would guide him to other friends.[115] Streight had been treated harshly by Confederates because he was believed to be, according to James M. Wells, "a notorious character charged with having raised a Negro regiment." Streight and two or three other officers were hidden by Miss Elizabeth Van Lew.[116]

Lt. Col. Harrison C. Hobart, of the 21st Wisconsin, claimed that he and Col. T. S. West were the last two out of the tunnel. They made their way through the streets of Richmond while Harrison, whose beard was long and his face pale, clung to the arm of West, and pretended to be a sick, decrepit old man with a "comsumptive" cough. They passed police, soldiers, and others to make their way out of the city down the Williamsburg Pike.[117]

Hobart and West had almost reached the Chickahominy when they saw bloodhounds tracking them. They jumped across a little brook, several times, to confuse the hounds. With the help of a slave, traveling at night, and hiding in the day, they reached Williamsburg.[118]

The first two Yankee officers reached the Federal pickets of Brig. Gen. I. J. Wistar on February 14. The former prisoners reported that Colonel Streight was on the road, but that Gen. Neal Dow "could not stand the fatigue of the trip," and so had remained in the prison. Wister sent out cavalry to look for more of the escaping officers.[119]

Capt. W. S. B Randall, of the 2nd Ohio Infantry, evaded being found by the bloodhounds by putting cayenne pepper on his trail. Someone had sent him the pepper in a bottle concealed in a roll of butter. He encountered a detachment of the 11th Pennsylvania cavalry, and was eventually sent to Washington to meet with Secretary of War Stanton.[120] Randall spoke at a reunion of the Ohio Association of Union Ex-Prisoners of War in 1890. He displayed the case knife which he had used in digging the tunnel.[121]

Another to reach safety was Lt. Albert Wallber, of the 26th Wisconsin Infantry. He wrote of his flight, the help of black people along the way, and the narrow escapes. He was rescued by the 11th Pennsylvania Cavalry under Col. Samuel P. Spear, only six miles out of Williamsburg. It had taken him and his companions five days.[122]

Recapture of Tunnel Escapees

The escape of the 109 Federal officers caused an uproar in Richmond. The newspapers had a field day and called it the greatest escape since John Hunt Morgan tunneled out of the Ohio State Penitentiary.[123]

The stories of the recapture of the prisoners are as bizarre as the initial escape. Two days after the escape, the Richmond *Whig* reported that only one prisoner had been recaptured. Another paper said four had been recaptured, two of them about 20 miles below Richmond, and two near Hanover Court House.[124] Couriers were sent in every direction, and pickets doubled on roads and bridges. Officials believed that the escapees were being hidden in or near Richmond by disloyal persons.[125] The citizens organized a vigilante committee to capture the prisoners.[126]

By Friday, February 12, 22 of the prisoners had been recaptured. Mr. John Ligon, Assistant Clerk, Orderly Hatcher, Warden R. R. Turner, and two policemen had captured eight of the fugitives along the roads. Fourteen others had been picked up on the Chickahominy.

The first eight recaptured were:

1st lieutenants— W. B. Pierce, 11th Kentucky Cavalry; H. Scroeter, 82nd Illinois Infantry; W. L. Watson, 21st Wisconsin; E. Schroeders, 74th Pennsylvania; F. Moran, 73rd New York; and C. H. Morgan, 21st Wisconsin.

Captains— J. Gates (Yates?), 3rd Ohio; and G. Starr, 104th New York.[127]

Morgan, Moran, and Watson were recaptured by Confederate cavalry within sight of the Federal lines.[128]

The 14 captured on February 11 were:

Colonel— S. P. Spofford, 97th New York;

Captain— F. Irch, 45th New York;

1st lieutenants— A. B. White, 4th Pennsylvania Cavalry; W. A. Daly, 8th Pennsylvania Cavalry, H. H. Hinds, 57th Pennsylvania; Engineer Isaac Johnson, of the gunboat *Sattelite;* A. Moore, Company E, 4th Kentucky; M. R. Small, 6th Maryland; C. S. Edmond, Company D, 67th Pennsylvania;

2nd lieutenants— J. P. Brown, 15th U.S. Regulars; G. S. Good, Company I, 84th Pennsylvania; G. P. Gamble, Company D, 63rd Pennsylvania; J. M. Sasson, Company H, 40th Ohio; and P. A. White, Company D, 83rd Pennsylvania.[129]

The Richmond *Whig's* list was slightly different, and included Col. J. P. Spofford, of the 97th New York, as remaining at large, along with Cols. Thomas E. Rose, and A. D. Streight.[130] On February 12, eight more were captured, making a total of 30 out of the 109.[131] Colonel Rose was recaptured near Williamsburg when he encountered some Confederate scouts.[132] After the two scouts captured him, they made him run a full mile. Then one of the scouts left, and Rose, exhausted and weak with hunger, attempted one last time to escape. He grabbed the scout by the neck and threw him to the ground. During the struggle, the scout's musket discharged, and that brought the other scout back.[133] Rose was placed in solitary confinement for 30 days on bread and water, according to one account.[134]

Three of the fugitives were recaptured near Fort Clifton on the Appomattox River. They had reached Port Walthall, and with a boat had started for Old Point. They got lost going down the James River, and turned into the Appomattox River by mistake. Utterly exhausted and almost frozen, they went ashore and surrendered to some men from Martin's Battery. The three taken to Petersburg and put in the provost marshal's guard house were: Frank M. Kreps, 77th Pennsylvania; Henry B. Freeman, U.S. Infantry; and C. Gay, 11th Pennsylvania.[135]

Another prisoner, Maj. J. N. Walker, of the 73rd Indiana, surrendered to Surgeon J. A. Slater, of the 15th Virginia Cavalry. Walker was tired and sick, had had nothing to eat since his escape, and was unable to travel further. He was returned to Richmond in an ambulance.[136] Four more were recaptured near Richmond: Lt. W. Clifford,

16th U.S. Infantry; Maj. Robert Henry, 5th Ohio; Lt. J. W. Hare, 5th Ohio Cavalry, and Lt. A. Garbett, 77th Pennsylvania.[137]

Sixteen more were recaptured by February 13: Lieutenant Colonel Ely, 18th Connecticut, Capt. E. S. Smith, 19th U.S. Cavalry; Lt. W. H. Wilcox, 10th New York Cavalry; Lt. Adam Hauf, 45th New York; Lt. Daniel Flausberry, 1st Michigan Cavalry; Lt. T. J. Roy, 49th Ohio; Lt. J. H. Gadsby, 19th U.S. Infantry, Lt. M. M. Basset, 53rd Illinois; Lt. M. Bedell, 123rd New York; Capt. N. Moore, 29th Indiana; Lt. J. D. Simpson, 10th Indiana; Capt. J. D. Phelps, 73rd Indiana; Capt. W. C. Rosman, 3rd Ohio; Colonel Rose, 77th Pennsylvania; Lt. H. P. Crawford, 2nd Illinois Cavalry; and Lt. S. D. Sutherland, 125th Ohio. Most of these were caught north of the Chickahominy.[138] Citizens aided in the arrest of several of the escapees. One was recaptured by a black man named Sambo, wielding a hoe for a weapon.[139]

One fugitive was recaptured in Richmond when he went to the ballroom at Concert Hall. He was recognized and arrested. Another prisoner encountered one of General Mosby's men in a saloon. Mosby's officer suspected he was an escapee, and took him in. A third tunnel escapee was recognized by a newsboy as he attempted to swap his Yankee uniform for a black man's greatcoat. It was noted that nearly all those who had been recaptured were wearing a Yankee greatcoat.[140]

With the capture of Lts. J. M. Fales, 1st R. I. Cavalry, and E. Cottingham, of the 35th Ohio, the total recaptured by February 15 was 52.[141]

Reported on February 17 was the capture of five more prisoners: Lt. C. D. Miles, 79th Pennsylvania; Lt. G. T. Hail, 112th Illinois; and Lt. E. C. Grable, 8th Michigan Cavalry; Capt. Thomas Hircy (?), 79th Illinois; and Capt. J. E. Wilkins, 112th Illinois.[142]

By February 20, 11 days after their escape, 58 of the 109 Yankee officers had been recaptured and returned to Libby Prison.[143] Twenty-one had eluded capture and made it to Fort Monroe and Williamsburg. Among them were Colonel Streight and Colonel McCready, of the 21st Michigan. Thirty were still unaccounted for.[144]

Some of those who reached safety were met 12 miles beyond Williamsburg by a party of scouts from the 11th Pennsylvania Cavalry. They told the Federal soldiers that they had been without any regular food for five days, and were exhausted from hunger and exposure. They told the cavalrymen of the tunnel. More would have escaped, but some were to large to pass through the narrow tunnel. Those that did get out were assisted by black people along the way who told them how to avoid rebel scouts and pickets, and directed them to the closest Federal lines.[145]

Several weeks later, 55 of the former inmates of Libby Prison had reached Butler's lines near New Kent Court House.[146]

The news of the escape soon reached Washington and New York. A deserter from the 14th Louisiana reported he had seen the news in the Richmond papers before he left. The deserter also noted that most of his regiment were barefoot (in February), and that their daily rations consisted of a fourth of a pound of meat and one pint of meal.[147]

Colonel Streight reached Washington about March 1. In August 1864, he wrote his official report of his capture, imprisonment, and escape. Many of his officers were still prisoners, and a number of them had died from disease, insufficient food, and their long confinement.[148]

Another who managed to evade capture after escaping through the tunnel was

Lt. Col. Harrison C. Hobart. He rejoined his regiment and was with General Sherman when he marched through Georgia.[149]

Col. W. P. Kendrick had many narrow escapes.[150] Once out of Libby Prison, he did not forget those he left behind. From the safety of the National Hotel in Washington, D.C., Kendrick wrote to President Lincoln to ask for his help in obtaining the release of Lt. Col. R. S. Northcott of West Virginia. Northcott, a colonel of the 12th Virginia, had been confined in Libby Prison since about June 20, 1863, and would have escaped with Kendrick but his health was "too bad to undertake it." Northcott's health would soon be destroyed if he remained in prison. He appealed to Lincoln to use his authority for a "special exchange."[151]

Capt. George H. Starr, of the 104th New York Volunteers, escaped through the tunnel only to be recaptured. He wrote from Libby Prison on February 16, 1864, to "Carrie":

> Last week 109 officers Escaped from Prison. I was one of them. We scattered but 50 or 60 of us were *retaken*. I was taken 9 miles from here; I had a hard choice *Lead* or *Libby* & I preferred to see Libby again as I knew under the circum' my *friends* would desire to have me. I had quite an adventure withal! Have been in a cell a few days but now at my old quarters all night.[152]

Captain Starr persisted in his escape attempts, and he was moved to Macon, Georgia, in August 1864. He continued to try to escape, and was transferred from Macon to Charleston, then to Camp Sorghum at Columbia, South Carolina. He finally succeeded and made it to Union lines.[153]

Lt. J. M. Wasson of Company H, 40th Ohio Volunteer Infantry, wrote of his experiences, imprisonment, escape, and recapture. He had crawled out through the tunnel and passed "leisurely by the guards," and even saluted them. By daylight, he and a Kentucky lieutenant were eight miles from the city. They hid out for a day, and at dark began to move again. However, they encountered a squad of Confederate cavalry, and "dodged into the brush." On their third day of freedom, they were suddenly discovered by five Confederate officers who fired at them but with no resulting injury. The two were taken to the headquarters of General Pickett, and then returned to Libby Prison. As punishment, they were put in a "dark, damp cell for eight days, the cell being so crowded that we could not lie down. Afterwards, Wasson made the rounds of southern prisons. He was sent to Camp Oglethorpe in Georgia, then transferred to Charlotte, then Salisbury. He was then transferred back to Danville and from there back to his "old room" at Libby. By then, the war was over, and he was sent to City Point for exchange.[154]

Capt. Frank E. Moran was one of those recaptured. He spent the next 10 months in various Confederate prisons in Georgia and the Carolinas, but survived to write his account of the tunnel.[155] Moran wrote that of the 109, "59 reached the Union lines, 48 were recaptured and 2 were drowned."[156]

The Aftermath

Some changes in security were made after the escape through the tunnel. After Rose and his group tunneled out in 1863, the cellar floor was "masoned over," and with tighter security arrangements, according to George Putnam, first lieutenant and adjutant, 176th New York Volunteers. Putnam had been captured October 19, 1864, at Cedar Creek in the Shenandoah Valley of Virginia, and taken to Libby Prison in Richmond. Putnam never got a chance to escape. It "would have been impracticable" to even attempt to reach the cellar floor. In addition, a guard walked a bloodhound around the prison. On occasions, the dog would circle the building, and stop occasionally to sniff at the foundations as if searching for tunnels. The dog had been trained to attack anyone wearing blue cloth. The big canine was captured when Weitzel's Federal troops entered Richmond and taken to New York, and sold at auction on the steps of the Astor House.[157] (The dog was the famous "Hero" or "Nero" kept previously by Capt. G. W. Alexander at Castle Thunder.)

Everyone, it seemed, wanted to be one of those who escaped through the famous tunnel. When a United States congressman claimed to have been one of the escapees, President Lincoln was not surprised. He jokingly replied, "I never saw or heard of a hole in this country so long or narrow that a member of Congress couldn't crawl through it."[158]

The Tables are Turned

When the Federal army marched into Richmond, they released all the prisoners in Libby and the other prisons, and installed prisoners of their own. Capt. W. B. Lowery, of the 62nd Ohio, had once been a prisoner at Libby. Now, he returned to Richmond as a guard over the 2,200 Confederate prisoners being held in Libby Prison and Castle Thunder. Among them was Richard R. "Dick" Turner.[159] Captain Warner, who had been the quartermaster at Libby, was held on charges of cruelty to prisoners. Lt. Col. Albert Ordway, commander of the 24th Massachusetts, was placed in control of the two prisons.[160]

Prison Commandant Fled

Both Maj. Thomas Turner and Capt. George Washington Alexander, former commandant of Castle Thunder and Salisbury, were on the Federals' "10-most-wanted" list. Both men would probably have met the same fate as Henry Wirz had they been captured.

The story of Turner's escape from capture by Federal authorities is every bit as tortuous as that of any of the prisoners who fled Libby and other prisons. On the day that the Yankees entered Richmond, April 3, 1865, Thomas Turner fled. He and several others joined General Lee, and when Lee surrendered, Turner wanted to join General Johnston's army. He made a wide detour to Augusta, Georgia, but when he could not get a ship from Florida, he traveled under an assumed name to the Mississippi River. He rowed a dugout canoe across the Mississippi. Walking across Arkansas, he finally reached Waco, and spent the summer in Texas. When Confederate Gen. Jubal A. Early arrived in Texas, the pair succeeded in getting passage on the bark *Liverpool* bound for Nassau. From Nassau, they took the English steamer *Corsica*, and arrived in Cuba on December 10, 1865.[161]

Years later, Thomas Turner returned to settle in Memphis where he practiced dentistry. Impoverished and broken in health, Turner died at the Odd Fellows Home in Clarksville, Tennessee, on December 26, 1901, just weeks after his second in command, "Dick" Turner, died.[162]

Richard R. Turner was with Lee at the surrender. He then returned to Richmond and went with his wife and son to the Capitol to give himself up. Since Maj. Thomas P. Turner could not be found, Federal officers arrested Richard Turner, the commissary/inspector of the Libby Prison. As the Federal officers were taking him away, one of them stabbed him in the hip with his bayonet.[163]

The Last Escape

Probably the last escape from Libby Prison was that accomplished by Confederate Capt. Richard R. "Dick" Turner. For his "alleged cruelty to Union prisoners," Turner was serving a term in solitary confinement at Libby Prison. Turner was confined to one of the underground cells, but the floor had been raised to keep him off the wet cellar bottom. He was given only bread and water.[164] His son, 5-year-old William Dandridge Turner, stood outside his father's cell. "Your father is starving," his mother told her son, as she urged the little boy to move closer to the window, and drop some food on the ground. She whispered for him to kick the food so that it would fall where his father could get it. Turner then would reach through the window and retrieve what food he could reach.[165]

Richard Turner escaped from his cell about midnight on May 11, 1865. The cell in which he had been placed had iron bars in the window that could be removed. While a Confederate prison, the bar had been removed by a Federal officer in order to escape. The bar was not replaced with iron, but with wood, then whitewashed to look like the rest. Turner wrenched the wooden bar out, and during a dark and rainy night, squeezed through the opening.[166]

Turner was free for about a month. He hid out in New Kent County, then went to his brother Samuel D. Turner's home in Charles City County, where he hid in the barn under the hay all day. One day, he decided to leave because he had had a dream that the Yankees had come to the barn and found him. According to his son, William, the Federal soldiers did come to the barn because a black girl had reported him. He escaped capture a day or so later by riding his horse into the Chickahominy River. He made it safely back to Richmond one night to see his wife. He planned to leave the next morning to join General Early and Major Turner in Canada. That night Federal troops came to the house. William remembered his father shouting, "Stand back! Stand back!" at the head of the stairs. "The first man that comes up these steps I shall kill." He told them if they would wait until he could put on his clothes, he would surrender. He was arrested and taken to the state penitentiary in Richmond, where he was held for the next eight months.[167]

One article published at the time of his death stated that Richard R. Turner was held in the state penitentiary for several days, then escaped and was hidden by a friend for several weeks.[168] (This may refer to his escape from Libby Prison when he was first arrested.) "Dick" Turner did spend some eight months in the state penitentiary, and was eventually transferred back to Libby for a second time.[169] This time, he was not allowed to escape, nor did he attempt to do so.

After Turner was paroled on June 18, 1866, he became a successful lumber merchant and lived in Smithfield, Virginia.[170] He died suddenly at the home of a friend, Mr. Hollowman, on December 5, 1901, where he had gone to look at a horse. Turner had recently been chosen county chairman of the Democratic Party for Isle of Wight County.[171] He was buried in Ivy Cemetery.[172]

The Tunnel Architects

After the war, Col. Thomas Rose, who supervised the tunnel, reenlisted in the 11th United States Infantry as a captain. Although he served another 26 years on the frontier until 1892, he only rose to the rank of major by brevet. Near the end of his career, Rose was finally promoted to lieutenant colonel. He died on November 6, 1907.[173]

Capt. A. G. Hamilton, who engineered the tunnel, was assassinated in Morgantown, Kentucky, in March 1895, by a man whose enmity he incurred during the war.[174]

The Demise of Libby Prison

After Federal troops occupied Richmond, Libby Prison was used to house Confederate prisoners. The sign, "L. Libby & Son," was shipped in May 1865 to Colonel Stetson, of the Astor House, New York City. It was then acquired by Col. F. E. Howe, of New York, who put it on display at the New England Rooms, No. 194 Broadway, New York.[175]

The West Building was sold to the Southern Fertilizer Company, Mrs. George S. Palmer continued to own the other two. In 1888, a syndicate purchased the property and the building was dismantled, to be reassembled in Chicago to become a tourist attraction. Each brick and each board were numbered, packed in 132 20-ton boxcars, and sealed.[176]

In transit, the train carrying the dismantled building wrecked near Maysville, Kentucky, on May 7, 1889. Parts of the building were scattered about and many who flocked to the scene came away with bricks or lumber as mementoes.[177]

A large building was reconstructed on the block of Wabash Avenue between 14th and 16th streets in Chicago to house the prison building. The Libby Prison Museum Association collected $400,000, and the extensive collection of Civil War artifacts of Charles F. Gunther to add to the exhibit. The building was completely rebuilt by September 1889. It was an attraction until 1899, when the venture was abandoned. The bricks were sold to collectors and souvenir hunters. The beams, timbers, and other wooden parts were sold to an Indiana farmer named Davis, who used the material to built a huge barn at Hamlet, La Porte County, Indiana. Many of the timbers have the names and initials of the prisoners. A door and keys and some other items are kept in the Confederate Museum in Richmond. Most of the records are housed in the National Archives in Washington, D.C.[178]

In 1906, Isaac N. Johnson, one of the successful escapees, put a notice in the *National Tribune* asking the other 15 who started the tunnel to contact him about a reunion at the next National Encampment.[179] Only a few remarkable stories exist in testimony to the skill, determination, and courage of the prisoners of Libby.

XXV

Camp Oglethorpe, Macon, Georgia

"Bolts and Bars can Never Chain the Mind."[1]
— Joseph Ferguson

Location: Macon, Georgia. **Established:** 1861–1864. **Type:** Converted buildings, and barren land enclosed by stockade. **Type of Prisoners:** Federal officers. **Capacity:** 600+. **Greatest Number Held:** 1,900. **Number of Escapes:** ?

History

Camp Oglethorpe, the official name of the prison at Macon, Georgia, was named in honor of James Oglethorpe, who was responsible for establishing a colony in Georgia.[2] Camp Oglethorpe had been a storage depot and a militia training camp, as well as the old state fairgrounds before the Confederate government decided to use it as a prisoner of war camp. The Macon city officials were not happy with the Confederacy's decision to gift the city with prisoners of war. Their sentiments were expressed in the *Macon Daily Telegraph:*

> At a time when it is difficult to feed our own population, we are to be *blessed* with the presence and custody of 900 prisoners of war. We have no place to hold them — no food to give them — nobody whose time can be well spared to guard them — nor, except in the mere matter of hostages for safety of our own prisoners in Lincoln's dominions, can we conceive of any object in holding them as prisoners.[3]

The mayor of Macon wanted to house the prisoners in the Market House, but the city council instructed him on May 2, 1862, to put the incoming prisoners in Camp Oglethorpe.[4]

The conversion of Camp Oglethorpe to a prisoner-of-war camp probably dates from the council's May 1862 decree.

The Site

The prison camp was established about a quarter of a mile southeast of Macon, Georgia, on the old fairgrounds. The area covered about 15 to 20 acres and already had a large building, and a number of small sheds and stalls. The camp was situated between a set of railroad tracks and the Ocmulgee River.[5]

The enclosed area was not entirely free of shade. At the northwest corner inside the stockade was a grove of pine trees. A small stream ran through the camp.[6]

The Facilities

At the entrance to the compound a sign was positioned over the gate, an arch bearing in big black letters the word, "Camp Oglethorpe."[7] A large frame building in the center had once served as the floral exhibit hall during the fair. It was now used to house prisoners, and as many as 200 slept there. The rest slept in the sheds and stalls or created their own shelter on the grounds.[8]

A stockade was built to enclose the prisoners. It was constructed of 12-foot pine boards, which were stood on end as close together as possible. On the outside of the fence, about four feet from the top, a platform was built for the sentries to walk on so they could watch for attempted escapes. Sentinels were placed about every 30 feet, with standing orders to shoot any prisoner who tried to cross the deadline. The deadline was clearly marked about 25 feet from the walls on the inside by a row of stakes.[9] When a prisoner approached close to the deadline, his fellow prisoners would shout, "Look out for the dead line!"[10] The prisoner would jump back as quickly as possible to avoid being shot. Fires were lit at night between the stockade and the deadline so the guards might watch the prisoners, and they had orders to shoot anyone who came even near the line.[11]

Two cannons were aimed at the prisoners; one was placed at the north side of the stockade near the gate, and the other on the east side. In June 1864, three more were placed in the woods.[12]

The Prisoners

In 1862, Camp Oglethorpe held 600 prisoners. That number had increased to 1,900 by 1864.[13] On May 17, 1864, the officers of the 12th New York Cavalry were ushered inside the gates of the stockade. They were joined by 800 officers who had been held at Richmond, and 21 others who had been held in the city jail at Macon.[14] This last group of prisoners would not remain at Macon very long.

Prison Personnel

Capt. W. Kemp Tabb was commandant at Camp Oglethorpe until he was replaced by Capt. George C. Gibbs in June 1864. Gibbs served until he was transferred to Andersonville in October 1864.[15] The guards were either very young or very old. The officer of the day entered the compound each morning and began calling roll. He was accompanied by 20 guards, who herded the prisoners to the north end of the pen to be counted.[16]

The prisoners were guarded by the 10th Georgia Battalion and the 59th Georgia Volunteers, according to a report of the "Position of Troops in the Department of South Carolina and Georgia, dated September 25, 1862." They were under the overall command of Gen. Pierre G. T. Beauregard. Colonel Brown was in charge of the 59th Georgia and Major John E. Rylander was in charge of the 10th Georgia Battalion.[17]

Treatment of the Prisoners

Although this camp was an open stockade, in some respects conditions at Macon were better because there was less crowding. Occasionally, the prisoners could even wash their clothing. Joseph Ferguson recalled that it was a sight to see "Officers [who] were put to great straits on washing-days, possessing no extra clothes an old blanket was wrapped around the person until the work was accomplished and the washed clothes dried."[18] Ferguson recalled that during his first month at the camp, he slept on the ground with no blankets or covering at all. Luckily, this was in the summer. For weeks he had worn no shoes, and he became accustomed to going barefooted.[19]

Ferguson believed conditions at Macon were better because the prisoners were given enough cooking utensils to cook their food, although the food was somewhat skimpy. For each 100 men, they were issued "5 iron skillets, with cover, 15 iron skillets, without covers, 10 tin pails, or buckets holding five quarts, 10 small tin pans, in which to mix meal, 5 wooden pails, or buckets." Axes and spades were also issued, which were to be turned in at the end of the day. Food was issued every five days. This consisted of six pints of cornmeal, a half pint of sorghum molasses, one half pound of rancid bacon, and two tablespoons of salt.[20]

Although they were given no eating utensils, knives, forks and spoons were whittled from wood. Wood was also used for plates and for the soles of shoes. The prisoners used their time and creativity to make "slap-jacks" out of cornmeal, coffee from burned cornmeal, vinegar from sorghum, and yeast from the cornmeal.[21]

James Pike, of the 4th Ohio Volunteer Cavalry, was not so pleased with his treatment at Camp Oglethorpe, and he complained to Federal authorities of a situation that was "most intolerable." After his release, former prisoner James Pike wrote from Murfreesboro, Tennessee, that he had been taken to Macon from Montgomery, Alabama, along with 1,200 other prisoners. The prison was surrounded by swamps. They were given seven pounds of corn meal and two and a half pounds of bad-quality bacon for a seven-day period. During the whole time he was at Macon, prisoners were fed a "foul and unwholesome diet, frequently left without any rations two or three days at a time...." He complained that his "exchange was delayed as long as possible" (something that was probably out of the hands of prison officials). "Our men fared badly, being punished severely for the most trifling offenses."[22]

Pike also reported that one prisoner named Cory was "tied up [for] three days by the wrists to a tree just so that his toes touched the ground," because he had helped other prisoners kill a calf that came into the camp.[23]

Pike also described how prisoners were "pegged" for minor offenses. A prisoner was put on the ground and his legs and arms stretched out, and a forked stick was driven into the ground over those limbs. Finally, a forked stick was placed over the prisoner's neck so that he was completely immobile.[24]

Pike was not happy with anything while he was at Macon:

> We were confined in bad quarters; our dead were left unburied for days [al]together; some were left unburied entirely, at least to our knowledge; we were denied medical attendance ... our men were shot without cause; an insane man was shot at Macon, Ga., for no offense; we were compelled to bury men in river banks where their bodies were liable to be washed out; ....[25]

Pike blamed Major Rylander specifically for issuing the order which forbade their chaplains from "preaching to us or praying for us."[26] Subsequently, after the war ended, Rylander was among several officials of southern prisons (including George W. Alexander of Castle Thunder and Salisbury, Dick Turner of Libby Prison, John H. Gee of Salisbury, and others) who were condemned for their treatment of prisoners and wanted for trial.[27]

Escape Plans and Preparations

It was quite easy, wrote B. S. Calef in an article for *Harper's Monthly Magazine*, for prisoners to bribe guards and get a gray uniform. It was pretty easy to get outside the prison grounds, but the distance to Federal lines was great, and many were caught along the way. The news of escaped prisoners spread quickly and the bloodhounds were soon on the trail. Very few managed to overcome all the obstacles, elude the dogs, and get away safely.[28]

At the first the prisoners sent to Macon were held in an open field. There, some of them were visited by local ladies who slipped notes in bouquets or in books to the prisoners. Lt. Alonzo Cooper mentioned in his diary that he received a note which gave a woman's address and promised that if a prisoner could manage to escape and get to her house, she would hide him until he could get away. Lieutenant Fish, of the 2nd Massachusetts Heavy Artillery, received a book with a note on one of the fly leaves. The prisoners were encouraged by these notes and by the fact that there were sympathetic persons living nearby willing to help them.[29]

Prisoners Organize

Several organizations were started among the prisoners for the purpose of breaking out of their prison pen. A plan was developed to gain their freedom and go to Andersonville, 50 to 60 miles away, to release the thousands of starving prisoners there. Their ultimate goal, although totally unrealistic, was to "break things up generally" inside the Confederacy, after they had freed the prisoners at Andersonville. It was believed that someone leaked the plan, because after that, the guards ceased coming into the yard for roll call.[30]

One of the best plans was developed shortly before the prisoners were transferred to Charleston in August 1864. A secret society was organized with "initiation oaths, pass-words, and grips," and those who joined were divided into companies and squads with proper officers. Maps of the country were obtained to help the men when they were free. It was decided that the best time to escape would be while they were on the train to Charleston. Tasks were assigned to each squad. A signal was to be given when the train stopped at some station along the way, and the guards inside and outside the cars were to be seized, and their guns taken. Another group of prisoners familiar with the operation of a train was designated to take command of the engineer, the fireman, and the guard. The train was to have been stopped near the Pocotaligo Bridge, and from there, Union General Foster's lines were only 10 or 12 miles away. The prisoners inside the cars waited for the signal to begin their escape plan, but the signal never came. It was later rumored among the prisoners that someone or something had alerted the guard, and that the train ran at top speed all the way to Charleston.[31]

Escapes

One prisoner escaped by submerging himself in the small stream that crossed the stockade yard. This stream was also used for the latrine or "sink." He braved the filth and the stench and escaped the hounds and his pursuers to reach Federal lines.[32]

Many others escaped but were caught and brought back to Macon. Some, according to Ferguson, had traveled hundreds of miles only to be caught "in the act of going through the lines."[33]

Three political prisoners (according to Pike), two from Kentucky and one from Florida, were confined to the jail in Macon for 22 days, and only given quarter rations. Their offense was to escape from the prison pen.[34]

Tunnels

Ferguson recalled that there was extensive tunneling at Camp Oglethorpe. Six tunnels were under excavation at the same time. A company was formed so that the work could progress systematically. One prisoner would stand guard, one would dig, and a third would haul the dirt from the tunnel in a bag or box. A fourth carried the dirt away to the sink, or scattered it in the yard. The work was slow and hard. During the hot summer months, several of the men digging the tunnel fainted from the heat and lack of air. To overcome this obstacle, the men worked in 15-minute shifts. At the slow pace required using only an old knife, in most instances, the tunnel took three to four weeks to complete.[35]

Three tunnels were found on June 27, 1864. Their location was probably pointed out by a traitor in the midst of the prisoners.[36]

Lieutenant Cooper described graphically how one tunnel was dug while he was in the stockade at Macon, Georgia. A spot in a shed close to the stockade was selected. Prisoners were allowed to build bunks 10 or 12 inches from the ground. When everyone had gone to sleep at night, the bunks were moved and a hole in the ground was begun. It would be cut downward for about five or six feet, with care being taken to conceal the freshly dug earth. A guard was stationed to keep a lookout. Another precaution was taken by sending out "pickets" who would engage anyone who approached in a conversation long enough for his voice to be heard by the tunnelers. They would stop digging until all danger was past.[37]

Someone was always moving around the camp in the night, going to or returning from the latrines. Therefore, whenever one of the diggers filled his haversack with the dirt from the tunnel and dumped it at a selected place, he did not attract attention. Sometimes, the dirt-filled sack was concealed under an overcoat or other garment.[38]

Once the tunnel had been dug to a depth of about five feet, digging would continue horizontal to the ground. When digging was finished for the night, boards were placed over the entrance and covered with some of the dirt that had been removed from the hole so that it appeared just like the surrounding ground. The ground would be swept so that all evidence of any new earth was removed. Then the bunk was returned to its original position.[39]

Night after night, the work continued, and the diggers were so quiet that those sleeping nearby never knew what was happening. A veil of secrecy was maintained to prevent the tunnel from being discovered by the guards. Only those actually involved in the digging knew about the tunnel. Cooper's memoirs mentioned that a tunnel was begun almost as soon as the officers were moved into the stockade. After working on it for 10 nights, it was discovered, and filled in. The camp was searched for additional tunnels, but none were found. However, by the next day, two tunnels had been discovered by Captain Tabb, who was in charge of the prison at that time. To prevent further resistance and escape efforts, Captain Tabb had two platforms built on which were placed 12-pound cannons.[40] Another prisoner described the platforms as being about 12 feet off the ground outside the walls. The cannon on the platforms could sweep the inside of the enclosure. At a moment's notice, the guards could fire on the prisoners with deadly grapeshot.[41] But even the presence of cannons did not stop the digging. Two new tunnels were begun, one in an old building on the east side of the camp and the other in No. 7 Squad on the opposite side. One was complete and the other nearly finished when both were discovered. The prisoners believed that someone had informed to Captain Tabb, because he did not have to search but knew where both were located.[42]

B. S. Calef recalled that two tunnels were brought nearly to completion. The prisoners were waiting until a third tunnel was completed to make their move. The third one was large, and the prisoners were confident that in a "few mornings some seven hundred of us would be running at large." However, that was not to be. Someone informed the commandant. All the prisoners were herded to one side of the camp while the guards made a thorough search and, naturally, the tunnels were discovered.[43]

Efforts to escape continued. Lt. H. Lee Clark, of the 2nd Massachusetts Heavy Artillery, escaped and sought the home of Miss Richardson, one of the ladies who had passed notes to the prisoners some time before. She made arrangements to get him out of Macon through Hartswell Silver, who boarded at her home. However, Silver betrayed Clark and the escapee was returned to the camp.[44]

Out in the Sutler's Box

One ingenious escape was managed by an Englishman, Lieutenant Wilson, who escaped by riding out on a cart concealed in the sutler's vegetable box.[45] This same incident was reported by Bernhard Domschcke and others. Every day a large quantity of food was delivered by the sutler. One day, the sutler came through the gates with a large wooden box on a cart. The box was soon emptied and a crowd gathered around the cart and the sutler's booth. As the sutler was busy with customers, the prisoner slipped into the box. Some of his friends, acting as if the box was empty, picked it up and replaced it on the cart. Once the sutler was finished, he and his driver drove back through the prison gates, with the prisoner in the box. Unfortunately, the prisoner was brought back after only a few days, captured just a few miles away from the prison.[46] The prisoner, who was "too scrupulous" to deny his identity, was accosted by a man who asked him, "Are you a Yankee officer?" The prisoner admitted he was, and gave himself up. From then on, his fellow prisoners called him "George Washington," for his inability to tell a lie.[47]

Another prisoner clung to the bottom of the sutler's wagon and was carried safely outside the gates.[48]

Prisoners Use Disguises

A group of Federal officers, including Lieutenant Frost, of the 85th New York, managed to obtain Confederate uniforms and escape.[49]

One Federal officer tried to disguise himself as a workman who had come into the stockade to fix the pumps. The officer, dressed in an old jacket and gray pantaloons, picked up the workman's pickaxe, and walked toward the gate. The gate was opened for him and he went outside. He was recaptured a hundred miles away.[50]

One prisoner blacked his face and passed out the gate as a black workman.[51]

Another Yankee prisoner, H. Bader, of the 39th Missouri Volunteers, managed to make a jacket and trousers from a gray woolen blanket. Dressed in gray "uniform," the prisoner confidently marched outside along with the guards when they finished roll call. He was recaptured, but he tried to escape several times.[52]

Under the Fence

While Union Capt. Bernhard Domschcke was imprisoned at Macon, Georgia, he said escape attempts never stopped. Most failed, but sometimes they succeeded. One evening, several prisoners "sneaked out the south side." It was dark, and the sentries did not see them. They made their way into the creek, crossed the deadline, then slipped through the main fence through a hole that admitted the creek into the compound. The prisoners thought they had succeeded in slipping unnoticed by the guards. However, the last man out made a noise and a sentry fired in that direction. Fortunately, no one was hit, but the alarm was raised, and in less than 10 minutes, the search was on for the missing prisoners. Torches were lit and the bloodhounds were brought out. The remaining prisoners were all ordered to stay in their quarters, and were not even allowed to visit the privy. The hunt for the escapees resumed at daybreak.[53]

Cooper recalled that two or three officers escaped by crawling under the stockade at the point where the stream entered the enclosure. They were seen and fired upon, and one was caught and brought back. Expecting a general breakout, orders were subsequently issued that "any one leaving their quarters, even to go to the sink, would be fired upon by the guard."[54]

When morning came, Captain Tabb placed two more cannons in the woods to the south, and hounds were brought to track and capture the escapees. However, the hounds could not find the scent, and only succeeded in treeing a raccoon.[55]

Usually, after roll call, the prison officials searched the camp. They found three tunnels that were almost completed. Although their efforts and long hours of digging were destroyed, the Yankee prisoners were not stopped. Another tunnel was begun on the north side of Domschcke's barracks. This tunnel did not have far to go to reach the wall, but it was reported by one of the prisoners, and the guards began to keep closer watch.[56] The guards routinely searched inside the barracks and under them for evidence of tunnels.[57]

Escape from the Macon Jail

Sgt. James E. Gillespie, of the First Kentucky Cavalry, had already made several escapes from the stockade at Andersonville. He had so exasperated Captain Wirz, the Andersonville commandant, that Wirz sent Gillespie to the jail at Macon.[58] The Macon jail was frequently visited by Union women, and from one of them Gillespie obtained an old spoon and a file. He fashioned the spoon into a key which he used to let himself and a Captain Whitlock out of the jail. The pair waited until dark, then made their way through the swamp where they encountered a runaway slave. The slave brought them some food, and they parted company. Near the Chattahoochee River, nearly faint with hunger, the fugitives approached a slave cabin and asked for food. While at the cabin, they heard the bloodhounds trailing them, and they asked how they could get the dogs off their trail. The black person gave them some asafoedita to rub on their feet and clothing, and told them that they would have no more trouble from the bloodhounds. They swam the river and made their way to Gen. John A. Logan's headquarters. Gillespie went on to Marietta, Georgia. He arrived there on August 17, 1864, where he was greeted by members of his old regiment, just as they were about to board the train home to Kentucky.[59]

Prisoners Moved to Other Locations

In June 1864, U.S. general Sherman was making his way to Atlanta. Thus, Confederate officials quickly transferred the Union generals, colonels, lieutenant colonels, and half the majors in custody at Macon to other facilities.[60] A number of officers were sent to Charleston, where they came under the fire of the Union siege guns bombarding the city.[61] Those prisoners who still remained were sent to Savannah as Gen. George Stoneman's troops approached.[62]

Escape from the Train in Transit

Six prisoners escaped on February 27, 1864, while being transported from Macon to Millen, Georgia. They did so by cutting a hole in the end of the boxcar. Six more escaped on March 20 near Windsor Station, South Carolina, by cutting a hole in the floor of the car. Four of the last group were recaptured, including Pvt. John A. Provines, Company H, 13th Indiana Regiment; John Ryan, a teamster with the 15th Army Corps; and Hy Johnson, also a teamster with the 15th Army Corps. The name of the fourth was unknown.[63]

Three prisoners escaped from the train on the way from Danville, Virginia, to

Macon, Georgia. On May 14, 1864, Lt. P. W. Houlihan and Walter Clifford of the 16th U.S. Infantry, along with James Butler, of the 2nd U.S. Infantry, escaped near Danville and were recaptured near Madison, Georgia. They arrived at the Macon prison on May 22.

Stoneman Approaches — Prisoners Moved

Those prisoners who arrived in May 1864 stayed only a brief time in the Macon stockade. That time was cut short because of the approach of Union General Stoneman, who was reportedly at Milledgevile, only 30 miles away. As the 642 prisoners were being moved by train to Charleston, three of them — Houlihan, Clifford, and Butler — jumped off the train as it crossed the Combahee River. They followed the river and got lost in a rice swamp. After two days of wandering, the trio found a boat and rode down the river to Federal lines. Although they saw Confederate pickets 10 miles from the mouth of the river, the fugitives passed unnoticed and continued on their way during the night of July 31. They arrived safely at St. Helena Sound, occupied by Federal troops, the next morning.[64]

On July 27, 1864, a number of the prisoners were ordered to get ready to move to Charleston because of the approach of Stoneman's Federal troops. Lieutenant Rogers of the Confederate Army revealed the interesting and almost humorous story of how some prisoners escaped during this move. Rogers was in charge of a detachment of guards detailed to escort the prisoners to Charleston. He had instructed his men to be very vigilant because this group of prisoners was "a shrewd, sharp lot of Yankee officers, and would need a heap of watching."[65]

The train passed by Savannah without incident, and the prisoners seemed to be enjoying themselves. When they arrived at Charleston, Lieutenant Rogers proceeded to turn his prisoners over to officials at the jail yard. He was just about to breathe a sigh of relief when, after a head count of the prisoners in the jail yard, he discovered that 34 Yankee officers and four guards were missing. Rogers could not believe it. He sat down on the curbstone in front of the jail to collect his thoughts. While he sat there, a Confederate captain rode up and asked him, "Are you Lieutenant Rogers?" The bewildered guard replied that he was, and admitted that he was in command of the guard who had escorted the prisoners from Macon. The captain then told him he was under arrest and was ordered to report immediately to the general's headquarters.[66]

The young lieutenant feared the worst, that he would either be shot or sent to prison for allowing so many to escape. However, the general only told him to go back to Macon with his remaining guards, and be sure "not to lose any" on the way back. Lieutenant Rogers complied and, although he never figured out how his prisoners got away, he still wanted his guards back. He had no idea whether the missing guards had been killed by the Yankee prisoners, or induced to desert along with them. Whatever the case, Rogers never heard from any of them.[67]

Stoneman Captured

Confederate officials were forced to move all of the prisoners from Macon because of the approach of Stoneman. However, Stoneman used very poor tactical judgment after he had requested and received permission to raid Macon and liberate the Union prisoners at Andersonville being held there. He left on June 27, but instead of moving south with his entire force, he split his forces and ordered Garrard to draw the Confederate cavalry away while he and 2,200 men headed by way of Covington for Andersonville. Garrard was attacked by Confederate Gen. Joseph "Fightin Joe" Wheeler, and withdrew to the north. When Stoneman reached the outskirts of Macon on July 30, he found the city defended by state militia. He attempted to circle to the south of the city across the Ocmulgee River but was cut off and surrounded by Confederate General Wheeler's cavalry. Stoneman and his cavalry attempted to fight, but he and 700 of his men were captured.[68]

Camp Oglethorpe served as a parole site at the end of the war, but was soon abandoned forever.[69]

Camp Macon Today

The exact location of Camp Oglethorpe is unknown today. The site of the stockade was taken over by the Macon and Brunswick Railroad, and the prison and fairgrounds buildings were removed, leaving only a barren area next to Seventh Street. Today, the Brosnan Yards of the Southern Railway Company occupy the site where the prisoners once lived.[70]

The Georgia State Fair was never again held at that location. It was moved several times before settling on a permanent location in 1870 at the Central City Park in Macon.[71]

XXVI

Salisbury Prison, Salisbury, North Carolina

There is considerable whispering going on among the prisoners about making a concerted rush for one of the gates, breaking it down and gaining our liberty if we can, or dying if we must.
— Benjamin F. Booth, prisoner, diary entry, November 24, 1864[1]

Location: Salisbury, North Carolina. **Established:** 1861. **Type:** converted cotton factory building, tents enclosed by high fence. **Type of Prisoners:** Federal prisoners of war, Confederate deserters, political prisoners, hostages, former slaves and free blacks. **Capacity:** 2,500 (as of August 1864[2]). **Most Held:** 10,321–15,000 (10,321 prisoners of war only[3]). **Largest Number Held at One Time:** 8,740.[4] **Known Escapes:** ±500.[5]

History

The Methodist minister A. W. Mangum described the evolution of a small cotton factory into one of the most notorious prisons in the South. In 1839, some Salisbury citizens decided to build a steam cotton factory. They formed a company and bought 16 acres of land in a "beautiful oak grove that bordered the town on the south."[6]

The Site

When the cotton factory closed, Davidson College bought the property, and on November 2, 1861, deeded the land to the Confederate government. The site would become a prison for Confederates under sentence of court-martial, citizens arrested for disloyalty, deserters from the Federal army, and captured prisoners of war.[7]

A local newspaper reported the transaction. The government had bought the "old Salisbury Factory," and was

> now preparing to fit it up for a prison to accommodate some thousands or more of Yankees who are encumbering the tobacco factories of Richmond. Our citizens don't much like the idea such an accession to their population, nevertheless they have assented to their part of the hardships and disagreeables of war....[8]

The Facilities

Initially, the building was ample shelter for several hundred prisoners, and the well furnished clean, refreshing water. Huge oak trees provided cool shade inside the compound.[9]

One Yankee officer described his quarters as "very undesirable, being about ninety by forty feet, with barred windows, dirty floors, partially occupied by rude bunks, and two broken stoves that gave out not heat" but only smoke from the green pine used as fuel. The men were not allowed any kind of light at night, but sat in the "thick darkness, inhaling the four vapors and the acrid smoke" while longing for morning.[10]

The main building, the former cotton factory was a four-story, brick building, about 40 feet wide, and 100 feet long.[11] It had an "elevator" at one end, and some of the prisoners discovered that they could go to the room above by climbing up the rope inside the elevator shaft. Those housed on the upper floors found that they could come down the rope, visit a while, and return. Prisoner William H. Jeffrey found that the "love of fun in some Yankees was greater than his love of Confederate bacon," and someone "spared enough from his ration to grease the rope." The next day, when some of the prisoners in the upper floor decided to visit, their cell-mates had great fun watching the boys "as they shot down through the other stories to the ground floor." Try as they would, they could not get back up, so had to get permission from the guards. Understandably, the rope was removed.[12]

Maj. Abner R. Small, of the 16th Maine, kept a diary during his stay at Salisbury Prison. He later wrote articles for newspapers, and published a short memoir. He described his first night at Salisbury Prison in the summer of 1864, and his encounter with thieves.

> We were forced up the factory stairway, step by step over nameless filth, to the monitor room under the roof. The fiendish "Muggers" crept in and robbed several of our number before an alarm was given. Two officers, then stationed at the door with billets of wood, will never be held accountable for the skull-crushing blows that beat back a "Mugger" as he attempted to force his way in. He fell backwards with a wild scream, and I heard him bound from stair to stair down, down, into what I hope was the Bottomless Pit.[13]

Near the main building were four or five tenement houses.[14] After Small and others in the factory building complained, they were transferred to quarters in one of the smaller outbuildings and were allowed the use of the grounds within the stockade. These huts were "close quarters for us, and were filled with vermin; yet they were preferable to the factory.[15]

Early in 1864, another frame building, about 20 x 70 feet, was constructed and used as a hospital. This two-story building was poorly ventilated, and uncomfortable both summer and winter. The main building, as well as the hospital building, a small building used as an office, about six Bell tents, plus six or seven log huts comprised all the available shelter.[16] The stockade was made by sinking 15-foot pine logs into the ground to a depth of about three feet. These were boarded up and down to form a solid wall. Along the outside of this enclosure, about three feet from the top, a platform was added on which sentinels were stationed about 10 paces apart. The sentinels paced back and forth, day and night.[17] At the northwest and northeast corners of the stockade, loaded howitzers were kept ready to fire inside at the prisoners in case they attempted to escape [18]

Officers and enlisted men were kept separated by a deadline vigorously guarded by Confederate sentries. The guards had standing orders to shoot everyone who dared cross the deadline, attempted to give any sign of provocation, or made any move to escape. The deadline was a ditch dug along the east, west and north sides of the stockade, three feet wide, and two feet deep. Any prisoner crossing this line, accidentally or on purpose, was shot without further warning.[19]

The Prisoners

The Confederate government hoped to move to Salisbury some of the thousands of Yankee prisoners who were filling to overflowing the tobacco factories of Richmond and Danville. Prisoners were soon transported to Salisbury from Richmond's Castle Thunder, Libby, and Belle Isle. Disloyal persons, especially those convicted of crimes against the Confederacy, also were sent to Salisbury.[20] In January 1862, 700 prisoners were transferred from Richmond to Salisbury.[21]

The Salisbury Prison held convicts, Confederate deserters, conscientious objectors, disloyal southern civilians, ex-slaves, captured Union soldiers, and Yankee deserters.[22]

The number of prisoners confined as of May 24, 1864, under the command of Captain George W. Alexander, consisted of "Confederates serving out sentences of court martial — 310; Yankee deserters — 95; Political prisoners — 164; Prisoners of war — 0," for a total of 569.[23]

This was about half the number of prisoners Captain Alexander usually had under his control in Castle Thunder. Alexander complained that a number of Yankee deserters being held at Salisbury Prison were "the worst prisoners we have in the whole place," and he requested that they be transferred to Andersonville, and treated as prisoners of war.[24]

In the spring of 1864, a large number of Castle Thunder prisoners were sent to Salisbury Prison. Fifty-eight were sent in mid–April.[25] In May 1864, 78 prisoners under sentence of court-martial were transported to Salisbury.[26] Thus, when Captain Alexander arrived at Salisbury Prison he was greeted by some of his "old friends."

The diverse prison population was noted on a report submitted for January 1865: 152 political prisoners, 121 convicts, 36 Federal deserters, 5,815 prisoners of war, 95 blacks captured in arms, and 25 free blacks, for a total of 6,244 [27]

Chaplain Mangum, a professor of English literature at the University of North Carolina, was a frequent visitor to the prison. In March 1862, he reported the condition and the treatment of the prisoners, the "fidelity of the officers, the care and attention of the Surgeons and the management of the hospitals." At the time, there were 1,427 prisoners, of whom 251 had received medical treatment, and only one had died. The prison doctor noted in his quarterly report for the period from December 1861 through March 1862 there had been 509 cases of sickness and only three deaths. There had also been much sickness among the guards."[28]

Famous Prisoners

While serving as a volunteer in Company H, 3rd Regiment New Hampshire, Robert Moffat Livingstone, son of the famous African explorer Dr. David Livingstone, was captured October 7, 1864, on the New Market Road in Virginia. The young Livingstone was 5 feet, 7 inches tall, with dark hair and complexion and hazel eyes. His personnel record stated that he was a sailor by profession, and he claimed to be 21 years of age, but was only 18, having been born in Africa in 1845. He preferred to use the alias "Rupert Vincent," rather than bring dishonor to his real name.[29]

Another famous prisoner was Col. Michael Corcoran, an Irish terrorist, who had arrived in the United States in 1849. He was captured at First Manassas, and was being held in Charleston, South Carolina, when he was selected as a hostage for the release of Confederate privateer William Smith. Corcoran was sent to Salisbury, but was released in August 1862. He used his book about his experiences, *The Captivity of General Corcoran*, to recruit men for the Union. Back in the service, Corcoran shot a fellow officer and was court-martialed, but found not guilty. On December 23, 1863, his horse stumbled and he was thrown and killed. A public funeral was held for him in New York.[30] Corcoran commented that civilian prisoners at Salisbury were "treated in the most heartless and brutal manner, much worse, in fact than ... their companion prisoners of war.[31]

News Reporters Held

By August 6, 1864, everyone knew that two New York *Tribune* correspondents, Junius Browne and A. D. Richardson, were prisoners at Salisbury.[32] The reporters had been captured at Vicksburg on May 3, 1863, and imprisoned.[33] They had already been confined at Libby Prison and Castle Thunder in Richmond. Richardson believed at first his removal to Salisbury Prison was a punishment. Yet, when he arrived at Salisbury, he found he could "exercise freely in the blessed open air," which he had not been able to for the previous nine months. [34] The two newsmen were held at Salisbury Prison from February 1864 until January 1865.[35] Richardson poetically expressed some of the universal truths about prison life:

> It is not hunger or cold, sickness or death, which makes prison life so hard to bear. But it is the utter idleness, emptiness, aimlessness of such a life. It is being, through all the long hours of each day and night—for weeks, months, years, if one lives so long—absolutely without employment, mental, or physical—with nothing to fill the vacant mind, which always becomes morbid and turns inward to prey upon itself.[36]

Wrote Junius Henri Browne, "we reached Salisbury, and entering the inclosure [sic] of the Penitentiary, we were warmly greeted by prisoners we had known at the Castle [Castle Thunder in Richmond]...." He described the prisoners as "Rebel convicts, Northern deserters, hostages, Southern Union men," and anyone the Confederacy wanted to hold. In late winter of 1864, there were 600–700 prisoners at Salisbury Prison. Browne preferred Salisbury over Libby or Castle Thunder because he could be outside and had the opportunity daily to "breathe the external atmosphere, and behold the overarching sky."[37] Both men escaped from Salisbury, and lived to write of their prison experiences.[38]

One of the civilian prisoners was Daniel Gerhart, a 60-year-old man from Miami County, Ohio. He had been captured in Winchester, Virginia, where he had gone to visit his son in the Union army. Another civilian, Frank B. Doran, was captured while visiting a sick brother in Oxford, Mississippi.[39]

Hostages

Except for the loss of freedom and confinement, during the early days of the war life for the prisoners at Salisbury was not bad, not even for the two or three officers being held in close confinement. These two were held in retaliation for two Confederate officers the Federal government threatened to execute in retaliation for the death of some criminals ordered executed by Confederate authorities. The situation of these hostages was "severe, but alleviated by the magnanimous treatment of the commandant."[40]

According to Richardson, some officers on the upper floor of the cotton factory building were "hostages for certain Rebel officers in the Alton, Illinois, penitentiary." The officers were Capts. Julius L. Litchfield, 4th Maine Infantry; Charles Kendall, Signal Corps; and Edward E. Chase, of the 1st Rhode Island Cavalry. These Federal soldiers had been sentenced to "confinement and hard labor during the war," but the "hard labor" part was seldom imposed.[41]

Eight hostages were sent from Libby Prison in Richmond, where they had been confined for 145 days in the dungeon, a cell so damp that "mold [had] accumulated on the beard of the Pennsylvania lieutenant." Richardson described the hostages as "plucky and enterprising," and remembered that they were always trying to escape.[42]

Prison Commandants

Salisbury Prison had nine commandants from December 9, 1861, to February 22, 1865.[43] They were: Braxton Craven, Maj. George Gibbs, Capt. Archibald Godwin; Capt. Henry McCoy, Capt. Swift Galloway; Capt. G. W. Alexander; Col. J. A. Gilmer, Maj. John Henry Gee, and Gen. Bradley T. Johnson.[44]

Captain Galloway was remembered by one prisoner as being kind and courteous to the captives.[45]

Captain Alexander, formerly in command of Castle Thunder in Richmond, was assigned to take charge of Salisbury Prison on May 1, 1864.[46] Alexander brought "discipline and order" to the prison to appease the fears of the citizens for their own safety. His tenure was short, and he was replaced by Colonel Gilmer, on Saturday June 18, 1864.[47]

When Gilmer assumed command, Salisbury Prison contained a total of 570 prisoners: 310 Confederate soldiers, each under sentence of a court-martial; 96 Federal deserters; and 164 political prisoners.[48] This number could be accommodated easily within the space of the prison compound. Two months later, the population increased to 777.[49]

An inspection of the prison on August 10, 1864, noted that Colonel Gilmer, of the 27th North Carolina Troops, was commandant of the post as well as prison commandant. He was seldom at the prison, and at the time of the inspection was on sick leave. In his absence, Capt. John A. Fugua, of the 13th North Carolina Regiment, was in command.[50]

On August 24, 1864, Major Gee took command.[51] Gee had the misfortune to be in command during the time when the prison became grossly overcrowded and conditions were at their worst. After the war, he returned to home in Quincy, Florida, and was arrested there in October 1865. Gee was imprisoned in the Old Capitol Prison in Washington on charges of cruelty and murder. Eventually, his trial was moved to Raleigh, North Carolina, and before a United States military commission he was unanimously acquitted of all charges.[52] A complete transcript of the trial of Major Gee was included in *The Captive*, a book by Annette Gee Ford, great-granddaughter of Major Gee's brother.

Prison Guards

William H. Jeffrey described the guards as "not very formidable fellows," and many were "unfit for field duty." The guards were generally "young boys, old men and cripples." One of the young boys performed his guard duty with a bayonet on the end of a broomstick. Once, some Yankee prisoners stole the bayonet from the gun of a sentinel while he was on duty. Even though a thorough search was made, the stolen bayonet was never found.[53]

Joseph Henry Foster, enlisted at age 13 as a fifer in Company E, 1st North Carolina State Troops. He later served as a guard at Salisbury Prison. (Courtesy of Mrs. Eva Baldwin.)

Yet, even the "motley crew" of guards suffered from sickness and depression. The morale of the guards was not helped by fact that they had no new uniforms, but all wore homespun clothing.[54] It was difficult to keep guards at Salisbury, and some deserted their post. They deserted almost as frequently as the prisoners. Beginning in the fall of 1862, notices appeared in the Salisbury *Watchman* offering $15 for the capture of guards who had deserted their posts, and $30 for their return to the prison. This was the same reward offered for escaped prisoners of war. While Captain Alexander was commandant, he added the names of the absent guards to the reward notices.[55]

An inspection of Salisbury Prison in June 1864, listed 200 guards on duty from three companies.[56]

However, during a routine inspection in August 1864, Maj. Garnett Andrews noticed that "discipline and instruction of the guard is extremely bad." He saw sentinels "reading and lounging on post." He found that only eight out of about 60 had ammunition, and guards were even on duty with "unloaded guns." The garrison at the prison was composed of three companies—one from an unattached unit from Alabama, and two from the local area that had been approved by Congress on August 21, 1862. Andrews reported that most of the guards were "active and able-bodied men, fit for field service." However, it was known that Captain Allen, who commanded one unit of the guards, had set up a barroom in the town. Major Andrews suggested that the present guards be sent to the field and replaced by other troops.[57]

Idyllic Days When Baseball Was Played at Salisbury Prison

During the summer of 1862, ladies and gentlemen from the town were permitted to visit inside the stockade. Both visitors and prisoners were entertained with a dress parade by the garrison troops. Afterward, some of the officers and men joined in a game of ball, a sight which was enjoyed by everyone.[58]

The prisoners played New York-style baseball, and Salisbury Prison soon became known for its leisurely baseball games.[59] The United States Sanitary Commission recommended the game to preserve the health of the soldiers. "Amusements, sports, and gymnastic exercises should be favored amongst the men," the commission advised. Baseball was one of the activities that was approved, and officers encouraged the men to participate to relieve the boredom of prison life.[60] Baseball was played almost every day, weather permitting. W. C. Bates wrote in his *Stars and Stripes:* "We have no official report of the match-game of baseball played in Salisbury between the New Orleans and Tuscaloosa boys, resulting in the triumph of the latter; the cells of the Parish Prison were unfavorable to the development of the skill of the 'New Orleans nine.'" Gray, a prisoner, noted that the baseball games at Salisbury were the first ever played in the South.[61]

Conditions Change

Before the great influx of prisoners in the fall of 1864, Chaplain Mangum reported that the prisoners could be heard singing hymns and songs of home in the quiet hours of a summer's night. These songs called up memories of a "Better Land, where peace is never broken and freedom has no foe or fear."[62] But the idyllic days at Salisbury Prison became a nightmare when the prison was overrun with thousands of new prisoners

From December 1861 through April 1864, Salisbury Prison contained fewer than 1,500 prisoners. This number permitted relatively comfortable living conditions.[63] As the war progressed, Brig. Gen. John H. Winder shifted prisoners from one prison to another, and more prisoners were transferred to Salisbury to relieve overcrowding at other facilities. When the exchange of prisoners was stopped, a once-comfortable prison turned into a nightmare filled with more prisoners than the facilities could accommodate.[64]

Prisoner Benjamin F. Booth, of the 22nd Iowa Infantry, stated in his memoirs

that he believed more Federal soldiers at Salisbury "were killed, died from starvation, and from numerous loathsome diseases and conditions, than in any other prison
in the Southern Confederacy." Steve Meyer, the editor of that book, corrected Booth's
statement. Many more Federal prisoners died at Andersonville than at Salisbury.[65]

Water Shortage

Prisoner William H. Jeffrey wrote that water for the prisoners came from two
wells, one with very good water, the other with "sulphur water." The water in the
good well soon gave out, and they were left with the sulphur water. Eventually that
well became so low that when the bucket was lowered, it returned partially filled with
mud."[66] Maj. Abner Small noted that when the number of prisoners increased, even
two wells were not sufficient. The prisoners were given "two worn shovels" and told
to dig a new well. They dug down for about 15 feet until they found water. They were
given an old wooden bucket, a rope, and a windlass was made from green firewood.
Mud and water were scooped up, and the water held "in dippers till the mud had
partly settled," and then the water could be drank. Small remembered how he was
often so thirsty that his "ears rang" and his "tongue swelled in my mouth." They were
not permitted to dig another well because the authorities feared the prisoners would
dig an escape tunnel.[67]

No stream ran through the stockade to carry away bodily waste and other filth.
Major Small described the ground as "reeking and the air was sour and heavy with
the stench of offal." It was on that filthy soil that the prisoners "lived, slept, and died."[68]

The prisoners soon became "overrun with vermin and reduced to mere skeletons."[69]

Food

A news correspondent who escaped from Salisbury reported that the "rations
were tolerable both in quality and quantity." He recalled that prisoners were allowed
to buy a variety of articles from civilians outside the prison. The correspondent
recalled that once his "mess had seventy-five dozen eggs." During the spring, summer, and fall, Salisbury citizens sent quantities of provisions to the prisoners.[70]

When prisoners were stricken with scurvy, a peck of Irish potatoes was given
to them. There were enough so that each could have one, or maybe two, and they
ate the potatoes raw. Once a woman visited the prison with sweet potatoes, and those
that had money bought them.[71] Prisoner A. D. Richardson recalled that he could purchase supplies of food from outside the prison.[72]

But the food supply dwindled as the war continued, and during the summer of
1864, the guards themselves committed "henroost robberies," a form of thievery
prevalent when food was scarce.[73]

Prison Overwhelmed in October

Early in October 1864 the first of 10,000 new prisoners arrived, and conditions
quickly became unbearable for all concerned. Conditions at Salisbury became far,

far worse than they had ever been at Libby Prison or Castle Thunder. One prisoner described conditions at Salisbury in the fall of 1864:

> nine or ten thousand scantily clad, emaciated, woe-begone soldiers— unnamed heroes … in an enclosure of five or six acres, half of them without other shelter than holes they had dug in the earth, or under the small buildings employed as hospitals. The weather is cold; perhaps a chilly rain is falling, or the ground is covered with snow. There are the soldiers— hundreds of them with naked feet, and only light blouses or shirts, hungry, feeble, despairing of the present and hopeless of the future— huddling over a small and smoky fire of green wood, in a crowded tent, whose very atmosphere is poisonous; or standing shivering against the outside chimney of the squalid hospitals, hoping to warm their blood a little from the partially heated bricks; or drawn up in their narrow caves....[74]

A Variety of Escape Attempts

Even during the best of conditions at Salisbury, prisoners tried to escape. Six sailors bribed a guard to let them escape in June 1862.[75] Several days later, the prisoners slipped through the fence where a slab had been loosened.[76]

Also in June 1862, after most of the prisoners of war had been exchanged, the remaining civilian prisoners plotted to escape. They did not succeed that month or in a second attempt the next month.[77]

Twelve officers, confined on the upper floor of the cotton factory building, devised a plan to escape. They tied their blankets together and hung them out the window. A deserter, who was to be their guide, was the first to slide down the blanket rope. It tore under his weight and he fell to the ground. The sentinels discovered him, and the escape was thwarted.[78]

In March 1863, eight prisoners escaped, but three were recaptured immediately. Two made it to Cool Springs in Iredell County, where they surrendered, unable to go on. The remaining three were never recaptured.[79] The citizens of Salisbury and the surrounding area were warned to keep their "guns ready and compel every suspicious traveler to give a good account of himself," or else have them arrested.

Two bold prisoners, Capt. B. C. G. Reed and Captain Litchfield, wrapped themselves in blankets and bluffed their way past the prison guards. They claimed to be members of the staff. They fooled the guards, and made it outside. They thought they were free, but were recaptured in the mountains of eastern Tennessee, after having traveled 120 miles.[80]

Captain Reed, of Zanesville, Ohio, was unhappy if he was not attempting to escape. However, all his attempts ended in failure, and he wound up being handcuffed or given a ball and chain to wear and confined in a filthy cell.[81] Reed continued his attempts and finally did escape from a railroad car in Charleston, South Carolina, and made his way to Federal troops on Battery Wagner. He returned to Thomas' Army, but was killed in the fighting at Nashville, Tennessee.[82]

One prisoner pestered a guard by throwing bricks at him until the guard shot and wounded the prisoner. He had wanted the guard to kill him to put him out of his misery and he failed.[83]

Another prisoner escaped by claiming he had was a Confederate "straggler," and when he was released, he made his way to Sherman's Federal forces near Fayetteville.[84]

Captain Ives, of the 10th Massachusetts Infantry, one of several prisoners being held as a hostage on the fourth floor of the cotton factory building, made a rope from blankets. He safely descended from a window to the ground. A Confederate deserter named Carroll tried to follow, but the rope broke, and he fell the whole distance. He was confined to the guard house over night, and other than having a "swollen head," was otherwise unharmed.[85]

One successful escape was carried out on burial detail. One of the prisoners helping carry the dead outside the stockade for burial was a ventriloquist. He used his talent to throw his voice so that it seemed to come from within the coffin. The sound so frightened the guards that they ran and the prisoner escaped.[86]

Another ploy was to get sent to the hospital because it was outside the stockade. The "smallpox ruse" was used by a number of prisoners. They heated needles over a fire to red hot and burned small holes in their faces and bodies so as to appear to have smallpox. They then went to the prison surgeon who ordered them sent to the hospital. Once outside the stockade, after a short time, the crafty prisoners soon managed to escape.[87]

In the 10 months he was a prisoner at Salisbury, Richardson knew of at least 70 prisoners who had escaped. Most were brought back, although a few were "shot in the mountains." He knew of only five who had actually reached the North.[88]

Tunnels

Tunnels were always being dug and some were not discovered until after the prisoners had escaped. One tunnel ran from the commissary building to the stockade, but the guards discovered this one, and foiled an escape.[89] The first tunnel was discovered in the spring of 1862. Its presence was reported by an English prisoner to gain favor with the Confederate jailors.[90] The 1862 tunnel was 670 feet long and 28 inches in diameter. It ran five feet below the ground.[91] Richardson remembered seeing six Yankee deserters tied to posts and whipped with a cat-o'-nine-tails as punishment for digging a tunnel.[92]

Escape Plot of October 1864

The great influx of prisoners in October 1864 motivated many to try to escape. Although the officers and men were still kept separate, the officers managed to communicate the plan to the enlisted men. By this method, all knew of the plot to batter down the stockade walls, while others threw rocks and mudballs at the sentries. Another group was to use clubs and sharpened sticks as weapons. The signal was to be the waving of a torch. Before the plot could be put into action, one of the officers told a guard, "Some of our officers have escape on the brain."[93]

The plan was not abandoned, and the prisoners continued to refine their plot. The prisoners organized a corps of two divisions, each led by a capable officer, under the direction of Gen. Joseph Hayes. Codes for signals were adopted, and quickly learned, orders were written and wrapped around stones. After dark, these orders were tossed over the heads of the sentries guarding the deadline inside the stockade. The plot called for an attack on the guard, the main gate, the batteries outside the stockade, the commissary, the railroad station, and the town. Everything was in place but on October 18, 1864, the day before the attack was to be launched, Lieutenant Gardner of the 13th Connecticut, threw his message-carrying stone too fast, and the note came off the stone and fell to the ground at the feet of a sentry. Whether by chance or on purpose, this particular message was not in code, and the guards knew immediately that a breakout was planned.[94]

The prisoners waited as if paralyzed, on both sides of the deadline. Before they could act, a Confederate officer shouted, "Turn out the guard! Man the guns!"[95]

A search was begun for Lieutenant Gardner, but no one knew what he looked like. When he could not be located, the prisoners were ordered to form in rank, and the roll was called. Each officer, upon answering to the call of his name, was passed out through a gate in the stockade. Lieutenant Gardner disguised himself with dirt on his face, and changing his uniform for a ragged one. He then answered to the name of an officer who had jumped from the train on the way to the prison. The next day, 306 officers were marched out and herded onto a train headed for Danville, Virginia, and yet another prison. They were to be exchanged for 500 privates.[96]

Another prisoner believed that the note which had put an end to this plot had been placed in a hollow bone, along with a complete outline of the plan, and he believed it had been "purposely thrown" to the guards.[97] Because he was believed to have been the officer who had thrown the note, Gardner was lucky to get out of the prison alive.

The prisoners did not abandon their efforts. Prisoner Ferris recorded that on thee days later on October 22, 1864, nine prisoners escaped by tunneling under the fence. Two days later, another tunnel was discovered when a prisoner informed the guards of its location for a "half a loaf of bread." Ferris believed that a hundred men had planned to use that tunnel. Eighteen men did escape on the night of November 1, 1864.[98]

The November Insurrection

The prisoners were getting desperate, but still another attempt at a mass escape met with disaster. Not only was the prison overcrowded, but a cold November rain had fallen all week, and then a cold snap froze the ground.[99] The prisoners at Salisbury were not issued any food on Thanksgiving Day, which had been proclaimed a national holiday in 1863 by President Lincoln.[100] Those conditions motivated the men to act, even if they died trying.

The prisoners began to think about rushing the gates. Once outside, they could arm themselves from the guns at the Salisbury arsenal, then march east to join Union General Sherman. There was much discussion and many thought it unwise, unless a definite plan of action could be agreed upon. However, hunger tipped the scales. After receiving only a pound of cornbread in a 48-hour period, the cry went up: "Those who are for liberty follow me." The time had been set for the moment when the guards were changing.[101] Unfortunately, the prisoners' timing was wrong. The Junior Reserves (the 67th North Carolina), scheduled to board the train, had not done so and the train was still at the depot.[102] When the prisoners rushed the large gate, they encountered two divisions of prisoners who were there getting their rations. This

Insurrection resulted in Massacre at Salisbury Prison. (Lithograph from A. D. Richardson, The Secret Service, The Field, The Dungeon, and The Escape. *Hartford, CN: American Publishing Co., 1865.)*

group knew nothing of the plan, and they were soon fighting at cross purposes—one group trying desperately to get their daily rations, the other group trying just as desperately to get out. The guards soon joined in the melee. The resulting massacre was remembered by all who survived, and accounts from various viewpoints can be studied in existing diaries, letters, and other writings.

According to prisoner Richard A. Dempsey:

> The signal was given, and a number, armed with clubs, sprang upon the relief guard of sixteen men as they were entering the yard, while others rushed on the guards stationed in the grounds. Weak and emaciated as the prisoners were, they performed their work well. They wrenched the guns from the soldiers, and those who resisted were bayonetted on the spot. Every gun was taken from them and they made their camp outside, where being reinforced by a rebel regiment on its way to Wilmington, together with the citizens, who turned out with shot guns, pistols, or whatever weapon was nearest at hand, we were overpowered though we had captured one of the field pieces. There was no organized action; several thousand prisoners rushing to one point only, instead of making attempts to break down the fence in different places, thus confusing the guards on the fence. The attempt was futile, as we had neither hammers nor axes with which to make an opening in the fence. At once every musket in the garrison was turned upon us, and two field pieces opened with grape and canister. The insurrection, which had not occupied more than a few minutes, was a failure, and the uninjured returned to their quarters.[103]

Another prisoner recalled that several hundred prisoners rushed toward the woods, but being too weak to outrun the guards, they were all recaptured. Some were tortured by being tied up by their thumbs, but no one told who the ringleaders were.[104]

The doomed escape attempt was reported in the Richmond *Enquirer,* and also picked up by the New York *Herald:*

> On Thursday last a serious attempt was made by the federal prisoners confined at Salisbury, N.C., to make their escape, which was rapidly and effectually quelled at the expense of considerable Yankee blood. It appears that a plot had been formed among the prisoners—of whom there are at Salisbury some thirteen thousand—to over-power the interior guard of the encampment, then break through the line of the parapet guard, and, after securing all the arms they could, to march through Western North Carolina into Tennessee, and make good their escape.[105]

The interior guards were overpowered and two were killed. Then the guards on the parapet were attacked, and two of them were killed, but not before they had alerted the garrison and two pieces of artillery were trained upon the prisoners. The guards fired upon the prisoners with grape and canister until they surrendered and pleaded for mercy. The final tally, according to the newspapers, was "about 40 killed and a large number wounded." This figure may have been too low.[106]

The guards were reluctant to fire on the prisoners, and many threw down their guns and ran. However, three rounds from the two six-pounders were fired, and this essentially quelled the riot. Grapeshot and canister were deadly, especially if fired at close range. The official report submitted by Major Gee of the incident reported the casualties: two guards killed, one mortally wounded; 13 prisoners were killed and three mortally wounded, and 60 others wounded to a lesser degree. The three ring-leaders of the insurrection were arrested and sent to Major Carrington in Rich-mond.[107] Richardson agreed with those figures.[108] Benjamin F. Booth believed that between "two and three hundred" may have died as the result of the insurrection.[109]

Results of the Insurrection

Two doctors were called to treat the wounded, and several arms and legs were amputated. One prisoner charged that the Confederates failed to care for the wounded. Rather than being used to carry the wounded to the hospital, the wagon was used to carry out the dead. On Sunday, 22 wounded were admitted to the hospital, and on Monday, 23 more.[110] Robert Livingstone was wounded and died in the hospital on December 5, 1864. His father, Dr. David Livingstone, did not learn of his death until June 1865.[111]

After the November 25 revolt, guards were not permitted inside the compound, and prisoners were not permitted to go to the latrines after dark.[112] Guards were placed in a line about 100 feet outside the prison walls.[113] The bloodhounds were daily taken around the prison stockade in order to detect the scent of any prisoners who might have escaped.[114]

After receiving the news of the insurrection, General Winder visited Florence and Salisbury prisons. Winder determined that both places were unfit. He believed that the mortality rates at both Florence and Salisbury exceeded that at Anderson-ville. The site at Salisbury was unsuitable because: (1) the water supply was insufficient for the number of prisoners; (2) there was no good place for the sinks (latrines), no stream, and with the sinks inside the walls, the "stench is insupportable both to the prisoners and the people in the vicinity; (3) the soil was sticky clay, and after even a slight rain, there was not a "dry spot within the enclosure;" (4) the prison was within the town, and defenses could not be erected without destroying much private property; (5) proximity to a town is "extremely objectionable and injurious," and (6) wood was so far away that 39 wagons and teams were required to obtain the 100 cords of wood each day, which, at a cost of $20 per cord, amounted to $720,000 per year. Winder also reported to Gen. Samuel Cooper that during the recent insurrection, three shots had hit the hotel in town. Winder recommended that the prison be moved to a wooded area to save money on wood. The Salisbury property could be sold for at least $150,000 (it had originally cost $15,000). This would pay for the purchase of a tract of 900 acres 14 miles from Columbia, South Carolina, with money left over to complete the prison and erect all necessary workshops.[115] Winder didn't impress the prisoners. When he reviewed the prison, Booth recorded that Winder's "face is a good index to his base heart." He noted that Winder had been promoted to be commander-in-chief of all prisons in the South because "he possessed the qualifications necessary for such a position—a brute nature in human form.[116]

Escapes Continue

Three prisoners who escaped on December 12, 1864, were recaptured and returned to Salisbury prison on January 14, 1865. These three had almost reached Federal lines when they were reported.[117] Eight prisoners were reported recaptured from January 16 to January 31, 1865.[118] The next month, a report for the period February 1–15, 1865, indicated that seven prisoners had escaped.[119]

A tunnel was discovered on January 16, 1865, but not before about a hundred prisoners had gone out through it. A group of about 25 prisoners had been working on the tunnel for about two weeks. They were bound by an oath not to reveal its location. When the decision was made to leave, each of the 25 was allowed to take two friends with him. Those who had worked on the tunnel would go out at midnight, their friends at 1 A.M. The next day, the tunnel was discovered, and the bloodhounds were sent in pursuit.[120]

On January 20, about a dozen of the prisoners who escaped through the tunnel were recaptured. They had traveled 40 miles before being caught. The prisoners had tried to avoid capture by splitting up into groups of about 10 to 12 men, each going in a separate direction. However, by January 26, about a dozen more had been recaptured. They had been captured through the combined efforts of bloodhounds and citizens. Booth remarked: "Every able-bodied man not in the Southern army is patrolling the country for rebel deserters and escaped prisoners, which makes escape almost impossible."[121]

Richardson, Browne and Others Escape

The two newspaper correspondents, A. D. Richardson and Junius Henri Browne, along with William E. Davis, correspondent for the *Cincinnati Gazette,* and a Captain Wolfe escaped on December 18, 1864. The men decided to escape on a rainy Sunday night of the day that a new prison commander was to take charge. Davis went first, because he had a pass to visit the hospital outside the fence to get medical supplies. Browne had frequently passed out of the gate and he knew he would be recognized, so he gave his pass to Richardson, so he could pass out of the gate. Richardson told the guard he would return with a box of bottles that were to be filled at the hospital.[122] Richardson described the details of his escape in his memoirs.[123]

Benjamin F. Booth noted in his diary on December 19, 1864: "This morning two of the escaped prisoners were returned to prison. They report that the other three got separated from them and the hunters were unable to discover their tracks." Booth recorded that the two that had been captured were kept in Major Gee's headquarters all night, "where every effort was made to extort from them the manner in which they escaped, and which of the guards

Albert D. Richardson, one of two New York Tribune *correspondents who escaped from Salisbury Prison. From lithograph in A. D. Richardson,* The Secret Service, The Field, The Dungeon, and The Escape. *(Hartford, CN: American Publishing Co., 1865.)*

aided them." The prisoners would reveal no information.[124] These men were probably from another group not with the party of Richardson and Browne.

Richardson and Browne and the other prisoners spent the first night in a barn only a few blocks north of the prison. The second night they stayed at the home of Lieutenant Welborn (Welborne), one of the prison guards.[125] Welborn was a member of a secret organization known as the "Sons of America," a network to help Union men, whether prisoners or refugees, escape to the North.[126] Before they left Salisbury, Welborn brought another prisoner out to join them, Charles Thurston of the 6th New Hampshire Infantry. Dressed in the uniform of a Confederate private, Thurston had simply walked out behind two Confederate detectives, and with a slouch hat over his face, sat down on a log outside the fence with other guards.[127]

Welborn gave the escapees a canteen of water with instructions attached as to how to reach a "staunch Union settlement" 50 miles away. It took the men six days to reach safety in a barn in Wilkes County. Lieutenant Welborn visited them there. Richardson revealed later that one of the six nights on the road had been spent in the home of the wife and daughter of a Confederate officer.[128] All along the way, they were helped by slaves who brought them food and provided shelter.[129] There was a network of Union supporters in Wilkes County who hid the escapees, fed and clothed them, then sent them on to the next safe house.[130]

Richardson's absence was not discovered until two days later, on December 20. When the prisoners learned how Richardson, posing as a hospital physician, had boldly walked out through the gates, they applauded his efforts and wished him and his group success.[131] Prison officials were not so pleased. The *Carolina Watchman* noted that the escape of Browne and Richardson was "very mortifying inasmuch as they were the most important prisoners at the garrison."[132]

On December 27, Richardson and his group learned that two other prisoners from Salisbury, Capt. William Boothby, a Philadelphia mariner, and Mr. John Mercer, a Unionist from New Bern, North Carolina, had escaped two nights after Richardson and Browne. Boothby had paid a guard $800 in Confederate money to let them out. Charley Thurston left Richardson and Browne to join them. For the rest of the journey, they sometimes traveled together, but when there was danger, they separated.[133]

Near Wilkesboro, they encountered the wife of Ben Hanby crossing a stream. The prisoners had been seen approaching and Hanby had joined others in the woods who were hiding out. After convincing Mrs. Hanby they were not members of the home guard, she took them to her home.[134] At the Hanby house, a number of his friends visited — Confederate deserters and Union bushwhackers — all armed to the teeth with rifles, navy revolvers, and Bowie knives. These men had fought several skirmishes with the Confederate home guard.[135]

The little band of escaped prisoners was told to find Dan Ellis, who had already become famous as a guide. Since the beginning of the war, Ellis reportedly had led 4,000 persons to safety behind Union lines. Richardson wrote that Ellis had probably seen "more adventure," in the form of "fights and races with Rebels, in long journeys, sometimes bare-footed and through the snow, or swimming rivers full of floating ice," than anyone.[136]

Dan Ellis, a Southerner who helped thousands of prisoners escape to Union lines. From a lithograph in A. D. Richardson, The Secret Service, The Field, The Dungeon, and The Escape. *(Hartford, CN: American Publishing Co., 1865.)*

Richardson's party encountered Ellis on January 8, 1865, as he was about to depart across the mountains to Strawberry Plains, Tennessee, with a large group of 70 men. This group included refugees, Confederate deserters, and Union soldiers returning to their homes, as well as escaping prisoners. Some of the men in Ellis' party were mounted, and once they were informed that Richardson and his group had escaped from Salisbury, they dismounted and let the Richardson party ride. There was a standing reward of $5,000 for Ellis' capture, and he never parted with his Henry rifle, which would fire 16 times without reloading.[137]

Their journey to freedom was approximately 340 miles, from Salisbury, North Carolina, to Strawberry Plains, Tennessee.[138] The trip took 27 days—December 18, 1864, to January 13, 1865. Once they reached safety, Browne and Richardson announced to the world that they were "Out of the Jaws of Death." They returned to work for the *Tribune,* and both men published articles on their experiences (see Appendices G and H, in Browne, *The Salisbury Prison,* pp. 197–209).

On a sad note, while A. D. Richardson was in prison, both his wife and son died. After the war, Mrs. Abbe Sage McFarland sought to obtain a divorce so she could marry Richardson. In a drunken rage, Mr. McFarland, the lady's husband, shot Richardson on November 25, 1869. He clung to life by a thread, and married the lady on December 2, 1869, just before he died. The jealous husband was tried for murder but found not guilty.[139]

Another Miraculous Escape

August Kissel, a German immigrant, who enlisted in Company B, 94th New York Infantry, was another prisoner contemplating means of escape. He was among 50 who dug a tunnel about 60 feet long, but someone informed on them. Determined to escape, Kissel became involved in trading with both prisoners and guards. He eventually collected $1,200 in United States currency, and he used that money to bribe a guard. With several friends, they made their escape on January 27, 1865. To avoid capture, the escapees submerged themselves in a pond, with only their mouths above water to allow them to breath. After wandering a bit, they reached Iredell County to the north of Rowan, and then Union sympathizers helped them to Wilkesboro. Along the way, they are said to have spend each night in homes of some of the Salisbury guards.[140]

The End of Salisbury Prison

The total number of prisoners held at Salisbury is controversial. Most of the prison records were lost when the camp was destroyed on April 12, 1865. On June 23, 1864, an inspector reported that since the prison had been established, 3,802 prisoners had been held, and at the time of his inspection, there were 550 present.[141] During the period October 5, 1864, to February 1, 1865, an official report stated that 10,321 prisoners had been held.[142] Without additional data on the number of prisoners received, exchanged, died and escaped, it is impossible to determine the exact number of prisoners who passed through Salisbury.

No accurate figures are available as to how many prisoners escaped from the Salisbury Prison. A. D. Richardson estimated that between February 3, 1864, and

December 1864, at least 70 escaped, but most of them were recaptured. Chaplain Mangum estimated that between 500 and 600 prisoners escaped *after* October 1864, but he had no idea how many of them reached safety behind Union lines. Most estimates place the number of escapees at around 300.[143]

By late February 1865, the days of confinement of prisoners at Salisbury ended. Prisoners were sent out in groups: 370 left on February 19 by train to Richmond (three died along the way). On February 20, the second group of 757 left by train. Of these prisoners of war, 400 were considered "well" and 357 sick. Under the care of Brig. Gen. Robert F. Hoke, 2,822 prisoners of war plus 48 citizens walked away on February 22. Another group of 938 soldiers were sent by rail to Richmond (12 died on the trip). The last group of 214, a mixture of 42 prisoners of war, 125 sick prisoners of war, 28 citizens, and 19 free blacks, left on March 3. The final count was 3,634 well prisoners of war; 1,420 sick ; 76 citizens; and 19 free blacks, for a total of 5,149 prisoners released.[144] At Greensboro, the majority were transported to Raleigh, and then to Wilmington, where they were transported by ship to Annapolis, Maryland.[145]

The demise of Salisbury Prison came a few weeks later with the arrival of United States cavalry. Gen. George Stoneman had come to Salisbury to release the prisoners, but found they had been moved. He destroyed the prison and the records of the prisoners, and other buildings during his occupation April 12–13, 1865.[146]

Salisbury Prison Today

All that remains of Salisbury Prison is the garrison house, located on the north end of the original prison site.[147] The approximately 11,700 soldiers who died are buried in the Salisbury National Cemetery, which is now a burial ground for veterans of all wars.[148]

XXVII

Camp Davidson, Savannah, Georgia

"From this prison there was no successful escape made to our lines."
— Joseph Ferguson

Location: Savannah, Georgia. **Established:** July 29, 1864–October 1864. **Type:** tents enclosed by a high fence, and open area surrounded by guards at the U.S. Marine Hospital. **Type of Prisoners:** Federal officers from Macon, enlisted men from Andersonville. **Capacity:** ? **Greatest Number Held:** 6,000–10,000. **Known Number of Escapes:** 0.[1]

History

As Sherman's Federal troops moved through Georgia, Confederate authorities had to shift prisoners to other locations. Those at Macon were transferred by rail to Savannah. In July 1864, 600 prisoners were transferred in closed boxcars under heavy guard. The train was almost captured by Federal cavalry a short distance out of Macon, when the train had to stop for wood and water. The Federal troops had destroyed the telegraph office, the rolling stock, and the buildings, and had torn up the track for hundreds of yards. One of the prisoners on that train, Union officer Joseph Ferguson, remembered that the prisoners were saddened to learn that they had just missed being liberated by Union soldiers.[2]

The Facilities — The U.S. Marine Hospital

In the summer of 1864, when prisoners were transferred to Savannah, Georgia, they were put in a stockade erected adjacent to the United States Marine Hospital. The new camp was officially named "Camp Davidson."[3]

The Marine Hospital was a large stone building. The hospital grounds included a large garden which was enclosed by a brick wall on three sides and a board fence on the fourth which connected to the hospital building. The prisoners were placed inside this area. A catwalk and boxes were added to the wall to enable sentries to watch the prisoners inside.[4]

Only a few days before the prisoners arrived on July 29, 1864, several little wooden huts had been completed to supplement the few tents. Some of the prisoners used scrap lumber to build platforms on which to sleep. Neither the tents nor the crude huts provided much protection against the storms that were common to Savannah in the summer.[5]

According to one of the prisoners, Capt. Bernhard Domschcke, some additional tents were provided after the prisoners arrived. Each tent could provide shelter for 16 prisoners and, although there were at least 600 tents, there were not enough to go around. However, the weather was warm and the huge oak trees shaded the grounds.[6]

Little "A" tents were issued, one for six or seven men. These were arranged in streets, and some were raised up off the ground to avoid flooding when it rained.[7]

Treatment of the Prisoners

One prisoner stated that he was treated far better at Savannah than at Macon.[8] The prisoners also received better rations. Divided into groups of 20, each group was issued one skillet. They were given one pint of cornmeal, a pound of fresh beef, and one gill of rice daily. An ounce of salt was issued every fourth day. Sutlers were allowed to sell items to the prisoners as well.

Captain Domschcke found conditions at Savannah, Georgia, a little better than at Macon. The prisoners were guarded by members of the 1st Georgia Regulars (Volunteers) under the command of Colonel Wayne. The colonel was strict but humane, and the sentries never randomly fired at the prisoners, and always gave a warning to anyone who got too near the deadline. During the daytime, the prisoners were allowed to hang clothing and blankets on the fence to dry.[9]

The officers were friendly to the prisoners, especially Major Hill, one of the prison officials. The guards tried to answer questions from the prisoners truthfully when they could. Major Hill also posted newspaper clippings that related to exchange of prisoners.[10]

Another Prison Pen Needed

The facilities at the Marine Hospital soon became overcrowded as prisoners continued to be transferred from Andersonville. Another stockade was hastily built near the city jail. This new site began accepting prisoners on September 7, 1864. This new "pen" had a high plank wall to confine the prisoners The prisoners could get a glimpse of the world outside through the spaces between the boards. This little pleasure ended on the second day when a 20-foot deadline was set up around the inside of the stockade. The interior was bare ground. These prisoners were guarded by sailors from the Confederate ships that sat at anchor in Savannah's harbor, unable to leave because of the blockade. Additional security was provided by 24 cannons placed around the pen.[11]

Problems at the Pen

Water became a problem for the prisoners. One pump supplied the entire prison with water. The water was bad and smelled like sulphur, similar to the water from

Sulphur Springs in Virginia. A hydrant was installed that pulled muddy water from the river, but it had to be filtered and purified to be used.[12]

There were problems with the sutler, who charged exorbitant prices for his wares. One of the Union officers who was a prisoner acted as the sutler's agent, and he received a cut from the enormous profits. The Union officer was greedy, and he saved all the Confederate money he could get to buy "greenbacks."[13]

However, some things were not as bad as at other prisons. Joseph Ferguson recalled that Savannah was the only place where the prisoners got "fresh meat, and any kind of decent treatment...."[14] In Savannah, Ferguson put on his shoes for the first time in months. The soles of his shoes were paper thin from the miles he had walked when he had previously tried to escape. He had gone barefooted in the summer in order to save his shoes for cold weather. Even though his shoes were in bad condition by the time winter arrived, it saved him much suffering from walking on the cold ground.[15]

Escape Attempts

According to historian Lonnie Speer, all accounts seem to agree that there were "no escapes from the Savannah facilities."[16] However, there were many attempts.

A Union officer dressed himself in a Confederate uniform and passed out through the gate and walked out, unnoticed by the guards. Once his absence was noted, he was soon recaptured, and was punished for his failed attempt. The next day, the prisoners' quarters were searched and all gray uniforms were confiscated.[17]

Two or three officers escaped from the train on the way from Macon to Savannah. One young officer jumped from the train and ran into the woods amidst a hail of bullets from the Confederate guards. He was later recaptured, and put in irons.[18]

Tunnels

Although the camp was inspected closely, the prisoners frequently dug tunnels in hopes of escape. One tunnel was almost completed and a black soldier was sent into it to open an exit at the end. When he stuck his head out, a Confederate guard ordered, "Go back, Yankee, or I'll shoot you." Sadly, the tunneler returned to his coconspirators with the news that the tunnel had been discovered. The next day, two of those who had been involved in digging the tunnel were taken to the city jail where they spent several days in a dark cell. One of those, according to Captain Domschcke, was Capt. Albert Grant of the 19th Wisconsin. Captain Grant was always attempting to escape and make his way to nearby Union-held Fort Pulaski, only 14 miles from the prison camp.[19]

Betrayed by a Cow

Another prisoner, Lt. Alonzo Cooper, recalled that almost the first thing he and his fellow prisoners did when they arrived at a new prison was to begin digging a tunnel. Two tunnels were started and had almost been completed when they were discovered and filled up. Cooper recalled that another tunnel was started soon after the first two had been discovered. This tunnel was nearly complete when the weight of a cow munching the grass above caused the ground to give way. A sentry happened to be watching and saw the cow almost disappear. He investigated and found the tunnel.[20]

This may be the same tunnel described by Ferguson which he helped excavate. This tunnel ran from a tent through an old well, and under the wall into the street. Fresh air was forced into the tunnel by a bellows so the digger could breathe. The loosened dirt was dumped in the old well. When the tunnel was complete, the first man through saw a guard waiting to nab them as they emerged. Quickly, he retreated backward through the opening into the prison. Ferguson remembered thinking that if he had gone out that night, he would probably have attempted to swim the wide, swift Savannah River.[21] And, if he had attempted it, he would probably have perished in the process.

The discovery of this tunnel resulted in an order from the prison commandant, Lieutenant Colonel Wayne. On August 28, 1864, Special Order No. 3 declared that the tent in which the tunnel was found would be taken from the Yankees, and that those inmates involved in the tunnel would be handed over to the provost marshal for "close confinement." Two prisoners were subsequently taken out and put in a "damp, unhealthy cell." They were allowed very little food, and were abused shamefully, for "*attempting to escape.*"[22]

One Gets Out

Lieutenant Cooper stated in his memoirs that only one prisoner escaped while he was at Savannah, and that was Captain Sampson, of the 2nd Massachusetts Heavy Artillery. Sampson crawled through a hole under the fence and tried to reach the fort on the coast six miles away from the prison. To get to the coast he had to make his way through the swamp. After two or three days of inching through knee-deep mud and water, Sampson decided to change direction. He was spotted and arrested by the patrol while he was trying to extract himself from the sticky mire of the swamp.[23] This may be the young artillery officer mentioned by Ferguson who, after "undergoing many hardships and adventures by 'flood and field,'" was recaptured and returned to the pen at Savannah. Upon his return to the camp, the young officer was only a "skeleton of what he once was, from the effects of the superhuman fatigues he had undergone."[24]

Closing the Savannah Prisons

On September 13, 1864, the prisoners held at Savannah were put on the train and transferred to Charleston and Columbia, South Carolina. There, they were sent to the jail yard.[25] Ferguson described the Charleston jail yard as one of the "uncleanest spots in the whole South. Six hundred of us were crowded into a small, filthy space, scarcely one acre."[26] Indeed, prisoners fared better at Savannah than they did before or after their incarceration there. By the end of October 1864, the few remaining prisoners at both the pen and the city jail were sent to Columbia and to a new prison pen at Millen, Georgia.[27]

Deaths at Savannah

Savannah served as a prison for only about six weeks, but it is believed that there were many deaths during the time. While only two officers died at the marine hospital, many more of the enlisted men died at the jail stockade or in the hospital tents there.[28] Many of those who died were undoubtedly prisoners transferred from Andersonville, and who were in very poor health when they reached Savannah.

Appendix

Number of Escapes from Federal Prisons, 1862-1865[1]

NR = no report found   NE = not yet established   Number of prisoners/escapes

Date	Alton	Camp Chase	Camp Douglas	Camp Morton	Elmira	Ft. Delaware	Ft. Lafayette
7/1862	795/27	1726/0	7850/45	4216/5	NE	3434/0	33/0
8/1862	1300/0	1961/0	7893/2	4254/0	NE	482/0	44/0
9/1862	1824/1	1367/7	7407/1	613/0	NE	2470/0	NR
10/1862	1191/0	1051/0	NR	NR	NE	2582/0	54/0
11/1862	1292/7	1043/0	NR	NR	NE	123/0	44/0
12/1862	794/0	756/0	NR	NR	NE	123/0	58/0
6 mths.	35	7	48	5		0	0
1/1863	1501/1	880/2	NR	NR	NE	17/0	41/0
2/1863	1500/1	1076/0	3881/6	NR	NE	30/0	52/0
3/1863	1519/0	1182/1	NR	NR	NE	38/0	62/0
4/1863	807/1	955/0	380/8	NR	NE	595/0	91/0
5/1863	1475/2	953/0	339/10	NR	NE	1255/0	63/0
6/1863	1704/0	1115/0	52/0	NR	NE	3737/1	110/0
7/1863	1468/0	3340/0	49/0	1276/2	NE	12505/0	122/0
8/1863	1298/6	332/0	3203/1	3060/6	NE	9136/8	70/0
9/1863	1267/0	2140/19	5133/0	1601/19	NE	8841/10	66/0
10/1863	1477/2	2333/1	6115/59	2522/10	NE	6498/4	36/0
11/1863	1691/4	2712/0	6018/27	3154/2	NE	3020/1	35/1
12/1863	1084/23	2828/0	5874/65	3372/0	NE	2859/1	74/0
1863	35	20	152	39	0	24	1
1/1864	1664/3	3047/0	5662/6	3279/3	NE	3767/0	122/0
2/1864	1646/0	2195/2	5607/11	3215/18	NE	2662/1	134/0
3/1864	1069/2	1604/0	5647/32	3122/0	NE	5818/1	133/0
4/1864	1186/6	1223/0	5462/2	2663/1	NE	6248/0	110/0
5/1864	1296/5	1546/3	5381/0	3209/2	NE	8289/0	109/0
6/1864	1372/6	1667/0	5277/4	4536/0	NE	9320/0	114/0
7/1864	1271/6	2015/0	6803/4	4999/0	4424/2	9274/10	110/1
8/1864	1280/2	4444/0	7655/2	4929/7	9606/0	9318/1	92/0
9/1864	905/4	5310/1	7554/8	4839/6	9480/0	8985/0	84/0
10/1864	975/1	5598/0	7525/17	4781/1	9441/11	7879/2	120/1
11/1864	1747/1	5610/0	8974/0	4752/31	8258/1	7671/1	135/0
12/1864	NR	5523/0	12082/6	4845/0	8401/2	7740/0	133/0
1864	36	6	94	69	16	16	2
1/1865	1891/1	9423/1	11711/0	4788/0	8602/0	7858/0	60/0
2/1865	1721/2	9416/0	11289/0	4215/2	8996/0	8045/0	55/0
3/1865	899/1	7861/0	9327/0	2868/0	7102/0	8899/0	49/0
4/1865	996/2	6339/0	7168/0	14080	5055/1	8575/0	NR
5/1865	632/2	5539/0	6107/1	1366/0	4885/0	8279/11	NR
6/1865	392/1	3353/0	4136/0	319/2	3610/0	7126/0	5/0
7/1865	62/0	48/0	4/0	7/0	1047/0	110/0	10/0
8/1865	closed	closed	closed	closed	closed	closed	9/0
9/1865	-	-	-	-	-	-	13/0
10/1865	-	-	-	-	-	-	10/0
11/1865	-	-	-	-	-	-	5/0
1865	9	1	1	4	1	11	0
Total	80	27	245	112	17	51	3

Total covers 41-month period from July 1862 through November 1865.

Number of Escapes from Federal Prisons, 1862-1865

NR = no report found   NE = not yet established   Number of prisoners/escapes

Date	Ft. McHenry	Ft. Warren	Gratiot	Johnson's Island	Old Capitol	Pt. Lookout	Rock Island
7/1862	NR	214/0	620/0	1184/0	NE	NE	NE
8/1862	NR	3/0	1183/6	1481/0	NE	NE	NE
9/1862	1 NR	3/0	NR	19490	NE	NE	NE
10/1862	NR	16/0	NR	911/0	99/0	NE	NE
11/1862	NR	15/0	NR	1258/0	NR	NE	NE
12/1862	NR	NR	NR	313/0	NR	NE	NE
6 mths.		**0**	**6**	**0**	**0**		
1/1863	NR	NR	NR	312/0	NR	NE	NE
2/1863	1 NR	NR	NR	36/0	NR	NE	NE
3/1863	NR	NR	NR	366/0	1063/0	NE	NE
4/1863	599/0	NR	NR	123/0	NR	NE	NE
5/1863	1550/4	NR	NR	72/0	1234/0	NE	NE
6/1863	1675/1	1/0	NR	806/0	1268/0	NE	NE
7/1863	6957/1	120/0	NR	1710/0	1260/1	136/0	NE
8/1863	328/0	114/4	836/2	2003/0	1467/0	1827/5	NE
9/1863	442/0	159/0	897/0	2186/0	1103/0	2942/11	NE
10/1863	380/14	154/0	1028/10	2627/0	1297/3	7585/1	NE
11/1863	407/1	131/0	905/1	2414/0	2783/0	9371/3	NE
12/1863	240/1	137/0	727/12	2653/0	1217/2	9153/4	5592/0
1863	**17**	**4**	**25**	**0**	**5**	**24**	**0**
1/1864	263/12	133/0	818/0	2635/3	1107/0	8621/0	7916/1
2/1864	142/0	162/0	822/7	2603/0	1215/1	8678/0	7600/2
3/1864	146/1	172/0	715/0	2206/0	904/0	8480/0	7233/0
4/1864	165/0	181/0	679/0	2251/0	529/0	6268/0	6946/0
5/1864	198/5	188/0	559/1	2144/0	797/0	12617/6	7190/0
6/1864	178/0	182/0	500/6	2313/0	825/1	15500/1	8607/3
7/1864	228/0	180/0	270/1	2411/0	1035/1	14747/2	8583/2
8/1864	335/0	147/0	219/1	2570/2	1061/2	11419/2	8398/1
9/1864	328/0	290/0	260/0	2717/1	540/0	8691/1	8273/10
10/1864	364/0	297/0	143/1	2697/3	684/1	13811/3	8181/9
11/1864	382/0	257/0	712/0	2754/0	595/2	11104/0	6394/1
12/1864	378/0	346/0	351/0	3231/1	529/0	10702/0	NR
1864	**18**	**0**	**17**	**10**	**88**	**15**	**29**
1/1865	350/0	332/0	104/0	3256/2	363/0	11860/0	6634/3
2/1865	239/0	394/0	186/0	3025/0	470/0	12231/0	6281/1
3/1865	208/0	380/0	210/0	2456/0	454/1	11332/2	5090/0
4/1865	217/0	333/0	98/0	2806/0	1531/0	20110/0	2772/0
5/1865	345/1	341/0	NR	2859/0	549/0	19818/0	2664/0
6/1865	172/0	320/0	12/0	2623/0	163/0	18836/0	1112/8
7/1865	18/0	26/0	3/0	119/0	55/0	closed	2/0
8/1865	5/0	5/0	2/0	7/0	41/1	closed	closed
9/1865	4/0	6/0	closed	91/0	29/0	-	-
10/1865	closed	closed	closed	closed	17/1	-	-
11/1865	-	-	-	-	-	-	-
1865	**1**	**0**	**0**	**3**	**3**	**2**	**9**
Total	**36**	**4**	**42**	**12**	**16**	**41**	**3**

Total covers 41-month period from July 1862 through November 1865.

Chapter Notes

Introduction

1. "Figures of Secretary Stanton," *Southern Historical Society Papers,* Vol. 1, No. 3 (March 1876), p. 216.

2. Nancy Travis Keen, "Confederate Prisoners of War at Fort Delaware," reprinted from *Delaware History* (Aril 1968), pp. 9–10.

3. Lonnie R. Speer, *Portals to Hell,* (Mechanicsburg, PA: Stackpole Books, 1997), pp. 323–339.

4. Mark M. Boatner, III, *The Civil War Dictionary,* Revised edition (New York: Vintage Books, 1988), p. 673.

5. Ibid.

6. Bernard Domschcke, *Twenty Months in Captivity: Memoirs of a Union Officer in Confederate Prisons* (Milwaukee, WI: W. W. Coleman, 1865. Reprint edition, editor and translator Frederic Tautmann (Cranbury, NJ: Associated University Press, 1987).

7. Boatner, *The Civil War Dictionary,* p. 854.

8. Ibid., p. 404.

9. Special Orders, No. 284, by L. Thomas, adjutant general, Washington, October 23, 1861, O.R., Ser. II, Vol. 3, p. 121.

10. W. Hoffman to Col. A. A. Stevens, Washington, November 12, 1863, O.R., Ser. II, Vol. VI, pp. 503–504.

11. Maj. Gen. John A. Dix and Maj. Gen. D. H. Hill to R. M. Stanton, secretary of war, Fort Monroe, Va., July 23, 1862, O.R., Ser. II, Vol. 4, pp. 266–267.

12. Ibid., cited in Boatner, *The Civil War Dictionary,* p. 271.

13. Boatner, *The Civil War Dictionary,* p. 271.

14. U. S. Grant to Benjamin F. Butler, City Point, Virginia, August 18, 1864, O. R., Ser. II, Vol. 8, p. 607.

15. Circular, July 7, 1862, Series II, Volume IV, p. 152. *The War of the Rebellion. A Compilation of the Official Records of the Union and Confederate Armies.* 70 vols., 130 parts. Washington, D.C.: Government Printing Office, 1880–1905, hereafter referred to as O.R., Ser.__, Vol. __.

16. "Abstract from monthly returns of the principal U.S. Military prisons," O.R., Ser. II, Vol. 8, pp. 986–1004.

17. Ibid.

18. Ibid.

19. Col. H. S. Burton to Bvt. Maj. Gen. E. D. Townsend, Richmond, Virginia, May 15, 1867, O.R., Ser. II, Vol. 8, p. 986.

20. Capt. J. W. DeForest, Veteran Reserve Corps, to Brig. Gen. James B. Fry, provost marshal general, Washington, D.C., November 30, 1865, O.R., Ser III, Vol. 5, pp. 543–567

21. Kenneth Radley, *Rebel Watchdog: The Confederate States Army Provost Guard* (Baton Rouge, LA: Louisiana State University Press, 1989), pp. 30, 33, 37–38.

22. DeForest, O.R., Ser III, Vol. 5, p. 543.

23. Ibid., p. 544.

24. Ibid., p. 549.

25. Ibid., p. 553.

26. "Abstract from monthly returns of the principal U.S. Military prisons," O.R., Ser. II, Vol. 8, p. 104

Chapter I

1. *Confederate Veteran,* Vol. XIV (1906), pp. 60–61, cited in Speer, *Portals to Hell,* p. 69.

2. Brig. Gen. William W. Orme to Edwin M. Stanton, December 7, 1863, O.R., Ser. II, Vol. 6, p. 663.

3. "Abstract from monthly returns of the principal U.S. Military prisons," July 1862–November 1865, O.R., Ser. II, Vol. 8, pp. 986–1004.

4. Speer, *Portals to Hell* p. 323; "Alton Civil War Prison," online at www.censusdiggins.com/prison_alton.html.

5. Patricia L. Faust, *Historical Times Illustrated Encyclopedia of the Civil War,* (New York: Harper & Row, Publishers, 1986), p. 9.

6. Speer, *Portals to Hell,* p. 68.

7. J. E. (Gene) Wheeler, "Infamous Alton Prison," online www.gwheeler.com/alton1.htm.

8. Speer, *Portals to Hell,* p. 68.

9. Galen D. Harrison, *Prisoners' Mail From the American Civil War,* (Dexter, MI: Thompson-Shore, Inc., 1997), pp. 121–122.

10. Col. Richard D. Cutts and Maj. John J. Key to Maj. Gen. H. W. Halleck, St. Louis, MO, April 3, 1862, O.R., Ser. II, Vol. 3, pp. 421–22.

11. Boatner, *The Civil War Dictionary,* p. 106; Speer, *Portals to Hell,* p, 57

12. Harrison, *Prisoners' Mail From the American Civil War,* pp. 121–122.

13. Cutts and Key, pp. 421–22.

14. Ibid.

15. W. Hoffman to Col. Thomas T. Gantt, October 13, 1862, O.R., Ser. II, Vol. 4, pp. 618–619.

16. W. Hoffman to Col. A. A. Stevens, November 12,

1863, O.R., Ser. II, Vol. 6, pp. 503–504; Speer, *Portal to Hell*, p. 3, 11.

17. Cutts and Key, pp. 422–423.

18. "Abstract from monthly returns of the principal U.S. Military prisons," July 1862–November 1865, O.R., Ser. II, Vol. 8, pp. 986–1004.

19. Maj. Franklin F. Flint to Colonel Hoffman, O.R., Ser. II, Vol. 6, p. 318, cited in Speer, *Portals to Hell*, p. 69.

20. *Daily Missouri Democrat,* December 23, 1861, December 24, 1861, December 25, 1861, cited in Speer, *Portals to Hell*, p. 48.

21. "Trial of Ebenezer Magoffin," O.R., Ser. II, Vol. 1, pp. 320–329.

22. Missouri Historical Company, *History of Saline County, Missouri* (St. Louis: Missouri Historical Company, 1881), p. 650, cited in Claycomb.

23. "Trial of Ebenezer Magoffin," pp. 299–301, 341–343.

24. "Trial of Ebenezer Magoffin," pp. 358–359.

25. "Trial of Ebenezer Magoffin," pp. 292–373.

26. Abraham Lincoln. *The Collected Works of Abraham Lincoln*, Vol. V (New Brunswick, NJ: Rutgers University Press, 1953), p. 170.

27. A. Lincoln to Major General Hallux, Washington, D.C., April 9, 1862, O.R., Ser. II, Vol. I, p. 276.

28. Speer, *Portals to Hell*, p. 68.

29. Harrison, *Prisoners' Mail From the American Civil War*, pp. 121–122.

30. Wheeler, "Infamous Alton Prison."

31. F. F. Flint, major, 16th Regiment, to Col. William Hoffman, Alton, Ill., July 26, 1862, in O.R., Ser. II, Vol. IV, pp. 317–318.

32. Speer, *Portals to Hell*, p. 69.

33. Speer, *Portals to Hell,* p. 69; Faust, *Historical Times Illustrated Encyclopedia of the Civil War*, p. 9.

34. W. Hoffman to Gen. L. Thomas, Detroit, July 31, 1862, O.R., Ser. II, Vol. IV, p. 317.

35. Edwin Stanton, August 20, 1862, O.R., Ser. II, Vol. IV, p. 317.

36. H. W. Freedley to Col. William Hoffman, Alton, IL, November 30, 1862, O.R., Ser. II, Vol. 4, pp. 740–741.

37. William Hoffman to E. M. Stanton, November 27, 1862, O.R., Ser. II, Vol. 4, p. 761.

38. H. W. Freedley to Col. William Hoffman, Alton, IL, November 27, 1862, pp.763–765.

39. "Proceedings of a Court of Inquiry Which Convened at Alton, IL, pursuant to the following Order, Special Order #207, Washington, D. C., August 26, 1862, O.R., Ser. II, Vol. IV, pp. 486–489.

40. N. S. Shaler, *Kentucky: A Pioneer Commonwealth* (Boston: Houghton Mifflin, 1895), p. 323, cited in Claycomb, "President Lincoln and the Magoffin Brothers."

41. James H. Carleton to E. D. Townsend, Department of New Mexico, September 1865, O.R., Ser. I, Vol. 48, Pt. II, p. 1233.

42. I. MacDonald Demuth, *The History of Pettis County, Missouri, Including an Authentic History of Sedalia, other Towns and Townships, Together with …biographical sketches….* (Clinton, MO: The Printery, 1882), p. 411–412.

43. H. W. Freedley to William Hoffman, Alton, Il., November 20, 1862, O.R., Ser. II, Vol. IV, pp. 740–741.

44. Ibid., pp. 740–741; Harrison, *Prisoners' Mail From the American Civil War*, pp. 121–122.

45. Speer, *Portals to Hell*, p. 70.

46. H. W. Freedley to Col. William Hoffman, Alton, IL, November 20, 1862, O.R., Ser. II, Vol. IV, p. 740.

47. H. W. Freedley to Col. William Hoffman, Il., November 27, 1862, p. 763.

48. F. A. Dick to Col. William Hoffman, Saint Louis, MO, January 9, 1863, O.R., Ser. II, Vol. 5, pp. 166–167.

49. "Abstract from monthly returns of the principal U.S. Military prisons," July 1862–November 1865, O.R., Ser. II, Vol. 8, pp. 986–1004.

50 H. W. Freedley to Col. William Hoffman, Alton, Il., November 27, 1862, p. 764.

51. Wheeler, "Infamous Alton Prison."

52. "Alton Prison Site Today," online at www.gwheeler.com/alton2.htm; "Alton Civil War Prison," online at www.censusdiggins.com/prison_alton.htm.

Chapter II

1. Henry, "Deposition of T. D. Henry," *Southern Historical Society Papers*, p. 279.

2. Speer, *Portals to Hell*, p. 324.

3. Ibid., p. 24.

4. Ibid.

5. Camp Chase Prison," online at www.census-diggins.com/prison_campchase.html, and "Camp Chase Prison," online at www.civilwarhome.com/campchase.htm

6. Robert E. Denny, *Civil War Prisons & Escapes*, (New York: Sterling Publishing Co., Inc., 1993), pp. 20–21.

7. "Camp Chase Prison," online www.censusdiggins.com/prison_campchase.html, and "Camp Chase Prison," online at www.civilwarhome.com/campchase.htm.

8. W. Hoffman to Hon. E. M. Stanton, Washington, D.C., July 24, 1862, O.R., Ser. II, Vol. 4, p. 278.

9. Wm. W. Orme to E. M. Stanton, Washington, D.C., December 7, 1863, O.R., Ser. II, Vol. 6, pp. 661–662.

10. B. R. Cowen to Hon. John Brough, governor, August 1, 1864, O.R., Ser. II, Vol. 7, pp. 528–529.

11. "Map of Camp Chase, drawn by A. Ruger, Co. H, 88th O.V.I," in *Confederate Veteran*, Vol. 6, No. 1 (January 1897), unable to obtain page number; online at www.geocities.com/Pentagon/Quarters/5109/map.html.

12. Milton Asbury Ryan, "Experience of a Confederate Soldier in Camp and Prison in the Civil War 1861–1865." Copy of this manuscript is located at the Carter House, a State of Tennessee Shrine commemorating the Battle of Franklin, 1140 Columbia Ave., P.O. Box 555, Franklin, TN 37065, an online at www.izzy.net/~michaelg/mar-text.htm.

13. Ibid.

14. Henry, "Deposition of T.D Henry," p. 279.

15. Ryan, "Experience of a Confederate Soldier in Camp and Prison."

16. Henry, "Deposition of T.D Henry," pp. 277–278.

17. Ibid., p. 276.

18. Ibid.

19. Ibid.

20. Ibid., p. 278.

21. Denny, *Civil War Prisons and Escapes*, p. 59.

22. Peter Zinn to Maj. Joseph Darr, Jr., November 21, 1862, O.R., Ser. II, Vol. 5, p. 139.

23. W. P. Richardson to Col. William Hoffman, Camp Chase, Ohio, March 8, 1864, O.R., Ser. II, Vol. 6, p. 1060.

24. Ryan, "Experience of a Confederate Soldier in Camp and Prison."

25. W. Hoffman to W. M. Stanton, March 17, 1864, O.R., Ser. II, Vol. 6, p. 1058.

26. Statement of G. W. Fitzpatrick, March 8, 1864, O.R., Ser. II, Vol. 6, pp. 1061–1062.

27. Isiah S. Taylor to E. M. Stanton, March 17, 1864, eyewitness reports from guards, prisoners and others about the shooting of five prisoners by the guard at Camp Chase November 5, November 16, and December 19, 1863, O.R., Ser. II, Vol. 6, pp. 1058–1067.

28. Statement of G. S. Barnes, O.R., Ser. II, Vol. 6, p. 1064.

29. Statement of H. P. J. Hathcock O.R., Ser. II, Vol. 6, p. 1065.

30. Denny, *Civil War Prisons and Escapes*, p. 144; W. P. Richardson to William Hoffman, March 8, 1864, O.R., Ser. II, Vol. 6, pp. 1058–1067.

31. W. Hoffman to E. M. Stanton, March 27, 1864, O.R., Ser. II, Vol. 6, pp. 1058–1067.

32. W. P. Richardson to Col. W. Hoffman, July 19, 1864, O.R., Ser. II, Vol. 7, p. 475.

33. Statement of Henry Grover, O.R., Ser. II, Vol. 6, p. 1066.

34. Statement of J. S. Sapp, O.R., Ser. II, Vol. 6, p. 1066.

35. W. P. Richardson to Col. W. Hoffman, July 19, 1864, O.R., Ser. II, Vol. 7, pp. 474–475.

36. W. Hoffman to Col. W. P. Richardson, commanding Camp Chase, Ohio, from Washington, D.C., July 27, 1864, O.R. Ser. II, Vol. 7, pp. 502–503; W. P. Richardson to Col. W. Hoffman, Camp Chase, Ohio, August 12, 1864, O.R., Ser. II, Vol. 7, pp. 584–585.

37. B. R. Cowen to Hon. John Brough, governor, August 1, 1864, O.R., Ser. II, Vol. 7 pp. 528–529.

38. "Abstracts from the Monthly Reports of Prisoners at Camp Chase, July 1862 through July 1865 (incomplete as of January 29, 2004), online at www.geocities.com/Pentagon/Quarters/5109/abstracts.html.

39. *Confederate Veteran,* Vol. XX (1912), pp. 296–297, cited in Speer, *Portals to Hell,* p. 223.

40. *Confederate Veteran,* Vol. XX (1912), pp. 296–297; A. H. Poten to Col. W. Wallace, O.R. Ser. II, Vol. VI, p. 855.

41. *Confederate Veteran,* Vol. XX (1912), pp. 296–297; Speer, *Portals to Hell,* p. 223.

42. W. P. Richardson to Col. W. Hoffman, July 19, 1864, O.R., Ser. II, Vol. 7, p. 474.

43. A. J. Morey, to the *Avalanche,* Memphis, TN, December 11, 1861, O.R., Ser. II, Vol. 1, pp. 544–546.

44. "Camp Chase Prison," online www.censusdiggins.com/proson_campchase.html.

Chapter III

1. "Just the Arti-Facts: A Prisoner's Diary," Chicago Historical Society, online at www.chicagohistory.org/AOTM/Apr98/apr98fact1a.html.

2. Speer, *Portals to Hell,* p. 324; *Medical Surgical Study,* p. 63, cited in George Levy, *To Die in Chicago: Confederate Prisoners at Camp Douglas, 1862–1865.* (Evanston, IL: Evanston Publishing, Inc., 1994), p. 271; Chicago Historical Society, "Douglas/Grand Boulevard: The Past and the Promise," online at www.chicagohistory.org/DGBPhoto Essay/DBG02.html.

3. "Illinois in the Civil War: Camp Douglas, Illinois," online at www.illinoiscivilwar.org/campdouglas.html.

4. Speer, *Portals to Hell,* p. 324.

5. Ibid., pp. 71–72.

6. Speer, *Portals to Hell,* pp. 71–72. The barracks were one-story frame buildings. A photo of the barracks may be seen at http://www.chicagohistory.org/DGBPhotoEssay/DGB02.html.

7. Levy, *To Die in Chicago,* p. 271.

8. Ryan, "Experiences of a Confederate Soldier in Camp and Prison in the Civil War 1861–1865."

9. *Site of Camp Douglas* (Chicago Historical Society, n.p., n.d.), p. 5, cited in Speer, *Portals to Hell,* p. 72–73

10. Tuttle, *The History of Camp Douglas,* p. 19, 21, cited in Levy, *To Die in Chicago,* p. 271.

11. Col. Joseph H. Tucker to Colonel Hoffman, Camp Douglas, Chicago, July 24, 1862, O.R. Ser. II, Vol. 4, pp. 279.

12. *Site of Camp Douglas,* cited in Speer, *Portals to Hell,* p. 72–73

13. Edward D. Kittoe, Surgeon, to R. C. Wood, assistant surgeon-general, January 18, 1864, O.R., Ser. II, Vol. 6, pp. 848–849.

14. Ibid., pp. 849–850.

15. Ibid., pp. 849–851.

16. L. C. Skinner to Col. B. J. Sweet, May 10, 1864, O.R., Ser. II, Vol. 7, pp. 142–143.

17. "Camp Douglas Prison," online at www.censusdiggins.com/prison_camp_douglas.html.

18. Levy, *To Die in Chicago,* pp. 124–125.

19. Ryan, "Experiences of a Confederate Soldier in Camp and Prison in the Civil War 1861–1865."

20. Ibid.

21. Lt. Col. W. Hoffman to Col. J. A. Mulligan, May 2, 1862, O.R., Ser. II, Vol. 3, p. 513.

22. Col. Joseph H. Tucker to Colonel Hoffman, Camp Douglas, Chicago, July 24, 1862, O.R. Ser. II, Vol. 4, pp. 279.

23. Maj. Gen. H. W. Halleck to Col. James A. Mulligan, April 8, 1862, O.R., Ser. II, Vol. 3, p. 433.

24. Gov. Richard Yates to General Halleck, April 8, 1862, O.R., Ser. II, Vol. 3, p. 433.

25. Col. Joseph H. Tucker to Colonel Hoffman, Camp Douglas, Chicago, July 24, 1862, O.R. Ser. II, Vol. 4, pp. 91–92.

26. Col. W. Hoffman to Gen. L. Thomas, July 1, 1862, O.R., Ser. II, Vol. 4, p. 111.

27. Col. W. Hoffman to E. M. Stanton, Secretary of War, August 1, 1862, O.R., Ser. II, Vol. 4, pp. 323–324.

28. Col. Joseph H. Tucker to Colonel Hoffman, Camp Douglas, Chicago, July 24, 1862, O.R. Ser. II, Vol. 4, pp. 278–279.

29. Col. W. Hoffman to E. M. Stanton, September 10, 1862, O.R., Ser. II, Vol. 4, pp. 503–504.

30. Col. Charles V. De Land to Colonel Hoffman, Camp Douglas, October 28, 1863, O.R., Ser. II, Vol. 6, p. 434.

31. Ibid.

32. Ibid.

33. Levy, *To Die in Chicago*, p. 129.

34. Ibid., p. 126.

35. Brig. Gen. William W. Orme to Edwin M. Stanton, December 7, 1863, O.R., Ser. II, Vol. 6, p. 661.

36. Levy, *To Die in Chicago*, p. 129.

37. Troy Taylor, "Camp Douglas: 'Eighty Acres of Hell' in a Confederate Prison Camp," online at www.prairieghosts.com/campd.html.

38. Levy, *To Die in Chicago*, pp. 124–125.

39. Boatner, *The Civil War Dictionary*, pp. 568–569.

40. Photograph, Chicago Historical Society, reproduced in Levy, p. 122.

41. Charles V. De Land to Colonel Hoffman, October 28, 1863, O.R., Ser. II, Vol. 6, pp. 434–435, cited in Levy, p. 129.

42. Col. Charles V. De Land to Col. William Hoffman, Camp Douglas, December 3, 1863, O.R., Ser. II, Vol. 6, pp. 637–638.

43. Ibid.

44. Brig. Gen. Wm. W. Orme to Col. William Hoffman, January 20, 1864, O.R., Ser. II, Vol. 6, pp. 860–861.

45. Col. Charles V. De Land to Col. William Hoffman, Camp Douglas, December 3, 1863, O.R., Ser. II, Vol. 6, p. 638.

46. Egbert L. Davis, "The James Henry Shore Family," in Frances H.Casstevens, ed., *Heritage of Yadkin County, North Carolina* (Winston-Salem, NC: Hunter Publishing Co., 1981), pp. 588–589.

47. Ibid.

48. B. R. Froman, "An Interior View of the Camp Douglas Conspiracy," *Southern Bivouac*, Vol. I, no. 2 (Oct 1882), p. 65, cited in Levy, p. 204.

49. R. T. Bean, "Seventeen Months in Camp Douglas," *Confederate Veteran*, Vol. 22 (June 1914), p. 311, cited in Levy, p. 204.

50. Levy, *To Die in Chicago*, p. 204.

51. B. J. Sweet to Col. William Hoffman, May 13, 1864, O.R., Ser. II, Vol. 7, p. 142.

52. Col. B. J. Sweet to Col. William Hoffman, June 2, 1864, O. R., Ser. II, Vol. 7, pp. 187–188.

53. Col. B. J. Sweet to Col. William Hoffman, August 15, 1864, O.R., Ser. II, Vol. 7, pp. 595–596.

54. Robert N. Scott, Assistant Adjutant General to Col. William Hoffman, October 31, 1864, O.R., Ser. II, Vol. 7, p. 1067.

55. Levy, *To Die in Chicago*, p. 203.

56. Ibid.

57. Col. B. J. Sweet to Col. William Hoffman, Camp Douglas, September 30, 1864, O.R., Ser. II, Vol. 7, p. 897.

58. Levy, *To Die in Chicago*, p. 203.

59. "Abstract from monthly reports of the principal U.S. Military prisons," O.R., Ser. II, Vol. 8, p. 998.

60. Levy, p. 213.

61. "Abstract from monthly reports of the principal U.S. Military prisons," O.R., Ser. II, Vol. 8, p. 998.

62. *Chicago Tribune*, 31 October 1864; Burke, October 29, 1864, cited in Levy, p. 213.

63. Levy, *To Die in Chicago*, p. 214.

64. Boatner, *The Civil War Dictionary*, p. 468.

65. Ibid., pp. 864–865.

66. Col. J. B. Sweet to Brig. Gen. W. Hoffman, November 7, 1864, O.R., Ser. I, Vol. 39, Pt. III, p. 696.

67. General Order No. 2, Headquarters, Cavalry Corps, A.N. Va., September 14, 1863, O.R., Ser. I, Vol. 29, Pt. II, p. 721.

68. "List of names of prominent members of Sons of Liberty in the several counties of the State of Illinois," Ser. I, Vol. 45, Pt. I, pp. 1082–1083; Jno. Cook, brigadier-general, commanding to Col. N. P. Chipman, Springfield, IL, November 10, 1864, O. R., Ser. I, Vol. 39, Pt. III, p. 739; Colonel B. J. Sweet to Col. N. P. Chipman, Camp Douglas, December 10, 1864, Ser. I, Vol. 45, Pt. II, p. 142

69. "Schedule of arms, ammunition, and equipment seized," O.R., Ser. I, Vol. 45, Pt. I, pp. 1081–1082.

70. J. Holt, judge-advocate general, to the president, June 29, 1865, O.R., Ser. II, Vol. I, pp. 684–689; 39th Congress, 2nd Session, House of Representatives, Executive Document No. 50, *The Case of George St. Leger Grenfel* (Washington, DC: U.S. Government Printing Office, 1867), p. 191, cited in Levy, p. 220.

71. Levy, *To Die in Chicago*, p. 275.

72. "Abstract from monthly reports of the principal U.S. Military prisons," O.R., Ser. II, Vol. 8, pp. 986–1003.

73. M. Briggs to Col. B. J. Sweet, Camp Douglas, Chicago, IL, December 25, 1864, O.R., Ser. II, Vol. 7, p. 1275.

74. Chicago Historical Society, "Douglas/Grand Boulevard: The Past & Present," online www.chigohistory.org/DGBPhotoEssay/DGB02.html.

75. "Camp Douglas Prison," online www.census-diggins.com/prison_camp_douglas.html.

Chapter IV

1. John A. Wyeth, "Cold Cheer at Camp Morton," *The Century*, Vol. 41, No. 6 (April 1891), p. 847.

2. Speer, *Portals to Hell*, p. 324.

3. W. P. A. *Indiana* (New York: Oxford University Press, 1941), pp. 210, 221, cited in Speer, *Portals to Hell*, p. 75.

4. Tim Beckman, "Camp Morton—Civil War Camp and Union Prison 1816–1865, Indianapolis, Indiana,"online http://freepages.history.rootsweb.com/~indiana42nd/campmorton.htm.

5. Thomas Sturgis, *Prisoners of War 1861–65: A Record of Personal Experiences, and a Study of the Conditions and Treatment of Prisoners on Both Sides During the War of the Rebellion* (New York: G. P. Putnam's Sons, 1912), p. 269.

6. W. Hoffman to E. M. Stanton, April 23, 1863, O.R., Ser. II, Vol. 5, pp. 511–512.

7. A. B. Feuer, "John Grady and the Confederate Prisoners at Camp Morton," *Civil War Quarterly* (September 1987), p. 43; Frost, *Camp & Prison Journal*, p. 255, cited in Speer, *Portals to Hell*, p. 75.

8. Col. Richard Owens to Col. W. Hoffman, Camp Morton, May 4, 1862, O.R., Ser. II, Vol. 3, p. 517.

9. Indiana State Archives, "Databases—Camp Morton," online www.in.gov/icpr/archives/databases/civilwar/camp/camp1862.html.

10. H. W. Freedley to Col. William Hoffman, March 24, 1863.

11. Speer, *Portals to Hell*, p. 76.

12. Sturgis, *Prisoners of War 1861–65*, p. 269.

13. Wyeth, p. 849.

14. Speer, *Portals to Hell*, p. 76.

15. Wyeth, "Cold Cheer at Camp Morton," pp. 844–847.

16. Ibid., p. 847.

17. Maj. Gen. H. W. Halleck to Governor O. P. Morton, February 18, 1862, O.R., Ser. II, Vol. 3, pp. 277, 333.

18. Noble to Edwin M. Stanton, Indianapolis, February 27, 1862, O.R., Ser. II, Vol. 3, p. 333.

19. *Indianapolis Journal*, March 4, 1862, quoted in W. H. H. Terrell, *Indiana in the War of the Rebellion: Official Report of W. H. H. Terrell, Adjutant General*, Vol. I (Indianapolis: Douglass & Conner, Printers, 1869), p. 548.

20. W. Hoffman to Gen. M. C. Meigs, March 5, 1862, O.R., Ser. II, Vol. 3, pp. 348–349.

21. Wyeth, "Cold Cheer at Camp Morton," p. 848.

22. W. Hoffman to Capt. James A. Ekin, assistant quartermaster, March 12, 1862, O.R., Ser. II, Vol. 3, p. 375.

23. Speer, *Portals to Hell*, pp. 76–77.

24. Col. Richard Owens to editor of *Indianapolis Journal*, April 18, 1862, O.R., Ser. II, Vol. 3, pp. 517–518.

25. Indiana State Archives, "Databases — Camp Morton," online.

26. Col. Richard Owens to editor of *Indianapolis Journal*.

27. "Rules for Camp Morton, O.R., Ser. II, Vol. 3, pp. 518–519.

28. Wyeth, "Cold Cheer at Camp Morton," p. 850.

29. Ibid.

30. Thomas E. Spotswood, "Horrors of Camp Morton," *The Memphis Commercial* online at www.csa-dixie.com/prisoners/t59.htm.

31. John Franklin Champenois, "For the Standard Life in Camp Morton, 1863–1865," online www.champenois.com/genealogy/campmorton.html.

32. Wyeth, "Cold Cheer at Camp Morton," p. 849.

33. Col. Richard Owens to Col. W. Hoffman, Camp Morton, April 18, 1862, O.R., Ser. II, Vol. 3, p. 517.

34. James A. Ekin to E. M. Stanton, July 15, 1862, O.R., Ser. II, Vol. 4, p. 225.

35. "Abstract from monthly returns of the principal U.S. Military prisons," Ser. II, Vol. 8, p. 986.

36. Col. A. A. Stevens, commanding Camp Morton, to Capt. W. T. Hartz, January 27, 1864, O.R., Ser. II, Vol. 6, pp. 884–885; A. A. Stevens to Col. William Hoffman, February 9, 1864, Ser. II, Vol. 6, pp. 941–942.

37. "Abstract from monthly returns of the principal U.S. Military prisons," Ser. II, Vol. 8, p. 994.

38. Wyeth, "Cold Cheer at Camp Morton," p. 849.

39. Ibid.

40. Capt. Robert M. Littler to Col. A. A. Stevens, February 12, 1864, O.R., Ser. II, Vol. 6, p. 946.

41. A. A. Stevens, February 15, 1864, Ser. II, Vol. 6, pp. 946–947.

42. A. A. Stevens to Col. W. Hoffman, October 3, 1864, O.R., Ser. II, Vol. 7, p. 916.

43. Testimony of First Lt. J. W. Davison, in report from A. A. Stevens to Col. W. Hoffman, October 3, 1864, O.R., Ser. II, Vol. 7, pp. 916–917.

44. A. A. Stevens, February 15, 1864, Ser. II, Vol. 6, pp. 946–947.

45. A. A. Stevens to Col. William Hoffman, March 13, 1864, O.R., Ser. II, Vol. 6, pp. 1043–1044.

46. Endorsement on report of A. A. Stevens by W. Hoffman, March 21, 1864, O.R., Ser. II, Vol. 6, p. 1044.

47. "Abstract from monthly returns of the principal U.S. Military prisons," Ser. II, Vol. 8, p. 994.

48. A. A. Stevens to Col. W. Hoffman, October 3, 1864, Ser. II, Vol. 7, pp. 915–916.

49. Feuer, *John Grady and the Confederate Prisoners at Camp Morton*, p. 47, cited in Speer, *Portals to Hell*, p. 223.

50. Sturgis, *Prisoners of War 1861–65*, p. 268.

51. C. T. Alexander to Col. W. Hoffman, August 6, 1864, O.R., Ser. II, Vol. 7, pp. 554–555.

52. H. B. Carrington to Lt.. Col. S. H. Lathrop, August 23, 1864, O. R., Ser. I, Vol. 39, Pt. II, p. 293.

53. Ibid., p. 296.

54. Wyeth, "Cold Cheer at Camp Morton," p. 849.

55. "Abstract from monthly returns of the principal U.S. Military prisons," Ser. II, Vol. 8, pp. 997–998.

56. A. A. Stevens to Col. W. Hoffman, October 2, 1864, Ser. II, Vol. 7, p. 911; George Wagner, Special Order No. 41, Ser. II, Vol. 7, pp. 911–912; testimony of Capt. Robert C. Hicks, O.R., Ser. II, Vol. 7, p. 912.

57. Testimony of Corporal De Witt, and Samuel Henderson, O.R., Ser. II, Vol. 7, p. 912.

58. Col. William Hoffman to Col. A. A. Stevens, October 3, 1864, O.R., Ser. II, Vol. 7, p. 919.

59. J. W. Davidson to Col. A. A. Stevens, January 8, 1865, O.R., Ser. II, Vol. 8, p. 44.

60. Wyeth, "Cold Cheer at Camp Morton," p. 850.

61. Ibid.

62. Ibid.

63. Sturgis, *Prisoners of War 1861–65*, pp. 271–272.

64. Champenois, "For the Standard: Life in Camp Morton, 1863–1865," online.

65. W. R. Holloway to Edwin M. Stanton, September 3, 1863, O.R., Ser. III, Vol. 3, p. 766.

66. Edwin M. Stanton to Governor Morton, September 19, 1863, O.R., Ser. III, Vol. 3, p. 824.

67. Wyeth, "Cold Cheer at Camp Morton," p. 849.

68. Beckman, "Camp Morton — Civil War Camp and Union Prison 1861–1865, Indianapolis, Indiana," online.

69. Abstract from monthly returns of the principal U.S. Military prisons," Ser. II, Vol. 8, pp. 1000–1003

70. Beckman, "Camp Morton — Civil War Camp and Union Prison 1816–1865, Indianapolis, Indiana," online.

71. Abstract from monthly returns of the principal U.S. Military prisons," Ser. II, Vol. 8, pp. 1000–1003

72. Holloway, "Treatment of Prisoners at Camp Morton," pp. 757–771.

73. John A. Wyeth, et al., "Rejoinder by Dr. Wyeth," *The Century*, Vol. 42, No. 5, (September 1891), pp. 771–776.

74. Beckman, "Camp Morton — Civil War Camp and Union Prison 1816–1865, Indianapolis, Indiana," online.

Chapter V

1. *Confederate Veteran*, Vol. XX (1912), p. 327, cited in Speer, *Portals to Hell*, p. 241; Taylor, "Prison Experience in Elmira, N. Y.," online.

2. Speer, *Portals to Hell*, pp. 241, 325,

3. Clay W. Holmes, *The Elmira Prison Camp: A History of the Military Prison at Elmira, N.Y., July 6,*

1864, to July 10, 1865 (New York: G. P. Putnam's Sons, 1912), p. 293.

4. Porter, G. W. D. "Nine Months in Northern Prison," online www.tennessee-scv.org/4455/9months.htm.

5. Ibid.

6. Pearson and Hoffsommer, "In Vinculis: A Prisoner of War, Part I," pp. 34–39, p. 29.

7. Ibid., p. 30.

8. Ibid.

9. *Confederate Veteran*, Vol. XX (1912), p. 327; Miles O. Sherrill, *A Soldier's Story: Prison Life and Other Incidents in the War of 1861–65* (sl:s.n., 1904?), pp. 5–10 (Electronic edition, University of North Carolina at Chapel Hill Libraries, online at http://docsouth.unc.edu/sherrill.menu.html), p. 15, both cited in Speer, *Portals to Hell*, p.241.

10. L. Leon, *Diary of a Tar Heel Confederate Soldier* (Charlotte, NC: Stone Publishing Company, 1913), p. 67.

11. Pearson and Hoffsommer, p. 33.

12. Pearson and Hoffsommer, "In Vinculis: A Prisoner of War, Part II," p. 26.

13. Pearson and Hoffsommer, Part II, p. 29.

14. Holmes, *The Elmira Prison Camp*, p. 301.

15. Sherrill, *A Soldier's Story*, pp. 5–10.

16. Porter, "Nine Months in Northern Prison," online.

17. Pearson and Hoffsommer, p. 32.

18. Porter, "Nine Months in Northern Prison," online.

19. Ibid.

20. S. Eastman to Col. William Hoffman, Elmira, N. Y., August 7, 1864, O.R., Ser. II, Vol. 7, p. 560; W. Hoffman to Lt. Col. S. Eastman, August 12, 1864, O. R. Ser. II, Vol. 7, p. 584; W. Hoffman to Col. B. F. Tracy, October 3, 1864, O.R. Ser. II, Vol. 7, pp. 918–9919; "Abstract from monthly returns of the principal U.S. Military prisons," O.R., Ser. II, Vol. 8, pp. 997–998.

21. Sherrill, *A Soldier's Story*, pp. 5–10.

22. Pearson and Hoffsommer, p. 31.

23. Holmes, *The Elmira Prison Camp*, pp. 254–255.

24. Ibid., p. 294.

25. E. F. Sanger, surgeon, to Lieutenant Lounsbury, Elmira, N. Y., August 13, 1864, O.R., Ser. II, Vol. 7, p. 604.

26. E. F. Sanger to Brig. Gen. J. K. Barnes, Elmira, N. Y., November 1, 1864, O.R., Ser. II, Vol. 7, p. 1092.

27. "Abstract from monthly returns of the principal U.S. Military prisons," O.R. Ser. II, Vol. 8, pp. 999–1001.

28. William F. Fox, *Regimental Losses in The American Civil War 1861–1865* (Albany, NY: Brandow, 1898; reprint edition. Dayton, OH: Morningside House, 1985), p. 51; Speer, *Portals to Hell*, p. 235.

29. "Abstract from monthly returns of the principal U.S. Military prisons," O.R., Ser. II, Vol. 8, pp. 997–1003; Holmes, p. 151.

30. Holmes, *The Elmira Prison Camp*, p. 167.

31. Michael Horigan, *Elmira: Death Camp of the North* (Mechanicsburg, PA: Stackpole Books, 2002), p. 105.

32. Holmes, *The Elmira Prison Camp*, p. 167.

33. Philip Burnham, *So Far From Dixie* (Lanham, MD: Taylor Trade Puablishing, 2003), p. 167.

34. Holmes, *The Elmira Prison Camp*, p. 151.

35. A. I. Schutzer, *Great Civil War Escapes* (New York: G. P. Putnam's Sons, 1967), pp. 138–142; Burnham, *So Far from Dixie*, p. 167.

36. Letter from M. T. Wade, Atlanta, GA, Oct. 23, 1911, to Clay W. Holmes, in Holmes, *The Elmira Prison Camp*, pp. 330–331.

37. Ibid.

38. Toney, *The Privations of a Private*, Commager, editor. *The Blue and the Gray*, p. 702.

39. Washington B. Traweek, "Recollections of Washington B. Traweek: Escaping Elmira," excerpted from transcription of Traweek's original memoirs, courtesy of R. Books Traweek, online at www.angelfire.com/ny5/elmiraprison/traweek.html.

40. Horigan, *Elmira: Death Camp of the North*, 110.

41. Letter from Mel Traweek, Ph.D., to Ms. Constance Barone, director of the Chemung County Historical Society, file 500–320, June 13, 1996, cited in Horigan, p. 106.

42. Holmes, *The Elmira Prison Camp*, p. 106.

43. Traweek, "Recollections,".

44. Ibid.

45. Ibid.

46. Ibid.

47. *Montgomery* (Alabama) *Advertiser*, June 22, 1902. cited in Horigan, p. 110.

48. Horigan, *Elmira: Death Camp of the North*, pp. 111–112.

49. Schutzer, *Great Civil War Escapes*, pp. 143, 173.

50. Schutzer, *Great Civil War Escapes*, pp. 175–186.

51. Ibid., pp. 186–190.

52. Burnham, *So Far From Dixie*, pp.135–151; Susan W. Benson, ed., *Berry Benson's Civil War Book: Memoirs of a Confederate Scout and Sharpshooter* (Athens, GA: University of Georgia Press, 1962). See also The Berry Greenwood Benson Papers, 1843–1922, no. 2636, Southern Historical Collection, University of North Carolina, Chapel Hill, North Carolina.

53. Burnham, *So Far from Dixie*, p. 139.

54. Horigan, *Elmira: Death Camp of the North*, p. 113.

55. Toney, *The Privations of a Private*, p. 95, cited in Horigan, p. 113.

56. "Sergeant Womack's Escape," Holmes, *The Elmira Prison Camp*, pp. 151–159; Burnham, *So Far from Dixie*, pp. 169–170.

57. Burnham, *So Far from Dixie* p. 167.

58. George R. Farr, "The Federal Confederate Prisoner of War Camp at Elmira," online http://www.rootsweb.com/~srgp/military/elmcivwr.htm.

59. "Elmira Prison Revisited," online www.rootsweb.com/~srgp/articles/elmirevis.htm; "Union Civil War Prison at Elmira, NY," online http://home.jamrr.com/rcourt52/cwprisons/elmiran.htm.

Chapter VI

1. W. Emerson Wilson, *Fort Delaware in the Civil War, Revised edition* (Delaware City, DE: Fort Delaware Society, n.d.), n.p.

2. *New York Times*, November 6, 1863, p. 1:2 cited in Speer, *Portals to Hell*, pp. 46, 325

3. Francis Trevelyan Miller, ed., *Photographic History of the Civil War*, Vol. 7, (New York: The Review of Reviews Co., 1911; reprinted, New York: Castle Books, 1975), p. 65.

4. Wilson, *Fort Delaware in the Civil War.*

5. Miller, *Photographic History of the Civil War*, p. 44.

6. "Welcome to the Official Fort Delaware Society Webpage," online.

7. Warren D. Reid, "Escaped from Fort Delaware," *Southern Historical Society Papers*, Vol. 36 (Richmond, VA: Southern Historical Society, 1908), pp. 271–272.

8. George W. Rivenbark, "Two Years at Fort Delaware," in Walter Clark, ed., *Histories of the Several Regiments of North Carolina Troops....*Vol. IV, p. 726. Note at the end of this article. "The above was written in 1874 and published in our "Living and Dead." It has now been revised by its author for this work."

9. Miller, *Photographic History of the Civil War*, p. 44.

10. Ibid., p. 65.

11. Barziza, *Decimus et Ultimus Barziza*, p. 89, cited in Speer, *Portals to Hell*, p. 145.

12. Tom Jenkins Journal, cited in Dale Fetzer and Bruce Mowday, *Unlikely Allies: Fort Delaware's Prison Community in the Civil War* (Mechanicsburg, PA: Stackpole Books, 2000), pp. 112–113.

13. Brown, "Fort Delaware," p. 37; Wilson, *Fort Delaware*, p. 11, both cited in Speer, *Portals to Hell*, 145.

14. Wilson, *Fort Delaware in the Civil War.*

15. Rich, *Comrades Four*, p. 94, cited in Nancy TravisKeen, *Confederate Prisoners of War at Fort Delaware*, p. 5.

16. Reid, "Escaped from Fort Delaware," pp. 271–272.

17. Ibid., p. 272.

18. C. H. Crane to Col. William Hoffman, "Inspection report of prisoners of war at Fort Delaware, September 3, 1863," Washington, D.C., September 11, 1863, O.R., Ser. II, Vol. 6, p. 281.

19. A. Schoepf to Brig. Gen. H. W. Wessels, Fort Delaware, Del., December 14, 1864, O.R., Ser. II, Vol. 7, p. 1221.

20. Frost, "Camp and Prison Journal," online www.civilwarstlouis.com/Gratiot/frost2.htm.

21. Wilson, *Fort Delaware in the Civil War.*

22. Brown, "Fort Delaware: The Most Dreaded Northern Prison," p. 36, cited in Speer, *Portals to Hell*, p. 46.

23. Wilson, *Fort Delaware in the Civil War.*

24. Ibid.

25. Rivenbark, "Two Years at Fort Delaware," pp. 725–726.

26. Ibid., p. 726.

27. Ibid.

28. Ibid.

29. Cashin, "Confederate States Naval and Other Maritime Prisoners Held at Fort Delaware," online; "Ships, Blockades & Raiders: Greyhound 'Short-lived Blockade Runner' 1863–1764, online; United States Naval War Records, Ser. I, Vol. 10, pp. 42–43. See also Bell Boyd, *Belle Boyd in Camp and Prison* (Baton Rouge: Louisiana State University Press, 1998).

30. W. Hoffman to Maj. Gen. S. P. Heintzelman, Washington, D.C., March 18, 1864, O.R., Ser. II, Vol. 6, p.1076.

31. A. J. Hamilton, *A Fort Delaware Journal: The Diary of a Yankee Private A. J. Hamilton, 1862–1865*, W. Emerson Wilson, ed. (Wilmington, DE: The Fort Delaware Society, 1981), pp. 50–51.

32. Fetzer and Mowday, *Unlikely Allies*, pp. 109, 156; Boatner, *The Civil War Dictionary*, p. 23;

33. Fetzer and Mowday, pp. 69–72.

34. Ibid., p. 72.

35. Ibid.

36. Ibid., p. 106.

37. Ibid., pp. 106–107.

38. Ibid., pp. 136–138.

39. Ibid., pp. 31, 67, 73.

40. Miller, *Photographic History of the Civil War*, p. 65; Speer, *Portals to Hell*, pp. 144–145; Fetzer and Mowday, *Unlikely Allies*, p. 94;

41. Tom Jenkins Journal, cited in Fetzer and Mowday, *Unlikely Allies*, pp. 112–113.

42. "New Diary Discovered," *Fort Delaware Society Notes* (Dec. 1975), pp. 2–3, cited in Fetzer and Mowday, *Unlikely Allies*, p. 130.

43. Rivenbark, "Two Years at Fort Delaware," p. 727.

44. Keen, *Confederate Prisoners of War at Fort Delaware*, p. 11.

45. Rivenbark, "Two Years at Fort Delaware," p. 728.

46. Keen, *Confederate Prisoners of War at Fort Delaware*, p. 23; Rivenbark, "Two Years at Fort Delaware," p. 727.

47. Keen, *Confederate Prisoners of War at Fort Delaware*, pp. 10–11.

48. Rivenbark, "Two Years at Fort Delaware," p. 730.

49. "Prison Rules at Fort Delaware," *Southern Historical Society Paper*, Vol. 1, No. 4 (April 1876), p. 292.

50. "Experience of Dr. I. W. K. Handy," *Southern Historical Society Papers*, Vol. I, No. 4 (April 1876), p. 272.

51. Ibid., p. 273.

52. Ibid., p. 64.

53. Wilson, *Fort Delaware in the Civil War.*

54. *The Papers of Randolph Abbott Shotwell*, in Henry Steel Commager, ed. *The Blue and the Gray* (New York: The Fairfax Press, 1982), pp. 697–700.

55. *Confederate Veteran* Vol. XIII (1905), p. 107, *Confederate Veteran*, Vol. XX (1212), p. 114, cited in Speer, *Portals to Hell*, p. 144.

56. *Confederate Veteran* Vol. XXI (1913), pp. 592–593, cited in Speer, *Portals to Hell*, p. 144.

57. Fetzer and Mowday, *Unlikely Allies*, p. 64.

58. Rivenbark, "Two Years at Fort Delaware," p. 721.

59. Ibid.

60. Wilson, *Fort Delaware in the Civil War.*

61. Fetzer and Mowday, *Unlikely Allies*, p. 109.

62. Wilson, *Fort Delaware in the Civil War;* Fetzer and Mowday, *Unlikely Allies* , p. 64.

63. Letters of Pvt. George M. Green, cited in Fetzer and Mowday, *Unlikely Allies* , p. 64.

64. W. Hoffman to Maj. Gen. B. F. Butler, Washington, D.C., June 13, 1864, O.R., Ser. II, Vol. 7, p. 368, and W. Hoffman to Brig. Gen. A. Schoepf, June 13, 1864, O.R., Ser. II, Vol. 7, pp. 368–369.

65. Hamilton, *A Fort Delaware Journal*, footnote 8, p. 55.

66. Fetzer and Mowday, *Unlikely Allies* , pp. 122, 156–157.

67. Col. Basil W. Duke, prisoner of war, to Brig. Gen. A. Schoepf, Fort Delaware, March 11, 1864, Ser. II, Vol. 6, p. 1036.

68. W. Hoffman to Brig. Gen. A. Schoepf, June 13, 1864, O.R., Ser. II, Vol. 7, p. 369.

69. Speer, *Portals to Hell*, p. 228.

70. "Abstract from monthly returns of the principal U.S. Military prisons," June 1863, in O.R., Ser. II, Vol. 8, p. 990.

71. Fetzer and Mowday, *Unlikely Allies* , p. 110.

72. *Delaware Gazette*, July 22, 1862, cited in Keen, *Confederate Prisoners of War at Fort Delaware*, p. 24.

73. A. A. Gibson to General Lorenzo Thomas, Fort Delaware, July 16, 1862, O.R., Ser. II, Vol. 226, p. 226.

74. Fetzer and Mowday, *Unlikely Allies*, pp. 67–68.

75. "Abstract from monthly returns of the principal U.S. Military prisons," O.R., Ser. II, Vol. 8, p. 986.

76. Hamilton, *A Fort Delaware Journal*, p. 1.

77. Ibid., p. 16.

78. Ibid., p. 42.

79. "Abstract from monthly returns of the principal U.S. Military prisons," November and December 1863, in O.R., Ser. II, Vol. 8, p. 993.

80. Rivenbark, "Two Years at Fort Delaware," p. 729.

81. *Richmond Dispatch*, August 28, 1863, cited in Fetzer and Mowday, *Unlikely Allies* , p. 110.

82. Ibid.

83. Speer, *Portals to Hell*, p. 228.

84. *Confederate Veteran*, Vol. III (1895), p. 172; Vol. XXII (1914), pp. 227, 279; Vol. XXV (1917), pp. 512–513, cited in Speer, *Portals to Hell*, p. 228.

85. "Abstract from monthly returns of the principal U.S. Military prisons," August 1863, in O.R., Ser. II, Vol. 8, p. 991.

86. Reid, "Escaped from Fort Delaware," pp. 273–279.

87. Fetzer and Mowday, *Unlikely Allies*, pp. 110–111.

88. Ibid., p. 110; diary of Joseph E. Purvis, cited in Fetzer and Mowday, *Unlikely Allies* , p. 110.

89. Hamilton, *A Fort Delaware Journal*, p. 36.

90. "Abstract from monthly returns of the principal U.S. Military prisons," November and December 1863, in O.R., Ser. II, Vol. 8, p. 992.

91. Hamilton, *A Fort Delaware Journal*, p. 50.

92. "Abstract from monthly returns of the principal U.S. Military prisons," February 1864, in O.R., Ser. II, Vol. 8, p. 994.

93. Hamilton, *A Fort Delaware Journal*, p. 52.

94. "Abstract from monthly returns of the principal U.S. Military prisons," March 1864, in O.R., Ser. II, Vol. 8, p. 995.

95. Hamilton, *A Fort Delaware Journal*, p. 55.

96. "Abstract from monthly returns of the principal U.S. Military prisons," July 1864, in O.R., Ser. II, Vol. 8, p. 997.

97. Hamilton, *A Fort Delaware Journal*, p. 56.

98. Dickinson, *Diary of Captain Henry Dickinson*, p. 54, cited in Keen, *Confederate Prisoners of War at Fort Delaware*, p. 22.

99. Handy, *United States Bonds or Duress by Federal Authority*, pp. 49–50, cited in Keen, *Confederate Prisoners of War at Fort Delaware*, p. 22.

100. Hamilton, *A Fort Delaware Journal*, p. 57.

101. "Abstract from monthly returns of the principal U.S. Military prisons," August 1864, in O.R., Ser. II, Vol. 8, p. 997.

102. Ibid., p. 998.

103. Ibid., p. 999.

104. Handy, *United States Bonds or Duress by Federal Authority*, p. 166, cited in Keen, *Confederate Prisoners of War at Fort Delaware*, p. 23.

105. McHenry Howard, *Recollections of a Maryland Confederate Soldier and Staff Officer Under Johnston, Jackson, and Lee*, 1914, cited in Wilson, *Fort Delaware in the Civil War*.

106. Rivenbark, "Two Years at Fort Delaware," p. 730.

107. Ibid., pp. 731–732.

108. Handy, *United States Bonds or Duress by Federal Authority*, p. 490, cited in Keen, *Confederate Prisoners of War at Fort Delaware*, p. 24.

109. Rivenbark, "Two Years at Fort Delaware," p. 732.

110. Ibid., p. 729.

111. Ibid.

112. Hamilton, *A Fort Delaware Journal*, p. 21.

113. Ibid., p. 69.

114. Keen, *Confederate Prisoners of War at Fort Delaware*, p. 22.

115. W. H. Moon, "Prison Life at Fort Delaware," *Confederate Veteran*, Vol. XV (1907), p. 213, cited in Keen, *Confederate Prisoners of War at Fort Delaware*, p. 24.

116. "Abstract from monthly returns of the principal U.S. Military prisons," May 1865, in O.R., Ser. II, Vol. 8, p. 1002.

117. Fetzer and Mowday, *Unlikely Allies*, p. 139.

118. Ibid., p. 146.

119. Wilson, *Fort Delaware in the Civil War*.

120. "Welcome to the Official Fort Delaware Society Webpage," online at http://www.del.net/org/fort/

Chapter VII

1. Zarvona to Mr. Benjamin, secretary of war, Fort Lafayette, December 7, 1861, O.R., Ser. II, Vol. 2, p. 441.

2. Speer, *Portals to Hell*, pp. 35–38, 326.

3. "Abstract from monthly returns of the principal U.S. Military prisoners," O.R., Ser. II, Vol. 8, pp. 986–1004.

4. Speer, *Portals to Hell*, pp. 35–36

5. Ibid.

6. Howard, *Fourteen Months in American Bastiles*, pp. 18–29, cited in Speer, *Portals to Hell*, p. 36.

7. Ibid.

8. Ibid.

9. Speer, *Portals to Hell*, pp. 37, 164.

10. E. D. Townsend to Major General Banks, Washington, July 15, 1861, O. R., Ser. II, Vol. 3, p. 10; *New York Times*, September 24, 1861, p. 1:5, cited in Speer, *Portals to Hell*, p. 35.

11. Speer, *Portals to Hell*, p. 37.

12. E. D. Townsend to Major General Banks, July 15, 1861, O.R., Ser. II, Vol. 3, p. 10.

13. William H. Seward to Major General Dix, August 6, 1861, O.R., Ser. II, Vol. 2, p. 43.

14. Speer, *Portals to Hell*, p. 37.

15. From Record Book, State Department, "Arrests for Disloyalty," O.R., Ser. II, Vol. 2, pp. 913–915.

16. George B. McClellan to Sir [Commanding Officer Fort Lafayette], February 8, 1862, O.R., Ser. I, Vol. 5, p. 342.

17. Charles P. Stone to Brig. Gen. S. Williams, February 9, 1862, O.R., Ser. I, Vol. 5, p. 342; Chas. P. Stone to Lt. Col. Martin Burke, April 5, 1862, O.R., Ser. I, Vol. 5, p. 342.

18. Geo. B. McClellan to E. M. Stanton, September 7, 1862, O.R., Ser. I, Vol. 5, p. 342.

19. Boatner, *The Civil War Dictionary*, p. 800.

20. Robert Murray to E. M. Stanton, July 16, 1863, O.R., Ser. I, Vol. 27, Pt. II, p. 927.

21. Edwin M. Stanton to Lt. Col. Martin Burke, July 16, 1863, O.R., Ser. I, Vol. 27, Pt. II, p. 927.

22. Speer, *Portals to Hell*, pp. 36–37.

23. *New York Times*, January 18, 1862, p. 2:5, cited in Speer, *Portals to Hell*, p. 36.

24. Speer, *Portals to Hell*, p. 38.

25. Marshal J. Smith to James A. Seddon, Richmond, Va., August 18, 1864, O.R., Ser. II, Vol. 7, pp. 612–613.

26. *New York Times*, January 18, 1862, p. 2:5, cited in Speer, *Portals to Hell*, p. 38.

27. William H. Seward to Maj. Gen. John A. Dix, October 19, 1861, O.R., Ser. II, Vol. 1, p. 699; John A. Dix to Hon. William H. Seward, October 21, 1861, O.R., Ser. II, Vol. 1, p. 699; William H. Seward to Maj. Gen. John A. Dix, October 21, 1861, O.R., Ser. II, Vol. 1, p. 699.

28. R. D. Lynde to Lieutenant Colonel Burke, October 19, 1861, O.R., Ser. II, Vol. 1, p. 699.

29. Algernon S. Sullivan, attorney at law, to J. R. Tucker, New York, July 19, 1861, O.R., Ser. II, Vol. 3, pp. 11–12.

30. Footnote, O.R., Ser. II, Vol. 3, p. 20.

31. C. H. Marriott, et al., to William H. Seward, Fort Lafayette, February 12, 1862, O.R., Ser. II, Vol. 3, p. 258.

32. John Mack to E. M. Stanton, February 24, 1862, O.R., Ser. II, Vol. 3, p. 312.

33. Martin Burke to Adjutant General Thomas, May 30, 1862, O.R., Ser. II, Vol. 3, p. 611.

34. Edwin M. Stanton, Order No. 8, February 13, 1862, O.R., Ser. II, Vol. 3, pp. 258–259.

35. Lord Lyons to William H. Seward, October 28, 1861, O.R., Ser. II, Vol. 2, p. 550.

36. William H. Seward to Lord Lyon, October 29, 1861, O.R., Ser. II, Vol. 2, pp. 550–551.

37. Ibid.

38. *Baltimore Sun*, July 9, 1861; information from members of the Thomas family, quoted in Charles A. Earp, "The Amazing Colonel Zarvona," *Maryland Historical Magazine* 34 (1939), p. 334.

39. R. to John, April 26, 1861, O.R., Ser. II, Vol. 2, p. 400.

40. Scharf, *History of the Confederate States*, p. 114, cited in Earp, "The Amazing Colonel Zarvona," p. 334.

41. Earp, "The Amazing Colonel Zarvona," p. 335.

42. United States Naval War Records Office. *Official Records of the Union and Confederate Navies in the War of the Rebellion*, Ser I., Vol. 4, p. 555, hereinafter cited as O.R.N.

43. James D. McCabe, Jr., *History of the War between the States (1861–2)*, unpublished MS, dated Vicksburg, 1862, p. 257, cited in Earp, p. 336.

44. Statement of George W. Alexander quoted in Scharf, *History of the Confederate States Navy*, p. 115, cited in Earp, "The Amazing Colonel Zarvona," p. 337.

45. Governor Letcher to G. W. Randolph, secretary of war, June 20, 1862, O.R., Ser. II, Vol. 4, p. 781; Governor Letcher to President Lincoln, January 2, 1863, O.R., Ser. II, Vol. 2, p. 401.

46. *Baltimore American*, July 9, 1861, July 10, 1861; *Baltimore, Sun* July 9, 1861, cited in Earp, p. 339.

47. John A. Dix to Col. W. W. Morris, December 2, 1861, O.R., Ser. 2, Vol. 2, p. 383; Martin Burke to Col. E. D. Townsend, December 3, 1861, O.R., Ser. 2, Vol. 2, p. 383.

48. John A. Dix to Col. W. W. Morris, December 2, 1861, O.R., Ser. II, Vol. 2, p. 383; Martin Burke to Col. E. D. Townsend, New York Harbor, December 3, 1861, O.R., Ser. II, Vol. 2, p. 383.

49. E. D. Townsend to E. M. Stanton, February 10, 1863, O.R., Ser. II, Vol. 2, p. 404.

50. E. D. Townsend to General L. Thomas, February 27, 1862, O.R., Ser. II, Vol. 2, p. 394; Lt. Col. Burke to General Thomas, March 5, 1862, O.R., Ser. II, Vol. 2, p. 395; Thomas to Burke, February 28, 1862, O.R., Ser. II, Vol. 2, p. 394; W. W. Morris to Brig. Gen. L. Thomas, September 28, 1862, O.R., Ser. II, Vol. 2, p. 399. also cited in Earp, "The Amazing Colonel Zarvona," p. 341.

51. D. T. Van Buren, by order of Major General Dix, to Lt. Col. Martin Burke, commander at Fort Lafayette, December 2, 1861, O.R, Ser. II, Vol. 2, p. 165; Zarvona to William H. Seward, secretary of states, December 22, 1861, January 9, 1862, O.R., Ser. II, Vol. 2, pp. 386–387, also cited in Earp, "The Amazing Colonel Zarvona," p. 341.

52. Thomas Ingram to Hon. James A. Pearce, Fort Lafayette, February 3, 1863, O.R., Ser. II, Vol. 2, pp. 387–388; R. W. Rasin to William H. Suydam, Esq., Fort Lafayette, February 6, 1862, O.R., Ser. II, Vol. 2, p. 389.

53. Edwin M. Stanton to Maj. Gen. John A. Dix, February 17, 1862, O.R., Ser. II, Vol. 2, p. 389; John A. Dix to William H. Seward, February 20, 1862, O.R., Ser. II, Vol. 2, pp. 389–390.

54. John A. Dix to Edwin M. Stanton, February 20, 1862, O.R., Ser. II, Vol. 2, p. 390.

55. L. Thomas, Adjutant General to Lieut. Col. Martin Burg, February 28, 1862, O.R., Ser. II, Vol. 2, p. 394; E. D. Townsend to [Adj. Gen. L. Thomas], February 27, 1862, O.R., Ser. II, Vol. 2, p. 394.

56. Mrs. R. Thomas to Colonel Burke, April 3, 1862, O.R., Ser. II, Vol. 2, p. 296.

57. E. D. Townsend to E. M. Stanton, February 10, 1863, O.R., Ser. II, Vol. 2, p. 404.

58. First Lt. Charles O. Wood to Lt. Col. M. Burke, Fort Lafayette, New York Harbor, April 22, 1862, O.R., Ser. II, Vol. 2, pp. 396–397; Earp, "The Amazing Colonel Zarvona," p. 341.

59. Scharf, *History of St. Louis City and County*, p. 121.

60. Zarvona to Hon. Mr. Benjamin, Secretary of War, December 7, 1861, O.R., Ser. II, Vol. 2, pp. 411–412; O.R., Ser. II, Vol. 4, pp. 774–776; Earp, "The Amazing Colonel Zarvona," p. 341.

61. E. D. Townsend to Lt. Col. Martin Burke, Washington, D.C., June 27, 1862, O.R., Ser. II, Vol. 2, pp. 397–398.

62. Barziza, *The Adventures of a Prisoner of War, 1863–1864*, pp. 79–81, f2, p. 79. Speer, *Portals to Hell*, pp. 237–238.

63. Martrin Burke to Brig. Gen. D. T. Van Buren, February 10, 1866, O. R., Ser. II, Vol. 8, p. 881.

64. "Abstract from monthly returns of the principal U.S. Military prisoners," O.R., Ser. II, Vol. 8, pp. 986–1004.

65. Speer, *Portals to Hell*, p. 311.

Chapter VIII

1. Speer, *Portals to Hell*, pp. 45, 326.

2. Scott S. Sheads to Frances H. Casstevens, personal communication, Baltimore, Maryland, June 19, 2003. A database of the names and other pertinent information is scheduled for completion in 2004.

3. "Archaeological Treasures at Fort McHenry: An Overview," online at www.nps.gov/fomc/archeology/overview.html.

4. Speer, *Portals to Hell*, p. 45.

5. National Park Service, "Fort McHenry—Facts," online at www.bcpl.net/~etowner/facts.html.

6. "Fort McHenry—Facts."

7. Speer, *Portals to Hell*, p. 45.

8. E. W. Andrews to Bvt. Brig. Gen. W. W. Morris, September 8, 1863, O.R. Ser. II, Vol. 6, pp. 255–256; 1863; Col. P. A. Porter to William Hoffman, December 19, 1863, O.R., Ser. II, Vol. 6, pp. 720–723.

9. Speer, *Portals to Hell*, p. 45.

10. William P. Jones to E. M. Stanton, Baltimore, MD, August 15, 1862, O.R., Ser. II, Vol. 4, p. 395.

11. E. D. Townsend to Major General Banks, July 15, 1861, O.R., Ser. II, Vol. 3, p. 10.

12. John A. Dix to William H. Seward, December 9, 1861, O.R., Ser. II, Vol. 2, p. 383.

13. "Memoranda of Various Political Arrests—From Record Book, U.S. Department of State, "Arrests for Disloyalty," O.R., Ser. II, Vol. 2, p. 291.

14. "List of Political Prisoners at Fort McHenry, Md., November 19, 1861," O.R., Ser. II, Vol. 2, p. 152.

15. John A. Dix to William H. Seward, secretary of state, Baltimore, MD, February 17, 1862, O.R., Ser. II, Vol. 2, 226; "Report of political prisoners taken, released and remaining since March 4, 1861, at Fort McHenry, Md.," by Col. W. W. Morris, Commanding Post, Fort McHenry, February 16, 1862, O.R., Ser. II, Vol. 2, pp. 226–228.

16. W. Hoffman to Brig. Gen. S. A. Meredith, Washington, D.C., August 1, 1863, O.R., Ser. II, Vol. 6, p. 164.

17. Col. P. A. Porter to William Hoffman, December 19, 1863, O.R., Ser. II, Vol. 6, pp. 720–723.

18. Ibid., p. 723.

19. Ibid.

20. John A. Dix to P. H. Watson, Baltimore, MD., March 10, 1862, O.R., Ser. II, Vol. 2, p. 259.

21. W. Hoffman to E. M. Stanton, July 24, 1862, O.R., Ser. II, Vol. 4, p. 278.

22. "Abstract from monthly returns of the principal U.S. Military prisons," O.R., Ser. II, Vol. 8, p. 989.

23. Speer, *Portals to Hell*, p. 143.

24. "Abstract from monthly returns of the principal U.S. Military prisons," O.R., Ser. II, Vol. 8, pp. 991–1004.

25. Marshall J. Smith to Hon. James A. Seddon, Richmond, Va., August 18, 1864, O.R., Ser. II, Vol. 7, p. 612.

26. W. Hoffman to Brev. Brig. Gen. W. W. Morris, March 25, 1865, O.R., Ser. II, Vol. 8, p. 429.

27. W. Hoffman to Brig. Gen. S. A. Meredith, Washington, D.C., August 1, 1863, O.R., Ser. II, Vol. 6, p. 164.

28. Ibid.

29. *Baltimore Sun*, September 9, 1861, September 10, 1861.

30. "Old Castle Thunder," *Richmond Dispatch*, March 3, 1895.

31. "A Brave Confederate," *Baltimore Sun*, February 22, 1895.

32. Ibid. See also S. Z. Ammen, compl. "Doings of Maryland Boys in Gray, From '61 to '65. Sketches of the War." Baltimore, *The Telegram*, 1879 (part of 180 pages of newspaper clippings found in a scrapbook of articles which appeared in a Baltimore newspaper in 1879), courtesy of John Wyman.

33. "A Brave Confederate," *Baltimore Sun*, 22 February 1895; see also Ammen, "Doings of Maryland Boys in Gray."

34. Ibid.

35. Ibid.

36. John Letcher to Richard Thomas Zarvona, July 2, 1861, O.R., Ser. II, Vol. 2, p. 399.

37. S. Bassett French, aide-de-camp to governor of Virginia, Richmond, July 3, 1861, O.R., Ser. II, Vol. 2, p. 399.

38. Ammen, "Doings of Maryland Boys in Gray, From '61 to '65.

39. J. T. Scharf, *History of the Confederate States Navy*, p. 114, cited in Earp, p. 334.

40. "A Brave Confederate," *Baltimore Sun*, 22 February 1895; George N. Hollins, "Autobiography of Commodore Hollins, C.S.A.," *Maryland Historical Magazine* (September 1939), pp. 237–239; Professor J. Russel Soley, "Early Operations on the Potomac River." *Battles and Leaders of the Civil War*, Vol. II (Secaucus, N. J.: Castle, 1982), p. 143.

41. Earp, "The Amazing Colonel Zarvona," f22, p. 338.

42. Commodore George N. Hollis, "A Daring Exploit: The Capture of the Steamer Saint Nicholas," *Southern Historical Society Papers*, Vol. XXIV, 1896, pp. 88–92.

43. Ibid., p. 89.

44. Ibid.

45. Scharf, *History of the Confederate States Navy*, p. 114, cited in Earp, "The Amazing Colonel Zarvona," p. 337.

46. "A Brave Confederate," *Baltimore Sun*, February 22, 1895.

47. Ammen, "Doings of Maryland Boys in Gray."

48. "Maryland Volunteers," *Richmond Dispatch*, July 6, 1861, page 2.

49. "A Brave Confederate," *Baltimore Sun*, February 22, 1895.

50. *Baltimore American*, July 9, 1861; *Baltimore Sun*, July 9, 1861, cited in Earp, "The Amazing Colonel Zarvona," p. 339.

51. Earp, p. 340.

52. Townsend to Edwin Stanton, Secretary of War, February 10, 1863, O.R., Ser. II, Vol. 2, p. 404; Scharf, *History of Confederate Navy*, p. 121, cited in Earp, p. 340.

53. N. P. Banks to the Secretary of War, Fort McHenry, July 8, 1862, and N. P. Banks to Col. E. D. Townsend, Fort McHenry, July 8, 1862, O.R., Ser. II, Vol. 2, p. 380.

54. N. P. Banks to Col. E. D. Townsend, July 13, 1861, O.R., Ser. II, Vol. 2, p. 380.

55. Major General Dix to Edwin Stanton, February 20, 1862, O.R., Ser. II, Vol. 2, p. 390; Extract from record book, State Department, "Arrests for Disloy-

alty," O.R., Ser. II, Vol. 2, p. 379, cited in Earp, "The Amazing Colonel Zarvona," p. 340; "Case of Richard Thomas (Zarvona), O. R., Ser. II, Vol. 2, p. 379.

56. Ammen, "Doings of Maryland Boys in Gray."

57. Personal communication from Scott S. Sheads, historian, United States Department of the Interior, National Park Service, Fort McHenry National Monument and Historic Shrine, Baltimore, MD, June 19, 2003.

58. Speer, *Portals to Hell*, p. 221.

59. "A Brave Confederate," *Baltimore Sun*, February 22, 1895.

60. Ibid.

61. Ammen, "Doings of Maryland Boys in Gray."

62. Ibid.

63. Ibid.

64. "A Brave Confederate," *Baltimore Sun*, February 22, 1895.

65. Ammen, "Doings of Maryland Boys in Gray"; "A Brave Confederate," *Baltimore Sun*, February 22, 1895.

66. Ibid.

67. Ibid.

68. "Old Castle Thunder," *Richmond Dispatch*, March 3, 1895.

69. Ammen, "Doings of Maryland Boys in Gray"; "A Brave Confederate," *Baltimore Sun*, February 22, 1895.

70. "A Brave Confederate," *Baltimore Sun*, February 22, 1895.

71. Ammen, "Doings of Maryland Boys in Gray"; "A Brave Confederate," *Baltimore Sun*, February 22, 1895.

72. Ibid.

73. G. W. Alexander to Hon. J. P. Benjamin, October 2, 1861, Ser. II, Vol. III, pp. 724–725; Frances H. Casstevens, *Captain George Washington Alexander and Castle Thunder: A Biography of a Prison Commandant* (Jefferson, NC: McFarland & Co., 2004), p. 26. See also Speer, *Portals to Hell*, p. 221.

74. *Selected Records of the War Department Relating to Prisoners of War — Fort McHenry Military Prison.* National Archives, Washington, D.C. Microfilm No. 596, Roll 96; W. W. Morris, "Report of political prisoners taken, released and remaining since March 4, 1861, at Fort McHenry, Md.," O.R., Ser. II, Vol. 2, p. 226.

75. "An Escape from Fort McHenry," *The Sun*, Baltimore, MD, September 9, 1861.

76. "The Escape of Lieut. Alexander from Fort McHenry — No More Passes." *The Sun*, Baltimore, MD, September 10, 1861.

77. John A. Dix to Capt. A. A. Gibson, Baltimore, MD, September 9, 1861, O.R., Ser. II, Vol. 2, p. 58.

78. Ammen, "Doings of Maryland Boys in Gray"; "A Brave Confederate," *Baltimore Sun*, February 22, 1895.

79. Speer, *Portals to Hell*, p. 221.

80. First Lt. G. W. Alexander to Judah P. Benjamin, October 2, 1861, O.R., Ser. II, Vol. 3, p. 725.

81. Ammen, "Doings of Maryland Boys in Gray."

82. G. W. Alexander, "Attention Marylanders!— Come one, Come all," *Richmond Dispatch*, October 3, 1861, p. 2, col. 4.

83. "Meeting of Marylanders," *Richmond Dispatch*, October 5, 1861, p. 3, col. 1.

84. "Zarvona Zouaves," *Richmond Dispatch*, October 21, 1861, p. 2, col. 4.

85. Ibid.

86. John A. Dix to Maj. Gen. G. B. McClellan, September 5, 1861, O.R. Ser. II, Vol. 2, p. 381.

87. E. D. Townsend to Maj. Gen. John A. Dix, September 10, 1861, O.R. Ser. II, Vol. 2, p. 381.

88. William H. Seward to Mr. R. Schleiden, December 11, 1861, O.R., Ser. II, Vol. 2, p. 384.

89. Robert Ould, no date, O.R., Ser. II, Vol. 2, p. 382.

90. Fort McHenry Prison Records, www.itd.nps.gov/cwss/fortdetail.cfm?RECNUMBER=545.

91. Ibid.

92. Col. P. A. Porter to William Hoffman, December 19, 1863, O.R., Ser. II, Vol. 6, p. 722.

93. "Abstract from monthly returns of the principal U.S. Military prisons," O.R., Ser. II, Vol. 8, pp. 990–1003.

94. Marshall J. Smith to Hon. James A. Seddon, Richmond, Va., August 18, 1864, O.R., Ser. II, Vol. 7, p. 612.

95. "Fort McHenry — Facts," online www.bcpl.net/~etowner/facts.html.

96. "Baltimore's Best Attraction," online www.bcpl.net/!etowner/best.html.

Chapter IX

1. J. W. Alexander, "How We Escaped from Fort Warren," *The New England Magazine*, Vol. 13, No. 2, (October 1892), p. 209; J. W. Alexander, "An Escape from Fort Warren," in Walter Clark, ed. *Histories of the Several Regiments and Battalions from North Carolina in the Great War, 1861–1865*, Vol. IV, (Goldsboro, NC: Nash Bros., 1901), p. 733.

2. George Morey to Gov. John A. Andrew, Boston, November 21, 1861, O.R., Ser. II, Vol. 2, p. 165; W. Hoffman to E. M. Stanton, July 24, 1862, O.R., Ser. II, Vol. 4, p. 278.

3. Speer, *Portals to Hell*, p. 326.

4. Alexander, "An Escape from Fort Warren," in Clark, p.735; see also Terry Foenander, "CSN Prisoners at Fort Warren: A Photographic Essay." Terry Foenander counts seven escaped, with four recaptured, and cites Alexander as the source of his information.

5. "Generals Buckner and Tilghman in Fort Warren — How They Pass their Time, and What They Say," *Boston Post*, reprinted in *Daily Richmond Examiner* April 10, 1862.

6. Rideing, "The Gateway of Boston," pp. 352–353.

7. Rideing, "The Gateway of Boston," pp. 353–356.

8. Speer, *Portals to Hell*, pp. 41–42.

9. Ibid.

10. Harrison Ritchie to Hon. Simon Cameron, secretary of war, Boston, MA, October 11, 1861, O.R., Ser. II, Vol. 3, p. 51; Thomas A. Scott, acting secretary of war, to John A. Andrew, Washington, D.C., October 17, 1861, O.R., Ser. II, Vol. 3, p. 53.

11. E. D. Townsend, "indorsement" October 17, 1861, O.R. Ser. II, Vol. 3, p. 51.

12. C. T. Alexander to Col. W. Hoffman, Fort Warren, June 24, 1864, O.R., Ser. II, Vol. 7, pp. 408–409.

13. Snow, *The Islands of Boston Harbor* (New York: Dodd, Mead & Company, 1936), p. 7.

14. For more information about the men of this company, see online article about "The Washington Grays," at http://thewashingtongrays.homestead.com/. See also *North Carolina Troops, 1861–1865: A Roster*, Vol. I, pp. 158–171.

15. George Morey to Gov. John A. Andrew, Boston, November 21, 1861, O.R., Ser. II, Vol. 2, p. 165.

16. J. P. Garesche, assistant adjutant general, to Col. J. Dimick, Washington, DC, November 8, 1861, O.R., Ser. II, Vol. 3, p. 128.

117. L. Thomas to Major General Wool, Washington, November 29, 1861, and L. Thomas, adjutant general, to Col. J. Dimick, Washington, DC, November 29, 1861, O.R., Ser. II, Vol. 3, p. 148.

18. J. Dimick "Total number of officers (commissioned and non-commissioned) and men ordered to be paroled by general orders, Headquarters of the Army, Adjutant-General's Office, Washington, November 29, 1861," Fort Warren, December 13, 1861, O.R., Ser. II, Vol. 3, p. 161.

19. H. A. Gilliam, major and senior officer 7th [17th] Regiment, Infantry, North Carolina Volunteers, Fort Warren, December 30, 1861, O.R., Ser. II, Vol. 3, p. 172.

20. J. Dimick to Gen. L. Thomas, Fort Warren, January 25, 1862, O.R., Ser. II, Vol. 3, p. 215, J. Dimick to Maj. Gen. B. Huger, January 31, 1862, O.R. Ser. II, Vol. 3, p. 233.

21. J. Dimick to Gen. L. Thomas, Fort Warren, June 4, 1862, O.R., Ser. II, Vol. 3, pp. 639–642.

22. W. Hoffman to E. M. Stanton, July 24, 1862, O.R., Ser. II, Vol. 4, p. 278.

23. Daniel Moran, "Suspension of Habeas Corpus: The Saga of Richard Henry Alvy," online http://www.us-civilwar.com/aldie/habeas%20corpus.html.

24. George Morey to Gov. John A. Andrew, Boston, November 21, 1861, O.R., Ser. II, Vol. 2, p. 165.

25. "Robert Renwick, a Cabinetmaker: Judge for Yourself," online at http://www.scots-in-the-civilwar.net/renwick.htm.

26. Thomas J. Claggett to Hon. Edwin. M. Stanton, Fort Warren, February 25, 1862, O.R., Ser. II, Vol. 1, p. 741.

27. W. Hoffman to Brig. Gen. S. A. Meredith, August 1, 1863, O.R., Ser. II, Vol. 6, p. 164.

28. A manuscript of prisoners held at Fort Warren from August 1861 to February 1862, kept by the prisoners themselves, can be seen at the Maryland Historical Society Library, 201 West Monument Street, Baltimore, Maryland 21201-4674. A description with some of the names in this manuscript can be seen online at http://www.mdhs.org/library/Mss/ms-0-1957.htm.

29. Shelby Foote, The Civil War: A Narrative, Vol. I, (New York: Vintage Books, 1986), pp. 156–157; and Boatner, The Civil War Dictionary, pp. 516, 765, 847.

30. John S. Keyes to W. H. Seward, Boston, April 18, 1862, O.R., Ser. II, Vol. 3, p. 461. John S. Keyes to William H. Seward, U.S. Marshal's office, Boston, April 18, 1862, O.R., Ser. II, Vol. 3, pp. 461–462.

31. T. T. Turnstall to W. H. Seward, Fort Warren, April 23, 1862, O.R., Ser. II, Vol. 3, pp. 473–474; Affidavit, sworn to April 23, 1862, and forwarded to the State of Massachusetts, O.R., Ser. II, Vol. 3, p. 475.

32. William H. Seward to Col. Justin Dimick, Washington, May 5, 1862.

33. Boatner, The Civil War Dictionary, pp. 95–96, 839–840.

34. H. W. Halleck to Colonel Cutts, Saint Louis, MO, February 25, 1862, O.R., Ser. II, Vol. 3, p. 320.

35. J. Dimick to Gen. L. Thomas, Fort Warren,

March 6, 1862, O.R., Ser. II, Vol. 3, p. 355; L. Thomas to Col. J. Dimick, Washington, March 6, 1862, O.R., Ser. II, Vol. 3, p. 355.

36. Boatner, The Civil War Dictionary, pp. 95–96.

37. "Generals Buckner and Tilghman in Fort Warren."

38. G. B. McClellan, to Generals Halleck, Buel and Rosecrans, and Gen. J. A. Dix, Washington, February 18, 1862, Ser. II, Vol. 3, p. 275.

39. J. Dimick to Gen. L. Thomas, Fort Warren, Boston Harbor, November 25, 1861, O.R., Ser. II, Vol. 3, p. 142.

40. H. A. Gilliam to W. N. H. Smith, Fort Warren, December 23, 1861, O.R., Ser. II, Vol. 3, p. 759.

41. C. T. Alexander, surgeon, acting inspector of prisoners of war, O.R., Ser. II, Vol. 7, pp. 408–409.

42. "Roster of the 43rd Battalion Virginia Cavalry, Army of Northern Virginia, Confederate States of America," online at http://www.mosocco.com/companyf.html.

43. Capt. Bruce R. Boynton, USN, "A Scottsville Teen in Mosby's Rangers: Henry G. Harris," online at http://scottsvillemuseum.com/war/harris/home.html.

44. E. M. Stanton to Colonel Dimick, Washington, D.C., May 24, 1862, O.R., Ser. II, Vol. 3, p. 588; J. Dimick to E. M. Stanton, Fort Warren, Boston Harbor, May 24, 1862, O.R., Ser. II, Vol. 3, p. 588.

45. Edwin M. Stanton to Major General McDowell, May 24, 1862, O.R., Ser. II, Vol. 3, p. 588.

46. "John R. Towers, Captain, Co. E, then Colonel, 8th Georgia Volunteer Infantry," online at http://home.earthlink.net/~larsrbl/towersphotopage.htm. This is part of the 8th Georgia Infantry Homepage.

47. A typed copy of the autograph book of John R. Towers transcribed by Andrea Towers Rohaly, can be seen on line at http://home.earthlink.net/~larsrbl/towersautograph.htm. This is part of the 8th Georgia Infantry Homepage.

48. Rebecca Blackwell Drake, "Portraits—Generals and Commanders," online at http://battleoffraymond.org/command2.htm.

49. S. C. Hawley to Hon. William H. Seward, New York, November 24, 1861, O.R., Ser. II, Vol. 2, p. 147.

50. George Morey to Governor John A. Andrew, Boston, November 21, 1861, O.R., Ser. II, Vol. 2, p. 165.

51. J. Dimick to General L. Thomas, Fort Warren, May 22, 1862, O.R., Ser. II, Vol. 3, pp. 573–574.

52. "Abstract from monthly returns of the principal U.S. Military prisons," O.R., Ser. II, Vol. 8, p. 991.

53. Ibid., pp. 986–1004.

54. Boston Herald 23 March 1864, 4:3.

55. United States Naval War Records Office, Official Records of the Union and Confederate Navies in the War of the Rebellion, Vol. XIV (Washington, D.C.: Government Printing Office, 1902), pp. 267–268.

56. John A. Bolles, "Escape from Fort Warren," Harper's New Monthly Magazine, Vol. 28, No. 167 (April 1864), p. 697.

57. J. W. Alexander, "An Escape from Fort Warren," in Clark, ed., Histories of the Several Regiments from North Carolina in the Great War, Vol. IV, pp. 733–743. This same account was also published in The New England Magazine, Vol. 13, No. 2 (Oct 1892), pp. 208–214.

58. Alexander, "An Escape from Fort Warren," pp. 735–736.

59. Ibid., p. 736.

60. Bolles, p. 697.

61. Alexander, "An Escape from Fort Warren," p. 737.

62. Ibid., pp. 737–738.

63. Ibid., pp. 738–739.

64. Ibid., pp. 738–741.

65. Ibid., p. 741.

66. Ibid., pp. 741–742.

67. R. Thomas Campbell, *Sea Hawk of the Confederacy: Lt. Charles W. Read and the Confederate Navy* (Shippensburg, PA: Beidel Printing House, Inc., 1999), pp. 132, 134.

68. Ibid., p. 126.

69. Dufour, *Nine Men in Gray* (1963), p. 147, cited in Campbell's *Sea Hawk of the Confederacy*, pp. 138–139.

70. Dufour, *Nine Men in Gray*, p. 147, cited in Campbell, p. 139.

71. Campbell, *Sea Hawk of the Confederacy*, pp. 139–141.

72. Ibid., pp. 141–142.

73. Alexander, "An Escape from Fort Warren," p. 742.

74. A. A. Gibson, endorsement on report submitted by Otis S. Wilbur, Fort Warren, December 3, 1864, O.R., Ser. II, Vol. 7, p. 1182.

75. A. A. Gibson, "Roll of prisoners of war at Fort Warren, Mass., in close confinement for plotting to escape," January 10, 1865, O.R., Ser. II, Vol. 8, p. 53.

76. Footnote, O.R., Ser. II, Vol. 8, p. 53.

77. Robert Willis Allen, "A Visit to Fort Warren," online at http://johnbrownsbody.net/Fort_Warren.htm.

78. Ibid.

79. Snow, *The Romance of Boston Bay*, excerpt online at http://jay.schmidt.home.att.net/ft.warren/ghost.html.

80. "Roster of the 43rd Battalion Virginia Cavalry, Army of Northern Virginia, Confederate States of America," online at http://www.mosocco.com/companyf.html.

81. Boatner, *The Civil War Dictionary*, pp. 268–269. See also Edward Rowe Snow's "History of Fort Warren: Some Famous Confederate Prisoners at Fort Warren," online at http://jay.schmidt.home.att.net/ft.warren/prisoners.html.

82. E. M. Stanton to Major General Halleck, May 19, 1865, O.R., Ser. I, Vol. 49, Pt. III, pp. 836–837; Boatner, *The Civil War Dictionary*, pp. 682, 795.

83. Alexander Hamilton Stephens, *Recollections of Alexander Hamilton Stephens: His Diary Kept When a Prisoner at Fort Warren, Boston Harbor, 1865, Giving Incidents and Reflections of His Prison Life and Some Letters and Reminiscence*, Myrta Lockett Avary, ed. (reprint Baton Rouge, LA: Louisiana State University Press, 1998).

84. For more information on visiting Fort Warren, contact Kelly Fellner, Supervisory Park Ranger, NPS, Boston Harbor Islands national park area, 408 Atlantic Avenue, #228, Boston, MA 02100, or telephone (617) 223-8668, E-mail-BOHA_Information@nps.gov; web page: http://www.BostonIslands.org.

85. "Historic Fort Warren: A Civil War Living History & Drill Competition, Boston Harbor, Boston, MA," online at http://www.geocities.com/ftwarren2004/index.html.

Chapter X

1. Frost, "Camp and Prison Journal," online.

2. Schuyler Hamilton to Colonel Tuttle, January 5, 1862, O.R., Ser. II, Vol. 3, pp. 185–186, Hesseltine, "Military Prisons of St. Louis, 1861–1865," *Missouri Historical Review* 23:3 (April 1929), p. 384, cited in Speer, p. 49.

3. Speer, *Portals to Hell*, pp. 49, 327.

4. D. H. Rule, "Gratiot Street Prison FAQ: Frequently Asked Questions about the Union Civil War Prison in St. Louis, Missouri," online at www.civilwarstlouis.com/Gratiot/gratiotfaq.htm.

5. J. Thomas Scharf, *History of St. Louis City & County*, p. 418; Speer, *Portals to Hell*, p. 47.

6. Ibid.

7. Scharf, *History of St. Louis City & County*, pp. 404, 418.

8. Speer, *Portals to Hell*, p. 88; Rule, "Gratiot Street Prison FAQ."

9. Bernard G. Farrar, provost marshal general, to Col. W. Hoffman, St. Louis, June 28, 1862, O.R., Ser. II, Vol. 4, pp. 95–96.

10. Frost, *Camp & Prison Journal*, pp. 29–32; Hesseltine, "Military Prisons of St. Louis," pp. 387 and 390; Henry M. Cheavens, "A Missouri Confederate in the Civil War: The Journal of Henry Martyn Cheavens, 1862–1863," ed. James E. Moss, *Missouri Historical Review* (October 1862), pp. 29–33, cited in Speer, *Portals to Hell*, p. 50.

11. Speer, *Portals to Hell*, pp. 50–51.

12. Frost, *Camp & Prison Journal*, excerpts relating to Gratiot Street Prison online at www.civilwarstlouis.com/Gratiot/frost.htm.

13. Speer, *Portals to Hell*, p. 88; D. H. Rule, "Gratiot Street Prison FAQ."

14. Schuyler Hamilton to Colonel Tuttle, O.R., Ser. II, Vol. 3, pp. 185–186.

15. William W. Orme to Edwin M. Stanton, Washington, D.C., December 7, 1863, O.R., Ser. II, Vol. 6, p. 662.

16. Hesseltine, "Military Prisons of St. Louis," 381–382; Speer, *Portals to Hell*, p. 48.

17. *Daily Missouri Democrat* December 23, 1861, p. 3:4, December 24, 1861, p. 2:3, December 25, 1861, p. 3:5, cited in Speer, *Portals to Hell*, p. 48.

18. Ibid., Speer, *Portals to Hell*, pp. 48–49.

19. W. Hoffman to E. M. Stanton, Washington, D.C., July 24, 1862, O.R., Ser. II, Vol. 4, p. 278.

20. W. Hoffman to Col. Thomas T. Gantt, October 13, 1862, O.R., Ser. II, Vol. 4, pp. 618–619.

21. William W. Orme to Edwin M. Stanton, Washington, D.C., December 7, 1863, O.R., Ser. II, Vol. 6, p. 662.

22. Gustavus Heinrichs, lieutenant colonel, inspector and superintendent of military prisons, St. Louis, Mo., November 19, 1864, O.R., Ser. II, Vol. 7, pp. 1141–1143.

23. Frost, *Camp & Prison Journal*, pp. 114, 119; Grimes, *Confederate Mail Runner*, pp. 168–169; Speer, *Portals to Hell*, p. 179.

24. H. L. McConnell to Lt. Col. B. G. Farrar, St. Louis, Mo., June 27, 1862, O.R., Ser. II, Vol. 4, p. 57.

25. Geo. Rex to Col. J. H. Baker, St. Louis, Mo., February 22, 1865, O.R., Ser. Ii, Vol. 8, pp. 291–292.

26. R. C. Allen to Maj. George Rex, office of the

Gratiot Street Military Prison, St. Louis, Mo., February 22, 1865, O.R., Ser. II, Vol. 8, p. 292,

27. "Extract from report of inspection of the Gratiot Street Prison Hospital, at Saint Louis, Mo, dated July 25, 1863, by Jon L. Le Conte, surgeon of volunteers, acting medical inspector, U.S. Army." O.R., Ser. II, Vol. 6, pp. 150–151.

28. "Abstract from monthly returns of the principal U.S. Military prisons," O.R., Ser. II, Vol. 8, pp. 986–998.

29. Rule, "Gratiot Street Prison FAQ."

30. Frost, "Camp and Prison Journal."

31. "Abstract from monthly returns of the principal U.S. Military Prisons," O.R., Ser. II, Vol. 8, pp. 986–998.

32. Frost, "Camp and Prison Journal."

33. Ibid.

34. William H. White to Doctor Davis, Glasgow [Ky.?], April 5, 1863, O.R., Ser. II, Vol. 5, p. 436.

35. Ibid.

36. Endorsement by Robert C. Buchanan on bottom of letter from William H. White to Doctor Davis, Glasgow [Ky.?], April 5, 1863, O.R., Ser. II, Vol. 5, p. 436.

37. Frost, "Camp and Prison Journal."

38. Grimes, *Confederate Mail Runner*, pp. 39–43, 87–93, *Missouri Democrat* September 2, 1862, p. 1:2, cited in Speer, p. 225.

39. Rule, "A. C. Grimes."

40. Scharf, *History of St. Louis City and County*, p. 420, cited in Speer, *Portals to Hell*, p. 225.

41. Grimes, *Confederate Mail Runner*, pp. 90–91, 93–96.

42. Ibid., pp. 171–172.

43. Frost, "Camp & Prison Journal"; Grimes, *Confederate Mail Runner*, pp. 172–173.

44. Grimes, *Confederate Mail Runner*, pp. 176–177.

45. Ibid. p. 172.

46. "Report of the Joint Committee Appointed to Investigate the Condition and Treatment of Prisoners," March 3, 1865, O.R., Ser. II, Vol. 8, pp. 337–351. Sebring is quoted on pp. 347–348.

47. Grimes, *Confederate Mail Runner*, pp. 421, 166–170; Gustavus Heinrichs to Major O. D. Greene, St. Louis, MO, June 24, 1864, O. R., Ser. II, Vol. 7, pp. 398–399.

48. Grimes, *Confederate Mail Runner*, pp. 90–91, 93–96.

49. Gustavus Heinrichs to Maj. O. D. Greene, St. Louis, MO, June 24, 1864, O. R., Ser. II, Vol. 7, pp. 398–399.

50. Rule, "A. C. Grimes."

51. Frost, "Camp and Prison Journal"; Speer, *Portals to Hell*, pp. 225–226.

52. Gustavus Heinrichs to Maj. O. D. Greene, Saint Louis, MO, June 24, 1864, O. R., Ser. II, Vol. 7, pp. 398–399.

53. Ibid.

54. Grimes, *Confederate Mail Runner*, pp. 188–191.

55. N. P. Chipman to Col. William H. McCowan, St. Louis, October 30, 1862, O.R., Ser. II, Vol. 4, p. 668.

56. Boatner, *The Civil War Dictionary*, p. 154.

57. Frost, "Camp and Prison Journal."

58. Ibid.

59. Ibid.

60. Ibid.

61. Grimes, *Confederate Mail Runner*, p. 173.

62. Grimes, *Confederate Mail Runner*, p. 173.

63. Frost, "Camp & Prison Journal."

64. Grimes, *Confederate Mail Runner*, pp. 173–174.

65. Ibid., p. 173.

66. Ibid., pp. 174–175.

67. Ibid., p. 175.

68. "The Retaliation: The Murder of Wilson and His Comrades," *St. Louis Democrat*, October 31, 1864; Howard Mann, "True Tales of the Tenth Kansas Infantry," online at www.civilwarstlouis.com/Gratiot/tenthkansas4.htm.

69. General Order No. 252, July 31, 1863, O. R., Ser. I, Vol. 33, pp. 866–867; Joseph Darr, Jr. to Col. John V. DuBois, October 29, 1864, O.R., Ser. I, Vol. 41, Pt. IV, p. 316; General Order #252, July 31, 1863, O.R., Ser. II, Vol. 6, p. 163; W. S. Rosecrans to Abraham Lincoln, St. Louis, November 11, 1864, O.R., Ser. II, Vol.7, pp. 1118–1119.

70. E. O. Wolfe to General Rosecrans, McDowell Prison, St. Louis, November 8, 1864, O.R., Ser. II, Vol. 7, p. 1111.

71. President Abraham Lincoln to Major General Rosecrans, Washington, D.C., November 10, 1864, O.R., Ser. II, Vol. 7, p. 115.

72. "Execution of Innocent Confederate POWs." online at www.geocities.com/Pentagon/Bunker/3802/prison.htm.

73. Ibid.

74. George Rex to Major General Dodge, St. Louis, MO, March 10, 1865, O.R., Ser. II, Vol. 8, pp. 376–377.

75. Rule, "Gratiot Street Prison FAQ."

76. "Abstract from monthly returns of the principal U.S. Military prisons," O.R., Ser. II, Vol. 8, p. 998.

77. Rule, "Gratiot Street Prison FAQ."

Chapter XI

1. Charles E. Frohman, *Rebels on Lake Erie* (Columbus, OH: The Ohio Historical Society, 1965), pp, 150–151,

2. Speer, *Portals to Hell*, pp. 77–79, 327

3. David Bush, "History of Johnson's Island Prisoner of War Depot," online www.heidelberg.edu/~dbush/jirev2.html..

4. Speer, *Portals to Hell*, p. 11.

5. Bush, "History of Johnson's Island Prisoner of War Depot."

6. Frohman, p. 4.

7. R. F. Webb, "Prison Life on Johnson's Island, 1863-'64," Walter Clark, ed., *Histories of the Several Regiments in the Great War, 1861–1865*, Vol. IV (Goldsboro, NC: Nash Brothers, 1901), p. 671.

8. Bush, "History of Johnson's Island Prisoner of War Depot."

9. Horace Carpenter, "Plain Living at Johnson's Island," *The Century*, Vol. XLI, No. 5 (March 1891), p. 710.

10. *Sandusky Register*, August 20, 1891; O.R., Ser. II, Vol. 3, pp. 56–57, cited in Frohman, p. 3–4.

11. Carpenter, p. 709.

12. J. F. Cross, "N. C. Officers in Prison at Johnson's Island, 1864," in Walter Clark, ed., *Histories of the Several Regiments and Battalions from North Carolina in the Great War, 1861–1865*, Vol. IV (Goldsboro, NC: Nash Brothers, 1901), p. 704.

13. Bush, "History of Johnson's Island Prisoner of War Depot."

14. Speer, *Voices from Cemetery Hill*, pp. 75–76.

15. Carpenter, p. 711.

16. Bush, "History of Johnson's Island Prisoner of War Depot."

17. Webb, "Prison Life on Johnson's Island, 1863–'64," p. 666.

18. Bush, "History of Johnson's Island Prisoner of War Depot."

19. Frohman, p. 5.

20. Webb, "Prison Life on Johnson's Island, 1863–'64," p. 668.

21. D. U. Barziza, *Decimus et Ultimus Barziza, Adventures of a Prisoner of War, 1863–1864*. R. Henderson Shuffler, ed. (Houston, TX: News Job Office, 1865, reprint edition, Austin, TX: University of Texas Press, 1964), pp. 77–78.

22. Bush, "History of Johnson's Island Prisoner of War Depot."

23. Frohman, p. 6.

24. Frohman, pp. 6–7.

25. *Sandusky Register*, April 11, 1862, cited in Frohman, pp. 7–8.

26. "Abstract of monthly returns of the principal U.S. Military prisons," O.R., Ser. II, Vol. 8, pp. 986, 993, 1000.

27. Cross, "N. C. Officers in Prison at Johnson's Island, 1864," p. 704.

28. Henry E. Shepherd, *Narrative of Prison Life at Baltimore and Johnson's Island, Ohio* (Baltimore: Commercial Printing and Stationery, 1917), pp. 11, 18–19.

29. Boatner, *The Civil War Dictionary*, pp. 477–478; see also Bowman, *Who Was Who in the Civil War*, p. 127.

30. W. Hoffman to Col. Joseph Roberts, Washington, D.C., November 10, 1863, O.R. Ser. II, Vol. 6, p. 495.

31. Barziza, pp. 93–94

32. Report of Brig. Gen. Junius Daniels, C. S. Army, commanding brigade, June 3–August 1, 1863 — The Gettysburg Campaign," O.R., Ser. I, Vol. 27, Pt. II, pp. 569–570.

33. Manarin and Jordan, *North Carolina Troops*, Vol. XI, p. 70.

34. Ibid., pp. 7, 70.

35. Report of Brig. Gen. Junius Daniels; Manarin and Jordan, *North Carolina Troops, 1861–1865: A Roster*, Vol. VIII, pp. 206–207; Casstevens, *The Civil War in Yadkin County, North Carolina*, p.267.

36. Allen P. Speer, *Voices from Cemetery Hill* (Johnson City, TN: Overmountain Press, 1997), pp. 30–31.

37. Speer, *Voices from Cemetery Hill*, p. 75.

38. Ibid.

39. Speer, *Voices from Cemetery Hill*, p. 76, 80. E. A. Speer (Ephraim Aquilla Speer, 1838–1893), was the son of Joshua Kennerly Speer and a brother to William Sheppard Speer (1822–1915), an abolitionist who was a diplomat during the Lincoln administration, and was the minister to South America for the U.S. government in 1862.

40. William M. Orme to Edwin M. Stanton, Washington City, D.C., December 7, 1863, O.R., Ser. II, Vol. 6, p. 661,

41. Letter from Lt. E. F. Spears, 2nd Kentucky Infantry, to Mrs. E. Nunn, Johnson's Island, April 18, 1862, *Camp Chase Gazette*, Vol. 10, No. 6 (April 1983), p. 18. Also available online at www.rootsweb.com/~orphanhm/spearsltr.htm,

42. William M. Orme to Edwin M. Stanton, Washington City, D.C., December 7, 1863, O.R., Ser. II, Vol. 6, p. 661,

43. William S. Pierson to Col. William Hoffman, October 17, 1863, O.R., Ser. II, Vol. 6, p. 391.

44. William M. Orme to Edwin M. Stanton, Washington City, D.C., December 7, 1863, O.R., Ser. II, Vol. 6, p. 661,

45. Bush, "History of Johnson's Island Prisoner of War Depot."

46. Carpenter, p. 709.

47. Speer, *Voices from Cemetery Hill*, pp. 75–76.

48. Ibid., pp. 78–80.

49. Ibid., pp. 75–76.

50. Ibid., pp. 83–84.

51. Ibid., pp. 78–80.

52. Ibid., pp. 30–31.

53. Manarin and Jordan, *North Carolina Troops*, Vol. VIII, pp. 110, 206–207; Casstevens, *The Civil War and Yadkin County, North Carolina*, p. 267.

54. William M. Norman, *A Portion of My Life* (Winston-Salem, NC: John F. Blair, Publisher, 1959), pp. 130, 156–162, 168–177, 182–189, 233–234.

55. Lt. M. McNamara, "Lieutenant Pierce's Daring Attempts to Escape from Johnson's Island," *Southern Historical Society Papers*, Vol. VIII (January-December, 1880), pp. 62–63.

56. David Bush, "Archaeology's Interactive Dig," online at www.archaeology.org/interactive/johnson/diaries/smith.html.

57. William Hoffman to Maj. Gen. A. E. Burnside, Washington, D.C., October 13, 1863, O.R., Ser. II, Vol. 6, p. 369.

58. General Order No. 38, Headquarters of the Department of the Ohio, Cincinnati, April 13, 1863, O.R., Ser. II Vol. 5, p. 480.

59. Barziza, pp. 96–97.

60. Speer, *Voices from Cemetery Hill*, pp. 83–84.

61. William S. Pierson to Col. William Hoffman, October 17, 1863, O.R., Ser. II, Vol. 6, p. 391.

62. Shepherd, pp. 10–11.

63. Ibid., p. 11.

64. Frohman, p. 51.

65. Lt. Col. E. A. Scovill to Col. Charles W. Hill, January 8, 1865, O. R., Ser. II, Vol. 8, p. 41.

66. Col. Charles H. Hill to Brig. Gen. H. W. Wessells, January 8, 1865, O.R., Ser. II, Vol. 8, p. 42.

67. "Abstract from monthly returns of the principal U.S. Military prisons," O.R., Ser. II, Vol. 8, pp. 1000–1004.

68. Cross, p. 704.

69. Frohman, p. 51.

70. Webb, "Prison Life At Johnson's Island," pp. 684–685.

71. Letter from J. P. Murphy to Maj. Edward Scoville, August 23, 1864, Western Reserve Historical Society, quoted in Frohman, p. 52.

72. Ibid., p. 685.

73. Col. Charles W. Hill to Brig. Gen. H. W. Wessells, Johnson's Island, January 8, 1865, and January 5, 1865, Ser. II, Vol. 8, pp. 42–43.

74. William S. Pierson to Col. William Hoffman, October 17, 1863, O.R., Ser. II, Vol. 6, p. 391.

75. Webb, "Prison Life at Johnson's Island," pp. 680–681.

76. Ibid., pp. 680–81.

77. Thomas S. Kenan, "Johnson's Island," in Walter Clark, ed. *Histories of the Several Regiments in the Great War, 1861–'65*, Vol. IV (Goldsboro, NC: Nash Brothers, 1901), p. 690.

78. Roger Long, "Out of a frozen hell," Part 1. *Civil War Times Illustrated*, Vol. 37, No. 1 (March 1998), p. 27.

79. William S. Pierson to Col. William Hoffman, October 1, 1863, O.R., Ser. II, Vol. 6, p. 333.

80. Ibid., October 16, 1863, O.R., Ser. II, Vol. 6, p. 385.

81. Endorsement dated October 19, 1863, by W. Hoffman on Pierson's letter of October 16, 1863, O.R., Ser. II, Vol. 6, pp. 385–386.

82. W. Hoffman to Lieut. Col. W. S. Pierson, Washington, D.C., October 19, 1863, O.R., Ser. II, Vol. 6, pp. 396–397.

83. William S. Pierson to Col. William Hoffman, near Sandusky, Ohio, October 28, 1863, O.R., Ser. II, Vol. 6, p. 435.

84. W. Hoffman to Brig. Gen. L. Thomas, Washington, D.C., November 11, 1863, O.R., Ser. II, Vol. 6, p. 500.

85. McNamara, p. 63.

86. Ibid., p. 64.

87. Ibid., p. 64; Frohman, p. 50.

88. McNamara, p. 65; Frohman, p. 50.

89. William S. Pierson to Col. William Hoffman, near Sandusky, Ohio, October 31, 1863, O.R., Ser. II, Vol. 6, pp. 448–450.

90. Ibid., October 28, 1863, O.R., Ser. II, Vol. 6, p. 435.

91. Long, "Out of a Frozen Hell," Part 1. *Civil War Times Illustrated*, Vol. 37, No. 1 (March 1998), pp. 26–27.

92. Col. B. J. Sweet to Col. William Hoffman, September 22, 1864, O.R., Ser. II, Vol. 7, p. 861.

93. Speer, *Portals to Hell*, p. 237.

94. Martin Burke to Brig. Gen. D. T. Van Buren, February 10, 1866, O. R., Ser. II, Vol. 8, p. 881.

95. R. Ould to President Lincoln, Richmond, March 11, 1865, O. R., Ser. II, Vol. 8, p. 400, cited in Speer, p. 293.

96. Shepherd, p. 11.

97. "Escape of Prisoners from Johnson's Island," *Southern Historical Society Papers*, Vol. XVIII (January-December 1890), pp. 428–429; see also Frohman, p. 52.

98. Maj. Thomas H. Linnell to Capt. J. F. Huntington, Johnson's Island, October 16, 1864, O.R., Ser. II, Vol. 7, p. 995.

99. "Escape of Prisoners from Johnson's Island," *Southern Historical Society Papers*, Vol. XVIII (January-December 1890), p. 428–429.

100. Maj. Thomas H. Linnell to Col. Charles W. Hill, Johnson's Island, December 25, 1864, O.R., Ser. II, Vol. 7, p. 1274.

101. Col. Charles W. Hill's endorsement on report of Thomas Linnell, December 25, 1864, O.R., Ser. II, Vol. 7, pp. 1274–1275; see also Charles W. Hill to Brig. Gen. H. W. Wessells, Johnson's Island, January 8, 1865, O.R. Ser. II, Vol. 8, pp. 42–43.

102. Shepherd, p. 10.

103. Bush, "History of Johnson's Island Prisoner of War Depot."

104. Long, "Out of a Frozen Hell," Part 1, p. 27; see also Frohman, p. 51

105. Speer, *Portals to Hell*, p. 139.

106. Long, "Out of a Frozen Hell," Part 1, pp. 24–31.

107. Ibid,, p. 29.

108. *Sandusky Register*, January 4, 1864, cited in Frohman, p. 55.

109. "Escape of Prisoners from Johnson's Island," *Southern Historical Society Papers*, Vol. XVIII (January-December 1890), p. 429.

110. Shepherd, p. 11.

111. Long, "Out of a Frozen Hell," Part 1, p. 27.

112. Ibid., p. 29.

113. Ibid., pp. 27–29.

114. Ibid., p. 29.

115. Col. Charles W. Hill to Brig. Gen. H. W. Wessells, Johnson's Island, January 8, 1865, and January 5, 1865, Ser. II, Vol. 8, pp. 42–43.

116. Long, "Out of a Frozen Hell," Part 1, p. 30.

117. Ibid., p. 31.

118. Roger Long, "Out of a frozen hell," Part II. *Civil War Times Illustrated*, Vol. 37, No. 2 (May 1998), pp. 42–45.

119. Ibid., pp. 46–47.

120. Ibid., pp. 47–48.

121. Ibid.

122. *Raleigh News & Observer*, September 21, 1958, p. 4:5, cited in Speer, *Portals to Hell*, p. 140.

123. Frohman, p. 51.

124. Barziza, pp. 104–113.

125. Ibid., pp. 114–120.

126. Frohman, p. 7.

127. Barziza, p. 78.

1128. *Sandusky Register*, June 16, 1864, quoted in Frohman, p. 13.

129. Extracted from official report of Lt. Col. W. S. Pierson, made January 18, 1864, on being relieved of command of Johnson's Island, by Brig. Gen. Terry, Commanding Third Division, 6th Corps, U.S. Army, cited in Barziza, p. 103.

130. Webb, "Prison Life at Johnson's Island," pp. 681–682.

131. "Abstract from monthly returns of the principal U.S. Military prisons," O.R., Ser. II, Vol. 8, pp. 986–1004.

132. Webb, "Prison Life at Johnson's Island," footnote, p. 687.

133. "Johnson's Island," online at www.deadohio.com/JohnIsl.htm.

134. Bush, "Archaeology's Interactive Dig," online.

135. "Johnson's Island, Ohio," U.S. Military Prison Collection, MS-22 mf, Center for Archival Collections, Bowling Green State University, Bowling Green, Ohio, online at www.bgsu.edu/colleges/library/cac/ms0022.html.

Chapter XII

1. W. Fred Conway, *The Most Incredible Prison Escape of the Civil War,* 2nd edition (New Albany, IN: FBH Publishers, 1994), p. 70.

2. William M. Orme to Edwin M. Stanton, Washington, D.C., December 7, 1863, O.R., Ser. II, Vol. 6, p. 662.

3. Speer, *Portals to Hell*, p. 329.

4. Works Progress Administration, *The Ohio Guide* (New York: Oxford University Press, 1940), pp. 252, 256–257, cited in Speer, *Portals to Hell*, p. 148.

5. Speer, *Portals to Hell*, p. 149.

6. J. N. Desellem to Capt. N. Merion, Warden Ohio Penitentiary, Columbus, November 30, 1863, O.R., Ser. II, Vol. 6, pp. 665–666.

7. Duke, *History of Morgan's Cavalry*, cited in Conway, pp. 19–22.

8. Conway, p. 19.

9. Lester V. Horwitz, *The Longest Raid of the Civil War.* (Cincinnati: Farmcourt, 1999), p. 390.

10. Boatner, *The Civil War Dictionary*, pp. 566–567.

11. Basil W. Duke, "A Romance of Morgan's Rough Riders. Part I. The Raid," *The Century*, XLI, No. 3 (January 1891), p. 403.

12. Conway, p. 9.

13. William J. Stier, "Morgan's Last Battle." *Civil War Times Illustrated*, Vol. XXXV, No. 6 (December 1996), p. 89.

14. Conway, pp. 11–12.

15. Ibid., p. 11.

16. Duke, "A Romance of Morgan's Rough Riders," p. 403.

17. Stuart W. Sanders, "A Little Fight Between Friends and Family." *Civil War Times Illustrated*, Vol. XL, No. 5 (October 2001), p. 66.

18. Horwitz, p. 19.

19. Ibid., p. 15.

20. Ibid., p. ix.

21. Ibid., pp. 403–404.

22. Ibid., p. 15.

23. Boatner, *The Civil War Dictionary*, pp. 566–569.

24. Orlando B. Willcox, "A Romance of Morgan's Rough Riders. Part II. The Capture," *The Century*, XLI, No. 3 (January 1891), p. 416.

25. Duke, "A Romance of Morgan's Rough Riders," p. 408.

26. Duke, *History of Morgan's Cavalry*, cited in Horwitz, p. 377.

27. *Ohio State Journal*, cited in Horwitz, p. 344.

28. *Cincinnati Commercial*, July 26, 1863, cited in Horwitz, p. 345.

29. *Cincinnati Gazette*, July 29, 1863, cited in Horwitz, p. 346; Duke, *Reminiscences of General Basil W. Duke, C.S.A.* (Garden City, NY: Doubleday, Page, 1911), pp. 365–366.

30. Horwitz, p. 346.

31. H. W. Halleck to Brig. Gen. S. A. Meredith, Washington, D.C., July 27, 1863, O.R., Ser. II, Vol. 6, p. 153.

32. A. E. Burnside to Governor Tod, Cincinnati, July 27, 1863, O.R., Ser. II, Vol. 6, p. 153.

33. David Tod to Major General Burnside, Columbus, Ohio, July 27, 1863, O.R., Ser. II, Vol. 6, p. 153.

34. Horwitz, p. 347.

35. *Cincinnati Commercial*, July 26, 1863, cited in Horwitz, p. 345.

36. R. A. Alston to James A. Seddon, Richmond, October 10, 1863, O.R., Ser. II, Vol. 6, pp. 375–376.

37. Photo of Morgan's men in prison, from University of Kentucky Library, Lexington, Kentucky, reproduced in Horwitz, p. C10.

38. Duke, *History of Morgan's Cavalry*, cited in Conway, pp. 19–22.

39. David Tod to Nathaniel Merion, warden of Ohio Penitentiary, Columbus, July 30, 1863, O.R., Ser. II, Vol. 6, pp. 420–421.

40. W. Hoffman to John S. Mason, Washington, D.C., October 21, 1863, O.R., Ser. II, Vol. 6, p. 404.

41. Jno. S. Mason to Col. William Hoffman, Columbus, Ohio, October 26, 1863, O.R., Ser. II, Vol. 6, pp. 419–420.

42. Ibid.

43. Ibid.

44. Wm. M. Orme to Edwin M. Stanton, Washington, D.C., December 7, 1863, O.R., Ser. II, Vol. 6, p. 662.

45. Jno. H. Morgan to Brig. Gen. J. S. Mason, Ohio Penitentiary, Columbus, Ohio, October 31, 1863, O.R., Ser. II, Vol. 6, p. 448.

46. Jno H. Morgan to E. M. Stanton, Ohio Penitentiary, Columbus, Ohio, November 9, 1863, O.R., Ser. II, Vol. 6, pp. 495–496.

47. Conway, p. 9.

48. Jno H. Morgan to E. M. Stanton, Ohio Penitentiary, Columbus, Ohio, November 9, 1863, O.R., Ser. II, Vol. 6, pp. 495–496.

49. Ibid.

50. Letter from John H. Morgan to Mattie Morgan, August 10, 1863, cited in Horwitz, pp. 350–351.

51. Conway, p. 24.

52. Conway, p. 35; Thomas H. Hines, "A Romance of Morgan's Rough Riders. Part III. The Escape," *The Century*, XLI, No. 3 (January 1891), pp. 417–418.

53. Conway, p. 131.

54. Duke, *History of Morgan's* Cavalry, p. 356, cited in Conway, p. 131.

55. Conway, pp. 39–40.

56. Hines, "A Romance of Morgan's Rough Riders. Part III. The Escape," p. 418.

57. Ibid., pp. 418–419.

58. Ibid., pp. 417–419.

59. Ibid., pp. 418–419.

60. George B. Wright to B. F. Hoffman, Columbus, Ohio, December 7, 1863, O.R., Ser. II, Vol. 6, p. 667.

61. William Wallace to Brig. Gen. George B. Wright, Columbus, Ohio, December 6, 1863, O.R., Ser. II, Vol. 6, pp. 670–671.

62. George B. Wright to B. F. Hoffman, Columbus, Ohio, December 7, 1863, O.R., Ser. II, Vol. 6, p. 666.

63. "General Morgan Escapes from the Ohio Penitentiary," in Commager, *The Blue and the Gray*, pp. 706–707.

64. N. Merion to Colonel Wallace, Ohio Penitentiary, November 28, 1863, O.R., Ser. II, Vol. 6, p. 671.

65. David Tod to E. M. Stanton, Columbus, Ohio, November 28, 1863, O.R., Ser. II, Vol. 6, p. 588.

66. P. H. Watson to David Tod, Washington City, November 28, 1863, O.R., Ser. II, Vol. 6, p. 588.

67. Edwin M. Stanton to Governor Tod, December 1, 1863, O.R., Ser. II, Vol. 6, p. 626.

68. Ibid.

69. Edwin M. Stanton to Major General Dix, December 1, 1863, O.R., Ser. II, Vol. 6, p. 636.

70. David Tod to E. M. Stanton, Columbus, Ohio, December 2, 1863, O.R., Ser. II, Vol. 6, p. 632.

71. Edwin M. Stanton to Governor Tod, December 2, 1863, O.R., Ser. II, Vol. 6, p. 632.

72. William Wallace to Col. William Hoffman, Columbus, Ohio, November 28, 1863, O.R., Ser. II, Vol. 6, p. 589.

73. William Wallace to Brig. Gen. George B. Wright, Columbus, Ohio, December 6, 1863, O.R., Ser. II, Vol. 6, pp. 670–671.

74. David Tod to N. Merion, Columbus, November 28, 1863, O.R., Ser. Ii, Vol. 6, p. 665.

75. P. H. Watson to David Tod, Washington City, November 28, 1863, O.R., Ser. II, Vol. 6, p. 589.

76. John S. Mason to Col. William Wallace, Steubenville, Ohio, November 30, 1863, O.R., Ser. II, Vol. 6, p. 670.

77. Excerpts from the warden's record book, submitted by George G. Wright to Gov. David Tod, December 7, 1863, Ser. II, Vol. 6, pp. 667–669.

78. George G. Wright to Gov. David Tod, December 7, 1863, Ser. II, Vol. 6, p. 669.

79. William Wallace to Brig. Gen. George B. Wright, Columbus, Ohio, December 6, 1863, O.R., Ser. II, Vol. 6, pp. 670–671.

80. Jno. S. Mason to Col. William Wallace, Steubenville, Ohio, November 30, 1863, O.R., Ser. II, Vol. 6, p.670.

81. J. N. Desellem to Capt. N. Merion, warden, Ohio Penitentiary, Columbus, November 30, 1863, O.R., Ser. II, Vol. 6, pp. 665–666.

82. Ibid.

83. Ibid.

84. Ibid.

85. Conway, p. 70.

86. George B. Wright to B. F. Hoffman, Columbus, Ohio, December 7, 1863, O.R., Ser. II, Vol. 6, p. 666.

87. Statement of Capt. Robert Lamb, December 7, 1863, O.R., Ser. II, Vol. 6, p. 672.

88. Statement of First Lt. M. W. Goss, December 7, 1863, O.R., Ser. II, Vol. 6, p. 672.

89. Affidavit of Jesse E. Watson, December 8, 1863, O.R., Ser. II, Vol. 6, p. 674.

90. Affidavit of John A. Gonce, December 7, 1863, O.R., Ser. II, Vol. 6, pp. 673–674; Affidavit of Nathaniel Merion, December 8, 1863, O.R., Ser. II, Vol. 6, pp. 676–677.

91. Affidavit of Nathaniel Merion, December 8, 1863, O.R., Ser. II, Vol. 6, pp. 676–677.

92. George B. Wright to Governor Tod, December 7, 1863, O.R. Ser. II, Vol. 6, pp. 677–678.

93. M. Merion to editor, Ohio State Journal, Ohio Penitentiary, Columbus, December 4, 1863, O.R., Ser. II, Vol. 6, p. 730.

94. O. A. Mack, major and aide-de-camp, to Brig. Gen. L. Thomas, Washington, D.C., December 19, 1863, O.R., Ser. II, Vol. 6, p. 725.

95. R. Lamb to Col. William Wallace, Columbus, Ohio, December 12, 1863.

96. Intercepted letter from Dick Morgan to Miss Sallie C. Warfield, of Lexington, Ky., December 5, 1863, O.R., Ser. II, Vol. 6, p. 732.

97. Ibid.

98. Jno. Brough to Col. William Hoffman, State of Ohio, Executive Department, Columbus, February 24, 1864, O.R., Ser. II, Vol. 6, p. 986.

99. Speer, Portals to Hell, p. 187.

100. Basil W. Duke, Reminiscences of General Basil W. Duke, C.S.A., (Garden City, NW: Doubleday, Page & Company, 1911), pp. 365–366.

101. David Tod telegram to E. M. Stanton, Columbus, Ohio, December 5, 1862, O.R., Ser. II, Vol. 6, p. 649.

102. Conway, pp. 81–83.

103. Hines, pp. 424–425.

104. Conway, pp. 81–83.

105. Ibid., p. 79.

106. Boatner, The Civil War Dictionary, pp. 566–567; Stier, "Morgan's Last Battle," pp. 83–92.

107. Stier, "Morgan's Last Battle," p. 87.

108. Boatner, The Civil War Dictionary, pp. 250–251.

109. Horwitz, p. 376.

110. Ibid. p. 374.

Chapter XIII

1. Col. N. T. Colby, "The 'Old Capitol' Prison," Annals of the Civil War: Written by Leading Participants North and South, 1878, Abridged Edition, Introduced by Gary W. Gallagher. (New York: Da Capo Press, 1994), p. 512.

2. Speer, Portals to Hell, p. 329.

3. John B. Ellis, The Sights and Secrets of the National Capital: A Work Descriptive of Washington City in all its Various Phases (New York: United States Publishing Co., 1869), p. 438.

4. James J. Williamson, Prison Life in the Old Capitol and Reminiscences of the Civil War (West Orange, NJ: no publisher, 1911), pp. 20–21; "Reminiscences of Washington," The Atlantic Monthly, Vol. 45, No. 267 (January 1880), p. 5 7.

5. Colby, "The 'Old Capitol' Prison," Annals of the Civil War, p. 502.

6. Ibid. pp. 502–503.

7. Philip Van Doren Stern, Secret Missions of the Civil War (New York: Wing Books, 1990), pp. 102–103.

8. William E. Doster, Lincoln and Episodes of the Civil War (New York: G. P. Putnam's Sons, 1915), pp. 65–66.

9. Williamson, Prison Life in the Old Capitol, p. 86.

10. Ibid., pp. 54–55, 86.

11. Speer, Portal to Hell, p. 82.

12. Colby, "The 'Old Capitol' Prison," Annals of the Civil War, p. 509.

13. Ibid., p. 511.

14. Williamson, Prison Life in the Old Capitol, p. 54.

15. Journal of D. A. Mahoney, cited in Belle Boyd, Belle Boyd in Camp and Prison, (Baton Rouge: Louisiana State University Press, 1998) p. 59.

16. Boyd, Belle Boyd in Camp and Prison, p. 131.

17. Ibid., p. 63.

18. Ibid., p. 138.

19. Ibid., pp. 138–139.

20. Stern, Secret Missions of the Civil War p. 107.

21. John S. Bowman, editor, Who Was Who in the Civil War, reprint edition (North Dighton, MA: World Publication Group, Inc., 2002), pp. 30–31.

22. Colby, "The 'Old Capitol' Prison," Annals of the Civil War, p. 507.

23. Ibid., p. 507; Speer, Portals to Hell, p. 289.

24. Boyd, Belle Boyd in Camp and Prison, pp. 138–139.

25. Bowman, Who Was Who in the Civil War, pp. 94–95; Boatner, The Civil War Dictionary, p. 356.

26. Janet C. Pittard, "Wild Rose," Our State (April 2004), pp. 25–26.

27. Bowman, Who Was Who in the Civil War, pp. 94–95; Boatner, The Civil War Dictionary, p. 356.

28. Pittard, p. 26.

29. Bowman, *Who Was Who in the Civil War*, pp. 94–95; Boatner, *The Civil War Dictionary*, p. 356.

30. "The Late Mrs. Rose A. Greenhow," *Wilmington Sentinel*, October 1, 1864, in Alexander Robinson Boteler Papers, Special Collections Library, Duke University, Durham, North Carolina, online at http://scriptorium.lib.duke.edu/greenhow/1864-10-01-a/1864-10-01-a.html.

31. Colby, "The 'Old Capitol' Prison," *Annals of the Civil War*, p. 502.

32. Doster, *Lincoln and Episodes of the Civil War*, p. 77.

33. Ibid., pp. 105–111.

34. Speer, *Portals to Hell*, p. 8;

35. H. H. Wells to Lt. Col. J. H. Taylor, Alexandria, Va., May 4, 1864, O.R., Ser. II, Vol.7, p. 112.

36. Endorsement to Wells' communication to Taylor, by C. C. Augur, Headquarters Department of Washington, 22nd Army Corps, May 4, 1864, O.R., Ser. II, Vol.7, p. 112.

37. Bowman, *Who Was Who in the Civil War*, pp. 150–151; Boatner, *The Civil War Dictionary*, pp. 569–570.

38. Colby, "The 'Old Capitol' Prison," *Annals of the Civil War*, p. 503.

39. Webb, "Prison Life on Johnson's Island, 1863–'64," in Clark, *Histories of the Several Regiments in the Great War, 1861–1865*, Vol. IV, pp. 662–663.

40. Colby, "The 'Old Capitol' Prison," *Annals of the Civil War*, pp. 504–505.

41. Diary entry, February 15, 1863, Williamson, *Prison Life in the Old Capitol*, pp. 53–54.

42. Williamson, *Prison Life in the Old Capitol*, pp. 52–56.

43. Doster, *Lincoln and Episodes of the Civil War*, pp. 74–78.

44. Williamson, *Prison Life in the Old Capitol*, p. 31.

45. Colby, "The 'Old Capitol' Prison," *Annals of the Civil War*, pp. 506–507.

46. Ibid., p. 507.

47. Capt. Bruce R. Boynton, USN, "A Scottsville Teen in Mosby's Rangers: Henry G. Harris," online at http://scottsvillemuseum.com/war/harris/home.html.

48. "Roster of the 43rd Battalion Virginia Cavalry, Army of Northern Virginia, Confederate States of America," online http://www.mosocco.com/companyf.html.

49. Williamson, *Prison Life in the Old Capitol*, pp. 36–37; Doster, *Lincoln and Episodes of the Civil War*, pp. 86–87.

50. Doster, *Lincoln and Episodes of the Civil War*, p. 86.

51. Williamson, *Prison Life in the Old Capitol*, pp. 63, 75.

52. H. H. Wells to Lt. Col. J. H. Taylor, Alexandria, Va., May 4, 1864, O.R., Ser. II, Vol.7, p. 112.

53. Doster, *Lincoln and Episodes of the Civil War*, p. 86.

54. Charles A. Dana, "The War — Some Unpublished History," *The North American Review*, Vol. 153, No. 417 (August 1891), p. 243.

55. Dana, "The War — Some Unpublished History," p. 244.

56. Ibid., pp. 244–245.

57. Boyd, *Belle Boyd in Camp and Prison*, p. 165.

58. Colby, "The 'Old Capitol' Prison," *Annals of the Civil War*, pp. 505–506.

59. Ibid., p. 510.

60. Speer, *Portals to Hell*, p. 310.

Chapter XIV

1. Speer, *Portals to Hell*, pp. 152, 329

2. Ibid., pp. 151–152.

3. Ibid., p. 151.

4. *New York Times*, October 16, 1864, p. 2:5, cited in Speer, *Portals to Hell* p. 151.

5. Luther Hopkins, "Luther Hopkins Recalls Prison Life at Point Lookout," in Commager, *The Blue and the Gray*, p. 695.

6. Ibid.

7. Speer, *Portals to Hell* pp. 151–152.

8. Keiley, *In Vinculis*, p. 59, cited in Speer, *Portals to Hell*, p. 152.

9. Speer, *Portals to Hell*, p. 152.

10. W. Hoffman to Brig. Gen. G. Marston, October 12, 1863, O.R., Ser. II, Vol. 6, p. 368; W. Hoffman to Brig. Gen. G. Marston, October 17, 1863, O. R., Ser. II, Vol. 6, 390; Barziza, *Adventures of a Prisoner of War*, p. 89, cited in Speer, p. 153.

11. C. T. Alexander, "Report of a medical inspection of the camp and prison hospital of the prisoners of war, commanded by Colonel Draper, Thirty-sixth Colored Regiment, made on the 1st day of July, 1864, by Surg. C. T. Alexander, medical inspector, U.S. Army," O.R., Ser. II, Vol. 7, pp. 448–449.

12. J. B. Traywick, "Prison Life at Point Lookout," *Southern Historical Society Papers*, Vol. XVIII (January-December 1890), p. 432.

13. Alexander, pp. 448–449.

14. C. T. Alexander, to Col. W. Hoffman, "Notes referred to this report," O.R., Ser. II, Vol. 7, p. 450.

15. W. F. Swalm to Dr. J. H. Douglas, Washington, November 13, 1863, O.R. Ser. II, Vol. 6, pp. 575–581.

16. "Abstract from monthly returns of the principal U.S. Military prisons," O.R., Ser. II, Vol. 8, p. 991.

17. Anthony M. Keiley, *In Vinculis; or The Prisoner of War, by a Virginia Confederate* (Petersburg, VA: "Daily Index" Office, 1866), p. 67; O.R. Ser. II, Vol. 6, pp. 132, 183, 214; O.R., Ser. II, Vol. 7, p. 859, cited in Speer, p. 152.

18. "Abstract from monthly returns of the principal U.S. Military prisons," O.R., Ser. II, Vol. 8, pp. 991–1004.

19. Traywick, "Prison Life at Point Lookout," p. 432.

20. Bartlett Yancey Malone, "The Diary of Bartlett Yancey Malone," in William Whatley Pierson, Jr., ed., *The James Sprunt Historical Publications*, Vol. 16, No. 2, (Chapel Hill, NC: University of North Carolina, (1919), p. 45.

21. Ibid., p. 5.

22. Leon, *Diary of a Tar Heel Confederate Soldier*, p. 1.

23. Ibid., pp. 60–63.

24. C. T. Alexander to Col. W. Hoffman, "Notes referred to this report," O.R., Ser. II, Vol. 7, p. 450.

25. Leon, *Diary of a Tar Heel Confederate Soldier*, pp. 64–65.

26. Malone, "The Diary of Bartlett Yancey Malone," pp. 43–45.

27. Leon, *Diary of a Tar Heel Confederate Soldier*, pp. 64–65.

28. Ibid.,, pp. 67,70.

29. Ibid., p. 64.

30. Malone, "The Diary of Bartlett Yancey Malone," pp. 48, 52–53, 55.

31. Traywick, "Prison Life at Point Lookout," p. 433.

32. Ibid., pp. 434–435.

33. Ibid.

34. Hopkins, "Luther Hopkins Recalls Prison Life at Point Lookout," p. 695.

35. Malone, "The Diary of Bartlett Yancey Malone," p. 46.

36. "Abstract of monthly returns of the principal U.S. Military prisons," O.R., Ser. II, Vol. 8, pp. 986–1004.

37. Ibid., p. 992.

38. W. Hoffman to Col. J. A. Hardie, July 27, 1864, O.R., Ser. II, Vol. 7, p. 502.

39. Hopkins, "Luther Hopkins Recalls Prison Life at Point Lookout," p. 695.

40. Burnham, *So Far From Dixie*, p. 47.

411. Ibid., pp. 48–49.

42. Ibid., p. 49.

43. Ibid., pp. 50–52.

44. Morris H. Church to Lieut. Col. S. Eastman, Barracks No. 3, Elmira, N. Y, July 22, 1864, O.R., Ser. II, Vol. 7, p. 489.

45. W. Hoffman to Secretary of War, July 26, 1864, O.R., Ser. II, Vol. 7, pp. 488–489.

46. A. Lincoln to Major General Butler, Executive Mansion, Washington, January 2, 1864, O.R., Ser. II, Vol. 6, p. 808.

47. Malone, "The Diary of Bartlett Yancey Malone," p. 53.

48. "Point Lookout Civil War Prison," online at www.censusdiggins.com/prison_ptlookout.html.

Chapter XV

1. Speer, *Portals to Hell*, p. 329.

2. "Rock Island Civil War Prison Barracks," excerpts from Clifford W. Stevens, *Rock Island Confederate Prison Deaths*, transcribed by Diana Hanson, online at www.rootsweb.com/~ilrockis/plac_hist/hist-cp.htm.

3. Charles Wright, "Rock Island Prison 1864–1865," Southern Historical Society Papers, Vol. 1, No. 4 (April 1876), p. 284.

4. Speer, *Portals to Hell*, p. 154.

5. M. C. Meigs to Capt. Charles A. Reynolds, Washington, July 11, 1863, O.R., Ser. II, Vol. 6, p. 115.

6. M. C. Meigs to Lt. Col. C. A. Reynolds, Washington, August 12, 1863, O.R., Ser. II, Vol. 6, p. 196.

7. Charles Thomas to Capt. C. A. Reynolds, Washington, September 11, 1863, O.R., Ser. II, Vol. 6, p. 198.

8. W. Hoffman to E. M. Stanton, Washington, D.C., December 3, 1863, O.R., Ser. II, Vol. 6, pp. 634–635.

9. A. M. Clark to Col. W. Hoffman, Chicago, Ill., February 13, 1864, O.R., Ser. II, Vol. 6, pp. 948–949.

10. Richard Bender Abel and Fay Adamson Gecik, ed. *Sojourns of a Patriot: The Field and Prison Papers of an Unreconstructed Confederate* (Murfreesboro, TN: Southern Heritage Press, 1998), p. 248.

11. W. Hoffman to E. M. Stanton, Washington, D.C., December 3, 1863, O.R., Ser. II, Vol. 6, p. 635.

12. A. M. Clark to Col. W. Hoffman, Rock Island, Ill., April 8, 1864, O.R., Ser. II, Vol. 7, pp. 23, 25.

13. A. M. Clark to Col. W. Hoffman, Rock Island, Ill., April 8, 1864, O.R., Ser. II, Vol. 7, p. 24.

14. W. Hoffman to Col. A. J. Johnson, Washington, D.C., April 16, 1864, O.R. Ser. II, Vol. 7, p. 59.

15. M. C. Meigs to Lt. Col. C. A. Reynolds, Washington, August 12, 1863, O.R., Ser. II, Vol. 6, p. 196; cited in Abel and Gecik, *Sojourns of a Patriot*, pp. 247–248.

16. W. Hoffman to Col. C. V. De Land, Washington, D.C., October 17, 1863, O.R., Ser. II, Vol. 6, p. 390.

17. William M. Orme to Edwin M. Stanton, Washington City, D.C., December 7, 1863, O.R., Ser. II, Vol. 6, , p. 663.

18. W. Hoffman to Col. C. Thomas, Washington, D.C., December 1, 1863, O.R., Ser. II, Vol. 6, p. 626.

19. "Rock Island Civil War Prison Barracks."

20. Clifford W. Stephens, compl., *Rock Island Confederate Prison Deaths* (Rock Island, IL: Blackhawk Genealogical Society, 1973), pp. 39–40, cited in Speer, *Portals to Hell*, p. 155.

21. Richard Bender Abel and Fay Adamson Gecik, ed. *Sojourns of a Patriot: The Field and Papers of an Unreconstructed Confederate* (Murfreesboro, TN: Southern Heritage Press, 1998), pp. 5–6.

22. Abel and Gecik, "Letter Number Seventy-Nine," May 31, 1864, p. 229.

23. Abel and Gecik, p. 235.

24. Abel and Gecik, pp. 242, 246.

25. Wright, "Rock Island Prison 1864–1865," p. 282.

26. "Testimony of a Federal Soldier," *Southern Historical Society Papers*, Vol. I, No. 4 (April 1876), p. 292.

27. Ibid., pp. 292–293.

28. L. McCormick, "Thomas R. McCormick," online at www.misscivilwar.org/persona/mccorm.html.

29. "Report of inspection of camp and field hospitals at Rock Island, Ill., February 4 to 7, 1864, by Surg. A. M. Clark, acting medical inspector prisoners of war," Ser. II, Vol. 6, pp. 939–940.

30. A. M. Clark to Col. W. Hoffman, Rock Island, Ill., February 10, 1863, O.R., Ser. II, Vol. 6, p. 938.

31. "Report of inspection of camp and field hospitals at Rock Island, Ill., February 4 to 7, 1864, by Surg. A. M. Clark, acting medical inspector prisoners of war," Ser. II, Vol. 6, p. 940.

32. Wright, "Rock Island Prison 1864–1865," p. 284.

33. C. A. Reynolds to Brig. Gen. M. C. Meigs, Rock Island, Ill, February 25, 1864, O.R., Ser. II, Vol. 6, pp. 1003–1004.

34. A. M. Clark to Col. W. Hoffman, Rock Island, Ill, March 1, 1864, O.R., Ser. II, Vol. 6, pp. 1001–1003; A. M. Clark to Col. W. Hoffman, Chicago, March 6, 1864, O.R., Ser. II, Vol. 6, p. 1022.

35. John F. Marsh to Col. James A. Hardie, Inspector General, U.S. Army, Rock Island Barracks, Ill., April 18, 1864, O.R., Ser. II, Vol. 7, p. 65.

36. "Rock Island Civil War Prison Barracks."

37. W. Hoffman to Col. A. J. Johnson, Washington, D.C., June 10, 1864, O.R., Ser. II, Vol. 7, p. 221.

38. A. J. Johnson to Col. William Hoffman, Rock Island, Ill., June 25, 1864, O.R., Ser. II, Vol.7, p. 415.

39. Otis Bryan England, *A Short History of the Rock Island Prison Barracks* (Rock Island, IL: Historical Office, U.S. Army Armament, Munitions, and Chem-

ical Command, 1985), pp. 17–18, cited in Speer, *Portals to Hell*, p. 230.

40. McCormick.

41. Testimony of Matthew H. Kollock, "Proceeding of a military commission convened at Rock Island Barracks, Ill., at 3 p.m., October 25, 1864," O.R., Ser. II, Vol. 7, p. 1038.

42. Testimony of Peter Cowherd, "Proceeding of a military commission convened at Rock Island Barracks, Ill., at 3 p.m., October 25, 1864," O.R., Ser. II, Vol. 7, p. 1039.

43. "Proceeding of a military commission convened at Rock Island Barracks, Ill., at 3 p.m., October 25, 1864," O.R., Ser. II, Vol. 7, pp. 1037–1040.

44. Wright, "Rock Island Prison 1864–1865," 285–286.

45. "Rock Island Civil War Prison Barracks."

46. Ibid.

47. Wright, "Rock Island Prison 1864–1865," p. 284.

48. "Abstract from monthly returns of the principal U.S. Military prisons," O. R., Ser. II, Vol. 8, pp. 1002–1003.

49. "Rock Island Arsenal," online www.ria.army. mil.riahistory.htm.

50. Ibid.

Chapter XVI

1. Bruce Catton, *John Ransom's Andersonville Diary: Life Inside the Civil War's Most Infamous Prison* (New York: Berkley Books, 1994).

2. Speer, *Portals to Hell*, pp. 260, 332.

3. Joseph Ferguson, *Life-Struggles in Rebel Prisons*, (Philadelphia, PA: James M. Ferguson, Publisher, 1865), p. 82.

4. Speer, *Portals to Hell*, p. 260.

5. Faust, *Historical Times Illustrated Encyclopedia*, p. 16.

6. Miller, *The Photographic History of the Civil War*, Vol. 7, pp. 74–75.

7. Ferguson, pp. 95–96.

8. Speer, *Portals to Hell*, pp. 259–260.

9. Miller, Vol. 7, p. 74.

10. Ibid.

11. Ferguson, pp. 95–96.

12. H. Wirz to Colonel Chandler, Camp Sumter, August 1, 1864, O.R., Ser. II, Vol. 7, pp. 521–522.

13. Miller, Vol. 7, p. 74.

14. Ibid., p. 76.

15. Speer, *Portals to Hell*, pp. 259–260.

16. R. B. Winder to Maj. P. W. White, Camp Sumter, Andersonville, February 20, 1864, O.R., Ser. II, Vol. 6, p. 977.

17. "Imprisonment of the 'Plymouth Pilgrim' Officers," online at http://home.att.net/~cwppds/officers.htm.

18. Alonzo Cooper, *In and Out of Rebel Prisons*, (Oswego, NY: B. J. Oliphant, 1988), pp. 32–35, 41–42.

19. Speer, *Portals to Hell*, p. 261.

20. H. Wirz to Capt. W. S. Winder, forwarded by Brig. Gen. John H. Winter to Gen. S. Cooper, adjutant and inspector general, C. S. Army, O.R., Ser. II, Vol. 7, p. 438.

21. Miller, Vol. 7, p. 76.

22. Ibid.

23. Ibid., Vol. 7, pp. 78–84.

24. H. Wirz to Colonel Chandler, Camp Sumter, August 1, 1864, O.R., Ser. II, Vol. 7, pp. 521–522.

25. Ibid.

26. Ibid.

27. Faust, *Historical Times Illustrated Encyclopedia*, p. 836.

28. Miller, Vol. 7, pp. 76–78.

29. O.R., Ser. II, Vol. 6, pp. 965–966, 993; O.R., Ser. II, Vol. 7, p. 438, John McElroy, *Andersonville: A Story of a Rebel Military Prison*, (Toledo, OH: D. R. Locke, 1879), p. 315; James Carson Elliot, *The Southern Soldier Boy* (Raleigh, NC: Edwards & Broughton, 1907), p. 40, cited in Speer, p. 260.

30. John H. Winder to Col. S. Cooper, Camp Sumter, June 14, 1864, O.R., Ser. II, Vol. 7, pp. 410–411.

31. Statement of Capt. R. C. G. Reed, August 4, 1864, O.R., Ser. I, Vol. 35, Pt. II, p. 1864.

32. Eliza Frances Andrews, *The War-Time Journal of a Georgia Girl, 1864–1865* (New York: Appleton, 1908, reprint Lincoln, NE: University of Nebraska Press, 1997), pp. 77–78.

33. Ferguson, *Life-Struggles in Rebel Prisons*, p. 82.

34. H. Wirz to Capt. W. S. Winder, forwarded by Brig. Gen. John H. Winter to General S. Cooper, Adjutant and Inspector General, C. S. Army, O.R., Ser. II, Vol. 7, p. 438.

35. Ferguson, *Life-Struggles in Rebel Prisons*, p. 83.

36. Eugene Forbes, *Death Before Dishonor: The Andersonville Diary of Eugene Forbes*. Edited by William B. Styple (Kearney, NJ: Belle Grove publishing Co., 1995), pp. 11–12.

37. Ibid., p. 56.

38. Ibid., pp. 62–63

39. John H. Winder to Gen. S. Cooper, Camp Sumter, June 24, 1864, O.R., Ser. II, Vol. 7, pp. 410–411.

40. "The Capture, Adventures, and Escape of Sergeant James E. Gillespie, of Company I," in E. Tarrant, compiler, *The Wild Riders of the First Kentucky Cavalry*, pp. 484–485, microfiche 157, Unit 4, KY# Regimental Histories, Library of Virginia, Richmond, Virginia.

41. Tarrant, *The Wild Riders of the First Kentucky Cavalry*, pp. 484–485.

42. Ibid., p. 486.

43. Ibid.

44. James Wolf, "In and Out of the Jaws of Death. Recollections of Fifteen Months Experience inRebel Prisons." The *Sciotio Gazette* 28 Feb. 1865, online www.89thohio.com/Prisoners/wolfe.htm..

45. "Archaeological Investigations at Andersonville Civil War Prison," online.

46. Forbes, *Death Before Dishonor*, pp. 66–67.

47. Ibid., pp. 69–70.

48. Ibid., p. 71.

49. H. Wirz to Capt. W. S. Winder, forwarded by Brig. Gen. John H. Winter to General S. Cooper, adjutant and inspector general, C. S. Army, O.R., Ser. II, Vol. 7, p. 438.

50. Forbes, *Death Before Dishonor*, pp. 89–90.

51. Ibid., pp. 91–92.

52. H. Wirz to Colonel Chandler, Camp Sumter, August 1, 1864, O.R., Ser. II. Vol. 7, pp. 521–522.

53. John McElroy, *Andersonville: A Story of a Rebel Military Prison* (Toledo, OH: D. R. Locke, 1879,

reprint, revised edition, Greenwich, CN: Fawcett, 1962), p. ix.

54. McElroy, pp. 178–181.

55. Ibid. pp. 181–183.

56. Ibid., pp. 183–85.

57. Speer, *Portals to Hell*, p. 220.

58. "Andersonville Civil War Prison," online www.censusdiggins.com/prison_andersonville, html.

59. Faust, *Historical Times Illustrated Encyclopedia*, p. 16

60. Boatner, *The Civil War Dictionary*, p. 15.

Chapter XVII

1. "The Narrative of James E. King, of Company A, of His Capture and Terrible Sufferings of Himself and Others on Belle Isle," in Sgt. Tarrant. *The Wild Riders of the First Kentucky Cavalry*, p. 479, Microfiche 157, Unit 4, KY# Regimental Histories, Library of Virginia.

2. Speer, *Portals to Hell*, p. 332.

3. "Yankee Prisoners," *Richmond Sentinel*, October 23, 1863.

4. *The Charleston Mercury*, August 7, 1862.

5. "Richmond Loop Site 010," online at http://www.greatamericantrails.co/nature_trains/virginia/richmond/richmond_loop_010.html

6. J. F. W., letter to the editor, from Camp Parole, Annapolis, MD, September 7, 1863, New York Sunday *Mercury*, September 13, 1863.

7. Richmond *Daily Dispatch*, July 9, 1862.

8. *Richmond Examiner*, September 24, 1862.

9. *Richmond's Civil War Prisons* (Lynchburg, VA: H. E. Howard, 1990), p. 15.

10. Richmond *Daily Dispatch*, July 9, 1862.

11. Parker, *Richmond's Civil War Prisons*, pp. 14–15.

12. "Enjoying Themselves," *Richmond Dispatch*, July 26, 1862.

13. Parker, *Richmond's Civil War Prisons*, p. 34.

14. "Prisoners on Belle Isle: How They Looked to the Eyes of a Libby Man. A Visit From Morgan, the Famous Raider—The Story of the Inception of the Two Tunnels out of the Old Warehouse," *New York Times*, March 1, 1891.

15. Parker, *Richmond's Civil War Prisons*, pp. 33–34.

16. George W. Kremer, Letter to the editor, *National Tribune*, February 14, 1884.

17. Parker, *Richmond's Civil War Prisons*, p. 15.

18. "Prisoners on Belle Isle."

19. Joseph Arnold, "Bell Island," in Domschecke, *Twenty Months in Captivity*, p. 136.

20. *Richmond Enquirer*, July 11, 1862.

21. J. J. Sneath, Harrison's Landing, Va., August 8, 1862, Shirleysburg, Pa., *Herald*, August 21, 1862.

22. Richmond *Dispatch*, January 17, 1863.

23. Tarrant, "The Narrative of James E. King," pp. 475–477.

24. W. W. Sprague, "Belle Isle: Something About the Dog Slayer and a Female Soldier," *National Tribune*, July 11, 1889.

25. "Prisoners on Belle Isle: How They Looked to the Eyes of a Libby Man." *New York Times*, March 1, 1891.

26. Ibid.

27. Parker, *Richmond's Civil War Prisons*, p. 34.

28. Ibid., p. 15.

29. "Enjoying Themselves," *Richmond Dispatch*, July 26, 1862.

30. "Belle Isle," *Richmond Dispatch*, September 1, 1862.

31. "Belle Island," *Richmond Examiner*, September 24, 1862.

32. "Belle Isle," *Richmond Dispatch*, January 17, 1863.

33. Tarrant, "The Narrative of James E. King," pp. 478–479.

34. "Prisoners on Belle Isle."

35. Parker, *Richmond's Civil War Prisons*, p. 52.

36. Ibid.

37. W. P. Kendrick, to President A. Lincoln, National Hotel, Washington, February 21, 1864, O.R., Ser. II, Vol. 6, p. 377.

38. William A. Carrington to Gen. J. H. Winder, Richmond, November 27, 1863.

39. Ibid.

40. Surgeon G. W. Semple to Surgeon William A. Carrington, March 6, 1864, O.R., Ser. II, Vol. 6, pp. 1087–1090.

41. Parker, *Richmond's Civil War Prisons*, p. 57.

42. H. C. Trumbull to Colonel Hoffman, Hartford, Conn., November 17, 1863.

43. W. S. Toland to the editor of the *New York Times*, "Prison Life at Richmond—Its Cruelties," *New York Times*, O.R., S. II, Vol. 7, pp. 80–81.

44. "Belle Isle Civil War Prison," online at www.censusdiggins.com/prison_bellisle.html.

45. "Change of Base," *Richmond Sentinel*, December 30, 1863.

46. Garnett Andrews to secretary of war, Richmond, September 24, 1864, O.R., Ser. II, Vol. 7, p. 870.

47. H. Wirz to Capt. Norris Montgomery, Richmond, Va., August 27, 1862, O.R., Ser. II, Vol. IV, p. 865.

48. Parker, *Richmond's Civil War Prisons*, p. 17.

49. H. Wirz to Capt. Norris Montgomery, Richmond, Va., August 27, 1862, O.R., Ser. II, Vol. IV, p. 865.

50. Parker, *Richmond's Civil War Prisons*, p. 36

51. Ibid. p. 34.

52. John W. Manning, "Brutal Murders at Belle Isle," *National Tribune*, September 2, 1882.

53. H. J. Peter, "Prison Experience," Toledo *Blade*, June 9, 1887.

54. Ira E. Gosby, "Belle Isle. The Sergeant at the Gate—Hite's Cavalry—The Cold New Year," *National Tribune*, April 16, 1903.

55. B. F. Jones, "Rebel Prisons, Belle Isle, Andersonville, Millen, Savannah, and Blackshear," *National Tribune*, May 19, 1904.

56. W. S. Toland to the editor of the *New York Times*, "Prison Life at Richmond—Its Cruelties," *New York Times*, date not given, probably April 1864, O.R., S. II, Vol. 7, pp. 80–81.

57. Gregory A. Coco, ed. *The Civil War Letters of Private Roland E. Bowen, 15th Massachusetts Infantry*. (Gettysburg, PA: Thomas, 1994), p. 173.

58. "Belle Island" *Richmond Sentinel*, May 13, 1863.

59. Boatner, *The Civil War Dictionary*, p. 323.

60. W. M. Gardner to Maj. Chestney, Richmond, October 23, 1864, Confederate Service Record of General William M. Gardner, Roll #102, M331-CSA Staff and General Officers; online at www.mdgorman.com/NARA/william_gardner_csr.htm.

61. Garnett Andrews to secretary of war, Richmond, September 24, 1864, O.R., Ser. II, Vol. 7, p. 870.

62. J. J. Sneath, Harrison's Landing, Va., August 8, 1862, Shirleysburg, Pa., *Herald*, August 21, 1862.

63. Tarrant, "The Narrative of James E. King," p. 478.

64. Arnold, "Bell Island," p. 136.

65. Ibid.

66. *Richmond Examiner*, October 5, 1863.

67. Tarrant, "The Narrative of James E. King," p. 478.

68. John W. Manning, "Brutal Murders at Belle Isle," *National Tribune*, September 2, 1882.

69. Louis P. Lienberger, "What Became of Dog Slayer?" *National Tribune*, January 6, 1887.

70. Ibid.

71. H. J. Peter, "Prison Experience," Toledo *Blade*, June 9, 1887.

72. Sprague, "Belle Isle: Something About the Dog Slayer and a Female Soldier," *National Tribune*, July 11, 1889.

73. Gosby, "Belle Isle. The Sergeant at the Gate — Hite's Cavalry — The Cold New Year," *National Tribune*, April 16, 1903.

74. J. M. Emery, "He Ate the Dog," *National Tribune*, June 25, 1903.

75. Arnold, "Belle Island," p. 136.

76. Gosby, "Belle Isle. The Sergeant at the Gate — Hite's Cavalry — The Cold New Year," *National Tribune*, April 16, 1903.

77. John W. Manning, "Brutal Murders at Belle Isle," *National Tribune*, September 2, 1882.

78. E. C. Culp, "To the Editor," *National Tribune*, March 11, 1888.

79. B. F. Jones, "Rebel Prisons, Belle Isle, Andersonville, Millen, Savannah, and Blackshear," *National Tribune*, May 19, 1904.

80. Parker, *Richmond's Civil War Prisons*, p. 54.

81. *The Charleston Mercury*, August 7, 1862.

82. Tarrant, "The Narrative of James E. King," pp. 479–480.

83. Orwin H. Balch, "Gettysburg Prisoners," *National Tribune*, August 11, 1904.

84. D. B. Curtis, "Diary of Henry H. Ladd," in *History of the Twenty-fourth Michigan of the Iron Brigade, known as the Detroit and Wayne County Regiment.* (1891, reprint ed. Gaithersburg, MD: Old Soldier Books, 1988), pp. 432–436.

85. "Belle Isle," *Richmond Sentinel*, November 9, 1863.

86. "The Yankee Prisoners," *Richmond Whig*, February 10, 1864.

87. Janet B. Hewett, Noah Andrew Trudeau, Bryce A. Suderow, *The Supplement to the Army Official Records*, Vol. 73, (Wilmington, NC: Broadfoot Publishing, 1996), pp. 585–587.

88. "Transfer of Yankee Prisoners," *Richmond Sentinel*. February 24, 1864.

89. "False Report," *Richmond Whig*, March 7, 1864.

90. "Four Prisoners Shot," *Richmond Sentinel*, August 27, 1864.

91. D. J. Martin, "'Jolly Fellows,' These. A Veteran Refutes one of the Characteristic Lies About Treatment in Rebel Prisons," *National Tribune*, June 13, 1895.

92. Ibid.

93. Ibid.

94. Coco, *The Civil War Letters of Private Roland E. Bowen*, p. 184.

95. Parker, *Richmond's Civil War Prisons*, p. 56.

96. "Prisoners on Belle Isle: How They Looked to the Eyes of a Libby Man." *New York Times*, March 1, 1891.

97. Boatner, *The Civil War Dictionary*, p. 57.

98. *Richmond Dispatch*, February 12, 1865; Parker, p. 65.

99. Ibid.

100. *Richmond Whig*, April 14, 1865.

101. Parker, *Richmond's Civil War Prisons*, pp. 68–69

102. Briscoe Goodheart, "Belle Isle Revisited. A Loudoun Ranger Taken in the Spot where He Starved and Suffered," *National Tribune*, November 10, 1892.

103. "Richmond Loop Site 010," online at www.greatamericantrails.co/nature_trains/virginia/richmond/richmond_loop_010.html.

Chapter XVIII

1. Jesse Hawes, *Cahaba: A Story of Captive Boys in Blue* (New York: Burr Printing House, 1882), p. 250.

2. Speer, *Portals to Hell*, p. 332.

3. William O. Bryant, *Cahaba Prison and the Sultana Disaster* (Tuscalossa: University of Alabama Press, 1990), pp. 17–20, cited in Speer, *Portals to Hell*, p. 256.

4. "Explore Old Cahaba," online.

5. Bryant, *Cahaba Prison and the Sultana Disaster*, pp. 17–20, cited in Speer, *Portals to Hell*, p. 256.

6. Speer, *Portals to Hell*, p. 255.

7. D. T. Chandler to Col. R. H. Chilton, Cahaba, Ala, October 16, 1864, O.R., Ser. II, Vol. 7, p. 998.

8. Speer, *Portals to Hell*, p. 255.

9. R. H. Whitfield to P. B. Scott, medical director, Cahaba, Ala., March 31, 1864, O.R., Ser. II, Vol. 6, p. 1124.

10. D. T. Chandler to Col. R. H. Chilton, Cahaba, Ala, October 16, 1864, O.R., Ser. II, Vol. 7, pp. 999, 1001.

11. R. H. Whitfield to P. B. Scott, Medical Director, Cahaba, Ala., March 31, 1864, O.R., Ser. II, Vol. 6, p. 1124.

12. D. T. Chandler to Col. R. H. Chilton, Cahaba, Ala, October 16, 1864, O.R., Ser. II, Vol. 7, p. 1000.

13. Speer, *Portals to Hell*, p. 256.

14. D. T. Chandler to Col. R. H. Chilton, Cahaba, Ala, October 16, 1864, O.R., Ser. II, Vol. 7, pp. 999, 1001.

15. Ibid., p. 1000.

16. Hawes, pp. 253–254, cited in Speer, *Portals to Hell*, p. 257.

17. Walker, *Cahaba Prison and the Sultana Disaster*, p. 13, cited in Speer, *Portals to Hell*, pp. 256–257.

18. Boatner, *The Civil War Dictionary*, pp. 940–941.

19. Jno. H. Winder to General S. Cooper, Camp Lawton, Ga., October 27, 1864, O.R., Ser. II, Vol. 7, p. 1051.

20. H. A. M. Henderson, captain and agent, to Colonel Surget, Cahaba, Ala., December 1, 1864, O.R., Ser. II, Vol. 7, pp. 1176–1177.

21. Ibid.

22. C. C. Washburn to H. A. M. Henderson, Memphis, Tenn., November 15, 1864, O.R., Ser. II, Vol. 7, pp. 1176–1177.

23. Boatner, *The Civil War Dictionary*, pp. 519–520.

24. Dabney H. Maury to Col. T. M. Jack, Mobile, AL, April 16, 1864, O. R., Ser. I, Vol. 32, Pt. III, pp. 787–788.

25. Brannon, "The Cahaba Military Prison, 1863–

1865," p. 165; Bryant, *Cahaba Prison and the Sultana Disaster*, p. 24, both cited in Speer, *Portals to Hell*, p. 257.

26. Brannon, "The Cahaba Military Prison, 1863–1865," pp. 32, 167–68, 171; Hawes, *Cahaba: A Story of Captive Boys in Blue*, p. 446, cited in Speer, *Portals to Hell*, p. 257.

27. S. Cooper to Brig. Gen. J. H. Winder, Richmond, Va., October 19, 1864, O.R., Ser. II, Vol. 7, p. 1014.

28. Hawes, pp. 210, 212, cited in Speer, *Portals to Hell*, p. 257.

29. John T. Young to Maj. Gen. C. C. Washburn, Memphis, TN, September 13, 1864, O.R., Ser. I, Vol. 32, Pt. I, p. 605.

30. Ibid.

31. Boatner, *The Civil War Dictionary*, p. 296.

32. John T. Young to Maj. Gen. C. C. Washburn, Memphis, TN, September 13, 1864, O.R., Ser. I, Vol. 32, Pt. I, p. 605.

33. John T. Young to Col. H. C. Davis, Cahaba Hospital, Cahaba, Ala., May 11, 1864, O.R. Ser. I, Vol. 32, Pt. I, p. 594.

34. Statement of John T. Young, Cahaba, Ala., May 16, 1864, O.R., Ser. I, Vol. 32, Pt. I, pp. 594–595.

35. John T. Young to Major General Forrest, Cahaba, Ala., May 19, 1864, O.R., Ser. I, Vol. 32, Pt. I, p. 595.

36. Ibid.

37. C. C. Washburn to Col. William Hoffman, Memphis, TN, September 30, 1864, O.R., Ser. II, Vol. 7, pp. 895–896.

38. Ibid.

39. Ibid.

40. Speer, *Portals to Hell*, p. 258.

41. D. T. Chandler to Col. R. H. Chilton, Cahaba, AL, October 16, 1864, O.R., Ser. II, Vol. 7, p. 1000.

42. Ibid.

43. H. A. M. Henderson, captain, commanding, to Gen. J. D. Imboden, Cahaba, AL, January 23, 1865, O.R., Ser. II, Vol. 8, p. 177.

44. "Evidence elicited at the headquarters of the post concerning the mutiny in Federal prison, Cahaba, Ala., January 20, between the hours [of] 3 and 4 a.m., O.R., Ser. II, Vol. 8, pp. 118–122 hereinafter cited as "Evidence of mutiny."

45. Ibid., pp. 118–119.

46. Ibid., p. 119.

47. Ibid.

48. Ibid.

49. Ibid.

50. Ibid.

51. Ibid.

52. Ibid.

53. Ibid., p. 120.

54. Ibid.

55. Ibid.

56. Ibid.

57. Ibid.

58. Ibid.

59. Ibid.

60. Ibid., p. 121.

61. Ibid.

62. Ibid.

63. H. A. M. Henderson to Gen. J. D. Imboden, Cahaba, AL, January 23, 1865, O. R., Ser. II, Vol. 8, pp. 117–118.

64. Ibid., Indorsement, J. D. Imboden, pp. 121–122.

65. Boatner, *The Civil War Dictionary*, p. 423; Bowman, *Who Was Who in the Civil War*, p. 112; Faust, *Historical Times Illustrated Encyclopedia*, pp. 378–379.

66. General Orders, No. 2, Augusta, Ga., February 15, 1865, O.R., Ser. II, Vol. 8, p. 122.

67. C. C. Washburn to Col. C. T. Christensen, Vicksburg, Miss., February 3, 1865, O. R., Ser. I, Vol. 48, Pt. I, p. 960.

68. *New York Times*, 8 April 1865, p. 3:3; Hawes, p. 448, cited in Speer, *Portals to Hell*, p. 258.

69. Speer, *Portals to Hell*, p. 259.

70. "Explore Old Cahaba" online www.selmaalabama.com/cahawbas.htm.

71. Ibid.

Chapter XIX

1. John W. Greene, *Camp Ford Prison, and How I Escaped* (Toledo, OH: Barkdull Printing House, 1893, reprint ed. Greencastle, IN: The Nugget Publishers, 19920, p. 29.

2. Speer, *Portals to Hell*, p. 333.

3. Swingle, "A Yankee Prisoner in Texas."

4. Speer, *Portals to Hell*, p. 216.

5. "A Brief History of Tyler, Texas," http://www.cityoftyler.org/8B1B70ADF71FEAB0BD93F041744A6EB/default.html.

6. A. J. H. Duganne, *Twenty Months in the Department of the Gulf* (New York: n.p., 1865), pp. 277, 286, cited in Speer, *Portals to Hell*, p. 132.

7. Tyler Economic Development Council Inc., "Tyler, Texas: Community Profile 2003," online at www.tedc.org/pdfs/profile.pdf.

8. Greene, p. 29.

9. A. A. Stuart, *Iowa Colonels and Regiments* (Des Moines: Mills & Co., 1865), p. 356, cited in Speer, *Portals to Hell*, p. 132; "Camp Ford Civil War Prison," www.censusdiggins.com/prison_camp_ford.html.

10. Richard S. Skidmore, "Introduction," in Greene, *Camp Ford Prison*, n.p.

11. Duganne, *Twenty Months*, pp. 335–336, cited in Speer, *Portals to Hell*, p. 132.

12. Speer, *Portals to Hell*, p. 132.

13. Duganne, *Twenty Months*, p. 408; Faust, *Historical Times Illustrated Encyclopedia*, p. 110; Speer, *Portals to Hell*, p. 217.

14. T. Scott Anderson to Capt. E. P. Turner, Tyler, Texas, August 11, 1864, O.R., Ser. I, Vol. 41, Pt. II, p. 1060.

15. Duganne, *Twenty Months*, p. 408; Faust, *Historical Times Illustrated Encyclopedia*, p. 110; Speer, *Portals to Hell*, p. 217.

16. Speer, *Portals to Hell*, pp. 129, 132.

17. James B. Tucker and Norma Tucker, "Great Escape from Rebel Prison," *America's Civil War*, Vol. 8, No. 1 (March 1995); Stuart, *Iowa Colonels and Regiments*, p. 356, cited in Speer, pp. 132–133.

18. Thos. F. Tucker to Maj. E. P. Turner, near Tyler, Texas, November 7, 1863, O.R., Ser. II, Vol. 6, p. 484.

19. J. B. Magruder's endorsement on letter from S. S. Anderson to Major General Magruder, Shreveport, November 10, 1863, O. R., Ser. II, Vol. 6, pp. 489–499.

20. Speer, *Portals to Hell*, p. 133.

21. Charles C. Nott, et al. to Gen. E. Kirby Smith,

Camp Ford, June 7, 1864, O.R., Ser. II, Vol. 7, pp. 208–210.

22. Frederick Crocker, "List of articles required for naval prisoners at Camp Ford, Texas, June 7, 1864," O.R., Ser. II, Vol. 7, p. 210.

23. William P. Coe Papers, Library of Congress, Manuscripts Division, entry 179, letter from William P. Coe, Camp Ford, to his wife, December 24, 1863, cited in Speer, *Portals to Hell*, p. 132.

24. Swingle, "A Yankee Prisoner in Texas."

25. "Xerxes Knox, Private," online.

26. Ibid.

27. Ibid.

28. Duganne, *Twenty Months*, p. 408; Faust, *Historical Times Illustrated Encyclopedia*, p. 110.

29. Duganne, *Twenty Months*, p. 334, cited in Speer, *Portals to Hell*, p. 133.

30. Duganne, *Twenty Months*, p. 415; J. E. Hougland, "The 19th Iowa," in *The National Tribune Scrap Book* (Washington, D.C.: National Tribune Publ., 1909), p.77, cited in Speer, *Portals to Hell*, p. 215.

31. Denny, *Civil War Prisons & Escapes*, p. 202.

32. Charles C. Nott, et al. to Gen. E. Kirby Smith, Camp Ford, June 7, 1864, O.R., Ser. II, Vol. 7, pp. 208–210.

33. J. M. McCulloch to colonel, Camp Ford, February 8, 1865, O.R., Ser. II, Vol. 8, p. 196.

34. Frederick Crocker to Rear Adm. D. G. Farragut, Camp Ford, June 7, 1864, O.R., Ser. II, Vol. 7, pp. 209–210.

35. "Camp Ford Civil War Prison," online.

36. Ig. Szymanski to Col. C. C. Dwight, Shreveport, La., November 18, 1864, O.R., Ser. II, Vol. 7, pp. 1138–1139.

37. William H. Sterling to Capt. C. H. Dyer, New Orleans, La., April 23, 1865, O.R., Ser. II, Vol. 8, p. 506.

38. Frederick Crocker to Commodore James S. Palmer, New Orleans, February 27, 1865, O.R., Ser. II, Vol. 8, pp. 316–317.

39. Richard S. Skidmore, "Introduction," in John W. Greene, *Camp Ford Prison, and How I Escaped* (Toledo, OH: Barkdull Printing House, 1893, reprint ed. Greencastle, IN: The Nugget Publishers, 1992), n.p.

40. Greene, *Camp Ford Prison*, p. 28.

41. Ibid., pp. 34–35.

42. Duganne, *Twenty Months*, pp. 346–354, cited in Speer, *Portals to Hell*, p. 217.

43. Swingle, "A Yankee Prisoner in Texas," www.greece.k12.ny.us/oly/herb.htm

44. Faust, *Historical Times Illustrated Encyclopedia*, p. 110; Tucker, Tucker, "Great Escape," p. 37, Speer, *Portals to Hell*, p. 217

45. Speer, *Portals to Hell*, pp. 217–218.

46. Richard S. Skidmore, "Introduction," in John W. Greene, *Camp Ford Prison; and How I Escaped* n.p.

47. Richard S. Skidmore, "Introduction," in John W. Greene, *Camp Ford Prison*, n.p.

48. Ibid.

49. Greene, *Camp Ford Prison*, pp. 35–38.

50. Ibid., pp. 40–42.

51. William H. Sterling to Capt. C. H. Dyer, New Orleans, La., May 6, 1865, O.R., Ser. II, Vol. 8, pp. 536–537.

52. Faust, *Historical Times Illustrated Encyclopedia*, p. 110; "Camp Ford Civil War Prison," online;

Swingle, "A Yankee Prisoner in Texas"; Tyler, Texas, Visitors Guide.

53. "Come to Camp Ford, C. S. A.: The largest Confederate Prisoner of War Camp west of the Mississippi River," online www.campford.org/.

Chapter XX

1. Albert D. Richardson, *The Secret Service, The Field, The Dungeon, and The Escape* (Hartford, CN: American publishing Co., 1865 Richardson), p. 396.

2. Sandra Parker, *Richmond's Civil War Prisons*, (Lynchburg, VA: H. E. Howard, Inc., 1990), p. 17.

3. Speer, *Portals to Hell*, p. 93

4. *Richmond Dispatch*, March 3, 1895; C. McRae Selph, A.A.G. and inspector general, to Col. R. H. Chilton, Richmond, June 6, 1864, O.R., Ser. II, Vol. 7, 204–205; Parker, *Richmond's Civil War Prisons*, p. 18.

5. *Richmond Daily Examiner*, August 12, 1862.

6. Frank B. Doran, "Prison Memories," *National Tribune* November 16, 1905.

7. Parker, *Richmond's Civil War Prisons*, pp. 17–18.

8. Speer, *Portals to Hell*, f120, p. 352.

9. Harrison, *Prisoners' Mail from the American Civil War*, p. 85.

10. *Richmond Dispatch*, March 3, 1895; C. McRae Selph, A.A.G. and inspector general to Col. R. H. Chilton, Richmond, June 6, 1864, O.R., Ser. II, Vol. 7, 204–205; Parker, *Richmond's Civil War Prisons*, p. 18.

11. Doran, "Prison Memories."

12. *New York Times*, May 24, 1865, p. 4:6; Putnam, *Prisoner of War*, p. 28, cited in Speer, p. 95.

113. Ferguson, *Life-Struggles in Rebel Prisons*, p. 40; Speer, *Portals to Hell*, p. 95.

14. Parker, *Richmond's Civil War Prisons*, p. 19.

15. Ferguson, *Life-Struggles in Rebel Prisons*, p. 40.

16. Ferguson, *Life-Struggles in Rebel Prisons*, pp. 35–36.

17. Richardson, *The Secret Service*, p. 382.

18. "The Camera and Pen Recall Bygone Days: A Weekly Pictorial Series of Events in Richmond's Past," *The Richmond News Leader*, March 30, 1935.

19. Bernard J. Henley,. "Col. George W. Alexander: The Terror of Castle Thunder," *Richmond Literature and History Quarterly*. 3(2) (Fall, 1980), p. 49.

20. Colby, "The 'Old Capitol' Prison," in *The Annals of the Civil War*, pp. 502–503.

21. Ronald W. Fischer, "A Comparative Study of Two Civil War Prisons, Old Capitol Prison and Castle Thunder Prison" (unpublished Master's thesis, Virginia Polytechnic Institute and State University, 1994), p. 26.

22. *Richmond Dispatch*, October 1, 1862, October 18, 1862, December 29, 1862, February 27, 1863, April 7, 1863, May 3, 1864, cited in Fischer, "A Comparative Study of Two Civil War Prisons," p. 28.

23. Parker, *Richmond's Civil War Prisons*, p. 17.

24. Harrison, *Prisoners' Mail*, p. 85.

25. Richardson, *The Secret Service*, pp. 381–382.

26. Parker, *Richmond's Civil War Prisons*, p. 26.

27. Parker, *Richmond's Civil War Prisons*, pp. 26–27.

28. "Good-looking Spy, "*Richmond Whig*, July 20, 1864, p. 1, c. 4.

29. Parker, *Richmond's Civil War Prisons*, p. 17.

30. P. Cashmyer to Col. N. P. Chipman, Richmond, October 12, 1865, O.R., Ser. II, Vol. 8, pp. 764–765.

31. [R.D.W.] "Old Castle Thunder: Death of Colonel Alexander, Who Was Superintendent of This Prison. The Splendid Dog Nero. History of the Noble Specimen of a Lordly Canine Race—Alexander as a Dramatist and Actor—How he Managed Those Under Him, *Richmond Daily Dispatch*, March 3, 1895; and Casstevens, *George Washington Alexander and Castle Thunder*.

32. Richardson, *The Secret Service*, p 381–382.

33. "Old Castle Thunder," *Richmond Dispatch*, March 3, 1895.

34. Ferguson, *Life-Struggles in Rebel Prisons*, pp. 35–36.

35. Ibid.

36. "Division of Detective Force," *Richmond Examiner*, April 9, 1863.

37. Parker, *Richmond's Civil War Prisons*, pp. 28–31; "Treatment of Prisoners in Castle Thunder, Richmond, Virginia," O.R., Ser. II, Vol. 5, pp. 871–924; Speer, *Portals to Hell*, p. 124.

38. Committee to Enquire into Treatment of Prisoners at Castle Thunder, *Evidence taken before the Committee of the House of Representatives, appointed to enquire into the Treatment of Prisoners at Castle Thunder* (Richmond, VA: House of Representatives, 1863); Casstevens, *Captain George Washington Alexander and Castle Thunder*, pp 122.

39. Fischer, "A Comparative Study of Two Civil War Prisons," p. 106.

40. Ferguson, *Life-Struggles in Rebel Prisons*, p. 39.

41. Parker, *Richmond's Civil War Prisons*, p. 30.

42. Richardson, *The Secret Service*, p. 382.

43. "Ring-leader of plot punished," *Richmond Enquirer*, December 29, 1862.

44. "Prisoner Shot," *Richmond Dispatch*, August 25, 1862.

45. "Proceedings of a general Court Martial convened at Richmond by virtue of the following order—General Orders No. 7," October 11, 1862, microfilm, Department of Henrico Papers.

46. Richardson, *The Secret Service*, p. 391.

47. Ibid.

48. Testimony of Frederick F. Wiley before the *Committee of Congress*, p. 46, cited in Golden, p. 58.

49. "A Delivery from Castle Thunder," *Richmond Enquirer*, November 19, 1862, p. 2, c. 4.

50. Ibid.

51. "Recaptured," *Richmond Dispatch*, October 9, 1862, cited in Fischer, p. 106.

52. "Escape," *Richmond Sentinel*, November 26, 1863, p. 2, c. 2.

53. "Attempt to Escape from Prison," *Richmond Dispatch*, October 17, 1862.

54. *Richmond Dispatch*, 5 January 1863, cited in Fischer, "A Comparative Study of Two Civil War Prisons," p. 1

55. "Stray Prison Birds Recaptured," April 18, 1863, *Richmond Examiner*, April 18, 1863.

56. "Castle Thunder Items," *Richmond Examiner*, April 4, 1863.

57. *Richmond Daily Whig*, April 6, 1863.

58. "Special Orders, No. 8," National Archives, Record Group 109, Chapter 9, Vol. 199 1/2, p. 50, online at http://www.mdgorman.com/NARA/rg_109,_ch_9,_vol_199_5,_p_50.htm.

59. "Killed While Attempting to Escape," *Richmond Examiner*, April 7, 1863, p. 1

60. "A Man Shot," *Richmond Sentinel*, April 7, 1863, p. 2, col. 3.

61. "Killed While Attempting to Escape," *Richmond Examiner*, April 7, 1863.

62. "Once More in Confinement," *Richmond Examiner*, July 21, 1863.

63. *Richmond Dispatch*, October 9, 1862; cited in Parker, *Richmond's Civil War Prisons*, p. 20; Speer, p. 125

64. "Attempted Escape," *Richmond Sentinel*, July 2, 1863.

65. "Attempt to Mine Out," *Richmond Sentinel*, October 1, 1863.

66. "Castle Thunder," *Richmond Sentinel*, November 16, 1863.

67. *Richmond Dispatch*, November 16 and 21, 1863, cited in Fischer, "A Comparative Study of Two Civil War Prisons," p. 108.

68. Junius Henri Browne, *Four Years in Secessia: Adventures Within and Beyond the Union Lines: Embracing a Great Variety of Facts, Incidents, and Romance of the War* (Hartford, CN: O. D. Case and Company, 1865), p. 299.

69. Ibid.

70. Richardson, *The Secret Service*, pp. 390–391.

71. "Restless," *Richmond Sentinel*, May 20, 1863.

72. "Attempt to Escape From the Castle," *Richmond Examiner*, May 21, 1863.

73. "An Impudent Scamp," *Richmond Enquirer*, August 14, 1863.

74. Richardson, *The Secret Service*, p. 392.

75. Ibid.

76. "Escape of Prisoners—Sentinel Killed," *Richmond Whig*, October 23, 1863.

77. Richardson, *The Secret Service*, p. 389.

78. "Escape of Prisoners—Sentinel Killed," *Richmond Whig*.

79. Ibid.

80. Richardson, *The Secret Service*, p. 389.

81. *Richmond Whig*, November 3, 1863.

82. "Broke Jail," *Richmond Sentinel*, April 15, 1863, p. 2, c. 2.

83. "Castle Thunder," *Richmond Sentinel*, November 14, 1863, p. 1, c. 7.

84. Richardson, *The Secret Service*, p. 391.

85. "The Winder Guards," *Richmond Examiner*, May 16, 1864.

86. "Ready for Work," *Richmond Dispatch*, July 6, 1863.

87. "Rewarded," *Richmond Examiner*, May 21, 1864.

88. *Richmond Examiner*, May 28, 1864.

89. "Deserters Recanting." *Richmond Sentinel*, April 28, 1864, p. 1, c. 6.

90. Parker, *Richmond's Civil War Prisons*, p. 24.

91. "Recaptured," *Richmond Sentinel*, June 27, 1863.

92. "A Scoundrel Caught," *Richmond Whig*, September 10, 1864, p. 2, c. 5.

93. Ibid.

94. Burrows, "Recollections of Libby Prison," *Southern Historical Society Papers* XI (1883), pp. 91–92.

95. "Stampede of Prisoners," *Richmond Sentinel*, February 11, 1864.

96. Tarrant, "The Narrative of James E. King," p. 480.

97. Burrows, "Recollections of Libby Prison," pp. 92–93; see also Fischer, p. 109.

98. Robert L. Willett, "Loyal to None," *The Civil War Times*, XLII (April 2003), pp. 43–44.

99. Ibid., p. 44.

100. Ibid.

101. Ibid.

102. Ibid.

103. Ibid., p. 46.

104. "Attempted Escape," *Richmond Sentinel*, March 30, 1863, p. 2, col. 3; Willett, p. 46.

105. Willett, p. 46.

106. Doran, "Prison Memories," *National Tribune*, November 16 1905.

1107. "Attempted Escape," *Richmond Sentinel*, March 30, 1863, p. 2, col. 3; Willett, p. 46.

108. Willett, p. 46.

109. Ibid., p. 47.

110. "Libby Prison Now and Then," *Dedham Gazette*, May 20, 1865, pg. 1, col. 3.

111. "Empty Prisons," *Richmond Whig*, May 31, 1865.

112. *Richmond Whig*, 19 May 1865.

113. Burrows "Recollections of Libby Prison," pp. 90–91.

114. *Richmond Whig*, May 19, 1865.

115. Putnam, *A Prisoner of War in Virginia, 1864–5*, pp. 28–29

116. Burrows, "Recollections of Libby Prison," pp. 90–91.

117. *Herald and Torch Light* [Hagerstown, Maryland], September 27, 1865.

118. Parker, *Richmond's Civil War Prisons*, pp. 67–68; "Blood Hounds!" Broadside, Virginia Historical Society; Fischer, "A Comparative Study of Two Civil War Prisons," pp. 116–117.

119. "Arrest of the Late Provost Marshal of Richmond," *Richmond Whig*, May 16, 1865.

120. "Location of 'Castle Thunder,'" *Richmond News Leader*, March 30, 1946.

121. Parker, *Richmond's Civil War Prisons*, p. 68.

Chapter XXI

1. Miller, *Photographic History of the Civil War*, Vol. 7 p. 161.

2. Speer, *Portals to Hell*, p. 334.

3. Edmund Ryan, "Cahaba to Charleston: The Prison Odyssey of Lt. Edmund E. Ryan," edited by William M. Armstrong, compiler, in William B. Hesseltine, *Civil War Prisons*, pp. 119–120, cited in Speer, *Portals to Hell*, p. 213

4. Cooper, *In and Out of Rebel Prisons*, p. 115.

5. Ibid., p. 260.

6. Ferguson, *Life-Struggles in Rebel Prisons*, pp. 125–127.

7. Miller, *Photographic History of the Civil War*, Vol. 7, p. 163.

8. Cooper, *In and Out of Rebel Prisons*, pp. 260–261.

9. John V. Hadley, *Seven Months a Prisoner, by an Indiana Soldier* (Indianapolis, IN: Meikel & Co., 1968), p. 83; Speer, *Portals to Hell*, p. 213.

10. Speer, *Portals to Hell*, p. 213.

11. Miller, *Photographic History of the Civil War*, Vol. 7, p. 163.

12. Domschcke, *Twenty Months in Captivity*, pp. 98–99.

13. Calef, "Prison-Life," pp. 143–144.

14. Ibid. p. 144.

15. Miller, *Photographic History of the Civil War*, Vol. 7, p. 161.

16. "Roper St Francis Healthcare," online at http://www.carealliance.com/about/index.asp.

17. Calef, "Prison-Life," p. 145.

18. Ferguson, *Life-Struggles in Rebel Prisons*, pp. 128–129.

19. Boatner, *The Civil War Dictionary*, p. 443.

20. Maj. Gen. J. G. Foster to Maj. Gen. Samuel Jones, Hilton Head, S., C., O.R., Ser. I, Vol. 35, Pt. II, pp. 134–135; also cited in Denny, *Civil War Prisons & Escapes*, pp. 206–207.

21. Boatner, *The Civil War Dictionary*, p. 837.

22. "Fort Delaware — Jeff Thompson," online at http://www.visitthefort.com/thompson.html.

23. Ibid.

24. J. G. Foster to Maj. Gen. Samuel Jones, Hilton Head, S. C., July 29, 1864, O. R., Ser. I, Vol. 35, Pt. II, p. 198.

25. J. G. Foster to Maj. Gen. H. W. Halleck, Hilton Head, S. C., June 22, 1864, O.R., Ser. I, Vol. 35, Pt. II, pp. 144–145; Denny, p. 205.

26. Sam. Jones to Maj. Gen. J. G. Foster, Charleston, S. C., August 2, 1864, O.R., Ser. I, Vol. 35, Pt. II, p. 210.

27. J. C. Foster to Maj. Gen. H. W. Halleck, Hilton Head, S. C., August 4, 1864, O.R., Ser. I, Vol. 35, Pt. II, p. 213.

28. Ibid., p. 213.

29. Speer, *Portals to Hell*, p. 214.

30. Miller, *Photographic History of the Civil War*, Vol. 7, p. 164.

31. John Ogden Murray, *The Immortal Six Hundred: A Story of Cruelty to Confederate prisoners of War* (Winchester, VA: Eddy Press, 1905), pp. 70, 72.

32. Speer, *Portals to Hell*, p. 249, f42, p. 368.

33. Charles M. Busbee, "Experience of Prisoners Under Fire at Morris Island," in Clark, *Histories of the Several Regiments and Battalions*, p. 621; Speer, pp. 249–250.

34. Murray, *The Immortal Six Hundred*, p. 272; Walter G. MacRae, "Confederate Prisoners at Morris Island," in Clark, *Histories of the Several Regiments*, Vol. 4, p. 715; Speer, p. 250.

35. Miller, *Photographic History of the Civil War*, Vol. 7, p. 164.

36. Ferguson, *Life-Struggles in Rebel Prisons*, pp. 128–129.

37. Murray, *The Immortal Six Hundred*, p. 268, cited in Speer, *Portals to Hell*, p. 252.

38. Sam. Jones to Maj. Gen. J. G. Foster, Charleston, S. C., September 10, 1864, O.R., Ser. I, Vol. 35, Pt. II, p. 279.

39. Friz Fuzzlebug, "Prison Life During the War of 1861: A Brief Narrative of the Miseries & Sufferings of Six Hundred Confederate Prisoners," (Singer's Glen, Va.: Joseph Funk's Sons, Printers, 1869; reprint Dahlonega, Georgia: Crown Rights Book Company, n.d.), pp. 5–37.

40. Miller, *Photographic History of the Civil War*, Vol. 7, p. 164.

41. Murray, *The Immortal Six Hundred*, pp. 97, 186, cited in Speer, pp. 252–253.

42. Cooper, *In and Out of Rebel Prisons*, pp. 117–118.
43. Ibid., p. 118.
44. Ferguson, pp. 130–134.
45. Ibid., p. 135.
46. Domschcke, *Twenty Months in Captivity*, p. 105; Calef, "Prison-Life," pp. 147–148.
47. Ferguson, p. 140.
48. Cooper, *In and Out of Rebel Prisons*, pp. 122–124.
49. "Roper Hospital St Francis Healthcare."
50. "Crew Burial to be April 17, 2004," online at http://www.thehunley.com/Crew/Crew%20Burial%20in%202004.htm.

Chapter XXII

1. John H. Winder to M. L. Bonham, governor of South Carolina, Columbia, S. C., December 3, 1864, O.R. Ser. II, Vol. 7, p. 1184.
2. Speer, *Portals to Hell*, p. 334.
3. Ibid., p. 271.
4. Capt. John C. Rutherford to Major Garnett Andrews, August 18, 1864, O.R., Ser. II, Vol. 7, p. 611.
5. Ibid.
6. Ibid.
7. Ibid.
8. Geo. W. Dodge to General Huger, Columbia Jail, January 20, 1862, O.R., Ser. II, Vol. 3, p. 227.
9. Ferguson, *Life-Struggles in Rebel Prisons*, pp. 142–143.
10. Ibid., p. 147.
11. Capt. John C. Rutherford to Major Garnett Andrews, August 18, 1864, O.R., Ser. II, Vol. 7, pp. 611–612.
12. Ibid.
13. Domschcke, *Twenty Months in Captivity*, p. 107; Hadley, *Seven Months a Prisoner*, p. 88; Glazier, *The Capture*, p. 169, cited in Speer, *Portal to Hell*, p. 270.
14. Calef, "Prison-Life," *Harper's New Monthly Magazine*, Vol. XXXI, No. 182, p. 148.
15. Domschcke, *Twenty Months in Captivity*, p. 107.
16. Speer, *Portals to Hell*, p. 271.
17. Hadley, p. 89, cited in Speer, *Portals to Hell*, p. 271.
18. Domschcke, *Twenty Months in Captivity*, p. 108.
19. Ibid., p. 109.
20. Ibid., p. 110.
211. Ibid., pp. 111–112.
22. Ferguson, *Life-Struggles in Rebel Prisons*, p. 148.
23. Ibid., pp. 145–146.
24. Ibid., p. 146.
25. Domschcke, *Twenty Months in Captivity*, p. 112.
26. Glazier, *The Capture*, p. 174, cited in Speer, *Portals to Hell*, p. 271.
27. Domschcke, *Twenty Months in Captivity*, p. 112.
28. Hadley, pp. 93–94; Glazier, *The Capture*, p. 184, both cited in Speer, *Portals to Hell*, p. 272.
29. Cooper, *In and Out of Rebel Prisons*, pp. 130–131.
30. Ibid., pp. 132–133.
31. Ibid., pp. 133–134.
32. Ibid., pp. 134–135.
33. Ibid., pp. 136–139.
34. Harrison, *Prisoners' Mail from the American Civil War*, p. 12.
35. Holmes, *The Elmira Prison Camp*, p. 300.
36. Speer, *Portals to Hell*, p. 272.
37. John H. Winder to M. L. Bonham, Governor of

South Carolina, Columbia, S. C., December 3, 1864, O.R. Ser. II, Vol. 7, p. 1184.
38. Speer, *Portals to Hell*, pp. 272–273.
39. Domschcke, *Twenty Months in Captivity*, pp. 113–114.
40. Ibid., p. 114.
41. Ibid., pp. 114–115.
42. Ibid., pp. 116–117.
43. Calef, "Prison-Life," p. 149.
44. Ferguson, *Life-Struggles in Rebel Prisons*, pp. 174–175.
45. Ibid., p. 176
46. Speer, *Portals to Hell*, pp. 272–273.
47. Boatner, *The Civil War Dictionary*, p. 167, Faust, *Historical Times Illustrated Encyclopedia*, p. 153.

Chapter XXIII

1. J. F. Hill, "To and From Libby Prison," Part 1, *The Scotio Gazette,* 26 Jan. 1864, online www.89thohio.com/Prisoners/hill.htm.
2. Speer, *Portals to Hell*, p. 334.
3. Ibid., p. 126.
4. Hill, "To and From Libby Prison," Part 1.
5. Speer, *Portals to Hell*, pp. 126–127.
6. Cooper, *In and Out of Rebel Prisons*, p. 209.
7. Speer, *Portals to Hell*, pp. 126–127.
8. Ibid.
9. Ibid., p. 127.
10. Cooper, pp. 208–209.
11. Ibid., pp. 210–211.
12. Abner R. Small, *The Road to Richmond*, Harold Adams Small, ed. (New York: Fordham University Press, 2000), pp. xii–xiii.
13. Ibid., p. 168.
14. Cooper, *In and Out of Rebel Prisons*, p. 211.
15. George Haven Putnam, *A Prisoner of War in Virginia, 1864–5*. Reprint, Second Edition (New York: G. P. Putnam's Sons, 1912), pp. 32–33.
16. Ibid., pp. 34–36.
17. Small, p. 261.
18. Putnam, pp. 32–33.
19. Cooper, *In and Out of Rebel Prisons*, pp. 211–212.
20. Putnam, p. 34.
21. Hill, "To and From Libby Prison," Part 1.
22. Ibid.
23. Ibid.
24. Hill, "To and From Libby Prison," Part 3.
25. Ibid.
26. Domschcke, *Twenty Months in Captivity*, p. 77
27. Putnam, p. 55.
28. Ibid., pp. 57–58.
29. Ibid.; Small, p. 175.
30. "The Great Escape," excerpts from the *Regimental History of the Seventy-Seventh Pennsylvania,* by Sergeant John Obreiter, onlinehttp://valley, vcdh.virginia.edu/HIUS403/77pa/Eric/escape.html.
31. Ibid.
32. Ibid.
33. Cooper, *In and Out of Rebel Prisons*, pp. 207–208.
34. Ibid., pp. 213–215.
35. Putnam, pp. 50–52.
36. Cooper, *In and Out of Rebel Prisons*, pp. 217–218.
37. Ibid., p. 218.
38. Ibid., pp. 223–225.

39. Putnam, pp. 53–55.

40. Small, p. 280.

41. Putnam, pp. 60–61.

42. Cooper, *In and Out of Rebel Prisons*, pp. 228–229; Small, p. 175.

43. Putnam, pp. 61–62.

44. Cooper, *In and Out of Rebel Prisons*, p. 229.

45. Ibid., p. 244.

46. Putnam, pp. 61–62.

47. Ibid.

48. W. H. Newlin, *Account of the Escape of Six Federal Soldiers from Prison at Danville, Va; Their Travels by Night Through The Enemy's Country to the Union Pickets at Gauley Bridge, West Virginia, in the Winter of 1863–64* (Cincinnati, OH: Western Methodist Book Concern Print, 1889), pp. 12–13.

49. Ibid., pp. 9–10.

50. Ibid., pp. 10–11.

51. Ibid., p. 12.

52. Ibid., pp. 17–19.

53. Ibid., pp. 4, 7–8.

54. Small, pp. 177–179.

Chapter XXIV

1. Ira K. Morris, "Col. Frederick Bartleson, The Poem He Wrote in Libby Prison on New Year's 1863-'64," letter to the Editor, *National Tribune*, September 15, 1904. Bartleson was killed in the Battle of the Wilderness, May 1864.

2. Speer, *Portals to Hell*, p. 336

3. "Lost Virginia — Vanished Architecture of the Old Dominion: Lost Civic Architecture," online at http://www.vahistorical.org/lva/libby.htm.

4. "Distressing Event," *Richmond Enquirer*, October 21, 1851; Robert W. Waitt, "Libby Prison," *Official Publication #12* (Richmond, Va.: Richmond Civil War Centennial Committee, n.d.), online at http://www.mdgorman.com/Libby/libby_prison_robert_w_waitt.htm

5. Waitt, "Libby Prison"; *Richmond Dispatch* June 27, 1861.

6. Bruce Klee, "They Paid to Enter Libby Prison," *Civil War Times Illustrated*, Vol. 37, No. 7 (February 1999), p. 32.

7. Ferguson, *Life-Struggles in Rebel Prisons*, pp. 33–34.

8. *Richmond Dispatch*, October 7, 1861.

9. Ibid.

10. "Significant Dates in the History of Libby Prison," online at http://www.mdgorman.com/Libby/significant-dates_in_the_history.htm

11. "Summary of Libby & Son file, M346, National Archives," online at http://www.mdgorman.com/NARA/summary_of_libby.htm.

12. Notice in *New York Daily News* reprinted in *Richmond Sentinel*, November 12, 1864.

13. Samuel H. Root to My Dear Wife, Libby Prison, Richmond, Va., May 14, 1865, online at http://www.mdgorman.com/samuel_h_root_letter.htm.

14. Frank E. Moran, "Colonel Rose's Tunnel at Libby Prison," *Century Illustrated Monthly Magazine* (March 1888), p. 770, online at http://www.mdgorman.com/Libby/colonel_roses_tunnel.htm.

15. Waitt, "Libby Prison."

16. Root letter.

17. Parker, *Richmond's Civil War Prisons*, p. 11; Speer, *Portals to Hell*, p. 90.

18. *Richmond Dispatch*, March 31, 1862.

19. "Promoted," *Richmond Dispatch*, October 23, 1862.

20. Parker, *Richmond's Civil War Prisons*, p. 58.

21. Ibid., p. 31.

22. *New York Times*, November 6, 1863, p. 1:2; Parker, *Richmond's Civil War Prisons*, p. 11; Speer, *Portals to Hell*, p. 90.

23. Moran, "Libby Prison — The Tunnel Diggers."

24. William Dandridge Turner, "The Libby Lion," in *The Black Swan*, August 1929, pp. 4–5, 29–35; September 1919, pp. 17–19, 20, 27–29; October 1929, pp. 22, 33–35, online www.mdgorman.com/Libby/libby_lion.htm.

25. Parker, *Richmond's Civil War Prisons*, p. 11.

26. *New York Times*, November 6, 1863, p. 1:2; Speer, *Portals to Hell*, p. 91.

27. Turner, "The Libby Lion," cited in Parker, *Richmond's Civil War Prisons*, p. 11.

28. *Richmond Dispatch*, December 28, 1870; *Richmond Examiner*, December 28, 1870.

29. "Memorial Services," *Richmond Dispatch*, December 31, 1870.

30. Richardson, *The Secret Service*, p. 365; Faust, *Historical Times Illustrated Encyclopedia*, p. 726

31. Whitlaw Reid to Colonel Hoffman, Cincinnati Gazette Rooms, Washington, August 6, 1863, O.R., Ser. II, Vol. 6, p. 183.

32. Jno. E. Mulford, assistant agent for exchange to Col. W. Hoffman, Fort Monroe, June 20,1864, O.R., Ser. II, Vol.7, p. 386.

33. Benjamin F. Butler to Hon. Robert Ould, August 10, 1864, O.R., Ser. II, Vol. 7, pp. 575–576.,

34. Robert Ould, "Indorcement," September 3, 1864, O.R., Ser. II, Vol. 7, p. 763.

35. Richardson, *The Secret Service*, pp. 365, 367;

36. Burrows, "Recollections of Libby Prison," p. 85.

37. "Arrived," *Richmond Dispatch*, August 15, 1864.

38. Boatner, *The Civil War Dictionary*, p. 245.

39. Richardson, *The Secret Service*, pp. 367–368; Faust, *Historical Times Illustrated Encyclopedia*, p. 726.

40. Boatner, *The Civil War Dictionary*, pp. 724–725; "Arrival of a Yankee General and Staff," *Richmond Examiner*, February 20, 1864.

41. *Walls that Talk: A Transcription of the Names, Inititals and Sentiments Written and Graven on the Walls, Doors and Windows of the Libby Prison at Richmond by the Prisoners of 1861–'65* (Richmond, Va: R. E. Lee Camp, No. I, CV, 1884), n.p., online www.mdgorman.com/Libby/walls_that_talk.htm.

42. "The Plymouth Prisoners," *Richmond Whig*, April 27, 1864.

43. Boatner, *The Civil War Dictionary*, pp. 901–902.

44. "Arrest of Rebel Officials," *Richmond Whig*. May 4, 1865.

45. Waitt, "Libby Prison."

46. *Walls that Talk.*

47. Thomas P. Turner, to Capt. W. H. Hatch, Richmond, Va., October 14, 1864, O.R., Ser. II, Vol. 7, pp. 987–988.

48. Sturgis, *Prisoners of War*, pp. 285–286.

49. Ibid., p. 287.

50. Thomas Simpson, "My Four Months Experience

as a Prisoner of War," in Rhode Island MOLLUS, Vol. IV, p. 54, online at www.mdgorman.com/rhode_island_mollus_voliv_p54.htm.

51. Ibid.

52. Burrows, "Recollections of Libby Prison," p. 87; Judah P. Benjamin to John H. Winder, Richmond, November 9, 1861, O. R. Ser. II, Vol. 3, pp. 378–379; J. H. Winder to Judah Benjamin, Richmond, November 11, 1861, O. R., Ser. II, Vol. 3, p. 379; Miller, *Photographic History of the Civil War*, Vol. 7, pp. 29, 34–36; Boatner, *The Civil War Dictionary*, pp. 265–266.

53. Domschcke, *Twenty Months in Captivity*, p. 24.

54. Ibid., p. 48; Richardson, *The Secret Service*, pp. 373–374.

55. H.C.T., letter to the Editor, *Springfield Republican*, April 24, 1865, reprinted in the *Dedham Gazette*, May 20, 1865, p. 1, col. 3.

56. Domschcke, *Twenty Months in Captivity*, p. 48; Richardson, *The Secret Service*, pp. 373–374.

57. Ferguson, *Life-Struggles in Rebel Prisons*, p. 37; Richardson, *The Secret Service*, p. 370.

58. Domschcke, *Twenty Months in Captivity*, p. 51.

59. "Emeute at the Libby," *Richmond Whig*, May 9, 1864.

60. Domschcke, *Twenty Months in Captivity*, p. 61; Ferguson, *Life-Struggles in Rebel Prisons*, p. 41; Wells, *With Touch of Elbow*, pp. 134–161, online.

61. Domschcke, *Twenty Months in Captivity*, p. 51, f2.

62. Boatner, *The Civil War Dictionary*, p. 270.

63. Domschcke, *Twenty Months in Captivity*, p. 50.

64. Jno. McEntee, to Major General Humphreys, headquarters, Army of the Potomac, July 22, 1864, O.R., Ser. I, Vol. 40, Pt. III, p. 386.

65. "Returned to Prison," *Richmond Dispatch*, August 7, 1862.

66. "Close Confinement," *Richmond Dispatch*, August 7, 1862.

67. *Richmond Dispatch*, August 8, 1862.

68. Domschcke, *Twenty Months in Captivity*, p. 62

69. "Attempted Escape from Libby Prison," *Richmond Examiner*, July 14, 1864.

70. Domschcke, *Twenty Months in Captivity*, p. 62

71. Ibid., p. 61.

72. Ibid., pp. 61–62

73. "The Escape: Daring and Suffering in the Rebel Country by Two 4th Pa. Cav. Men," *National Tribune*, December 14, 1893.

74. "The Rescuer of Capt. Porter," *Richmond Sentinel*, April 18, 1864.

75. Linus Pierpont Brockett, "Narrative of Captain John F. Porter, Jr., Fourteenth New York Cavalry — Particulars of His Escape," *The camp, the battle field, and the hospital: or, Lights and shadows of the great rebellion. Including adventures of spies and scouts, thrilling incidents, daring exploits, heroic deeds, wonderful escapes, sanitary and hospital scenes, prison scenes, etc., etc., etc.* (Philadelphia, PA: National Publishing Co., c. 1866), pp. 280–282.

76. Richardson, *The Secret Service*, p. 379.

77. "The Rescuer of Capt. Porter."

78. "Another Report," *New York Times*, February 15, 1864.

79. Brockett, "Narrative of Captain John F. Porter, Jr.," pp. 280–282.

80. *Richmond Whig*, January 21, 1864.

81. Thomas P. Turner to Capt. G. W. Alexander, C. S. Mil. Prison, Richmond, Nov. 19, 1862, National Archives, Record Group 109, Chapter 9, Vol. 199 1/2, p. 33, online at http://www.mdgorman.com/NARA/rg_109,_ch_9,_vol_199_5,_p_33.htm.

82. Thomas P. Turner to Capt. W. S. Winder, C. S. M. Prison, Richmond, February 17, 1863, "Letters & Orders Issued, Confederate Military Prison, 1862 — December, 1863," p. 68, National Archives, Record Group 109, Chapter 9, Vol. 199 1/2, p. 33, online at http://www.mdgorman.com/NARA/rg_109,_ch_9,_vol_199_5,_p_68a.htm.

83. "Escaped from the Libby," *Richmond Whig*, May 2, 1864; "Escape of Prisoners," *Richmond Sentinel*, May 2, 1864.

84. William H. Jeffrey, "The Escape of Colonel Charles A. De Villiers," *Richmond Prisons 1816–1862*, (St. Johnsbury, Vt.: The Republican Press, 1893), pp. 116–117.

85. Jeffrey, *Richmond Prisons*, pp. 117–118.

86. Ibid., pp. 118, 121.

87. Boatner, *The Civil War Dictionary*, p. 416.

88. Jeffrey, *Richmond Prisons*, p. 122.

89. Moran, "Colonel Rose's Tunnel at Libby Prison."

90. "Prisoners on Belle Isle: How they Looked to the Eyes of a Libby Man," *New York Times*, March 1, 1891; Wells, *With Touch of Elbow*, pp. 134–161, online www.mdgorman.com/Libby/with_touch_of_elbow.htm.

91. "Stampede of Prisoners," *Richmond Sentinel*, February 11, 1864.

92. "Escape of One Hundred and Nine Commissioned Yankee Officers from the Libby Prison — A Scientific Tunnel — Their Underground Route to Liberty," *Richmond Examiner*, February 11, 1864.

93. "Extraordinary Escape from the Libby Prison — One Hundred Officers Homeward Bound," *Richmond Enquirer*, February 11, 1864.

94. *Richmond Enquirer*, February 11, 1864.

95. "Escape of One Hundred and Nine Commissioned Yankee Officers," *Richmond Examiner*, February 11, 1864.

96. *Richmond Whig*, February 11, 1864; Domschcke, *Twenty Months in Captivity*, pp. 63–64.

97. "Escape of One Hundred and Nine Commissioned Yankee," *Richmond Examiner*, February 11, 1864.

98. *Richmond Examiner*, February 11, 1864.

99. Domschcke, *Twenty Months in Captivity*, p. 62, f3.

100. Earle, "In and Out of Libby Prison," 1:247–292.

101. Thomas Ellwood Rose, *Col. Rose's Story of the Famous Tunnel Escape from Libby Prison: A Thrilling Account of the Daring Escape of 109 Union Officers from Libby Prison Through the Famous Tunnel* (Bethesda, Md.: University Publications of America. Microfiche, Civil War Unit Histories, Part 3, The Union — Mid-Atlantic; PA:486 1992), p. 9.

102. Hamilton, *Story of the Famous Tunnel Escape from Libby Prison*, online.

103. Rose, "Libby Tunnel. An Interesting Account of Its Construction,"*National Tribune*, 14 May, 1885, online www.mdgorman.com/National_Tribune/national_tribune_5141885.htm.

104. Bvt. Brig. Gen. Harrison C. Hobart, "Libby Prison — The Escape," papers read before the Wis-

consin Mollus, Vol. I, Milsaukee, 1891, pp. 394–409, online at http://www.mdgorman.com/Libby/Libby_Prison_The_Escape.htm.

105. W. S. B. Randall, "Libby Prison. The Experience of One of the Successful Tunnelers," *National Tribune*, 27 March 1890, online www.mdgorman.com/National_tribune/national_tribune_3271890.htm.

106. Rose, *Col. Rose's Story*, pp. 2–3.

107. Hamilton, *Story of the Famous Tunnel Escape from Libby Prison*, online.

108. Ibid.

109. I. N. Johnson, *Four Months in Libby, and the Campaign Against Atlanta*. Cincinnati, OH: privately published, 1864; see also Moran "Colonel Rose's Tunnel at Libby Prison," p. 784–785.

110. Domschcke, *Twenty Months in Captivity*, p. 63.

111. Root letter.

112. Hobart, "Libby Prison — The Escape," online.

113. Wells, *With Touch of Elbow*.

114. Domschcke, *Twenty Months in Captivity*, pp. 63–64.

115. Rose, *Col. Rose's Story*, pp. 4–5; Moran "Colonel Rose's Tunnel at Libby Prison," p. 787.

116. Wells, *With Touch of Elbow*, pp. 134–161.

117. Hobart, "Libby Prison — The Escape," pp. 394–409.

118. Ibid.

119. I. J. Wistar to Col. J. W. Shaffer, O.R., Ser. I, Vol. 33, pp. 559–560.

120. Randall, "Libby Prison. The Experience of One of the Successful Tunnelers," online http://www.mdgorman.com/National_tribune/national_tribune_3271890.htm.

121. "Digging Out of Libby," *National Tribune*, April 21, 1892, online at http://www.mdgorman.com/National_tribune/national_tribune_4211892.htm.

122. Albert Wallber, "The Escape from the Libby," in Domschcke, *Twenty Months in Captivity*, pp. 125–134.

123. "The Recent Escape from the Libby Prison — Recapture of Twenty Two Officers," *Richmond Enquirer*, February 12, 1864.

124. *Richmond Whig*, February 11, 1864; *Richmond Examiner*, February 11, 1864; *Richmond Examiner*, February 11, 1864.

125. *Richmond Examiner*, February 11, 1864.

126. Brockett, "How the Prisoners Escaped from the Richmond Jail — Incredible Underground Work, — Friendship of Negroes," *The camp, the battle field, and the hospital: or, Lights and shadows of the great rebellion*, pp. 285–292.

127. *Richmond Enquirer*, February 12, 1864.

128. Moran "Colonel Rose's Tunnel at Libby Prison," p. 770.

129. *Richmond Enquirer*, February 12, 1864.

130. *Richmond Whig*, February 12, 1864.

131. *Richmond Sentinel*, February 13, 1864.

132. Rose, *Col. Rose's Story*, pp. 5–6.

133. F. F. Cavada, *Libby Life: Experiences of a Prisoner of War in Richmond, VA, 1863–1864* (Philadelphia, PA: J. B. Lippincott, 186). Mirofiche, Ann Arbor, MI: University Microfflms, 1992. www.rose-hulman.edu/~delacova/book/libby-10.htm.

134. Wells, *With Touch of Elbow*, pp. 134–161. Boatner, *The Civil War Dictionary*, p. 708, states that Rose retired in 1894 as a major.

135. "Recapture of More Yankee Officers," *Richmond Enquirer*, February 13, 1864.

136. Ibid.; *Richmond Whig*, February 13, 1864.

137. "Recapture of More Yankee Officers," *Richmond Enquirer*, February 13, 1864.

138. Ibid.; *Richmond Sentinel*, February 15, 1864.

139. "The Escaped Yankee Officers— Interesting Incidents," *Richmond Whig*, February 15, 1864.

140. "The Re-Captured Yankee Officers," *Richmond Examiner*, February 15, 1864.

141. "Two More Yankees Recaptured," *Richmond Enquirer*, February 16, 1864.

142. "The Escaped Yankees," *Richmond Sentinel*, February 17, 1864.

143. *Richmond Examiner*, February 20, 1864.

144. "More Capture of Escaped Yankees," *Richmond Sentinel*, February 20, 1864.

145. "The Libby Jail Delivery," Franklin (PA) *Repository*, February 24, 1864.

146. Domschcke, *Twenty Months in Captivity*, pp. 65–66.

147. "Interesting News from Richmond," *New York Times*, February 15, 1864.

148. A. D. Streight to Brig. Gen. William D. Whipple, Chattanooga, Tenn., August 22, 1864, O. R., Ser. I, Vol. 35, Pt. I, pp. 285–286.

149. "Report of Lieut. Col. Harrison C. Hobart, Twenty-first Wisconsin Infantry, Georgia, April __, 1864, O.R., Ser. I, Vol. 52, Pt. I, pp. 83–84; Hobart, "Libby Prison — The Escape," pp. 394–409, online.

150. Brockett, "How the Prisoners Escaped from the Richmond Jail — Incredible Underground Work, — Friendship of Negroes," *The camp, the battle field, and the hospital: or, Lights and shadows of the great rebellion*, pp. 285–292.

151. W. P. Kendrick to President Lincoln, National Hotel, Washington, D.C., February 21, 1864, O.R., Ser. II, Vol. 6, pp. 377–387.

152. Harrison, *Prisoner's Mail from the American Civil War*, p. 12.

153. Ibid.

154. J. M. Wasson, "Letter from Lieutenant J. M. Wasson — Adventures in Southern Prisons," in Beach, *History of the Fortieth Ohio Volunteer Infantry*, pp. 132–136.

155. Moran, "Libby Prison — The Tunnel Diggers"; Moran, "Colonel Rose's Tunnel at Libby Prison," pp. 770–790.

156. Moran, "Colonel Rose's Tunnel at Libby Prison," p. 785.

157. Putnam, *A Prisoner of War in Virginia, 1864–5*, pp. 4, 19, 27–29.

158. Moran, "Libby Prison — The Tunnel Diggers."

159. W. B. Lowery, "A Prisoner's Story," letter to the editor, *National Tribune*, January 2, 1902.

160. H.C.T., letter to the editor, *Springfield Republican*, April 24, 1865, reprinted in the *Dedham Gazette*, May 20, 1865, p. 1, col. 3.

161. "Major Turner's Escape: How the ex–Commandant of Famous Libby Prison Fled to Cuba." the *New York Times*, July 7, 1895, online at http://www.mdgorman.com/NYC-Papers/new_york_times_771895.htm.

162. Parker, *Richmond's Civil War Prisons*, p. 68.

163. Turner, "The Libby Lion."

164. H.C.T., letter to the editor.

165. Turner, "The Libby Lion."

166. "Escape of Dick Turner from the Libby," *Richmond Whig*, May 13, 1865; Root letter.

167. Turner, "The Libby Lion."

168. "Had a Peep at Death," *Richmond Dispatch*.

169. Parker, *Richmond's Civil War Prisons*, p. 68, *Richmond Dispatch*, December 6, 1901.

170. Ibid.

171. "R. R. Turner's Death. Was County Chairman of Isle of Wight," *Richmond Dispatch*, December 7, 1901.

172. Parker, *Richmond's Civil War Prisons*, p. 68, *Richmond Dispatch*, December 6, 1901.

173. Wells, *With Touch of Elbow*, pp. 134–161.

174. "The Assassination of Major A. G. Hamilton," *Kentucky Explorer*, March 2001, pp. 36–?

175. "The Libby Prison Sign," *Richmond Whig*, May 12, 1865.

176. Waitt, "Libby Prison."

177. "Libby Prison in Ruins," *New York Times*, May 18, 1889.

178. Waitt, "Libby Prison."

179. "Survivors of Libby Tunnel Party," *National Tribune*, March 8, 1906, online at http://www.mdgorman.com/National_Tribune/national_tribune,_3_8_1906.htm.

Chapter XXV

1. Ferguson, *Life-Struggles in Rebel Prisons*, p. 95.

2. Speer, *Portals to Hell*, p. 266.

3. *Macon Daily Telegraph*, 3 May 1862, reprinted from Richard W. Lobst, *Civil War Macon — The History of a Confederate City* (Macon, GA: Mercer University Press, 1999), p. 126, online at http://georgiastatefair.org/CampOglethorpe.htm.

4. "Camp Oglethorpe — Georgia military facility," online at http://georgiastatefair.org/CampOglethorpe.htm

5. Speer, *Portals to Hell*, p. 266.

6. Ibid.

7. Hadley, *Seven Months A Prisoner*, p. 59, cited in Speer, *Portals to Hell*, p. 266.

8. Hadley, *Seven Months A Prisoner*, pp. 67–68; Glazier, *The Captive*, pp. 103, 106, 111, P. Cashmyer to Col. N. P. Chipman, Richmond, VA, October 12, 1865, O.R., Ser. II, Vol. 8, p. 765, cited in Speer, *Portals to Hell*, p. 266.

9. Cooper, *In and Out of Rebel Prisons*, p. 97.

10. Ferguson, *Life-Struggles in Rebel Prisons*, p. 89.

11. Ibid.

12. Ibid.

13. Speer, *Portals to Hell*, p. 266.

14. Cooper, *In and Out of Rebel Prisons*, p. 51.

15. Hadley, *Seven Months A Prisoner*, pp. 67–68; Glazier, *The Captive*, pp. 103, 106, 111, P. Cashmyer to Col. N. P. Chipman, Richmond, VA, October 12, 1865, O.R., Ser. II, Vol. 8, p. 765, cited in Speer, *Portals to Hell*, p. 266.

16. Hadley, *Seven Months A Prisoner*, p. 70, cited in Speer, *Portals to Hell*, p. 267.

17. "Camp Oglethorpe — Georgia military facility," online.

18. Ferguson, *Life-Struggles in Rebel Prisons*, p. 91.

19. Ibid., p. 90.

20. Ibid., p. 92.

21. Ibid., pp. 92–93.

22. James Pike, "Eleven Months Among the Rebels," Murfreesborough, Tenn., March 23, 1863, O. R., Ser. II, Vol. 5, pp. 418–419.

23. Ibid.

24. Ibid., p. 419.

25. Ibid.

26. Ibid.

27. J. Holt to E. M. Stanton, November 3, 1865, O. R., Ser. II, Vol. 8, pp. 782–783.

28. Calef, "Prison Life," p. 143.

29. Cooper, *In and Out of Rebel Prisons*, pp. 44–45.

30. Ferguson, *Life-Struggles in Rebel Prisons*, pp. 103–104.

31. Calef, "Prison Life," pp. 142–143.

32. Ferguson, *Life-Struggles in Rebel Prisons*, p. 104.

33. Ibid.

34. James Pike, "Eleven Months Among the Rebels," p. 419.

35. Ferguson, *Life-Struggles in Rebel Prisons*, pp. 106–107.

36. Ibid., p. 107.

37. Cooper, *In and Out of Rebel Prisons*, p. 80.

38. Ibid., pp. 80–81.

39. Ibid., pp. 81–83.

40. Ibid., pp. 84–85.

41. Ibid., pp. 86–87.

42. Ibid., pp. 86–87.

43. Calef, "Prison Life," p. 143.

44. Ibid.

45. Ibid., pp. 88–91.

46. Domschcke, *Twenty Months in Captivity*, p. 89; Ferguson, *Life-Struggles in Rebel Prisons*, p. 104.

47. Cooper, *In and Out of Rebel Prisons*, pp. 91–92.

48. Calef, "Prison Life," p. 143.

49. Cooper, *In and Out of Rebel Prisons*, pp. 88–91.

50. Ferguson, p. 104.

51. Calef, "Prison Life," p. 143.

52. Domschcke, *Twenty Months in Captivity*, p. 89.

53. Ibid., p. 88.

54. Cooper, *In and Out of Rebel Prisons*, pp. 87–88.

55. Ibid., p. 88.

56. Domschcke, *Twenty Months in Captivity*, pp. 88–89.

57. Ibid., p. 89.

58. Tarrant, "The Wild Riders," pp. 484–486.

59. Ibid., pp. 486–488.

60. Domschcke, *Twenty Months in Captivity*, p. 89.

61. Domschcke, *Twenty Months in Captivity*, pp. 89–90, f25.

62. Speer, *Portals to Hell*, p. 268.

63. F. T. Miles to Gen. S. Cooper, Branchville, S. C., March 24, 1864, O.R., Ser. II, Vol. 6, p. 1091.

64. Statement of Lt. P. W. Houlihan, Walter Clifford and James Butler, submitted by Lt. Col. James F. Hall, August 6, 1864, O.R., Ser. I, Vol. 35, Pt. II, p. 221.

65. Cooper, *In and Out of Rebel Prisons*, pp. 106–107.

66. Ibid.

67. Ibid., p. 107.

68. Boatner, *The Civil War Dictionary*, pp. 801–802.

69. Speer, *Portals to Hell*, p. 298.

70. Lobst, *Civil War Macon*, pp. 143–144.

71. Ibid.

Chapter XXVI

1. Booth and Myer, *Dark Days of the Rebellion*, p. 131

2. Garnett Andrews to Brig. Gen. W. M. Gardner, Richmond, August 12, 1864, O.R., Ser. II, Vol. 7, p. 586.

3. Louis A. Brown, *The Salisbury Prison: A Case Study of Confederate Military Prisons, 1861–1865*, revised ed. (Wilmington, NC: Broadfoot Publishing Co., 1992), p. 86.

4. J. L. Tyerly to Capt. G. W. Booth, Salisbury, February 1, 1865, O.R., Ser. II, Vol. 8, p. 254.

5. Speer, *Portals to Hell*, p. 338

6. Chaplain A. W. Mangum, "Salisbury Prison," in Walter Clark, ed. *Histories of the Several Regiments and Battalions from North Carolina in the Great War*, p. 745.

7. Mangum, "Salisbury Prison," p. 745.

8. Robert E. Eberly, Jr., "Prison Town," *Civil War Times Illustrated*, No. I, Vol XXXVIII (March 1999), pp. 30–31.

9. Mangum, "Salisbury Prison," pp. 751–752.

10. Browne, *Four Years in Secessia*, cited in Yearns and Barrett, *North Carolina Civil War Documentary*, p. 121.

11. Booth and Myer, *Dark Days of the Rebellion*, p. 95.

12. Jeffrey, *Richmond's Prisons*, p. 157.

13. Small, *Road to Richmond*, p. 164–165

14. Booth and Myer, *Dark Days of the Rebellion*, p. 95.

15. Small, *Road to Richmond*, p. 165.

16. Booth and Meyer, *Dark Days of the Rebellion*, p. 95–96.

17. Ibid., p. 95.

18. Ibid.

19. Ibid.

20. "Interrogation Statements," Record Group 249, Entry 131, National Archives, Washington, D.C.; *Richmond Dispatch*, July 19, 20, 1864, August 24, 1864.

21. *Richmond Dispatch*, January 30, 1862.

22. Booth and Meyer, *Dark Days of the Rebellion*, p. 87

23. Mangum, "Salisbury Prison," pp. 753–754.

24. G. W. Alexander to Col. John Withers, Salisbury, N.C., June 11, 1864, O.R., Ser. II, Vol. 7, p. 227.

25. "Castle Thunder," *Richmond Sentinel*, April 14, 1864; "The Castle," *Richmond Whig*, April 14, 1864.

26. "Castle Thunder Items," *Richmond Examiner*, May 7, 1864.

27. Jno. H. Gee, "Consolidated return for C. S. Military prison, Salisbury, NC., for 1865, from January 16 to 31, inclusive," O.R., Ser. II, Vol. 8, p. 255.

28. Mangum, "Salisbury Prison," pp. 746–747

29. Brown, *The Salisbury Prison*, pp. 74–75.

30. *New York Tribune*, August 19, 1862; *New York Tribune*, December 24, 1863, cited in Brown, *The Salisbury Prison*, p. 72–73.

31. Corcoran, *Captivity of General Corcoran*, p. 97, cited in Brown, *The Salisbury Prison*, p. 79.

32. Statement of Capt. R. C. G. Reed, Third Ohio Infantry, August 6, 1864, O.R., Ser. I, Vol. 35, Pt. II, p. 220.

33. Brown, *The Salisbury Prison*, p. 76.

34. "A. D. Richardson's Experiences in the Confederacy," cited in Brown, *The Salisbury Prison*, pp. 198–199.

35. Browne, *Four Years in Secessia*, pp. 315–361, cited in Yearns and G. Barrett, *North Carolina Civil War Documentary*, p. 121.

36. Richardson, *The Secret Service*, p. 402.

37. Browne, *Four Years in Secessia*, pp. 315–361, cited in Yearns and Barrett, *North Carolina Civil War Documentary*, p. 121.

38. Brown, *The Salisbury Prison*, p. 76.

39. Benjamin F. Butler to Robert Ould, Fort Monroe, Va., April 30, 1864, O.R., Ser. II, Vol. 7, p. 101.

40. Mangum, "Salisbury Prison," p. 752.

41. Richardson, *The Secret Service*, pp. 404–405.

42. Ibid., p. 406.

43. Brown, *The Salisbury Prison*, p. 190; "Prison Personnel Commandants," online at http://www.salisburyprison.org; Salisbury Confederate Prison Association, "Prison History," online at www.salisbury prison.org.

44. "Prison Personnel Commandants," online.

45. Richardson, *The Secret Service*, p. 401.

46. O.R., Ser. II, Vol. 7, p. 227, cited in Louis A. Brown, *The Salisbury Prison*, p. 190.

47. Cleve Horton Cox, "Salisbury: The Confederate Prison of General Stoneman, 1860–1865," typescript, n.d., Rowan Public Library, Salisbury, North Carolina; "New Commandant of the Prison," *Carolina Watchman*, June 18, 1864.

48. Mangum, "Salisbury Prison," in Clark, *Histories of the Several Regiments*, Vol. 5, pp. 753–754.

49. Garnett Andrews to Brig. Gen. W. M. Gardner, Richmond, August 12, 1864, O.R., Ser. II, Vol. 7, p. 586.

50. Garnett Andrews to Brig. Gen. W. M. Gardner, Richmond, August 12, 1864, O.R., Ser. II, Vol. 7, pp. 586–587.

51. O.R., Ser. II, Vol. 7, pp. 674–675, cited in Louis A. Brown, *The Salisbury Prison*, p. 190.

52. "The Court-martial of Major John H. Gee, Commandant Salisbury Confederate Prison," online at http://www.geocities.com/ageeford2002/index.html.

53. Jeffrey, *Richmond's Prisons*, p. 155.

54. *Carolina Watchman*, July 25, 1864; diary of William Francis Tiemann, Rowan County Public Library, p. 13, cited in Brown, *The Salisbury Prison*, p. 31.

55. Brown, *The Salisbury Prison*, p. 30.

56. Archer Anderson, "Report of inspection of the C. S. Military Prison and post at Salisbury, N.C.," June 23, 1864, O. R., Ser. II, Vol. 7, pp. 401–402.

57. Garnett Andrews to Brig. Gen. W. M. Gardner, Richmond, August 12, 1864, O.R., Ser. II, Vol. 7, pp. 586–587.

58. Mangum, "Salisbury Prison," p. 747

59. Eberly, "Prison Town," pp. 30–31.

60. George B. Kirsch, "Bats, Balls, and Bullets: Baseball and the Civil War," *Civil War Times Illustrated* No. II, Vol. XXXVII (May 1998), pp. 32–33.

61. "Salisbury Confederate Prison," online at http://www.ci.salisbury.nc.us/prison/csprison1.htm.

62. Mangum, "Salisbury Prison," p. 751.

63. "Interrogation Statements," Record Group 249, Entry 131, National Archives, Washington, D.C.; *Richmond Dispatch*, 19, July 20, 1864, August 24, 1864.

64. Eberly, "Prison Town," pp. 30–31.

65. Booth and Myer, *Dark Days of the Rebellion*, pp. xi, viii.

66. Jeffrey, *Richmond's Prisons*, p. 154.

67. Small, *The Road to Richmond*, p. 166.
68. Ibid.
69. Jeffrey, *Richmond's Prisons*, p. 154.
70. Mangum, "Salisbury Prison," pp. 751–752.
71. Jeffrey, *Richmond's Prisons*, p. 158.
72. "A. D. Richardson's Experiences in the Confederacy," cited in Brown, "*The Salisbury Prison*, pp. 198–199.
73. Brown, *The Salisbury Prison*, p. 31.
74. Browne, *Four Years in Secessia*, pp. 318–319.
75. Mangum, Letters from 1861–1865, October 31, 1864, Southern Historical Collection, Chapel Hill, NC, cited in Brown, *The Salisbury Prison*, p. 90.
76. Charles Carroll Gray diary, June 30, 1862, p. 20, cited in Brown, *The Salisbury Prison*, p. 90.
77. Gray diary, pp. 195, 210, cited in Brown, *The Salisbury Prison*, p. 90.
78. Mangum, "Salisbury Prison," pp. 751–752.
79. *Carolina Watchman*, March 17, 1862.
80. Richardson, *The Secret Service*, p. 406.
81. Ibid.
82. Ibid., p. 407.
83. *Carolina Watchman*, May 6, 1864.
84. *Carolina Watchman*, July 11, 1864.
85. Richardson, *The Secret Service*, p. 406.
86. Mangum, "Salisbury Prison," pp. 752–753.
87. Ibid. p. 753.
88. Richardson, *The Secret Service*, p. 428.
89. Mangum, "Salisbury Prison," pp. 751–752.
90. Brown, *The Salisbury Prison*, pp. 89–90.
91. *Carolina Watchman*, June 30, 1862.
92. *Richardson, The Secret Service*, p. 409.
93. Brown, *The Salisbury Prison*, p. 91.
94. Small, *Road To Richmond*, pp. 167–168; Brown, *The Salisbury Prison*, p. 91.
95. Ibid.
96. Ibid.
97. William Francis Tiemann Diary, pp. 14–17; Sprague, *Lights and Shadows*, pp. 60–67, cited in Brown, *The Salisbury Prison*, p. 91.
98. Ferris diary, October and November 1864, cited in Brown, *The Salisbury Prison*, pp. 91–92.
99. Brown, *The Salisbury Prison*, p. 92.
100. John P. C. Shanks, chairman, *Report of Committee of the House of Representatives Made during the 3rd Session of the 40th Congress, 1869* (Washington, D.C.: Government Printing Office, 1869), pp. 72–73, cited in Brown, *The Salisbury Prison*, p. 92.
101. O.R., Ser. II, Vol. 7, p. 1230; Browne, *Four Years in Secessia,* pp. 328–329; Ferguson, *Life Struggles in Rebel Prisons*, p. 60; Brown, *The Salisbury Prison*, p. 93.
102. Brown, *The Salisbury Prison*, p. 93.
103. Dempsey, "An Account from the Ranks," pp. 180–181; "Diary of George S. Bixby, Boston *Globe*, November 28, 1909, cited in Brown, *The Salisbury Prison*, p. 93.
104. Brown, *The Salisbury Prison*, p. 93.
105. "They are Surrounded and Overpowered," *Richmond Enquirer*, November 26, 1864, reprinted in the *New York Herald*, December 1, 1864.
106. Ibid.
107. Jno. H. Gee to Gen. J. H. Winder, O.R., Ser. II, Vol. 7, p. 1230.
108. Richardson, *The Secret Service* p. 420.
109. Booth, *Dark Days of the Rebellion*, pp. 147, 198.
110. Ferris diary; War Department. Collection of Confederate Records. *The Original Register of Federal Prisoners of War of the United States Army Confined in Prison Hospital, Salisbury, N. C., 1864–1865*, pp. 38–39, cited in Brown, *The Salisbury Prison*, p. 95; Booth, *Dark Days of the Rebellion*, pp. 140–141.
111. George Seaver, *David Livingstone: His Life and Letters* (London: Lutterworth Press, 1957), p. 455, cited in Brown, *The Salisbury Prison*, p. 93.
112. Kellogg, *Life and Death in Rebel Prisons*, pp. 380–381; Browne, *Four Years in Secessia*, pp. 328–329; Dempsey, "An Account from the Ranks," pp. 80–81; T. W. Hall to Gen. S. Cooper, February 27, 1865, O.R., Ser. II, Vol. 8, p. 248; cited in Brown, *The Salisbury Prison*, p. 93.
113. Richardson, *The Secret Service*, pp. 425–426.
114. Booth, *Dark Days of the Rebellion*, p. 129.
115. Jno. H. Winder to Gen. S. Cooper, Salisbury, N. C., December 13, 1864, pp. 1219–1221.
116. Booth, *Dark Days of the Rebellion*, p. 157.
117. Ibid., p. 167.
118. Jno. H. Gee, "Consolidated return for C. S. Military prison, Salisbury, N. C., for 1865, from January 16 to 31, inclusive," O.R., Ser. II, Vol. 8, p. 255.
119. Ibid., p. 253.
120. Booth and Myer, *Dark Days of the Rebellion*, pp. 169–170.
121. Ibid., p. 173, 179.
122. Brown, *The Salisbury Prison*, p. 98.
123. Richardson, *The Secret Service*, pp. 432–509.
124. Booth and Myer, *Dark Days of the Rebellion*, p. 152.
125. Richardson, *The Secret Service*, pp. 453–454; Brown, *The Salisbury Prison*, p. 98.
126. Richardson, *The Secret Service*, p. 429; Faust, *Historical Times Illustrated Encyclopedia*, p. 629.
127. Richardson, *The Secret Service*, p. 438.
128. Richardson, *The Secret Service*, pp. 453–454; Brown, *The Salisbury Prison*, p. 98.
129. Richardson, *The Secret Service*, pp. 440–445.
130. Ibid., pp. 450–454.
131. Booth and Myer, *Dark Days of the Rebellion*, pp. 152–153.
132. *Daily Carolina Watchman*, quoted in the New York *Tribune*, March 21, 1865, p. 4, c. 4; cited in Brown, *The Salisbury Prison*, p. 99.
133. Richardson, *The Secret Service*, pp. 456–457.
134. Ibid., pp. 464–465.
135. Ibid., pp. 465–466.
136. Ibid., p. 487.
137. Ibid., p. 488.
138. Ibid., p. 509.
139. Brown, *The Salisbury Prison*, footnote 52, p. 99.
140. Ibid., p.100.
141. "Report of inspection of the C. S. Military prison and post at Salisbury, N. C., June 23, 1864," O.R. Ser. 2 Vol. 7, pp. 401–402.
142. J. L. Tyerly to Capt. G. W. Booth, Salisbury, N. C., February 1, 1865, O.R., Ser. II, Vol. 7, p. 254.
143. Brown, *The Salisbury Prison*, p.105.
144. John H. Gee, "List of prisoners sent from this post on exchange," O.R., Ser. II, Vol. 8, p. 455.
145. Brown, *The Salisbury Prison*, pp. 159–161.
146. Ibid., p. 161.
147. "The Salisbury NC Confederate Civil War Prison," online at http://www.gorowan.com/salisburyprison/.

148. "Salisbury National Cemetery," online at http://www.interment.net/data/us/nc/rowan/salis-nat/index.htm.

Chapter XXVII

1. Speer, *Portals to Hell*, p. 268, 338
2. Ferguson, pp. 113–114.
3. Speer, *Portals to Hell*, p. 268.
4. Domschcke, *Twenty Months in Captivity*, pp. 91–92.
5. Ibid.
6. Ibid., p. 92.
7. Ferguson, *Life-Struggles in Rebel Prisons*, p. 117.
8. Hadley, *Seven Months A Prisoner*, p. 78; Glazier, *The Capture*, p. 128, both cited in Speer, *Portals to Hell*, p. 268.
9. Domschcke, *Twenty Months in Captivity*, p. 94.
10. Ibid., pp. 94–95.
11. McElroy, *Andersonville: A Story of Rebel Military Prisons*, p. 401, cited in Speer, *Portals to Hell*, p. 269.
12. Ferguson, p. 118.

13. Ibid., pp. 118–119.
14. Ibid.
15. Ferguson, p. 114.
16. Speer, *Portals to Hell*, pp. 267–270.
17. Ferguson, p. 122.
18. Ibid., p. 116.
19. Domschcke, *Twenty Months in Captivity*, p. 95.
20. Cooper, *In and Out of Rebel Prisons*, pp. 108–109.
21. Ferguson, p. 119.
22. Ibid. pp. 120–121.
23. Cooper, *In and Out of Rebel Prisons*, p. 114.
24. Ferguson, *Life-Struggles in Rebel Prisons*, p. 122.
25. Cooper, *In and Out of Rebel Prisons*, p. 115.
26. Ferguson, p. 125.
27. Speer, *Portals to Hell*, p. 269.
28. Ibid., pp. 267–270.

Appendix

1. "Abstract from monthly returns of the principal U. S. Military prisons," O.R., Ser. II, Vol. 8, pp. 986–1004.

Bibliography

Primary Sources

NEWSPAPERS

Baltimore (Maryland) *American*
Baltimore (Maryland) *Sun*
Boston (Massachusetts) *Herald*
Boston (Massachusetts) *Post*
Chicago (Illinois) *Tribune*
Cincinnati (Ohio) *Commercial*
Cincinnati (Ohio) *Gazette*
Daily (St. Louis) *Missouri Democrat*
Indianapolis (Indiana) *Journal*
Macon (Georgia) *Dairy Telegraph*
Montgomery (Alabama) *Advertiser*
National Tribune (Washington, D.C.)
New York (New York) *Times*
New York (New York) *Sunday Mercury*
Richmond (Virginia) *Daily Dispatch*
Richmond (Virginia) *Enquirer*
Richmond (Virginia) *Examiner*
Richmond (Virginia) *Sentinel*
Richmond (Virginia) *Whig*
Saint Louis (Missouri) *Democrat*
The Sandusky (Ohio) *Register*
The Scioto (Ohio) *Gazette*
Shirleysburg (Pennsylvania) *Herald*
The Sun (Baltimore, Maryland)
Toledo (Ohio) *Blade*
Wilmington (North Carolina) *Sentinel*

ARCHIVES

Bowling Green State University, Bowling Green, Ohio, Center for Archival Collections
Fort Delaware Society Archives, Delaware City, Delaware.
Indiana Historical Society, Indianapolis, Indiana.
Library of Congress, Washington, D.C.
Library of Virginia, Richmond, Virginia
Maryland Historical Society Library, Baltimore, Maryland
Museum of the Confederacy, Richmond, Virginia
National Archives, Washington, D.C.
North Carolina Department of Archives and History, Raleigh, North Carolina
Rowan County Public Library, Salisbury, North Carolina
Southern Historical Collection, University of North Carolina, Chapel Hill, North Carolina
Virginia Historical Society, Richmond, Virginia

PUBLIC AND OFFICIAL RECORDS

Committee to Enquire into Treatment of Prisoners at Castle Thunder, *Evidence taken before the Committee of the House of Representatives, appointed to enquire into the Treatment of Prisoners at Castle Thunder* (Richmond, VA: House of Representatives, 1863)
Hewett, Janet B., Noah Andrew Trudeau, and Bryce A. Suderow. *The Supplement to the Army Official Records.* 100 vols. Wilmington, NC: Broadfoot, 1994–2001.
Office of Naval Records and Library. *Register of the Confederate States Navy, 1861–1865: As compiled and revised by the Office of Naval Records and Library, United States Navy Department, 1931, from all available data.* Washington, D.C.: Government Printing Office, 1931, reprint Mattituck, NY: J. M. Carroll, 1983.
Selected Records of the War Department Relating to Prisoners of War—Fort McHenry Military Prison. National Archives, Washington, D. C. Microfilm No. 596, Roll 96.
Shanks, John P. C., chairman. *Report of Committee of the House of Representatives Made during the 3rd Session of the 40th Congress, 1869.* Washington, D.C.: Government Printing Office, 1869.
Terrell, W. H. H. *Indiana in the War of the Rebellion: Official Report of W. H. H. Terrell, Adjutant General.* Vol. I. Indianapolis: Douglass & Conner, Printers, 1869.
Thirty-ninth Congress, 2nd Session, House of Representatives, Executive Document No. 50, *The Case of George St. Leger Grenfel.* Washington, DC: Government Printing Office, 1867
United States Naval War Records Office. *Official Records of the Union and Confederate Navies in the War of the Rebellion.* 27 Vols. Washington: 1894–1922.
United States War Department. *The War of the Rebellion. A Compilation of the Official Records of the Union and Confederate Armies.* 70 vols., 130 parts. Washington, D.C.: Government Printing Office, 1880–1905.
Works Progress Administration. *The Ohio Guide.* New York: Oxford University Press, 1940.

UNPUBLISHED MANUSCRIPTS

Benson, Berry Greenwood. Papers, 1843–1922, no. 2636. Southern Historical Collection, Wilson Library, University of North Carolina, Chapel Hill, North Carolina.

Boteler, Alexander Robinson. Papers. Special Collections Library, Duke University, Durham, North Carolina.

Coe, William P. Papers. Library of Congress, Manuscripts Division, Washington, D.C.

Ferris, Augustus Harvey. Diary. In the possession of the granddaughters of Sergeant Ferris who lived in St. Louis, Missouri.

Fischer, Ronald W. *A Comparative Study of Two Civil War Prisons: Old Capitol Prison and Castle Thunder Prison.* Master's thesis, Virginia Polytechnic Institute and State University, 1994.

"Fort Warren Prisoners' Records, 1861–1862." Maryland Historical Society, Baltimore, MD, 1957.

Golden, Alan Lawrence. "Castle Thunder: The Confederate Provost Marshal's Prison, 1862–1865." Typescript, master's thesis, University of Richmond, 1980.

Gray, Charles Carrol, Diary and revised copy, Southern Historical Collection, University of North Carolina, Chapel Hill, North Carolina.

Harris, Henry M. "A History of the Harris Family of Virginia and West Virginia," unpublished manuscript, 1967.

Roberts, B. E. Manuscript about Gen. John Hunt Morgan's escape from the Ohio State Penitentiary. The Filson Historical Society, Frankfort, Kentucky. 1886.

Ryan, Milton Asbury. "Experience of a Confederate Soldier in Camp and Prison in the Civil War 1861–1865." Copy of manuscript at the Carter House, a State of Tennessee Shrine commemorating the Battle of Franklin, 1140 Columbia Ave., P. O. Box 555, Franklin, TN 37065.

Tiemann, William Francis. Diary. Rowan County Public Library, Salisbury, North Carolina.

PUBLISHED DIARIES, LETTERS AND MEMOIRS

Abel, Richard Bender, and Fay Adamson Gecik, eds. *Sojourns of a Patriot: The Field and Prison Papers of an Unreconstructed Confederate.* Murfreesboro, TN: Southern Heritage Press, 1998.

Andrews, Eliza Frances. *The War-Time Journal of a Georgia Girl, 1864–1865.* New York: Appleton, 1908. Reprinted, Lincoln, NE: University of Nebraska Press, 1997.

Annals of the Civil War: Written by Leading Participants North and South. 1878, Abridged Edition, Introduced by Gary W. Gallagher. New York: Da Capo Press, 1994.

Barziza, D. U. *Decimus et Ultimus Barziza, Adventures of a Prisoner of War, 1863–1864.* R. Henderson Shuffler, ed. Houston, TX: News Job Office 1865. Reprinted, Austin, TX: University of Texas Press, 1964.

Beach, John N. *History of the Fortieth Ohio Volunteer Infantry.* London: Shepherd & Craig, 1884.

Benson, Susan Williams, ed. *Berry Benson's Civil War Book: Memoirs of a Confederate Scout and Sharpshooter.* Athens, GA: University of Georgia Press, 1962.

Booth, Benjamin F., and Steven Myer. *Dark Days of the Rebellion.* Revised. Garrison, IA: Meyer, 1995.

Boyd, Belle. *Belle Boyd in Camp and Prison.* Baton Rouge: Louisiana State University Press, 1998.

Brockett, Linus Pierpont. *The camp, the battle field, and the hospital: or, Lights and shadows of the great rebellion. Including adventures of spies and scouts, thrilling incidents, daring exploits, heroic deeds, wonderful escapes, sanitary and hospital scenes, prison scenes, etc., etc., etc.* Philadelphia: National, c 1866.

Browne, Junius Henri. *Four Years in Secessia: Adventures Within and Beyond the Union Lines: Embracing a Great Variety of Facts, Incidents, and romance of the War.* Hartford, CN: O. D. Case, 1865.

Catton, Bruce. *John Ransom's Andersonville Diary/Life Inside the Civil War's Most Infamous Prison.* New York: Berkley Books, 1994.

Cavada, F. F. *Libby Life: Experiences of a Prisoner of War in Richmond, VA, 1863–1864.* Philadelphia: J. B. Lippincott, 1865. Microfiche, Ann Arbor, MI: University Microfilms, 1992.

Clark, Walter, ed. *Histories of the Several Regiments in the Great War, 1861–1865,* 5 vols. Goldsboro, NC: Nash Brothers, 1901.

Coco, Gregory A., ed. *The Civil War Letters of Private Roland E. Bowen, 15th Massachusetts Infantry.* Gettysburg, PA: Thomas, 1994.

Commager, Henry Steele, ed. *The Blue and the Gray.* 2 volumes in 1. New York: Fairfax Press, 1982.

Cooper, Alonzo. *In and Out of Rebel Prisons.* Oswego, NY: R. J. Oliphant, 1888.

Corcoran, Michael. *The Captivity of General Corcoran. The Only Authentic and Reliable Narrative of the Trials and Suffering, Endured, During His Twelve Month's Imprisonment in Richmond, and Other Southern Cities, by Brigadier General Michael Corcoran, Hero of Bull Run.* Philadelphia: Barkely & Co., 1862.

Cross, J. F. "N. C. Officers in Prison at Johnson's Island, 1864." In Walter Clark, ed., *Histories of the Several Regiments and Battalions from North Carolina in the Great War, 1861–'65,* Vol. IV. Goldsboro, NC: Nash Brothers, 1901, pp. 703–712.

Curtis, D.B. *History of the Twenty-fourth Michigan of the Iron Brigade, known as the Detroit and Wayne County Regiment.* 1891. Reprinted. Gaithersburg, MD: Old Soldier Books, 1988.

Domschcke, Bernhard. *Twenty Months in Captivity: Memoirs of a Union Officer in Confederate Prisons.* Milwaukee, WI: W. W. Coleman, 1865. Reprinted. Frederic Toutmann, editor and translator. Cranbury, NJ: Associated University Presses, 1987.

Duganne, A. J. H. *Twenty Months in the Department of the Gulf.* New York: n.p., 1865.

Duke, Basil Wilson. *History of Morgan's Cavalry.* Cincinnati: Miami Printing and Publishing Co., 1867.

_____. *Reminiscences of General Basil W. Duke, C.S.A.* Garden City, NY: Doubleday, Page, 1911.

_____, and Don D. John. *The great Indiana-Ohio raid by Brig.-Gen. John Hunt Morgan and his men, July 1863: An authentic account of the most spectacular Confederate Cavalry raid into Union territory during the War Between the States — the Capture and Subsequent Escape of Brig.-Gen. Morgan.* Louisville, KY: Book Nook Press, 1955.

Elliot, James Carson. *The Southern Soldier Boy*. Raleigh, NC: Edwards & Broughton, 1907.

Ellis, Daniel. *Thrilling adventures of Daniel Ellis, the Great Guide of East Tennessee for a Period of Nearly Four Years during the Great Southern Rebellion, Written by Himself*. New York: Harper Bros., 1867.

Ferguson, Joseph. *Life-Struggles in Rebel Prisons*. Philadelphia: James M. Ferguson, 1865.

Forbes, Eugene. *Death Before Dishonor: The Andersonville Diary of Eugene Forbes*. Edited by William B. Styple. Kearney, NJ: Belle Grove, 1995.

_____. *The Diary of a Soldier and Prisoner of War in the Rebel Prisons*. Trenton, NJ: Murphy & Bechtel, Printers, 1865.

Frost, Griffin. *Camp & Prison Journal*. Quincy, IL: Quincy Herald Book and Job Office, 1867.

Glazier, Willard W. *The Capture, The Prison Pen, and the Escape, Giving an Account of Prison Life in the South*. Albany, NY: J. Munsell, 1866.

Greene, John W. *Camp Ford Prison; and How I Escaped*. Toledo, OH: Barkdull Printing House, 1893. Reprinted. Greencastle, IN: Nuggett, 1992.

Greenhow, Rose. *My imprisonment and the first year of abolition rule at Washington*. London: Richard Bentley, 1863.

Grimes, Absalom. *Confederate Mail Runner*. M. M. Quaife, ed. New Haven, CT: Yale University Press, 1926.

Hadley, John V. *Seven Months a Prisoner, by "An Indiana Soldier."* Indianapolis: Meikel, 1868.

Hamilton, A. J. *A Fort Delaware Journal: The Diary of a Yankee Private A. J. Hamilton, 1862–1865*, W. Emerson Wilson, ed. Wilmington, DE: The Fort Delaware Society, 1981.

Hamilton, Andrew G. *Story of the Famous Tunnel Escape from Libby Prison*. Chicago: S. S. Bogs, 1893?

Hamilton, J. G. De Roulhac, ed. *The Papers of Randolph Abbott Shotwell*. Vol. II Raleigh, NC: North Carolina Historical Commission, 1931.

Handy, Isaac W. K. *United States Bonds; or Duress by Federal Authority: A Journal of Current Events During an Imprisonment of Fifteen Months, at Fort Delaware*. Baltimore: Turnbull, 1874.

Hawes, Jesse. *Cahaba: A Story of Captive Boys in Blue*. New York: Burr Printing House, 1888.

Holmes, Clay W., *The Elmira Prison Camp: A History of the Military Prison at Elmira, N. Y., July 6, 1864, to July 10, 1865*. New York: G. P. Putnam's Sons, 1912.

Howard, Francis K. *Fourteen Months in American Bastiles*. Baltimore: Kelly, Hedian, Piet, 1863.

James, Frederic Augustus, *Civil War Diary: Sumter to Andersonville*, Jefferson J. Hammer, ed. Rutherford, N. J.: Fairleigh Dickinson University Press, 1973.

Johnson, I. N. *Four Months in Libby, and the campaign against Atlanta*. Cincinnati: privately published, 1864.

Kellogg, R. H. *Life and Death in Rebel Prisons*. Hartford, CT: 1865.

Kenan, Thomas S. "Johnson's Island," in Walter Clark, ed., *Histories of the Several Regiments and Battalions from North Carolina in the Great War, 1861–'65,* Vol. IV. Goldsboro, NC: Nash Brothers, 1901, pp. 689–696.

Keiley, Anthony. *In Vinculis; or, The Prisoner of War*. New York: Blelock, 1866.

King, John R. *My Experience in the Confederate Army and in Northern Prisons*. Clarksburg, WVA: United Daughters of the Confederacy, 1917.

Leon, L.L. *Diary of a Tar Heel Confederate Soldier*. Charlotte, NC: Stone, 1913.

Malone, Bartlett Yancey. "The Diary of Bartlett Yancey Malone." *The James Sprunt Historical Publications*. Vol. 16. No. 2. Chapel Hill, NC: University of North Carolina, 1919.

Mangum, Chaplain A. W. "Salisbury Prison." in Walter Clark, ed., *Histories of the Several Regiments and Battalions from North Carolina in the Great War, 1861–1865, Written by Members of the Respective Commands*, Vol. V. Goldsboro, NC.: Nash Brothers, 1901, pp. 745–772.

McElroy, John. *Andersonville: A Story of Rebel Military Prisons*. Toledo, OH: D. R. Locke, 1879. Reprinted, abridged, Greenwich, CN: Fawcett, 1962.

Moran, Frank E. *A Thrilling History of the Famous Underground Tunnel of Libby Prison*. New York: Century, 1889.

Murray, John Ogden. *The Immortal Six Hundred: A Story of Cruelty to Confederate Prisoners of War*. Winchester, VA: Eddy Press, 1905.

Newlin, W. H. *An Account of the Escape of Six Federal Soldiers from Prison at Danville, Va; Their Travels by Night Through The Enemy's Country to the Union Pickets At Gauley Bridge, West Virginia, in the Winter of 1863–64*. Cincinnati: Western Methodist Book Concern Print, 1889.

Norman, William M. *A Portion of My Life*. Winston-Salem, NC: John F. Blair, 1959.

Obreiter, John, and David W. Reed. *The Seventy-Seventh Pennsylvania at Shiloh: History of the regiment; the battle of Shiloh*. Harrisburg, PA: Harrisburg, 1905.

Putnam, George Haven. *A Prisoner of War in Virginia, 1864–5*. Reprint, Second Edition, New York: G. P. Putnam's Sons, 1912.

Ransom, John. *John Ransom's Andersonville Diary/Life Inside the Civil War's Most Infamous Prison*. Edited by Bruce Catton. New York: Berkley Books, 1994.

Richardson, Albert D. *The Secret Service, The Field, The Dungeon, and The Escape*. Hartford, CN: American, 1865.

Rose, Thomas Elwood. *Col. Rose's Story of The Famous Tunnel Escape from Libby Prison: A Thrilling Account of the Daring Escape of 109 Union Officers from Libby Prison Through the Famous Tunnel*. Bethesda, MD: University Publications of America. Microfiche, Civil War Unit Histories, Part 3, The Union — Mid-Atlantic; PA:486, 1992.

Scharf, J. T. *History of the Confederate States Navy*. New York: Rogers & Sherwood, 1887.

Shepherd, Henry E. *Narrative of Prison Life at Baltimore and Johnson's Island, Ohio*. Baltimore: Commercial Printing and Stationery, 1917.

Sherrill, Miles O. *A Soldier's Story: Prison Life and Other Incidents in the War of 1861— 65*. sl:s.n., 1904? Electronic edition, University of North Carolina at Chapel Hill Libraries. http://docsouth.unc.edu/sherrill.menu.html.

Small, Abner R. *The Road to Richmond*. Edited by Harold Adams Small. New York: Fordham University Press, 2000.

Speer, Allen Paul. *Voices from Cemetery Hill.* Johnson City, TN: Overmountain Press, 1997.

Stephens, Alexander H. *Recollections of Alexander H. Stephens; His Diary Kept when a Prisoner at Fort Warren, Boston Harbor, 1865.* New York: Da Capo, 1971.

Stuart, A. A. *Iowa Colonels and Regiments.* Des Moines: Mills,1865.

Sturgis, Thomas. *Prisoners of War 1861–65: A Record of Personal Experiences, and a Study of the Conditions and Treatment of Prisoners on Both Sides During the War of the Rebellion.* New York: G. P. Putnam's Sons, 1912.

Tarrant, Sgt. E., compiler. *The Wild Riders of the First Kentucky Cavalry, A History of the Regiment, in the Great War of the Rebellion, 1861–1865.* Louisville, KY: A Committee of the Regiment, 1894. Microfische 157, Unit 4, KY# Regimental Histories, Library of Virginia.

Toney, Marcus B. *The Privations of a Private.* Nashville, TN: Methodist Episcopal Church South, 1905.

Tuttle, Rev. E. B. *The History of Camp Douglas; including Official Report of Gen. B. J. Sweet; With Anecdotes of the Rebel Prisoners.* Chicago: J. R. Walsh, 1865.

Walker, John L. *Cahaba Prison and the Sultana Disaster.* Hamilton, OH: Brown & Whitaker, 1910.

Wells, James M. *With Touch of Elbow; or Death Before Dishonor.* Philadelphia: Winston, 1909.

Williamson, James J. *Prison Life in the Old Capitol and Reminiscences of the Civil War.* West Orange, NJ: n.p., 1911.

Wyeth, John A. *With Sabre and Scapel: The Autobiography of a Soldier and Surgeon.* New York: Harper & Brothers, 1914.

Secondary Sources

Boatner, Mark Mayo III. *The Civil War Dictionary.* Revised. New York: Vintage Books, 1991.

Bowman, John S., general editor. *Who Was Who in the Civil War.* Reprinted. North Dighton, MA: World Publication Group, 2002.

Brown, Darren. *The Greatest Escape Stories Ever Told.* Guilford, CT: Lyons Press, 2002.

Brown, Louis A. *The Salisbury Prison: A Case Study of Confederate Military Prisons, 1861–1865.* Revised. Privately published by the author, 1992.

Burnham, Philip. *So Far From Dixie: Confederates in Yankee Prisons.* Lanham, MD: Taylor Trade Publishing, 2003.

Campbell, R. Thomas. *Sea Hawk of the Confederacy: Lt. Charles W. Read and the Confederate Navy.* Shippensburg, PA: Beidel Printing House, 1999.

Casstevens, Frances H. *Captain George Washington Alexander and Castle Thunder: A Biography of a Prison Commandant.* Jefferson, NC: McFarland & Co., 2004.

Conway, W. Fred. *The Most Incredible Prison Escape of the Civil War.* 2nd Edition. New Albany, IN: FBH, 1994.

Demuth, I. MacDonald. *The History of Pettis County, Missouri, Including an Authentic History of Sedalia, other Towns and Townships, Together with ... biographical sketches....* Clinton, MO: The Printery, 1882.

Denny, Robert E. *Civil War Prisons & Escapes.* New York: Sterling, Inc., 1993.

Donnelly, Ralph W. *The Rebel Leathernecks: The Confederate States Marine Corps.* Shippensburg, PA: White Mane, 1989.

Doster, William E. *Lincoln and Episodes of the Civil War.* New York: G. P. Putnam's Sons, 1915.

Dufour, Charles L. *Nine Men in Gray.* (New York): Doubleday & Company, Inc., 1963.

Ellis, John B. *The Sights and Secrets of the National Capital: A Word Descriptive of Washington City in all its Various Phases.* New York: United States Publishing, 1869.

England, Otis Bryan. *A Short History of the Rock Island Prison Barracks.* Rock Island, IL: Historical Office, U. S. Army Armament, Munitions, and Chemical Command, 1985

Faust, Patricia L., ed. *Historical Times Illustrated Encyclopedia of the Civil War.* New York: Harper & Row, 1986.

Fetzer, Dale, and Bruce Mowday. *Unlikely Allies: Fort Delaware's Prison Community in the Civil War.* Mechanicsburg, PA: Stackpole Books, 2000.

Foote, Shelby. *The Civil War: A Narrative,* 3 vols. New York: Vintage Books, 1986.

Fox, William F. *Regimental Losses in The American Civil War 1861–1865.* Albany, NY: Brandow, 1898. Reprinted. Dayton, OH: Morningside House, 1985.

Frohman, Charles E. *Rebels on Lake Erie.* Columbus, OH: Ohio Historical Society, 1965.

French, Joseph Lewis. *Thrilling Escapes.* New York: Dodd, Mead, 1924.

Harrison, Galen. D. *Prisoners' Mail From the American Civil War.* Dexter, MI: Thompson-Shore, 1997.

Hesseltine, William Best. *Civil War Prisons.* Kent, OH: Kent State University Press, 1972.

Hicken, Victor. *Illinois Camps, Posts and Prisons,* (Monograph, Series No. 10), in Civil War Centennial Commission of Illinois. *Illinois Civil War Sketches.* Springfield, IL: Civil War Centennial Commission, 1971.

Horigan, Michael. *Elmira: Death Camp of the North.* Mechanicsburg, PA: Stackpole Books, 2002.

Horwitz, Lester V. *The Longest Raid of the Civil War.* Cincinnati: Farmcourt, 1999.

Jeffrey, William H. *Richmond Prisons, 1861–1862.* St. Johnsbury, VT: Republican Press, 1893.

Knauss, William H. *The Story of Camp Chase.* Columbus, OH: General's Books, 1990.

Levy, George. *To Die in Chicago: Confederate Prisoners at Camp Douglas, 1862–1865.* Evanston, IL: Evanston, 1994.

Lobst, Richard W. *Civil War Macon — The History of a Confederate City.* Macon, GA: Mercer University Press, 1999.

Miller, Francis Trevelyan, ed., *Photographic History of the Civil War,* 10 vols. New York: The Review of Reviews Co., 1911. Reprinted. New York: Castle Books, 1975.

Missouri Historical Company, *History of Saline County, Missouri.* St. Louis: Missouri Historical Company, 1881.

Parker, Sandra V. *Richmond's Civil War Prisons.* Lynchburg, VA: H. E. Howard, 1990.

Radley, Kenneth. *Rebel Watchdog.* Baton Rouge, LA: Louisiana State University Press, 1989.

Reed, Thomas J., W. Andrew McKay, Rev. Anthony R. Wade. *Untying the Political Knot.* Wilmington, NC: Broadfoot, 2001.

Schutzer, A. I. *Great Civil War Escapes.* New York: G. P. Putnam's Sons, 1967.

Scharf, J. T. *History of the Confederate States Navy.* New York: Rogers and Sherwood, 1887.

Scharf, J. Thomas. *History of St. Louis City & County.* Philadelphia: Louis H. Everts, 1883.

Shaler, N. S. *Kentucky: A Pioneer Commonwealth.* Boston: Houghton Mifflin, 1895.

Sifakis, Stewart. *Who Was Who in the Civil War.* New York: Facts on File, 1998.

Snow, Edward R. *Historic Fort Warren.* Boston: Yankee, 1941.

_____. *The Islands of Boston Harbor.* New York: Dodd, Mead, 1936.

_____. *The Romance of Boston Bay.* Boston: Yankee, 1944.

Sriver, Philip Raymond. *Ohio's Military Prisons in the Civil War.* Columbus, OH: Ohio State Press for the Ohio Historical Society, 1864.

Speer, Lonnie R. *Portals to Hell: Military Prisons of the Civil War.* Mechanicsburg, PA: Stackpole Books, 1997.

Starr, Louis M. *Reporting the Civil War: The Bohemian Brigade in Action, 1861–65.* New York: Collier Books, 1962.

Stern, Philip Van Doren. *Secret Missions of the Civil War.* New York: Wing Books, 1990.

Stephens, Clifford W., compiler. *Rock Island Confederate Prison Deaths.* Rock Island, IL: Blackhawk Genealogical Society, 1973

Toy, Sidney. *Castles: Their Construction and History.* London, William Heinemann, 1938. Reprinted. New York: Dover, 1985.

Wilson, W. Emerson. *Fort Delaware.* Newark, NJ: University of Delaware Press, 1957.

Winslow, Hattie Lou. *Camp Morton 1861–1865: Indianapolis Prison Camp.* Indianapolis: Indiana Historical Society, 1940.

Yearns, W. Buck, and John Gilchrist Barrett. *North Carolina Civil War Documentary.* Chapel Hill, NC: University of North Carolina Press, 2002.

Articles, Booklets, and Pamphlets

Alexander, J. W. "An Escape from Fort Warren." In Walter Clark, ed. *Histories of the Several Regiments in the Great War, 1861–1865*, Vol. 4. Goldsboro, NC: Nash Brothers, 1901, pp. 733–743.

_____. "How I Escaped from Fort Warren." *The New England Magazine*, Vol. 13, No. 2 (October 1892), pp. 208–214.

Bixby, George S. "Diary of George S. Bixby." *Boston Globe,* November 28, 1909.

Bolles, John A. "Escape from Fort Warren." *Harper's New Monthly Magazine,* Vol. A28, No. 167 (April 1864), pp. 697–701.

Brown, Ann L. B. "Fort Delaware: The Most Dreaded Northern Prison." *Civil War Quarterly*, Vol. 10 (September 1987).

Burke, Curtis R. "Civil War Journal." *Indiana Magazine of History.* Vol. 65 (December 1969), pp. 283–327; Vol. 66 (June 1970), pp. 110–172; Vol. 66 (December 1970), pp. 318–361; Vol. 67 (June 1971), pp. 129–170.

Burrows, J. L. "Recollections of Libby Prison." *Southern Historical Society Papers,* Vol. 11, Richmond, VA: Southern Historical Society, 1883, pp. 83–92.

Calfe, B. S. "Prison Life." *Harper's New Monthly Magazine,* Vol. 31, No. 182, pp. 137–150.

Carpenter, Horace. "Plain Living at Johnson's Island." *The Century,* Vol. 41, No. 5 (March 1891), pp. 705–718.

Cheavens, Henry Martyn. "A Missouri Confederate in the Civil War: The Journal of Henry Martyn Cheavens, 1862–1863." Edited by James E. Moss. *Missouri Historical Review* 57:1 (October 1962), pp. 29–33.

Cook, S. N. "Johnson's Island." *Ohio Magazine* Vol. 1, No. 3. (September 1906), pp. 225–232.

Dana, Charles A. "The War — Some Unpublished History." *The North American Review,* Vol. 153, No. 417 (August 1891), pp. 240–245.

Davis, Egbert L. "The James Henry Shore Family," in Frances H. Casstevens, ed., *Heritage of Yadkin County, North Carolina.* Winston-Salem, NC: Hunter, 1981, pp. 588–590.

Dempsey, R. A. "An Account from the Ranks," *121 Regiment Pennsylvania Survivor's Association Review Edition.* Philadelphia: Press of Catholic Standard and Times, 1906, pp. 180–181.

Doran, Frank B. "Prison Memories. Castle Thunder, the Rebel Bastille for Deserters, spies and Criminals — Repeated Attempts at Escape — Execution of Webster, the Union Spy — Merciless Shooting of Deserters — Responsibility for the War." *National Tribune,* November 16, 1905.

Duke, Basil W. "A Romance of Morgan's Rough Riders. Part I. The Escape." *The Century,* Vol. 41, No. 3 (January 1891), pp. 403–412.

Earp, Charles A. "The Amazing Colonel Zarvona." *Maryland Historical Magazine,* Vol. 34 (1939), pp. 334–343.

"The Escape: Daring and Suffering in the Rebel Country by Two 4th Pa. Cav. Men," *National Tribune,* December 14, 1893.

"Escape of Prisoners from Johnson's Island." *Southern Historical Society Papers,* Vol. 18 (January-December 1890), p. 428–431.

"Figures of Secretary Stanton." *Southern Historical Society Papers,* Vol. 1, No. 3 (March 1876), pp. 216–218.

Flora, Samuel R. "'I consider the Regiment my home': The Orphan Brigade and Letters of Capt. Edward Ford Spears." *Register of the Kentucky Historical Society,* Vol. 94, No. 2 (Spring 1996), pp. 134–173.

Foenander, Terry, "CSN Prisoners at Fort Warren: A Photographic Essay." http://hub.dateline.net.au/~tfoen/fortwarren.htm.

"Had a Peep at Death. Memorable Incident in the Life of R. R. Turner, A Libby Prison Official." *Richmond Dispatch,* December 8, 1901.

Henley, Bernard J. "Col. George W. Alexander: The Terror of Castle Thunder," *Richmond Literature and History Quarterly.* 3(2) (Fall, 1980), pp. 48–50.

Henry, T. D. "Deposition of T. D. Henry." *Southern*

Historical Society Papers. Vol. 1, No. 4 (April 1876), pp. 276–279

Heseltine, William B. "Military Prisons of St. Louis, 1861–1865." *Missouri Historical Review* 22:3 (April 1929).

Hines, Thomas H. "A Romance of Morgan's Rough Riders. Part III. The Escape." *The Century,* Vol. 41, No. 3 (January 1891), pp. 412–417.

Holloway, W. R. "Treatment of Prisoners at Camp Morton." *The Century.* Vol. 42, No. 5 (September 1891), pp. 757–771.

Hougland, J. E. "The 19th Iowa," in *The National Tribune Scrap Book.* Washington, D.C.: National Tribune, 1909.

Keen, Nancy Travis. *Confederate Prisoners of War at Fort Delaware.* Booklet, reprinted from *Delaware History,* April 1968, pp. 1–27.

Klee, Bruce. "They Paid to Enter Libby Prison," *Civil War Times Illustrated,* Vol. 37, No. 7 (February 1999), pp. 32–38.

Long, Roger. "Out of a Frozen Hell." Part I. *Civil War Times Illustrated,* Vol. 37, No. 1 (March 1998), pp. 24–31.

_____. "Out of a Frozen Hell." Part II. *Civil War Times Illustrated,* Vol. 37, No. 2 (May 1998), pp. 42–48.

"Major Turner's Escape: How the ex–Commandant of Famous Libby Prison Fled to Cuba." *New York Times,* July 7, 1895.

McNamara, M. "Lieutenant Pierce's Daring Attempts to Escape from Johnson's Island." *Southern Historical Society Papers,* Vol. 8 (January-December, 1880), pp. 61–67.

Moran, Frank E. "Colonel Rose's Tunnel at Libby Prison." *Century Illustrated Monthly Magazine* (March 1888), pp. 770–790.

_____. "Libby Prison — The Tunnel Diggers. Capture of Yankee Gunboats by Rebel Cavalry." *National Tribune,* March 17, 1892.

"New Diary Discovered." *Fort Delaware Society Notes* (December 1975), pp. 2–3.

"The Old Capitol Building and Its Inmates." *New York Times,* April 19, 1862, p. 2.

Pearson, Priscilla, and Robert D. Hoffsommer. "In Vinculis: A Prisoner of War." Part I. *Civil War Times Illustrated* Vol. 23, No. 8 (December 1984), pp. 34–39

_____, and _____. "In Vinculis: A Prisoner of War." Part II. *Civil War Times Illustrated* Vol. 23, No. 9 (January 1985), pp. 26–33.

Pittard, Janet C. "Wild Rose." *Our State* (April 2004), pp. 25–26.

Porter, John F. "Narrative of Captain John F. Porter, Jr., Fourteenth New York Cavalry — Particulars of His Escape." In Linus Pierpont Brockett, *The camp, the battle field, and the hospital: or, Lights and shadows of the great rebellion. Including adventures of spies and scouts, thrilling incidents, daring exploits, heroic deeds, wonderful escapes, sanitary and hospital scenes, prison scenes, etc., etc., etc.* Philadelphia: National, c 1866, pp. 280–282.

Reid, Warren D. "Escaped from Fort Delaware." *Southern Historical Society Papers,* Vol. 36. Richmond, VA: Southern Historical Society, 1908, pp. 271–279.

"Reminiscences of Washington." *The Atlantic Monthly,* Vol. 45, No. 267 (January 1880), p. 5 7.

"The Retaliation: The Murder of Wilson and his Comrades," *St, Louis Democrat,* October 29, 1864; October 31, 1864.

Rideing, William H. "The Gateway of Boston." *Harper's New Monthly Magazine* Vol. 69, No. 411 (August 1884), pp. 352–361.

Sanders, Stuart W. "A Little Fight Between Friends and Family." *Civil War Times Illustrated.* Vol. 40, No. 5 (October 2001), pp. 40–44, 66.

Stier, William J. "Morgan's Last Battle." *Civil War Times Illustrated.* Vol. 35, No. 6 (December 1996), pp. 83–92.

Traywick, J. B. "Prison Life at Point Lookout." *Southern Historical Society Papers,* Vol. 18 (January-December 1890), pp. 431–435.

Tucker, James B., and Norma Tucker, "Great Escape from Rebel Prison." *America's Civil War* Vol. 8, No. 1 (March 1995).

"Tunneling Out of Libby Prison." *Confederate Veteran.* Vol. 17 (1909), p. 114.

Turner, William Dandridge. "The Libby Lion." In *The Black Swan.* August 1929, pp. 4–5, 29–35; September 1919, pp. 17–19, 20, 27–29; October 1929, pp. 22, 33–35

Wasson, J. M. "Letter from Lieutenant J. M. Wasson — Adventures in Southern Prisons." In John N. Beach, *History of the Fortieth Ohio Volunteer Infantry.* London: Shepherd & Craig, 1884, pp. 132–136.

Webb, R. F. "Prison Life on Johnson's Island, 1863–'64," Walter Clark, ed., *Histories of the Several Regiments in the Great War, 1861–1865,* Vol. 4 (Goldsboro, NC: Nash Brothers, 1901), pp. 657–687.

Willcox, Orlando B. "A Romance of Morgan's Rough Riders. Part II. The Capture." *The Century,* Vol. 41, No. 3 (January 1891), pp. 412–417.

Wyeth, John A. "Cold Cheer at Camp Morton." *The Century,* Vol. 41, No. 6 (April 1891), pp. 844–852.

_____. "Rejoinder." *The Century.* Vol. 42, No. 5 (September 1891), pp. 771–776.

Wright, Charles. "Rock Island Prison 1864–1865." *Southern Historical Society Papers,* Vol. 1, No. 4 (April 1876), pp. 281–292.

ONLINE ARTICLES

"A Brief History of Tyler, Texas." http://www.city-oftyler.org/8B1B70ADF71FEAB0BD93F041744A6EB/default.html.

"Abstracts from the Monthly Reports of Prisoners at Camp Chase, July 1862 through July 1865 (incomplete as of January 29, 2004). http://www.geocities.com/Pentagon/Quarters/5109/abstracts.html.

Allen, Robert Willis. "A Visit to Fort Warren." http://johnbrownsbody.net/Fort_Warren.htm.

"Alton Civil War Prison." http://www.censusdiggins.com/prison_alton.html.

"Alton Prison Site Today." http://www.gwheeler.com/alton2.htm.

"Andersonville Civil War Prison." http://www.censusdiggins.com/prison_andersonville.-html.

"Archaeological Investigations at Andersonville Civil War Prison." http://www.cr.nps.gov/seac/archinvt.htm

"Baltimore's Best Attraction." http://www.bcpl.net/~etowner/best.html.

Beckman, Tim. "Camp Morton — Civil War Camp and Union Prison 1816–1865, Indianapolis, Indiana." http://freepages.history.rootsweb.com/~indiana42nd/campmorton.htm.

"Belle Isle Civil War Prison." http://www.censusdiggins.com/prison_bellisle.html.

Boynton, Bruce R. "A Scottsville Teen in Mosby's Rangers: Henry G. Harris." http://www.scottsvillemuseum.com/war/harris/home.html.

Bush, David. "Archaeology's Interactive Dig." http://www.archaeology.org/interactive/johnson/questions/2.html.

_____. "History of Johnson's Island Prisoner of War Depot. http://www.heidelberg.edu/~dbush/jirev2.html.

"Camp Chase Prison." http://www.censusdiggins.com/prison_campchase.html.

"Camp Chase Prison." http://www.civilwarhome.com/campchase.htm

"Camp Morton — Civil War Camp and Union Prison 1861–1865." freepages.history.rootsweb.com/~indiana42nd/campmorton.htm.

Cashin, Don. "Confederate States Naval and Other Maritime Prisoners Held at Fort Delaware." http://hub.dataline.net.au/~tfoen/delaware/htm.

Cavada, F. F. *Libby Life: Experiences of a Prisoner of War in Richmond, VA, 1863–1864.* Philadelphia: J. B. Lippincott, 1865. Microfiche, Ann Arbor, MI: University Microfilms, 1992. http://www.rose-hulman.edu/~delacova/book/libby-10.htm.

Champenois, John Franklin. "For the Standard: Life in Camp Morton, 1863–1865." http://www.champenois.com/genealogy/campmorton.html.

Chicago Historical Society. "Douglas/Grand Boulevard: The Past & Present." http://www.chigohistory.org/DGBPhotoEssay/DGB02.html

Claycomb, William B. "President Lincoln and the Magoffin Brothers." http://www.morningsidebooks.com

"Civil War Prison Camps," (for various prisons), http://www.censudiggins.com.

"Digging Out of Libby," *National Tribune*, 21 April 1892. http://www.mdgorman.com/National_tribune/national_tribune_4211892.htm.

Drake, Rebecca Blackwell. "Portraits — Generals and Commanders." http://battleofraymond.org/command2.htm.

"Elmira Prison Revisited." http://www.rootsweb.com/~srgp/articles/elmirevis.htm

"Explore Old Cahaba," http://www.selmaalabama.com/cahawbas.htm.

Farr, George R. "The Federal Confederate Prisoner of War Camp at Elmira." http://www.rootsweb.com/~srgp/military/elmcivwr.htm

"Fort McHenry- Facts." http://www.bcpl.net/~etowner/facts.html.

"The Great Escape." *From the regimental history of the Seventy-seventh Pennsylvania, by Sergeant John Obreiter.* http://valley.vcdh.virginia.edu/HIUS403/77pa/Eric/escapel.html.

Hamilton, Andrew G. *Story of the Famous Tunnel Escape from Libby Prison.* Chicago: S. S. Bogs, 1893? http://www.mdgorman.com/Libby/story_of_the_famous_tunnel_escap.htm.

Hanson, Diana, translator "Rock Island Civil War Prison Barracks." Excerpts from *Rock Island Con-federate Prison Death,* by Clifford W. Stephens. http://www.rootsweb.com/~ilrockis/plac_hist/hist-cp.htm.

Hill, J. F. "To and From Libby Prison." Part 1, *The Scotio Gazette,* January 26, 1864. http://www.89thohio.com/Prisoners/hill.htm

"Historic Fort Warren: A Civil War Living History & Drill Competition, Boston Harbor, Boston, MA." http://www.geocities.com/ftwarren2004/index.html.

Hobart, Harrison C. Hobart, "Libby Prison — The Escape." Papers read before the Wisconsin Mollus, Vol. 1, Milwaukee, 1891, pp. 394–409. http://www.mdgorman.com/Libby/Libby_Prison_The_Escape.htm

"Imprisonment of the 'Plymouth Pilgrim' Officers." http://home.att.net/~cwppds/officers.htm

Indiana State Archives. "Databases — Camp Morton," http://www.in.gov/icpr/archives/databases/civilwar/camp/camp1862.html.

"John R. Towers, Captain, Co. E., then Colonel, 8th Georgia Volunteer Infantry." http://home.earthlink.net/~larsrbl/towersphotopage.htm.

"Johnson's Island, Ohio," U. S. Military Prison Collection, MS-22 mf, Center for Archival Collections, Bowling Green State University, Bowling Green, Ohio. http://www.bgsu.edu/colleges/library/cac/ms0022.html.

"Just the Arti-Facts: A Prisoner's Diary," Chicago Historical Society, online http://www.chicagohistory.org/AOTM/Apr98/apr98fact1a.html.

"The Late Rose A. Greenhow." *Wilmington Sentinel,* October 1, 1864, in Alexander Robinson Boteler Papers, Special Collections Library, Duke University, Durham, North Carolina. http://scriptorium.lib.duke.edu/greenhow/1864-10-01-a/1864-10-01-a.html

"Lost Virginia — Vanished Architecture of the Old Dominion: Lost Civic Architecture." http://www.vahistorical.org/lva/libby.htm

"Major Turner's Escape: How the ex–Commandant of Famous Libby Prison Fled to Cuba." *New York Times*, July 7, 1895, http://www.mdgorman.com/NYC-Papers/new_york_times_771895.htm.

Mann, Howard. "True Tales of the Tenth Kansas Infantry." http://www.civilwarstlouis.com/Gratiot/tenthkansas4.htm.

McCormick, L. "Thomas R. McCormick." http://www.misscivilwar.org/persona/mccorm.html

Moran, Daniel. "Suspension of Habeas Corpus: The Saga of Richard Henry Alvy." http://www.us-civilwar.com/aldie/habeas%20corpus.html.

Moran, Frank E. "Colonel Rose's Tunnel at Libby Prison." *Century Illustrated Monthly Magazine* (March 1888), pp. 770–790. http://www.mdgorman.com/Libby/colonel_roses_tunnel.htm.

_____. "Libby Prison — The Tunnel Diggers. Capture of Yankee Gunboats by Rebel Cavalry." *National Tribune*, March 17, 1892. http://www.mdgorman.com/National_Tribune/national_tribune_3171892.htm.

"Point Lookout Civil War Prison." http://www.censusdiggins.com/prison_ptlookout.html.

Porter, G. W. D. "Nine Months in Northern Prison." http://www.tennessee-scv.org/4455/9months.htm.

Randall, W. S. B. "Libby Prison. The Experience of

One of the Successful Tunnelers." *National Tribune,* 27 March 1890. http://www.mdgorman.com/National_Tribune/national_tribune_3271890.htm.

Reno, Linda Davis. "Richard Thomas Zarvona." Part I, Part II, St. Mary's Families, February 2003 and May 2003. http://stmarysfamilies.com.

"Robert Renwick, a Cabinetmaker: Judge for Yourself." http://www.scots-in-the-civil-war.net/renwick.htm.

"Rock Island Arsenal." http://www.ria.army.mil.riahistory.htm.

Rose, Thomas E. "Libby Tunnel. An Interesting Account of Its Construction." *National Tribune,* 14 May 1885. http://www.mdgorman.com/National_Tribune/national_tribune_5141885.htm.

"Roster of the 43rd Battalion Virginia Cavalry, Army of Northern Virginia, Confederate States of America." http://www.mosocco.com/companyf.html.

Rule, D. J. "Gratiot Street Prison FAQ: Frequently Asked Questions about the Union Civil War Prison in St. Louis, Missouri." http://www.civilwarstlouis.com/Gratiot/gratiotfaq.htm.

Ryan, Milton Asbury. "Experience of a Confederate Soldier in Camp and Prison in the Civil War 1861–1865." Copy of manuscript at the Carter House, a State of Tennessee Shrine commemorating the Battle of Franklin, 1140 Columbia Ave., P. O. Box 555, Franklin, TN 37065. http://www.izzy.net/~michaelg/mar-text.htm

"Salisbury National Cemetery." http://www.interment.net/data/us/nc/rowan/salisnat/index.htm

"The Salisbury NC Confederate Civil War Prison." http://www.gorowan.com/salisburyprison/

"Ships, Blockades & Raiders: Greyhound 'Short-lived Blockade Runner' 1863–1864." http://civil.war.bluegrass.net/ShipsBlockadesAndRaiders/greyhound.html.

Snow, Edward Rowe. Excerpts from "The Romance of Boston Bay." http://jay.schmidt.home.att.net/ft.warren/ghost/html.

_____. "History of Fort Warren: Some Famous Confederate Prisoners at Fort Warren." http://jay.schmidt.home.att.net/ft.warren/prisoners.html.

Spotswood, Thomas E. "Horrors of Camp Morton," http://www.csa-dixie.com/csalprisoners/t59.htm.

Swingle, Herb, "A Yankee Prisoner in Texas," http://www.greece.k12.ny.us/oly/herb.htm.

Taylor, G. T. "Prison Experience in Elmira, N. Y." http://www.tarleton.edu/~kjones/ElmiraDocs.html.

Turner, William Dandridge. "The Libby Lion." In *The Black Swan.* August 1929, pp. 4–5, 29–35; September 1919, pp. 17–19, 20, 27–29; October 1929, pp. 22, 33–35, http://www.mdgorman.com/Libby/libby_lion.htm.

Tyler Economic Development Council, Inc., "Tyler, Texas: Community Profile 2003." http://www.tedc.org/pdfs/profile.pdf

"Union Civil War Prison at Elmira, NY." http://home.jam.rr.com/rcourt52/cwprisons/elmiran.htm

Waitt, Robert W. "Libby Prison." *Official Publication #12* (Richmond, VA: Richmond Civil War Centennial Committee, n.d. http://www.mdgorman.com/Libby/libby_prison_robert_w_waitt.htm

Walls that Talk: A Transcription of the Names, Initials and Sentiments written and graven on the Walls, Doors and Windows of the Libby Prison at Richmond by the Prisoners of 1861–'65. Richmond, VA: R. E. Lee Camp, No. I, C.V., 1884. http://www.mdgorman.com/Libby/walls_that_talk.htm.

"Washington Grays." http://thewashingtongrays.homestead.com/.

"Welcome to the Official Fort Delaware Society Webpage." http://www.del.net/org/fort/.

Wheeler, J. E. "Gene." "Infamous Alton Prison." http://www.gwheeler.com/alton1.htm.

Wolf, James, "In and Out of the Jaws of Death/Recollections of Fifteen Months Experience in Rebel Prisons." *Sciotio Gazette* February 28, 1865. http://www.89thohio.com/Prisoners/wolfe.htm.

"Xerxes Knox, Private, Company G, 3rd Iowa Cavalry in the Civil War." http://www.oz.net/~cyndihow/xerxes.htm.

Index